ANYTHING COULD HAPPEN

GRANT ROBERTSON

ANYTHING COULD HAPPEN

A MEMOIR

ALLEN&UNWIN
AUCKLAND • SYDNEY • MELBOURNE • LONDON

First published in 2025

Allen & Unwin Aotearoa New Zealand
Level 2, 10 College Hill, Freemans Bay
Auckland 1011, New Zealand
+64 (9) 377 3800
auckland@allenandunwin.com
www.allenandunwin.co.nz

83 Alexander Street
Crows Nest NSW 2065, Australia
+61 (2) 8425 0100

EU Authorised Representative: Easy Access System Europe, Mustamäe tee 50, 10621 Tallinn, Estonia, gpsr.requests@easproject.com

A catalogue record for this book is available from the National Library of New Zealand.

ISBN 978 1 99100 687 5

Design by Kate Barraclough
Printed and bound in Australia by the Opus Group
1 3 5 7 9 10 8 6 4 2

MIX
Paper | Supporting responsible forestry
FSC® C001695

To my darling Alf, the love of my life,
for always keeping it real

Anything could happen
And it could be right now
And the choice is yours
To make it worthwhile

'Anything Could Happen', The Clean

CONTENTS

1.
BEGINNINGS

Mum and Dad sat me and my two older brothers down on the old yellow sofa in our Hastings living room. Dad looked excited; Mum looked like she had been crying.

The three of us, Stephen aged nine, Craig eight and me six, could easily fit on the creaky couch. The room itself was as 1970s as it was possible to get — a symphony of beige, yellow and orange. The very new 26-inch colour TV took pride of place.

That living room was the centre of my universe. I had spent hours and days in there. Home with Mum after my brothers went to school, I would nag her to sit with me on the floor to play my favourite card game — Memory. I usually won, probably because she was doing three other things at the same time, but I loved it.

I was in the living room the day the kitchen caught fire after Mum cooked homemade chips and we all had to run out onto the road. I don't remember who put the fire out, but when Dad came home from work he was not happy. The whole house still stank of smoke, oil and burnt net curtains.

It was also where I freaked out after Dad walked in dressed as Santa Claus before the kindergarten Christmas party. I was scared of Santa Claus because of the enormous 20-foot-high Santa outside Fantasyland across the road. It was just too big for me.

I remember being scared a lot. At night, often running into my parents' room and jumping into the bed, I was worried all the time — about what might happen, about not knowing, about whether I could do what my brothers could do. When you're the youngest of three boys, you always want to do what your older brothers are doing. But what if I couldn't?

'We are moving to Dunedin,' said Mum.

'Why?'

'Because your father is going to become a minister and he has to go to training college.'

My eldest brother started to cry too.

I knew where Dunedin was because that was the home base of the Otago rugby team. I could have told the rest of the family that they played at Carisbrook, and that one of my favourite players, Bevan Wilson, was the fullback. But even at six I knew this probably was not the right time.

'Things are going to be different down there. Dad will be a student so we will not have very much money. If we are going to have Kentucky chicken [as my mother still calls it] then someone else is going to have to pay for it.'

I could see why Mum and my brother were crying now. Why would anyone actively put themselves in the position of not being able to have KFC? But what would moving there mean, apart from limitations on my preferred dinner?

It would mean a new school, and moving away from my best friend Peter, and going to a different church. In short, it would mean breaking away from everything I knew.

I don't remember being particularly upset by this. But memory is a funny thing. Why do I remember sitting on that couch so clearly? I think it was because somehow I knew this news was momentous.

We had comfortable, settled lives in Hastings. Dad was an accountant with the Eastern & Central Savings Bank, heavily involved in rugby refereeing and in the church. Mum was active in the church too, and in the local community, having recently helped to establish the first Parents Centre in Hastings. She made all our clothes, our dinners — she made our world.

Our extended family were there, including Mum's grandmother and aunts; Dad's grandmother, who also lived there, had only recently passed away. We were within easy reach of beaches, rivers and the stockcars at Meeanee Speedway where Dad would take us to buy chips and drink Coke and we would pretend to care about the stockcars.

We were leaving the endless summers of Hawke's Bay for a city where it snowed. I knew that — because they once had to call off club rugby in Dunedin because of it. I had read about it in the *Rugby News* that Dad brought home from the newsagents every week. Did I mention I liked rugby?

It should not have been a surprise that Dad would want to become a minister. He had been a lay preacher for some time, and we were used to trailing around after him to various remote parishes in Hawke's Bay. His grandfather, born in Tasmania to Scottish migrants, had come to New Zealand to be a Presbyterian minister; he died suddenly in the 1950s, but had spent his whole working life with the church. Dad's father, my Poppa, had been involved in every conceivable committee of the Presbyterian Church.

The only reason Dad had not become a minister earlier, he would later tell me, was because his mother Olive (Nana to me) had sat him and his two brothers down when they were in their early teens and instructed them on what they would become. Dad's twin Graham was to be an engineer, and his younger brother Neil was to be a lawyer. Dad was to be an accountant. It was not what he wanted. Becoming a church minister or a teacher would have made him happy. But in the Robertson household what Olive said was what happened.

The church in fact lay at the centre of the lives of both sides of the family. It was the social and spiritual sun around which Mum and Dad orbited. Mum, too, had been brought up in the Presbyterian Church, with her father briefly training to be a minister, and her mother active in the Women's Fellowship and later in the Association of Presbyterian Women. And it was through the church that Mum and Dad first met — at one of the many enormous youth camps held in the 1950s and 1960s. By 1977 they were both serving as elders in the Hastings East parish where we went to church every Sunday.

That was us. Three boys sitting quietly and politely in church. Waiting to be told afterwards how good we had been. That was just about the highlight of my week — the praise after church that we had been good boys. I knew it was important to be a good boy.

Our (and I suspect Dad's) favourite part of the service when he was lay preacher was the children's talk. All the children were brought up the front of the church shortly before being dispatched to Sunday school. Dad had a rotation of talks, all of which seemed to revolve around food. One involved him making two batches of pikelets, one beautiful and golden, the other misshapen and slightly burned. He would ask the children which one they wanted. The other kids would instantly go for the attractive-looking ones, but the Robertson boys were in on the trick and took the less appealing pikelets, safe in the knowledge that they had sugar in them while the others had salt. An important moral lesson in not judging a book by its cover, but most likely a good excuse to make and eat pikelets.

The decision to leave such a settled life seems odd, but moving around had been part of both our parents' upbringing.

Mum is the eldest of four. Her father Bob Wilkie was training to be a Baptist minister when Mum was born in Oxford in rural Canterbury. He fell out with the Baptist Church and switched to being an extramural student for the Presbyterian Ministry, based in Knapdale in Southland. This was a financial stretch, and so, having nearly completed a BA degree, he became a teacher in Gore. Postings followed in Northland and eventually in the Hutt Valley. All the while, her mother Muriel was a dedicated parent who in later years worked as a boarding school matron and in various other roles.

The Wilkies were all around us growing up — Mum was close to her aunts and her cousins from that side. Muriel's family were not a presence, and we later found out she had been adopted. Our grandmother, conscious of status and shame in equal measure, would never discuss it.

On her father's side, Mum had similar Scottish roots to Dad, the Wilkies and the Stewarts all finding their way here in the mid-to-late 1800s. Even then there were politicians in the family — on the Stewart side at least. William Downie Stewart, who was Finance Minister in the Reform governments of Coates/Forbes, is a great-great-uncle.

Poppa Bob carried on the Stewart political tradition as the Labour candidate for the Wairarapa in the 1954 and 1957 elections. His pitch was an amalgam of traditional Labour values — family, community and equality. I quoted from his 1957 campaign material in my maiden speech in Parliament in 2008:

> *I believe it is the responsibility of all in prosperity to care for those in adversity; that the welfare of the nation in the future depends on the children of today, and every assistance financial and otherwise should be given to those who have undertaken the responsibilities of parenthood.*

He ran close the second time but missed out, and the call of a young family meant his ambitions were put to one side. It's worth noting that Bob stayed involved in politics his whole life. He fell out with the Labour Party, as many did in the Rogernomics years, and served in branch leadership roles for the National Party in Auckland and Blenheim. We had some decent debates in his later years, finding much more in common than either of us imagined, and it meant a lot that Bob was able to be in Parliament for my maiden speech.

Dad's father Murray was a Customs officer for his whole working life. He married Olive Gascoigne in Blenheim, but the family moved often — to Whanganui, Auckland, Timaru and eventually Upper Hutt. His greatest moment, captured by the global press, was being the first person to welcome The Beatles to New Zealand in 1964 thanks to his role as the officer who sprayed the aeroplane (yes, they used to do that) that brought them here. He features in several iconic images of the Fab Four wearing massive plastic tiki. Murray could not resist an opportunity to show off the pictures and accepted the title 'The Fifth Beatle' from his workmates with pride.

There is some evidence of political activity on this side of the family — Olive's father served on the Blenheim Borough Council. Olive also had the habit of listening to Parliament most days — though exactly what she made of it was anyone's guess, as she kept her politics very much to herself.

With the benefit of hindsight, my parents Doug and Yvonne were probably not the best of matches. Don't get me wrong, I am very grateful that they did get together and for the life they built and gave my brothers and me. But both of them married at least in part to fulfil the wishes of their respective strong-willed mothers.

Dad told me in his later years of a young Catholic woman he had met and been very attracted to. This relationship was nipped in the bud, and an active search for a 'good Presbyterian girl' was undertaken with some urgency. For her part, Mum had a difficult end to her high school years, with her parents separating and her great dislike of authority clashing with the culture of Queen Margaret College in Wellington. Her mother, too, wanted her to find stability in the form of a church boy. In the early 1960s Mum would not conceive of going against her mother's wishes.

The Presbyterian Bible Class Easter camps of the early 1960s acted as an extended courting session for them, and on 10 October 1964

Doug and Yvonne were married at Knox Church in Lower Hutt. They settled into life in the Hutt Valley. Stephen came along in 1968, and by the time Craig arrived in 1969 and I arrived in 1971, the family was in Palmerston North, with Doug, as his mother instructed him, having become an accountant and working for a bank. A transfer to the Eastern & Central Savings Bank saw the move to Hastings — welcomed by all, given it was home ground for the Wilkies and the Robertsons.

But by the late '70s the ministry was calling, and the family duly moved south at the beginning of 1978.

We settled on the hill in St Clair in a home rented from a church minister. Apparently, we went to pick up the keys from another man Mum and Dad knew from Bible Class days — Robin Bain. The house had glorious views of St Clair beach and the Forbury Park trotting track. In the early days we stayed up way past our usual bedtime as the long southern days fooled my parents as to what the time was.

The tight unit that was our family re-created itself, with Dad off to study, Mum looking after us, and the three boys trooping down the hill each day to school.

But Dad's time as a student and his dream to follow in his grandfather's footsteps came to a crashing end. The story I was told was that Dad found the academic side of the programme tough. He struggled so much that he gave it away in his second year of study and turned back to accountancy, first for Fletchers and then for an established law firm. The truth is a bit more complicated, but that was only to emerge for me a decade or so later.

Dad dropping out of training college changed our course as a family. Rather than continuing the nomadic lifestyle that my parents had grown up with and heading off somewhere in New Zealand to be a 'manse family', we started to settle into living in Dunedin.

We moved down to Pretoria Avenue 'on the flat' and South Dunedin with its working-class roots, close-knit community and narrow streets was our home. It felt easy to make friends — first at church, then at school. We all lived within a stone's throw of each other, spending our after-school time in and out of each other's homes. But the Robertson boys had to be back by 5pm — no exceptions. I would get nervous as the hour drew near and sprint home to make sure I made it on time.

Summer and some school holidays we would go camping or drive to our aunt and uncle's farm in rural Marlborough. The huge family tent — green, brown and orange stripes — was always a struggle to put up, and it did not like the rain. One summer in Te Anau it rained the whole time. 'Don't touch the sides!' Dad shouted at us as the tent began to leak. In the middle of the night I woke to find him outside in his undies fruitlessly trying to dig a trench around the tent. The rain still came in. 'I told you boys not to touch the sides,' Dad roared. We went home early from that holiday.

In the early 1980s Mum began to set about her own path. She wanted more economic independence and enrolled in Teachers College. It was for her a massive turning point. In addition to gaining a career, she had the opportunity to do papers at university. Her lifelong love of history had an outlet. Mum had left school after an unsuccessful crack at School Certificate. There is not much doubt that she was clever enough to have passed, but the strictures of Queen Margaret College clashed badly with her strong will and hatred of airs and graces.

Mum qualified as a teacher — and in fact taught at my intermediate school as well as a number of others around Dunedin. But it was her university study that she really loved. And through that her circle of friends grew and her strong opinions, never far from the surface, became even more strident.

It was from Mum that I got my first lessons in politics. Her upbringing had left her with strong egalitarian views, and she regarded the social justice work of the church as its main attraction.

She had a particular distaste for people showing off wealth. Whenever an advertisement for expensive carpet came on TV, Mum would shout 'Class distinction!' at the screen. As a youngster I took this in. One day we were visiting friends when the door opened to reveal what looked to me like very expensive carpet. I pointed and yelled '*Class distinction*!', much to the embarrassment of my mother and amusement of her friends.

In 1981 when the Springbok tour came to town, Mum and Dad's differences were to the fore. Dad, a rugby referee, was all for it, and went to the game in Dunedin. Mum, a student at the time, went on the protest. It was not quite civil war in our house, but the different trajectories of our parents were obvious.

Mum and Dad argued constantly. My bedroom in later years was next to theirs. I would lie in bed and score their arguments. Mum was louder and easier to hear, but Dad would give as good as he got. It was usually a draw. I don't know if I worried that they might break up — but I knew I did not like it.

But whatever they were saying to each other, Mum and Dad showered us kids with love. Admittedly, Dad was somewhat more distant, always busy at work or with something else on. We sought out time with him. We would tail along with him to rugby games and then afterwards to the Rugby Referees rooms. Dad did not really drink, so they would not be long nights or give us much insight into who he was around others, though I do recall being shocked when I first heard him swear to one of his fellow referees. Some nights he and I would wander down to Forbury Park for the night trots. I loved it. The lights, the sights and sounds felt exotic. Dad would bet a dollar each way on horses 7 and 9. I think this was an act of rebellion in some way for him, straining away at his Presbyterian roots.

In late 1979 he came off his motorscooter on the way to work and injured his back. This caused him a great deal of pain, and he was grumpy a lot of the time. He also seemed to always be at work. At various times he would take us with him to help with a task or see what he was doing, but his dedication to his work, as well as his many clubs, church and other activities, meant he felt a step removed.

Mum on the other hand was more emotionally engaged with us. She loved teasing people — to the point that some of our friends would end up in tears, not quite getting the joke. But she was full of love and concern. She was very keen not to be too strict, as her mother had been with her. She had a saying that children are lent to you, and that your job is to do your best to raise them before handing them back to the world.

She instilled in us early three important attributes. To treat others as we wished to be treated, to know that we are our brother's/sister's keeper and that we should work hard to achieve our goals.

She gave us responsibility early on. When we each turned 13 she gave us the universal Family Benefit money so that we could buy our own clothes. She would take responsibility for socks and undies, but anything else was up to us. I think I bought more lollies than clothes, but it was a good education in how to make money stretch.

She also had an innate love of learning that was instilled in all three of us.

I was a relatively shy boy until I hit puberty. School reports from the end of my time at St Clair primary school praise my ability but suggest I need to contribute more in class. Be careful what you wish for!

By intermediate I was coming out of my shell somewhat, and in Form Two I had Harry Kerr as my teacher. Harry was an institution at Macandrew Intermediate. He was the kind of teacher you dream about having — fun, clever and intuitive. In my year he had become a father at the age of 49. Our class celebrated that event for about a week and did no schoolwork as Harry nursed a hangover and sleep deprivation. He was not a huge fan of rules. He would send students most days to trek across Bathgate Park to the shops near the Hillside

Workshops to buy his lunch. He let us organise our own school camp, with somewhat disastrous consequences when we ran out of food on the last day and one boy shot another in the foot with an arrow, requiring a trip to the doctor. But, it was brilliant fun.

Harry was also responsible for the library. In reality, this meant finding students each year who could run it for him. My friend Linden and I were among those lucky students. We spent days in there. Harry was not bothered that we missed classes. He could see how much we loved it. That year, too, I started writing stories. I was very influenced by a children's author named Alan Garner, who wrote a kind of sci-fi/fantasy genre. One night the phone rang at home and it was Harry. He had read a story I had contributed for an assignment. He was calling at 7.30 at night to tell me it was 'shit hot'. It's hard not to be inspired by someone like that.

Harry encouraged me to do public speaking. I was incredibly nervous. I can remember standing in the Science Room at Macandrew to speak in the school speech contest. I had written a speech with some jokes in it that I had tried out on Mum. She had laughed, but I was not so sure about this audience of fellow students and teachers. When I got up to talk, my terror disappeared and I found my voice. I made people laugh, and they seemed to listen. I never looked back on that account.

School provided plenty of opportunities to get involved in sport too. It has always been an important part of my life. My earliest memory and concrete evidence of this is a scrapbook we made of the 1977 British Lions tour of New Zealand. It's not exactly historically accurate with its pasted-in photos of random rugby games claiming to be from the tour. But the intent is definitely there. My parents told me that one of their party tricks when I was four or five was to get people to ask me to name the All Blacks, what province they played for and, bizarrely, what their job was. (This was the amateur era after all.) Before I was 10 I constructed a mini scorer's and commentator's box in our back shed at Pretoria Avenue. I listened to *Sports Roundup*, scored the cricket games and at the lunch break headed out to re-create them, complete with running commentary.

Over the next couple of years I played both rugby and cricket — and showed a little promise in the latter. At age 11 I went off to a trial of sorts for a Dunedin Metropolitan team and played out a long session in the nets under the watchful eye of Billy Ibadulla, a legend of cricket in Dunedin. At the end of my session, he complimented me on my defensive technique but noted that I might be a bit limited by the fact that I did not seem to know how to play any attacking shots. Higher honours were not to be.

Around this time, in fact, I reached my sporting peak. Through watching my brother Craig, I knew that our school, Macandrew Intermediate, provided ballboys for the club, representative and international rugby games at Carisbrook, just a stone's throw from the school. In my Form One class was a bright, sporty and cheeky lad named Tony Ballantyne (later to be Deputy Vice-Chancellor of Otago University). We hit it off, and became fast and firm friends, whiling away hours and days at the cricket nets or just talking about sport. Tony and I determined to approach the teacher in charge of rugby to ask if we might become ballboys that year, and cornered him one day after rugby practice. He seemed relieved that someone was interested, but we sensed we probably needed to find some Form Two boys who would like to do the job too. Enter some of Tony's fellow Zingari Richmond clubmates, and we had the job.

That year the British Lions were touring again, and the third test was scheduled for Dunedin in early July. After serving our apprenticeships on the sidelines of many club and Otago games, Tony and I were told we were to be ballboys for the game. It was the big time. We were presented with Adidas tracksuits at the school assembly. Our names appeared in the match-day programme. We were even given our own dressing room under the main stand.

On the day itself, we were extraordinarily excited — so excited that a polar blast hitting Dunedin was no deterrent. It was freezing. Some of the players wore mittens. We were issued with giant oilskin parkas that got heavier and heavier in the wet. By halftime I resembled a drenched, rotund, bespectacled Ewok.

But I didn't care, it was a great day. The All Blacks won, Stu Wilson scored a try to become the then record test try scorer for New Zealand and we got a scalding hot pie after the game.

In Form Three I joined my brothers at King's High School, which (with its sister school Queen's) served the South Dunedin community. It had been through a few ups and downs. The roll had dropped dramatically in the years just before my eldest brother Stephen arrived. But a new Rector, Ian Simpson, began to turn the reputation of the school around. By the time I got there in 1985 the roll was growing, and my class had pupils from all over Dunedin, including from the Otago Peninsula and out at Fairfield.

It still had its rough edges. We jokingly referred to the school as the Bay View Road Academy for Young Gentlemen. It was anything but. The bogans, the surfies and the tough South Dunedin lads were a potent cocktail. But my brothers and I thrived.

The three of us did well academically and were heavily involved with sport, debating and other cultural activities, including seeking the non-singing parts in musicals. The Robertson boys looked the same, and we all got called 'Robbie' or a variant thereof by staff and students alike.

In my Third Form year my brother Stephen was Dux of the school. He was, and is, the brightest of us. Our Classics teacher, Bryan Frost, stole Stephen's notes at the end of Seventh Form and was still teaching from them when I got there five years later. Mum, whose innate self-deprecation meant she had not really worked out just how bright Stephen was, tells the story of being invited to the school prizegiving in Stephen's Fifth Form year and being blown away as he won a succession of awards.

Craig, too, was bright and right near the top of his year. He was also very social. He ended up getting on the Dunedin Junior Council, an initiative from the City Council to engage more with young people. Through this Craig found an outlet for his love of music.

Despite Mum being a great piano and guitar player, none of her children had inherited the musical performance gene, though Stephen did get as far as playing the saxophone for a while. But we all loved listening to music. In the early 1980s Mum joined the family up to the World Record Club. This was like a pre-internet version of Spotify. You had to order a certain number of records a year, and each of us was allowed to choose some. My early efforts are embarrassing (I think there was a Chicago album in there, featuring 'Hard to Say I'm Sorry'), but it was a great way to discover what we liked.

Craig had shown his interests early, even at the age of 12 getting Mum and Dad to let him go to see Split Enz at the Town Hall — on his own. He started to listen to the bands of the so-called Dunedin Sound, the likes of The Clean, The Chills, Sneaky Feelings, The Verlaines and Straitjacket Fits. Somehow, he managed to convince the Dunedin City Council to let him organise 'dances' at the Town Hall with these bands as entertainment. When I went along to one of them and saw The Chills, the music and the energy were like nothing I had ever experienced before — I loved it. Craig kept pursuing this interest and made friends with an eclectic group of people. One day I came home to find The Dance Exponents in the living room as they prepared for one of the Junior Council shows.

For my part I battled away to try to match my brothers. I found the arts subjects to my liking. History, social studies, English — I loved them all. I kept writing stories and worked on the school magazine.

My friends were mostly on the geekier side of the line, but I played cricket, rugby, squash, volleyball and basketball, essentially joining in with whatever was going on. Following on from my early speech-making, I also got into debating. In the Fifth Form I was in the senior team and we did pretty well in the local competitions. My mother was teaching at an intermediate school and took her class along to watch us debate against a Logan Park High School team. She told me later that she was amazed to see me in my element, speaking with a confidence she didn't know I had.

By this point my brothers and I had managed mostly to get ourselves out of church activities. As teenagers we all still attended the church youth group, but as time went on it offered more of an insight into social rather than religious matters. But we were still good boys, doing as our mother told us, working hard and looking out for people.

It was a middle-class, middle New Zealand life. But I was harbouring a secret — one that as my Sixth Form year arrived would nearly cost me my life.

2.
GIN AND INDULGENCE

During my Fifth, Sixth and Seventh Form years I kept a diary. Reading it back as an adult is a humiliating experience. The level of self-indulgence and grandiose self-importance is appalling.

The diary has each day rated out of 10 and descriptions of what happened. There was never a 10. The odd 8 or 9 was reserved for an epic party or a good exam result at school. Mostly I find myself in the 5s and 6s — digging deeply into my worries about my friends, what they thought of me, what I could see was upsetting them.

They also show that the scared boy in Hastings was a teenager still frightened of so many things. The biggest fear of them all was something that, as I began writing the diaries, I knew but no one else did. I am gay.

I don't particularly recall a moment when I knew I was gay. From my early teens I do remember being much more interested in boys than girls. Hilariously, I initially assumed that this must be how it was for everyone and that soon enough I would like girls the way most of my friends did. But by my Fourth Form year the word 'gay' was one I understood, and I was pretty sure that was what I was. I was also very sure that it was not something I should be telling people.

One of the reasons for this was the widespread public debate about the Homosexual Law Reform Bill. Introduced by Labour MP Fran Wilde in 1985, it divided New Zealand. The campaign against the legislation was as vile as it was vigorous. Opponents pitched it as a battle for the moral soul of the country.

Unsurprisingly it was a topic for discussion in church circles. I remember going to a church youth group raft-building competition with churches from across Dunedin. Amid the bad Hawaiian shirts and less than buoyant structures, the anti-decriminalisation petition was circulated. It led to a blistering argument at home. Mum was outraged, but Dad seemed to think a church event was a more than appropriate place for such a petition, although he did not sign it.

When the Bill passed, I must have cut out of the newspaper the names of who voted for and who voted against it, because years later I found the clipping in a box in my room. Something told me that this legislation mattered, and that maybe it was okay to be gay.

Still, I was committed to keeping it all to myself. As I entered Fifth Form, I tried for 'normality'. I went with friends to a ball at one of the all-girls schools. My partner for the evening was a nice young woman from the boarding part of the school, and we got on well. We started seeing each other every Sunday for a few months. There might even have been a kiss. But it did nothing to change the tune playing in my head.

That same year I became part of a new, less geeky circle of friends. My interest in listening to music that had been tweaked by the Dunedin bands saw me hanging out with people who were buying records and starting bands. My friends Alex, Graeme, Grant and John formed a band called Reference to England — a name drawn from Grant's obsession with The Beatles. I would go along to their practices and thought they sounded great. My obvious lack of musical ability meant I was never going to join them, but I wanted to be useful, so I appointed myself as their manager.

I had no idea what a manager actually did, but I carried some gear around, and one night I had to negotiate with the Sea Scouts over getting paid for a gig which ended in disarray when the audience began demanding to hear the 'Birdy Dance' rather than the diet of Beatles, Talking Heads and Mockers covers. And through my brother

Craig I helped get them a gig at a police-run Blue Light Disco at the Town Hall, a staple of 1980s police outreach. It felt grown up and special to be up the front, dressed in what was now my signature outfit of an op-shop trench coat, ripped jeans and poorly chosen sweater.

I also discovered alcohol and parties. I was useful to my friends in this respect. At 15 I looked pretty much the same as I do now, which meant lax bottle-store owners didn't bat an eyelid when I came in with an order that was clearly more than I was going to be able to drink on my own. I recall when a big group of us were in Wānaka for New Year's Eve in 1987 I ordered $130 worth of alcohol (roughly $325 today), and was not even asked for ID. We stayed in the camping ground feeling very adult and drinking in the sun until the money or our capacity to absorb the drink ran out.

I loved being part of a group like this — and my diary records all the machinations of our relationships, spats, tiffs, escapades and more. My intense analysis of it all suggests just how much it meant to me to be connected to people in this way.

As 1988 arrived, my intensity was spilling over into something more like an obsession. The diary records that I was starting to field questions about whether I was gay. Initially, of course, I denied it to almost everyone. Eventually I did confide in a couple of friends and, intentionally or not, the news spread. One day I opened my school bag to find a workbook had been filled in by someone with suggestions about who I wanted to 'root' and marking out various days as 'gay days'.

I tried to ignore this and carried on with hanging out with my friends. But there was tension in our group, and this only fuelled my obsessions and anxieties. My diary records that I was warned by friends to stop making everything about me, but I could not see it.

One April Saturday, word spread after my team's rugby game that there was to be a party at the home of one of our circle of friends who was also in the team. I expected I would get a call from someone about going. In the days before cellphones this was how it was done. But nothing happened. I stayed at home stewing, and began ringing around. It was hard to get hold of anyone, but at last I talked to the younger brother of one friend who innocently confirmed that the party was on.

I set out to walk the 45 minutes or so to the party. But first I went to the bottle store at the Waterloo Hotel at the end of Hillside Road and bought a 750ml bottle of Gordon's gin. The owner, who had been serving me for more than a year by this stage, barely even looked at me as he handed over the bottle.

I am not sure if my plan had been to drink the whole bottle as I walked to the party. I suspect I was just getting enough inside of me to get up the courage to go. However, I do remember that after a few awkward sips I began taking huge mouthfuls as I walked up to Concord. At one stage I had a lie-down on a grass verge. A person came out of a nearby house and asked if I was all right. I carried on to the address and took my final swig just as I reached the steps down to the house. All 750 millilitres gone in 45 minutes.

I could hear the music from the party. I stumbled down and discovered on the mat outside the house a note in handwriting I recognised: 'NO POOFTERS'. I collapsed on top of the note. My next memory is of being carried into the house. I was ranting and raving about how one of my friends 'needed me' and no one else. I was put into a bed, but that did not last long. I was up again shortly thereafter and this time my ranting was replaced by projectile vomiting. The party-goers soon realised they were not up to handling this and called my parents.

I have no memory of this — but my diary recalls that Mum and Dad did eventually arrive to pick me up. Apparently all the while I was alternating between giving everyone a piece of my mind and vomiting.

When I got home Mum rang the hospital to ask what she should do with her son. For someone who rarely, if ever, drank, I must have been a frightening sight. The hospital advised that if I had consumed any more than a hip flask then I should have my stomach pumped. Somehow Mum had gained the impression that I had indeed drunk just a hip flask. She settled on propping me up in the bath and sitting with me as the vomiting continued.

Again, I remember none of this. My first memory is of waking up in my brother's old bedroom, trying to work out why I was there. Just how sick I had been, and how close I had come to something much worse, only dawned on me over the following few days. I could have ended up anywhere, choking on the vomit I could not control.

Looking back, I was like a lot of young LGBT people. I was depressed and using alcohol — for others it is drugs — as a form of escape. I had been getting drunk most Fridays and Saturdays since my Fifth Form year. There had been other nights when, but for a bit of luck, I might have hurt myself badly. My relationship with alcohol would continue to be destructive for several years until I became truly comfortable with who I am.

I stayed home from school for a few days, apologised to the party host and learned courtesy of my now sister-in-law Delwyn that fish and chips (or at least salt and fat in some form) are the best hangover cure. And I put my head down with schoolwork and migrated to a different group of friends — for the time being.

Sadly, I also decided to put my sexuality into a box. I confided in a few people over that year, and through a friend met my first actual gay person. I even went to a couple of gay parties. But for public purposes I was careful.

The year ended with most of my old friendships repaired, and as the Seventh Form year dawned I was elected head boy of King's High School. I even had a girlfriend for a spell. It was a year full of fun and achievements, and at the end of it I was awarded runner-up to the Dux. The prize was $75 cash. I promptly went out and bought a

50-litre keg, and we had a raucous party at our friend Ryan's house on the hill in St Clair to celebrate the end of school and exams.

In the early hours of the morning, several of us were headed back down the hill to get home to my place in time to watch the All Blacks play a test in the UK. We got to Jacobs Ladder — the same long concrete stairway that my brothers and I used to walk down to school each day when we first moved to Dunedin. My friend Nick was doing an impression of Uncle Arthur from the Australian TV comedy series *The Comedy Company*. He was moving pretty fast and started to lose control, so veered off on to a grass strip — but there was a tree ahead. He went back onto the steps, tripped, and began somersaulting down.

I can still see him mid-flight as he went past one of the lights on the stairs. And I can hear the thud as he hit the ground. We sprinted down to find him conscious, bleeding from his head and leg, and complaining about his ribs. One of our group, Morvan, lived nearby and rushed home to get her car, which we figured would be quicker than an ambulance. We bound up Nick's wounds and bundled him into the car.

He was not looking good when we arrived at the hospital and was quickly rushed into surgery. He had smashed his kidney, and his complaint about his ribs was serious internal bleeding. He had also broken his leg. The doctor came out and asked me to sign a form allowing them to operate. I called Nick's mum and told her the news. We sat in the waiting room for hours, hoping to hear that he was okay. The news finally came through — and my friend Aaron and I went home to my place at about 5am exhausted and upset.

Experiences like this drew us closer together as friends. The importance of friendship is something I think about often. Many of my friends today are those same people I grew up with, fell out with, made up with in those years. Through all the ups and downs of our teenage escapades, I found my people.

Politics was starting to feature as an interest too. From about the age of 12 I had followed politics closely, and I was especially delighted to see and hear David Lange. It was a no-brainer that I was going to be drawn in by a big guy with glasses who made people laugh. I now fancied myself a debater and marvelled at his oratory at the Oxford Union in 1985. He was a hero, though I came to realise soon enough that such worship would be challenged.

My own 'political' journey began in my time on the School Council during most of my years at King's. And as head boy I led a campaign on the most serious of political issues — to get a common room for senior students. I was interested enough in the outside world to join Greenpeace, mostly thanks to the nuclear-free issue. I was also selected to be a part of a Youth Parliament in Wellington in 1989. Sadly, fog at Dunedin Airport curtailed our participation. History records that my question to the ministers was asked on my behalf. 'Why are all votes in Parliament not conscience votes?' seems on reflection equal parts naïve and valid. When at last we got the chance to go to Wellington and visit Parliament, it was 8 August 1989. I know this because it was the day David Lange resigned. That explained why everyone was just a little distracted.

Also in 1989 I went on my first protest. Two students from the Otago University Students' Association (OUSA) came to King's to tell us about the government's plan to introduce user pays into tertiary education. The Labour government, via Minister of Education Phil Goff, was proposing to introduce up-front fees for tertiary students for the first time.

In July a group of us were given permission to join a march through the main street of Dunedin against tertiary fees. Thus, my first protest chant was a three-word slogan ending in 'off Goff'.

I came to greatly admire Phil as a politician and public servant in later years, but I knew then the damage that was being done by the policies of the Fourth Labour Government. Dunedin was reeling from the loss of manufacturing jobs. The closure of the local freezing works had seen the parents of a number of classmates forced on the dole. Whatever changes were required in the New Zealand economy — and no doubt they were needed after the quasi dictatorship of Rob Muldoon — they went too far and too fast for our community.

We lost the battle on fees — and 1990, my first year at university, saw a 1000% increase in the cost of going to university. This curtailed the ambitions of some people from my part of town. There was no loan scheme, and taking on other forms of debt was out of the question.

In the end, when I voted in a general election for the first time in 1990, I did vote for the local Labour candidate Clive Matthewson, because I had met him on the Youth Parliament trip the year before and liked him, but it was with no passion.

What the Fourth Labour Government had done, and the incoming neoliberal Bolger/Richardson government that followed would do, was turn my interest in politics into activism.

At university I enrolled to do a Law degree and chose other subjects on the basis that I had never done them before: Legal Systems, Russian, Philosophy and Political Studies. The first club I signed up with was the organisation dedicated to fighting fees, the Education Action Group (EAG). From there, the next few decades of my life were set in motion.

I felt at home at the University of Otago from the moment I arrived. I knew a fair bit about the place from my brothers and my mother. I knew the names of lecturers, had heard the stories of Orientation gigs and had even studied a bit in the university library preparing for exams in Seventh Form.

I threw myself straight into it, including a 10-night Orientation programme built around the Flying Nun bands. I could not have scripted it better myself. I went to gigs every night. By the end, I had developed a twitch, so I went to Student Health. The doctor asked me how much of Orientation I had been to. When I told her, she sent me away with an instruction to get some sleep and ease up on the drinking for a bit.

A friend from Queen's High School, Susan Brook, asked me one day if I would be interested in being part of her team for the weekly quiz run by OUSA. I was keen. Susan and I had been in the TV show *It's Academic* which pitted high school students against each other. The King's team had beaten our arch-rivals from Otago Boys' High in our heat, and were feeling full of ourselves until Susan and her Queen's team put us in our place in the semi-final. Any quiz team she was in would be worth being a part of. I was even more enthusiastic when she told me that her friend Andrew Geddis would be in the team as well. I knew who Andrew was, as he had been the deputy head boy at Otago Boys'. He was very smart.

On the night of the first quiz I arrived early to find Andrew was the only team member there. We nervously said hello. Eventually Andrew told me that he was celebrating that night, because he had been awarded the Lissie Rathbone Scholarship for the Otago student who had received top combined marks in the Bursary History and English exams. He told me what his marks were. As others arrived and he shared the news with them, I sat and wrote down Andrew's marks, then mine, and added them up. They were exactly the same total. I stewed over this for a while, wondering how Andrew had won the prize and I had not. Still, a good night was had and I think our team — geekily named the Spiro Agnew Support Society — came second, surprising some of the older teams.

I headed home to Brockville, where Mum and Dad had moved earlier that year, to find a large envelope on my bed. Inside was a letter informing me that I, too, had been awarded the Lissie Rathbone Scholarship. Andrew and I had shared it — and so began a competitive friendship that has never gone away. Andrew is of course much more clever than me and is a Professor of Law who these days can easily beat me in any argument.

University life agreed with me, even if I was still struggling with my sexuality and drinking a lot. I made new friends, stayed in touch with old ones and loved my studies. It was a good and relatively comfortable life. But a devastating twist lay just around the corner.

3.

A WORLD TURNED UPSIDE DOWN

At the end of my first year at university, I left home for a flat on Castle Street: 620C to be precise, the upstairs of two weatherboard flats built down a driveway. It was, at best, utilitarian. There was nothing to speak of in terms of insulation. Creeping black mould rose up the walls in the living room and kitchen. Each of the five bedrooms had a built-in divan bed in some state of repair. We became intimately familiar with the downstairs neighbours as the absence of any kind of soundproofing became clear.

My friend Nathan had identified the flat, but when the time came to move in he was nowhere to be seen, having also sensibly identified the shortcomings. That left me, Andrew and Justine (also from the quiz team), and we recruited two others, Teresa and Sarah, from the university noticeboards.

I was happy to be away from home. There was an underlying tension between Mum and Dad. They went about their largely independent lives, only occasionally intersecting at home, and I'd been spending most of my time elsewhere, at university, or out and about at the pub or seeing bands. I had settled into life as a second year having decided that Law School was not for me. I was doing the Political Studies Honours programme, was active in the EAG and had started volunteering at Radio One, editing the news for the breakfast shows — which consisted of reading out sections of the *Otago Daily Times* (*ODT*) on air. I made an unsuccessful run at being elected to the

OUSA Executive for the following year. Six candidates were to be elected to the general executive positions; I came seventh and was a bit gutted at missing out. Looking back, the picture I chose for my poster (me holding a wine glass while wearing a suit — I think from the Arts Ball that year) might not have quite been the image I was looking for.

Despite still being partly in the closet, it was proving to be an enjoyable year. I was even getting good marks in all my papers. And then my world fell apart.

One Thursday morning in August my mother rang the flat. That was unusual in itself. Her near-hysterical state was even more so. She said she was coming down to talk to me. My mind was racing. I had already organised to go home for dinner the following Sunday, determined to tell her and Dad that I was gay. I was pretty sure she knew, but the time had come to front up. But even if she'd guessed, she wouldn't be this upset, surely?

I barely recognised the person who arrived at my door. We sat in my room on the uncomfortable bed, surrounded by my clothes strewn about the floor, and she told me that my father had been arrested the previous evening for theft as a servant. At this stage it was for just over $20,000, stolen from the law firm he worked for, but there was already an indication that there might be more charges.

I was dumbstruck. It did not make sense. Nothing made sense. Dad was in a pretty well-paid job, though I had never really asked him what he earned. Earlier in the year the National government had announced they were introducing means testing for student allowances based on parental income, and I'd asked Dad if this meant we would be ineligible. He said we would — but that he would provide me with some extra support on top of what I could borrow from the soon-to-be introduced student loan scheme. The truth was that his salary was below the threshold, but his stealing put his actual income above that. It was a sure sign of his state of mind that he told me we were ineligible.

Dad was desperate to be needed by his family. I had learned a couple of years earlier that he had had an affair about 10 years previously. This was a major factor in why he had left his training to be a minister. Mum had wanted to leave him but did not feel financially independent enough to do so. That was one of the reasons she set about studying to be a teacher. As time wore on, she and Dad reconciled their lives enough to stay together, but it was a fragile peace — and Dad knew it.

What he stole moved him from a modest but reasonable salary to one that provided room for some comfort: the odd holiday, dinner out for birthdays, a full pantry and fridge. There was no sign of obvious wealth. We had two cars — both second hand. There were no flash clothes or watches. But we never went without, and Dad could be relied on to front up for whatever costs we had.

For my mother this situation was even more bewildering. After five years teaching, she had recently returned to university to finish her History degree and was working as a research assistant in the History Department. Further postgraduate study beckoned. She had no idea Dad had been stealing, no understanding of why and what this would mean.

'What are we going to do?' she asked.

Mum was facing a future of next to no money, and of dealing with a husband from whom she had long been distant but who would need to be supported, and children all at university with limited income.

After a bit of time we agreed that I should go and find my brothers on campus to let them know. In those pre-cellphone days, if someone was not at home that was your best bet.

I walked there in a daze. I knew Stephen would spend lunchtimes outside the main cafeteria. Sure enough, he and his wife Delwyn were there. I pulled them aside and shared the news. Further shock and tears ensued. Before long we found ourselves at Craig's flat; his girlfriend Sally was there as well. The five of us sat there trying to figure out what this all meant. At one point someone asked me if I had anyone that I could talk to or who could support me. I fell apart, sobbing that there was no one, and that I felt more alone than ever. I made the call not to say what really lay behind that — there was enough drama for one day.

Eventually we headed up home to Brockville. It was a surreal scene. Dad was in the laundry taking clothes out of the washing machine to transfer to the dryer. It could have been any day at all. I rushed into the room and gave him a hug. He shook with his sobbing but could not say anything. He did not really say much from that moment on, shutting down on what he had actually done.

In the days that followed we faced a dilemma. It was not clear exactly what the next steps would be. We made the decision not to widely share the news until we knew more. But Dunedin is a small town.

My flatmate Andrew had inherited some money and had, on my suggestion, invested it with Dad's law firm. A few days after Mum had broken the news of Dad's arrest to us, he received a letter from the firm, telling him that his money was safe but that they had dismissed Dad after an investigation revealed theft from the business. Andrew left the letter on my bed. I went for a walk with him and told him all that I knew. He, like each and every friend, was amazingly supportive.

When it all added up, Dad pleaded guilty to stealing $120,000 over a period of 10 years. He was adamant that he did not think he was responsible for all of that. But he had no proof, and the law firm said there was no other explanation for the missing money. And what did it matter really? The breach of trust was the same whatever the amount.

As the shock sank in, life had to keep moving on. Stephen had a scholarship to go to Rutgers University in the USA to do his PhD. He and Delwyn left shortly before Dad's sentencing. The scholarship was not enough to live on, and Dad had told them he would be their financial backstop. The next few years, short on money and with only letters and expensive toll calls to keep in touch from so far away, would be very tough for them.

Come late September it was time for sentencing. We were realistic that a prison term was likely. Perhaps six months, we were told, or maybe some kind of community sentence if he was lucky. In the historic surroundings of the Dunedin District Court, Judge Ron Young made clear his distaste for what Dad had done. But when he handed down the sentence it was still a shock — two years in prison.

In that moment I wondered if my father would survive that long. Dunedin Prison (right next door to the court) was a Victorian era relic. Cold, sterile, lacking in almost any outdoor space, it was home to a wide variety of prisoners from murderers to minor drug users. White-collar criminals like Dad were regarded by the other inmates as second only to paedophiles in the order of disgust.

The first phone call we had with Dad the morning after sentencing he sounded almost excited. He was clearly delirious and trying to reassure us that he would be okay. My first visit with Mum (Craig had an exam that day) a few days later laid bare the reality. Going into the prison through a series of vault doors set into cold brick, huge sets of keys jangling in the wardens' hands to open them, each corridor getting ever darker, was frightening. The visiting room was a strange airless hallway. Dad looked terrible and sounded worse. He had already been roughed up and had begun eating his meals standing up with his back to the wall to avoid giving anyone a chance to surprise him. He tried to put a brave face on, but this was going to be a long lag.

Over the next year and a half, much of my life revolved around visiting Dad. I tried to go every week, sometimes twice a week. It was falling more and more to me to see Dad through his sentence. At the end of 1991, Craig left Dunedin to go to journalism school in

Christchurch. Mum was increasingly and understandably starting to distance herself from Dad. Their marriage had been in name only for several years, and his betrayal of her was the final straw. She discussed the timing of divorce with me — but agreed it should wait a little. In his very frequent letters to me and during my visits, Dad would talk about his counselling and some of the things that had led to his offending. But mostly he would talk about Mum, and how he wanted to be a better husband when he got out. It was heartbreaking — but also frustrating. It felt like he was minimising what he had done and simply spending his time plotting his return. My visits sometimes ended in me walking out. But I always went back.

On Saturdays and Sundays I worked in the fruit and veggie department at the New World supermarket in South Dunedin, as I had done since school days. I had inherited one of the family's second-hand cars. My route to work took me past the prison. Dad knew the timing of the trip and would look out the window for me. As he saw the car approach, he would reach his hand through the bars on his second-level window and wave. I would toot the horn — and start to cry.

As time wore on, Dad began to feel more at home in prison. His knowledge of computers saw him employed in the office, rearranging the systems and schedules. He worked in the kitchen, which in turn led to him enrolling in a cooking course at the polytechnic where he would occasionally be able to step out the back of the room and say hi if you, ah, happened to be there.

He also began working with other prisoners. I had been at school with some of them. Dad's pastoral care had him writing letters to girlfriends, filling in forms, drafting parole applications. The more he told me, the more it became clear that prisons were not providing much, if anything, to help rehabilitate the inmates. A lot has changed in the intervening 30-odd years — and a lot has not.

Bill English once said that prisons are a moral and fiscal failure, and he is right. On the fiscal side it costs over $100,000 a year to house a prisoner. But with a recidivism rate of over 35%, and over 50% for those who have already had a conviction, much of that money is wasted. The money could be far better spent keeping people out of prison — investing in education, training and programmes for substance abuse and anger management.

The morality question is more complex. Crimes have been committed, and a punishment is expected. But the critical issue for me is that too many politicians (and the public) think people should be sent to prison *for* punishment rather than *as* a punishment. The loss of freedom and liberty is the punishment. With the exception of a very small number, everyone in prison is going to re-enter society at some point. It would, then, make sense for the whole time spent in prison to be an exercise in rehabilitation. Sadly, that is not the case. In New Zealand rehabilitation mostly means providing some form of alcohol and drug addiction counselling and mental health support. In my time in government we increased resources for these programmes, but more needs to be done. The Alcohol and Other Drug Treatment Courts are a good start. Community sentencing that focuses on the source of the addiction is vital.

Dad did get some counselling, and strong support from the prison visiting programme run through one of the local churches. His counselling drew out a range of issues that he shared with me. Most shocking was the story of sexual abuse in his early teens at the hands of a grocer he worked for in Timaru. He also highlighted some difficulty in his relationship with his mother. It was clear Dad had huge trust and self-esteem issues. Of course, none of this justifies his offending, but his stories started to give me an insight into what had shaped his character.

The other major insight was into the impact of imprisonment on perpetrators' families. Dad's conviction was front-page news in Dunedin. Some of Mum's friendships withered away as people, either judgemental or frightened, backed off. The same applied for Dad. Ian Simpson, the Rector of King's High where Dad had chaired the Board of Trustees, was a frequent visitor, as were some others from the church. In recent years I have been a strong supporter of the charity Pillars, which provides support to the children of prisoners. The isolation and stigma that children and families face is immense, and little thought is given to it by authorities. Pillars is remarkable in what it has achieved and would be a valid candidate for some government support.

For my family, and especially for Mum, it was also hard going financially. She scraped by for several years before getting the role as archivist for the Presbyterian Church, a job she loved and stayed in until her retirement. Her extraordinary resilience during this time still blows my mind. She did as she always had told us to do: she worked hard, and kept looking out for others, especially her children.

Dad's imprisonment meant I was now most definitely eligible for student allowances, but proving this presented a challenge. When I visited the student support staff at Otago they could not believe that my father's income was zero dollars. I was reduced to photocopying the front-page story from the *ODT* to take in as proof.

Dad's spell in prison would finish at the end of 1992. He was released on parole six months ahead of his sentenced time. He had in many ways been a model prisoner — so much so that the prison had issues working out what to do without him, and asked him to come back and work a few hours a week to keep the systems running. He also volunteered with PARS (the Prisoners Aid and Rehabilitation Service).

This apparent successful transition from prison was not, however, the full story. Mum went through with her divorce plans, leaving Dad devastated. Reintegration was tough from a financial and emotional perspective. He stayed in a series of small and cold flats, and found it difficult to get work. Moreover, he struggled to find a network of people to accept him. The church was his comfort zone and provided him the solace he needed. He eventually entered into a relationship with Viv, whom he met through Knox Church. With her help Dad began to address some of the issues that underlay his offending. And, importantly, through her work in health education he got a job as the administrator for a trust that ran programmes in schools.

My relationship with Dad never fully recovered from what had happened. I never stopped loving him of course, but his breach of trust and his frequent regression into self-destructive behaviours (especially in his relationships) would frustrate and upset me.

But there is much I am grateful for, not least that he was fully accepting when he learned I was gay. I had told Mum a few months after Dad went to prison. As I'd suspected, she had, like most mothers, known it in her heart and had been waiting for me to tell her. In keeping with the times, her first words were 'Please don't get AIDS.' I told her I would try to avoid it. There was another dynamic at play here too. In going through with her divorce from Dad, Mum was finally able to accept herself as a lesbian, something she had known deep down for most of her adult life. She would not actually come out to me or my brothers for a couple more years, but when she did it certainly filled in the picture of our parents' relationship.

I decided not to bother Dad with the news that I was gay while he was in prison, and then never quite got round to telling him. One day Viv said to him that folks at work were delighted that I had been elected OUSA president for 1993 because 'having a gay man means they will take safe sex messages seriously'. Not quite how it was meant to happen!

Dad and I spent a lot of time together on my frequent visits to Dunedin over the following years, and when my partner Alf arrived on the scene Dad, with his infinite reservoir of love, made sure he felt very much part of the family. He was the same with Mum and her partner and their son. With Dad, there was so much love to go around. His pride in his family was enormous. He could barely be restrained when I was elected to Parliament in 2008, and beamed throughout my maiden speech. He beamed even more when Alf and I had our civil union in early 2009.

One afternoon in June that year a phone call came through to my Parliament office from Dad's home number. Like Mum's call 18 years earlier, this was unusual. I interrupted the meeting I was having to answer it. The caller was a young policeman who told me that my father had been found dead in his flat an hour or two before. He'd had a massive heart attack at some time in the previous 24 hours.

Again, it fell to me to call my brothers — one now in Sydney, the other in Boston. We were devastated, but there was also some relief. Dad had had a stroke in 2007 following an operation to remove a tumour from his optic nerve. Life had been a struggle from then on.

At his funeral we celebrated the loving father we knew, the man who doted on any children he came into contact with, who served his community and his church. And we acknowledged his flaws, his foibles and problems. 'No more suffering now', I said as I finished my speech.

Dad died at 68. In my fifties, I think often about the kind of man he was. He had a huge heart that he struggled to control. His upbringing had seen him hide away his feelings and take paths that were not his own.

I have taken lessons from both my parents as to how to live my life. When you're a child you do not think of your parents as individuals with feelings and failings. They are ever-present, indestructible forces. But they are, in the end, just people trying to make it through life and do their best by you. As an adult I have appreciated Mum and Dad more and more. They set us up as best they could — and stayed with us through whatever happened. And I could not love them any more than I do.

4.
THE MAKING OF A POLITICIAN

After my unsuccessful tilt at the OUSA Executive, I decided that 1992 would be a year to focus on study. I expanded my BA studies to a double major, adding History, in line with the family tradition, to my Political Studies focus. Andrew and I struck out to find a new flat.

Once again the noticeboards at the university did us a favour. We found 29 Malvern Street, the ground floor of a sprawling old pub. The living area had been the main bar, a huge space with 13-foot ceilings and no obvious heating source. At some point during that year our flat was chosen for a study on heating and insulation. It came as little surprise to us that on several days in winter it was warmer in our fridge than it was in our living room. The place was run down, and so very cold, but we loved it. We were joined by Kendra and Jo, old school friends of mine, but we needed to advertise for one more flatmate.

One January day, not long after we moved in, there was a knock on the door. A lean, good-looking guy, sweating from a run, stood there clutching the ad we'd put up at the university. His name was Terence. He was from Invercargill. He loved music and seemed like good fun, and after a brief interview with Jo and I we agreed he could move in.

We quickly discovered lots of mutual connections, and the flat became a hub for parties and gatherings, including my 21st later in the year when we had a couple of bands play, including Dunedin music stalwarts The Puddle. They were fronted by the vastly talented and somewhat chaotic personality that was George Henderson.

On the day of my 21st I went to pick up the PA for the band and came home to find George operating the stove, using every available pot to boil up some plants he had found in the garden for a 'tonic'. The party itself was such a raucous affair it was visible and audible from the Northern Motorway. It certainly caught the attention of the local branch of White Power, who rode their bikes to see what was happening. Their presence caused quite a stir. George offered to stop playing in the hope that they would leave. My flatmate Kendra was particularly aggrieved by their presence. She stormed up to me and uttered a phrase I never thought I would hear: 'White Power ate my tangelos.' Eventually they got bored and left. George and The Puddle played an incredible 25-minute version of their song 'Too Hot to Be Cool' and the night ended about 5am when I finally convinced the band to go by offering to drive them home.

While the year had begun with my political aspirations on the back burner, fate intervened. At the start of the first semester, one of the people elected to the OUSA Executive got a scholarship to the USA and resigned before they could start their term. A by-election was held. I threw my name in, but decided against campaigning, relying on the previous year's recognition to get me through. I was a bit surprised when I got the news that I had won, and became the Information and Publicity Officer. This was, in reality, a fancy name for the person who organised speakers to come to campus and generally tried to drum up interest in the affairs of the Association.

I was somewhat thrown in at the deep end. It had been decided the year before that, in the interests of providing balance, representatives from the Israeli government would be invited to give a lunchtime address after representatives of the Palestinian community had been given a similar slot. The Israeli Ambassador took up the invitation, and it was agreed I would pick him up from his motel and take him down to the campus.

I arrived at the motel and made my way to the Ambassador's unit. The door was ajar, and as I pushed it open I caught a glimpse of him in the bathroom mirror, putting what looked to me like a pistol in a holster inside his jacket. This was not in the job description.

I greeted him nervously, we got into my car and I drove him to the university. The Palestinian Human Rights Group, a strong presence on campus, had positioned themselves right in front of the stage in the main common room. As I entered the hall, I tried to engage with my fellow Executive members. I exaggeratedly mouthed, 'He's got a gun' at Kirsty Graham, the OUSA president. She looked at me blankly.

On stage I was beside myself. I introduced the Ambassador and sat awkwardly, scanning the audience for anyone who might understand the potential disaster that could unfold. When he finished his talk, I briefly considered ending the whole event then and there but reasoned that would cause more trouble than it solved. I invited questions.

Up shot the hand of Matt Farry, a leader of the Palestinian Human Rights Group and a man who had once broken my nose in a schoolboy rugby game. He meant business. He marched up to get as close as possible to the Ambassador. I would like to say that I courageously stood between them, but the truth is I stepped so far back I nearly fell off the stage. Fortunately, Matt made his contribution briefly and stepped back. The Ambassador relaxed his pose, answered a few more questions and then finished. We hustled him out the door, and it was with great relief I agreed to his suggestion that he could walk back to his motel.

The other forums I organised throughout the year were less eventful, but I really enjoyed getting speakers down and being a part of the debate. On top of this, I was still active in the EAG. This was the first proper year of the Student Loan Scheme, which had been put in place by the National government to allow students to borrow for fees and for living and course costs. It had an interest rate initially struck at 8%. To make matters worse, borrowers were charged interest from the moment they drew down the loan, even though they clearly had no way of paying it back. National had not only broken their promise to get rid of fees, which they now passed to institutions to set, but had also limited students' access to allowances, which meant most were now having to borrow from the scheme.

Needless to say, we protested these changes hard. We marched in the main street, followed around any government politician we could find and generally tried to keep the issue alive. A particular target was anyone to do with the National Party. In fact, it was an incident involving a National minister in 1991 that helped galvanise my interest in getting onto the OUSA Executive. That year Bill Birch, who was Minister of Labour, had come to town and held a forum at the university about the upcoming Employment Contracts Act. Those of us who worked at the supermarket knew all about the Act. Our boss had already told us that he was going to put us all on individual contracts and get rid of our penal rates for weekend work. I heckled the Minister with my colleagues and, when his forum ended abruptly, followed him out to his car. The crowd were really riled up by this point, and several people surrounded the car. Felix Geiringer, who was one of the protest leaders, lay down in front of it. I was a couple of steps back when I heard the car engine rev and realised the driver was about to move forward. I rushed forward to put my hands on the bonnet, but the driver carried on so that the car's front tyres were up against Felix. It was frightening. People remonstrated with the driver and the Minister. After a few seconds Felix emerged from under the car and it took off. But we were outraged.

The 1992 Executive were a lot of fun to spend time with. President Kirsty Graham was a shrewd thinker, focused on getting people engaged with our work. We were a diverse bunch, but everyone was on board with the free education campaign.

Part way through 1992 I decided to put my hat in the ring for president for the following year. My reasoning was that I was highly unlikely to win, but putting myself forward would signal to people that I was serious about what we were doing, and it would put me in a good position to stand the following year when I'd have completed my degree.

My main opponents were the vice-president Anishka Jelicich, who had just finished a term on the Dunedin City Council and was the undoubted frontrunner, and another Executive member, Bevan Tipene. I was pretty good friends with Anishka and would have been happy to work with her. I decided to have fun with my campaign. I mocked up posters of myself in historic contexts — as one of the Kennedy brothers, as Martin Luther King's dream. Friends and I plastered the posters everywhere. I also earnestly wrote up a 10-point plan for our campaigns inside and outside the university.

It was a good lesson in electoral politics. Sizzle will usually beat the sausage. No one cared about the 10-point plan — but the posters were a hit. People laughed about them everywhere I went. They were also a target. One night almost all of them were covered up by another poster that alleged I was a National Party plant. It was so ridiculous as to be hilarious. I had a fair idea who had done it, as the font used on the poster was identical to the one the International Socialists used. They had their own candidate in the race and seemed to see me as too moderate. I dramatically produced one of the vandalised posters at a forum for candidates and challenged whoever had done it to front up. No one did, but it made for even more publicity. I was having fun without expecting to be elected.

And then, without warning, two weeks before voting opened, Anishka withdrew from the race. The possibility of winning suddenly became a reality. Two weeks of frenetic campaigning followed.

On polling day I headed to the Captain Cook Tavern to await the result. After a couple of hours of nervous drinking, one of the Executive came over to inform me that I'd won. Dad was still in prison at this point — and so learned the news when a photo of me appeared on the front page of the *ODT* the next morning. My feet on the desk, two thumbs up. I looked very happy.

Becoming student president was a big deal. I would be not just the face and voice of students, but in charge of a multimillion-dollar organisation. I was 20 years old, and was responsible for multiple staff, a radio station, a newspaper, a bookshop, half of a gym and several other buildings, and for organisations like Student Job Search. Not for the first or the last time I wondered if I was really up to it. It was a daunting prospect, but also an opportunity to have experiences few others of my age would have.

I and the rest of the Executive were not alone, of course. The OUSA secretary was a formidable woman named Bridget Rennie. She had been there for nearly 20 years and knew everyone and everything about the university. She was scary, gruff and a true blue National supporter, but she loved students and was fiercely protective of what we did at OUSA. She also had a wicked sense of humour and a great love of gin (admittedly, still not my favourite drink). She made sure we all showed up to our meetings, were fed and did not swear too much. We were in good hands.

As 1993 began, Andrew, Terence and I took a flat in Queen Street. We were joined by our good friend Phil Edgar, whom we had met via mutual friends and who shared our passion for seeing bands and having a good time. Phil was tall and angular — physically the opposite of me, but kindred in spirit. We made a fearsome combination on the dance floor at gigs. Phil had a unique dance move that involved 'getting low'. I swooped around, often still wearing a trench coat, lunging towards the band. People kept their distance as we tore up the floor.

Going to gigs inevitably meant hanging out with some of the bands. One of these was a loose, cartoon-rock band called Kid Eternity. They had modelled themselves on the 3Ds, one of the best of the latter phase of the Dunedin Sound. The Kids were a bit younger than us, but we enjoyed their irreverence. What they lacked in musical acumen, they made up for with endless energy. They started getting gigs and decided they needed a manager. We were at all the gigs in any case, so it made sense that I took on the role.

My main idea was to get them in front of schools, where their boyish good looks and cheekiness would go down well. I set about organising a tour of the North Island. In the earliest days of the internet this was quite the undertaking. The fax machine at OUSA got a hammering, but the tour came together well. And then, a week or two before we were due to leave, one of the Kids was unable to go. The rest of the band did not seem too concerned that the whole tour had to be cancelled, but by this stage I was $200 out of pocket. I was not impressed. I of course never got the money back, but years later, when one of the band members, Matt Heath, made himself famous via radio, it was a staple gag on my appearances on Radio Hauraki's breakfast show that he owed me money. I am still waiting to be paid back.

Meanwhile, 1993 was massive politically. It was an election year, and there was a chance to change the policy direction that was putting students into high levels of debt. We were trying absolutely anything. There was a loophole in the student allowance rules. If you were under 25, you were means-tested on your parents' income, meaning the vast bulk of students were ineligible for support. If you were married, however, the parental means-testing did not apply. Apparently, matrimony made you independent in a way that leaving home did not.

Students cottoned on and started to marry each other for the money. At OUSA we were a bit concerned that this might go pear-shaped if it was not done properly. So we set ourselves up as a kind of matchmaking service, figuring it was better in many ways if people did not get married to a boyfriend or girlfriend, given what could go wrong there. By the end of 1993 we had managed to get over a hundred couples married. We also counselled those who had less than two years to go on their degree to immediately file for divorce, which took two years to come into effect. It was a bizarre time. We knew we had made it a couple of years later when *Shortland Street* characters Rachel and Nick got married so as to be eligible for allowances. Suffice to say the loophole was eventually closed.

The chief target of our campaigns was Education Minister Lockwood Smith. He was the face of the broken fees promise and an unabashed defender of the new right.

We invited him to come to campus, but he was having none of it. We drove to Christchurch to find him, and joined with students from Lincoln and Canterbury in following him about the city. Eventually he was barricaded into a room at Canterbury University where he famously had to climb out the window to get away. When at last he came to Dunedin, we took a hundred or so students down to the Southern Cross Hotel where he was staying, and made a lot of noise and disturbance. Eventually Lockwood agreed to meet a delegation of us. Photos recall that we did not think much of his defence of what he was doing — and we left even more frustrated.

What was becoming clear was that after four years of action against fees, the number of students showing up to protests had started to wane. What had been close to five thousand in 1989 was now just a few hundred. We needed to turn things around.

That year we had appointed full-time campaign coordinators to make the most of election year. Joss Debreceny and Mark Grindlay were doing a good job, but we were still not getting the numbers we wanted to pressure the government. Joss's dad worked in PR and we asked him for some ideas. He came up with the idea of a theme about Budget Day Sweeteners. We bought hundreds of dollars' worth of jellybeans and began handing them out with the promise of more at a rally on Budget Day. We also hatched a plot that once we got a decent crowd on the day, I would deliver a hellfire and brimstone speech and we would do a 'spontaneous' march to the National Party HQ on George Street. It was a gamble, but somehow it worked. I channelled every ounce of anger and righteousness I could muster, and with no traffic plan in place, no support from police, between two and three thousand students marched down the road and took over the National Party HQ in the Harvest Court Mall. I suspect I visited that office more than most National Party members over the years. The poor woman who worked there had about as much influence over National's policies as we did, but that did not stop us handing over our demands and disrupting her day.

That protest kick-started our campaigns. The next focus was the university itself. The government had given it the power to set fees but had cut its funding. It was left with little option but to significantly increase fees to make the books balance. While we understood this, we wanted the university to make a stand.

The fees-setting meeting was to be held in late July. With the Budget Day event in recent memory, nearly five hundred students arrived for the University Council meeting. Only a small portion of students could get in — the rest sat in the hallway outside. We made our case, and the students made a lot of noise. The Council took the decision to increase fees by up to 15% on average and then promptly shut down the meeting. As Council members left, there was some pushing and shoving with angry students, but overall I felt the protest had been peaceful.

Not wanting to admit defeat, we managed to get the issue of fees back on the agenda of the next Council meeting, via one of the committees. I was desperate for the Council to consider a different fee structure and the creation of a hardship fund. There was sympathy around the Council table, and I felt we had a chance of achieving this.

When the September meeting came around, about a thousand students showed up for a rally and march to the Registry Building where the meeting would be held. This time the Proctor (in charge of University discipline), a genial former Northern Irish policeman named Ron Chambers, was ready for us. The doors of the Registry Building were locked and surrounded by police officers. Only Council members could get inside. Nick Braithwaite, the other student rep, and I went in to voice the concerns of students.

Meanwhile some students set about finding other ways to get into the building. Half a dozen tried getting in through a basement window and were taken into custody. There was increasing police presence around the perimeter of the building, and plenty of pushing and shoving took place at each door. Inside the meeting things did not go well. One by one the Council members who had expressed support for our position said that they were reluctantly re-affirming the agreement to increase fees as the only way for the university to meet budget in the face of the government funding cuts. They did agree to a sizeable hardship fund, but the vote for a fee increase was confirmed.

It was a pretty good political lesson for me. A few councillors had given me their commitment they would support our proposals on fees and then took a different position on the day. In later years I would always operate a discount principle when it came to a vote — knocking off at least 10% of people who had committed their vote as likely not to be telling the truth.

As disappointed as I was in the Council, I knew that the real enemy here was the government. They had created a system that forced councils to carry the can for the funding cuts they were making.

The rest of the meeting's business was completed in short order.

I had been communicating with Ron Chambers throughout, and at the conclusion he came over to say that more than half the students who had started the protest were still at various entrances of the building. I agreed to go outside and talk to them about what had happened in the meeting. The police were still there, and I knew there was a risk of major confrontation. I went out to the two main areas where students were gathered and gave the same speech: that while fees had gone up, we had made our point loud and clear, we had got the increased hardship fund and we lived to fight another day, especially in light of the upcoming election.

The message I got from the fifty or so students who were sitting at the front steps, blocking the entrance, was that they wanted to know what had happened to the group who had been taken into custody. I went inside to find out. They were still in the building waiting to be transported to the police station. I told Ron Chambers that I thought that if they were let go it would effectively be the end of the protest. He spoke to the police, but they were adamant that was not going to happen.

As we discussed alternative strategies, Council members were getting restless. They wanted to go home. One or two, including Mayor Richard Walls, were advised that they could get out via the basement (the same route that the students had tried to get in). They hustled off and left without anyone caring or possibly even noticing. Other Council members, however, demanded that they be allowed to leave through the front door.

About this time a large number of police reinforcements arrived with riot gear, accompanied by the head of the Dunedin police, Superintendent Bert Hill. I urged him to wait. Students were drifting away, and in time it would be relatively easy to leave. To his credit, Ron Chambers said the same thing.

But the police were on a mission. In 1990 a full-blown riot had occurred on Castle Street during an Easter sports tournament, and a policeman was injured when a dart hit him in the neck. In 1992 a group of students coming from a party had caused a fair bit of damage in the main street and had scuffled with police. And in July 1993 a post-Bledisloe Cup rugby game night saw a further confrontation with riot police outside the Captain Cook Tavern. On that occasion the police had given me a cellphone (the first time I had seen or held one) to keep in contact. I had been to the game and had gone to a party in town afterwards. I was pretty surprised, and slightly the worse for wear, when the phone rang and I was asked to come down to see what I could do.

I told them to take the riot squad around the corner and out of sight. I got on the megaphone and told the students that it was time to go home, the police had gone and the pubs were shut. There were probably a few swear words thrown in. Amazingly, everyone did as they were asked. An article in the *ODT* the following Monday noted the police as saying my intervention was 'very effective'.

But the bad blood ran deep. Now, as I remonstrated with the police in the Registry building, one of them turned to me, and said, 'This is for Castle Street.' Little did it matter that the protesting students had nothing in common with the Easter Tourney attendees.

The riot police opened the door and started to literally beat a path through the students sitting on the steps. It was a horrific scene. Students were scattered in all directions; some of them received heavy blows. A van pulled up to take the Council members away. Students regrouped and began sitting in front of the van. They were hit with batons and pulled away by their hair. It was violent, ugly and totally unnecessary.

Eventually the van was able to get away. By another door the arrested students were also whisked away to the police station. The carnage was evident, as was the anger of students. I returned to OUSA to call our lawyer and to start answering the media calls that were coming in. The redoubtable Mrs Rennie headed over to the Registry and began administering first aid and ferrying students who had been hurt to the hospital.

All of the students were eventually released on bail, and I finally got home after dark, feeling angry but also very sad. I knew that the focus would be on the actions of the police rather than the issue of free education.

The next day just happened to be a pre-arranged student forum with a guest speaker: a politician named Winston Peters. This was the first election for New Zealand First. They did not have a lot of policy, and the New Zealand University Students' Association (NZUSA) had in fact written the party's tertiary education policy, so he was, at this point, a pretty welcome visitor.

The forum in the Union Hall was attended by roughly the same number of people as had been at the protest. Before we could get under way, some students identified an undercover cop who had been at the protest in the audience. They were right. He was called out and eventually had to leave as students chanted him off.

There were calls for us to go back to the Registry Building. I had quickly come to the view that we had the moral high ground. Images of the police violence had featured on the TV news the previous night. People believed we were justified in our concerns about the fee increases. I believed that a return to the Registry Building would inevitably see the story change focus. And the university was actually not our target. I assured the forum that we had other ways of getting our message across. In fact, I was to appear on the *Holmes* show that night to talk about our issues. This was heady stuff. Paul Holmes's nightly current affairs show, viewed by more than a million people, was at the peak of its powers. TVNZ were flying me to Christchurch for the interview.

With this news the crowd settled down and we got on with the forum. It was clear that most people were there to see Winston in any case.

The chair of the forum was former *Mastermind* winner and later Mayor of Whanganui Hamish McDouall. Ever the showman, Hamish decided to warm up the crowd, finishing with a final flourish: 'And now, ladies and gentlemen, the world's greatest rock and roll band, The Rolling Stones.' Everyone cheered, and Winston, somewhat bewildered, walked out onto the stage, took the microphone and in his best Elvis impression said, 'Thank you very much.'

Shortly afterwards, I had to leave to go to Christchurch. I rushed into the office to find my jersey, a brown homespun number I pretty much wore every day, but it was nowhere to be seen. Mrs Rennie would later admit to hiding it, telling me, 'Your mother would not want to see you on TV in that.' When I arrived at the studio I realised I had not eaten all day and asked the crew if they had any food. They rustled up a chocolate ice cream, which I promptly spilt on my shirt. There was no jersey to cover it up.

But the show itself went well. Vice-Chancellor Sir Robin Irvine was the other guest, speaking from the Dunedin studio. He was flat-footed in the interview, and I was able to make all the points I wanted. Towards the end Sir Robin surprisingly said the government was the real culprit, and for the first time voiced a view on the funding cuts. I swiftly agreed with him and said that we needed to present a united front. It was just the outcome we had wanted.

TVNZ put me up in a flash hotel in Christchurch. My room even had a spa. I called my old school friend Nick, who was studying engineering at Canterbury. He arrived with a box of beer and we sat in the spa and toasted my day. I rang Mum to see if she had seen me on TV. 'Yes,' she replied, 'and you had a stain on your shirt.'

The protest had two postscripts. The general election was close, with the government almost tipped out after only one term in office. But they clung on. They would, however, dial back some of their reforms of tertiary education in the next few years after Lockwood Smith was moved on to a new role.

The second was a knock on my door a month or so after the protest. My visitors were two police officers. They told me that I was under arrest for the charge of incitement to riot and that I was required to accompany them to the Dunedin Police Station. They had executed about half a dozen other arrest warrants to add to the seven who had been charged on the day.

I called Mrs Rennie and asked her to get our lawyer to meet me at the station. The interview was relatively brief. It was clearly an attempt to scare me: the charge, the police told me, had a 10-year prison term attached to it. But mainly they wanted to talk to me about a couple of other incidents that had occurred that day. After what seemed like only a few minutes I was told I was free to go and they would not be pressing charges.

The police did carry on with charges against a few other students. We knew that we needed more help to defend them. Enter a fearsome lawyer named Judith Ablett-Kerr. She was ably assisted by her junior Greg King, who would later go on to his own fame before his tragic early death.

The saga dragged into the next year. Eventually only four people were sent to trial. One of them, not a student, was convicted of assault on a police officer. For the other three, Judith and her team mounted a brilliant display. I was one of many witnesses who made the case that a relatively peaceful protest had turned violent only when the police arrived in numbers.

One of those charged was Felix Geiringer — he of the Bill Birch incident a few years earlier. Felix was not really involved in protests anymore and he had simply been in the area. He had been charged with intentional damage of a police vehicle — that is, he'd thrown a rubbish bin at the van.

In court, Greg King represented Felix.

He put on the stand an officer who had taken detailed notes on the day of the protest. The exchange went something like this:

'Officer, did you see Mr Geiringer throw the rubbish bin at the van?'

'Ah, no, he actually threw it away from the van.'

'Officer, so did the rubbish bin hit the van?'

'Well, ah, no it didn't.'

Judge Carruthers, who was presiding, let out an audible groan.

'No further questions, your Honour.'

As we left the court that day, Judith walked past and under her breath said to me, 'One–nil.'

It turned out to be three–nil. All of the students got off their charges. Judge Carruthers in his findings was scathing of the police and said that they had used 'gratuitous and unnecessary force'.

My year as president of OUSA made me grow up fast politically. I had learned about running an organisation, how to campaign and how to work with the media. There was still a degree to finish, but the world of politics was opening my eyes.

5.

I WISH I WAS IN WELLINGTON

In 1994, freed from the full-time presidency, I focused on completing my Honours in Political Studies. I did well and achieved a First Class grade. Academic life loomed as a possibility, but I was still neck deep in student politics and stayed on the University Council as a student representative. The university had got wise and moved the fee-setting meeting to November, just after exams. There were only minor protests and again the fees rose by 17%.

In August I headed to Hamilton for the NZUSA conference and sought one of the head office jobs. I was elected as vice-president for the following year. This would mean a move to Wellington — a change that was long overdue from a personal perspective.

I had quietly come out to family and my circle of friends. I had moved into a flat that year with Jason, another gay guy, and had met a few guys through him. But the scene in Dunedin was small, and it was my hometown. I remember going to a gay dance party one night, nervous as hell, and the first person I saw when I walked in the door was one of my old schoolteachers. I freaked out, and as soon as it was socially acceptable to do so I took off. I needed to go somewhere bigger — and Wellington was perfect for that.

Before I left there was one further foray into band management. Among the musicians and bands I had got to know in recent years was a band called Tin Soldiers. They were pretty good — and had been runners-up in the nationwide Battle of the Bands a couple of years earlier. But they had broken up, and two of their members, John Howell and Mark Orbell, had joined my friend Phil and Terence's friend Nick Vient to form a band called Too Many Daves. It is fair to say that while John and Mark were accomplished musicians, Phil and Nick were novices. The band was more joke than serious, but the lads put in the effort to write a few songs. It was punk meets mod. An ode to all the influences that had gone before — played fast.

I was lingering around and took on the role of manager. All the band had alter-egos with the first name Dave. As their manager I was Ronald D. Ponce. It was the ultimate in-joke. The boys recorded a single that was pressed in Geraldine and had an outrageous release party at the Empire Tavern. They were also supported at a gig at Sammy's by the 3Ds and The Verlaines after the two well-known bands could not agree who would play last. They just said the Daves should do it. We told the audience that the Daves were an American indie band who had come over secretly for the gig. Some of them believed it.

Too Many Daves typifies so much about my time at Otago. Student politics was my focus, but so too were friends and flatmates. Everything seemed possible, and even if it wasn't we would have a go at it. But our lives were also pretty precarious. There was nowhere near the focus on the mental health of young people that there is today. We were self-medicating through various means and rarely, if ever, did we discuss each other's wellbeing.

I feel this particularly about Terence. He was a big personality, always up for fun and adventures. We went to the forest and took mushrooms; he and I designed a racing prediction system that saw me back at Forbury Park on cold afternoons watching trials. One night we pretended to be Russian sailors and almost took to sea when we snuck onto a boat. But Terence would also have bouts of what I now know was possibly depression. He would get very dark in his moods, say hurtful things and occasionally treat people badly. He stayed in

Dunedin after I left, and eventually moved with his girlfriend to Australia. We kept sporadically in touch, swapping musical discoveries and sending each other stupid clips from the internet.

One day in 2013 I got a message from a mutual friend to tell me that Terence had taken his life in Brisbane. I flew over for his funeral with a couple of other friends. It was hard going — especially seeing his two young children trying to make sense of it all. We got some answers and filled in a few gaps ourselves.

Terence was a magical, wandering soul — and he could not make the world around him fit his dreams and desires. At the funeral I told his early-teenage son that if he ever wanted to know more about his dad he should get in touch with me. I wanted to tell him that Terence was a crazy, creative, loving, sensitive guy, who lived a little bit on the edge and was part of a group of friends who meant the world to me.

At the end of 1994 I packed up my Datsun Sunny station wagon, which I had purchased from Terence's father in Invercargill, and headed for Wellington. I remember farewelling Phil and his girlfriend Rebecca, the incoming OUSA president, and heading out on the Northern Motorway. I drove straight through to Ashburton and stopped at the KFC for dinner. I sat down in the restaurant and burst into tears. I was leaving Dunedin, the most comfortable of hometowns, for the unknown.

Wellington was, and is, a big Dunedin. It shares the same topography of hills and harbour, and it acts a bit like a finishing school for Otago University. My initial nervousness fell away almost as soon as I arrived. After a bit of a false start I ended up living in an eight-person flat at the end of The Terrace. Several flatmates were in an Irish band, and there was a never-ending flow of visitors. I settled into the gay scene too, helping out at the NZ AIDS Foundation and spending way too much time at Casper's, the gay bar.

One night I went there with two friends from student political days, Rochelle and Natasha, after a party with other ex-Otagoites. We were in high spirits, and I didn't notice a guy veering towards me as we left the bar and started along the road. Before I knew it, he had punched me in the mouth and I was on the ground, on top of Rochelle. He stood over me and said, 'You fucking faggot' before walking off into the night.

I was dazed, but the police soon arrived and suggested we drive around with them to see if we could find my attacker. Amazingly enough, we found him a few minutes later having a scrap with a security guard outside another nightclub.

I was shaken and needed a bit of dental work. It was a reminder that just because I was in a bigger city, there was still plenty of prejudice out there. Over the years I have heard so many stories of queer people being abused and beaten up just for being themselves. It's one of the reasons I have continued to fight for Rainbow communities and spoken to Rainbow groups whenever I can. Many young people coming out today still face the same issues I and my contemporaries did.

I got stuck into organising NZUSA. Essentially our job was to lobby and advocate for students, and to help organise campaigns. The president Paul Williams and I shared a political view that we needed to both challenge the status quo and look for ways to get immediate wins for students. We did this, including by successfully arguing that the accommodation benefit needed to be increased, particularly for students in Wellington and Auckland. We kept up the protests around the country, and felt that when Lockwood Smith was relieved of his role we had scored a victory.

By the end of 1995 I believed I was in a good position to lead NZUSA in the election campaign the next year. I stood, and was elected co-president with Alayna Ashby from Waikato.

We had an amazing year. By 1996 it was hard going to get students out on the streets. User-pays education was well and truly set in, and the new generation of students knew nothing else. Once again Joss Debreceny, who had been the campaign coordinator at OUSA, joined us in Wellington as the nationwide campaign coordinator. We decided to go for smaller, more impactful actions.

The previous year at Otago there had been an occupation of the Registry Building. It seemed like a great model. As each university moved to discuss fees, we set up rolling occupations of university buildings. We started small at Lincoln, grew significantly at Otago and by the time we got to Victoria University in Wellington, hundreds of students stayed in the Hunter Building for six nights, until the university decided to shut the power off. We kept user-pays education in the news, secured commitments from Opposition parties to more support for students and generally tried to keep hope alive. On one occasion we managed to disrupt Prime Minister Jim Bolger's plans to visit a campus. Later, when asked to comment on something I had said about the incident, he described me as a 'full-time paid troublemaker'. It was just the kind of performance review I was looking for!

As the next general election drew closer, it was not looking good for a change of government. In Wellington Richard Prebble and the ACT party were making a play for the seat of Wellington Central. ACT had been created by Roger Douglas a couple of years earlier to try to keep his neoliberal experiment rolling. I could not imagine anything worse than their succeeding. I decided to volunteer for the Labour campaign in the seat. It was a big moment for me. I had never properly forgiven the Labour Party for Rogernomics and what that had meant for my communities. But I liked Helen Clark, who was now leader, and I could see the party returning to traditional progressive politics. And I was desperate to stop Prebble.

Sadly, the local Labour campaign was a bit of a train wreck. The candidate Alick Shaw was an old-school Labour bloke, who had a load of old-school Labour blokes around him. As I door-knocked in Karori, I could sense that he, and Labour, would not pull it off. Alick was well beaten. And despite some heroics from Helen during the campaign, Winston Peters went with National to form New Zealand's first Mixed-Member Proportional (MMP) government.

But something had changed for me in that moment. As my term at NZUSA ended, I reflected on half a decade of student activism. I was proud of what I had been a part of. But I was also tired of fighting for change from the outside with limited impact. I had seen enough of how politics worked to be able to think about other ways of making change.

Early the next year I sat in the Backbencher pub with ex-NZUSA president Paul Williams and Michael Gibbs, the current NZUSA president and a good friend and long-term Labour member. They produced a Labour Party membership book, and I signed on the dotted line.

Things happened fast after that, as they do in the Labour Party.

I went to the AGM of my local branch in Thorndon. It was a sparsely attended affair. Our host was the branch president. He looked at me. I had brought a pad and pen to the meeting. A rookie mistake. I was immediately, unanimously, elected secretary of the branch. In 1998, Michael took a shot at a seat on the Wellington City Council, and I took on the role of campaign manager. Sadly, Michael missed out, but I got to know a heap more Labour people in Wellington.

They included Labour stalwarts like Pat Webster, Lynn Middleton and list MP Marian Hobbs. I had met Marian years earlier through her niece and former OUSA president Kirsty Graham, and we reconnected when she arrived up from Christchurch as a list MP after the 1996 election. She had been a school principal, was a former member of the Communist Party, had started a commune, was just in the process of leaving husband number two, had two great kids and was a huge amount of fun. We had a few memorable nights out on the town. I was also impressed by Marian's principled approach to politics. She wore her heart on her sleeve, and she was there for all the right reasons.

One day in 1998 I sat at the Ministry of Food cafe out the back of Parliament with Michael, Lynn and Pat. We knew if Labour was to beat Richard Prebble in the Wellington Central seat we would need a very particular type of candidate. We made a list of the attributes: a woman, with an existing profile, who was demonstrably left wing and would have the personality to capture the public mood. We all looked at each other and knew that person was Marian. It would take a year, a fight with Labour Party Head Office and a tense selection meeting, but Marian became the candidate for Wellington Central for the 1999 election.

For me, life had taken another significant turn. I had applied for a few jobs after I left NZUSA, some with unions, some with corporates and at the Ministry of Foreign Affairs and Trade (MFAT). I thought my political activism would be a major negative. But I was fortunate Kirsty Graham had joined MFAT a year or two earlier and had impressed people. Even so, I was surprised I was offered a position. The day before my interview I had been part of an NZUSA-organised protest that had briefly occupied the steps of Parliament. But somehow I got through the interview process, and in January 1997 took up the role of managing the Official Development Assistance (ODA) programme in Samoa.

This was a fantastic job — looking after twenty or so projects ranging from forestry to primary education, women's empowerment to tourism promotion. I travelled to Samoa numerous times over the next 18 months. It was fun, the people and islands were amazing, and I felt I was doing genuine good. I also learned a few lessons. We had a project providing training to support women in dealing with family violence. One attendee had gone home to tell her husband that she was not going to put up with his beatings any more. He proceeded to give her an even more severe beating, and she was hospitalised. The intentions of the project were admirable, but it was delivered without the cultural sophistication to make it work and didn't give the women in the programme the tools to help change their lives. A successful aid programme is one that is driven by locals and understands how to make change in their context. We did far better in other areas, including supporting small businesses making coconut soap and beauty products that were picked up by The Body Shop.

At MFAT, the focus is always on postings. That is why most people are there: to get the chance to work overseas on behalf of the country. After 18 months or so I looked to see what was available. I knew, given my role in Samoa, I would have a fair chance at the posting in Suva that was focused on ODA. Also up for application was one in New York at the United Nations. This seemed a bit out of reach, but I expressed interest in it too.

When Jeff from personnel called one afternoon and asked for a chat, I was busy. I was sure it would be Suva he wanted to talk about. I asked if I could come and see him the following morning. He said I would probably want to come over now. He offered me the posting in New York to commence early in 1999. He also said that I would be moving to the Environment Division to work on UN-related issues during my remaining time in Wellington. It was the stuff of dreams. By this stage both of my brothers were studying in the USA. And New York — I had only seen it in the movies.

There was about eight months to go before the posting began, and while my mind was on my big shift, there was one more life-changing event ahead. I got a phone call from Dean Knight, nowadays a Law professor at Victoria University but then a young lawyer about town. I didn't know Dean, but he was the friend of a friend. He was setting up New Zealand's first gay rugby team. While in London on his OE he had played for a gay team and thought it would be fun to start one here. I said no. I hadn't played for several years, and the memories of my final playing days were not great. I had been involved in social rugby in my first year at university, but the culture was homophobic and misogynist and I just felt out of place. Plus, playing prop had taken a toll on my body.

Dean was persistent and called back another couple of times. He was desperate to have people who had played rugby before to join the many interested novices. Eventually I relented but insisted that I had to be able to pick my position. I think Dean would have said yes even if I said I wanted to be halfback, but he was happy to agree to me playing No. 8.

I was relatively fit at the time, courtesy of playing squash, social netball and touch rugby. But contact rugby is a whole other thing and I could hardly walk after each game. But the team was so much fun. A lot of the guys were exorcising the demons of high school, where they'd been the butt of the first fifteen's abuse. Others were doing as I was, playing the game they loved but in a totally different atmosphere. The changing rooms were a bit different. First, they smelled amazing. The banter was different too. After one game we were slumped totally exhausted in the changing rooms. No one could speak, and then someone said, 'That halfback in the other team was cute.' And suddenly everyone joined in with their reckons.

As fun as it was off the field, we were initially a catastrophe on the field. We lost our first game by about 80 points. It was shaping up to be a long season.

However, we got a bit of publicity, and a few more people joined the team. One of them was a short, very cute Ngāti Porou lad named Alf Kaiwai, who played halfback. As I would later joke, I first met Alf when he had to reach between my legs to pick up the ball.

As a team we got better and better, and some quite skilled players emerged. We even won a game! The big event of the season was a Labour Weekend game against a gay team from Auckland that had been formed in the wake of the publicity around our team. They looked a lot bigger than us, bolstered by some large Samoan drag queens, who were a lot more scary without their make-up than with it. The game was a hard-fought affair. We had a few chances but eventually lost 17–15. That night as the two teams celebrated, danced, drank and told tales, I felt what it must have been like for straight rugby players. To feel part of a team and a culture that I related to. I felt at home.

In the wake of that weekend, I started seeing more of Alf. He and I were both in relationships which we had to extract ourselves from, but in short order we were a couple. I had wanted a longer-term relationship for some time but had not met anyone I really connected with. From the beginning I felt differently about Alf. He was so warm, friendly and loving. He instantly relaxed me and made me a better person to be around.

He had lived a life already. After leaving school at 17, he went to work at the Treasury, where he still was 16 years later. He had two beautiful kids, Hayley, 12, and Abe, 8. From our first meeting I liked hanging out with them too. Alf asked me if I wanted to have kids. I said no, it was not something I had ever considered. He was relieved, and said the two he had were enough. He also said that his kids came first. And that was the foundation of our relationship.

He knew when we met that I was going to New York in a few months' time. We agreed just to have fun and see what happened. What happened was that we fell in love — fast.

But New York is a long way from Ruatōria where Alf was raised, and a very long way from his children. In April 1999, when I moved to New York permanently, Alf was at the airport to see me off. We were both distraught. He had a plan to come over and see me later in the year, but we both knew that for now we were going our separate ways.

6.

IF YOU CAN MAKE IT HERE — NEW YORK AND THE UN

When I was living in New York there was a subway driver who used to announce our arrival at the 42nd Street station by saying, 'Next stop Times Square, the centre of the universe.'

It certainly felt like that to me when I arrived to take up my posting at the UN. The city that never sleeps was still mostly awake. Rudy Giuliani had arrived as mayor a few years earlier and had cleaned up the city a bit, but it still had plenty of rough edges. When I went downtown to some of the gay bars there was always someone outside wanting to sell me a range of drugs. Locals were often concerned when I explored bars and restaurants in Alphabet City, which they still saw as the Badlands. I never felt really in danger — partly because, day or night, there were almost always other people around.

I settled into an apartment building on the Upper West Side of Manhattan. I was very fortunate that fellow MFATer Sarah Paterson was a few floors above in the same building. This was our Kiwi home away from home.

It took 45 minutes to get across town to the UN, no matter what form of transport. If I walked, I made use of the finest New York jaywalking to cut across the avenues when the traffic lights went red. When it was too hot, or too cold, the bus crawled through traffic until it got to 42nd Street where it could get on one of the half-dozen two-way cross streets. But my preferred method was the subway. Filthy, smelly and always too full, it was everything I felt living in New York should be. I made it my job to memorise all the subway lines and connecting stations — and set about exploring this extraordinary city.

I found speakeasies in the West Village, amazing food in Harlem and Queens, and quirky galleries in the East Village. I loved the Met and MOMA and the Guggenheim. On my own, I threw myself into the gay scene, the alternative music scene, the theatre scene and the diplomatic world. There was not a lot of crossover between them, but I made friends in them all and had a ball.

But there was a big gap. Alf and I were in almost daily contact through the newfangled invention that was email. We talked on the phone every weekend. I thought about that phone call all week. No matter what I was doing, I found the time to talk. Just hearing his voice made me feel better.

By September, when he came over for a visit, I was so ready for us to spend time together. We had the most brilliant couple of weeks as I showed off everything the city had to offer. And then, on the last night, Alf told me he could not move over. It was just too much. Leaving his kids and his whānau, adjusting to the big city — it was too big an ask.

I was devastated. I understood what he had at home, but the connection felt as strong as ever. On the train back after dropping him off at JFK I was a mess. I just knew the relationship could not be over.

In the months that followed we kept talking and emailing. No promises, no strings. Alf felt the same as I did and was talking to a counsellor. Eventually, after a few months of hesitancy, he confirmed that in the New Year he would come and join me.

Meanwhile, the work at the UN was fascinating. I was assigned to the not very imaginatively named Second Committee. This mostly dealt with development and environmental issues, and covered everything from climate change to the work of the Population Fund.

The committees do the grunt work of the UN. They contain

representatives of every member country and deal with all of the business created by the General Assembly. In each subject area there are also related bodies, and if you come from a small country like New Zealand these are managed by the same people. For me this meant the UN Development Programme (UNDP), UN Population Fund (UNFPA) and the Economic and Social Council (ECOSOC) among others.

It was incredibly busy work. A large mission such as the United States had up to sixty diplomats working on the Second Committee. New Zealand had me. It was daunting and frankly a bit ridiculous, but it also meant that I was involved in work that in other countries it would take years and years to be responsible for.

One of my first tasks in 1999 was to support Simon Upton as Minister for the Environment as he took on the chairing of the UN Commission on Sustainable Development (CSD). I had been working on this in Wellington for a few months before I arrived. This was a relatively new UN body charged with getting action following on from the Rio Earth Summit in 1992. From Minister Upton's perspective, the commission did not seem to be getting much traction at all. He wanted to inject some energy and real outcomes into the CSD when rotation dictated that New Zealand would become the chair.

I learned quickly that if you were to enjoy work at the UN, you needed to be a fan of test-match cricket. It was slow going, punctuated by short periods of activity. And it all often ended in a draw. Simon Upton did not appear to be a fan of test cricket. While I was still in Wellington, he had brought in an old MFAT hand, Bill Mansfield, to come up with a work programme that would have proper outcomes for the CSD. The main focus of this was on oceans — in particular, governance of oceans and measures to reduce over-fishing. Bill and Minister Upton hustled around the globe to drum up support for the Minister's ideas.

As is the way for Wellington-based staff, my job was to book the Minister into hotels and set up meetings (with the aid of our overseas posts). Minister Upton had some very specific requests for hotels. I remember getting a call from South Africa, where the Minister was travelling, because he had been booked on a floor that allowed smoking when he had expressly asked not to be.

By the time I was in New York, the CSD itself was meeting. Months of preparation had gone into this, and the Minister was determined it would be a success. Back then UN committee meetings were scheduled to commence at 10am each day. The reality was that most meetings got under way considerably later, with various corridor conversations usually taking precedence over the meeting itself. Minister Upton was having none of it. At exactly 10am on the Monday of his first week as the chair of the CSD, he banged his gavel down to begin the meeting.

Instead of representatives of the 185 member states, there were approximately half a dozen people sitting in front of him. Minister Upton pressed on — gave a brief introduction on the first topic of the day and called for any country that wanted to make a statement on it. There was silence. No one was ready — especially not the ministers, who would normally read any statements at a meeting such as this. I sprinted around the room trying to find one of my colleagues who could speak. I was promising lunches, dinners, drinks — anything I could think of to get someone to say something. Eventually my Chinese colleague, who was an impressive operator, put her country nameplate in the air and saved me. I carried on like a demented conductor, finding speakers until we settled into a rhythm.

For the next two weeks Minister Upton kept up the pace. To his credit, he wanted an outcome and he kept going till he got one. After New York, the Minister was heading to Washington DC to deliver a speech. He was working on it in the car to the airport when he announced his need for a highlighter pen. I said I did not have one with me. When it became clear he was not going to accept this answer, I asked our brilliant driver Benny to stop the car on a busy 2nd Avenue. I got out, and in typical New York fashion there was a stationery store across the road. I ran across the traffic, dodging cars, bought the highlighter pen, and repeated the same journey back, raising the ire of the ever-so-patient New York drivers. I triumphantly handed the pen to the Minister, who took it and said nothing. Such was the exciting and valued life of a diplomat.

Managing ministers is indeed one of the key roles of diplomats. One minister who came to New York was far more interested in shopping than in working. That minister's private secretary quit their job while they were there.

Mike Moore came through during his term as World Trade Organisation (WTO) Director-General. He gave an impassioned speech about free trade, including references to his growing up in Northland, walking barefoot to school. The assembled diplomats were finding him a little hard to follow when, all of a sudden, he shouted 'Back up the truck' and started off on a new tangent. I asked my friendly Chinese colleague what the translator was making of Mike and this particular phrase. She said the translator had paused, listened to Mike and said, 'The speaker is referring to heavy vehicles.' In fact, the main problem for New Zealanders at the UN was that we almost always spoke too fast. We all got a special visit from the translator service at the beginning of our time there to ask us to slow down.

The work that I most enjoyed while I was in New York was for UNDP and UNFPA. There is a lot to criticise about the UN and how it does or, more rightly, does not do its work. But the Funds and Programmes, as they are known, do the real work on the ground, alleviating poverty, and defending the rights of women and children. UNFPA, for example, was the only organisation in the world allowed into strict Muslim countries to talk about contraception. I have absolutely no doubt that their work saved lives.

The UN might not have started on time, but it did sit late. The hours were often mad. If we were negotiating an agreement, we would simply meet until we had an agreement. More than once I saw the sun rise on the East River as we worked through the night. But I learned a huge amount about negotiations.

Two lessons stand out. The first came from a Mexican colleague who, when all seemed lost, would always remind us: 'The last minute of the last hour of the last day still has 60 seconds in it.' No matter how late in the day it is, you can always get an outcome. Time and again at the UN it would seem there would be no result from our discussions, and then at the last moment we would find a way.

The second lesson was that negotiations are as much about what you agree to remove as what you agree to include. At the UN language mattered, and to get agreement we would often have to include all manner of things that a particular country wanted before it signed up. But at the very end of a negotiation, when two opposing countries could not find a way through, the suggestion that each of them remove a sentence was often the route to a successful result.

I stayed in touch with the political scene at home, including the build-up to the 1999 election. From afar, it felt very close-run. Michael Gibbs and others gave me regular updates on the Wellington Central race. One day I emailed Michael to ask how it was going. He said Marian was making the headlines, and sent through a story about the launch of some kind of fun run. Richard Prebble was quoted as saying he loved any kind of race and he was sure he would win the one for Wellington Central. Marian was quoted as saying, 'The last time I went jogging I got pregnant.' It was classic Marian: true, in a sense, funny and very real.

On election night I went to bed not knowing if Marian had won but confident that Labour and Jim Anderton's Alliance had secured a majority to govern, bringing to an end nine long years of a National government. Marian's victory was confirmed the following day — it was a thrilling, momentous achievement.

The political bug was not subsiding in me. I very much enjoyed the diplomatic work in New York, but I was not a great fan of the Wellington-based part of the MFAT job. Prior to my departure I had been asked to represent new recruits on a working party looking at the career structure at MFAT. We met with the management consultant who was running the review, and she asked each of us to describe what it was like starting at MFAT, beginning with me as the most recent arrival. I paused, and, perhaps unwisely, said, 'It's like being shown into a dark room full of furniture. No one ever switches on the light, so you keep bumping into the furniture until you learn to navigate it. Then, after 18 months you're picked up and put into another dark room with the furniture differently arranged. And no one ever turns on the light.' There was total silence in the room until my manager in the Environment Division did a slow clap. But that is how I felt — it was dreadfully hierarchical, and time served appeared to mean much more than ability. I wondered if I was really cut out for the diplomatic life.

The New Zealand Permanent Representative at the UN (the head of the mission) was Michael Powles. Michael was a lifetime diplomat, wise, thoughtful and, especially after a whisky or two, devilishly good fun. He had a young daughter from his second marriage, and when he was on the UN TV channel he would delight in wearing a bright yellow and red plastic watch from McDonald's, or a plastic brooch of hers, as a way of saying hello to her.

Michael was due to retire at the beginning of 2001. Not long before he left, we were the last two remaining at a function at the magnificent New Zealand residence in Gracie Square on the Upper East Side. We were having a whisky when conversation turned to my future at MFAT. Michael looked at me hard and said, 'Grant, I think you're in the wrong part of the food chain. You're too political for this organisation. It will drive you mad. Go away and become Minister of Foreign Affairs. That's where you will be happy.'

Hearing someone I respected so much say this was a real moment of clarity. I began to think about how such a future might play out.

In 2000 both Prime Minister Helen Clark and Phil Goff, the relatively new Foreign Minister, visited. I did not know either of them well, but I had met them both through Labour Party circles. One day it was my job to take Helen to an early-morning TV interview. On the way back we got stuck in a classic New York traffic jam. There was no way out, we just had to wait.

After a while I mentioned to Helen that I was still a Labour Party member. We reminisced about the Taranaki–King Country by-election that I had helped out with in 1998. I made her laugh with my story of five gay boys, including me, heading up to Stratford for a day's door-knocking. Everything had been fine until we got to a pub at the end of the day for a drink. It was Saturday and an entire rugby team was there. I reasoned that I could pull off ordering drinks at the bar better than the rest could, so asked the others what they wanted. 'Ooh, I'll have a gin and tonic,' said Stuart, one of the group, and the others agreed they'd like one too.

I walked to the bar. 'I'll have a pint of Speight's, and, um, four gin and tonics.'

At that moment Stuart, at full volume, yelled, 'Can I have an umbrella in mine, girl?'

Somehow, we avoided being beaten up.

Helen and I gossiped for the remaining 45 minutes we were stuck in the traffic together.

When Phil arrived in New York a few weeks later, his first words on seeing me were, 'So when are you going to come home and run for Labour?'

That was not where I was at, but the stars were starting to align for some change. Alf was also finding New York tough going. He was working as the sole systems administrator for the UK government offices in the city, with 170 staff. It was a huge job and was starting to get to him. He also missed his kids terribly.

As 2001 got going, Marian Hobbs passed through New York. She was not in a good way. She was struggling as a Minister and was miserable. I checked in with her regularly after she got back, and one day she told me her senior private secretary had quit. She asked, hesitantly, whether I would be prepared to come back to take the role. I talked to Alf, and we agreed that this was probably the last push we needed to come home.

I was not sure about the role, but I knew I could help Marian. I got hold of Heather Simpson, Helen Clark's Chief of Staff. She said that senior private secretary was not the right role for me, and not what Marian needed either. She felt Marian needed a political advisor. This was a relatively new position. Independent of the public service, he or she would be the political eyes and ears of the Minister. That sounded very like me.

After a bit more soul searching and a brief delay as Marian dealt with an expenses investigation, my job was confirmed. We would be leaving at the beginning of May 2001.

It was pretty unheard of for someone to leave a posting in New York early. I had loved living in the city, and had grown up a lot in the two years there, but I just knew that this was the right direction to go in. A new life awaited in Wellington.

7.
THREE EXTRAORDINARY WOMEN

We landed back in Wellington on a grey day in early May 2001. We initially stayed in Ngaio at Labour stalwarts Pat and John Webster's place. I would get up in the morning and trudge to the train station for the commute into town. I spent a bit of time wondering quite what I had done leaving New York. But the air was breathable, tomatoes had actual flavour and even though all the restaurants were shut by 9pm, the pies tasted just how I remembered them.

Over the next few months Alf went back to his old job at Treasury, we took a flat on Molesworth Street and we began hunting for a house, using savings from our time in New York as the deposit. We were busy and happy to be settling back in, and I was pleased to be making new friends at the Beehive and connecting with old ones.

On 12 September, our peaceful return from New York was rocked by a 1.30am phone call. It was our friend Jeremy in Sydney. He had just got home and had turned on the television to see the World Trade Center on fire. Jeremy had stayed with us in New York, and he and Alf had gone together to see Alf's old friend John Lozowsky at his workplace in the North Tower. We turned on the TV as the first tower collapsed. Alf rang John's cellphone. It rang but went to his voicemail. Over the next few hours we checked that our other friends in New York were safe. Everyone was. But we could not get hold of John. Eventually the calls started going straight to voicemail.

John had been a great friend to us in New York. He had come

to New Zealand a decade or so earlier and had worked with Alf at Treasury. He was a barrel of laughs, loved a drink, and Alf loved running with a short-legged companion. John had returned to New York, and when we moved there he was a frequent visitor to our apartment. He would always tell the doorman that David Lange was here to see us, and would arrive upstairs chuckling away at his joke. In 2001 he was putting in extra hours at the insurance company he worked for so that he could go over to celebrate his son's birthday in Ireland, where he lived with his mother. That was exactly what he was doing on the morning of September 11. John's body was never found, although his family did eventually get back some fragments of clothing identified via DNA from his twin sister Michelle.

In early 2002 we returned to New York to check in on friends, and to visit John's family who lived upstate. It was heartbreaking. The city we loved so much felt like a shell of itself. John's family were devastated. We spent time with them all, remembering John for his unique and hilarious approach to life. One day we sat with his father, whom we had only just met. Not too much was said, but as we got up to leave he grabbed us and hugged us. It was like he wanted to hold on to people who could somehow help him reach his son.

We returned to New Zealand sad for the city and its people but glad we were in safe Aotearoa.

As I began work in Marian's office in Bowen House, it was clear there were problems. Marian had a very busy set of portfolios — Environment and Broadcasting in particular. She also had associate roles in Biosecurity and Education, and oversight of the National Library and Archives. On top of this, she was a first-term electorate MP in the political hotspot of Wellington Central.

Even the roles that should have been easy somehow became hard.

National had severely undermined the Library and Archives. Marian, determined to do her best by these institutions, set about getting new legislation that would modernise and protect them. As the son of an archivist I can tell you that librarians and archivists are a passionate bunch. There were plenty of people wanting to give us advice. The Friends of the Turnbull Library, or FOTTL as they were better known, looked for all the world like a kindly group of retirees. In reality, their lobbying style was that of a paramilitary group, who waged relentless email attacks and meeting ambushes. It was exhausting, even when we were working with people who liked us!

Marian had far too much on her plate. Labour had a detailed policy programme in each of her portfolios, but setting the agenda was nigh on impossible as issues came firing at us from all directions. Marian was tired, stressed and lonely. She was struggling in Parliament and struggling to keep up with a huge volume of paper (and it was all paper back then). Most significantly, her confidence when speaking in Parliament's debating chamber had been severely eroded.

Marian is one of the most intelligent and considered politicians I have ever worked with. But these qualities did not always translate to a coherent speech in the House. Under pressure, her hilarious penchant for forgetting everyone's name and calling them 'darling' or 'dearest' or 'thingy' did not quite work. On one occasion she went down to Question Time straight from the airport. As she fumbled an answer, she said, 'Sorry darlings, I have just flown off a plane.' Endearing on one level, but not for someone feeling the pressure. She had also been very hurt by some of the name-calling that went on in the House. And then there was the expenses inquiry that had delayed my arrival. It was launched into her claims for allowances as she was transitioning from being a Christchurch-based MP. She was ultimately cleared of any wrong-doing, but it added to a miserable vibe in the office.

The staff did not really know how to approach her or understand her way of working. She and I knew each other pretty well — and I was clear that the first job was to boost her confidence. She has a great sense of humour and is a potent debater on her day. My mantra was to make Marian the best Marian she could be, not to try to turn her into some caricature of a politician.

We put hours and hours into Question Time preparation. I created a filter to reduce the dozens of bits of paper she would normally take with her to just a few with key points and arguments on them. And we would practise. I would assume the role of whichever Opposition politician was gunning for her. I did a pretty good Rodney Hide impression. I tried to make it as fun as possible, getting her to laugh and relax, practise some jokes. It was not perfect, but by the end of 2001 Marian was performing solidly in the House, and able to focus more on her portfolio areas — and on being out and about in Wellington Central.

In the Broadcasting portfolio Marian had come in all guns blazing. The previous National government had effectively abandoned the portfolio — disbanding the policy group in the Ministry for Culture and Heritage, and working behind the scenes to prepare TVNZ for sale. There was zero commitment to public broadcasting, and the main issue was the sale of spectrum rights.

When I arrived in early 2001, there was an ambitious new policy programme under way, but no focus on how to achieve it. I quickly realised that we needed to pick a couple of areas where we might show some progress. One chose itself — the creation of a charter for TVNZ. Under National, TVNZ had taken an almost fully commercial stance. The salaries of presenters were the main story in the media, and they were huge — but this belied a much bigger cultural problem. TVNZ was a public broadcaster in name only — and from their Auckland offices could see no further than the Bombay Hills.

Marian's solution was a legislated charter that would compel TVNZ to act as a public broadcaster and promote New Zealand content. The idea was popular with the public but vehemently opposed inside TVNZ. The battle was in full swing. TVNZ CEO Rick Ellis was defiantly trying to tell us he could and would make the changes without the charter. Board chair Ross Armstrong, a former Auckland chair of the National Party, was ingratiating himself to the Labour government but seemed utterly ineffectual when it came to pushing the government's agenda.

It was frustrating, but we pushed on. Of course, with Marian there were lighter moments. At a Board meeting in Auckland, Marian was making her point about the need for TVNZ to exist outside of that city. She so wanted to tell them that film and television were the 'bread and butter' of the Wellington economy — but instead declared in no uncertain terms that they were the 'bed and breakfast'. The Board were stony-faced as Marian realised her mistake and the two of us laughed till we cried.

The charter would eventually make its way into law, but not before there was a change of leadership at TVNZ and former broadcaster Ian Fraser took charge. Ian had a difficult time making the cultural changes that were needed at the organisation, and TVNZ has never really succeeded in putting the public broadcasting ethos into practice.

We had a great deal more success in the other chosen priority — a quota for New Zealand music on commercial radio. This had long been Labour Party policy but was staunchly opposed by the radio sector. Not only that — the policy had caught the eye of the US Embassy, ever alert for a chance to play New Zealand at its own game on issues of protectionism. We felt on safe ground, as arts and culture had always had fairly strong exclusion from trade matters. Nevertheless, the US concern led to Marian and me being included in the WikiLeaks documents several years later, as the notes of a fractious meeting on the subject were included. New Zealand was threatened with trade sanctions and various reprisals if we pursued this approach. I am not sure that our 20% quota had much potential to bring down the US music industry, but the US government was pretty fired up about it.

We pressed on. Again, the policy had some public popularity, and the music scene in New Zealand was in a good place. The Fifth Labour Government's cultural recovery package in late 2000 had created a New Zealand Music Commission, increased funding for NZ On Air and generally fostered a climate of interest in the arts. I took on the role of meeting with the industry to try to get some agreement on a quota for New Zealand music. It seemed to me they were happy to call our bluff. So, I got busy writing up how a legislated code would work and presented this to them. The head of the Radio Broadcasters Association was Brent Impey. Brent was fairly sympathetic to the policy but knew his bosses were not. Over weeks we toed and froed until eventually, with the threat of a mandatory code looking more likely, they agreed to a voluntary code with a stepped programme to reach 20% over the next few years. This was a big reach given that the previous year around 10% of the music played on commercial radio was New Zealand music. The policy also included limits as to when the music had to be played (that is, it could not all be put in the graveyard shift) and transparent reporting requirements.

We were ecstatic and headed to Auckland for the launch — in a pub halfway down Dominion Road. I wrote Marian's speech, using the venue as the start of a series of musical allusions. Marian was in fine form and spoke with gusto until she reached a line about some of the great musicians who we would now hear far more of on the radio: 'artists like Neil Finn, Dave Dobbyn and Ric Bunga'. I felt the world stop. There were audible gasps. Marian sailed on and afterwards told me how well she thought the speech had landed. When I explained the spoonerism, Marian was horrified, but nothing could take away from the success of the code. The 20% target was met a year ahead of schedule in 2005 — and the flow-on benefits were huge. I remember talking to one radio station manager who had been reluctant to play

Kiwi music but soon found listeners loved it, and the artists were right here to do promotions with.

We had another big idea — a nationwide Youth Radio Network. Modelled on a Triple J-type approach from Australia, it was backed by Neil Finn, who was prepared to fund a touring recording studio bus. It was hard going to get support for this among Marian's Cabinet colleagues. I recall Michael Cullen asking, 'Isn't all radio youth radio?' But eventually Michael relented, and we prepared for the announcement. I can still tell you what day the Youth Radio meeting was — 10 June 2002. Because the next day, Helen Clark announced a snap election.

I was nowhere near senior enough to know this was coming, but the move did make sense. The coalition with the Alliance was under strain, largely because the Alliance itself had collapsed, in part because of the government's decision to commit SAS troops alongside a provincial reconstruction team in Afghanistan. Jim Anderton had backed the position, against the will of many in his party and a number of his MPs. It was an ugly split, with Laila Harré and Matt McCarten leading the core of the Alliance away. Parliament was getting messy, and Helen had no desire to be dragged down by the in-fighting of another party. Another factor might have been the very strong poll ratings she was reading. National was struggling badly, having replaced Jenny Shipley with Bill English, who was not resonating with the public. Helen gambled on an early election and a clear mandate for Labour.

Among many more important things, that was the last we heard of Youth Radio, lost in the midst of an election campaign.

One Tuesday evening a few weeks into the campaign I went out with my friend Michael Gibbs to fix up some of Marian's hoardings. It is one of the thankless and frankly pointless tasks of any campaign to keep the hoardings upright and free of graffiti or, in that particular campaign, to prevent them from becoming a pile of ash thanks to someone repeatedly setting fire to them. I am not sure that in the history of campaigns a hoarding has won or changed a vote, but visibility does matter, most especially to your own supporters.

Michael and I had stopped for a drink at Magills, a long-lost bar in Thorndon near the Wellington stadium, before heading home. About 8pm my cellphone rang. It was Heather Simpson, Helen Clark's Chief of Staff and therefore my boss.

'Have we released an OIA [Official Information Act] response about genetic modification recently?'

Genetic modification (GM) or genetic engineering had been a hot-button topic for the government. It was strongly opposed by many in the environmental movement who feared that cross-contamination from GM could damage crops and human health. Labour had established a Royal Commission to investigate how the technology could or should be used, and it had recommended proceeding with caution on GM. Many in the public were not convinced.

'Um,' I said. 'Not that I know of. Why?'

'Helen has just been asked about the unauthorised release of GM crops in Gisborne or Northland. She is not happy.'

This was a terrific piece of Southland understatement. In fact, Helen had been ambushed by John Campbell in a pre-recorded interview for TV3 and was, as the New Zealand public would later see, incandescent with rage.

I told Heather I'd see what I could find out, farewelled Michael and headed to my office in Bowen House to make some calls.

The first of these was to one of our Environment private secretaries, who knew nothing. The second was to the senior Environment private secretary, who also did not know of any recent OIA release. He casually said, 'To be honest it sounds more like a Biosecurity issue. Perhaps you should call David.'

David was Biosecurity Minister Jim Sutton's private secretary. Marian had previously held the portfolio.

I called him and explained what Heather had told me. His reply made my heart stop.

'I have been waiting for this phone call.'

David then proceeded to tell me his version of the story that we all now know as Corngate. In short, concern had been raised that GM corn had been released in New Zealand in late 2000 in contravention of the law. After intense discussions between officials and scientists, it was concluded that there was not sufficient evidence to say that this had occurred. But it was clear from David's tone that there was a lot more to the story than this. I quizzed him further, and he said there was an extensive paper trail of conflicting views. Many people inside and outside of government had been involved. When I asked him how much ministers knew, he said they had some awareness of the situation, and the issue had been mentioned in a media release that Marian had put out in late 2000. That seemed a little odd to me: why would something that had apparently not happened end up in a ministerial statement?

But before I could get much further, Marian's press secretary Trevor Henry called to say that RNZ political editor Al Morrison wanted to interview Marian the next morning about the issue of unauthorised release of GM material. He refused to give Trevor any more information other than to say it would be after 9am. At this point I surmised that it was no coincidence that John Campbell and Al Morrison were pursuing the same story. It felt big. I decided to call Al. I knew him a bit. His partner Kate was a friend of Marian's, and we'd had a very enjoyable dinner together a few months earlier.

Al refused to say exactly what he knew, or how, though repeated that the story concerned the unauthorised release of GM material. He said all would be revealed at nine the next morning. I said that if it had anything to do with events at the end of 2000, this was effectively a false alarm. Al said that he had information that this was a serious issue. I think he might even have used the word 'cover-up'. Our call ended with me saying there was no way Marian was going on radio without more background. He said he had made a commitment to someone that he would not give it. I finished with the words, 'There are two sides to every story, Al.'

I finally spoke to Marian late in the evening. She said she had a vague recollection of some issue with regard to GM but that it had all been sorted at the time. She, too, remembered a media release saying just this. She was a bit nonplussed, to be honest, and we agreed to catch up in the morning.

As a former MP and Minister, one of the things I know now is that trying to remember what you did last week, let alone 18 months ago, is just about impossible when so many issues are constantly competing for attention. Vague recollections and an absence of exact detail are the norm, especially if an issue has concluded with a 'nothing to see here' finding.

Marian and I were due to drive to Whanganui the next day to campaign with Labour MP Jill Pettis. Suffice to say, that never eventuated. At nine that morning the first words on the RNZ news bulletin were: 'In December 2000 GM corn was released into the environment . . .' No 'allegedly', no 'it is claimed'. Just stated as a fact. The absence of any mitigating words would eventually be a mistake that Al would admit.

We were then introduced to the book *Seeds of Distrust* and its author Nicky Hager. Nicky had already published a couple of books looking at the murky world of New Zealand's security agencies. He would go on to do more in another election (discussed later). But for now he had chucked a corn cob-shaped grenade into the election campaign.

There was in fact no OIA release. The book was based on a series of leaked papers that outlined the twists and turns of this tale, with allegations of cover-up after cover-up. It drew on eight drafts of a Cabinet paper that lurched from acknowledging a full-on breach, to nothing to see here, to everything in between. There was conflicting scientific evidence; explanations of confidence-level testing and false positives; correspondence and meetings with pro-GM lobbyists and companies; draft media releases written by those companies. And eventually the media release that everyone remembered which said it was all a false alarm.

Like all of Nicky's books, *Seeds of Distrust* was a triumph of great sources, dogged research and an unwavering view that truth should be spoken to power. Unfortunately for us, the book was missing a few vital documents, and had at its heart an assumption that ministers were aware of the many drafts of the Cabinet paper and were therefore guilty of a cover-up. I can see why Nicky made that assumption.

The question of whether GM corn had been released occupied officials for weeks. What I knew already after my short time in Parliament was that it was fully possible, and in fact very common, for ministers to know very little of the work that went on before they saw only the very final draft of a paper or a press release. In a busy meeting they might be told that there was some investigation under way; later, they might be told it was all sorted. Good job — onto the next thing.

The next two weeks were full-on, full-tilt defence. The Ministry for the Environment had recently hired a new Chief Executive. The aptly named Barry Carbon was a straight-shooting Australian. He was direct, abrasive and, as it turned out, a good man in a crisis. Within 24 hours he had got his head around the enormous volume of material and fronted a press conference at which he essentially said the facts in the book were correct but the conclusion was not. It deflated the outrage a little, but GM was now well and truly the centrepiece of the election campaign. Those billboards that Michael and I were trying to fix were plastered with corn-cob stickers. The campaign had started with Labour hovering around 50% in the polls. We had already shed about 5% by the time Corngate arrived. Two weeks later we were on 40%.

For me, this was a huge test as an advisor. Marian had quickly lost her relaxed demeanour as the accusations of a cover-up hit home. She was upset by attacks on her integrity, and had some pretty ropey media appearances. But as ever there were moments of levity. She had been struggling to talk about confidence levels and false positives, which lay at the heart of the scientific debate. In an interview with John Campbell she attempted to use an analogy. She said she had recently had a breast scan that looked like it could be cancer and had been referred for further tests. She had been very worried, she told Campbell, but it turned out there was no cancer and 'my breasts are totally fine'. Not completely convinced of this analogy, but wanting to sound sympathetic, Campbell blurted out, 'I am so happy about your breasts, Marian.' We later discussed whether it was a great thing to be talking about her breasts in the media, but she seemed happy to have made her point.

Corngate was also a lesson in political management. Nicky Hager had received a huge number of documents, but there were even more that showed how the whole situation had played out. Early on I felt we would be best served by getting all the documents out there. In particular I was keen to release the documents that showed ministers being told that any early concerns that there had been an unauthorised release were in the end not found to be true and there had been no cover-up. A critical one of these, and easily the clearest of them all, had been written by a Department of the Prime Minister and Cabinet (DPMC) advisor to the PM.

One evening, as we began to gather the materials for release, Heather came to see me in Bowen House. She wanted to look through the pile of paper. After doing this she told me some documents needed to be withheld, in particular the DPMC note. Now, in fairness, it is not normal practice to release notes written by DPMC policy advisors. There have been numerous Ombudsmen's rulings accepting that this is a stream of free and frank advice that needs to be protected. But it is not a cast-iron rule, and I thought it was such an important document that its release was justified. Heather told me firmly that this was not going to happen and walked out of my office. Tired, and slightly bewildered, I followed her out to the lifts, saying (maybe shouting) that Marian needed the note because it vindicated her comments. Heather fixed her gaze on me and said, 'Helen is not getting dragged into this, end of story.'

In later years I came to understand that one of the first rules of politics is to protect the leader. Corngate was engulfing the government, and Heather was doing exactly as she should to keep Helen as distant from it as possible after the first fractious John Campbell interview. She was right, but it sure did not feel that way at the time.

There were a lot of lessons from Corngate on all sides. It was the subject of a lengthy select committee inquiry in the next Parliament. A first-term MP, David Parker, chaired that inquiry because the chair of the Environment Committee, Green MP Jeanette Fitzsimons, felt conflicted. He and I worked hour after hour going through material to explain our positions. It was clear to me right back then that David was a details man with a stronger political streak than many gave him credit for.

Corngate also taught me the lesson that I have since tried to impart to everyone I worked with in the Beehive. Your worst enemy in politics is panic. Once you start that, you're toast, especially if you're an advisor. If your minister senses that you're panicking, they lose confidence fast.

Three weeks after *Seeds of Distrust* was published, the election was held. Labour's vote had stabilised at 40%. National, with a tepid and colourless campaign led by Bill English, tanked to their worst ever result of 21%. Minor parties made huge strides, with ACT, the Greens, New Zealand First and Peter Dunne's United Future (backed by the studio audience 'worm' and a collection of crazy Christians) all gaining a large number of MPs. Labour could easily govern again, but what had been one coalition agreement became a series of agreements in different forms with the Progressives, United Future, the Greens and New Zealand First.

It would be fair to say that in some sense the traumatic experience of Corngate was the making of me politically. Despite having had a stand-up row with Heather, or perhaps because of it, I was well and truly on her radar screen. Her call to me just after the 2002 election to ask if I would join her in the PM's office to help manage the now more complex arrangements was the turning point in my political career.

This of course meant the end of my direct working relationship with Marian. I had reasoned that it was probably time for me to leave. I remember I sat in on an interview she did in early 2002. A couple of times in the interview she turned to me to check facts; another time I corrected something she said. When the interview was written up, the reporter made much of my role and suggested that I was the one running the show. That wasn't the case, but it was true that Marian and I were friends, our relationship was probably too familiar and my own political views were never far from the surface.

Marian continued as a Minister for the next three years — ditching Broadcasting and performing well when she took on the MFAT Official Development Assistance role. When I left to go to Helen Clark's office, Alastair Cameron became her advisor and really brought out the best in her.

I remember Helen saying to me that she had always wanted Marian in Cabinet because she valued her brain. Marian read every Cabinet paper. She always asked searching questions. She always brought her rock-solid Labour values to bear on any issue. As the years went by we became even closer, and my admiration for her only increased. She is principled, passionate and honest, and has been my political touchstone for 25 years. She is a guiding light for many in the Labour movement, especially young women.

And above all she is amazing fun. There was never a situation where Marian and I could not find something to laugh about. One Saturday when she was Minister for the Environment I accompanied her to an MP electorate clinic. She picked me up in our electorate van — an ageing Toyota. Marian was a fairly chaotic driver at the best of times, and the van was not the easiest to drive. We were chugging up Bowen Street when we noticed a strange smell, followed by billowing black smoke from the exhaust. We made it to the lights at Tinakori Road and sat there as the smoke continued. We were by now drawing a bit of attention. I turned to Marian and asked if she had read the paper from the Ministry for the Environment on emissions standards for cars. We laughed so hard, she had to pull over.

Heather Simpson's reputation well and truly preceded her. She was Helen Clark's right-hand woman, and by the time Labour got into government, she had been in this role for more than a decade. Heather came from Southland and had been an Economics lecturer at the University of Otago. She cut her political teeth on the campaign that began in the early '80s to stop the building of an aluminium smelter at Aramoana, near Dunedin. Her activism in the Labour Party saw her connect up with Helen, and she was an advisor when Helen first became a minister in the late 1980s.

Heather was not without her own political ambitions, twice running unsuccessfully for Parliament, once in 1987 in the unwinnable seat of Awarua, and again in 1993 in the very winnable seat of Heretaunga, near Wellington. She had also sought the Labour nomination in 1990 for Eastern Hutt. The candidate who got that nomination and became MP was Paul Swain. In later years Paul told me that his boss at the Public Service Association (PSA) had given him leave to go and convince Labour members to select him. Heather, on the other hand, had been given only one day a week to campaign.

When Helen took the party leadership after the 1993 election, Heather as Chief of Staff was there right through the tough years of the 1990s to the highs of three election wins. Her intense loyalty to Helen, and indeed to Labour, combined with her formidable intellect and personality, made people afraid of her. I came to believe that Heather wanted people to be scared of her but did not respect anyone who really was.

This was never more evident than in the weekly meeting of ministerial advisors. These meetings were held at 11am on a Friday. Heather reasoned it was a good way of making sure advisors showed up to work on a Friday (ministers left on a Thursday night) and that by 11am most of us nursing hangovers would be fully recovered. Certainly, Thursday nights were huge in my early days in the Beehive. The bar known as 3.2 would hum from the moment the ministerial limos headed to the airport. There was still smoking in the bar, and the Press Gallery would show up en masse. Several nights I found myself heading into Courtenay Place and the likes of Café Brava after 3.2 closed, occasionally in the company of Winston Peters and half the gallery. It was what they call character forming — mostly for my liver.

At the end of one of those long evenings I stopped off at the KFC in Manners Street for a late-night snack before catching a taxi home. I was pleased to be feeling okay when I woke the next morning — but that was before I discovered that I'd come home without my briefcase full of draft Cabinet papers. I was beside myself. The KFC was due to open at 10am, and I was outside that door when it did. An initial search found nothing, and then a staff member appeared from the toilets holding up my battered satchel. I was overcome with relief, pausing only briefly to note that the toilet-cleaning regime at KFC was somewhat questionable.

While Heather was disapproving of much of this kind of behaviour, she was grateful for the gossip and insight that might come out of it.

And come 11am I was expected to be there along with other advisors for a grilling about what had gone well and, more often, what had not gone well in the past week. Woe betide any advisor who could not explain what their minister was up to — or exactly where they were. This was challenging at the best of times, but even harder if you were a little the worse for wear. There was enormous relief among the advisors when after a couple of years Heather largely turned the running of the meeting over to me. I could be tough — but I was never going to match Heather's intensity.

Going up to join the 9th-floor team felt like a huge move. They were a tight crew, most of whom had been with Helen since she'd been in Opposition. The media team was Mike Munro, David Lewis and Mark Watts; Dot Kettle ran comms; and Alec McLean was the senior private secretary. I felt like a bit of an outsider, and folks were a bit surprised that Heather had decided to bring someone else in. No one was particularly sure what my job description was.

Her reasoning was that running the government with a number of partners was sure to be a challenge. I never got a job description in written form, but Heather told me once that it was 'to count to 61' — the number of votes needed to progress legislation. Those 61 votes could come from a combination of Labour and Jim Anderton's Progressive Party, who were in coalition, and United Future, New Zealand First and the Greens, with whom we had a variety of arrangements.

Multi-headed coalition agreements are the norm now, but back then Heather was writing the book as she went. She had learned from the mistakes of the first MMP government that too much detail will trip you up. The 1996 New Zealand First/National Party agreement ran to 73 pages of policy detail. So our agreements were essentially about ways of working together, with a nod to the main issues or areas of work we wanted to cooperate on. This meant that legislation was worked through on a case-by-case basis. This is where I came in. I also supported Heather and Helen with Question Time preparation, had a go at speech writing, dealt with the backbench, supported advisors in other offices and generally did whatever I was asked to do.

I also discovered that Heather quite liked having someone she could delegate difficult issues to. The rule of thumb for other offices was that if I arrived in their office, something bad was brewing; if Heather arrived, something bad had happened; and if Helen arrived, it was to say goodbye. Helen told a story after we went out of government about sending Heather down to sort out a minister who had been misbehaving. He was outraged at being growled at by Heather, and the next time he saw Helen he bitterly complained about Heather's treatment of him. Helen murmured along and said, 'Really? Gosh, that's no good, I will be sure to talk to Heather about that.'

With ministers' every step made in the public arena open to scrutiny, every decision analysed, every conversation monitored, one of the inevitabilities of being in government is that eventually some will resign or be forced to resign. Mistakes happen and things go wrong.

Lianne Dalziel was Minister of Immigration when she was caught up in a scandal about a young Sri Lankan migrant. Lianne is one of the most passionate politicians I have met. She was very aggrieved by the way the media treated this incident, and she attempted to correct what she saw as unfair coverage by getting material to media in support of her actions. I had the job of reading everything she had said about the issue to gauge if she had misled the public or Helen about her role. I did find contradictions, and reported them to Helen as requested. Lianne offered her resignation, which Helen accepted. (She would later return to Cabinet.) I was dispatched to her office to support the staff. Her senior private secretary was at a one-day cricket game at the stadium. The phone reception there was terrible, and we could not get hold of her. In the end we got a message relayed over the public address system for her to call us. Being an advisor meant being resourceful.

My core job was still occupying my attention. I installed Microsoft Project and began tracking all our legislation. At Heather's direction, I came in to support individual ministers and advisors with particularly tricky discussions and negotiations. One of the first was the Responsible Gambling legislation that was looking to stop further casinos being developed and control the growth of pokie machines. It was a good example of how we had to work.

The relevant Minister had not been able to make progress on the legislation. I came in and started working with the Greens, who had identified the issue as important to them. The researcher on their side was Russel Norman, later to become Greens co-leader. They were adamant about provisions of the Bill that went further than Labour was comfortable with. We tried to find ways through, but when it appeared unlikely we could make progress, I switched to working with United Future to see if they could agree. Oddly for a Christian-based party, they wanted a more liberal regime. We moved a few things around — held onto the core objective of preventing more casinos, and compromised a bit on pokie machines — while still tightening up the regime. I had to go back to the Greens and say thanks, but we have found another way through. The net result, I might say, was that the Responsible Gambling Bill ended up being called just the Gambling Bill. Perhaps not something to be remembered for!

Heather was extraordinary in how she could look ahead to trouble spots. Her combination with Mike Munro, and later David Lewis as chief press secretary, was superb. They would often come at issues from a very different perspective, but they gave Helen the ultimate backstop and protection. Helen was at her finest when she looked at what was usually a long-term versus short-term dilemma and picked a path through. Heather was instrumental in making Helen one of our very best PMs.

Helen Clark is the reason I joined the Labour Party. Having come to my political consciousness in the later years of the Fourth Labour Government, I was not in a mood to join up, despite feeling aligned with the history of the party. But once Helen took over I sensed the old Labour Party coming back, and it was her effort in the 1996 election that convinced me to finally sign up. Down and out at the beginning of that year, she fought hard. Her version of social democracy resonated with me as a chance to achieve something rather than shouting from the outside.

Admiring her from afar was one thing; going to work for her was another. She was formidable. She was across every issue, and has a crystal-clear memory and finely attuned bullshit detector. She was extremely direct when she was not happy. On one occasion in the later years of her time in office she was sent a copy of a draft speech by a new staff member. She put red pen through most of the speech and faxed it back with a note written on the top of it: 'I don't know who you are, or what your job is, but you are not very good at it.'

In 2002 I was very much thrown in the deep end. On some days Helen could get up to six oral questions in the House. She was meticulous in her preparation, and we had to be too. We would be advised of the details of the question somewhere between 10.30am and 11am. There was usually a quick conversation about likely angles and answers, and then a sprint to around 12.30pm when I would pull the material together for Heather to look at and final tweaks to be made. At 1pm we would brief Helen.

Sometimes I would leave her and Heather to it, but more often than not I would sit with them in the PM's boardroom. Most days a relevant minister would be called or summoned to the office. Helen would usually have an egg sandwich, a banana and a cup of tea as she prepared herself. I never told her that I was allergic to eggs, but I was very glad for the size of the boardroom table.

In my time with Helen there was only one issue I think she got wrong, and that was the Foreshore and Seabed legislation. Timing is everything in politics, and the Foreshore and Seabed issue arose when the Opposition was beginning to push race as a debate. Don Brash, the new leader of the National Party, delivered the famous Ōrewa speech in early 2004, scratching a political itch about so-called privilege for Māori. I saw this as a diabolical speech, full of exaggeration, lies and dog whistles. But it worked for him, giving National a massive boost in the polls.

Labour grappled with the issue of race from then on. Helen even appointed Trevor Mallard as Minister Coordinating Race Relations. It did not have the calming effect intended. Trevor declared himself indigenous to Wainuiomata in his usual diplomatic style.

The issue of ownership of the foreshore and seabed had been debated through a court case brought by iwi from the upper part of the South Island. It had found its way to the Court of Appeal who ruled there was a right for iwi to pursue an interest in ownership. Rather than let the issue go through the courts, Helen and the Cabinet judged that they needed to legislate over the top of the court to get the outcome they wanted — a ruling that the seabed and foreshore was publicly owned — rather than risk a negative outcome or a drawn-out debate that would play into Brash's hands.

This is one of the only times I believe panic took hold. Helen felt that she could not hold middle New Zealand without putting this issue to bed. It felt wrong — and when tens of thousands of people descended on Parliament Grounds, it proved to be a turning point in New Zealand politics. At that moment the Māori Party was born, and the strong hold that Labour had had over the Māori vote began to wilt. Helen might argue that her plan worked, because Labour would win again in 2005, having seen off Don Brash. That is true, but the collateral damage was significant.

That 2005 election campaign was one of the more bizarre in New Zealand's history, in large part because of the role of the Exclusive

Brethren. This odd religious sect was not a fan of the Labour government, women, gays or liberals in general. It poured money into an anti-government, pro-National campaign. Hundreds of thousands of leaflets were delivered to homes across New Zealand. As chronicled in Nicky Hager's *The Hollow Men*, Don Brash, John Key and others in National were well aware of the campaign, and some even gave it their tacit support. That, however, was not what Don Brash was telling the world. When confronted about the campaign, he claimed to know nothing about it.

Our team on the 9th floor were able to play a small but important role in giving the story momentum. We had a pretty sophisticated operation in place in 2005. We had a rapid response group which included me, later Labour Party General Secretary Rob Salmond, a newly arrived advisor named Jacinda Ardern and others. One of our jobs was to monitor the media. We heard an interview with Don Brash on bFM, the Auckland student station, in which he appeared to acknowledge that he had met with members of the Exclusive Brethren. We listened to the audio several times and concluded that he did indeed say this. We released an interview that few had heard out to the mainstream news media, and the rest is history. Brash was caught out, and while he pushed hard in the election campaign, the inkling that he could not be trusted took hold.

For us, the winning moment in that election was the policy to introduce interest-free student loans. This was a huge issue for my generation, who had encountered interest rates of up to 8%. The interest rate created a phenomenon called 'flat-spotting', where you met the threshold to pay back your loan, but were not keeping up with the interest, so found the size of your loan staying the same or getting bigger. We were able to assure Helen that there was a massive constituency who would benefit from interest-free student loans: graduates with growing loan balances, current students looking to many years of debt ahead, and parents and grandparents worried about the future of their children and grandchildren.

Labour had already removed interest from loans while studying, but the next step — making them interest free for the life of the loan — was a huge one to take. We had to progress the idea largely in secret. A team was formed called the Thursday Group (imaginatively named after the day on which we first met). It included Jacinda Ardern, Rob Salmond and fellow advisors Chris Hipkins and David Choat. Rob had grasped the value of the internet to campaigning. He came up with the idea of an online calculator that would allow you to punch in the size of your loan and calculate what you would now save as a result of the policy. The communications nous of Jacinda was also clear. She wanted to be able to show what the policy would mean to people. She went out with her sister's Handycam and 'vox-popped' people in Cuba Mall about loans and what a policy like this would mean. It was not exactly hi-tech, but it worked.

On the day of the reveal I called in NZUSA co-presidents Camilla Belich and Andrew Kirton to tell them what was to be announced. Camilla burst into tears. I was very emotional too. All the efforts we had made in the student movement in the 1990s to keep the fight against user-pays education alive finally felt worth it. We had started to turn the tide.

The announcement was made over at Victoria University's Pipitea Campus. We handed out packs to the media before Helen arrived, and at first people could not get their heads around the scale of what we were doing. They kept asking if it really meant zero interest.

As Helen began to make the announcement, Camilla texted Bill English, now the National Party Education spokesperson, to tell him what was happening. He texted her back something to the effect of 'Rubbish, they haven't?' Everyone was caught by surprise. By the end of the day stories were filtering through from offices around the country where graduates were huddled over computers, entering their balances into Rob's calculator and cheering as the savings popped up.

The policy was a triumph, and we excitedly sent Helen out on the road on a tour of universities to promote it. Popular as it was, the anti-government grouping was vocal this time around. At Canterbury University in particular Helen got a very hard time from a group of mostly male ACT supporters. She was not happy, and we had to pull out all the stops to make her next visit at Victoria University work smoothly. It did, and the reason it did was thanks to Jacinda Ardern.

Jacinda had come to our attention early in the term. She had started working in Phil Goff's office, but relatively quickly ended up as the advisor in Associate Energy Minister Harry Duynhoven's office. Harry was an idiosyncratic character, loyal to the core to Labour, but somewhat on the right of the party and particularly keen on anything that involving digging or drilling. He was capable of the odd faux pas. He once accidentally lost his New Zealand citizenship by too enthusiastically embracing his Dutch heritage and taking up citizenship, thereby voiding his New Zealand one. We had to pass an emergency law to save him. So, he could be a bit of a handful. And yet Jacinda managed him with apparent ease.

She was active in Young Labour, and seemed like the kind of person we should have around. When a vacancy in our office emerged, Heather asked me who I thought would be good to approach. Jacinda came to mind right away. I took her for coffee (which she did not drink) and asked her if she would come to work with us. She was very loyal to Harry but was already thinking about moving on from his office. She agreed to join me in a fairly cramped, messy office on the 9th floor.

From day one her political instincts, incredible work ethic and absolute Labourness shone. It was great to have someone with her capability to share the load. We became fast friends. I have often taken credit for taking Jacinda from sober Mormon to the whisky-loving, sailor-level swearer that she is today. That might be a bit of an exaggeration, but I think we were pretty good for each other.

A major turning point in Jacinda's relationship with the Mormon Church was the Civil Union legislation. Labour had grappled with a position on the issue of marriage equality for several years. I had been the Rainbow Sector representative on the party's Policy Council for a number of years, and we had floated a few options. Despite a strong desire to achieve equality, Tim Barnett, Chris Carter, Maryan Street and other leaders in our sector concluded that we had the numbers only to get civil unions across the line. Helen, despite being a tremendous ally for the Rainbow community, had judged the public not ready for full marriage equality, and that essentially curtailed our options.

A bill was drafted that would create civil unions and give civil-union partners the same rights as those who are married. We had to leave issues around related matters, such as adoption rights, to one side in order to hold support for the Bill.

It was decided to adopt it as a government Bill but allow a conscience vote by the Labour Caucus. This would avoid debate being dragged out over a long period and enable better management of the process of amendments. I worked on it as the point person from the PM's office.

Tim Barnett, the Labour MP for Christchurch Central, was an incredible organiser. We used to laugh when accusations of the government having a 'gay agenda' were made. Tim had a policy document that was literally called 'The Gay Agenda' on the wall of his office. We knew we could not pass the Bill with Labour votes alone, and needed to make up for a handful of Labour MPs who would vote against. Tim and his office managed a spreadsheet to track the positions of MPs from all parties. I had a job to make sure the votes of our likely coalition allies held firm. It was hard going.

In the public arena, debate was furious. The proponents of the Bill were well organised, with the Campaign for Civil Unions led by some experienced political operators, such as Tim's former staff member Hoani Lambert, later to become a senior public servant; Margaret Mayman, the minister from St Andrew's on the Terrace; lawyer Cameron Law; and Auckland-based activist Michael Wallmannsberger.

The opponents were not so organised, but they were vocal. The most vocal of all was Brian Tamaki. His Destiny Church was growing across the country. His form of evangelism had a particular draw for Māori and Pasifika populations, and Destiny had a large supply of funds, partly drawn from the tithe put on their parishioners. The peak of their opposition to the Bill was the 'Enough is Enough' rally in August 2004 against the so-called moral decay of the country under Labour. Dressed in black trousers and black T-shirts emblazoned with 'Enough is Enough', he and his mostly male followers marched down Lambton Quay punching the air, chanting and looking like an army of hate.

At Parliament I stood on the steps with several staff and MPs holding a Rainbow flag. A reasonable-sized crowd of counter-protesters had gathered too but were well and truly outnumbered by Brian's army, who performed haka and made angry speeches about 'filth' and 'perversion'. Alf attended the counter-protest — an unusual political act for him — and was deeply disturbed to see so many Māori faces screaming in anger at him.

Georgina Beyer, the world's first transgender MP, and a Labour list MP, was with us on the steps. She had had enough. She marched down to confront the protesters. I genuinely thought she was going to get beaten up. I took off after her, alongside Tim's partner Ramon Maniapoto and others, clutching the Rainbow flag. God knows what we thought we were going to be able to do! Georgina walked up and down the front of the protesters, challenging how they could claim to be Christians and Māori when they were filled with such hate. It was courageous and raw and wonderful, and so very Georgina.

A day after the protest I checked in on a couple of our wavering supporters in New Zealand First. One of them was Brian Donnelly, a schoolteacher from the far north. He and I had developed a good working relationship over the previous few years, and I had written him a letter explaining my own circumstances — I essentially came out to him — and reasons for supporting the Bill. He had responded by saying he was in something of a moral dilemma about the legislation but he would seriously consider what I had said. In the wake of the Destiny Church rally, Brian told me his position had hardened. There was no way he was going to let the hatred he had seen that day win. I heard of a number of other MPs and many members of the public who felt the same way. We probably owe Brian Tamaki a lot, even if it did not feel so great at the time.

In the end the Bill passed 65–55. It felt a lot closer than that. I had also worked on a companion Bill, the Relationships (Statutory References) Bill, which changed 108 pieces of legislation to make civil unions equivalent in law to marriage. It was a reminder to me that in all campaigns there is a mixture of public and private, direct and indirect work that makes for success.

The 2005 election saw Labour secure enough votes to be the largest party, though National performed significantly better than in 2002. Again the combined forces of United Future, the Greens and New Zealand First would enable us to govern. I did quite a bit of work behind the scenes of the coalition negotiations. My natural instincts were that there was now an opportunity to work more closely with our closest allies, the Greens. I think Helen and Heather felt the same. But the maths did not quite work. Labour and the Greens together could not form a majority. We would need the agreement of either New Zealand First or United Future to support that arrangement. They were not interested in that at all. Helen, ever the pragmatist, knew what she had to do, especially given her hope that Labour could be the equivalent of Sweden's Social Democrats, who had governed for close to 20 years. The numbers did add up if we went with both New Zealand First and United Future. We put in place some unique arrangements to allow the government to benefit from Jeanette Fitzsimons's knowledge in the environment and energy area, with Greens co-leader Rod Donald in the area of Buy NZ Made. Rod tragically died before he could properly take up that role, which passed to Sue Bradford.

I was tiring a bit of the advisor's role, and there was little prospect of career progression with Heather so firmly in her position. Besides, that was not where I saw my future. Prior to the 2005 election I had approached Helen and Heather to say I was considering putting my name forward for the Labour nomination for the Ōhāriu-Belmont electorate. The seat was held by Peter Dunne, and was considered unwinnable, but standing there would be a clear signal of my interest in becoming an MP. My time as an advisor had only served to sharpen my desire to do so. I now actually knew what an MP did. I had seen up close how Marian had worked as Wellington Central MP and the enormous contribution that an MP like her could make.

Helen and Heather counselled me against seeking the nomination. Their reasoning was a combination of self-interest, in that they wanted me around the PM's office for the campaign, and their knowledge that Charles Chauvel, a long-term Labour member, was putting himself forward. The timing was not right. And timing, as I was to discover, is everything in politics. I eventually agreed.

But post-election I felt differently. I needed a change, and I also knew if I was going to be an MP it would be useful to expand my political experience and do something else for a while. My decision to leave the advisor's role was made even easier when Marian told me that this was going to be her last term. She wanted to have one more crack at teaching, and to do an OE she had never had the chance to do. She also told me she thought I was the right person to follow on from her in the Wellington Central seat.

In mid-2006 I was approached by the head of the Research and Enterprise Office of the University of Otago to see if I would be interested in a position representing my alma mater in Wellington. It was just about the perfect role for me. It connected me back to home in Dunedin, but had me living and working in the capital, using all that I had absorbed over the previous few years.

At my farewell I was presented with a signed copy of the latest Budget by Helen and Michael Cullen. In her speech Heather noted that she and I had had our moments, but that once she worked out that I wanted Helen's job, not hers, we got on fine. She, as ever, was right. The lure of politics and Parliament that I had felt since a young age was well and truly in place. I had learned from three extraordinary women what it was really about, how to succeed and why it all mattered. Now it was time to try to do it for myself.

8.

THE CAMPAIGN FOR WELLINGTON CENTRAL

In the Labour Party, as in most political parties, the first step to becoming an MP is to be selected as a candidate by party members. In the politically conscious Wellington Central electorate, this group is made up of long-term older party members from working-class backgrounds, university students, young professionals, urban liberals and, yes, even a few public servants.

I knew I would have a decent amount of support for the nomination. My involvement in Wellington Central that had begun at the fateful Thorndon Branch meeting years earlier had continued. On returning from New York I had not only worked in Marian's office but also served as a branch chair and member of the Electorate and Campaign Committees. I had, as the saying goes, made the policy and made the tea. But I also knew there would be others interested in the seat. Richard Prebble's win for ACT in 1996 had shown it was definitely not a safe Labour seat, but Marian had held it for nine years and Fran Wilde for a number of terms before that.

Once Marian made her decision public in late 2006, various people started to show an interest. One of them was Helen Kelly. I had worked with Helen in the electorate for five years. She was a terrific organiser and leader, and was always prepared to get her hands dirty. She totally revamped our pamphlet delivery system for the electorate, creating a block system, with lead deliverers and a clear plan for each delivery. That is still the system used today. Equally she pushed hard inside the party for wins for working people — increased annual leave, health and safety, and fair bargaining laws. Helen had grown up in the electorate, tutored in the ways of unions and politics by her wonderful parents Pat and Cath. I knew that if she wanted the nomination for the seat she would almost certainly get it.

But she was on a different trajectory. She was the head of my union at the time — the Association of University Staff — and was rumoured to have her eye on the presidency of the Council of Trade Unions. I met Helen for coffee and told her I was interested in the seat. She was, as always, direct. She told me it was the seat she had always wanted but that she had in fact made her mind up to go for the CTU presidency. Without me even having to ask, she said she would back me for the nomination, and we started to draw up a campaign plan. Helen and I stayed close over the following years. Like so many others, I was devastated when she revealed her cancer diagnosis in February 2015. She faced this with huge courage and integrity. She kept fighting for working people even when gravely ill — for the families of the men killed in the Pike River mine collapse, for the forestry workers injured and killed at work and their families, and for locked-out meatworkers. I was able to present her Labour Party Life Membership certificate to her shortly before she died in October 2016. We missed a great deal by her never making it into Parliament. She would have been an incredible minister.

When it all shook down, there was one other person who had a decent chance of winning the Wellington Central nomination: Charles Chauvel.

I knew Charles pretty well. He was a fellow member of the Rainbow sector. He had been around the Labour Party since he was a teenager and had fashioned a successful career as a lawyer in one of the big firms. He had been the candidate in Ōhāriu-Belmont in the 2005 election, doing exactly as I had considered doing, and had just missed being elected off the list on election night. He came into

Parliament midway through 2006. My observation was that Charles was ambitious, and from the moment he entered Parliament he began seeking promotion. I was warned by various people not to take him on. 'Even if you win you could make an enemy for life,' a mutual friend confided.

Charles initially had the backing of the party leadership (including Helen Clark) and had strong support from the union leadership too. However, he had not been active in Wellington Central itself. I definitely had the upper hand among active members whom I had worked alongside for the last five years. Marian's endorsement mattered as well. She was not going to be public about it but was happy to tell anyone who asked who her preference was.

Through 2007 the jostling for the nomination intensified. The Labour Party's selection rules are like the rules of Monopoly. Only a few people have actually read them, they cause a lot of fights and, in truth, you do not want to know them unless you really have to. But in short, and in the case of Wellington Central, in each selection committee the Labour Party Council has three representatives and local members have three representatives (one of them elected by the people who show up to the selection meeting). A seventh vote comes from a straw poll of members after candidates have spoken at the selection meeting.

Given the support for Charles from the party leadership, I knew that I had to win over the members and secure the four votes on offer. So, I set myself the job of personally talking to every one of the five hundred or so members in the electorate. It meant drinking a huge number of cups of tea. Still, as the selection meeting approached in November 2007, nomination was looking like an uphill battle. I was determined to stay in the race. I felt like Wellington Central was my place, and I owed it to Marian to try to carry on her hard work.

The Labour Party conference that year was held on the North Shore in Auckland. Helen Clark had done a small Cabinet reshuffle in the days leading up to it. Charles had been in Parliament for just over a year but had high expectations he would be made a minister. He was not, but issued a press release welcoming his own 'promotion' to the role of parliamentary private secretary (PPS) to Attorney-General Michael Cullen. This is a role for a Caucus member who provides support to a minister; they are not in the Executive and there is no extra pay for the position. It was obvious that this was Charles trying to pre-empt the fact he had not been named a minister. The PM's office made clear its dissatisfaction by telling the media that consideration was being given to the PPS role but no final decision had been made.

As I headed to Auckland, I did not think too much about what had happened, knowing that Charles was prone to this kind of outburst. But on the first day of the conference I was walking along past the various stalls when I felt myself being pulled sideways. I looked around to see Helen's hand on my shoulder, forcefully guiding me to where she was lurking behind a screen. She pulled me into an alcove for a chat. Helen indicated that she was no longer expressing a preference in the contest for Wellington Central. She noted that my background in student politics showed that I must have something about me that would be helpful in campaigning. Then she sent me on my way.

For the next few days nothing much seemed to change. Charles carried on campaigning, and so did I. My focus moved to ensuring that I had a big turnout at the selection meeting to be held later in the month. The competition was intense, and my feeling was that the nomination could go either way.

Then, a week before the selection meeting, Charles emailed local party members to say he was withdrawing from the contest. Nominations had well and truly closed, so it meant I would be uncontested for the seat and would be the candidate.

There was, however, one more hurdle to cross. I got a call from Labour Party General Secretary Mike Smith to tell me that he intended to re-open nominations for the seat. I called my friend, lawyer Alastair Cameron, and asked him to come to meet with me, Mike and Party President Mike Williams.

We met in a cafe in Wellington, and Mike Smith said that given Charles's late withdrawal he considered that they should re-open nominations to give a chance to others who might have entered the race if Charles had not been involved. I reacted strongly and told Mike that he would have a legal battle on his hands if he tried to do that. I had followed all the constitutional rules, and there had been plenty of uncontested selections. Mike Smith then indicated that he was concerned about my inexperience as a candidate for such a high-profile seat as Wellington Central.

At that point I'd had enough, and told both Mikes in no uncertain terms that we were going ahead with the meeting the following Sunday. I let them know that for five years I had been showing up for Wellington Central and I would keep doing that. I don't remember everything I said that day, but Mike Williams has told me subsequently that what he saw in those moments convinced him I had what it took to be an MP.

Mike Smith backed off (and subsequently became a strong supporter of mine), and on a sunny Sunday afternoon at the St John's Church hall on Willis Street, I was endorsed as Labour's Wellington Central candidate. I was elated, and very aware of the mountain I had to climb. While I was pretty well known in Labour circles, I had zero profile in the wider electorate.

Wellington Central always attracts a lot of attention. It's the home of Parliament, and of the public service, and it's where many of the Press Gallery live. In the MMP era, the electorate is also likely to have a number of resident MPs. This was going to be the case in the 2008 election. And while the Greens and ACT held little hope of winning the seat, they had sitting MPs Sue Kedgley and Heather Roy as their candidates.

For the National Party it was an interesting situation. Their candidate in 2005 had been former Mayor of Wellington Mark Blumsky. During the campaign he was found bloodied and unconscious on the stairwell leading to his inner-city apartment. This was front-page news, and the rumour mill went into overdrive. He lost the election to Marian but came into Parliament on the list. He never found his groove and was not standing at all in 2008.

Enter Stephen Franks. Stephen had been an ACT MP for a couple of terms but had lost his seat in 2005 when ACT's vote tanked. He was a long-time resident of Mt Victoria in Wellington, but a few eyebrows were raised when he popped up as a National candidate in 2008. He was representative of the Don Brash part of the party that was now all but defunct under the new leader John Key. Nevertheless, he became National's candidate for Wellington Central, and an intense election campaign began.

The Labour Party in Wellington Central under Marian's guidance was an impressive team. But I knew I needed to lift my profile. I asked Alastair to be my campaign manager. We had known each other since the late 1990s when he started working on Labour campaigns as a 16-year-old. Alastair has always been wise beyond his years, and is one of the most organised and meticulous people I know.

We went back to the basics — days and days of door-knocking. Wellington Central is hilly, and weekend after weekend some hardy volunteers and I set about covering the electorate. As I stared at another set of steps or massive driveway, I would remind myself that the election could come down to a handful of votes. A couple of times when, puffing and cursing, I made it to the door of the house, the person who greeted me said that no politician had ever knocked on their door before. That made it all worthwhile.

We also deployed an old staple of Wellington Central campaigns — cottage meetings, where a supporter invites their neighbours and friends to meet the candidate and ask questions. In Wellington Central this is an especially hazardous experience. On one occasion I was asked to explain a particular part of our early childhood education policy. I thought I was doing a reasonable job until I saw the expression on the questioner's face. It dawned on me that this person might well know a bit more about the topic than me. It turned out they did — they were a policy advisor in the Ministry of Education. But meetings like these were character forming — and honed my skills for the candidate debates that lay ahead.

We also began street-corner meetings early in the campaign. These involved leafleting an area to say I would be on the corner of a particular street at a particular time, and inviting all and sundry along. These were designed as whistle-stop meetings, 15 to 20 minutes each. We developed a formula that I used for every election thereafter. A person with a megaphone arrived 10 minutes before I did, marching up and down the street to remind people that I was on my way. I would swoop in, grab the megaphone, and do a three- to five-minute speech, by the end of which a crowd had usually gathered. I would then pass the megaphone back, and the advance party would head off to the next stop while I engaged with whoever had gathered. Sometimes it was only a couple of people, sometimes it was 20 or 30. It didn't matter: people knew we were there. Marian used to talk about the 'curtain twitchers' who would never come outside but watched and listened carefully.

In that first campaign I did over a hundred street-corner meetings. They went ahead even if the weather turned against us — as it did several times. On one occasion the wind was blowing so hard at the top of Northland that one of my volunteers lost control of their sign, which almost decapitated another volunteer. On another it was so wet we stayed in the branded car to see if anyone showed up. A couple did just that, and I hopped out to say hello. They told me they had come along only because they were convinced I would not be there. One of them said he would vote for me on that basis alone.

But showing up on people's doors and street corners was not going to be enough. I needed a couple of local issues. One of those somewhat fell into my lap. While working for the University of Otago I had been renting office space from a company called MediaLab (later to be renamed Harmonic). The CEO, Phil Shepherd, was a Mt Victoria resident and involved in the community house and crèche known as Crossways. They were in a battle with the owners of their premises, the Presbyterian Church, and the City Council over whether they could stay and, if not, where they could go. I took up the cause, first to try to save the premises, and then to help find new ones. I lobbied everyone I could think of, and helped drum up publicity around the importance of community spaces. We were initially unsuccessful in saving the Centre, but people in the community saw that that I cared, and I made some terrific contacts — and a year or so later we found new premises for the Centre too.

The second issue was one I created myself. I had friends who lived in the central city, and through Marian I knew that residents had a number of ongoing concerns, with rubbish, safety, noise and parking top of the list. I decided to call a meeting for people interested in inner-city issues. I knew I could get a few people to come along, but was pretty surprised when close to a hundred people showed up. They included the local Wellington city councillors and a somewhat peeved-looking Stephen Franks.

There was a lot of energy in the room — and at the end of the meeting I asked if there were volunteers who might want to pull together an Inner City Residents Association. There were. I dragooned my friend Gus Charteris to be the chair, and the association formed that evening. It continues today as Inner City Wellington, a very active lobbying and advocacy group. For years people assumed I lived in the inner city because of my involvement in its establishment.

As the election loomed, I knew Wellington Central would be close. Labour was polling consistently behind National. After nine years the public were tiring of the government, and the economy, which had been going gangbusters, was starting to slow down in the face of the Global Financial Crisis (GFC). In Wellington itself the mood was a little better, but it was still not great.

Among its other traditions Wellington Central always hosts a number of public meet-the-candidates gatherings. The most famous of these is in the Aro Valley, where candidates are sprayed by water pistols and general mayhem ensues. There are more when there are new candidates in the mix, and in 2008 there were 21 of these meetings. The audience is almost always made up of decided voters, so there is little to be gained from participating. But there is always a lot to be lost if you make a mistake and the media are there to report it.

The first gathering in 2008 was in Wadestown, the bluest bit of the electorate, although home to some hardcore Labour supporters too. All 14 candidates, representing all the major parties as well as a clutch of independents, were present. When we drew lots to speak, independent Al Mansell drew number one. He stood up, surveyed the good and the great in the audience, nervously laughed and said, 'It's great to be back in Wadestown. The last time I was here it was to steal your opium poppies.' Al was not too long out of prison for various drug offences. He had decided to become a candidate after discussing his rehabilitation with his probation officer. I became quite fond of him and tried to help him navigate the complexities of the election. He baked me a cake for my birthday which fell midway through the campaign. On balance I decided not to eat it given Al's well-stated views about the use of certain 'herbs' in cooking!

We were in Kelburn for the final candidates meeting. Al decided that this would be a good night to talk about just how far he had come. He brought with him a taser gun that he had used to enforce the payment of drug debts. He also brought a hammer that he used to smash the taser to show this was all in the past. Unfortunately, the taser was switched on and as Al began to smash it, the weapon sparked and started moving of its own accord across the floor. I was up on my seat as Al manically chased the taser around the church hall.

The candidates meetings had made me understand something about myself. I loved them. The debate, the interjections, the Q & A were all to my liking.

That was clearly not the case for Stephen Franks. I had seen this at our very first event, a debate organised by students at Wellington College. They had chosen two left-leaning and two right-leaning pupils to join Stephen and me in teams. Stephen spoke first. I had expected that as a lawyer and former MP he would be comfortable speaking in public. But he was not. His voice was not strong, and he seemed diffident, almost uninterested in having to explain himself to voters. Part of the issue was that he was not really able to be his authentic self. In ACT he had been able to say and do pretty much anything. In a mainstream party he found he was restricted. Early on in the campaign he spoke favourably about nuclear-powered ships. National had to come in over the top of him and say this was not party policy. But his greatest slip-up in the campaign came in the most innocuous of surroundings.

A group of students had somehow convinced all the major party candidates to join them for a meeting at their Aro Valley flat — I think it might have been the flat of the students' association president.

We candidates were sandwiched onto a couple of sofas while the students sat on the floor. We got to a question about same-sex marriage. Stephen had opposed civil unions on what I thought were spurious technical grounds. I noted he had actually said some offensive things. Stephen asked if that was when he said he was sick of 'grumpy Christians and whining gays'. I said no, it was when you said, 'I love my dog, but that doesn't mean I should be able to marry it.'

The reaction in the room was one of shock, and cries of 'shame'. Stephen kept trying to explain himself, claiming that love was not enough to justify a law change, but the damage was done. Stephen's remark was played on a weekly current affairs show that asked for people to send in clips they had filmed on the campaign trail, and then went viral. The issue came up a few more times in candidates meetings. Whatever justification Stephen had for his view, it didn't work.

Despite all of this, the election remained too close to call. We did a poll with a couple of weeks to go, and I was in front by about 2%. Sue Kedgley for the Greens was assuring people she was only after the party vote but was still getting a solid percentage of the electorate vote. Heather Roy from ACT was not making the same inroads into Stephen's vote.

On election day itself I was a wreck. I spent much of it wondering what work I could do if I lost. I had been placed at number 46 on the party list — an absolute guarantee that if I did not get the seat I was not going into Parliament.

We had our election-night party at the Basin Reserve grandstand. It was *very* stressful. Booth results came through slowly, and at first the lead switched between Stephen and me. I got my nose in front from mid-evening and stayed there. The last couple of big booths from Mt Victoria and the Aro Valley saw me pull further ahead to an on-the-night majority of 1500 (later to rise to 1904 after special votes). We were jubilant that a year of hard work had paid off and we had held the seat.

But the picture nationwide was as the polling had indicated it would be. Moments after I delivered my victory speech, Helen Clark was on TV conceding the election and announcing that she would be stepping down as Labour leader. It was the definition of a night of conflicting emotions.

The Class of 2008 who were elected that night included some kindred spirits. Down the road from me Chris Hipkins, or Chippy as he was known to everyone, another advisor from the Clark era, had romped home to win Rimutaka. Others whom I had got to know such as Clare Curran in Dunedin South and Phil Twyford off the list in Auckland were in Parliament too. And then there was Jacinda Ardern.

Jacinda had begun the election period campaigning from London where she was living. The Wellington region nominated her for the Labour list. We ensured that she was placed as high as possible, knowing that there was no seat for her to fall back on. In the end she was asked to come home to contest the unwinnable Waikato seat. Inevitably, she got nowhere there, but as a 28-year-old she entered Parliament via a strong list position.

I was thrilled to have Jacinda alongside me as a new MP. We had stayed in touch after our time working together in the Beehive and caught up a few times while she was overseas. We thought very similarly about politics — sharing a strong core of progressive politics mixed with a desire to achieve real change. It was a philosophy we would later coin as 'pragmatic idealism'. Now we had a chance to put it into practice.

Straight after the election, she and Alf (accompanied by TV cameras) took me shopping for a new suit, the beginning of a fruitless journey to try to spruce me up!

We walked into a Caucus that was still stacked with former ministers and senior MPs from the previous government. The Cabinet had what was described as a cathartic last meeting, out of which emerged a consensus that Phil Goff would be nominated as leader. The motivation for this was clearly to avoid a messy leadership fight, but as new MPs we felt like we were being railroaded. I was not sure that there was anyone I especially preferred to Phil, though a few of our intake were keen on David Cunliffe. Helen Clark called us in to talk through our concerns. I remember Brendon Burns, the new Christchurch Central MP, and I tried to raise the concerns. But Helen was not interested. For the very first time I saw her emotional, as she fought back tears asking us to please not re-litigate the decision of the outgoing Cabinet.

In the end we agreed, and Phil was elected leader and Annette King as deputy leader. As is often the case, there was an odd feeling of optimism at the beginning of the term. The new Prime Minister John Key was relatively inexperienced and after nine years there were few ministers with experience either. The country was also plunging headlong into the GFC, caused in part by the greed of finance people just like John Key. We began to convince ourselves that the public would see through his likeable image soon enough. We were most definitely guilty of underestimating Key, as National would later be with Jacinda. Politics is often tribal, and it is hard to accept that the other side are in the ascendancy. With Key, National was very much on the up.

9.
NINE LONG YEARS

My maiden speech in Parliament, delivered in early December 2008, was the result of a lot of work. I researched the speeches of a number of my heroes and predecessors. I was very aware of the likes of Peter Fraser and Fran Wilde in Wellington Central, and of course of Helen Clark and Michael Cullen who were still in the House. New MPs were advised to show our speeches to at least one senior colleague in advance, so I chose Michael. He very kindly came back with only one suggestion, which was to dial back the joke I made about Alf being a halfback while I was the No. 8. He was right, and the version I did put in, minus references to balls and legs, still got a laugh.

My speech was an attempt to put together my vision for a socially just New Zealand by returning to the influences that had made me who I am: an upbringing that put fairness, compassion and hard work at the centre; a belief that education matters; and my pride in our nation as we stood up in the world. I finished the speech by saying:

> *I say quite simply the reason I entered the political arena was my belief in social justice. My desire is to play a part in making my community, city, country and world a fairer and more equal place, because it is that equality that will drive aspiration, opportunity and success for all. In my time in this Parliament, it is my commitment that I will work to build an ever better, fairer New Zealand, where we seek to ensure that achieving one's potential is not just the preserve of the privileged, but possible for all.*

I also said in that speech that I was first and foremost the MP for Wellington Central. Right from the start I was focused on winning the seat again. I carried on attending as many events as possible, visiting schools, businesses, NGOs and more. I held electorate clinics on Saturdays around the city and persisted with many of Marian's projects as well as a few of my own.

In all of this I was aided by the most exceptional electorate staff you could ever want. The people who work in electorate offices around the country are heroes of democracy. In my case, Sheila Linton and Anna Locker-Lampson were carry-overs from Marian's time. They were incredible. Sheila was already well on the way to being a resident expert on immigration (by far the most commonly raised topic by constituents) and was connected into communities across the electorate. Anna knew everyone. She had previously worked for the community newspaper *City Voice*, and her personality helped too. She had a number of friends from the right of politics, and she played tennis. Frequently her conversations would begin with, 'We were talking at tennis last night . . .' I added to the staff by bringing ex-Young Labour folk to help with our communications, starting with Kurt Sharpe. I thought the office was a great training ground for a younger group interested in politics, but the truth is we learned as much from them as they learned from us.

Our philosophy in the office in Willis Street was that our doors were always open. Over the years, Anna would often say that her friends were staggered by what we did there. I knew that I wanted to be an advocate for those who did not normally have a voice, and this meant that all kinds of characters became part of our lives. We saw a lot of the residents of the nearby social housing complexes. I would visit them at places like Vincents Art Workshop and made many friends among them. Many lived fragile lives, not working and barely making ends meet.

Work and Income was across the street from our electorate office.

Day after day we would watch people leave there and come across the road to us. The new National government had issued instructions to Work and Income to not automatically grant beneficiaries access to all of their entitlements. It was cruel, and led to some terrible outcomes which we did our best to rectify.

People who come to an MP's office are often at their wits' end. My heart used to sink when I saw someone arrive at the door with massive files, usually for an ACC or Inland Revenue case. Introducing myself with the question, 'What can I do to help?', I decided early on that my job was to do all I could to try to find a positive outcome for them. Sometimes, as with an ACC case that had been appealed at every level, it was impossible. Other times, such as with immigration issues, we could spend years and years advocating for someone, only for the process to end in disappointment. But when we did succeed, it was hugely rewarding. I remember one of the so-called *Tampa* boys, a refugee from Afghanistan, who spent years trying to get his family to join him in New Zealand. There were always barriers — they did not have birth certificates, they could not prove anything about their identities to the officials. We worked hard to support him through all of that — and the day he came into the office with his parents, we all cried.

Of course, not all encounters with the electorate were happy. We had someone try to overdose in the office, a couple of people try to pull the door off its hinges in anger and rage. But Sheila, Anna and Sophia Shanks, who later joined them, kept helping out anyone they could.

I continue to believe that a physical electorate office presence is an essential part of our democracy. People need somewhere to go, to feel that their representative is a real person. For an MP, it is also the best way to stay grounded. I despair at those who are elected who do not see this as important. It is the bedrock of our system and needs to be taken seriously by every MP.

There were opportunities, too, to pursue some significant community projects. One such example was a piece of legislation to protect Wellington's Town Belt. Marian had begun work on this, including on how to ensure that land that was once in the Town Belt but had been requisitioned for public works would be returned. This proved very difficult given the current ownership arrangements. I took a different tack. The Town Belt was established via Deed in 1873 for use as a recreation ground for the inhabitants of Wellington. I wanted to give this purpose some legislative protection. There had already been some building on the area, and there were frequent calls for various parts of the Town Belt to be opened up for commercial use. A vigilant and active lobby group, Friends of the Town Belt, campaigned for years on these issues and provided the first draft of the legislation.

On becoming an MP I set about working with the Wellington City Council to make progress on the issue. Drafting legislation was a laborious process, with both local and central government bureaucracy to navigate. A pause was also needed to allow Treaty settlements to be finalised with Taranaki Whānui and Ngāti Toa Rangatira. The mission was clear, though: codify in law the purpose of the Town Belt, create a management plan that would be jointly implemented with mana whenua and create a process for land to be added to it. It took eight years, but on the day the Bill passed 120 hectares of land was added to the Town Belt and its future was secured. It was a proud achievement.

When we began in Opposition, I asked Phil if I could be the spokesperson on State Services. It made sense, given that Wellington Central is where many of the public services are based. I also knew that National had plans to make significant cuts to public services and that this would open up plenty of opportunities to show what I could do as an MP. I also picked up the Associate Foreign Affairs and Arts spokespersons' roles, shadowing Helen who was sticking around in Opposition for the time being.

The State Services role was immediately busy. The 2009 Budget saw significant cutbacks in many departments, including in the Department of Conservation, the Ministry of Justice, Ministry of Economic Development, Ministry of Social Development and the Tertiary Education Commission. All told, by early 2010 almost 1500 jobs had gone from the public service.

It was here I honed some critical skills to run an issue. I had a large number of contacts in the public service, so I was often able to be ahead of the cuts. I also worked with the Press Gallery to get stories ready. My experience in the PM's office meant that I knew many Gallery staff already, and felt confident wandering their corridor to gossip and share information. Much of what I did involved perfecting the 10-second sound bite. In reality, that was all I was going to get in a TV or radio story. I learned quickly that if the interviewer kept asking me the same question two or three times, I was not quite giving them the answer they wanted.

By mid-2009, both Helen and Michael Cullen had gone. There were plenty of issues to campaign on, but we were not getting a lot of traction. I inherited the Tertiary Education portfolio in 2010, and at the beginning of 2011 was promoted to the frontbench to be Health spokesperson.

By this stage Phil Goff had become aware that he needed to bring forward fresh energy. I was asked to put some pressure on National's Health Minister Tony Ryall. It was a big ask. Ryall was an accomplished performer in the role, a total control freak, and would be hard to outmanoeuvre. Then there was the small matter of my knowing nothing about health — and I was not really a picture of it either. I did my best, but as 2011 carried on I could see that an election win was far out of reach.

Despite my first impressions of Phil when I was a student politician, I became a great admirer of his work ethic and his core Labour values. But timing is a huge factor in politics, and Phil's was a bit off when it came to leadership. It was going to be hard for anyone to dent John Key's popularity in that first term, and even harder for someone who had been a major player in the government that had been voted out. Phil also struggled to deliver crisp, focused messages. It became a bit of a staple at Caucus that I would ask Phil what the *messages* were we were trying to get across that week. He would reply with a list of *issues* of the day. There is a huge difference between the two.

We did misfire somewhat too. In 2010 John Key, despite explicitly saying that he would not increase GST, did exactly that, raising it from 12.5% to 15%. We made a huge deal of this — including launching an 'Axe the Tax' bus tour from north to south to draw attention to National's policy and show us as connected to an issue that voters cared about. There was only one problem: we did not have a policy to axe the tax, either GST itself or the increase. We were well aware that extra revenue was badly needed by the government, and did not want to tie our hands so early in the term. Nevertheless, the bus tour rolled on. I joined it for the lower part of the North Island. We lacked focus, and organisation was loose, depending on the whim and the strength of the local party. There were regular mishaps and miscommunications, and the whole venture felt very amateur. I was not part of the South Island leg, but a combination of fatigue and general malaise about the value of it all made the final stages a bit more *Goodbye Pork Pie* than *Goodbye GST*.

By 2011, Phil was pretty miserable about the prospects of winning. He was also starting to be the subject of leaks out of Caucus. This was to set the tone for the next few years as we committed the cardinal sin of disunity — something the public can smell a mile away and judges harshly. Our polling dipped below 30%. A few months out from the election, Phil called his frontbench together and asked if we thought he should resign. I suspect it was mainly done to flush out any conspirators. We rallied around him, but the damage of the leaks was very clear.

The election was a predictable shellacking. In defeat Phil showed just what a professional he is. The threat of asset sales by the government had been a feature of the campaign. At our first Caucus meeting after losing the election, Phil was after petition forms against the sales so he could go to weekend markets to get signatures. He and Annette King stepped down but gave the Caucus a month to choose a successor.

A few of the Class of '08 wanted me to put my name forward for the leadership. This was largely because the most likely candidate seemed to be David Cunliffe. David was a mercurial figure. Prodigiously bright, he had been a bit of a rising star at MFAT. He had just left for a career in management consultancy when I arrived there, but people still talked about him. I felt that David was not burdened with modesty, and his move into politics in 1999 was a surprise to very few, though some wondered about his choice of party given some of his views.

When he arrived, he was seen as a business-friendly face for the party. His ambitions grew rapidly, and during my time in Helen Clark's office I found myself dispatched from time to time to try to quell those ambitions or point out to David how he was resonating with his colleagues. Helen liked David — well, certainly admired his intellect — and through her largesse he found himself as a minister outside Cabinet, and then in the later years of the Clark administration, inside Cabinet. I vividly remember him becoming Minister of Health and announcing to the House like some kind of sheriff that there was a new kid in town running the show. I wanted to crawl under my desk. By the time we were in Opposition, David had transformed himself into the standard-bearer of the left of the party. There seemed to be a degree of inauthenticity about this, but nevertheless he had attracted a following.

I knew that I was not ready for the leadership. The first three years had been fun, and instructive, but I was well aware that I lacked experience. I ruled myself out.

Other contenders soon emerged. Among them were more Davids: Parker, a strong performer in Opposition after a solid showing as a minister in the Clark government. He threw his hat in the ring as the Caucus began taking informal soundings. And the third David: Shearer. He had been elected at a by-election to replace Helen Clark as MP for Mt Albert in 2009. By-elections, when the eyes of the public are on a single contest rather than many, have a habit of propelling candidates into the public consciousness. He also came with a terrific backstory. He had for many years worked for the UN in trouble spots all over the globe, leading teams in humanitarian and construction efforts from the Middle East to Rwanda. He was not a complete stranger to Labour, having run as a candidate once before and worked for Phil Goff when he was Foreign Minister. He had performed well in 2009 and had maintained a profile throughout the first term.

David Parker eventually decided to pull out of the contest for personal reasons. This left us with a two-horse race. All that I knew told me that David Cunliffe was not the right person for the job. He was clever, but I felt he lacked the EQ needed to win over the New Zealand public. And we appeared to have a candidate from central casting in David Shearer.

I threw my lot in with David S. Recognising his lack of experience in the party, he asked if I would run as his deputy to show a united ticket. David C had chosen Nanaia Mahuta as his running mate. Nanaia was even then an experienced hand and brought with her the support of the Māori Caucus.

The result would come down to a Caucus vote. Labour had not yet adopted a system of electing a leader that directly involved party members, though there was a strong push for members to be consulted, and the candidates criss-crossed the country to meetings of members to put their case. In the first few meetings I became pretty concerned about David S. He was not a brilliant public speaker, and his limited parliamentary experience meant he struggled with some of the questions put to him. He was at his best using his background to give a flavour of the kind of leader he would be: compassionate, values driven, with a pragmatic streak.

My own local electorate committee was very much split. David C's strong pitch for a more explicitly left-wing approach was popular among members, and I was put in the position of having to talk to them privately about my misgivings. It was awkward, but I made my voting intentions clear to them.

In the end, David S and I won the Caucus vote convincingly though certainly not unanimously. The campaign had been respectful, and David S decided it was important to give David C a frontbench role to try to build the Caucus team. For my part, I was pleased to be in the engine room of the Opposition. I threw myself into the role of deputy which I had seen so expertly handled by Annette King. I was there to back the leader, but also to deal with problems or issues before they got away from us.

I was successful in the first of these tasks but most definitely not in the second. David initially appointed Stuart Nash as his Chief of Staff. Stuart had been part of the Class of '08 but had lost his seat at the 2011 election. He had been a good MP and was an excellent politician who held ambitions to return as an MP. These were not good qualifications to be a chief of staff. Within months, he had to go. Not for the first time I approached my friend Alastair Cameron to see if he would help us out by taking on the role. He and David met and hit it off, and Alastair joined the team. On reflection, Alastair's strong association with me did not help him. He was viewed with a bit of suspicion by some, and as too young and inexperienced by others. That was far from the truth, but he had a tough run and would eventually quit and leave the political world altogether.

Caucus, meantime, was continuing to leak regularly. Policy positions were being debated in the media, and various rivalries were playing out in the public arena. We tried our best to rein it in, but in truth we were hopelessly divided.

I recall going to a meeting in New Lynn organised by David Cunliffe in 2012. I was, by this stage, the party's Environment spokesperson, a role I had taken on alongside the deputy leadership in part to show that we were taking environmental and conservation issues seriously. West Auckland had long been a place where voters strongly supported such causes. David C, however, had another agenda that day. He delivered a long speech bizarrely titled 'The Dolphin and the Dole Queue'. He was our spokesperson on Economic Development, but the speech had all the hallmarks of a leadership bid — including a backstory about his growing up and the presence of the media. More than this, the atmosphere that day was toxic. I have never felt less welcome at a Labour Party event. David C's electorate crew were passionate in their support of him, and the scars of the leadership contest had clearly not healed one bit.

This tension continued to play out throughout the year, until our conference in November 2012 at the Ellerslie Racecourse in Auckland. There the issue occupying most attention was the new system of electing a leader for the party. I had been involved from the parliamentary end in establishing the system, though change was being driven by members and the Party Council, and by now most of the issues had been agreed. The voting was to be in three electoral colleges: the Caucus (making up 40%), the party membership (40%) and the affiliated unions (20%).

The outstanding issue was around what triggers other than the resignation of the leader would be required to hold a vote. It had been agreed that the leader would need to be endorsed by the Caucus each year. The debate came down to whether 50%+1 of the Caucus or 60%+1 of the Caucus was needed for endorsement. David C and his people were after the latter — with a pretty clear motive.

The conference became a circus. The media were well aware of the issues and subplots at play, and took every opportunity to present the disunity. On the Saturday we voted on various amendments. David C made a rockstar-style entry to the packed main hall, accompanied by a posse of TV cameras and journalists. He was asked to endorse David S as leader and declined to do so. It was horrific. The debate on the floor pitted Caucus members against each other for all to see. I hid down the back of the hall with Jacinda and a few others. At one point Jacinda, now fully lapsed from her Mormonism, produced a hip flask of whisky to help us manage our emotions.

The Cunliffe grouping won the vote and were ecstatic. They knew it meant they had a reasonable chance of taking David S out early the next year. That evening, I was the auctioneer at the official conference dinner. Most people skipped it, but David C and his crew were there celebrating. I wanted to get out as soon as I could. When it came time for the auction, I began by simply pointing at him and his friends and announcing that they had to bid on items whether they were interested in them or not. In the spirit of the moment, they could hardly say no, and the auction was over in record time, having generated a decent return.

The next day was make or break for David Shearer. Half the membership had essentially voted him down the day before. He needed something special in his address to the conference. And he delivered. His speech showed a level of energy and passion none of us had seen before. He was helped by a bold policy announcement. The next Labour government would build 100,000 homes, working with both state and private-sector developers. The audience took to their feet multiple times. By the end, David S had won over the crowd and left his detractors scurrying away from the cameras.

Building on the strength he took from the conference, David S moved against David C. The behaviour he had seen at the conference was just the tip of the iceberg, and there was no sign that the leaking or manoeuvring would stop. David C was sacked from the frontbench. Everything looked good going into the Christmas break.

However, it was a short-lived victory. David S survived the Caucus vote in the New Year, but not by much. The rumblings and leaks continued. Working in this kind of environment is exhausting. When your focus should be on the government and holding them to account, you are instead constantly fighting internal battles and second-guessing everyone.

There was further upset to follow with the death of our Caucus colleague and leader of the Māori Caucus, Parekura Horomia. Parekura had been very unwell for some time. He was a huge man, and not a healthy one either. Over the years he had attempted to lose weight with some temporary success, but by 2013 a host of health issues were impacting him. Never one to go to the doctor, he battled on. He would often fall asleep in Caucus meetings. One day he dozed off during an intervention I was making. Several further agenda items went through, and then I spoke on another item just in time for Parekura to wake up and assume it was the same speech from earlier. 'Are you still talking? Shut up, Grant,' I heard him say.

Parekura was responsible for some brilliant moments in Parliament. Once when he was a Minister for Māori Development, he was being quizzed about the contradiction between a letter he had written and the final outcome of an issue. He was asked to justify the letter. He rose and said, 'That's easy, Mr Speaker, it was a pre-letter.' And sat down, with the House in hysterics and none the wiser.

He was an amazing character. His time in the Community Employment Group in the Department of Labour meant he knew a lot of people across Aotearoa, and he knew absolutely everyone on the East Coast. I remember being paired up with him to go door-knocking in the Mana by-election that brought in Kris Faafoi as an MP. We were dropped off at one street, and Parekura suggested we each take a side of the road. I reasoned I might move a bit faster than him, so when I finished my side of the street I started working my way down his side until I met up with him. I made it all the way back to the first house on his side of the street to find Parekura sitting at a table laden with morning-tea treats. He waved at me to come inside, and I met a lovely family he had shared whakapapa and a very pleasant morning with. I told him not many people had been home when I had knocked at their doors. He smiled, and produced a list written by one of his relatives that covered the likely voting intentions of everyone in the street!

Alf was related to Parekura, and his mother had helped out with some of Parekura's election campaigns. We were very moved when he came to Alf's sister's place just after she died, as he did in so many homes up and down the coast, such was his connection with his people.

In April 2013 David Shearer went on a work trip to the USA. I knew Parekura was not well and he told Chippy, Labour's Whip, that he was going to go back home to rest. He drove north, stopping in each major town. It was clearly his final trip, and he knew it. He eventually made it home to Tolaga Bay where, surrounded by his family, he passed away.

In David's absence it was my job to front the media about Parekura's death. It was one of the most challenging pieces of media work I had ever done. He was a great man, a leader for our team and for his people, and all of us felt his loss deeply. His tangi was an enormous event, with members of the army brought in to help with catering and logistics — a sign of just how much he meant to people.

There were some positive achievements during this period. Several years earlier I had drafted a Bill to ensure that Anzac Day and Waitangi Day, the only two legislated public holidays that were not transferred to a Monday if they fell on the weekend, would become fully recognised as public holidays. Our staff member Marcus Ganley had raised this with me as a possible Member's Bill after a year in which they both fell on the weekend. We christened it the 'Mondayisation Bill'. It was a very popular piece of legislation — and we had the numbers to get it through Parliament because Peter Dunne supported it. However, it languished in the members' ballot before I handed the Bill off to Darien Fenton and then David Clark. David had particularly good luck in the ballot, the Bill was drawn, and he did the heavy lifting to get it through the parliamentary process. But he was away in the US on an Eisenhower Fellowship when it came time for the final reading, so I moved it and put it through its process. At last New Zealanders got the full value of their public holidays every year, not just five out of every seven.

The same night the Mondayisation Bill passed, the Marriage Equality legislation, put forward as a member's Bill by my colleague Louisa Wall, had its final reading. It was still a conscience vote, but attitudes had moved on considerably in the decade since civil unions had passed. A critical moment for the Bill was when Prime Minister John Key said he would vote for it, giving licence to more socially liberal National MPs to support the Bill too. I helped Louisa out where I could with the cross-party group that was established to support the legislation, and supported some of the community groups who were promoting it.

Despite some vocal opposition, the numbers in favour were much stronger than they had been for civil unions. That night I gave the speech that I am most proud of in my time in Parliament. I was very emotional. I was able to hark back to how I had felt as a teenager when the Homosexual Law Reform Act passed, and to link it to the journey of Rainbow causes back to Harvey Milk, the gay US politician who was assassinated in the 1970s. I finished the speech by saying:

> *For all the victories that there are to celebrate when this bill passes — the victory for families, for fairness, for equality, for inclusion, for commitment and for love — there is to my mind a greater win. If there is a 14-year-old young man in Dunedin who is watching this, like I did 27 years ago, and he is wondering how he will cope with being a bit different from his mates, and he is going to struggle a bit over the next few years, today goes some way to fulfilling Harvey Milk's plea. This Bill is not going to solve all his problems. It is not going to prevent him from being discriminated against. It is not going to prevent him from getting hurt. But it will do something of huge value, because what we will do in this House tonight is give him some hope. Because tonight hope has won.*

When the Bill passed, the public gallery sang 'Pōkarekare Ana'. The moment went viral globally. Louisa, rightly, received high praise for her courage in leading the legislation. We headed into town to celebrate. At S & M's Bar in Cuba Street, the owners Scotty and Mal let us behind the bar to give speeches. National MP Nikki Kaye was there, and it felt like we had come such a long way from the days when people like me were scared to be who we wanted to be. Later, I joined the Young Labour crew at another bar. Many of them were LGBT, and their joy and confidence were so incredibly heartening. We had done good.

Meanwhile, things were not looking good for David Shearer. He was a conviction politician, and not a fan of political games. His media and public performances were not improving and arguably getting worse. I was there to help manage the party, and I was not succeeding either. There was even more chatter among the media that his days might be numbered.

This came to a head one day when he and his office decided that a good way to highlight changes to fisheries regulations that would harm recreational fishers would be to bring two dead snapper into the House. David was an experienced fisherman and he felt he could connect with voters on this issue. The opposite effect occurred — a dead man walking held up dead fish in Parliament. It was not instant, but that was the turning point. There were further rumbles, and eventually a story broke that a coup was about to be mounted. As deputy, I dug in and tried to identify who had spoken to the media; I even went as far as getting Caucus members to sign a pledge that it was not them, which they all signed!

Dealing with David C's supporters was one thing, but eventually some of David S's frontbench came forward to say that they had lost confidence. It was in some ways unfair: Labour's polling was higher than it had been in 2011. But this group could no longer see how David S could lead us to victory and felt he would struggle in a campaign.

By this stage my own relationship with David S wasn't great either. I felt he wasn't listening to my advice, and he in turn felt that I was not fully supportive of him. Looking back, I think both of these things were partly true. I was never disloyal to David, but I probably was not as full throated as I could have been in my endorsement of him.

As Whip, Chippy let David S know that there was the possibility of a no-confidence motion coming forward. He told David he thought it could be defeated and it was still possible to stare down those who were seeking to have him removed. I recall a conversation one evening when I told David S I backed him but that he needed to show that he really wanted the role.

The next day, David S called a media conference to announce his resignation. I don't have many regrets in politics, but one I do have is that I did not attend that press conference. I wanted to go, but I knew that the media would immediately ask if I was in the running to replace him and I did not want to be a distraction. But not showing up made me look disloyal.

Once again we were in the spiral of a leadership contest. This time the choice to run was easier. I felt more prepared and, crucially, I knew that David C was going to push hard to win. Just three days after David Shearer's resignation, I announced my run with concurrent interviews on the two 6pm news channels. TV3 led with the story. Their headline would become one of the features of the contest: 'Is New Zealand ready for its first gay Prime Minister?' In the interview I expressed the view that I did not think New Zealanders cared too much about my private life and were much more interested in the policies I would promote. In reality, I knew it was likely to be an issue and one that might be too tough to get past.

David C and I were joined by Shane Jones in the contest. I was pretty convinced that I would have the majority support among the Caucus: they were the people who knew us best, and there was a strong feeling that David C was not the one to lead Labour to a win in the 2014 election. I got organised, gathered some of those closest to me — Jacinda, Phil Twyford, Megan Woods and Kris Faafoi, among others — and formed a campaign team.

This was the first leadership contest to be run under the new rules. Twelve meetings were organised across the country, and we candidates hit the road to convince party members to vote for us. This proved a double-edged sword for the party. It meant we got a lot of media coverage, but it also meant most of that coverage was about our divisions, not about why we would be a better government.

Over the course of the roadshows, we got used to each other's style and stump speech. Shane's was colourful, full of anecdote and florid phrasing, often harking back to the First and Fourth Labour Governments for inspiration. David's was a life story that highlighted his left-wing credentials and ended every night with the same phrase: 'My name is David Cunliffe and I am ready to lead.'

My speech was an attempt to take the work of the Fifth Labour Government to the next stage. I harked back to the values of the Labour Party around work, opportunity and equality, and put them into modern contexts with issues like climate change and the digital economy. I found that it landed pretty well most nights. But the cloud of my sexuality loomed large. After the meeting in Christchurch, which I felt I had 'won', a gay couple I knew a little came up to congratulate me on my performance. Then they stunned me by saying, 'But we are not going to vote for you.' I was speechless as they went on to say, 'We just don't think New Zealanders will vote for a gay Prime Minister.'

Hearing this from a gay couple was hard to take. Meanwhile, I got wind of a Labour stalwart from the West Coast who was openly going to branch meetings to push the line that the party could not have a gay leader. I called him up to ask what was going on. He was a bit remorseful and then said that he had been asked by someone in David's campaign to do this. I was incensed. I called David, who denied all knowledge of it. From my perspective, this did not ring true, especially after a former Labour Party staffer went on TV and said pretty much the same thing. In fairness to David, he did stand her down from his campaign.

The same problem existed in the union movement. I had strong support from the Service Workers Union, thanks to my close links with them in Wellington. But I did not have the same connections with others. One leader of an affiliated union went to his members and explicitly ruled me out as a candidate because I was gay.

It was an uphill battle, and in fairness David's line about his experience and readiness to lead was a factor as well. He had been an MP for nine years longer than me, and this mattered to members.

I was hoping against hope when the results came in. In the end, David scored a decisive victory. I had won the Caucus vote, but he had prevailed among the members and the unions. I was upset — for myself, of course, but also for the party. I had an inkling of the chaos and calamity that was about to occur, but even I did not realise just how bad it would get.

David C had a bit over a year to lead us into the election. I was given the roles of Economic Development and Shadow Leader of the House, and got to continue in the Skills and Training and Arts areas that I enjoyed.

The shadow leader's role proved to be a good fit. I liked the cut and thrust of debate, and had spent a bit of time in the first couple of terms learning about the standing orders, so could support the Whips in making Parliament as challenging as possible for the government. But my work in the House became useful for another reason.

We had some very good researchers in the team — one of them was Karl Beckett. He had in turn learned his craft from Don Badman, a long-time staffer. One of their tactics was to build files on the business interests of each National MP. Another tactic was to do OIA requests on every ministerial trip, mostly to hold the government to account on the costs. One day, Karl came to see me when these two pieces of work intersected. Judith Collins, as Minister of Justice, had taken a trip to China, during which she had visited the China headquarters of Oravida Ltd. The company had three directors, one of whom was Collins's husband. The media had found a photograph of Judith Collins's visit on the Oravida website. This was interpreted by many people to be an endorsement of the company. This was a no-no for a minister in any event, let alone for a company they were connected to.

I took up the baton and began asking questions in Parliament about the visit. I had learned from watching the likes of my colleagues Trevor Mallard and Pete Hodgson that you needed to take a long-run view of these kinds of inquiries. The initial questioning would elicit information, and it was important to keep the questions up day after day. Meanwhile, we peppered all the agencies involved in the visit with OIA requests.

While Judith Collins insisted that she had not done anything wrong, we pieced together what we considered to be a number of damning pieces of information. The Chairman and Executive Director of Oravida had also travelled to China at the time of her visit. She had dined with them and an unnamed Chinese official. Briefings about the dinner were prepared by MFAT, although the content of them was withheld. Her original programme as Minister of Justice had her attending a different event at the time she visited Oravida.

She continued to maintain that she had just 'popped into Oravida' on the way to the airport in Shanghai and there was nothing here to see. I still remember the day when Karl, not the most demonstrative of people, skipped down the hallway to my office to tell me that Oravida's offices were in fact 45 minutes in the other direction from the Minister's hotel than Shanghai Airport. I suggested we print off a map to show her circuitous journey, and produced the map in the House — much to the Minister's chagrin.

Eventually the Prime Minister had to take a proper look at what had happened. He concluded that there was the 'perception of a conflict of interest', and that Collins was on her final warning. I felt it was clearly more than that, but such was Collins's power within National, and the likelihood that she could go rogue, that this was as far as he would go.

In short order Judith Collins faced more difficulty. That was caused by the release of emails that highlighted her involvement in another story. As the 2014 election neared, Nicky Hager appeared with a new book called *Dirty Politics* that detailed the workings of a number of right-wing politicians and political operatives. Judith Collins's name was peppered through the book, and as material drip-fed about her role in these activities John Key was forced to persuade her to resign as a minister. She would of course return later to play a pivotal role in her party.

In the Labour team, meanwhile, David C had brought Matt McCarten in to be his Chief of Staff. Matt had been a leading light in the Alliance, and had established the Unite Union. He was an organiser of the highest order. I had a lot of respect for him, though we had never worked closely together.

Initially it seemed Matt was going to be able to focus David and our campaign team. He was clear that our path to victory was as part of a left coalition that would have both the Greens and New Zealand First involved. Matt was a pragmatist at heart, and he did not have a lot of concern about the exact percentages involved. The important thing was for a Labour-led coalition to get over the line. The situation was complicated, however, by the emergence of Kim Dotcom as a political force.

Dotcom, a Finnish-German internet entrepreneur, had come to New Zealand after his file-sharing website Megaupload drew the attention of US authorities. He had flexed his political muscle a little along the way and had part-funded John Banks's campaign to be Mayor of Auckland. After he became the target of a raid on his mansion in Auckland by the SIS and police, he was on a collision course with the government.

As it happened, I briefly met with Dotcom during this period. In 2013 I had led the questioning in Parliament around the appointment of Ian Fletcher as head of the SIS, having received a tip-off that all was not what it had seemed. I did some digging via the OIA, and found that a shortlist of candidates for the role had been rejected by ministers, and that Ian Fletcher had been identified as a candidate by the Prime Minister. Under questioning in Parliament, John Key acknowledged a family association with Fletcher. It eventually emerged that the PM had in fact shoulder-tapped Fletcher, who was working for the Queensland government at the time, to head the SIS. This was serious stuff. At that time the only real check and balance on the SIS came from the PM. I was pleased to have been able to put the PM under some pressure in the House, though as often happens the issue eventually died away without an immediate consequence.

Kim Dotcom, however, was very interested. The raid on his house on behalf of the US government had taken place with heavy SIS involvement. He was pursuing the legality of the raid through the courts. Meanwhile, the Prime Minister was desperately trying to distance himself from the case. He famously said that he did not even know who Kim Dotcom was before the raid happened — a far-fetched claim, as Dotcom's sprawling mansion was in Key's electorate. When pressed, Key said that he did not know Dotcom but was aware 'there was a German in the mansion'. This was too much for me, and I made it the centrepiece of a General Debate speech on a *Dad's Army* theme about John Key's 'memory lapses'.

Kim Dotcom, for his part, kept telling New Zealanders that he had information that would prove John Key was lying about what he knew. Eventually, through his lawyers, I agreed to meet him. He was a strangely engaging man. He was tall and large, and dressed entirely in black. This, combined with his thick German accent, made him appear like a Bond villain. Our meeting was full of covert claims but no evidence to back them up. I soon lost interest, but Dotcom carried his campaign into a full-blown electoral attempt with the establishment of the Internet Party. It eventually joined forces with the Mana Party, which included Hone Harawira and the remnants of the Alliance in the form of Laila Harré and others.

The 2014 campaign proved one of my theories of politics — about the commodity of political oxygen. Political junkies have an endless interest in the machinations of politics. The general public do not. They can take on only so many issues or stories before switching off. In 2014 the Internet Mana Party gained only 1.42% of the vote. The presence of Kim Dotcom and his outrageous claims, however, gathered a huge amount of attention. They sucked up the available political oxygen for the Opposition, and we struggled to register with voters.

When we did it was for the wrong reasons. David Cunliffe had a habit of putting his foot in his mouth. Most famously in this campaign it was his comment that he was 'sorry for being a man'. He also found numerous ways to lose focus on his message. A major misstep came at the *Press* debate in Christchurch where John Key confronted him with detailed questions on Labour's capital gains tax policy and whether it would impact the family home. David had been one of the architects of the policy during Labour's first term, and knew that it would not, but for some reason he was unable to answer.

His behaviour was erratic as well. The next day I was undertaking visits with him in Christchurch. He and I were doing a lunch event with the local business community. It was classic David. He spoke well and cogently to a less than friendly audience. When we got to question time, he seemed distracted. At one point a question was put to me as the Economic Development spokesperson. David excused himself, saying he needed to take a phone call. And he never came back. I answered a couple more questions before the host called the whole thing off. I went outside to find David in his car. His press secretary was standing outside and gave me a pained look. I'd had enough and left him to it.

On election night, Labour slumped to its worst result since 1922, with 24% of the vote. You would not have known it from David's speech that night. It was as if he had grabbed the wrong speech on the way out the door and was doing his victory one, not his concession. It was embarrassing.

In the wake of this defeat, our first Caucus meeting was always going to be bad, but it was by far the worst I have attended. For seven hours the Caucus let rip. There was a lot of pent-up emotion in the room. We had genuinely tried to support David, but he had done all the damage himself. The comments made were brutal, but he just seemed to absorb them all. At various points in the meeting people threatened to go outside and say their piece to the media. But somehow, probably through exhaustion, we emerged saying that we would review our campaign. David said he wanted to stay but would go away and think about the result.

The idea of David staying was beyond my comprehension. I resolved to have one last go at the leadership. After some public jostling, David eventually announced that he would resign the leadership but would run again to test his mandate. I immediately announced that I would be a candidate. It was now or never, I said at that time.

This time around David Parker was more sure that he wanted the job, having done heroic work as David C's deputy leader. There was pressure for there to be a candidate from the Māori Caucus, too, and eventually Nanaia Mahuta put up her hand.

Once again I began the task of ringing around my colleagues. Once again the majority of them expressed their support. One person who prevaricated was Andrew Little. Andrew, the former Labour Party President, had come into the Caucus in 2011. He had been a solid contributor and his leadership skills from his time as a union leader were evident. Andrew is a straight-up person, and I knew his prevarication meant he was considering his options.

Within a couple of weeks he was in the race and David Cunliffe was out. That was the first goal achieved. But by now I wanted to win, and I thought I would have a good shot at the 2017 election against a third-term National government.

There was one person who was polling well for the job but did not want it, and that was Jacinda. Even by that stage she was resonating well with the New Zealand public. She was adamant that she did not want the leadership but said she would do whatever she could to help me in my campaign. I asked her to be my official running mate. She agreed, albeit a little reluctantly. From then on we worked on a campaign to reflect that our team would represent a shift in gear. We coined the phrase 'A New Generation to Win'. The media coined the term 'Gracinda'. Whichever way you looked at it, we were a good combination.

A large number of party members wanted to support us. We decided to run a fully fledged campaign: daily phone calls, key messages, phone canvassing of members, letters to others. We even had a launch at the King's Arms pub in Auckland on a sunny Sunday afternoon. Jacinda was clearly unwell (she would end up in hospital with something called quinsy) but gave a rousing speech, and I was able to get a few good grabs for the news.

We were feeling good, and as the inevitable roadshow took place, I began to think our team was in front. Even so, the lingering doubts and homophobia of the 2013 campaign were there — I knew that, in what would inevitably be a close race, this could be crucial.

This was particularly the case with the unions. Andrew's background there was always going to make him a favourite. My strongest allies, the Service Workers Union, had merged with Andrew's old union, the Engineers Union, to form E tū. They took a position that their votes would be made by the Executive rather than rank-and-file members. And there was pressure on to vote for their preferred candidate as a block. At almost every stop I would engage with union members who supported me, but that was not going to count for anything.

In fairness to Andrew, he performed well in the campaign. He had definitely picked up support from David Cunliffe's loyalists, and his passionate delivery of solid Labour values was there for all to see.

The Labour Party's leadership contests use an STV-style proportional representation system.

On the day of the announcement the candidates were taken into the Whip's office beside the Labour Caucus room. Party President

Moira Coatsworth gave us a printed sheet. Nanaia had been the first to be eliminated, followed by David Parker. The final result between Andrew and me was as close as it could be — 50.52% to 49.48%. Nanaia's votes had largely fallen to Andrew, but David's split more evenly than I had hoped. Overall, I had won both the Caucus and the party members, but Andrew had got 75% of union support. I was one Caucus member's vote, or just a hundred or so party members' votes, away from victory.

To say I was gutted is an understatement. I felt I had let a host of people down — including Jacinda, who had pinned her colours to my mast so selflessly. I was also acutely aware of the hundreds of volunteers, especially the younger members, many of whom had worked with me since my first campaign in 2008. But when I stood up to speak in the Caucus room after Andrew had given his victory speech, there were two things I knew for sure. One was that Andrew would have my complete loyalty as leader. The second was that I would never again run for the leadership. I said both of those things. The mental toll of putting myself forward and losing twice was enormous. Alf had never really been a fan of the idea of me being leader and knew what it would mean for us. I had told him that this was it — and I wanted to keep my word to him.

Andrew set about putting his team together. I said I would do whatever role he considered useful. I was aware that David Parker had taken the result hard as well. When Andrew asked him to carry on as Finance spokesperson, he declined. Annette King, whom Andrew had wisely asked to be his deputy, suggested to Andrew that he offer the role to me. It was a massive call. I had been in the economic team for the past year or so as Economic Development spokesperson but had never touched Finance. Annette reasoned that I was one of the stronger performers both in the House and in the public arena, and I would be able to pick up the technical side of the role, with support from the likes of Michael Cullen.

I was gobsmacked when Andrew proposed the idea, and I asked him for some time to think about it. I called Michael, and he urged me to take on the role. In our very first conversation he pointed out that he, too, had had little or no experience in the Finance space before taking on the position for Labour.

More or less convinced, I told Andrew I was happy to take the job if that was what he needed, but I asked him to check with David Parker once more to make sure he didn't want it. He did so, and came back to me to say David had not shifted his view.

Andrew and I talked on that first day about the project that was to become known as the Future of Work. In the leadership campaign we had both talked about the importance of Labour, as the traditional party of workers, understanding more about the changing nature of work and particularly the place of technology. He encouraged me to take on the project, and I think we even sketched out at that first meeting the Commission approach we would end up using.

From the very start Andrew set about healing the wounds of the previous few years. He worked hard to bring us together and to use the talents of the full team.

For me, taking on Finance was daunting, but I quickly felt a sense of relief that the whole question of leadership was behind me. I could focus now on the issues that had driven me to be an MP in the first place — fairness, opportunity — and I could do so from the box seat of the Finance role.

I also felt that 2017 was probably my last shot. I knew I could not do 12 years in Opposition. This was it — we had to make it work.

10.
IT COULDN'T BE DONE

I was in Dunedin in late 2016 when John Key announced he was going to resign as Prime Minister. A day of meetings was planned with businesspeople as part of my Opposition Finance role. Every one of them became an exercise in speculation about what it all meant.

From Labour's point of view, it was exciting news. John Key, while less popular than in his early years in the job, was a trusted figure as PM. Conventional wisdom was that he wanted to go one better than Helen Clark and win a fourth term. Our leadership travails had given him ample room to further entrench his reputation as a steady pair of hands. But he clearly wanted to go out on top, and some indications in the more detailed polling we had done gave a hint that for him it was only downhill from here. The so-called 'rockstar economy' of the mid-2010s was beginning to wane, and there was a feeling that issues like housing affordability, the availability of mental health services and rates of child poverty were getting worse, not better. There was also a sense that Key's energy for the day-to-day of politics was reducing.

The prospect of an internal National Party war over who should be his successor was tantalising. After all, we more than anyone else knew how corrosive that could be. Judith Collins and Jonathan Coleman both expressed an interest in the role, and we thought our wishes would be granted. Our excitement about that died away fairly quickly. Key anointed Bill English as his successor, and it was pretty clear his wishes would be acted upon by the National Caucus.

Still, Bill English had been there, lost that before. His tepid performance as Opposition leader in 2002 gave us hope that we could bridge the very significant gap between National and Labour in the polls. He was a respected Finance Minister but had a dull and diffident persona. In Parliament I had, perhaps cruelly, described his previous leadership as being sponsored by Mogadon, a drug that puts you to sleep. But as 2017 began, Labour's hope started to fade. What seemed like ridiculous attempts to humanise Bill English somehow seemed to work. He created memes about his favoured choice of pizza toppings (for the record, not a fan here of pineapple on pizza) and his favoured form of exercise, the walk-run.

Meanwhile, we were struggling. Andrew Little had achieved a significant amount internally within Labour. Years of warring factions centred around David Cunliffe's suitability were put to bed. Andrew created a team in which all views were represented. Intentionally or not, his decision to give David Cunliffe the role of spokesperson on Superannuation even felt right: many of us had thought for a while that David should go away and think about retirement. We felt more focused and cohesive than we had at any time during our years in Opposition. But externally Andrew was not resonating. He had always been a passionate advocate of Labour causes. His time as a union boss had hardened an already adversarial default setting. The National Party labelled him 'Angry Andy', and it stuck. The contrast with the seemingly laid-back John Key and Bill English was blindingly clear.

Jacinda's star, however, was on the rise. The resignation from Parliament of David Shearer, who returned to his UN work, finally gave her the safe seat her talent warranted. The Mt Albert by-election in February 2017 was a cakewalk, and the positive vibe and buzz around Jacinda was the polar opposite of that around Andrew. Not long after the by-election, it was obvious something needed to change. I did not feel the first move was necessarily the right one.

Annette King was the glue of the Labour Caucus. Apart from her enforced three-year sabbatical after the 1990 election, she had been an MP since 1984. She was a force of nature, with energy greater than those decades her junior. As Caucus went about our regional visits to drum up support, Annette could be found hurtling down the main streets of provincial towns, ducking in and out of shops, indulging in what she called 'practical regional development', i.e. shopping for bags and clothes. On policy she was sharp and attuned to what would and would not work. She was wise, direct and essential. But she was also tired after 30 years of politics.

When the time came to assess if she had another three or six years left in the tank, Annette had some second thoughts. Simultaneously, public speculation about a leadership role for Jacinda was reaching fever pitch among the media. Annette and Andrew talked, and she decided it was the right time to step aside — and for Jacinda to come forward as deputy. Annette announced her retirement from politics. At a personal level I was sad. Annette was my neighbouring electorate MP, and a good friend and confidante. She gave her life to Labour and to New Zealand. In hindsight we could have done with her experience in government — but we found many ways to draw on that experience as time wore on.

Initially, the change looked like a great move. Jacinda offered a significant contrast to her leader. But that contrast quickly became a problem rather than an advantage. We staggered on through 2017, trying to put together a campaign that would reach the public, and relying on MMP to deliver a potential alternative government made up of Labour, the Greens and New Zealand First. By mid-year Labour was drifting down into the mid-to-high 20s in most polls, with our two potential support partners at around 10% each.

We hit the road to drum up support in the provinces. Jacinda travelled with Andrew and introduced him at each event. As the days went by, it was clear who the people were warming to.

One night in Whanganui encapsulated where we were at. I was there in my role as buddy MP for the area. A fairly decent crowd of three hundred or so came along to the racecourse function centre. It was roasting hot in the room but attempts to open the doors were foiled by a howling gale that was blowing furniture around outside. At one point a distraught audience member collapsed, either from the heat or other causes, and Jacinda leapt from the stage to assist her from the building. Despite the distractions, she hit all the right spots in pushing the campaign themes in her speech of introduction. The crowd were onside as Andrew stood at the podium to deliver his 15-minute stump speech. Over the course of the next 40 minutes he put Labour's case at full volume. He went on frequent diversions from the campaign script, and by the end the crowd's energy had dissipated. The night ended with a whimper.

As we gathered for a drink in a local bar with our terrific Whanganui volunteers, Jacinda and I decided to talk to Andrew about his speech. Before we could get going, he said, 'Look I know I went a bit over time.' We asked him how long he thought he had spoken for. 'Twenty or 25 minutes, I guess.' He was as shocked as we were dismayed that it was twice that length.

A couple of months out from the election, our prospects were looking dire. Most polls put us in the mid-20s, and there was a very real chance that not only would we lose the election but both New Zealand First and the Greens would also get close to us on election day.

On 24 July, Jacinda was the guest speaker at the annual Peter Fraser lecture, a fundraiser we had created for the Wellington Central Labour Party. As Arts spokesperson she talked about Fraser's legacy and the place of the arts in our society. She was brilliant, as ever. Party stalwarts Geoffrey and Margaret Palmer were there. As we finished, Margaret grabbed Jacinda by the arm and said, 'You have to take over.' What neither Margaret nor any of us knew was that Andrew would tell Jacinda two days later, on her birthday, that he was considering stepping down. Jacinda told Andrew he should not do it — but she also knew that Andrew's misgivings meant the prospect of her becoming leader was getting more real.

The following Saturday, just two months out from the election, a Labour Party fundraising art auction was to be held in Auckland. I flew up from Wellington early in the day, then received a message that Andrew wanted to talk to me and several other colleagues. We decided to meet at Jacinda's place in Point Chevalier. It was an odd scene. Andrew, Phil Twyford and I were dressed up to the nines for the auction, sitting on couches and sipping tea. For some reason Jacinda was sitting on the floor. Andrew told us that he had been interviewed for a poll that was coming out on Sunday night on TV1. Labour had dipped to 24%. We were miles behind National, but, even more worryingly, both the Greens and New Zealand First were now in the mid-teens. It was disastrous news at this point in the campaign.

Andrew asked us what we thought he should do. Without pausing for breath, Jacinda said, 'You have to carry on. It's too late to change, and as your deputy I support you.' Phil took the opposite stance. He said he felt for Andrew, that he had given it everything, but we were staring down the barrel of a catastrophic result and he needed to resign.

Everyone turned to me. I said to Andrew I needed to know the answer to three questions. Did he still want to do the job? If he did, what was he going to do differently to turn things around? And what would he do if we went down further in the next poll?

Andrew said he did still want to be leader. He thought that the more people he met face to face the better. He talked about a reset of the campaign that would play to his strengths in smaller groups. His other ideas, too, all sounded good. But it was his answer to the third question that left me cold. If we did drop further in the next poll, he said, he would seriously think about going.

That was the worst possible answer from my perspective. First, we would be even closer to the election. Second, it seemed to undermine his first answer. What we did not know, but would see on TV on Sunday night, was that his second-guessing of himself was also now a matter of public record.

We left Jacinda's house with Andrew thinking further. The auction that night was a surreal event. I had offered to Barbara Ward, the amazing Labour fundraiser, to be one of her bidders to get the items up to reserve price. To do this I stood near the back of the room behind the tables and in line of sight of the auctioneer. I kept moving so as to appear to be a different person for the benefit of those at the tables. This also meant I ended up talking to a lot of people. Everyone was worried about where we were at. Some people knew what the TV poll the next night was going to say. Those conversations were even more fraught. Could we change leader this late? It seemed crazy, but were we now looking at finding someone to 'save the furniture'? I was a bit distracted and at one point lost track of where we were in the bidding, only to discover that I was about to be the proud owner of a $20,000 sculpture. A genuine buyer rescued me in the nick of time.

I caught Jacinda's eye several times that night. She was in another place. She was well aware of what might unfold if Andrew stepped down. She was the only choice. And she was desperate for that not to happen.

I returned to Wellington the next day and went out door-knocking with the Wellington Central team. We still had good numbers showing up, but morale was low. The reaction on the doors as we chased down possible swing voters was almost identical: We will vote for you, Grant, but the party vote is going somewhere else.

When the polling news aired, the phone started to ring. Not so much about the numbers, but about what Andrew had said in the interview. This was what led the story. In response to the inevitable question about whether he had considered stepping aside, Andrew answered like the good guy he is. He said he had considered it but had decided to carry on.

His own seeds of doubt, however small, fuelled those who felt a move had to be made. I spoke to Chief Whip Kris Faafoi. He had already been advised by other senior colleagues that he needed to ring around the Caucus to check if Andrew still had their confidence. I told him that while I knew we were in a hopeless position, I thought it was too late to change — and that doing so now would expose Jacinda to being leader in an unwinnable situation and might damage her prospects long term. Kris reported a range of reactions but that there was a core of people who thought Andrew needed to step aside.

By Monday morning speculation was mounting. I had planned to spend the day out in the electorate, but texts and calls flying in from the media made that impossible, however much I tried to ignore them. I retreated to my electorate office. At one point I saw that a TV3 News car had pulled up outside, and bolted into the back part of my office, where I lay down on the floor beside one of the sofas so as not to be seen from the front part. I listened as reporter Jenna Lynch asked my electorate secretary where I was. Sheila said she didn't know. Jenna said they would wait.

Still lying on the floor, I rang Andrew. It took me a while to get hold of him. Eventually he called me back. I repeated the question I'd asked on Saturday night. Do you want to carry on? If the answer was yes, I said, I would go out and tell Jenna that I supported him to stay on. He said he was still thinking, but yes, he did still want to carry on.

I went outside and did the interview. Sadly, other MPs had done interviews and were more forthright in saying that Andrew should consider stepping down. It was a terrible news bulletin that only fuelled the calls for change.

By this point Jacinda had decided that she needed to cover her bases. She set about preparing herself for the inevitable questions if she became leader. To be clear, she still did not want the job at this point and most definitely would not be contesting Andrew for it. But, as she had always done and would do so often in the future, she was thinking through every angle and wanted to be prepared.

That evening Kris Faafoi's calling was complete, and Andrew was in trouble. There was no avoiding the fact that if someone called a confidence vote the next day, he might very well lose. Among the many phone calls I took that night, the one I remember most was from Annette King. Hers was the wisest head we had. One that had seen it all. She was clear. We were not going to win the election with Andrew as leader. We had nothing to lose. Jacinda was popular and capable, and you just never knew what might happen.

I knew then that a change was coming, whatever Jacinda might have felt. But it was Annette's next words that were most unexpected. She guessed that I would want to be Jacinda's deputy. She knew how close we were, that Jacinda would probably want me by her side and that as Finance spokesperson, it would also be a good idea. But, she said, it was just not going to work. We needed better balance at the top. Jacinda and I were too similar as urban liberals. We also needed to keep the Māori Caucus onside and stop any more bleeding to the Māori Party. Annette said that Kelvin Davis should be Deputy.

I knew that Annette's call would not have been random. We were friends as well as electorate neighbours, and she would have put her hand up to ring me. My first reaction was one of quiet anger — not so much at the fact I would not be Deputy, but that there was manoeuvring going on that I was not part of, and that my fate was in others' hands. I did want to be there beside Jacinda, and I was upset that this was not going to happen. But as the evening wore on, I recognised the logic of the argument. Late in the evening I left Kelvin a message saying I wanted to catch up with him the next morning. I knew he would be reluctant to take on the role and wanted him to know that I would support him. I had also determined that if this was going to happen, then I wanted to nominate him.

The next morning Jacinda was desperately trying to talk to Andrew, but he was not returning her calls. I managed to get hold of Neale Jones, Andrew's Chief of Staff, on the phone just before he and Andrew took off from Auckland to return to Wellington. He said Andrew was refusing to confirm what he was going to do but Neale thought it was over.

In Parliament we wondered what to do. We knew we would need to deal with the matter as soon as possible. I went to find Kelvin. Before I could, Jacinda texted from the car — Neale had called and told her Andrew would step aside.

My conversation with Kelvin became very real. I reassured him that he was the right guy for the job and that he would have no trouble at all from me. He looked utterly shell-shocked.

Emotions ran high as the Caucus gathered. Andrew came in and gave an extraordinarily gracious speech, but he was clearly hurting. He told Caucus that he would nominate Jacinda to be his replacement at a meeting later that morning. He then left the room. Andrew truly put the party before himself. Jacinda would never have challenged him, so it had to be his decision. I was very pleased for Andrew as he fashioned a career as one of our most capable ministers. In Caucus, Kris Faafoi started outlining the next steps — and a couple of Caucus members let rip. I was accused of having set the whole thing up to get Jacinda in place. It was tough, and some harsh words were said. I was thrilled to see my friend as the leader, a role I knew she was destined for, but my view was that now was not the right time. Seven weeks just did not feel like enough time for her to overturn the yawning deficit in the polls. But those who were feeling hurt chose not to believe me.

When we gathered again a few minutes later, some Caucus members still could not accept what had happened. But again Andrew showed real class, nominated Jacinda and smoothed some of the ruffled feathers. I did as I said I would and nominated Kelvin for Deputy. They were both elected unopposed.

We hustled off to the Legislative Council Chamber for the press conference. The full Press Gallery was there. Jacinda spoke confidently about what she wanted to do as leader and then opened the floor for questions.

First impressions matter in politics as much as they do anywhere, and Jacinda knocked this out of the park. In response to a question from an experienced reporter about whether she could be a credible leader of the government she noted she had been an MP since 2008, and then said, 'And would you mind telling me why you don't think I am?' She was clear, feisty and funny.

The media were one audience to win over; the public was another. Labour Party General Secretary Andrew Kirton put out a fundraising email off the back of the press conference. A number of us gathered in Kris's office to watch the news. The change had landed well. The 'vox pops' were all positive about Jacinda. As we sat there, Andrew kept refreshing his computer, and each time we could see that dozens more donations had come in to the party. In a few hours more than $100,000 was donated. Right then, there was the hint that something very special was about to occur.

The campaign itself was turned on its head. There were logistical problems to deal with, of course. Our billboards featuring Andrew and Jacinda were already up. Campaign materials had been printed and all the planning had been around Andrew. But the National Party seemed ill-prepared for Jacindamania and were flat-footed in response to Labour's new and fresh face. The positive stories around her just kept coming.

At the end of the week a group of senior MPs and Labour campaign staff gathered in Wellington. Jacinda and Andrew Kirton led us through what we now needed to do. Andrew was calm and had already begun the work required to get new materials made. Jacinda was again clear and clinical. We were grappling with a slogan. Andrew Little's had been 'A Fresh Approach'. It was probably more accurate now but could not be used. Jacinda had written a social media post on the day she was elected which had finished with 'Let's Do This!' She suggested we use it. It was not a normal political slogan, but it was not a normal campaign. It had the urgency and the energy that we were feeling.

From then on, that urgency and energy never left the campaign. The first polls saw a massive bounce for Labour. First we went up by 9 points, then by another 5, and then we hit 40%. Jacinda was mobbed wherever she went. Young women, in particular, went crazy. Success still seemed very unlikely, but we were starting to believe.

One night as we were preparing for Labour's formal campaign launch Jacinda called to ask if I had any ideas about what song we should play. She knew that as a total music nerd this would be right up my street. I pondered the idea for a while, then recalled some of the commentary on the day we had taken over. A journalist had said that the change had come too late and there was no way we could pull off the win. A song by Tim Finn came into my head:

We had no idea that it couldn't be done
And we needed to find a like-minded someone
Who had no idea that it couldn't be done

I sent Jacinda a link to the song.

She came back to me instantly: 'YES! THOSE LYRICS!'

Thanks to Barbara Ward's connections in the music industry, we got the rights to use the song — just the once.

The launch itself was remarkable. The Auckland Town Hall could have been filled three or four times over. We had an overflow theatre which overflowed. Crowds gathered in Aotea Square. And again Jacinda stepped up to the challenge and went beyond it. Her speech was note-perfect and inspiring — she called climate change her generation's nuclear-free moment and got the headline she wanted.

When the speech finished, we headed out to Aotea Square. People came from everywhere, wanting autographs, photos, just to get a glimpse of Jacinda. By this stage she had the support of the Diplomatic Protection Squad (DPS). I stood next to its long-serving head as he cast his eyes around and said, 'I have never seen anything like this — we are going to have to re-think everything.'

As in all election campaigns there were ebbs and flows. Our support plateaued a little. As Finance spokesperson I knew that the economy, or more specifically people's confidence in our handling of the economy, was going to be a major factor. I was up against Steven Joyce, a relatively new Finance Minister but a wily and experienced campaigner.

By this stage I was being ably assisted by Craig Renney as my economic advisor. Craig had come on board 18 months earlier from working in government at MBIE and the Treasury. He is a gifted economist and, a rare breed, a left-wing one. The son of an English coal miner, he had, remarkably, a lifelong ambition to help write a government Budget.

Craig and I had created a credible fiscal plan. We had managed to bring together a number of significant campaign commitments, and still meet our fiscal targets of keeping net debt at 20% of gross domestic product (GDP) and the books in surplus. It's true that there was limited room for new spending beyond our core commitments. But it added up. We had the figures checked by Ganesh Nana and his team at Business and Economic Research Limited (BERL), who concurred.

Steven Joyce, however, did not agree. He called the Press Gallery to his office and announced that Labour had an $11 billion 'fiscal hole' over the four years of our plan. He had tables and charts, and pressed his case.

As is the way of modern politics and journalism, the first reporting was simply his claim. The words 'FISCAL HOLE' screamed out from the websites. We scrambled together our response. It is not especially relevant now, but the essence of Joyce's argument stemmed from us presenting our fiscal plan in a slightly different format from how the Budget was presented. Essentially, we had included in our plan a whole load of future spending that was still to be allocated in an upcoming Budget.

I went downstairs and did a stand-up, denying Joyce's claim and patiently explaining how our numbers added up. I was helped not only by the fact that BERL had backed us but also by the fact that fairly quickly the most financially literate members of the Press Gallery, particularly Bernard Hickey and Vernon Small, agreed that there was no hole. A tight budget but, yes, it did all add up.

Over the following days, the argument turned on Steven Joyce. As more and more voices agreed that there was no hole, he was challenged to find one economist who backed him. Memorably, in a RNZ debate between the two of us, Guyon Espiner repeatedly asked him to name an economist who backed him. Espiner then shifted the question to anyone who backed him. Joyce said Bill English agreed with him. Perhaps a less than impartial observer.

As helpful as this was, Steven Joyce had scratched an itch. For as long as the Labour Party has done polling, we have lagged behind National on trust in our handling of the economy. I can recall Michael Cullen telling me that at one point during the Fifth Labour Government, when net debt was at a record low, and unemployment was the second lowest in the OECD, we still polled behind National on managing the economy. Our support started to move backwards.

We also encountered more problems on the issue that has vexed many Labour campaigns — tax. Under Andrew's leadership, we had decided to establish a Tax Working Group to investigate changes to make the tax system fairer. Andrew, sensibly as it turns out, had said we would not implement any outcomes from the group in the first term. When Jacinda became leader, we agreed that we would carry on the working group but decided not to rule out change in our first term. We both believed it was essential that a capital gains tax (CGT) be introduced. New Zealand's tax system is highly unbalanced. We barely tax assets and wealth at all. Wage and salary earners bear the load disproportionately to almost any country we would care to compare ourselves to. We also felt that it would be better to get the work over and done with in our first term. However, we had not given ourselves time to make the case, nor land on the fine details.

This left too much room for our opponents. We found ourselves constantly being asked to rule things out (which we did for a CGT on the family home and an inheritance tax). But it was a game of whack-a-mole, and it was hurting us in the polls; the focus groups were also reporting back nervousness about our tax plan. We knew we had to cauterise the wound.

Once again I found myself on the black-and-white tiles at Parliament, explaining Labour's economic position. I committed that no new taxes would be implemented during our first term, meaning that the public could judge our policies at the 2020 election before they came into force. It was a backdown, for sure — but the commitment was reported fairly, and stabilised us in the polls.

Come election night, expectations were still high. Despite a few bumps, Jacinda was still the star of the campaign. Our policy platform was solid. We were reversing National's tax cuts, which provided room for boosts to Working for Families, a new child support payment (Best Start), a Winter Energy Payment for low-income people, first-year tertiary fees free and a boost to student allowances. We also had our flagship, highly ambitious housing policy, Kiwibuild, for the construction of 100,000 affordable homes over 10 years, and a commitment to reductions in doctors' fees and other health costs.

When the results rolled in, Labour was the only party whose percentage of the vote increased, but it landed just below 36%.

National had polled just under 46%. They were going to need both ACT and New Zealand First to be able to govern, but they were in the box seat.

As the results became clear, Jacinda called me. She felt she had let people down. She had written a couple of versions of her speech and was preparing to deliver what sounded to me like a concession. I counselled her against it. We knew that in the latter stages of the campaign we had enrolled a large number of voters who had cast special votes, and these, along with the votes from overseas where Jacinda had resonated, had not yet been counted. We were not entirely convinced they would make a difference, but it was worth just holding back a little. Besides, it was an incredible result in many ways — we had lifted our vote from the low 20s to the mid-30s in just seven weeks. It was in fact something to celebrate. Jacinda gave the more upbeat version of her speech, and we waited for the final results.

Interestingly, Winston Peters said right away that he was not going to be doing anything until the special votes had been counted. Two weeks later they came in, and we had gained a seat, as had the Greens. National, while still well ahead as the preferred party, had lost two seats, and this created a little room for us.

While the Greens were not an absolute given to be in a formal coalition with Labour, they certainly were not going to go with National. We began our preliminary discussions with them about what an agreement might look like. On the right, David Seymour was on his own as an ACT MP and he was locked in for the Nats. That left, as it has before, Winston Peters in the driver's seat. And what a ride it would be.

We thought carefully about who we wanted in a negotiating team with New Zealand First. Jacinda, Kelvin as deputy and I as Finance spokesperson represented the Caucus. We also wanted people Winston would relate to. Annette King had a respectful relationship with him and was happy to add her experience to the team. Michael Cullen also joined us in the early stages. Jacinda had already approached former Helen Clark chief press secretary Mike Munro to be her Chief of Staff, and he was added to the team.

New Zealand First booked a meeting room on the second floor of the Beehive, accessible from Parliament House and far enough away from the Executive offices to be seen as neutral ground. They would alternate morning and afternoon meetings with National and Labour.

On the first day we arrived under the full glare of the media. Jacinda brought along a ginger loaf baked by her friend Julia and a copy of the New Zealand First manifesto. The New Zealand First team that day was Winston, his Chief of Staff David Broome, his friend Paul Canard, Ron Mark MP, Tracey Martin MP, and her sister Kirsty who had been a New Zealand First staffer. People came and went on their side, but the pattern set on that first day stayed the same for many days after.

Jacinda noted at the outset that our 100 Day Plan was the core of what we wanted to do, but that we understood that New Zealand First would have priorities too, and we wanted to hear them. Winston spent much of the first meeting talking about the need to do things differently, the state of the global economy and how trickle-down economics had not worked. He then said that he wanted to work through New Zealand First's manifesto policy area by policy area. And that is what we did. Day after day. We went into some excruciating detail. New Zealand First wanted a New Zealand Jazz Orchestra. They had a problem with rumble strips on roads, and drone regulation. There were also bigger-picture issues, especially about areas like regional development. And there was, thankfully, some common ground too: the need to review defence spending, reform the Reserve Bank Act, ban foreign buyers of existing housing and more. We would eagerly note these areas as common to our view. Winston, it felt to me, did not seem especially interested, however, in what Labour's policy might be.

Each day we would mark issues as either agreed, needing more discussion or not agreed. Many issues would fall into the middle category simply because we really didn't know exactly what New Zealand First wanted, or how what they wanted could be implemented. But the process was respectful and detailed, and seemed to be the discussion that New Zealand First had in mind.

As the days stretched on, nothing was ever given away about how discussions between New Zealand First and National were progressing. One day we arrived early for an afternoon meeting and New Zealand First were not there. There were papers on the table, some with the National Party logo on them. The temptation to pick them up was huge. But Jacinda, ever the responsible one, told us to leave them where they were.

Eventually we ran out of policy to discuss. Jacinda broached the need for us to get the Greens on board with whatever Labour and New Zealand First were agreed on. We had already begun a series of talks with the Greens who had a long list of policies they wanted included in an agreement. Winston made clear that the Greens were for us to deal with. He was negotiating only with us, end of story. This made life difficult and meant that we reduced the number of meetings we had with the Greens on the grounds that there was not a lot of point in going further until we knew more of what Winston wanted.

We decided to bring to what appeared likely to be our last meeting with New Zealand First a summary of the key matters we thought we had agreed across the negotiations. I drafted it with the help of Neale Jones, who had stayed on to work with Jacinda. Winston seemed quite positive when he got the document. He had not asked for it, so it was a risk giving it to him, but he said he would take it away and they would work through it.

The days that followed were random. Every now and then there would be a follow-up to something that was in the document. One of the ideas that had been discussed early on was giving a portion of GST back to the regions for regional development purposes. I was not keen on the idea. I felt that once we started mucking around with GST and its collection, we would lose considerable control of our spending. I also had very limited confidence in some of the local authorities which would end up with a fair amount of cash. We countered with the idea of a significant Regional Development Fund. Shane Jones, now a New Zealand First MP, having left Parliament and Labour in 2014, wanted an amount that would be equivalent to the returned GST, which had been estimated to be around $3 billion a year. There was no way we could do that, but a $3 billion fund across the term of Parliament we could (just) make work. It would be funded by stretching out our debt profile a bit, and by repurposing some other infrastructure funding.

Probably the biggest policy sticking point was immigration. New Zealand First wanted a cap, and changes to various categories. Winston had raised these issues early in the negotiations. Jacinda had held her ground in the room, saying that we were not prepared to set numerical caps. New Zealand First via Shane Jones, who still had friends in the Labour Caucus, pushed and said that this could be a deal breaker. Jacinda would not budge. She was, and is, an internationalist, and this kind of nationalistic politics she judged to be not in line with Labour values. Her resolve was impressive and scary all at once.

Having got some kind of acknowledgement of the policy list from New Zealand First, we could at last go into discussions with the Greens with more intensity. We had a lot more common ground with them, of course, but we were wary of some big-ticket items and some social policy areas that New Zealand First would not back. These would need to be negotiated separately when the time came. One of these was marijuana law reform. The Greens had been thinking about this too, foreseen there might be a problem, and so put forward the idea of a referendum on the issue. They acknowledged this would be a challenge to get through. We nodded sagely — knowing that only a day or two earlier New Zealand First had said that the furthest they could go was a referendum on the issue. Sometimes the strange game of three-handed poker worked well!

Having witnessed just how much distance Winston wanted from the Greens, we became stronger in our belief that rather than trying for a three-way coalition, we would be better off having a confidence and supply agreement with the Greens. This would also give them more freedom to disagree and manage their internal battles. We were clear that there would be ministerial roles for them, and policy agreements, but the formalities of a coalition could be dispensed with. We were grateful that after some consideration the Greens took this view too.

Meantime, Jacinda also met privately with Winston to discuss personnel issues. We had deliberately kept these to the last. As we later learned, National had somewhat crassly put ministerial roles and appointments on the table in the first few days of their discussions. Jacinda came back from those meetings frustrated but resolute. Winston had suggested that all nine of his MPs, including some who had just arrived in Parliament, should get Executive roles. She pushed back, eventually agreeing to four ministerial roles. This was eventually added to with an under-secretary position. We mirrored this in our discussions with the Greens, suggesting three ministerial roles and one under-secretary. Towards the end of the discussions, as we wondered what else to do, we offered Winston the role of Deputy Prime Minister. We knew the risk, and I mused that he might not want to take it up.

The New Zealand First Board began discussing the possible agreements on 16 October, some 23 days after the election. Three days later, word emerged that a decision was imminent. That day we did not hear at all from New Zealand First. We assumed the worst. Surely they would have been in contact to get more details about policies or particular roles? We waited much of the day in our offices. Jacinda fretted that she had been too stubborn. Then sometime after 6pm, TV news coverage switched to footage of Winston making his way to the Beehive Theatrette. We gathered in Jacinda's office.

Winston began by talking about the need for change in the economy — the very same speech he had started with in our discussions. Jacinda and I shot each other a glance. Could he be about to go with us? Winston meandered for a bit — and then finally announced that the government would be a coalition between New Zealand First and . . . New Zealand Labour.

We erupted with ecstatic relief. All the hard times of nine long years of Opposition, the disastrous Cunliffe saga, the Hail Mary of Jacinda taking over, came pouring out in the form of tears of joy. We still had the Greens' Special General Meeting to approve our agreement with them, but their co-leader James Shaw was confident his party would not give up a shot at government.

We had done it.

Now the coast is clear and the case has been won
And we lost our fear that it couldn't be done
All we needed to find was a like-minded someone
Who had no idea that it couldn't be done.

11. GOVERNING BEFORE COVID

After so long in Opposition, the prospect of becoming a minister was at once thrilling and overwhelming. I had grown in confidence in the Finance field, but the step up to Finance Minister felt huge. It was a moment of imposter syndrome. The only way I knew through it was to follow that advice my mother had given me: if I worked hard, then good things would happen. I had worked very hard — and now I was going to have to work even harder.

The most surreal experience of all was going to Government House to be sworn in. Jacinda started as she meant to go on by telling ministers that they would be travelling there by bus rather than in the Crown cars.

As we sat in the massive ballroom waiting to be sworn in, I reflected on the journey from South Dunedin to there. I had been interested in politics from a young age, but I am not sure I really appreciated what it all meant until that moment. My mother had come up from Dunedin for the day. Her — and Dad's — interest in making a better world had shaped me so much. Surrounded by the grandeur of Government House, there was plenty of reason to yell 'Class distinction!' today, but we both resisted the opportunity. That day, the privilege of my new role was top of mind.

I also invited my long-time parliamentary Executive Assistant Jen Toogood to attend the ceremony. She had no desire to work in a minister's office so was not joining me in the Beehive, but it felt right to have her there. Jen was a force of nature. She had been in and around the Labour Caucus since the 1980s, though had left Parliament before I became an MP. I knew her socially, lured her back, and for nine years she kept me on the straight and narrow. She could be tough on her colleagues but she was so loyal to me. Jen passed away from cancer while we were in government, and right to the end she was giving me great advice — and great gossip.

My other guest at the swearing-in was of course Alf. By this stage he was a bus driver, having left the Treasury a few years earlier. It had become increasingly difficult for him to work there when Labour was in Opposition. And in any case, 29 years at the Treasury felt like long enough for him. He came to Government House straight from a shift, in his bus driver's uniform. As ever, he was keeping things real for me.

As each of us was given the opportunity to swear our allegiance, there were many moments of emotion. For Jacinda, it was an extraordinary occasion: in just a matter of months she had become party leader, then New Zealand's youngest ever Prime Minister, and only the third woman to hold the position.

I sat next to Winston. He shuffled his papers nervously. He signed his warrant before he took his oath and generally gave off a less than comfortable vibe.

As we were sworn in, Cabinet Secretary Michael Webster read out our portfolios. When he came to Chris Hipkins and said, 'Minister of Education', I noticed Chippy wipe tears from his eyes. This was his life's ambition, and here we were.

We got back on the buses and returned to Parliament. We were greeted by an unbelievable scene. Hundreds of people had come to the grounds to wish us well. There was a band playing on the steps — that had never happened before. Jacinda said a few words and acknowledged the support. Echoing the campaign slogan, she signed off by saying we had to get to work — 'Let's do this!'

—

We were desperate to get going. The core of our campaign had been the 100 Day Plan, and the clock was ticking. It was a highly ambitious document and from the get-go officials were concerned that we would not meet our deadlines. The centrepiece was the Families Package. This involved the creation of the new Best Start Payment, the Winter Energy Payment, and boosts to Working for Families and the Accommodation Supplement. It was paid for by reversing National's proposed tax cuts.

The first meeting on the package hit home the big difference between making policy in Opposition and implementing it in government. It no longer involved a handful of MPs and a couple of staff. My office on the 7th floor of the Beehive was packed with about 40 officials from every conceivable agency. People perched everywhere; some were standing. Each of them had come with some issue or other to be resolved. The interaction between the payments, what that meant for eligibility for other support — would anyone actually end up worse off?

At this point I remembered the best piece of advice I ever got about being a Minister. Annette King had told us that our job was to make decisions. The system was full of people who would give advice, write reports and provide opinions, but it was our job to decide. The ministers who would succeed, she said, were those who were prepared to make the calls and to do so in a timely manner. Everything I observed for the next six years proved this point. Some ministers just could not shift paper along. They prevaricated, sought more advice and lost momentum.

The 100 Day Plan meant we just did not have time for that. So we pushed on, and got the new payments established and the legislation passed. This was, in effect, a mini-Budget, and I treated it as such. Very quickly I found myself in the Beehive Banquet

Hall, explaining to the Press Gallery what we were doing, and how 385,000 families were going to be better off by an average of $75 per week. Those on benefits and Superannuation were going to get an income boost in winter to the tune of $450 per person. It was all a bit daunting, but it felt so good to be achieving some of what we had campaigned on.

The 100 Day Plan was more than the Families Package. A long-time Labour policy was finally implemented — paid parental leave would increase to 26 weeks. And our commitment to fees-free tertiary education began with legislation and funding to make the first year of study free, with the promise of further years in later Budgets. We also boosted student allowances and living-cost payments by $50 per week.

On top of this, the 100 Day Plan made good on some long-term policy work. One of the most important to me was the establishment of a Royal Commission into Abuse in State Care. My involvement with the survivors of abuse had started when the remarkable Keith Whiffen came to see me in my electorate office in 2010.

Keith had for years been battling the system for recognition of and compensation for abuse he suffered at the Epuni Boys' Home in the 1970s. I could scarcely believe what he told me about the sexual, physical and emotional abuse that took place there and in other institutions. Its impact on Keith and other survivors was lifelong. What I was also appalled by was the inaction, and indeed obstruction, from government agencies about getting proper resolution. After several years of trying to help Keith in his personal case, it was clear to me that a systemic response was needed.

I spoke to Jacinda, who was our Children's spokesperson. She, too, had been working with survivors. We put forward the policy that Labour in government would initiate a Royal Commission of Inquiry. Keith and his fellow survivors had been let down so many times, they did not really believe we would do it. The National government had flatly turned down the idea. I'm sure this would have been because of the same advice we got: the cost of redress and compensation was going to be huge. All that did for me was confirm that the problem was large enough to justify a Royal Commission.

We set it up inside those first 100 days. It is a sign of the complexity and extent of the abuse that the final report was not handed down until 2024. There were many times when we wondered how it would ever get finished, and I am immensely proud that we got it done. But that pales in insignificance to the pride I have in Keith and other survivors. This is a dark chapter in New Zealand's history that needed to have light shone on it. There is more to do to find the redress that survivors deserve, but getting the process started was a highlight of our first 100 days.

Part of our agreement with New Zealand First was a review of the Reserve Bank Act. Winston Peters had long had issues with the Reserve Bank and its slavish attachment to conventional monetary policy. This was not an area in which I was particularly well versed before becoming Finance spokesperson, but I had set about learning all I could, and talking and meeting with people in the sector. While it was easy to be intimidated by the 'high priests' of monetary policy, I came to the view that in many ways the issue boiled down to psychology with numbers. It was an attempt to use the tool of the official cash rate to influence behaviour.

Since 1989 New Zealand had preached the virtue of a bank with a sole focus on inflation targeting. Little had changed in that time, with the exception of the target of 1% to 3% inflation being codified. It was simply how it was done.

The more I learned, the more I realised that while New Zealand had once led the way, we were now out of step with many jurisdictions in terms of the objectives of the bank and how we made decisions. With Craig Renney's help, I developed an alternative policy and used its release as a chance to push my bona fides with the financial community. It was risky, but I also genuinely believed that there needed to be change.

One of two core elements of our change proposal was the addition of a new objective for the Reserve Bank to support employment outcomes. My basic belief here was that while inflation control was vital, it was also essential that all the apparatus in the economy was supporting a productivity focus. Employment outcomes felt like the best proxy for this. Such a change would also put us in line with others such as the Federal Reserve and the Reserve Bank of Australia.

We also proposed a move to a Monetary Policy Committee to make decisions, rather than leaving them entirely to the Reserve Bank Governor. In addition, we wanted the committee to include some external appointees to provide a broader perspective. The minutes of the committee would be made public as well, providing more transparency on the decisions. This model was based on the Bank of England.

Our proposals went down like a cup of cold sick with the purists, who included the outgoing Governor Graeme Wheeler. I had clashed with him a number of times as Opposition spokesperson. I was concerned at the impact of some of the bank's decisions and its reluctance to act that had been evident in 2015/16 when the economy slowed significantly.

We were clear that while we wanted to review the Act overall, the core proposals were going ahead, with advice sought on how to implement them, rather than whether to do so. Right to his final days in the job, Graeme Wheeler tried to convince us not to go ahead, particularly on the change to the bank's objectives. This continued with the Acting Governor Grant Spencer when we were elected. I knew we had to have someone with a more pragmatic attitude take over, and that none of the current leadership would be able to offer that.

As the search for a Governor began, one person came up from many quarters — NZ Super Fund CEO Adrian Orr. I did not know Adrian, but I had admired his work at the Fund. He was also a straightforward communicator who I hoped would bring some of those skills to the bank. When he was brought forward as the nominee after the selection process, I had only one question. Would he be able to work with the new arrangements? The message came back that he was not only comfortable with them but also thought they were sensible changes.

His appointment in December 2017 was warmly welcomed, though some of those supporters later became less complimentary. The announcement of the appointment was a moment of hilarity and clarity for Jacinda and me. We were getting conflicting advice: that we needed to make the announcement when the markets were closed and that we had to do it right away, as soon as we had made the decision. As we sat there angsting about whose advice to take, Jacinda said, 'Hang on, I'm the Prime Minister, you're the Minister of Finance, we get to decide.' 'Yeah', I said, 'we get to decide.' We were at the grown-ups' table now.

In our first 100 days we also restarted government contributions to the New Zealand Superannuation Fund. In the midst of the GFC, Bill English had decided that contributions should be paused, and he never restarted them. He claimed he would wait till the books reached a surplus, but even when they did, no contributions were made. To me this was the height of irresponsibility. Michael Cullen's Super Fund was designed to defray the cost of a retirement bulge that we could all see coming. It would start paying out by the mid-2030s, reducing the burden on future taxpayers. Meantime, the Fund was making strong returns (over 10% per annum). By pausing contributions, the government had cost taxpayers $17 billion of earnings.

In December 2017 Jacinda and I went over to Treasury to physically restart the contributions. It was a slightly weird scene as we hovered over the keyboard of some poor Treasury official and ceremonially pushed the enter key to deposit the money. What the moment lacked in pizazz it made up for in a real manifestation of our commitment to responsible fiscal management.

Establishing our fiscal credentials, given the inbuilt bias against Labour governments' handling of the economy, had been an essential part of our election campaign. I had been working with Craig Renney on an idea based on former UK PM and Chancellor of the Exchequer Gordon Brown's 'fiscal golden rule' when it emerged that James Shaw was thinking along similar lines. Working together on this would kill two birds with one stone. It would quell nervousness about a potential coalition with the Greens and push Labour's own credentials. We worked hard to produce five rules that would still allow us to advance our policy agenda. Both James and I had some very reluctant colleagues, but we knew that we had to deal with our Achilles heel.

We jointly announced the rules with a major splash in the *New Zealand Herald*. These were:

- achieve a sustainable operating surplus across an economic cycle;
- reduce the level of net core Crown debt to 20% of GDP within five years of taking office;
- prioritise investments to address the long-term financial and sustainability challenges facing New Zealand;
- maintain government expenditure to within the recent historical range of spending to GDP ratio, which has averaged around 30% over the last 20 years;
- ensure a progressive taxation system that is fair, balanced and

promotes the long-term sustainability and productivity of the economy.

The debt level was chosen solely because that was the target of the current National government. We had given ourselves a bit longer to get there to accommodate some of the investments we wanted to make. But setting it at 20% gave limited room for our opponents to attack us.

The final commitment on tax was the most general and reflected the issues we had with a capital gains tax. We pulled together a Tax Working Group that covered business, unions and various tax experts, and I prevailed on Michael Cullen to chair it. We gave them a wide brief. Michael had not been a fan of a CGT when in office, but in latter years was coming around to the idea. He was respected, and the perfect person to kick things off.

Once in government, New Zealand First was mostly happy to go along with our fiscal approach. Winston fancied himself as a fiscal conservative, but he had no shortage of ideas on how he and his colleagues could spend money. On tax, he was highly sceptical. He was happy to let the Tax Working Group do its work, and said his party were open to its recommendations, but was no fan of CGT. I don't think his position was highly principled; he just knew the politics were awkward.

We ticked off all of the 100 Day Plan items and felt very satisfied with our beginning as a government. The vast bulk of what we did was Labour policy, and we knew that there was a big list of commitments in the two agreements that needed attention. But there seemed to be a fairly strong reservoir of goodwill among the coalition partners as we looked towards 2018.

In early January 2018 Jacinda and I agreed that I would head to Auckland to spend a day or two with her doing some planning for the year ahead. When I got there, she suggested we go for a walk. As we wandered along, with the DPS a few steps in front and behind, she told me she was pregnant. It's quite hard to stifle your emotions in a moment like that. This was huge. I knew that she and her partner Clarke had been trying to have a baby for a long time and it had not been an easy road.

Jacinda pointed out I had missed a few clues. For example, she did not have a drink on the night we became the government (I thought she was being a goody two-shoes). Or the day not long after the election when we were flying to Auckland together and she produced some anti-nausea pills from her bag when I told her I wasn't feeling well (okay, I was just being self-absorbed that day). But I was so happy for her and Clarke. They were going to be amazing parents. It would be a tough balance for Jacinda, given her workload, but I also knew that as a team we would rally around. I did wonder how Winston would go as PM when she took parental leave, but that was far enough off not to take the gloss off the news.

As we got ready for the Budget that year, I essentially ruled out bids for funding that were not in coalition and confidence-and-supply agreements. It was tight, but we met all of our fiscal rules. I coined the Budget title *Foundations for the Future*, given that the bulk of the new spending went towards shoring up public services in areas such as Health, Education and Housing. We did establish the Provincial Growth Fund and the Climate Commission, and honour several other important commitments. For now, everyone was playing ball.

For me the most significant announcement at Budget 2018 was to signal that the Budget the following year would take a Wellbeing approach. For a long time I had been concerned at GDP being used as the sole barometer of the health of the economy. Certainly, it is a standard and consistent way of measuring the output of the economy, but it does very little to measure or understand the quality of that output.

This was not a new concern. Bobby Kennedy gave a famous speech on the shortcomings of GDP (or GNP in this instance) in 1968. He spoke about how it measured all manner of things, from bombs to jails and other undesirable items, and finished with the devastating critique:

> *Yet the gross national product does not allow for the health of our children, the quality of their education or the joy of their play. It does not include the beauty of our poetry or the strength of our marriages, the intelligence of our public debate or the integrity of our public officials.*
>
> *It measures neither our wit nor our courage, neither our wisdom nor our learning, neither our compassion nor our devotion to our country, it measures everything in short, except that which makes life worthwhile.*

It has often been said that the best thing for GDP is a war and the second-best thing is a natural disaster. Both are sources of immense activity in the economy but offer little or nothing that makes life worthwhile.

As I looked at how we could shift to a different set of measures, I realised that part of the answer was on our doorstep. As far back as 2011, Treasury had been working on a Living Standards Framework (LSF). It in turn had been based on the OECD's Better Life Index. It looked through the lens of increasing standards of living in four domains (or capitals in economists' speak): financial, human, natural and social — or, as I came to talk about them, money, people, the environment and our communities.

This was exactly what I wanted: a framework with some theoretical basis that could change the approach to how we did Budgets. Treasury were already working on a suite of indicators to support the framework, and I asked that this work be brought forward. We then turned our attention to how to actually refocus the Budget process to look at Wellbeing. A significant element for me was to break down the silos of government that were reinforced by the current approach to the Budget and the broader public finance system.

The Public Finance Act and its twin sister the State Sector Act were products of the 1980s. They did have their advantages. They had given some much-needed transparency to government spending and decision-making. They also had instilled a sense of fiscal discipline. But they did this by creating a series of unconnected silos. Ministry and departmental CEOs operated virtually in competition with one another, with shared funding actively discouraged. Minor tinkering had taken place over the years, but little had actually changed. This siloed approach actively worked against the government addressing the 'messy' problems of the world — such as climate change, child poverty or other inequalities. Meeting these challenges in government required cooperation and collaboration, not competition.

At Budget 2018 we were able to confirm that a piece of legislation Jacinda had written in Opposition to create a child poverty reporting framework would now be a feature in future Budgets as well. This fitted perfectly with the new approach. We added climate reporting and an overall Wellbeing Report that would now be required at each Budget.

The other significant issue was the short-term focus created by the annual Budget process. Without a consistent framework, Budgets became reactive and were essentially a contestable fund with arbitrary decision-making. We set about establishing an enduring set of Budget priorities that focused on the intergenerational challenges New Zealand was facing. We used evidence from the LSF, and tested it with experts, including academics and Māori business and union leaders. There emerged a fairly consistent list of the kinds of issues that would need sustained attention if we were to lift outcomes across the board. The priorities were:

- creating opportunities for productive businesses, regions, iwi and others to transition to a sustainable and low-emissions economy;
- supporting a thriving nation in the digital age through innovation, social and economic opportunities;
- lifting Māori and Pacific incomes, skills and opportunities;
- reducing child poverty and improving child wellbeing, including addressing family violence;
- supporting mental wellbeing for all New Zealanders, with a special focus on under 24-year-olds.

We listened to the experts. We knew we wanted to focus on child poverty. Our experts told us that a critical determinant in the wellbeing of children was the presence (or absence) of violence in their household. We tweaked the priority to reflect this. All Budget bids for new funding now had to align with these priorities. Extra support was available where agencies could show they were working together.

While other countries had been working with concepts of Wellbeing, New Zealand was the first that we knew of to create an end-to-end Budget process using those concepts. We were deciding what to invest in on the basis of a Wellbeing analysis, and would then use Wellbeing indicators to measure our success. It was groundbreaking stuff, and some quality work was done by staff at the Treasury to put in place the framework in time for Budget 2019.

As 2018 ended, Jacinda and I received an invitation to the World Economic Forum at Davos at the start of the following year to talk about Wellbeing. There was also an invitation for me to speak at the London School of Economics about our Budget process. I had come a long way from taking the portfolio on in 2014, and it felt like we were right at the cutting edge.

The day of 15 March 2019 was set to be busy. The first big School Strike for Climate march was ending at Parliament. It had already been a big week. Driving to work the day before, I had noticed an ambulance on Glenmore Street opposite the entrance to the Botanic Gardens. I soon found out that it was there for James Shaw, my friend, fellow minister and Green Party co-leader, who had been assaulted on his way to work by an angry conspiracy theorist. I had known James since the 1990s when he was in and around student politics. We had caught up in London a couple of times when he worked there, and we had been through a few Wellington Central campaigns together. I even drove James to campaign events before he got his driver's licence. Only a morning or two earlier I had picked him up as he walked down the hill from his house.

It was a real shock to see James at a Cabinet committee meeting later that morning, so soon after the assault. It was even more of a shock to see blood coming out of his mouth and eyes. We urged him to go to hospital, where he discovered he had a fractured eye socket.

James showed up to the rally the next day looking much the worse for wear. It should have been no surprise he was there. Climate change is his driving passion. He was 18 months into an extraordinary run as Minister responsible, and was bringing parties across the House together in that cause.

The rally was massive. It felt like something very special. Young people had had enough of the talk on climate change and wanted climate action. I was really proud to see a number of students from the schools in my electorate in the crowd. I remember going back to my electorate office after the rally and saying to my staff that this would be a big story on the news tonight.

Next up, a meeting with the head of Wellington Free Ambulance, Mike Grant. As he walked in, he was on the phone. He told me there had been a shooting in Christchurch. He did not know the details, but it had been picked up by his communications people. We settled into a conversation about funding for the amazing service that is Wellington Free.

I had a rule that the only phone calls I would take when I was in a meeting with a constituent were from Alf, Mum or Jacinda. A few minutes into the conversation, I saw Jacinda's name flash up. Straight away I could tell from her voice that something terrible was unfolding. I made my apologies to Mike, who rushed away to find out more. Some of his staff would later re-deploy to Christchurch to help out.

I decided I should head to the Beehive. I spoke with Jacinda again from the car and she told me this was a shooting unlike any other. We did not know how many people were dead, but it was likely to be dozens. And they were almost all members of our Muslim community. At that point there was still some question as to whether the shooter had been acting alone.

Jacinda was in New Plymouth and was preparing to make her first comments to the media. I was struck in that moment by how clear her thinking seemed. She ran past me some of what she wanted to say, and uttered the now famous phrase, 'They are us.' I asked her what she wanted me to do. She asked me to head to support the team in her office at Parliament. And that is where I basically stayed for the next few days.

This was what I did during the many crises we would have to deal with. While there was always a financial element to any crisis, I saw my role as providing whatever support I could to Jacinda. In this case, it was really a matter of helping get the messages right, and of liaising with our Christchurch MPs. Megan Woods had a very close relationship with the Muslim community, and in particular with Gamal Fouda, the imam of the Al Noor Mosque. Megan showed incredible strength over this period, as she knew many of the dead but pushed on to be their advocate. The scale and horror of the terrorist attack was there for all to see, but through Megan and Gamal I learned so much about the personal trauma of so many families. It was heartbreaking, as they had to grieve so publicly.

I still regard Jacinda's handling of the days after the terrorist attack as one of her finest moments. I sat in the back as she told a shocked Press Gallery and nation that 49 people were dead and others critically injured. She was compassionate, clear and resolute. When she said the words, 'I can tell you one thing right now, our gun laws will change', it was a pivotal moment. The ban on semi-automatic weapons is an extraordinary legacy. It was a measure that had been talked about for years, and we were able to do it within weeks. Her description of the shooting as a terrorist attack was also a major turning point in how the situation played out at home and across the world.

When the memorial service for the victims was held in Christchurch two weeks later, and Jacinda walked onto the stage to speak, the crowd stood and just started clapping. As she tried to begin, she had to pause as people stood and kept applauding. The public, in their grief, felt they had a real leader — decisive and caring.

When I look back, I'm reminded that even while reeling from that horrendous event, we were still trying to govern. Already, it felt like we had to be ready for anything to happen because it probably would. But the day-to-day work of government had to go on as well.

As we headed towards our first Wellbeing Budget in May, there was the matter of the report of the Tax Working Group to deal with. Sir Michael and his group had managed to find a consensus around the need for a CGT. It was what we needed to push ahead with much-needed tax reform. The Greens were already on board, but to get it through we needed the support of New Zealand First.

I had been in discussions with them for some time. They gave the impression of wanting to engage, albeit with misgivings. We discussed various versions of a CGT, including how to discourage the ownership of multiple properties. I shared a number of different proposals in writing and met with staff. I was, in fact, being strung along. In the background, New Zealand First were working with others who were strongly opposed to the change. In early April I finally received in writing what I already knew — that New Zealand First were not prepared to support a CGT.

While this meant the government was not going to be able to pursue the tax change, it was still open to Labour to do so. However, Jacinda had come to the view that the issue would act as an electoral drag on us. She felt that we would bleed votes to New Zealand First, the very people we would have to convince to support it if we were back in government. We had campaigned three times on a CGT and it had never worked. The right of politics continued to oppose it, and she reasoned that electorally it was poison. She made the call to say that as Prime Minister she would not introduce a CGT. I understood the politics of it, but I was gutted. This was one of the most significant issues I wanted to deal with as Finance Minister. I totally understood where Jacinda was coming from — and that we had so much more we were trying to do as a government. I hoped I might be able to come back to it another day, but the definitive statement left me with few options for now.

My focus turned to the Budget. Economic growth had been maintained, so the fiscal picture was good. We were able to make some very significant investments in our first Wellbeing Budget, keep debt under the 20% figure and run a surplus. It was the balanced economic management I had been working towards.

As was tradition, on the Tuesday morning prior to the Budget on the Thursday I went out to the printers in Lower Hutt for a photo opportunity. I was excited and happy to joke around with the Press Gallery. On the way back into town I took a phone call. It seemed that the National Party had somehow got hold of parts of the Budget.

By the time I got back and headed to Caucus, National had published a section of the Defence budget. This was serious. Secrecy and confidentiality around the Budget are sacrosanct. Once upon a time this was because a change in the price of booze and cigarettes would cause a run; now it was more to prevent market movements.

We did not know how much of the Budget National had seen. I stepped out of Caucus to discover that a further section of it had now been put online. There was the risk that National was going to drip feed the whole thing. It was a disaster.

I got Jacinda out of Caucus, and we stood in the Members' Billiards Room discussing what to do. Should we bring the Budget forward and release it that afternoon? Treasury were still trying to work out what had happened and could not offer any certain answers. Trying to remember the message I used to give to others to not give in to panic, we decided to wait to find out more.

Around five o'clock that evening I got a message that Treasury Secretary Gabs Makhlouf was coming over to see me. He had asked for it to be a one-on-one meeting. He looked sombre when he came into the room, and in one of a handful of moments as Minister that made my heart stop he said, 'Minister, the Treasury server has been hacked. I have already spoken to the police. I believe this is a deliberate, criminal act.'

Trust me, these are not the words that you want to hear 48 hours before the Budget. He went on to say that their initial inquiries had found that the 'hack' had been undertaken from a parliamentary IP address. Eventually Gabs agreed to staff including my advisors and press secretaries, and Andrew Campbell from the PM's Office, coming in to join us. We talked through the next steps, one of which was that the Government Communications Security Bureau (GCSB) and others would look into exactly what happened. The media were clamouring for information, and there was still the risk that National would release more material, potentially for the next morning's news.

We took the decision to try to flush National out. We put out a media release saying that I had been advised of a hack and called National out on being a party to it. National responded swiftly, vehemently denying this was the case. Their response gave me pause for thought. They seemed very sure of their ground.

Late in the evening I got an indication that those who had been looking into the leak had found that it was not as sinister as first thought. Over the course of the night and the next morning it emerged that a dummy version of parts of the Budget had been put up to test the website. It seemed a National Party researcher had typed into the search bar the address for sections of the previous Budget, had changed the date to 2019 and had struck gold. Clearly the researcher had some knowledge of how the Treasury worked at Budget time, but this was not, in anyone's language, a hack.

The next 24 hours are a bit of a blur, but it became apparent National did not have much more to put out. We held our nerve and reasoned that public interest would turn to the content of the remainder of the Budget as soon as we put it out. I did make one change to the normal order of events. I suggested to Gabs that perhaps he not join ministers on the stage at the Budget lock-up.

Budget Day itself went very well. The Wellbeing focus was clear for everyone to see: a massive injection into mental health not just in Health, but also in the Corrections and Social Development budgets; a new multi-agency approach on family violence that saw eight agencies come together to act as one. We made major capital spending plans in health, education, rail and more. This was also part of a change to multi-year capital allowances. Previously we had been hamstrung by working to an annual capital allowance as per the operating budget. Creating a four-year window allowed for more long-term planning. It was a no-brainer for a government eager to get on with some well-overdue infrastructure investment.

At our traditional Budget night party, Winston Peters complimented me on the Budget. He had struggled a bit with the Wellbeing concept but had concluded that it all made sense while he listened to my speech.

The two months from the Tax Working Group decision to the reaction to the Budget summed up how it was to work in the coalition. The relationship could swing from fractured to cohesive and back again on a daily basis. Ministers would frequently believe they had sign-off from their New Zealand First counterparts for a policy, only to find it being re-litigated.

I came to the view that Winston hated making decisions. The long weeks he had put New Zealanders through when forming MMP governments seemed to me to be reflective of a person who was incredibly nervous about putting his penny down. He was also wary of his own Caucus, given the experience he'd had in the 1996–99 government, when Tau Henare and others abandoned New Zealand First when the coalition with National collapsed. He did, from time to time, seem to give way to his Caucus's views, even if it came after a ministerial-level decision. And then there was what I saw as the chaotic nature of New Zealand First. Tracey Martin was a voice of sanity, and was meticulous and organised. From my point of view the same could not be said for all the others.

We mostly sat in rank order at Cabinet committee meetings, which meant I sat next to Winston at many of them. I could not always tell if he had read the papers. But some days, it seemed to me at least, if he was feeling curmudgeonly or tired or he needed a smoke, he could seize on a minor point and derail a paper. Often this would be on a matter related to the Treaty of Waitangi or to an issue he saw as 'too green'. Sometimes it was as though an issue would trigger a memory of a past event. It was exhausting, and sometimes debilitating for the government.

Particular ministers really copped it. Iain Lees-Galloway in Immigration and Andrew Little in Justice seemed to raise Winston's ire more than most. Of course, these were areas in which New Zealand First also had strong views. On an issue like repealing the Three Strikes law, the mixed messaging played out in public, with Andrew Little announcing agreement, swiftly followed by New Zealand First saying there was not. There is always an element of people hearing what they want to hear in a negotiation, but this matter had actually been discussed at a Cabinet committee.

On Immigration the reality was that New Zealand First had not got what they wanted in the coalition agreement. Jacinda's staunchness meant that they were always on the back foot on one of their core issues. Thus, every time Iain bought a paper forward, he was stonewalled. This in turn infected his other portfolios, especially Employment Relations.

As 2019 went on, relations were fraying badly. The Greens for their part were incredibly frustrated with New Zealand First's feet-dragging on issues such as climate change and light rail. There were some difficult discussions and heated exchanges, and limited progress in those areas.

We ended the year together, but with a close eye on the election.

There were signs that the global economy was going to slow down in 2020. We wanted to get ahead of that and steal a march on election year. The government's balance sheet was strong, and debt levels below our target.

As we began the process of putting the 2020 Budget together, an idea emerged that we should start election year with a bang — by announcing a major nation-building infrastructure investment package. Work began in around October on which projects might be included in what became known as NZUP, the New Zealand Upgrade Programme. A teaser was announced at the Labour Party conference in Whanganui in early December with a $400 million fund for schools to use to upgrade their facilities. Work was also done to look at projects in the health area that could be brought forward. But the main focus was on transport projects.

On this issue the differences in views among the government parties were stark. We had to make some deals to reflect those views. It's important to note that every project that was eventually in NZUP was already part of the New Zealand Transport Agency (NZTA) work programme. The additional funding ($12 billion in total) would allow projects to be brought forward. This meant some re-ordering of existing regional transport projects. It was a fraught process, made worse by needing to be finalised over the Christmas holiday period. NZTA produced some solid costings and background materials to back the projects, and I felt reasonably comfortable with it proceeding. But changes were being made right up until the last minute. It was, as it turned out, too much for the public service to deal with. We were moving too fast and making too many changes for the normal processes to work properly.

Nevertheless, in late January 2020, we all gathered in Auckland to make the announcements. The programme looked, on the surface, to be a success. It was clear, and most questions about funding and financing could easily be answered. All the leaders and relevant ministers spoke.

At the end of the announcement, Andrew Campbell attempted to corral the media for a series of stand-ups with Jacinda, Winston and James. Winston only wanted to do one on his own. As I stepped back from the melee, I saw three separate stand-ups under way from Labour, Greens and New Zealand First. It was obvious we were only papering over the cracks in the government.

But within a matter of weeks, none of that would matter one bit. The biggest shock to our society and economy since World War Two was about to hit.

Doug and Yvonne on their wedding day. To Doug's left are his parents Murray and Olive, and to Mum's right, her mother Muriel. 10th October 1964.

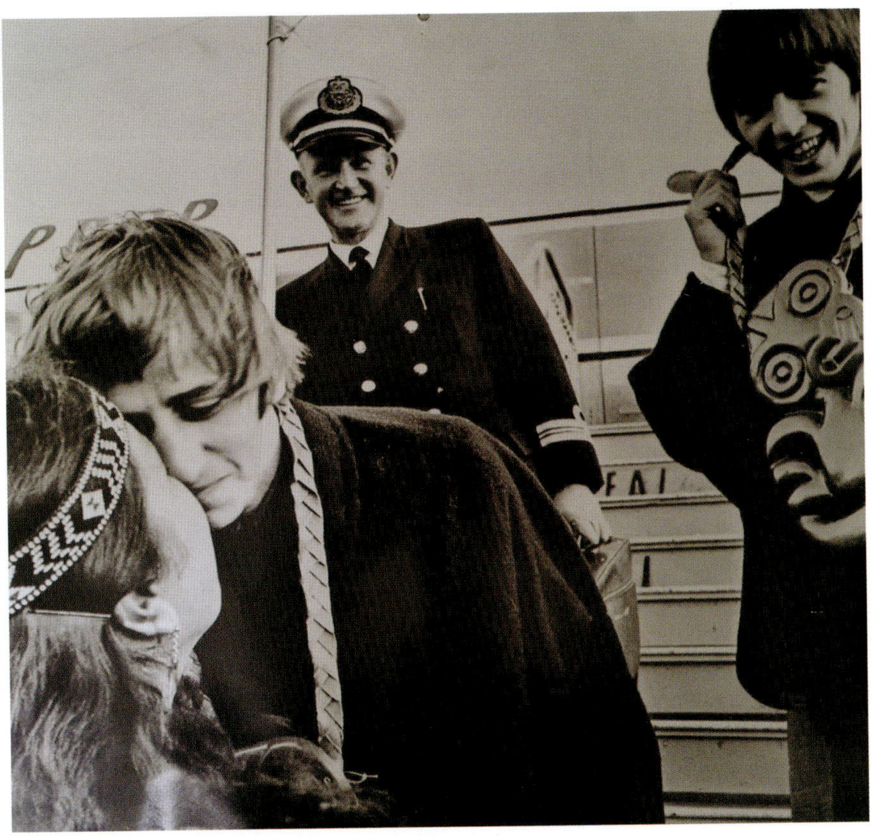

Dad's father Murray as the Customs officer who had sprayed The Beatles' plane when they landed in Wellington. June 1964.

RIGHT Me, aged approx 3 years old, with my favourite soft toy, the imaginatively named Doggy.

BELOW Stephen (left), Craig (right) and me at a family photo shoot, 1975.

RIGHT The giant Santa Claus at Fantasyland in Hastings, in all its 28-feet frightening glory. Me with my brothers, around 1976.

BELOW A very excited me (far left), ballboy at the 1983 All Blacks v Lions test, Carisbrook, Dunedin. From left, touch judge Tom Doocey, All Blacks winger Stu Wilson and Australian referee Dick Byres. © Peter Bush, *All Blacks v Lions test, Carisbrook, Dunedin 1983*. Collection of Te Manawa Museum, Courtesy of the Bush Family.

With my father, Doug, early 1990s.

Protest outside the National Party HQ in Harvest Court Mall in Dunedin. 1 July 1993. © Otago Daily Times

The Queen Street flatmates: Terence, Phil (seated), me and Andrew. 1993.

New York, September 1999, with the Twin Towers in the background.

Campaigning with my friend and mentor Hon. Marian Hobbs. Wellington, 2008.

Alf and I on the evening of our Civil Union. January 2009. © Mason Chidgery

Election night, 2008, explaining to Alf that I have indeed won the Wellington Central seat, and our lives are about to change. © John Lake

Receiving the congratulations of colleagues, and the apparent laying on of hands from Helen Clark, after my maiden speech in Parliament. December 2008. © The Post

The Robertson boys still looking alike, in selfie mode. Washington DC, 2016. Stephen (rear) and Craig (to my right) for the avoidance of doubt.

With my dear friend and comrade Helen Kelly at a climate change rally. Wellington, February 2016.

The anticipation and the relief – Winston Peters addresses the nation to say who he has chosen to form a government with. October 2017. © Clarke Gayford

Wellington Labour MPs victorious in the annual croquet challenge against Wellington City Councillors. From left, Chris Hipkins, Annette King, the late Paul Skinley (Wellington Croquet Club), me and Kris Faafoi.

Hard to believe we found something to laugh about on this day — with James Shaw at Schools Out climate protest, March 15 2019. The previous day James had been assaulted on the way to work, and just a couple of hours later we would learn of the terrorist attack in Christchurch.

Laying wreaths at the Kilbirnie Mosque for the March 15 victims.

Being Minister for Sport was 'boys' own' stuff for a cricket nerd like me. With the Black Caps prior to the Boxing Day Test at the MCG. December 2019.

A huge honour, and a slightly terrifying occasion, speaking (in te reo Māori) at the politicians' pōwhiri. Waitangi, February 2021.

A very Wellington Central scene — campaigning in the Aro Valley. October, 2020.

Telephone (03) 477-4760 INDEPENDENT VOICE OF THE SOUTH $2.20

Otago Daily Times

New Zealand's first daily newspaper. Est 1861

TUESDAY, November 3, 2020

INSIDE TODAY

DUNEDIN • 4 Ready to roll on Cup day — Wingatui fields • 14

REGIONS • 7 Christchurch air link returns

TRAVEL • 10 Scenic ride a challenge

'Boy from South Dunedin' deputy PM

MIKE HOULAHAN
Political reporter

GRANT Robertson has had a few moments in his career when he has wondered: "How has a boy from South Dunedin ended up here?"

Mr Robertson added another one to the list yesterday, when Prime Minister Jacinda Ardern named him as deputy prime minister.

"I'm proud, humbled and looking forward to carrying on the work," Mr Robertson said.

"You don't forget your roots, as Six60 might say."

Mr Robertson has been Finance Minister for the past three years. He retains that portfolio and also assumes responsibility for infrastructure.

That places Mr Robertson, who was central to the emergency response to Covid-19, at the forefront of the economic recovery from the effects of the pandemic.

"It's about being a backstop for her [Ms Ardern] and filling in for her occasionally, but she was also very clear with me to ensure we deliver on the commitments we have made and do the things we said we would as part of our overall Covid response and rebuild."

The health and economic impact of Covid-19 was continuing worldwide and made forward planning an uncertain science, Mr Robertson said.

With major European economies entering lockdown again, New Zealand's economy would no doubt suffer another buffeting, he said.

"We need to see New Zealand through this, and I think the plan we put out during the election was a good, balanced one, making sure we are aware of Covid-19 but also building back better.

"We have got a massive infrastructure programme under way with more to come, and my job is making sure that we are building on the foundations laid in the last term."

Mr Robertson's ascension to the deputy prime ministerial role was enabled by Labour's deputy leader, Kelvin Davis, ruling himself out for the post.

Mr Davis said yesterday he had told Ms Ardern before the election that while he wanted to remain deputy leader of the party, that role was the limit of his ambitions.

Ms Ardern said yesterday she had asked Mr Davis to reconsider, but he stuck to his decision.

"Grant has been given the seniority and portfolio mix required to drive our economic recovery," she said.

"I am excited by the opportunities we have here.

"It will be hard, but the legacy that we can leave the next generation in the way we choose to rebuild, is immense."

Mr Robertson's mother, Yvonne Wilkie, of Brockville, laughed when she answered the phone yesterday afternoon.

She said she was "very proud" of her son but declined to be interviewed.

Ms Ardern managed to spring several surprises in a far-reaching reshuffle of her team.

Nanaia Mahuta was a name few thought was in the running for Foreign Affairs and Andrew Little was an unexpected choice for Health.

Senior MP Phil Twyford retains a ministerial rank but plummets out of Cabinet, as does Jenny Salesa, who will be nominated to be Assistant Speaker.

Newly-elected list MP Ayesha Verrall, a one-time president of the Otago University Students Association and a specialist in infectious diseases, soars straight into Cabinet.

"It is not without precedent to bring new members straight into Cabinet," Ms Ardern said.

"In the middle of a global pandemic, I believe we would be foolish not to use the considerable expertise Dr Verrall brings in infectious diseases into our response."

Chris Hipkins retains education, but takes on a new portfolio of Covid-19 response, building on the work he has done recently as temporary Health Minister.

Former Otago MP David Parker remains Attorney-general, and Dunedin MP David Clark returns to Cabinet.

Te Tai Tonga MP Rino Tirikatene becomes an under-secretary, helping Mr Parker in a new portfolio of Oceans and Fisheries and also promoting Maori trade in the Trade portfolio.

mike.houlahan@odt.co.nz

New role .... Grant Robertson speaks in Wellington yesterday after being named deputy prime minister. PHOTO: GETTY IMAGES

Clark forgiven and back in the Cabinet

MIKE HOULAHAN

DUNEDIN MP David Clark, out of favour for his Covid-19 walkabouts, has found his way back into the affections of his colleagues and returned to the Cabinet.

The former health minister quit that role in July as penance for two breaches of pandemic lockdown regulations, Prime Minister Jacinda Ardern having earlier said she would have sacked him but for the health emergency.

The Labour caucus elects its Cabinet-ranked MPs, and yesterday Dr Clark was grateful his colleagues had forgiven him.

"It's nice that a vote of confidence from my colleagues has come my way, and having been a minister previously I know how challenging the role can be and how satisfying it can be."

Dr Clark, ranked 10th in the Cabinet when Labour took office in 2017, is now ranked 18th out of 20.

The former Treasury analyst and one-time associate finance minister, has new roles as Minister of Commerce and Consumer Affairs and State Owned Enterprises.

He also becomes Minister of Statistics, the Digital Economy and Communications, and Minister in Control of the Earthquake Commission.

"There is a lot of work to do and the portfolios I have been given all have their own challenges . . . It is a pretty full workload which has been put my way."

Ms Ardern said while there were issues when Dr Clark was health minister, he presided over the beginning of what had ultimately been a successful response to Covid-19.

"On this occasion, my view is that we have given a better match to his skill set in areas where he has enormous value to add, particularly in the space around growing the digital economy and digitising the public service."

WHO GETS WHAT • Page 2

VIDEO: www.odt.co.nz

Anything can happen — a long way from Pretoria Avenue to the Beehive. November 2020.

With Alf and Mum at our swearing in as ministers, Government House in Wellington. November 2020.

The 'Five Finance Ministers' meeting in Washington DC, April 2023. From left, Australian Treasurer Jim Chalmers, Canadian Minister of Finance Chrystia Freeland, me, UK Chancellor Jeremy Hunt and US Treasury Secretary Janet Yellen.

Sad to see my friend go — Jacinda's farewell function after her valedictory speech. April 2023.

Keeping up the Budget Day traditions for Prime Minister Chris Hipkins, with both cheese rolls and sausage rolls. May 2023.

Absolute scenes. Celebrating with the Football Ferns after their 1–0 victory over Norway in the opening game of the FIFA World Cup. July 2023.

Trying to keep my energy and enthusiasm for the debating chamber going right to the very end of our time in government. I am speaking in the Adjournment Debate of the 53rd Parliament, September 2023, surrounded by colleagues, (clockwise) Hon Megan Woods, Hon Nanaia Mahuta, Angie Warren-Clark, Hon Duncan Webb and Hon Kelvin Davis. © The Post

Being a GG (Grandad Grant) is one of the delights of my life – 3 of our 4 mokopuna pictured.

12.
THE COVID YEARS

Waitangi celebrations in 2020 were in full swing. Jacinda had kept her word to the people of the North and had five full days of visits and events. One of those was the opening of Te Rau Aroha, the museum dedicated to the Māori Battalion, which had been an early commitment of the coalition government. It is a superb memorial. Bom Gillies, the last surviving member of the Māori Battalion, was in attendance, along with whānau of other veterans from around the motu. Despite my differences with Shane Jones, I had to acknowledge that this was a project he had driven, and it was a raging success.

That evening the Waitangi National Trust Board held its annual dinner in the new venue. It was a balmy night and people were in good spirits after the opening. At one point I saw that I had missed a call from Rodney Jones. I had met Rodney some 10 years earlier at a University of Otago Foreign Policy School. He was a Dunedin boy made good — most specifically in China, where his investment firm Wigram Capital Advisors was extremely successful. A chunk of that success was built on Rodney's understanding of the Chinese system, its leadership, its people and its economy. We had stayed in touch, and he had given me many valuable insights into one of our largest trading partners.

I stepped out onto the deck and called Rodney back. He asked me what officials were telling us about the virus outbreak in China. We had been following it, of course, since just before New Year. It was spreading fast in and around Wuhan, and there were now cases in other countries. By the end of January, we had chartered a plane to get New Zealanders out of Wuhan. Just a few days before Waitangi, we had restricted entry by foreign nationals coming from China and asked others to self-isolate.

Rodney's message to me was that his sources in China were saying that the spread and seriousness of the virus was much larger than had been reported, and that the economic impacts were going to dwarf the earlier bird flu outbreak. He had been analysing data from several sources in China — hospital admissions, transport, consumer spending and so on. In what would normally be a busy period leading into Chinese New Year, these indicators were in a spiral. He said his staff in China were aware of thousands of people affected by the virus. His modelling was showing that the outbreak would result in a large number of deaths and a massive economic shock that would reverberate all around the world.

I asked Rodney to email me what he could. I got off the phone, called the relatively new Secretary to the Treasury Caralee McLiesh, and forwarded Rodney's emails to her. Treasury had been monitoring the situation but had not seen the data. I organised for Rodney to come to Wellington that week to talk through his material with officials.

When we returned to Wellington, officials had already begun to develop economic scenarios for what might happen. I gave my annual speech to the Massey University/Auckland Chamber of Commerce lunch a couple of weeks later. In it I outlined the three central scenarios. They ranged from what was considered the most likely — a hit to the Chinese economy that might affect some particular export sectors in New Zealand — to a year-long economic slowdown across the globe if the virus spread more. I was at pains to stress just how unlikely the extreme scenario was. How wrong we were — though in fairness this was the assessment of most people and governments at the time.

Events moved quickly. By the end of February the first case was identified in New Zealand. As the virus began to spread around the world, and there were an increasing number of deaths reported, the World Health Organisation christened it COVID-19 and by March had declared a global pandemic.

Economically the sectors most exposed to China were the first to start to feel the impact — rock lobster, tourism, forestry. But as the impact spread and countries such as Italy put themselves into lockdown, the fears of a significant recession grew. Stock markets began to shed value at a rapid rate. Countries were beginning to pull together economic support packages.

We knew that it was highly likely that we would need to close New Zealand's borders to some degree. It was our only chance of avoiding what the rest of the world was experiencing, and we had the benefit of being an isolated island nation. But if we went ahead with it, we also knew the economic consequences would be huge.

To me this was exactly the moment our careful management of the economy was meant for. If you are saving for a rainy day, you have to be prepared to spend when it starts to pour down. It would be expensive, but in a crisis like this there were no costless decisions. The growing death toll around the world made it obvious that the cost of not going hard and early would be lives, not dollars.

We hastily prepared an economic support package. We treated it like a mini-Budget and took proposals over a couple of days before refining it for announcement. All parties in the coalition understood the enormity of the situation, even though we were going into the complete unknown.

On 17 March I went down to the Legislative Council Chamber with a team of ministers and announced a $12.1 billion package, representing 4% of GDP. It was a larger package than Australia's (which was around 1%) and it covered a lot of ground. I signalled clearly that our debt position would worsen and had Treasury forecasts that were already predicting a recession. I also made clear that we would not be able to save every business. We were there to cushion the blow for business and position ourselves to recover. There was additional funding for the health system, with a $500 million boost for the urgent public health response.

Our business and worker support package totalled $8.7 billion, including a targeted wage subsidy scheme, alongside a new Covid leave payment scheme to provide incentives to self-isolate if unwell, worker redeployment schemes and tax relief. There was also $2.8 billion to support recovery, including a $25-a-week increase to main benefits, the doubling of the 2020 Winter Energy Payment and the removal of the hours test from In Work Tax Credits. It was clear that, as in any crisis, those on the lowest incomes would be hit the hardest.

The numbers were mind-boggling. We would normally have an operating allowance for new spending of $3 or $4 billion in a Budget. Here we were doing triple that, outside of our normal cycle. We also knew this was only the beginning, and I made it clear that the Budget in May would include further measures. In Parliament that day I finished my speech by saying:

> *Today is not the day to go into further detail about the recovery and rebuilding phase. But for now let me say this. In New Zealand we have been here before with major economic and social crises. In my lifetime we have seen governments respond with austerity — an ideology that has done enormous damage to the fabric of our society.*
>
> *We also have other examples such as the first Labour Government who responded with investment, pragmatism, optimism and kindness. It is from them that I take my lesson on how we recover and rebuild in a just, fair and far-sighted manner.*

Mr Speaker we are in for a fight. A fight against a virus, an outside force beyond our control that is wreaking havoc around the globe. We are up for the fight. There is no better defensive line than the All Blacks and it is just the same with our people as we face this virus.

We are in as good a position going into this as we can be, with net debt so low.

We are taking bold and decisive actions to respond to uncertain and unprecedented times.

My message to New Zealanders is simple. Look after yourself, look after your family, look after our elderly. Look out for each other.

There are tough days ahead, but we will get through this together.

I meant every word of it (except perhaps the corny All Blacks analogy). We did know that this was a pivotal moment. The modelling we had started to see showed that the spread of the virus was bad for the economy and even worse in respect of the number of cases and potential deaths. We were talking tens of thousands of deaths, and before that a health system that would simply be overrun. We also wanted to look ahead and to give some hope, not just in our ability to deal with the virus, but also to reset the economy as part of the rebuild.

From that moment on we moved at a speed I had not thought possible. It seemed like the dimensions of time changed. What used to take a month took a week. What used to take a week took a day, and what used to take a day took an hour. It is hard to believe that so much happened in such a short space of time.

Here's how the rest of that week played out.

Two days after the package, Cabinet made the decision to close the country's borders. We had already made the decision that anyone coming into New Zealand would be required to do 14 days of self-isolation, but this was not going to be enough to protect us. All of New Zealand's 30 or so cases were linked to overseas travel. Director-General of Health Ashley Bloomfield was now joining many of our meetings. He told us that there was probably still no community transmission of cases, but it was really only a matter of time before that happened. We would lose control of the spread of the virus unless we took more action.

Jacinda wanted to make sure that everyone understood the significance of what we were about to do, so got each person at the meeting to give their agreement out loud. After the decision had been made, she and I looked at each other, knowing the gravity of the moment. I tried to lighten the mood. 'Well, I knew when we went into coalition with New Zealand First our immigration policy would change, but I did not think it would go this far!' Jacinda did not seem to find it as funny as I did.

The next day we finalised a bail-out package for Air New Zealand. The company had approached us with concerns about their future earlier in March. Countries were closing their borders and limiting flights. Bookings had collapsed. The new CEO Greg Foran (who had taken over from Christopher Luxon only weeks earlier) and chair Dame Therese Walsh said that if things kept going in the same direction, the airline would be insolvent in months. Air New Zealand had significant debt-servicing requirements and was for all intents and purposes a cash business reliant on the bookings that were now drying up. They wanted a backstop, and with the financial sector struggling would rather work with the government as 52% shareholder than go to the banks or to a crumbling market. At one level, the decision was simple. Did we need a functioning national airline? Of course, especially as we looked towards recovery. But the amount of money that was going to be needed as a guarantee was significant. We had established a team including some external support from people familiar with the sector, and after some very intense negotiations agreed to a $900 million loan package.

The day of the Air New Zealand announcement also happened to be the day that Beehive staff were asked to start working from home. The days leading up to this were chaotic, as people tried to access screens, printers and all the other paraphernalia of work. No one had any idea how long this was going to be our way of life.

On the Friday morning, there was no one else left in my office. My amazing press team put the media release together remotely and got it out just before 9am. I hand-wrote some talking points and went down to the theatrette on my own to deliver the news. A handful of Press Gallery journalists had gathered. I finished speaking, and the first question was something along the lines of why the bail-out was necessary. I replied that if we did not do it, Air New Zealand would be insolvent within months. The journalists nodded. It was very surreal. I walked out of the media conference with Pattrick Smellie, a vastly experienced journalist. He said to me that on any other day this would be the biggest business story of the year. But already it felt like a footnote as we stood in the Beehive foyer while staff scurried past carrying their belongings into the unknown.

The next day, Saturday 21 March, Jacinda announced the Alert Level framework to the nation. The framework had been under development for a week or two. We were desperate for an easy way to communicate where the country was at, and what was required of people. Having the Prime Minister directly address the country is not something we do in New Zealand. But we knew how essential it was to get everyone's attention, and made the decision to have Jacinda do a broadcast to the nation via both main TV channels. It was high-stakes stuff. We needed to show the enormity of the situation but also show confidence and not a hint of panic.

Jacinda's office was set up like a TV studio. I was standing a little off camera when, as recording was about to commence, I realised that the door to her office was unlocked. Paranoid that someone would burst in during this critical moment, I stood with my foot against the door to prevent it opening. It was a unique spot to witness history from, and a sign that over the next few months I was going to have to turn my hand to anything and everything.

Jacinda announced that the country was at Level 2, which meant restrictions on travel and gatherings, and asked those over the age of 70 to stay home. She signalled that it was likely we would soon need to move up the alert levels.

Her approach was a masterclass not just in communications but in how to build confidence. We were under pressure from some, including in the business community, to move straight to a lockdown. Jacinda's judgement was that the public needed to be brought to that as a position, and to be given some brief time to prepare. I suggested to her the phrase 'team of five million'. As we came to say often in the following weeks and months, we were all in this together — He Waka Eke Noa.

On the Monday, the announcement was made that we were moving to Alert Level 3 in the light of more cases that could not immediately be linked to overseas travel. Jacinda told the country that in 48 hours we would be moving to Level 4 and total lockdown.

We had worked through scenarios of what this might mean, including working with supermarkets to make sure that they had enough stock. They did, but only if people shopped normally. No matter how much we said this, people behaved as they had across the world — by buying toilet paper in bulk. One day someone will write a psychology thesis on how people respond in these moments!

On that same Monday, we announced further economic measures. Remember, we were still not a full week on from our $12 billion package. Time had evaporated. It was obvious that we would need to do more when Level 4 arrived. The wage subsidy scheme had been based on what was delivered in Canterbury after the earthquakes. It had tight eligibility criteria and was capped at a total payment of $150,000 per business. I told Treasury officials that this was simply not going to be enough.

The mantra for the health response was to go hard and go early. We had to take the same approach with the economy. What was needed was cashflow and confidence. Businesses large and small, and workers, needed to know that we would have their backs, and that they would not need to make any precipitous decisions about their staff. We opened up the wage subsidy to all businesses for an initial 12 weeks and no per-business cap. The amount paid per worker was decided by taking what had been paid in Canterbury and adding a bit for inflation. We struck a part-time rate as well. It was never going to be enough to cover all costs, but we made the main criteria for receiving the subsidy a commitment from businesses that they would keep their staff employed and pass on at least the full value of the subsidy to those workers. We considered making direct payments to workers, but as we discovered with the later cost-of-living payment, doing this is extremely challenging. Meantime, we had the systems in place with businesses to make the payments in a short space of time.

Critically we included sole traders and contract workers. Artists and self-employed creatives, for example, were eligible. This was not the case in many other countries, and it meant a large number of vulnerable workers had income security. We also made the decision to freeze rents. This decision was literally made at the Cabinet table that Monday. We were moving so fast that the idea was raised and decided on all within an hour.

This Cabinet meeting was already a smaller than normal group. Many ministers had already returned to their home base to be with their families. Winston Peters soon retreated to his place at

Whananaki in Northland. His age put him in the highly vulnerable category whom we had already asked to stay at home. It was the right thing to do, but in the long run his isolation from the government's inner workings would hurt the coalition. We took a photo of the Cabinet meeting, not knowing when we would gather again. There were hugs and tears.

The following day, the Olympic Games in Tokyo were postponed for a year, and New Zealand went into lockdown at 11.59pm. Jacinda told New Zealanders, 'You may not be at work, but that doesn't mean you don't have a job. Your job is to save lives, and you can do that by staying home and breaking the chain.' We had an opportunity that almost no other country did: to break the chain of transmission.

On most days in Level 4 I headed into the Beehive. We had decided that Alf and I would effectively join the Ardern-Gayford bubble. This was a considerable sacrifice for Alf, because it meant he could not have any immediate contact with his kids or grandkids. But it made sense, as it enabled me to be there in person as the government and officials made one big call after another.

It was a bizarre scene in the Beehive. There were a small group of staff in Jacinda's office, and there was me alone on the 7th floor. On his way to work on the first morning Andrew Campbell was stopped by police wanting to know what he was doing. After that, all of us carried letters to prove our status as essential workers. Throughout the country, the only food outlets open at Level 4 were supermarkets. There were huge queues to get in, and Alf had not yet braved them. I realised I did not have any food. The fridge in my office was empty. I searched the rest of the floor like some kind of latter-day Bruno Lawrence in *The Quiet Earth*. I stole some bread from Kelvin Davis's fridge, and Marmite and toast became my staple for the next few days.

My days, as they were for many people, were a whirlwind of Zoom meetings, with ministers, officials, business and union leaders, the Reserve Bank Governor, bank CEOs and more. They started early and finished late. We began to use Zoom for Cabinet meetings. A dollar for every time I said, 'Damien, you are on mute', and the deficit would have been wiped. We quickly realised that we needed more decision points than a once-a-week Cabinet meeting. We created a Covid committee with power to act as Cabinet. It met at least a couple of times a week. The public service had organised itself into a focused Covid unit, and Treasury threw all its resources towards Covid work.

The public service did some truly heroic things in those first few weeks. Wellington eliminated street homelessness. It was a remarkable achievement. Government agencies such as the Ministry of Social Development (MSD) and Housing New Zealand worked with NGOs like the Downtown Community Ministry to find housing for everyone. The critical ingredient was empowering those at the coalface to make decisions. I was told, for example, that there was a longstanding policy that no emergency housing places were to be in houses down a shared driveway. No one really knew the origin of this but it probably stemmed from a single adverse incident. The policy was waived, and people were housed.

When it came to the wage subsidy, MSD were in overdrive. Once we had given the signal that we would accept a high-trust model, they moved fast. I kept hearing stories from people who applied for the subsidy one day and had the money in their bank account the next day. At one point MSD were processing more than 20 applications a minute. This was the cashflow and confidence we were after.

We also had to be flexible. I started getting feedback that the changes we had made to the wage subsidy around part-time work were creating confusion for those who perhaps worked only 10 hours per week. Some people thought they would be paid the part-time rate, rather than a pro-rata of it. The issue needed to be resolved. That day I could not get access to the parliamentary network from home. I threw on a pair of track pants and drove to Parliament. I parked in the Beehive basement, pulled out my laptop and wrote an email to MSD to tell them to issue a directive that the payment could be made pro-rata. And I drove home.

We kept the initiatives coming. We worked with the Reserve Bank and the retail banks to create a Business Finance Guarantee Scheme to ensure that businesses could access capital. In early April we announced a string of changes to the Companies Act to provide 'safe harbour' facilities to avoid companies going into bankruptcy or insolvency.

I announced that initiative at a Friday 1pm press stand-up. These had become compulsory viewing, and were mainly fronted by Jacinda and Ashley Bloomfield. They provided clear information and updates and were watched by millions each day. But it was a huge effort, and we realised that we needed to give Jacinda and Ashley a break. It made sense for me to be one of those to front the briefings, given the amount of economic news to share. On Fridays I was usually joined by Caroline McElnay, the Director of Public Health. Caroline and I were the 'substitute teachers', no doubt, but we knew it mattered to keep the shows going and the information flowing. This did not mean that Jacinda was slacking off. I learned to keep my phone on the lectern, anticipating that she would frequently send me through facts, stats and answers. In fairness, I would do the same for her when she was on the podium.

Jacinda had made a decision early on that if she was going to lead the country through the virus she would understand every aspect of it. With the help of Ashley, Chief Science Advisor Juliet Gerrard and an army of officials, she got on top of the science, the testing process, the development of vaccines. Anything and everything. I tried to keep up, but watching Jacinda absorb and process information was something else. On one occasion she found herself correcting officials at Environmental Science and Research about elements of the testing process. Little wonder her staff gave her a stethoscope as a birthday present that year. In all seriousness, I do not believe there was another world leader who understood COVID-19 the way she did. And it showed in New Zealand's response.

Under Level 4 my life settled into a pattern like that of many New Zealanders. Occasionally I would come home to find Alf having Zoom drinks with friends. We went for walks around the neighbourhood, keeping our two-metre distance. Anzac Day was very different. At dawn I headed down from our house to the street. I took my phone and played the Anzac service broadcast on Radio New Zealand. Across the road, in the half-light, I could make out my neighbour, army veteran Jeremy Seed. He was in his uniform. Not for the first time in those few weeks, tears welled up.

Towards the end of April we could see that our efforts were paying off. The number of cases was declining. Nineteen people had died — a tragedy, but so much better than it might have been. We felt confident to move to Level 3 — which, most importantly for many, meant access to takeaways. We signalled that if all went well, two weeks later we would be at Level 2 again.

There were so many decisions to be made about how we lived at each alert level. As we were about to move to Level 3, there were desperate pleas for golf courses and bowling greens to be allowed to cut their grass. The media were on to it and kept making inquiries. With my Sports Minister hat on, I felt we could probably do this safely. Officials were not so sure. It was Friday afternoon, and I got it into my head that the matter had to be resolved before the weekend. After a series of phone calls, I finally told the exhausted and bewildered officials that this just had to happen. They relented, and I went home happy. I might have lost a bit of perspective that day.

Likewise, at Level 3 we concluded that hunting and fishing would be okay as these were mainly outdoor pursuits and could be done with adequate social distancing. There was limited time to get this organised before we hit Level 3, so with help from the amazing Holly Donald from Jacinda's office I sat down and wrote the first draft of the Cabinet paper on hunting in a day. Neither of us had ever been hunting. It was complete madness.

By this stage I was deep in Budget preparations. We had been working on the normal Budget since late 2019, and I made the decision that we would largely keep this intact. Then, in the course of a month, we effectively wrote an additional Budget to deal with Covid. We established the Covid Response and Recovery Fund (CRRF) with $50 billion set aside. This was an enormous sum of money — more than 10 times the operating allowance we had for the whole of the previous Budget, and the largest financial commitment by a New Zealand government in modern history.

Our plan was a three-stage one — response, recovery and rebuild. The first stage was the one we were in — shovelling money into the health response and the immediate support packages. We also knew that coming out of the emergency response phase was going to be challenging. We set up funds and programmes that could support this, including targeted support for the arts, sports, tourism, the environment and job creation. We used the fund to push forward projects that would support employment and industry development. The mantra of cashflow and confidence remained.

We wanted the rebuild phase to be one in which we could also deal with longer-term issues facing the country. One of these was our infrastructure deficit. A major downside of the fiscal approach adopted by successive governments was a failure to adequately invest in critical systems. NZUP had been a chance to shift the dial. We went further in the Budget by setting aside $3 billion for what became known as the Shovel-Ready Programme. This was designed to give confidence to the construction sector, and to start to deal with the infrastructure deficit. There were, we were told, public and private infrastructure projects ready to go but for some funding.

In many ways the Shovel-Ready Programme was a microcosm of both the value and the dangers of our speedy response. We created an external reference group to manage the process of applications, making use of the already established Crown Infrastructure Partners whom the previous government had established to manage the rollout of ultrafast broadband. They came back to us with a shortlist of nearly eight hundred projects that were, according to the applicants, ready to go.

The process of whittling those down became politicised. James Shaw, Shane Jones and I tried to work through the proposals and provide some criteria. We also wanted there to be a good geographical spread of projects — more than the targeted approach we had for the Provincial Growth Fund. Truth be told, it got very messy, and by the time of the announcement in July there had been some deals to get the full package over the line. It also emerged fairly quickly that many of the projects were, despite what their proponents had said, nowhere near shovel ready.

The Budget itself was delivered on the day we went into Level 2. We called it *Rebuilding Together*. It was the first time the Speaker had allowed outsiders into the building since late March. Level 2 allowed gatherings of up to 100 people, so there was the traditional Budget lock-up, but Trevor Mallard decreed that food would not be allowed — a dangerous call. Hungry journalists are second only to hungover journalists as a group to be avoided.

Rebuilding Together had to eschew the Wellbeing Report and a number of other Budget documents. Everyone understood why, but this omission highlighted the difficulty of implementing the changes required to create a true Wellbeing Budget in a sustained way. 'Events, dear boy, events,' as Harold Macmillan said, that is what politics really is about. But it was still in many ways a Wellbeing Budget. In the absence of information or certainty, we were making decisions based on our values. When you are hurtling into the unknown, you need to rely on your instincts and intuitions.

This saw us take an approach that focused on people, and indeed on their wellbeing. We knew that the best health approach was also going to be the best economic approach. If people stayed healthy, they could work and be productive. Specifically, on the economic front this approach meant a focus on jobs — keeping people in them, supporting people when they lost them and helping create sustainable jobs for the future.

In April I had received a report from Treasury outlining scenarios for what might happen with unemployment. The worst-case scenario, with limited government intervention and a long-lasting pandemic, was a peak of 13.5% unemployment. It would mean more than 350,000 people unemployed. This would be devastating for communities and for the country. My politics had been shaped in the 1980s and '90s by government policies that created unemployment. I was determined that would not be our legacy.

As I prepared to deliver the Budget, unemployment in the USA was at its worst since the Great Depression. Global and New Zealand growth forecasts were for a significant recession. There was red ink everywhere, with deficits forecast for the foreseeable future and net debt forecast to reach 53% in the coming years. It was a long way from our original targets, but it was broadly accepted as necessary by Opposition parties and commentators alike. We were still a lot better off than most other countries that had started with higher debt levels. Both the US and UK were looking at well over 100% net debt levels.

Our focus on jobs also included extending out the wage subsidy scheme, albeit with a higher threshold for loss of income. We also created a small business cashflow scheme, and provided additional support for exporters and small businesses alike. We established the Jobs for Nature programme and other conservation-related employment measures. A special focus was on apprentices. This was a lesson from previous economic downturns, when apprentices were often the first to be let go. My stepson was in exactly this position when the GFC hit. Six months into his apprenticeship, he was gone. We invested heavily not only to support firms to keep their apprentices on but also to create new training opportunities. These were measures we had looked at as far back as the Future of Work Commission; now the future had advanced towards us and we needed to act. In addition, we massively extended the school lunches programme and provided a multimillion-dollar boost to community groups which were already seeing the strain on vulnerable families from Covid. All up, it was a monumental Budget.

I used to joke that one thing that Covid had spurred was a new branch of economics called Hindsight Economics. Looking back from 2025, it is easy to see ways we could have acted differently if only we had been able to predict the future. In the moment we wanted to look after people and support them through the shock of their lifetimes. And, fundamentally, to keep them alive.

Through our intervention, particularly with the wage subsidy scheme, we were able to not just cushion the blow, but also save businesses and jobs. One day in 2020 when I was campaigning in Featherston I saw a guy in a ute cruise past me, then do a u-turn and come back. I was initially a bit wary, but he marched up to me and shook my hand. He told me the story of how when COVID hit, his building business began taking calls from customers cancelling work. He told his staff that he thought he was going to have to let them go. He and his wife looked into the wage subsidy. They filled in the application one evening and were gobsmacked when the money went into their bank account the next day. They were able to keep all their staff employed. This was the result of heroic work by a group of dedicated public servants. In the end unemployment never went above 5.1%, and in that first year business closures were actually lower than in a normal year. I understand that people look back and see that a lot of money was spent. There were no costless decisions in COVID — and I am proud that we prioritised the lives and wellbeing of our people.

In any case, what we were doing clearly had the public's support. This hit home for me when I convinced Jacinda to have a night out in early June. We were in Level 2, and restaurants and bars were operating with restrictions. Nadia Reid, a Dunedin-based musician who Jacinda and I both liked, was playing at San Fran in Cuba Street. Jacinda took the night off, and joined Alf and me for dinner and the gig. We went to Loretta, a restaurant just down the road from the venue. It's a long, narrow place, and we had a table down the back. As we entered, I could see eyes turn as other diners saw Jacinda. And table by table they stood and applauded. By the time we got to our seats near the back, the whole restaurant was on its feet. It was hugely emotional.

On 3 June we celebrated 11 days with no new cases. A few days later we were able to announce that we would move to Level 1. At 11.59pm on 8 June we switched. I remember seeing a video of a countdown in a bar. When the clock struck midnight, patrons invaded the dance floor and celebrated wildly. If it were not for complete exhaustion, I would have joined them. We had done what we set out to do.

13.
A MAJORITY GOVERNMENT

2020 was of course an election year. Our initial response to Covid had worked, and we were polling well. The National Party were doing their best to help us too. Simon Bridges had taken over from Bill English as leader, and by the time the pandemic arrived seemed fairly well settled into the job, despite the best efforts of Jami-Lee Ross and others.

I always quite liked Simon. Apart from anything else, he has a sense of humour and does not seem to mind too much having the mickey taken out of him. But he is a Christian conservative, and many of his colleagues disliked the similarly conservative-minded group who surrounded him, who they dubbed the 'Taliban'.

Simon struggled as Opposition leader in the pandemic. Finding the sweet spot to hold the government to account without looking disloyal was never going to be easy. He got in trouble for commuting to Wellington during the lockdown, and for most of the public was out of the blocks way too fast in calling for restrictions to be eased. When we returned to Parliament after the Budget, a few rumours had started to spread that there could be a move against him. It soon happened. After a messy couple of days, Bridges called out his opponents and invited them to challenge him. Todd Muller obliged, and was soon elected in what we understood to be a very close vote.

As veterans of Caucus splits and divisions and disunity, we knew that Todd was not going to be in for a good time. His start was disastrous. His deputy was Nikki Kaye, the hyper-intelligent and just generally hyper MP for Auckland Central. They were fresh faces, and their inexperience showed. In just the first few days they had created one of the best television moments of my time in politics after they were criticised for the absence of Māori MPs in their frontbench line-up. When Nikki claimed that Paul Goldsmith was Māori, he came forward to vehemently deny it. TV3's Tova O'Brien deserved an Emmy for the story that went to air that night. Nikki was an MP who many of us across the aisle liked, and her cancer diagnosis and untimely passing robbed New Zealand of a talented politician.

In early July, Alf and I took our first break since the pandemic had begun and went to stay at Waimārama Beach in Hawke's Bay. It was idyllic; we read books and drank wine and relaxed for the first time in months. We were there when the news broke that Todd Muller had resigned after just seven weeks in the job.

It was obvious he had been struggling. His team were a bit of a shambles and he was not projecting any confidence. What we know now is that Todd's mental health was spiralling downwards. I had known Todd since student politics days and saw him as a decent man — just in the wrong party! It took enormous courage for him to speak out about his mental health struggles, and he only went up in my estimation for doing so.

National meanwhile went looking for their third leader inside a few months. Up stepped the one person who actually wanted the job: Judith Collins. I don't think there were any other circumstances in which she would have got the role, given the very mixed view of her in her own Caucus. But there she was, full of vim and vigour in front of some strained-looking Caucus colleagues as the National leader.

If we had not been so preoccupied with Covid we might have taken some satisfaction in these travails. But, sadly, the pandemic was far from done with us. We had to put Auckland back into Level 3 in August as cases with no obvious link to the border were found. The public once again largely rallied behind the idea, and we went back out with further support in terms of the wage subsidy. Our Covid Fund was still doing the heavy lifting.

Jacinda had set the election date in January before Covid took hold. We were now just on a month out from the election scheduled for 19 September. We knew we had to postpone it, and the other political parties agreed. They had to, really, as both National and New Zealand First had been calling for the election to be delayed for some months. The election was rescheduled for 17 October.

Our relationship with New Zealand First was at breaking point by this stage of the cycle. In many ways, the fact we held it together to the extent we did is remarkable. Covid was taking up all the political oxygen and Winston was sidelined. It felt like that on every issue he fought and scrapped and shifted and changed his position. We were over it. I told Jacinda there was no way I wanted to work with New Zealand First again.

By late September the outbreak in Auckland was under control, and we eased restrictions there and around the country. But the first inklings of strain were showing. Towards the end, anti-lockdown protesters had gathered in defiance of the prescribed crowd limits. They were still at the fringe, but it was an early sign of what was to come.

The election campaign itself had continued to run. It was, of course, mostly dominated by Covid. After the tax contortions of the previous election, and with Jacinda's ruling out of a CGT, we kept it simple, with a commitment to return the top rate of tax to 39c for those earning more than $180,000 per year. This would impact only 2% of taxpayers, and was met with only mild criticism given the need to pay for the Covid response. Otherwise, it was a matter of campaigning on our record. On 29 September the global death toll from Covid passed one million. *The New York Times* reported that the virus had taken more lives in the past 10 months than HIV, malaria, influenza, cholera and measles combined. In New Zealand the death toll was 25.

As the restrictions lifted and the campaign continued, it was clear Labour was going to do well. Everywhere I went I found a grateful public. Jacinda was mobbed at every event.

Our pollster, David Talbot, had a rule of thumb that the result of an election is only ever likely to change by a couple of percentage points from where the polls are a month out. Exactly a month out from the election, our internal poll had us at 48%. This was an unheard-of MMP result. I checked with David whether he thought his rule still applied — and he said he thought it did. I refused to believe it.

Again, National were doing everything they could to help us. In late September they produced their fiscal plan. We had been calling for it for some time, knowing the challenges of producing such a document in Opposition. They had to get it out before their campaign launch, otherwise the media would not believe any of their policy commitments. It finally came out on a Friday in advance of their campaign launch on the Sunday. I had been using the phrase 'fiscal Bermuda Triangle' for a while, and it began to get some traction. National were promising to reduce taxes, increase spending and lower debt all at the same time. There was no way it could add up.

I was campaigning in Palmerston North and took the time to look at the tables National had released. They were partly paying for their promises by, again, stopping contributions to the Super Fund. But something was off. I called Craig Renney, and within minutes he came back to say that National had used the wrong figures and there was a $4 billion mistake. We could scarcely believe our luck. Craig headed over to Greytown where I was meeting Jacinda later that day for a campaign stop. In a room upstairs at the White Swan Hotel, Craig took us through his calculations. They looked right to me.

We could have gone out then with National's mistake — but we knew that the maximum impact would come if we could disrupt the campaign launch. We drafted up a release, checked our numbers again. It went out on Sunday morning, and an hour or so later I drove down to Parliament and walked out onto the forecourt to meet the Press Gallery to talk it through. National's Finance spokesperson Paul Goldsmith had already admitted the mistake. One of the journalists asked me if this was revenge for Steven Joyce's fiscal hole exercise in 2017. I failed miserably to cover up my satisfaction. The National launch was totally overshadowed by the error. Paul Goldsmith dropped his notes on the way to the podium, and the TV images for the night were set. And there was worse to come. Within days we had identified further errors that took the fiscal hole to around $10 billion.

There was no coming back for National. Judith Collins compounded the situation through a series of bizarre campaign appearances, including a bungled staged walkabout in Ponsonby, kneeling at prayer in an empty church and an outburst about people being to blame for their own obesity. In light of all of this, a week before the election David Talbot put to me the idea of a video in which I pitched to disillusioned National voters that Labour was the safest and most responsible bet at this election. It was an audacious plan that we could only really pull off in the current circumstances. I did the video staring straight down the barrel of the camera. I told those very voters that National was not the party of John Key and Bill English any more (a favourite phrase): 'There is too much at stake right now to vote for National. They're unstable. They have had three leaders in four months, 19 resignations, a string of different positions on the border and they published a budget full of mistakes.' It was a measure of the strength of our position that I could say this and that it might actually resonate with voters.

On election night I was on the way to our election headquarters at the Wharewaka Function Centre on the Wellington waterfront when the first results came through. We were in fact on 48%. By the time

I got settled in, we were up around 50%, and we stayed there for the whole night.

If that was not enough, we began to take the lead in — and win — the truest of blue seats. Jo Luxton in Rangitata was one of the first. Then came news that Labour was in front in Gerry Brownlee's blue-ribbon seat of Ilam.

Jacinda rang me: 'Do you know who our candidate is in Ilam?'

I thought I'd met her once at an event in Christchurch but was not sure. 'It's Sarah someone,' I replied. No offence to our excellent candidate Sarah Pallett, but Ilam was not a seat we had focused on or even imagined winning.

For me there was enormous personal excitement that night too. My good friend and campaign worker for several elections, Ibrahim Omer, was on track to be Labour's first MP with a refugee background and the first MP of African descent to enter Parliament. Ibrahim's journey from arriving as a refugee in 2008 to becoming an MP 12 years later was nothing short of remarkable.

When the dust settled, we had won an outright majority — with 65 seats, including Ibrahim coming off the list. It was a staggering result. The next morning, I headed to Auckland to meet up with Jacinda and our senior leadership team. I was feeling euphoric and sleep deprived. Jacinda seemed a bit more reserved, and she soon revealed that the country had yet another unexplained Covid case.

We had won the battle — but the war against the virus was far from over.

We were well aware that Covid was going to be the dominant issue for the immediate future. Around the world new variants of the virus were causing yet more waves of death and disruption. We were saved the need for any immediate lockdown measures post-election, but knew we were likely to have to come back to them soon enough.

When it came time to form the government, Jacinda asked me to be Deputy Prime Minister. Kelvin Davis had made it clear that he did not want the job. He disliked the stress of regularly standing in for the PM and was keen to focus on his passions in Māori–Crown Relations and the Children's portfolio as he had long wanted to do. Jacinda tried a couple of times to see if he would reconsider, but he was adamant.

In addition to the new role, I took on Infrastructure, which really was part of the Finance role. I also took on the Racing portfolio. That was a bit of a surprise. I had said to Jacinda that I was very keen to retain Sport (more of which in Chapter 14) but thought I needed to drop something to make up for taking on the Deputy PM position. I did this by not carrying on my Associate Arts role. On the morning of the Cabinet announcement, Jacinda rang me to say that Racing had not been allocated to anyone and she thought I would enjoy it. She knew that Alf and I liked going to the races. That did not feel like much of a qualification, but I agreed to do it.

At Government House for our swearing-in on 6 November, I looked around the table to a mostly Labour line-up. We had signed a cooperation agreement with the Greens, so their co-leaders James Shaw and Marama Davidson were at the table too. We did not need the Greens to govern, but it was an investment in the future, as we would be sure to need them for a further term. James's expertise on climate issues was also going to be essential if we were to make real progress during the term.

Mum and Alf again joined me at Government House, along with Sheila from my electorate office. This swearing-in had less emotion attached to it, but it marked an important moment in my political relationship with Jacinda. We had always been close, and now that partnership was as tight as it could be. As her deputy, I knew I could take some of the pressure off her, particularly around commitments like media appearances. I'd had a ringside seat to the work of the most extraordinary leader I had ever worked with. I could see the pressure that every decision was putting on her, and I decided my future political contribution was to ease that. It felt like the best service I could do.

As the year ended, we were still feeling good. New Zealand was 'having a summer', which could not be said in the rest of the world. There was cricket, music festivals and more. Alf and I headed south on a bit of a road trip just before Christmas, prior to a planned holiday in the Coromandel. The public mood towards us was still very positive. In the supermarket I was hugged by elderly people who thanked me for saving their lives. More than once I was not allowed to pay in a shop, or had a drink ordered for me. But the gratitude was not universal. We stopped in Christchurch and caught up with colleague and friend Megan Woods. We were out at brunch when I noticed people at the next table paying us a lot of attention. Eventually a guy in his forties came up and politely inquired if he could ask me a question. He wanted to know if I had heard of The Great Reset. I had not. He said he found that hard to believe. He then asked about Agenda 30 and the World Economic Forum, and whether I was a follower of them. By this point it was clear he was not happy, and I tried to shut the conversation down. He kept going, getting angrier and angrier. I can still picture his eyes blazing. Eventually we just got up and left. The encounter felt odd and disturbing. Megan mentioned she'd had a couple of similar experiences. I put it down to something in the water in Christchurch.

We headed to Dunedin. On Christmas Eve we had some drinks with friends in town. Early in the evening there was a lot of love around, and more free drinks, but towards the end of the night a young man made a beeline for me. He was way more aggressive than the guy in Christchurch — he was ranting and raving about 5G, the Pfizer vaccine we had recently purchased and the Chinese

Communist Party. We, and others, told him to get lost, but he kept coming back. Eventually we decided to go, but he followed us up the road and grabbed my shoulder. By this point Alf had had enough, and despite being on crutches after a hip replacement, pushed our pursuer who stumbled and fell over in front of some amused onlookers.

It was a reminder that no matter how popular the government was, Covid was creating an angry grouping who had all of their hatred and conspiracy theories backed up online.

As 2021 began I had the honour of speaking for Labour at the pōwhiri for political parties at Waitangi. Kelvin Davis had worked hard to re-engineer the events at Waitangi to give them a bit more dignity and had negotiated to have all politicians welcomed in one ceremony. He also wanted to make sure that it was not just Māori MPs who spoke. He pushed me to do the kōrero that year.

My reo journey owed an awful lot to meeting Alf. Not too long after we got together, he told me my Māori pronunciation was terrible. I decided to do a night class through Victoria University. It helped me a lot, and over time I became comfortable doing a mihi and had a pretty good vocabulary, even if my grammar was a bit lacking. But the idea of speaking on the Treaty Grounds was something else. I practised over and over, refining my kōrero so that I could speak without notes. I talked about the world I wanted for my mokopuna and the role the government was playing to, as Kelvin would say, build the bridge between Pākehā and Māori. It was a massive relief to get it done and receive some positive feedback.

There was a lot of talk about what we would do with the extraordinary mandate the New Zealand public had given us. I found this a curious observation. Our mandate was what we had campaigned on. First and foremost, it was Covid and carrying on the job we had started to get us through the pandemic. Beyond that it was to rebuild the economy and push forward on the big issues of climate change and child poverty that we had started in our first term. There was a notion among some that we could do whatever we liked with our majority, and this led to some very high expectations.

We had attracted the votes of a wider range of New Zealanders than usual, and we felt that we needed to keep them in the tent and build on that majority for future terms. This would require a continuation of the balanced approach that had got us this far. Ruth Bader Ginsburg, the inspirational US Supreme Court judge, had died during the election campaign. My favourite of her many sayings is: 'Fight for the things you care about, but do it in a way that will lead others to join you.' We had an opportunity to build a strong case for progressive change that would endure.

I had a plan for my Budgets over the term which I pitched to Jacinda. The first one would inevitably focus on Covid, but also on reducing inequalities, drawing on the recommendations of the Welfare Expert Advisory Committee we had established in the previous term, and following through on a number of initiatives for Māori and Pasifika communities. The second Budget, hopefully with Covid less of a factor, would focus on strengthening public services, including a significant boost to health spending in the wake of the substantial reforms of the health sector we had under way. The third Budget, to be delivered in election year, would be one in which we gave something back in the form of targeted tax cuts — or, as I hoped it would be, 'a tax switch'.

While I had got over my disappointment about the CGT debacle with New Zealand First, I still believed that the imbalance in our tax system was a massive problem and was continuing to cause inequalities, particularly in the housing market. Knowing that Jacinda had ruled out a CGT, I was looking for another way through that would tax wealth and assets, and provide us the revenue to deal with the obvious issue of 'bracket creep'. This occurs when salaries are rising but tax rates do not change commensurate with them.

I was aware of rumblings in this area. We had lifted the pay of teachers and nurses, and this had pushed them into a new tax bracket. The way marginal tax rates work (i.e. that you are taxed at that higher rate only for the proportion of your income that is over the amount at which the rate kicks in) means the impact is not as high as people might think, but I was hearing an undercurrent of concern. I told Jacinda that we could legislate for a change at the time of the Budget in 2023, but that it would not need to come into force until after the election, meaning we would not get accused of acting outside our mandate from 2020. She agreed that we could start work on the issue, acknowledging the need for reform. It was the practical politics that were in the way, but we resolved to work through them.

More immediately, we did need to deal with housing issues. These came up even more often on the campaign trail. I remember speaking to a group of about thirty to forty people at one of the street-corner meetings near to where I lived. There is an interesting dynamic in these meetings: a crowd this size can become emboldened if there is an issue they are unified on. In this case, it was the cost of housing. A youngish guy told the story of how he and his wife, both in professional jobs, simply could not get a deposit together, let alone buy a house, after years of savings. Others joined in — grandparents on behalf of grandchildren, a solo parent and more. As happy as this group were with how we had handled Covid, it was a great illustration of the bread-and-butter issues that matter in people's lives — a house to live in, the state of the health and education systems, transport networks.

We knew we had to act on housing early in the term. The supply and demand problem in the housing sector had been present for many years. Successive governments had simply had not built enough affordable homes that first-home buyers could access.

There were a number of elements at play here. Around that time, I often included a statistic in my speeches to explain part of the problem. New Zealand's population had grown from 3 million to 4 million over the course of 30 years (1973 to 2003); it had then grown from 4 million to 5 million over 17 years (2003 to 2020). We just had not built the infrastructure to handle that rate of growth.

Then there was the inbuilt tax advantage for housing that governments had failed to resolve over so many years. This was a major factor. A whole industry had arisen to help people take advantage of it by buying rental properties, flipping houses and generally absorbing all the benefits of speculation. The monetary and fiscal response to Covid had the effect of locking in this advantage. To keep the economy going, the Reserve Bank had pumped in money. This was the right thing to do, but because the remaining settings stayed the same, property became the go-to. Interest rates were very low, and the value of property just kept rising. If you were already an owner, there was an enormous wealth effect. If you were not, you didn't just not experience that wealth, you felt ever more locked out.

Early in 2021 we acted on this. We increased the bright-line test which National had brought in to deal with some of the property-flipping issue. If you sold a property that was not your family home within two years, you paid tax on the profit you made. We had extended the period to five years in our first term, and now we took the opportunity to double that to 10 years. We also announced the end of interest deductibility. This was the key to the property seminars that were being run all around the country: landlords could deduct the interest from mortgage and related payments for rental properties. No one else in the economy could do that, including of course those owning their own home. It was a tax advantage for landlords, and we wanted to level the playing field.

Before that package, in late 2020 I had also made a change to the agreement with the Reserve Bank that meant it had to explicitly consider the impact that its official cash rate (OCR) decisions had on house prices. This was not a popular call inside the Reserve Bank. It had always jealously guarded its independence when setting monetary policy. But there had always been an agreement that governed this, and I wanted the bank to take into account our desire for sustainable moderation in house prices. The bank, with some justification, did not want to be seen as the arbiter of house prices that were affected by many issues. It was the only time in my term as Finance Minister that I clashed with Adrian Orr as Governor. We had been joined at the hip on the Covid response, and I admired greatly the way he had helped navigate us through the crisis. But I believed we needed to put all the tools to work to burst the housing bubble.

The reality remained that, in any case, the biggest issue was housing supply, and particularly the supply of affordable homes. We had been doing our bit with state houses. We built at a faster rate than any government since the 1950s. But that was only part of the market. Kiwibuild had been our major move on home ownership in our first term of government. The policy announced by David Shearer to build 100,000 affordable homes all those years ago had survived. But when it came time to implement the policy, the market was radically different. Developers were busy with their own large private projects and were not very interested in partnering with us. Housing Minister Phil Twyford pushed and pushed the project, but the numbers being built in the first three years were pitifully small.

This was not just a policy failure. It was also an enormous political weight around our necks. Kiwibuild was becoming an emblem of a failure to deliver. This was ultimately unfair — Covid had caused all manner of problems. But the narrative was taking hold.

In mid-2019, Megan Woods had become Housing Minister. A no-nonsense politician, she had been tutored by Jim Anderton in the Alliance and the Progressives, and had returned to Labour when those vehicles folded. She was our troubleshooter and she was brought in to sort out housing. This meant backing away from Kiwibuild as the main policy and trying new ways of working with the private sector. A critical part of this was an infrastructure support package to get large-scale developments built. Megan had a measure of success with this, and changing market conditions started to bring housing supply and affordability more under control, but housing remained a thorny issue throughout our time in government.

The 2021 Budget was still paying the Covid bills. By this stage we had come up with a more structured approach to giving assistance to businesses and workers when we went up and down alert levels. We instituted a Resurgence Support Payment to deal with Level 2, where some businesses were heavily restricted by the gathering limits, and kept the wage subsidy for Level 3 and above. It gave some certainty, but the strain on businesses that had been doing it tough was obvious. We kept pushing out support via the Small Business Cashflow Loan Scheme and advisory services. The big new cost was vaccines.

The fact we even had vaccines was extraordinary. When the pandemic first hit, I was involved in a conversation with a group of epidemiologists and health experts. The conclusion was that a vaccine for COVID-19 would be three years away at a minimum. Instead, in October 2020, less than a year after the outbreak, we were purchasing from Pfizer. It was not easy, and there was still some concern that the vaccine that became the most widely used and available might not be the first one we purchased. Our vaccine strategy involved spreading our bets and purchasing three or four before settling on the one that would be rolled out for most New Zealanders.

It was a very challenging market to be in. Of course, everyone wanted the vaccines, and in a hurry. We used every lever we could to get New Zealand up the queue, while also being part of the international consortium helping to get vaccines for developing countries. Jacinda was frequently on the phone to fellow world leaders, trying to source more, but it was hard going. We rang New Zealanders we knew who worked at Pfizer, got phone calls with the CEO. As much as some in the community were hesitant to use the vaccine, there was a huge demand that we were struggling to meet. On top of the cost of vaccines, there was the cost and effort of just keeping the Covid response going — testing, PPE, community support.

All of this meant that the amount of headroom for new spending in Budget 2021 was limited. But I was determined to use this Budget to right some wrongs. It was the thirtieth anniversary of Ruth Richardson's 'Mother of All Budgets' that slashed benefits, cut government spending in education and health, and generally paved the way for an unravelling of New Zealand's social fabric. The intergenerational impacts of the cuts to benefits were still being felt.

In our first term, Carmel Sepuloni as Minister for Social Development had established a Welfare Expert Advisory Group (WEAG), chaired by Cindy Kiro (later to become Governor-General). It included a cross-section of experts, and representation from business and unions. It identified a system that was not allowing people to live in dignity and that was failing to meet government expectations. It made a series of recommendations — some of which we had already implemented, such as indexing benefits to wage increases and increasing abatement rates for benefits when people found work. We had increased benefits above the normal inflation adjustments in the March 2020 Covid package, but they were still well below the WEAG recommended levels.

The centrepiece of the Budget was a package that saw main benefits rise by up to $55 per week. I asked my staff to check whether we had restored benefits to or above the inflation-adjusted level they were in 1990. We had done that. And they made an appreciable difference. After the payments came into force, I received an email from a recipient saying that for the first time in a very long time they could buy meat with their groceries. We had already reduced the cost of going to the doctor for low-income people, and this, combined with the Winter Energy Payment, meant the lowest-income New Zealanders were better off by hundreds of dollars a week.

There was another important change that had massive symbolic value. We reinstated the Training Incentive Allowance. This was the payment that allowed those on benefits to undertake degree-level study and not lose their benefit. It was personal for Carmel: she had been a recipient of the allowance as a young parent. So had Paula Bennett, the Minister who had cancelled the allowance when National was in government. I knew Paula well from our time together in student politics. I was incredulous that she would pull the ladder up behind her in this way. Restoring the allowance would allow another generation of Paulas and Carmels to succeed.

The Budget changes meant a lot to me personally, but none so much as the funding for a new railway workshop and wagon assembly at Hillside Workshops in South Dunedin. The enormous investment in rail that had been made in league with New Zealand First justified a further facility. When I was a child, the workshops were the length of a couple of rugby fields away from my intermediate and high schools; we used to queue up with the workers from Hillside when Harry Kerr sent us out to get his lunch. The workshops had closed as investment in rail declined and offshore manufacturing was preferred. Clare Curran, my friend and Dunedin South MP, had been campaigning tirelessly for their re-establishment.

Jim Kelly was a local member of the Rail and Maritime Transport Union, a stalwart of Labour, whose son Steve had been in my year at school. Jim was very unwell by 2021, and it was a real highlight post-Budget to head down to Dunedin and visit him. He died not too long after. Jim was the absolute epitome of the spirit of the working class of Dunedin, always looking to help others and a massive believer in the powerful opportunity that decent work could provide. I was so happy we could do this for him and his fellow workers.

We returned to the Wellbeing format for the Budget and had

received updated data to show that New Zealanders' wellbeing had survived Covid well, with 86% of people reporting high levels of satisfaction with their own wellbeing. This was a great result. Satisfaction was of course not evenly distributed, and our focus on Māori and Pasifika families, and solo parents, was well and truly justified by their lower rates of satisfaction.

Economically we were doing better than the dire forecasts of the previous year. Unemployment was at 5.2%; there was solid economic growth predicted; and while predicted debt levels were high, at 52%, they were still low relative to the rest of the world. But alongside the Budget I was determined that we should start to plan ahead to deal with more economic shocks. I had been thinking for some time that the way we established the wage subsidy scheme was not sustainable long term for managing the loss of jobs. Around the world most developed countries had some form of social or unemployment insurance, usually funded by a mix of employer and employee levies. New Zealand had nothing, and redundancy coverage was patchy in employment agreements. We used the Tripartite Forum that we had established with Business NZ and the Council of Trade Unions to gauge their support for such a scheme. It was full throated, and in February that year they wrote jointly to ask us to develop the scheme. We made the announcement at Budget 2021 to limited fanfare. Over time, the project would get significantly more attention — especially as economic conditions deteriorated in 2022 and 2023. But for now it seemed like a piece of work whose time had come.

We also announced the establishment from Budget 2022 of the Climate Emergency Response Fund. This saw the proceeds of the Emissions Trading Scheme automatically directed to climate action work. It would allow us to undertake the long-term investment needed to meet our climate goals in the Emissions Reduction Plan that was foreshadowed in the Zero Carbon Act which had passed almost unanimously in 2019.

This was the first Labour-only Budget since 1990 — and we made it one to be proud of. It was big and reflected the incredibly busy programme we had set ourselves. In addition to dealing with Covid, we were involved in major reforms of the vocational education sector, the health system, the planning system (via Resource Management Act reform) and Three Waters reform. Taken individually, each of these was a mammoth nation-building project; taken together they pushed our capacity, and that of the public sector, to breaking point. Ultimately, hindsight would tell us the programme was too big to handle. But as a progressive government we were never going to be happy just managing the shop. Whatever people wanted in terms of our mandate, we had a lot to keep us busy.

In many ways it felt like we were governing twice — once for normality, and once for Covid. It was exhausting, and whenever we felt like we were getting somewhere, the virus would come back.

At the end of March 2021, the first case of the Delta variant was detected in New Zealand in a managed isolation facility. Delta was a virulent strain that was always going to be hard to contain once it took hold. Auckland had spent some time at higher alert levels in February, but the quarantine system was giving us the levers to manage outbreaks. It was, however, beginning to cause strain.

In the meantime, we did have some success. Australia had adopted a similar strategy to New Zealand and achieved excellent outcomes. Accordingly, both countries agreed to set up a Quarantine Free Travel (QFT) zone. Alf and I made a trip to Tasmania during this time. He had friends there, and I wanted to trace the Robertson ancestors who had stopped there on their way to New Zealand. It was a great trip to a beautiful place. But while there we became aware of increasing outbreaks in various states of Australia. As we waited at Hobart

Airport to return to New Zealand I was part of a conference call that would almost certainly decide we would be ending the QFT. I am not sure if any of the other returning New Zealanders knew what was going on, but my continual pacing up and down and furrowed brow might have been a giveaway.

A return to a full quarantine arrangement placed huge pressure on us. New Zealand has a vast diaspora. Over a million New Zealanders are estimated to live overseas. Those of us who are here look outwards and like to travel. Over the decades we had all become very used to coming and going from our country, and suddenly that movement was heavily restricted.

We were continuing to take the best health advice, which was that people needed to isolate for 14 days after contracting the virus. To make sure that happened, the quarantine requirement had to be compulsory.

Our Managed Isolation and Quarantine (MIQ) system was sophisticated and large. But however many MIQ places we had, they were never sufficient to meet demand. We tried a variety of ways of allocating places. Whatever we tried had drawbacks, and as time went on the measures became increasingly unpopular. The ballot approach brought in during September was particularly disliked, and coincided with a wave of restrictions in Auckland following the first community case of the Delta variant.

These restrictions lasted in one form or other through until Christmas 2021. It was during this period that the social licence for our Covid response began to fray. What had been a unified response felt fractious. We were acutely aware of what was happening, but vaccination levels were simply not where they needed to be before we could remove those restrictions.

While we set about getting people vaccinated, we tried everything to deal with the growing frustration. This included introducing half steps in the alert levels to allow for small outdoor gatherings. It did not work. When I filled in for the PM at the now less regular media conferences, the questions were niggly, playing gotcha games with particular rules, or chasing up stories of poor or illegal behaviour. This was matched by the niggliness in the community. I went to Auckland to meet with members of the business community. They were all angry and worried. People in hospitality and retail who could not fully operate in Level 3 were particularly upset.

In August 2021 we tried to set out a plan to open up the borders. It was well received, but the full opening was not scheduled until May the next year. And the tools that we were deploying to enable us to remove restrictions, such as mandated vaccinations for some parts of the workforce, the wearing of masks on public transport and the Covid tracer app, were having the perverse effect of making a small but growing percentage of the population furious.

There were still signs of the 'team of 5 million'. Super Saturday, held in October to try to achieve even higher vaccination levels, was an amazing day — and absolutely unthinkable in any other circumstances. More than 120,000 people nationwide were vaccinated that day. This was the lead-in to a new system — the traffic light system that we hoped would provide a long-term way of managing the need for restrictions.

At the time I flagged with Jacinda my view that we should look to use the success of Super Saturday to set an earlier time for the lifting of restrictions to encourage a final push for vaccination. I could see that the runway for our approach to Covid was running out. I know that Chris Hipkins as Covid Minister felt the same way. Jacinda rightly pointed out that our vaccination rates were highly variable, both by geography and by ethnicity. Many of the District Health Boards that were responsible for vaccinations were failing to get uptake among Māori. In many ways, of course, this reflected problems with the delivery of healthcare generally. The mainstream mechanisms for vaccination were simply not reaching parts of the population. Jacinda felt it would just be irresponsible to open up too soon and risk losing all that we had fought for in terms of lives saved. She was right, we had to keep the focus on saving lives — particularly those of our most vulnerable. But it was getting harder to keep people together.

Later, in October, we did in fact set a target for vaccination, and for lifting restrictions. We also announced a major package to directly fund iwi- and hapū-led organisations to undertake the vaccination programmes. This had the impact we wanted, albeit late in the day. It was a huge vindication for Te Aka Whai Ora, the Māori Health Authority that we were in the process of establishing. By December 2021 we had achieved 90% vaccination coverage, a remarkable achievement. This paved the way for us to ease ourselves out of the approach we had taken to Covid.

But for a small but growing group of New Zealanders, it was too little, too late.

14. WĀHINE TOA — SIX YEARS OF SPORT

In 2017, not long after the coalition agreements were signed off, I sat with Jacinda in her office in front of a whiteboard with the names of potential ministers, and cards with the names of potential portfolios to stick next to the names.

Jacinda had been canvassing ideas with people and had already developed a pretty good idea of who should be doing what. We had a long conversation about various combinations and roles. Towards the end I looked up at the board and said, 'I guess you want me to be Minister of Finance then?'

'Absolutely!'

'Great — it's on one condition though.'

'What's that?'

'I want to be Minister for Sport and Recreation.'

'Ah, a few people have expressed interest in that job.'

'Hmm, well, how many of them have you asked to be Minister of Finance?'

I got the job.

In the Labour Caucus there was not much room for anyone else in the Sport portfolio when Trevor Mallard was there. Trevor was, and is, a sports tragic like me. He had spent a long spell as Minister, and in Opposition carried on as our spokesperson. While he was never going to give up that role, he did introduce me to the Black Ferns and women's rugby. Trevor's daughter Beth had been in the Black Ferns, and he was their number one fan. I went to a couple of games with him, and greatly admired the skill and commitment the Black Ferns brought to the game.

The team were in my head when, with Trevor moving to the Speaker's Chair, I took up the Sport portfolio. I wanted to make women and girls in sport a priority.

This also came from spending time with my stepdaughter Hayley, and seeing just how much sport meant to her. She was a great netballer, if challenged a little by inheriting her father's stature. She, Alf and I were part of a trophy-winning social indoor netball team which involved almost entirely her downing two-pointers from everywhere. She stopped playing after she had kids but returned to the game once they got older. She once told me that playing was so important to her because for an hour or two a week she was just Hayley, not Mum, and needed to do nothing other than focus on playing and on having fun. Her netball club was also her community — friends, babysitters and more.

I could see New Zealand was not doing all it could to support women into sport and recreation. All aspects of sport were male dominated. There was little focus on improving participation of girls and women outside of traditional sports like netball, and there was an appalling lack of interest or support in elite-level women's sport. This was the case despite heroic efforts by women over many decades to promote and develop their sports. I felt strongly that with sport such an important part of New Zealanders' DNA we needed to make it work for more than half of the population.

Just a matter of weeks after I was sworn into the role of Minister for Sport and Recreation, Alf and I travelled to Brisbane for the Rugby League World Cup finals. Our men's team had a shocker in the tournament and were knocked out in the quarter finals but the Kiwi Ferns women's team were there in the final.

On the day of the game we got a taxi to the ground. The driver, having found out why we were there, launched into a passionate speech about how much he loved the fact that women's sport was now featuring more on television in Australia. He talked about WNRL, the Big Bash Cricket League and AFLW. He knew the players' names, and said they played with such freedom and joy, it reminded him why he loved sport. I remember thinking if a blokey Brisbane taxi driver could be a convert, then there was an audience out there for what I was planning.

Meantime, in February 2018 I headed to the Winter Olympics in South Korea. I arrived on the day New Zealand won its first Winter Games medals for 26 years — with teenagers Nico Porteous and Zoi Sadowski-Synnott both winning bronze.

At these major events there is usually an opportunity for a fair bit of diplomatic work, and I met with a number of my fellow ministers. I even bumped into Ivanka Trump several times. But there was one person MFAT was determined I should avoid. South Korea had made a major effort to get North Korea to participate in the Games. It was a huge story, and from the Koreans' point of view a great success. But MFAT felt it was better I did not give the North Koreans any reason to think New Zealand was on their side, so we made sure not to make contact. One day, we were waiting for a lift after visiting the International Olympic Committee base. When the lift doors opened, out poured a large delegation. They looked at us — all wearing the New Zealand team-issued gear — and, amid much excited talking and waving of arms, a Korean man stepped forward and thrust his business card into my hand. He was indeed the North Korean Minister, but the English translation of his card described him as 'Supreme Sports Leader'. As we hastily made our excuses to get into the lift, I told the sports officials that this was a name change I wanted to seriously consider. Strangely, it never happened — all I got was a desk plaque with the title on it!

Back in Wellington, Sport New Zealand got to work on New Zealand's first ever Women and Girls in Sport Strategy. The hard work of previous generations meant there was a great foundation to build from.

We settled on three themes: Leadership, Participation, and Value and Visibility. Early on there was controversy. We made the decision, after much angsting, that as part of the Leadership theme we would require all national sporting organisations (NSOs) to ensure that at least 40% of the membership of their governing bodies would be female. 'Quotas' such as this were unpopular. But I felt that if we were to achieve change, it needed to come from the top of the organisations in charge of our sports. We gave them two years to get there and, crucially, we tagged achieving the goal to their funding. A failure to meet the target in time would see 10% of the Sport NZ funding withheld.

Despite the initial gnashing of teeth, the NSOs began to get on board — with one exception. NZ Rugby had a complicated governance structure even then, and when our policy came in the board of eight contained one woman. They doubled the number by the time the policy came into force. I felt NZ Rugby had taken the women's game for granted for years, and this proved to be the case for some time to come. But other codes thrived. At the New Zealand Golf Open a couple of years later, one of the board members thanked me for the decision, and said he felt the board was making far better decisions as a result of the increased diversity around the table.

In terms of Participation, we invested significant resources to support clubs and codes to grow the number of female participants. A particular focus was at the secondary school level, where there has long been significant player dropout.

But it was in the Value and Visibility space that we knew we could make a big difference. The mantra that you can't be it if you can't see it was obvious to me.

Sport NZ ran a survey of media coverage of women's sport. In 2018 it was less than 10% of the total. I could see why. That year I attended the annual Sports Media Awards. While I waited patiently to present the award sponsored by NZ Sport for the best coverage of women's sport, I looked around the room. In an audience of hundreds, there was a handful of women. Two were nominees for our award. Even worse, as I got up to present it, I looked out into the audience. The lack of interest was nearly matched by the underlying hostility. I presented the award to one of the two women and got out of there as quickly as I could.

We knew that the key to lifting the value and visibility of women's sport was putting quality sport in front of New Zealanders. There were so many people way ahead of me on this. I discovered the most extraordinary network of wāhine toa who had been plugging away for years, supporting each other and making great things happen. Women in Sport Aotearoa, in particular, was making sure that elite-level sportspeople had a network of support and advocacy.

We purposefully set about supporting the hosting of three major events: the World Cups in cricket, rugby and, audaciously, football. The path to hosting each of them was very different.

In 2018 we worked with NZ Rugby to get the hosting rights for the 2021 Rugby World Cup. All previous tournaments had been held in the Northern Hemisphere, and there was a view that it was time for a Southern Hemisphere host. Australia was also interested. The chances of a joint bid were low, especially after I approached the Australian Sports Minister about it during the 2018 Commonwealth Games on the Gold Coast. We had a meeting on the margins of a tense trans-Tasman hockey game. I put the idea on the table. She said no. The conversation ended.

The government backed NZ Rugby, in the end to the tune of around $10 million. Even then the proposal was a fairly narrow one: to keep costs low, only two or three host cities would be used. Australian rugby has never been the most united force, and eventually its bid faltered. New Zealand was announced as the host.

The International Cricket Council (ICC) has a less open way of allocating tournaments, and NZ Cricket indicated to me that they thought the hosting of the Women's ODI World Cup was likely to come to New Zealand after we had expressed interest. In 2019 that hunch was confirmed, and we were announced as the hosts, again with government backing care of the Major Events Fund crucial to the success of the bid for the tournament.

The FIFA World Cup was another matter entirely. I had watched the 2019 tournament held in France and seen the huge crowds and growing interest in women's football. It was likely the 2023 tournament would be the only chance New Zealand might have of hosting the event before it got too big, but we also knew the tournament was too massive for New Zealand to host on its own.

We had approached Australia several times to co-host with us, but once again they were determined to go it alone. Australia is big enough to do that, and had the requisite number of stadia and the infrastructure across several cities to make it possible. But their relationship with FIFA was strained. In 2017 FIFA had threatened to take over Football Australia in the wake of governance concerns. I was told that the Australians were regarded as both pushy and disorganised. On the other hand, NZ Football enjoyed a good relationship with FIFA. We had successfully hosted age-group tournaments and, despite some challenges, had kept the Oceania Federation afloat when Australia had departed to join the more competitive Asian Federation. A joint bid was our only hope.

Behind the scenes, it was a torturous process to bring the bid together. It had never been done across federations. Though we needed each other, we also had our own goals to meet. For New Zealand that meant maximising what we could get from the early stages of the tournament, knowing that we did not have a large enough stadium to host the final.

It was not cheap either. Minister of Economic Development

Phil Twyford and I took a paper to Cabinet requesting an initial $20 million to finance the hosting. Many of my colleagues were bemused when I told them that if we were to pull it off it would be the biggest sporting event ever in New Zealand. If we won the rights, the economic benefits would dwarf the $20 million price tag — but that was hard for many to grasp. In the end we got the paper through and set about finalising the shape of the bid.

Before we could get to the final stages of doing this, Covid arrived. In March 2020, as the virus spread, sporting events around the world were impacted. In Australia the Black Caps were playing a three-match one-day series. The first game was played in front of an empty stadium. At home we were preparing to shut our borders. I had been in regular contact with NZ Cricket CEO David White about where we were at. I called him to tell him that we were moving to put in place a mandatory 14-day self-isolation period for people coming from Australia. It would come into force the following day. If the team left Australia right away, they would avoid it. If they played the next scheduled game, they would be caught up in the new rules. David was shocked. He said he would talk to the team management. He called me back a few minutes later to say the series was off and the team were on the way to the airport with just hours to spare.

That was just the beginning of the Covid chaos. At every level, sport was set to be decimated by Covid restrictions. Local sports clubs which relied on income from clubrooms or sponsors were in trouble. At the elite level the loss of crowds and sponsors would be catastrophic.

I worked with Sport New Zealand on a rescue and recovery package. I remember saying to CE Peter Miskimmin that my goal was that not one sports club would have to fold because of Covid. We set about establishing a fund to support this. By the time we came to announce it at Budget 2020, it was worth $270 million. Some of that went to local clubs to pay rates or insurance. Small grants of $5000 were, literally, to keep the lights on. For professional sports it was crisis funding. We paid millions of dollars to Super Rugby franchises, netball, league and the Wellington Phoenix just to keep them alive. It was a stark lesson for me in how fragile the financial model for professional sports in New Zealand is. These franchises and clubs are essentially cash businesses. If they don't play, they can't pay.

New Zealand's success in combatting the first wave of Covid saw a rapid return to professional sport, even as most of the rest of the world remained under lockdown. By June 2020 Super Rugby was back. The first game was in my old hometown of Dunedin where the Highlanders played the Chiefs. The Highlanders franchise had organised for essential workers to be celebrated before the game. Representatives of emergency services, defence forces, supermarket workers and others were brought out onto the field. The crowd rose to cheer and thank them. It was very emotional.

I was given the opportunity to speak, essentially to thank the crowd for getting through lockdown. It was the first and only time a politician appearing at a rugby game has been cheered. An epic night was completed with a last-minute drop goal that gave the Highlanders the win — and me bragging rights over Chiefs fan and Prime Minister Jacinda Ardern.

But much harder was to come. Our ability to control Covid relied on border controls. This in turn meant managed isolation and quarantine. There were only a limited number of beds in MIQ, and it was a hard ask to prioritise sports teams over the many New Zealanders who wanted to return home. As well as any visiting sports teams, we had individual New Zealand athletes to think about, including those trying to qualify for the Olympics.

I worked with the ministers responsible to find some solutions. My argument was that sport remained one of things that was giving some joy and connection to our communities. If we could get a small number of places in MIQ, then we could make something happen. It was hard going, but with some extreme prioritisation, and incredible work from Sport NZ and national sporting organisations, we began to make some visits work. International teams were not fans of managed isolation, but they knew if they wanted to play this was what they had to do.

But there was no way we could make that work for whole tournaments. First the Cricket and then the Rugby World Cup due to be held in 2021 would have to be postponed. I vividly remember the day I drove out to the hotel in Kilbirnie where the Black Ferns were in camp, preparing for the Cup, to tell them we were postponing the event. I looked around the room and realised that what I was saying would likely mean some players would not have a chance to play in the Cup when at last it was rescheduled. It was tough, but it connected me to the team in a way that made what would happen the next year even more special.

Cricket was in fact the first of the World Cups to get going in early 2022. We were still progressively removing restrictions around travel and gatherings. We created a category for special events to allow visas for teams to be granted. The organising team, led by the exceptional Andrea Nelson and organising committee chair Liz Dawson, had multiple scenarios in place. They knew there was a risk that at any moment we could have a Covid outbreak, and restrictions would be re-imposed and crowds not allowed. It was touch and go almost every day leading into the tournament. But they made it work. This included dealing with anti-mandate protesters who spray-painted their concerns on Hagley Oval. Such was the dedication of the people who brought the tournament together, I don't think anyone even noticed. We funded the construction of lights at the ground, and I bowled to Sir Richard Hadlee at the opening — a boyhood dream fulfilled, even if he clouted me to the boundary and made me chase after the ball.

It was not a great tournament for the White Ferns. They had

their chances in a number of games but were knocked out in the group stages. A lot of our planning (and budgeting) had been for the White Ferns to at least make the semi-finals. Ending the tournament without New Zealand involved was unknown territory. But the quality of play had captured the cricketing public. The final at Hagley Oval in Christchurch on a balmy April night was extraordinary. The lights splashed out over a full house for Australia to play England. I walked around the ground with Megan Woods. Every now and then we would stop and just stare at the crowds: a packed house and amazing atmosphere for a women's cricket game not involving New Zealand. We knew we were part of something special.

With the Rugby World Cup, we already had an inbuilt rugby public to attend the games. But no one had seen much of the Black Ferns, who had played on New Zealand soil only sporadically in recent years. We were also limited by the tournament being played only in Auckland and Whangārei.

Once again a remarkable group of women were running the show. The organising committee was chaired by Dame Julie Christie, with Michelle Hooper as the CEO. They had reasoned that we needed to get the tournament off with a bang if there was to be any hope of success. This meant attracting a full house at Eden Park for the opening game against Australia — essentially, the biggest ever crowd at a women's sport event in New Zealand. The committee decided they needed star pulling power. They got British superstar Rita Ora (now married to Taika Waititi) on board and organised a massive cultural performance. We came up with some extra funding, and they went for it. Ticket sales were good — but not enough to fill the ground. A lot of tickets were given away, but in the day or two before the game we began to believe that a packed stadium might just be a possibility.

It was a tough run-in to the tournament for the Black Ferns. They had played poorly through much of the previous year, with limited game time to get things right. An end-of-year tour to the UK and France in 2021 had been a disaster on and off the field. The coach was sacked. The team, who had won five World Cups before, were at their lowest ebb just before their biggest moment.

Enter Wayne Smith. The Professor, as he is known in rugby circles, had an extraordinary coaching record but had never coached women's rugby before. He entered the camp only five months before the tournament and brought former All Blacks coach Graham Henry with him. They rebuilt the team brick by brick, with superb leadership from new co-captains Ruahei Demant and Kennedy Simon. Crucially, they were able to draft in some of the highly successful Black Ferns Sevens players. The likes of Ruby Tui, Portia Woodman-Wickliffe, Sarah Hirini and Stacey Waaka were already household names and skilful, hardened competitors.

I was at a wedding in Melbourne the day of the opening game. At the reception I sat at a table in the corner to watch a stream of the game. The ground wasn't full, but it was near enough. The rugby itself was stressful. The Black Ferns went behind in the first half but clawed back to win. In between spells on the dance floor, I watched the team grow in confidence. They were playing an exciting, running and open brand of rugby.

Over the next few weeks interest in the tournament grew. I flew to Whangārei for the Black Ferns' quarter-final against Wales. It was the same night that the All Blacks were playing a test in Japan. The only senior representative of NZ Rugby I could find at the game was the former Black Ferns captain and now board member Dame Farah Palmer. I was livid. This was one of the most significant moments for the Black Ferns and women's rugby, and NZ Rugby did not seem to care. I did my best to host the World Rugby representatives, and sat next to chair and former England international Bill Beaumont, who was treated to one of my bad habits. I have watched a lot of rugby games over the years and tend to provide a running commentary on the players and the performance of the referee. I'm sure he really appreciated my insights.

The team won convincingly, setting up a semi-final against France at Eden Park. The buzz around the tournament suddenly exploded. I started fielding calls from friends asking if they could get tickets to the game. It was a sell-out. Again it was stressful to watch the team struggling to get control but somehow, remarkably, winning after the French captain missed a final kick at goal that would have won the game.

In the halftime break I confronted NZ Rugby CEO Mark Robinson in the big reception room at Eden Park about the absence of senior NZ Rugby people in Whangārei. Our conversation grew a bit heated. Mark was very defensive about how much work they had put into the tournament. I felt that the investment was not being matched with deeds. After a few minutes I looked up to see that other people in the room had stepped several metres away! On reflection I was probably being overly harsh, and I actually like and respect Mark. But I was desperate that we would not waste the opportunity we had.

As it happened, I was not the only one thinking that things could be done differently. I am told that, during that same halftime break, a coup was being mounted to remove the chair of the board. The arrival of Dame Patsy Reddy as chair sometime later was a welcome shift. In fairly short order, NZ Rugby was compliant with the 40% governance rule too.

All of this drama was put to one side for the final against England. By now public interest was unprecedented, and the ground was bursting at the seams. England had been dominant in the tournament, mainly through their forwards who seemed unstoppable. The Black Ferns were massive underdogs.

The game was, and is, one of the greatest sporting events I have attended. It was full of drama, with Portia Woodman-Wickliffe knocked out in the first few minutes and the England player responsible sent off. Even so, England looked in control and led handsomely at halftime.

One of the privileges of being Sports Minister is being hosted at games like this. There is always a good feed, an open bar and plenty of people to talk to. This can lead to an extra-long halftime break that makes it very easy to miss a fair bit of the second half. As a tragic fan, I very rarely fell for this trap — especially on a night like this.

When I went outside for the start of the second half, the VIP section was mostly empty. I looked around and saw the Mayor of Auckland Wayne Brown. The ball was kicked off. Ruby Tui caught it in front of us with her foot millimetres from touch. The Black Ferns began a passing movement from inside their own half. They surged forward, and after a remarkable run Stacey Waaka scored behind the posts. I was delirious. It was the try of the season. I looked around for someone to celebrate with. I hugged my private secretary Jack Lane, and even had an awkward embrace with Wayne, as well as a realisation that the Black Ferns could do this.

The second half see-sawed, but with a few minutes to go the Black Ferns were in front, though England were hard on attack. The crowd was at fever pitch. History tells us that the final lineout five metres out was won by the hand of replacement forward and public servant Joanah Ngan-Woo. The referee's whistle blew — and the impossible had happened. The Black Ferns had won.

I ran towards Mark Robinson and gave him a massive bear hug. All arguments were forgotten in that moment. I hugged Farah Palmer — the trailblazer for women's rugby. And then I just stood and looked out at the crowd and this remarkable group of women.

Jacinda for her part was travelling to Vietnam. She was getting live updates via the pilots of the Defence Force plane and reading them out to the Press Gallery. She made it to the hotel for the final minutes of the game, which she watched on a grainy cellphone. Her staff sent me footage of them all in the foyer, jumping up and down and yelling and dancing when we won — while other bemused world leaders walked by.

The celebrations at Eden Park were epic. A few years earlier NZ Rugby had tried to get crowds to sing 'Tūtira Mai Ngā Iwi' as a way of countering British Lions supporters. It fell flat. Well, on this night, the irrepressible Ruby Tui grabbed the microphone after the game, and 43,000 people sang that Ngāti Kahungunu tune with gusto. It was more than we could have imagined.

Hosting the FIFA World Cup was an altogether more contested affair. When New Zealand first started pulling together a bid, there was already significant interest from Brazil, Japan and Colombia among others. It is an extensive process to be selected. The twin federation bid took the title 'As One'. It was a sophisticated and cohesive bid that relied on the ongoing tricky relationship between New Zealand and Australia.

Part of the process was site visits from the FIFA team who travelled the country looking at grounds and meeting key people. Along with the team from Te Papa, local iwi and NZ Football, we hosted the FIFA delegation at Te Papa, and gave them a mihi whakatau, demonstrating some of what would make New Zealand a special venue if our bid was successful. I knew we were making an impact when I noticed one of the FIFA staff wiping away tears as we sang our waiata. The ratings given by the visiting team were released only after the vote — New Zealand's had been far and away the best.

As time wore on first Brazil and then Japan pulled out. This left a straight contest with Colombia. They were pushing hard, and it was clear that UEFA, the European Football grouping, were going to be critical in securing the votes. We used our diplomats and every ministerial engagement, no matter what the portfolio, to make our case. At last, in June 2020, I woke to a text from my Sports private secretary Ollie Thurston: 'WE DID IT!' The joint bid had won by 22 votes to 13.

That, however, was just the beginning of a three-year journey punctuated by Covid. There were times when it felt as if we were very close to losing the rights to host, and relationships with our Australian co-hosts were sorely tested.

Dealing with FIFA is like dealing with a small, very wealthy, slightly dodgy nation. Its president, Gianni Infantino, had been elected as the man who would clean FIFA up after Sepp Blatter's controversial reign. He is a larger-than-life character who has a very particular way of doing things. We soon came to learn that FIFA were all over every detail of the tournament. The overall organising committee was led by New Zealander Dave Beeche, and in New Zealand by Jane Patterson. We were also working with NZ Football chair and FIFA board member Dr Johanna Wood, and NZ Football CEO Andrew Pragnell. Throw in MBIE as the Major Events organisers, Sport NZ, half a dozen local councils and football organisations, and there was a heap of chefs in the kitchen.

Our major battle with the Australians was over the allocation of matches and the pools. Initially Australia would only agree to give us a very narrow set of games, and none of the semi-finals or finals. We pushed back hard and also held out to be the hosts of the draw, which we knew attracted nearly as many viewers as the final. It was a knock-down, drag-out negotiation. After several calls with the Federal Minister of Sport, who was also trying to deal with state leaders, we got a deal. New Zealand would host the draw, the opening game and one of the semi-finals, as well as 40% of the pool games. It was a good outcome.

Meanwhile, FIFA were flexing their muscles in every direction. Every ground, every training pitch was pored over. We had set significant funding aside to upgrade facilities, and we had to find more as various details were required to be changed. FIFA controlled the grounds from weeks before the games. All commercial signage had to go, including the giant SKY symbol from the side of the Wellington stadium. They controlled everything down to where buses would stop and, especially, what food and drink would be available at the grounds. We were incredibly lucky that the stadia across New Zealand went along with all of this. That said, they all had ground upgrades courtesy of us and FIFA, so had every reason to be happy. It actually became a running joke as I went around the country opening all-gender changing rooms here, there and everywhere.

A few weeks before the opening game, just when it seemed we had got there with FIFA, a request came through to create smoking lounges for VIPs in the main stadia. Harry Tod-Smith, a handy footballer himself and now my private secretary, kept many of FIFA's more unusual requests from me, but this one he had to share. I told him to write back and say this would be illegal and we were not doing it. Predictably, the response was to ask how long it would take to change the law to allow for it! We held our ground and eventually the request was dropped.

The draw was a massive event, not just because of the audience size but because the result would determine several critical factors. First was who the Football Ferns would be playing. We needed a helpful draw to boost the team's chances of making it out of the group stage and keep fan interest in the tournament going. Second, we were keen to host some teams in pool play who would have big travelling supporter groups. The word was that there would be between 15,000 and 20,000 US fans coming to the tournament.

The pōwhiri for the FIFA crew was held on the Auckland waterfront. Gianni was given a beautiful korowai to wear and was fussed over at every point. Everything was looking good for the draw, which Jacinda along with many other dignitaries attended. I was incredibly nervous as the balls were drawn for each group, and kept a close eye on the ones New Zealand was hosting. When the Philippines were drawn in the Football Ferns group, there was a whoop of delight from the Ferns coach. The chances of beating Norway or Switzerland were slim, but the Philippines were beatable. Eventually, the US was drawn in a group that would be hosted in New Zealand. I shouted 'YES!' just a bit too loudly, earning stern looks from the FIFA officials. When the Netherlands, another country with a major supporters' crew, was drawn in the same group, I limited myself to a silent fist pump. It could not have gone better.

A small group of officials went into a room to sort out the timing of games, and the rest of us went back to the Park Hyatt Hotel, which FIFA had taken over. It was to be their base for the full tournament the next year. It is an opulent place, very well suited to FIFA's largesse. Nothing was too much trouble, with food and booze laid on. By the time the tournament came around, I was increasingly uncomfortable with the whole arrangement. The cost of the presidential suite was $21,000 per night. It was reserved for the president for the full three weeks of the tournament, but for a variety of reasons he ended up staying there for only three nights. That money could have paid for a year's football programme in a developing country. But this was FIFA.

Once the draw was confirmed, we set about trying to drum up a crowd. We knew we would get decent crowds for New Zealand games, and those involving the USA, but the rest were unknown. In my weekly meetings I pestered officials to give me the ticket numbers. Sales were painfully slow. I was particularly worried about a game on a Monday night in Hamilton between Costa Rica and Zambia, and whether anyone would show up. I became a bit obsessed about the whole thing, at one point threatening that I would make my parliamentary colleagues fly up for the game. FIFA do not allow discounting or giveaways of tickets, so we had to sell most of them. I found myself on the phone to local mayors, imploring them to push sales. I did media in every host city. The FIFA and NZ Football teams did a great job, and week by week the sales started to grow. Soon we were ahead of target, and some games, such as the USA v Netherlands game, were sell-outs.

As the tournament drew near, excitement took over from nervousness. This was indeed the largest sporting event that New Zealand had ever hosted, with a TV audience in the billions, tens of thousands of travelling fans and teams from around the globe.

On the morning of the opening game between Norway and the Football Ferns I was due to attend and speak at the blessing by Te Ātiawa elders of a new building adjacent to the parliamentary precinct before flying to Auckland. As I got up to make my remarks, I noticed the CE of Precinct Properties, Scott Pritchard, go outside to take a call. That was a bit unusual, but I assumed he'd heard enough from me over the years. But Scott returned looking grey. He told me there was an active shooter at one of their building sites in Auckland — in Lower Queen Street, a couple of hundred metres from the FIFA HQ, and literally across the road from the hotel where the Norwegian team were staying.

I have had a few heart-stopping moments as a minister, and this was one of them. Every possible scenario rushed through my head. Surely this couldn't relate to the tournament? But what if any of the teams were caught up in the situation? How would this be reported across the world . . . what if we had to postpone the opening game?

I headed back to Parliament to get the latest information from the Minister of Police. It soon emerged that the shooter was a solo gunman who had worked at the site. As tragic as the situation was — two people were killed and six injured — it was unrelated to the tournament. Nonetheless, it took considerable effort to calm the worst fears of FIFA. Many of the teams were in hotels inside the cordon set up by police, and they were unable to leave. Harry and I rushed to the airport to get an early flight north.

Of all the things I thought I would be worried about that day, a shooting was not high on my list. We went straight to the hotel and met with the FIFA team. We assured them that security would be bolstered for the game. We even got the Police Commissioner on the phone to talk them through our plans. Eventually it was agreed that the game would go ahead.

One of the issues I had been worried about was Auckland's traffic. And on this night it played up. Harry and I headed to the game early but ended up arriving just 10 minutes before kick-off. Gianni Infantino got there about a minute beforehand. This was a bad outcome. His team had been pestering us about him having a motorcade for games. We had told him that we don't really do motorcades in New Zealand. His team were not convinced. The police had even told them motorcades are such a rarity they tend to slow the journey down because of rubberneckers. The only reason we would have one was if there were security concerns. And despite Gianni's view of his place in the world, most New Zealanders would not have picked him in a line-up, let alone wanted to do him any harm. But matters were made worse that night because US Second Gentleman Doug Emhoff had arrived, and there were legitimate security concerns for him, so he did get a motorcade. When Gianni had to pull over for him, the insult became an injury.

Getting the game kicked off felt like a relief. We had the capacity crowd we wanted, even if no one gave the Football Ferns a chance against the former champions Norway. But the Ferns rose to the occasion, playing solidly in the first half and even creating a couple of chances. They went in at nil–nil.

At the halftime break I met Barbara and Michelle Cox, the mother and daughter duo who had played for New Zealand. Both were hugely emotional that this day had come. Barbara had been in the first ever New Zealand women's team. She told me about the fundraising they had done for their first overseas trip. There was no funding from NZ

Football at all. They did everything, including an event at which they sold kisses from the players. I thanked her for being a trailblazer.

Remembering my experience from the rugby, I excused myself and went back outside to the mostly empty VIP seats. One of the only people there was Auckland Mayor Wayne Brown. An omen, perhaps?

Three minutes into the second half, a sweeping move from inside the Football Ferns' half ended with a perfectly weighted cross into the six-yard box where Hannah Wilkinson swept the ball home. There was delirium in the stadium — and this time I ran and embraced the Mayor in a full bear hug.

The rest of the second half felt like an eternity, but at the end of it Jacinda, who was enjoying a rare post-politics outing, Chippy and I were simply ecstatic. We made our way down to the changing rooms. The atmosphere was astounding. Everyone was crying — former Ferns, the current team and coaching staff, and us. Each of us spoke to the team about our pride in them and what the win meant for us.

Ticket sales exploded after that game. There were full houses everywhere, with record crowds for any football game in New Zealand, men's or women's. At one Wellington game three male friends separately sent me pictures of them at the stadium with their daughters. The tournament had done exactly what we wanted. It was an inspiration, it was entertaining and the football was of the highest quality. And that Costa Rica v Zambia game in Hamilton? Just over 8000 people made it along!

Sadly, the Football Ferns, having done the unthinkable against Norway, lost to the Philippines and drew with Switzerland to miss out on progressing further. But if you had told the team earlier that they would beat one European team and draw with the other, they would have taken that result.

When the sums were done after the tournament, it had returned a net benefit to New Zealand of $109 million. Close to 27,000 international visitors had come, and they had a 97% satisfaction rate for the experience. Player numbers for girls' football have continued to grow, with many reporting the World Cup as the motivation for new players.

And on numbers — at the end of 2023, mainstream media coverage of women's sport was 26%. We still have a long way to go, but given the global average is around 4%, we can be proud of the progress we have made.

There have been some dark times alongside the positive ones that come with the role of Minister for Sport. The darkest of all for me was the death of Olivia Podmore while she was part of Cycling NZ's High-Performance Programme. Olivia took her own life during the delayed Tokyo Olympics.

She had travelled to Rio in 2016 but had not been selected for the Tokyo games. I was aware of issues in the Cycling NZ programme thanks to the report Mike Heron, KC had done into the culture of the programme in 2018. I was assured that improvements had been made, key coaching staff had been let go and that greater efforts were being made to look after the athletes in the programme. When I attended Olivia's funeral in Christchurch, there was no shortage of people wanting to share with me their thoughts about what was happening in Cycling NZ and what had happened to Olivia. I spoke with her parents and agreed we needed to take another look at what was going on.

We got another review under way at Cycling NZ, again utilising the skills of Mike Heron, joined this time by Massey University academic Sarah Leberman, former Silver Fern Dr Lesley Rumball (née Nicol) and Genevieve Macky. Their 104-page report was a damning indictment of the organisation's culture and practices, particularly at the Cambridge HPSNZ base. It spoke of a power imbalance, gender bias and unresolved trauma from the previous review.

Sadly, similar reviews had in the previous few years come to similar conclusions about a number of sports, albeit without the tragic outcome in Olivia's case. In sports ranging from football to kayaking, from hockey to gymnastics, we uncovered abuse, bullying, sexual misconduct, racism and more. This was particularly marked in female-dominated sports, and often involved male coaches and leaders. It was clear to me that some systemic change was needed. We were playing a game of 'whack-a-mole' with individual sports. Victims of the abuse did not feel they could come forward without compromising their position; there was little consistency across sports as to how complaints could be handled, and limited training for administrators and coaches alike.

We looked around the world for some models and noted Australia's relatively new Integrity Commission. It was clear that in a small country like New Zealand we would need to bring together our work on drug-free sport, anti-corruption and anti-bullying into one entity. Some excellent work was done by a preparatory group, and the outcome was a proposal for a Sport Integrity Commission. It would be able to hear complaints, undertake investigations and, crucially, develop codes that sports could sign up to in order to protect their athletes. In the hectic run-up to the 2023 election we managed to get the legislation passed and the body established under the astute leadership of former NZ cricketer Rebecca Rolls. It is an achievement I am immensely proud of.

The enormous dedication of our athletes deserves to be backed up by a system that supports and protects them. Some would say that we are wrapping our sports stars in cotton wool, and that coaches must have the right to be tough to get the best out of the athletes. I utterly reject that notion. Coaches can push their athletes hard without crossing over into abuse and bullying. The long-term damage of that approach is enormous. Sport is such a unifying force — I hate the idea that it can put people in a position where they lose their confidence, or, worse, choose to take their own life.

After six years as Sports Minister, I have a renewed appreciation for the effort and dedication it requires to be at the elite level. I also remain in awe of how much is achieved by a small nation like ours. I watched the 2024 Paris Olympics with such pride in our athletes, especially our female athletes. They are backed by some terrific administrators. Working alongside the likes of Raelene Castle, Steve Tew, Kereyn Smith and others has been a massive privilege.

The highs and lows of the Sports job have been extraordinary. I still can't write properly about what happened at the 2019 Men's Cricket World Cup final. I know I flew there (paying for myself) because I was not sure New Zealand would ever be in a final again. I know I witnessed an incredible game and got to meet Clive Lloyd and Steve Waugh. But I still can't fathom a game we could tie twice and still lose.

The next morning, I took a train to Liverpool to see the Silver Ferns netball team playing in the World Cup tournament. I'd had no sleep and was feeling down. The minute I met up with the team, CEO Jennie Wyllie, and coaches Noeline Taurua and Debbie Fuller, I felt instantly uplifted. I saw only a couple of games before I had to head back to New Zealand, but as I left I said to myself that they felt like a team that could win. And so they did, providing yet another of our most nail-biting sporting occasions.

Being Minister of Finance was the most important job I have ever had. Being Minister for Sport and Recreation was the most fun and fulfilling.

15.
NO FUEL IN THE TANKS

2022 was a hard year. The whole country was tired of Covid and the restrictions that had gone with it. Most of these had been removed by the beginning of the year, but the issue of vaccine mandates was provoking protests, as it was in other countries. I had been following the extreme voices closely for some time. Partly it was self-preservation. The online hate was reaching fever pitch. I was receiving threats through most social media channels, and any attempt to communicate about Covid was futile as rational advice and argument gave way to the increasingly vociferous views of conspiracy theorists. It was clear from monitoring that the local extremists were closely following the actions of overseas groups such as the Canadian truck convoy that closed off central Ottawa for some time.

On Waitangi weekend, a New Zealand protest convoy set off for Wellington. We were in Queenstown for Alf's birthday. In between celebrating with him and enjoying Zoi Sadowski-Synnott's gold medal at the Winter Olympics, I was keeping an eye on Facebook and Twitter. It seemed clear to me that the numbers involved were larger than even the organisers expected. By the time I made it back to Wellington, I was concerned. I rang a couple of colleagues to ask what measures were in place to manage them. I was told the police were monitoring the situation, but it quickly became obvious they, and Parliament, were thoroughly ill-prepared for what would happen next.

The convoy arrived at Parliament on 8 February — and never left.

The occupation was well planned: a number of tents immediately sprouted up in the grounds. More challenging again were the vehicles — dozens of campervans, utes and cars that blocked the roads around Parliament. It was clear they were going to be impossible to shift.

As the days turned to a week, then two weeks, then three weeks, the occupation grew in size and in determination. As the local MP, I was involved in regular discussions with police as to how we might bring it to an end. It was tense. We knew the government could not tell the police how to do their job, but they seemed unable to find a way to end the protest.

I worked with the Wellington City Council to see if we could get tow-truck companies to agree to move the vehicles that were demonstrably illegally parked. Their resistance to this idea was explained only when one of the companies told us about the phone calls and emails that threatened them with what would happen to their business if they cooperated with the police. Some of the calls came from Canadian numbers. This was a global effort.

The occupation was the worst period of my time in politics. I had led protests onto the grounds of Parliament as a student leader; I have participated in and spoken at dozens of protests on the grounds. I believe strongly in peaceful protest. The occupation in 2022 was not a peaceful protest. It was a toxic environment. People trying to go to and from work were regularly being spat on or abused simply for wearing masks. I started getting calls from concerned local residents struggling to access their homes. My electorate office staff worked to find alternative accommodation for some who could not handle the stress — older residents, people with medical conditions, even a pregnant woman worried she would not be able to get to hospital. Businesses were forced to shut up shop and public transport routes were significantly disrupted. One day midway through the protest I saw from a Beehive office window a group of St Mary's College pupils being escorted by security guards just to get to school. This was not New Zealand. Parents began to withdraw their kids from school.

At a personal level, the occasional threatening email became a more regular torrent of abuse. One day early in the occupation I found a note in the letterbox at home which made it clear that someone had visited the house to express their views. From then on, I was driven to work each day and the police began regular patrols of our street.

At Parliament, nooses were hung in the trees and speakers at the protest regularly called for the arrest, trial and execution of politicians and journalists. It was not, as some commentators suggested, a festival atmosphere.

While there was no doubt a core of protesters for whom the issue of mandates was a particular concern, the extent of the backlash against mandates was grossly overstated. The government had responded to the urging of the police and military, and included their personnel in mandated vaccination, along with health workers and teachers. Other mandates, such as they were, came from employers themselves, with no involvement from the government.

The protesters constantly claimed that children were being forced to be vaccinated. Again, not true. And in any case, the argument against vaccination was nothing more than quackery. Of course, the protest captured a whole range of people with any number of conspiracy theories and views. But it had a violent, sinister undercurrent. At one point the offices of the Taranaki Whānui Rūnanga were vandalised. It was an anti-authority, anti-science, pro-chaos shit show.

After an early unsuccessful attempt to break up the protest, the police were still working on the idea that eventually numbers would drop and they would be able to move people on. When the protesters installed toilets and plumbed them into the Wellington sewerage system, I did not share the optimism. Eventually, after 23 days, I got a very early call from the police to suggest that today I might choose to come into Parliament a bit later on, and that my driver would come up later in the day to pick me up.

The police had massed significant numbers of officers from around the country. I later learned that they chose a Wednesday to take action because numbers at the protest tended to drop midweek. It was a large and sophisticated operation, but it was never going to be easy.

The battle to remove the protesters took all day. From our offices in the Beehive we could view the skirmishes as police moved the protesters along. Late in the afternoon I was called into Chippy's office. A fire had been lit and had engulfed the children's playground that Trevor Mallard had installed a few years earlier. The huge trees that have long stood in front of Parliament buildings were also on fire. The scene was apocalyptic and it was upsetting. Jacinda could not take it any longer and retreated upstairs. Later I watched the live news coverage of protesters throwing bricks and paving stones at police. It felt like watching another country.

It became clear to me that while the immediate battle was at last over, the impact of the protest was long lasting. I thought of myself as thick-skinned after 13 years in politics, but I now found myself wondering if I really had it in me to carry on. I was literally scared to leave my house. Did I really want to spend all my time looking over my shoulder? I confided in some friends that I thought I might have had enough. Most of them felt it would get better. There was so much I still wanted to do, and I still wanted to be there to support Jacinda. I resolved to carry on.

Over the next few weeks there was a return to a kind of normality. Much of our work preparing for Budget 2022 focused on public services, and in particular on funding the creation of Te Whatu Ora (Health New Zealand) and Te Aka Whai Ora (the Māori Health Authority). These changes to our health system were overdue. The District Health Board model which had sought to bring services closer to the communities they served had outlived its usefulness. There were inequities everywhere you looked. It was a postcode health system — where you lived dictated the quality of service and care you received. It was also a system that was failing to respond to the needs of Māori and Pasifika populations — the very people with the greatest health needs. We knew that the reforms would take years to turn around New Zealand's poor health outcomes. But we put in significant new funding, a $14.9 billion package over four years, and pushed money to areas where we thought we could see some immediate benefit, including the drug-buying agency Pharmac and mental health services.

Meanwhile, the global economy was heading into troubled waters. Russia's invasion of Ukraine in February had sent the EU into a tailspin. Post-Covid inflation was already on the rise, and the conflict sent it spiralling — eventually up to double digits in the UK and elsewhere in Europe. New Zealand is never immune in such circumstances. From late 2021, the Reserve Bank, concerned about an overheating economy, had begun lifting interest rates.

This did not stop the incoming National leader Christopher Luxon from making one of his first announcements a call for more support for businesses affected by Covid. Not for the first time National wanted us to spend more money — a fact that has been forgotten by those majoring in Hindsight Economics.

In early 2022 we shut down the Covid Response and Recovery Fund. In two years we had allocated $58.4 billion. It was a huge sum of money — and there were inevitably instances of the funds not having delivered what we wanted. But the spending was needed to get New Zealanders through the crisis. The Wage Subsidy scheme paid out a total of $19 billion and supported more than a million people to stay in their jobs. It was a lifeline, along with other investments, that kept people alive and working. Our management of the economy was lauded from the outside. New Zealand had been one of very few countries to have a credit ratings upgrade from the international ratings agencies during Covid. I was able to say at Budget 2022 that we were one of only 12 countries with two Triple-A ratings. Those ratings were maintained throughout our time in government.

But in politics there is never time to rest on your laurels. We had a massive political issue on our doorstep in the form of the cost of living. The economic cycle post-Covid had seen the New Zealand economy do well while others were still in lockdown, but the global inflation pressures and Reserve Bank monetary tightening started to take its toll.

In every interaction, it was the cost of living that would dominate conversation. As a country we had become very used to inflation at low levels, and the increasing cost of everything was unsettling and unwelcome. In addition, people who had purchased homes thanks to the rock-bottom interest rates of the Covid period were facing interest-rate hikes that absorbed all of their discretionary income. They stopped spending in the shops, cafes and bars, and this in turn hammered sectors trying to recover from the pandemic.

It was a toxic economic and political cocktail. We knew we had to respond. As 2022 rolled on, we moved to stop increases to petrol taxes and introduced half-price public transport fares (which also helped with climate targets), but we knew that these indirect measures were only scratching the surface. Throughout Covid we had toyed with the idea of direct payments to New Zealanders as a way of providing support. We had never gone through with them, largely because they would take too long to implement and because the logistics of making a payment were deemed too challenging.

This time round we pushed officials to see what was possible — and to do so in time for the Budget. The calls for some kind of intervention and support were getting louder. The group that was missing out was those on middle incomes who were not eligible for state support. We needed a policy that could target those people and be modest enough in total spend that it would not draw the ire of the Reserve Bank, which was trying to dampen the economy. Inland Revenue bravely took on the job of making the payment. It was targeted to those earning less than $70,000 who were not already getting the Winter Energy Payment. The payment of $350 per person was announced on Budget Day to be delivered in three instalments from 1 August.

When it came time for delivery, a National Party that had been calling for support for exactly this group were able to capitalise on some wayward payments to people who no longer lived in New Zealand to show the scheme as a failure. In fact, 98.3% of payments went to exactly who we wanted them to — but the damage was done.

The Budget did see us return to making progress on the Wellbeing approach. The multi-year funding for Health was added to by the first Climate Emergency Response Fund which we had foreshadowed the previous year. We also trialled two clusters — one in the Justice area and the other in Natural Resources — where we funded for three years rather than the traditional one year. The trade-off for that level of budget certainty was that the agencies had to work together on an agreed set of shared goals and policy objectives. We had teams of ministers and officials working on these clusters throughout the Budget process. It was groundbreaking stuff that got to the heart of breaking down the siloed, annualised basis for putting Budgets together.

It would be fair to say that one cluster worked a lot better than the other. The Justice cluster came together well, with very clear goals. It was really encouraging to see ministers actively supporting others getting funding. The police were keen for the courts to get more funding to speed up access to justice; in turn, Justice officials advocated for police resources to be boosted in particular areas. The approach was less successful in Natural Resources. Environment, Conservation and Primary Industries ministers and officials do not share a sufficiently common vision to make development of a cluster a worthwhile exercise. In the end it was a cluster in name only.

But I felt pleased we had tried something different, and I remain convinced that we need these kinds of approaches if we are to deal with issues that do not conveniently sit inside the boundaries of a particular agency.

My usual post-Budget roadshow suffered from the hangover of the parliamentary occupation. On a swing through the Wairarapa electorate with MP Kieran McAnulty we encountered trouble. At a public meeting in Dannevirke it was particularly bad. A group of twenty or thirty Covid conspiracy protesters interjected throughout my presentation. They were calmed down by locals, but when question time began, they took over the meeting. Their first question was what role Klaus Schwab and the World Economic Forum had in writing the Budget. It went downhill from there, and even with local businesspeople trying to keep the protesters quiet, I eventually had to cut the event short.

The protesters pursued me as I went to leave. The small number of police officers who were present managed to get between me and the mob. I had made it to the local Council offices when one young guy yelled, 'I am going to get you, you fucking faggot.' After that we needed a police escort to the car, and eventually had to cancel other events in the Wairarapa electorate as the group followed us around.

A month or so later, protesters in Whangārei were similarly disruptive and threatening. One of their number had brought along a lamington to 'present' to (i.e. throw at) me. All I knew at the time was that I was bundled into an unmarked police car to get away from a group the police deemed a sufficient threat that hasty retreat was necessary. The same group blocked the entrance to Whangārei Airport at the end of the day. The DPS were with me that day and ensured that I got directly onto the tarmac. As I waited in my car, I could hear the megaphone-toting protesters' abuse: I was a 'pervert and a paedophile' who 'deserved to die'. The homophobic element of the abuse I received was always strong. I am very comfortable in who I am, but I continued to worry that such a strand of bigotry existed in New Zealand and what it still meant for future generations. This might explain me losing my sense of humour when at the end of 2022 Massey University judged that David Seymour's quip that 'I would have thought Grant Robertson would be a much bigger threat to lamingtons than lamingtons would be a threat to Grant Robertson' was the quote of the year. The danger was real — and the stress that went with it was enormous. I was mentally and physically exhausted from the crises of the past few years, and was struggling to find the joy in the job that meant so much to me.

I am aware that there is little sympathy for politicians, who are indeed well paid. However, even the everyday intensity of work is ridiculous. During the week, most days would start before 7am with either morning media or helping a colleague with their morning media. A combination of meetings, Parliament sitting till 10pm two days a week, work as Wellington Central MP and reading would see me on the go till late in the evening. In the weekends I tried hard to keep Friday night and Saturday as free as possible to spend some time with Alf, but there were often events to attend. On Sunday I got up as early as I could to work through the folders (paper and electronic) that had been provided by my seven private secretaries, four advisors and two administrative staff. These would inevitably mean conversations with other ministers, and I was usually still at the table late in the evening. At one point a school class asked me to keep a diary of my hours for a project they were doing. That week was typical — it was 71 hours.

For Jacinda, the pressure was much greater. As a young (or as she would say, youth-adjacent) female politician, she had endured untold abuse and denigration. She had deliberately kept away from watching or reading most media for years, and was unaware of the number of specific threats made against her. But still the pressure of years of life-and-death decisions, crises and disasters had taken their toll. And through it all she was a mother to the boundless ball of energy that was Neve. I worried about her — a lot.

So it was not a huge surprise when around August or September 2022 she shared with me and her Chief of Staff Raj Nahna that she did not think that she had it in her to carry on for another electoral cycle.

I was not surprised, but I was shocked — and very worried. As her friend, I wanted what was best for her. As her colleague, I knew what she meant for the government, for Labour and for New Zealand.

Over the next couple of months I thought about how I could persuade her to stay. I offered to do more of her media. I talked about the kind of campaign we could run in 2023 that would reserve her energy and protect her from the worst of the extremes. There were times when it seemed possible. At the Labour Party conference in November, we had our first in-person gathering as a party since Covid. Jacinda felt the aroha of her people. She saw what it meant to them and the people we represented. I watched her start to believe again. She started smiling. She physically opened up.

On the final day, it was my job to introduce her to the conference for her keynote speech. I gave it everything to hype up the crowd and to pay tribute to my friend for all that she had done. I gave her a hug as she came on the stage, and whispered, 'Have fun.' After that, I stood at the side of stage and watched in awe. It was one of her very best speeches. She grew in confidence as she spoke. The magic was there, and I could tell she was feeling it might be possible to go on.

As we left the hall to go to the post-speech press conference, I was on a high. Then Andrew Campbell told us that there was a poll out that night. Labour was down, and Jacinda had suffered a big hit to her preferred PM numbers. You could almost hear the air go out of the balloon.

A couple of weeks after that conference, in late November, I aggravated a back issue that had been with me since my rugby-playing days. I was in significant pain, unable to sit for any length of time. Scans revealed a ruptured disc. All the while, Jacinda, Raj and I discussed various scenarios. Jacinda had suggested that if she did go, then I was the right person to take over. She knew I had my own misgivings about carrying on, and we found ourselves both saying, 'I want you to do this, but I will support you if you decide you can't.' In the end we agreed to take time out over summer before making any final decisions.

By late December we knew we needed to tell Chippy. Not only was he our friend and a senior colleague, but he was also a person who might take over if our summer considerations went the way we thought they probably would. A couple of days before the end of the working year, Jacinda asked him to come to Premier House for a chat about the next year. Raj and I were there as well. In the downstairs sunporch where we'd gone to get some privacy and uninterrupted time, Jacinda told Chippy that she wanted to step down as PM. She said that she was keen for me to take over, but that I, too, was undecided about what I wanted to do. We thought it best to take summer to think over options but felt he deserved to know where we were at. It was a lot to take in. Chippy just stared at the ground. His first words were, 'Well, you can't both go.' We talked through the thinking and the options. My back, meantime, was killing me. I was on the floor doing back stretches, and throwing in my two cents' worth from the lotus position.

We left and went our separate ways for the summer break. Chippy called me that night to try to get my assessment of how likely it was that Jacinda would change her mind and carry on. I told him it was a less than 10% chance. As for me stepping in, I said I really didn't know, but it was wise for him to have a think about his own position. We agreed to touch base again in early January.

The next day — the last working day of the year — I had scheduled a spinal cortisone injection at one of the private hospitals in Wellington to give me some pain relief. These are a very normal course of action for dealing with disc problems. The procedure was booked for about lunchtime. I had meetings from 3pm that day and was assured by my specialist that I would be able to attend them. However, in a one-in-10,000 event, the anaesthetic that is used as part of the CT-guided injection was put in the wrong place. As I went to stand up after the procedure, my legs felt incredibly heavy. I tried to get up and could not. I had lost all the feeling below my waist.

The next few hours were frightening. I had no idea how long the paralysis would last, or if indeed I would get feeling back at all. I got hold of Alf and asked him to come and join me. It was Friday afternoon and there were not a lot of hospital staff around, but I was given scans to see if they could shed light on what had happened. They showed nothing that would explain my predicament. I was running through in my head the idea that maybe this was permanent.

Eventually my back specialist called through and said, 'I know this is scary but you will walk out of the hospital tomorrow morning.' He was right. After an awful night, the feeling slowly came back and I was discharged.

That, however, was not the end of the matter. I was in a highly strung state in any case, given the decisions that had to be made about the leadership. This, combined with the stress of the temporary paralysis, caused me to experience real anxiety for the first time in my life. I wasn't sleeping and I developed a condition called esophagitis that meant I was struggling to swallow. I was unable to have a proper conversation about why with anyone apart from Alf and Jacinda, because I could not reveal the truth about what might be about to happen.

Just after New Year 2023 I was in Dunedin, as my brother Stephen and sister-in-law Delwyn were over from the States. I was completely paranoid that I was going to aggravate my back. Somehow, I had also managed to convince myself that this would make me lose the feeling in my legs again. When I was driving, I became convinced that I might not be able to apply the brakes. My mind was playing some terrible tricks on me.

I was visiting one of my best mates, Alex, and his girlfriend one afternoon when they confronted me about how worried they were about me. They told me I needed to see a doctor. I knew they were right, called the emergency doctor and for the first time ever played the 'I am not sure if you know who I am . . .' card. The clinic told me to come down right away.

I was taken in the side entrance to the after-hours clinic. A very kindly doctor looked me over, did a few tests and then sat me down. He said what I knew to be true but had not been able to accept: 'You are suffering from extreme stress, compounded by the trauma of the temporary paralysis.' He gave me some anti-anxiety medication and told me that I really needed to talk to someone.

I was relieved. That night I went home to my mother's house and confided in her about Jacinda's likely decision and my own misgivings about what I should do. Mum's reaction was interesting and very similar to my own. She understood my reluctance, but as a political person she wondered what would happen if I did not take on the role.

I went back to the hotel where I was staying. I had a shower and went to bed. I decided not to take the medication. I'm a bit of a wuss when it comes to pills, and I felt a bit better after talking with Mum. About 2am I woke up and began shaking uncontrollably. I could not stop. I got up, made a cup of tea and sat on the couch, hoping for it to pass. After what felt like hours, my heart began to slow a bit and the shaking stopped. I had no idea what a panic attack was, but it is clear to me now that this is what it was.

I flew home the next day, still feeling anxious and incredibly worried that more uncontrollable shaking would happen on the plane. I sat next to a lovely American couple on the flight. I have no idea what they made of me as I asked them question after question to take my mind off how I was feeling.

I made it home and collapsed into Alf's arms. I called my colleague Ayesha Verrall, a qualified doctor, and asked her if she knew of a counsellor or therapist I could talk to. She came back with some names. Contacting them was the best decision I made in many years in politics. I had conversations with a couple of people, and settled on a therapist who would help me through my remaining time in Parliament.

But the final decision about what to do in terms of the leadership still had to be made. Having run for leader a couple of times, and failed, I had already said I would not put my name forward again. I still felt that way. Watching Jacinda up close, and acknowledging how uncertain I was feeling, I knew in my heart that I did not want the job. You have to be able to give it 110%, and I did not have that in me. But I was feeling a sense of obligation. There was much more for the government to do. All of the things that Covid had put on hold were still very much there. I knew my colleagues and the party would want me to take over.

I talked it over again with Alf. He was very reluctant to see me put myself through the stress of leadership. He knew what it would mean for me and for us. But he said he would support me whatever I decided. Then one night he said to me, 'Even though you don't want to do this, you're not going to be able to say no, are you?'

It hit me like a thunderbolt. For the first time in my political career I needed to put myself and Alf and my health first. I was not going to be able to do the role justice when I was doing it out of a sense of obligation and was mentally and physically exhausted.

I called Jacinda, and she confirmed what I already knew: that she had made her mind up to go. I told her that I was not going to put my name forward, but that I would carry on as Finance Minister. I reasoned I knew the job well and could handle that — and, frankly, both of us going would be too much for the government and the party.

Jacinda rang Chippy to tell him of her decision, then I called him to let him know mine. He was surprised. He had been expecting a very different call. The job of PM would of course have been an incredible experience. But I was not in politics to have experiences, I was there to do the right thing, however hard that decision might be.

My first session with the therapist was the next day. When I started to tell my story, I said that it would need to stay confidential. She laughed and said that was in her job description. I then told her that in just over a week's time the Prime Minister was going to resign, that I was not going to be a candidate for the role and I needed a plan for how to navigate whatever time I had left in politics. Her eyes widened, she took a deep breath and said, 'Well, that is a lot.'

When I look back, I don't think I ever really dealt well with the stress of politics. Jacinda and I used to joke that we had the polar opposite reactions to stress. She would be unable to eat, and I would eat compulsively. When there was a crisis — seemingly a permanent state — people would bring food into the office. I would eat my share and then ask her, 'Are you going to have that?' I had also hidden away from my own stress by looking after others. I was always happy to help people, and in many ways that became my coping mechanism. I neglected my own health in both a physical and mental sense. We had managed Covid on adrenaline, but now it was taking its toll.

The other thing I have learned is that I am somewhat lucky in that the worst symptoms of my anxiety were short-lived. I have never suffered another panic attack. The temporary paralysis was almost certainly the trigger for what occurred. Others who have to go through these crises on a regular basis have my empathy. My friend Beth gave me the best possible advice when I confided in her how I was feeling.

She said, 'When you're overwhelmed and anxious, remember you will not always feel this way.' I hung onto that thought more than once.

Even after deciding against taking on the PM role, I knew I had to ease the pressure. One way to do that was to step back from being the Wellington Central MP.

I still loved the constituency work and felt a deep sense of loyalty to the people of the electorate. At the 2020 election I had a majority of nearly 19,000 votes, almost 10 times what I had had in 2008. But being Minister of Finance and an electorate MP was too much. Both Michael Cullen and Bill English had worked that out. I resolved to announce I would not run in the seat again once the dust had settled on Jacinda's resignation.

In mid-January 2023 we all headed to Napier for our annual Caucus retreat. The National Party had also decided on Napier as the venue for their event. Even so, a fair few media outlets were wondering whether it was worth attending. By this stage the PM's chief press secretary Andrew Campbell was one of the very few who knew what would be announced, and did his best to say it would be worth their while attending.

Alf came with me to provide support. We stopped in Waipukurau for a coffee and pulled up next to *New Zealand Herald* journalist Claire Trevett on her way north. She looked at me and exclaimed at how much weight I had lost. I was still not really eating properly but assured her this was not the weight-loss mechanism I would recommend for anyone. My physical state was a good distraction from other questions she might have asked.

The first night at our Caucus retreats had become a traditional night for MPs and their whānau to come together for a meal. This one was held at Ocean Beach. It was a beautiful night. Jacinda was due to make her announcement the next day and could not face going along. She called in sick. I was incredibly distracted. It was noticeable and a couple of colleagues came up to ask if I was all right. There was a bit of chatter about what might be wrong with Jacinda. Carmel wanted reassurance that Jacinda was not dying. I was at least able to give her that.

She had in fact called and asked if I could get senior colleagues Kelvin Davis and Megan Woods to see her after the event. The dinner ran late, and eventually we had to leave before it had finished. Driving back into town, everyone knew something was badly amiss. We gathered in Jacinda's hotel room, and she shared the news that she was stepping down. Straight away Kelvin said that he would resign as deputy leader too. He had never enjoyed the role and had done it out of loyalty to Jacinda. He was also unsure about running again. After a bit I indicated to my colleagues that I would not be contesting the leadership. No one in the room wanted the job either, and the mood was sad and sombre.

I could not sleep that night. I was sure of my decision but the reality of it was hitting home. I had been in politics a long time, I had fought hard to be the leader, and when I had parked that idea I had given everything I had to support Jacinda. I had always had at the back of my mind that I would go when she went. I really had no idea what being in politics would be like without my mate.

The next morning, we gathered the Cabinet and ministers early at the venue on the pretext of doing some pre-Caucus planning. Jacinda shared the news again. There were more tears. Each minister in turn spoke of their love and admiration for her. Towards the end, I told them that I would not be a candidate in any leadership contest.

We then went into Caucus. By this stage I was emotionally exhausted from all of the reveals. Jacinda told everyone of her decision, and again the tributes flowed. We took a break as Jacinda prepared herself for the media conference that would shortly follow. During the break colleagues began coming to me saying that I had to take over. I could barely speak. I just shook my head.

When we reconvened, I stood in front of Caucus and told them that I would not be standing as leader. I reassured them I was not going anywhere and that I was prepared to be Finance Minister if that was what the next leader wanted. I shared something of my health challenges and asked that they please not try to talk me out of my decision. I had in fact pre-empted this by giving Jacinda and her team a media release to say that I would not be standing that would go out at the same time as hers.

We sat in the main room of the centre and watched the live stream of Jacinda's media conference next door. It was impossible to focus on anything else. As always, her resignation announcement struck just the right note of the political and the personal. Jacinda had given every bit of herself to the job and to the nation. In normal circumstances she would have been a standout Prime Minister; in the shadow of Covid she emerged as one of our very best. She did so in an environment where misogyny towards a successful woman in her early forties was ever present. I was upset watching her speak, but also incredibly proud that I had served alongside her.

Once that was over, it was time to get out. I grabbed a couple of friendly colleagues and made my way through the media. I managed to get by with only a few comments, headed to the hotel room and collapsed on the bed. There were already hundreds of messages on my phone from people urging me to take on the leadership. I started trying to reply to them but gave up after the first few and switched the phone off. For the first night that year I went to sleep without a sleeping pill. I have not used one since.

The rules for the Labour Party leadership had, sensibly, been tweaked a few years earlier so that if a person could get two-thirds of the Caucus to support them, the party-wide election process would not be triggered. This would save the party a lot of heartache.

Before we left Napier, it was pretty much decided that Chippy would be the candidate for leadership. A couple of other people flirted with the idea of running, but this close to the election we needed stability, and a leader the public already knew and liked. Chippy ticked all the boxes. His role as Covid Minister after the 2020 election had made him a household name, not least when at a 1pm press conference he famously misspoke and encouraged New Zealanders to 'spread their legs'. It quickly became a meme, and was on T-shirts, mugs and more. He took it all with good humour.

He was, and is, my mate. We came into Parliament together in 2008, and have been there for each other through many ups and downs. I was even best man at his wedding. We are both political nerds in the best sense. Chippy's bookshelf is a library of political books. He understands how Parliament works better than any other current politician. He is a great dad, a handyman and has almost no fashion sense. Perfect PM material.

I had already made my deal with him — I would stick around as Finance Minister, do whatever other jobs he wanted me to do, but I was going onto the party list. Not needing to be present in Wellington Central made me feel I could carry on. I told Chippy that if Labour won, I would do him one more Budget and then re-assess whether I would continue. If we lost, I would stick around long enough to support the transition to Opposition and then I would go. Having that plan in place made it possible to get through the next few months.

Chippy was duly elected by the Caucus just a couple of days later. Jacinda had a mini farewell tour at Rātana Pā, and announced that she would leave in April, late enough to avoid a by-election before the scheduled October election.

Chippy asked me to be Leader of the House, managing the business of Parliament for the government. We were blessed by having Peter Hoare on the staff. Peter had been in the Office of the Clerk of Parliament and knows everything about how Parliament works, so I reasoned I would be in safe hands doing that job. Peter is also a fellow cricket tragic, who managed magically to create a parliamentary timetable that never clashed with a cricket test in Wellington. Genius.

The first polls after the leadership change were very good for Labour and Chippy. He got the bounce you would expect for a new leader and gave a nervous Caucus a boost. He was well aware of the tough times the country was experiencing. As people struggled with the cost of living, he felt we needed to jettison some of the more ambitious policies we had been working on. This was not just for fiscal reasons. It had become very clear that we were just trying to do too much.

For me this meant having to let go of the social insurance project. While the cost to the government was limited, it was to be funded by levies on employers and employees. The payoff for these was income security in the worst of times — but selling that to people who were financially struggling was tough. I reluctantly agreed to let it go, knowing all the while that a scheme like this is a missing strand in our social safety net, and one that I am sure we will return to. Also on Chippy's policy bonfire was the TVNZ/RNZ merger and the Clean Car Upgrade. In addition to the savings from ditching these policies, the Three Waters programme was revamped, freeing up some money that we were going to give local councils to support the change.

Three Waters was a classic example of a government doing the right thing but at the wrong time and losing the communications battle to bring the public on board. One element of the reforms was that mana whenua in the areas where we were creating combined water authorities would have 50% of the membership of the group that appointed the governing board. Not the board itself: that board still had to be appointed on a skills basis. Opponents of the change, joined by others who wanted to stir up race as a political issue, called it co-governance. Within some bodies there were actually co-governance arrangements emerging from Treaty settlements that National had set up. But Three Waters was not about co-governance. Alas, we lost that battle early on — and could never get the focus back to the very necessary reforms to deliver safe and clean drinking water and well-managed waste water and storm water.

In the spirit of our time in government, Chippy soon found himself facing a crisis. The Auckland Anniversary weekend floods were followed just a couple of weeks later by Cyclone Gabrielle, which ripped through the North Island, causing deaths, injuries and massive damage to land, buildings and businesses.

Chippy stepped up, and provided the calm, reassuring leadership that people need in moments of crisis. He asked me to be Cyclone Recovery Minister. It was not a job I wanted. My back was still not in good shape, and I was only just out the other side of my anxiety. But I knew he needed an experienced pair of hands, and as Finance Minister I was going to need to be involved in every major decision in any case.

My first visit to Hawke's Bay and Tairāwhiti was devastating. In orchards where decades of work had been obliterated, generations of the same family wept in front of us. I flew in a helicopter up the coast. The only fibre-optic cable keeping the area connected was strung between the trees because the road and rail lines were wiped out. This was going to be a long and expensive recovery.

Meanwhile, we had the job of putting together our election-year Budget. True to my original plan, I had been working on a Budget that gave something back. With Jacinda having ruled out a CGT, I had been looking at alternatives. David Parker had long wanted us to examine how we taxed wealth. When he became Revenue Minister, I approved funding for a piece of work that looked to estimate how much tax the wealthiest New Zealanders paid. It made for depressing reading. Inland Revenue had analysed the details of more than three hundred of our highest-income people. On average they were paying 8.9% of their income, including capital gains on investments, in tax. In contrast, a person earning $80,000 per annum on a salary alone paid 22% of their income in tax.

This was a world-leading study, and it proved what we knew already — New Zealand's tax system is unfair and unbalanced. David had hoped that it would provide the evidence needed to make change possible. Jacinda had supported us working up a proposal for the Budget, and we began work on a possible wealth tax. As 2022 ended, she and I had delayed decisions, knowing that there would likely be a leadership change.

A week or so after his election as leader, I went to Chippy to ask him what he wanted to do with our work. He was keen to see it finished so he could judge the idea of a wealth tax against CGT or any other options. He seemed genuinely open-minded.

The plan we had come up with was to put our proposals into the May Budget and legislate the tax cuts, but have them come into effect after the election, thereby keeping our promise that we would not introduce a new tax in this term. Through some heroic work by David Parker, Inland Revenue and our offices, particularly my advisor Toby Moore, we were able to pull off a fully formed proposal. It would have seen couples pay a 1.5% levy on their assets over $10 million. Our estimates were that it would have impacted about 46,000 people and raised $3.4 billion. We were planning to use this, initially, to fund a tax switch that would see a $20-a-week cut to wage and salary earners.

At this point Chippy became nervous. He was doing well in the polls and felt that the best contest at the election would be between his experience and stability and the inexperience of National's relatively new leader Christopher Luxon. He initially said that we could pick up the wealth tax as Labour policy for the election but he just did not feel ready to put it into the Budget.

I thought this was a mistake. My view of the election was that we were in trouble and we needed a circuit breaker. The Covid years had been hard on governments around the world, and we, too, were struggling. The cost-of-living crisis was evident in people's daily lives. If we could give them certainty of tax cuts that were paid for by the top 1% paying a bit more, maybe that could get us through.

In fairness, to sell an idea like this we needed more time. The public would have had to undertake a crash course in taxation policy that would have had a high chance of failure. There was no operational wealth tax anywhere in the world, and those who had tried it had encountered significant implementation issues.

After weeks of wrangling, Chippy ruled out the wealth tax not only for the Budget but for the campaign as a whole. I was gutted — but I also knew that I was the one who had stepped away from the leadership and Chippy was the one who stepped up, and I had to support his decision.

I remain convinced that New Zealand needs to tax wealth and assets better to help create the fairer society we need and desire, and to pay for the things we want to have — like world-class health and education systems. I am agnostic as to the exact way to do this. CGT remains a good, easy-to-understand option but reform needs to happen, and it needs a measure of cross-party support so that whatever is implemented is given the chance to work.

In April, as our response to the cyclone settled into a more business-as-usual approach, I headed to the USA for meetings of the World Bank and the International Monetary Fund (IMF) and, significantly, the first face-to-face meeting of the five Finance ministers from the USA, UK, Canada, Australia and New Zealand. This group had started during Covid as a forum for sharing ideas on how to deal with the pandemic. So far, all of its meetings had been virtual, and I had only ever met some of its members online.

In DC we were hosted by US Treasury Secretary Janet Yellen, a former chair of the Federal Reserve, chair of the Council of Economic Advisors in the Clinton era and generally an exceptional person. I'd had a couple of phone conferences with Janet over the previous year or so, and we had got on well. She had a huge reservoir of experience and insight. Also there was Australian Treasurer Jim Chalmers. We had got to know each other during long spells in Opposition. I really like Jim. He is a thoroughly decent human being, and incredibly smart. At one of our first meetings in Wellington, I earnestly told him about the Future of Work project and the importance of understanding the impact of technology on working people. He nodded and seemed very interested. A month or so later he sent me a card thanking me for the visit. It was tucked inside a book he had already written on the future of work. Modest, but very smart — politically and economically.

Canadian Minister of Finance Chrystia Freeland and very recently appointed UK Chancellor Jeremy Hunt completed the ministerial line-up. Jeremy was the latest addition, having come to the role in the dying days of the debacle that was Liz Truss's term as UK PM and the very short-lived career of Kwasi Kwarteng as Chancellor. As I sat with them in the incredibly grand surroundings of the US Federal Treasury building, I realised I was the longest serving of the Finance ministers. It was an odd moment, and a testament to the troubled political times around the world. The half-life of a Finance minister was shrinking in front of my eyes.

Back home, I once again found myself preparing a Budget that needed to take account of an unexpected event. Paying for the cyclone recovery was going to set back the post-Covid fiscal restoration job that we had begun in 2022. The cost was estimated to be between $9 and $14 billion, more than half of which was for public infrastructure. It had to be dealt with; it was the right thing to do. The lives of people in the cyclone-affected regions had been devastated. Our fiscal picture was still relatively strong compared to the rest of the world.

At the Budget lock-up for media I said:

> *In all of my Budgets, I have put them together so they are appropriate for the time we are in. You'll see from what we are announcing today that this is a practical Budget that gives Kiwis a helping hand now when times are tough, while laying strong foundations for the future.*
>
> *This is a Budget that does what it says on the tin, or in this case, the cover: Support for Today, Building for Tomorrow.*

In terms of support for today, the tax switch was off the table, but there were a number of other initiatives to help deal with the continuing cost-of-living pressures. We worked hard to find initiatives that could also help achieve other goals. We extended the twenty hours free early childhood education to cover two-year-olds so that more people could return to the workforce earlier; we scrapped the $5 prescription charge in the hope of keeping more people well and taking pressure off hospitals; and we made public transport free for kids under 13 and extended half-price public transport to under-25s to help with our climate goals. We also continued other programmes that supported the cost of living, like free school lunches and the Warmer Kiwi Homes insulation programmes.

It was a strong package, and each of the policies was individually popular. But the scale of the cost-of-living pressures was such that even together they fell short of what people felt they needed.

We had already extended the fuel excise duty cut a couple of times after first implementing it in the 2022 Budget. It was popular, but expensive. That money goes directly to road maintenance and building. We were having to top that fund up, and it could not go on forever.

The Building for Tomorrow element was important to me. The impacts of climate change were there for all to see. More regular serious weather events are now the norm for New Zealand. We had to keep responding in an emergency mode, but I was keen for us to get ahead of the game. My solution was a National Resilience Plan that could give communities investment to support climate adaptation and resilience measures. In the immediate aftermath of the cyclone in Hawke's Bay, we had done our first media conference on the stopbanks built at Taradale with Provincial Growth Fund money. That area had not flooded at all and stood in stark contrast to the devastation elsewhere. The Fund would be a chance to get projects like this built nationwide. I also wanted to see it used for even more long-term thinking. There was some great work under way in my old hometown about how to protect and support the community of South Dunedin where I had grown up. This was a 20- to 50-year project to deal with both flooding and sea-level rise and maintain the community. We need to be looking this far ahead if we are to deal with the very real impacts of climate change.

For now, the first part of the package was aimed at supporting the recovery and rebuild from the floods and cyclone. It was tough and slow going in these communities. One of the biggest issues was how to deal with properties that were in areas that really should not be rebuilt on — and arguably should never have been.

We did our best on the fiscal picture. We found $4 billion in savings and flagged that there would be more to come. This included sacrificing any notion that fees-free tertiary education could be extended beyond the first year. The Trustee tax rate was aligned with the top personal rate at 39c. The medium-term picture was not all bad, with growth coming in the years ahead. Inflation, which had peaked at 7%, was already coming down and was forecast to go inside the RBNZ 1–3% band in the September quarter of 2024 (which it did).

The Opposition played up the level of government expenditure, but the reality remained that faced with Covid, the cost-of-living crisis and the cyclone, there was little we could do. Of the new government spending in Budget 2023, 79% was on core activities. The government, like everybody else, was dealing with the impact of inflation. Overall, in our time in government core Crown expenses peaked at 34.6% of GDP in response to Covid, and had come down to 32% by the time of the 2023 Budget. The peak was only a fraction higher than during the Canterbury earthquakes.

Our attention post-Budget turned to the election. On the day she resigned in January, Jacinda followed normal practice at the beginning of election year and set the date for polling day. We had picked 14 October in the time-honoured way of looking at the dates of All Blacks tests. It was Rugby World Cup year. The All Blacks had not been in great form in 2022 and we did not want to risk going after a loss, so we picked the day before the quarter finals, reasoning that the team should make it that far. As a rugby fan I always felt at my most useful at times like this.

This timeline gave us a decent run-in from the Budget. We also hoped that the feel-good factor of hosting of the FIFA Women's World Cup would give us a bit of a lift, though the tournament did absorb a good deal of my time. Sadly, none of that really mattered, as the impacts of the cost-of-living crisis persisted. The global economy was not recovering quickly, and I was aware that the pre-election fiscal update was likely to present a worse picture than the Budget had done.

Chippy was clear that we needed to present ourselves as not only effective economic managers through Covid but also capable of taking tough decisions when we needed to do so. It had been obvious for some time that finding savings as we had done in the Budget would need to be a regular feature of Budgets to come as we tried to move to a more sustainable fiscal position.

We set about developing a fiscal package for the election. This involved most government agencies having to find 1% or 2% baseline savings. I thought this was a realistic ask. Every agency would have some areas in which they could work more efficiently or a programme or two they could drop. The public service found this a tough adjustment after a period in which resources had been readily available. We exempted some agencies, but it was a demanding exercise.

We had begun work on this package immediately after the Budget so that it could be released in August. While it did speak to a responsible economic approach, it landed with a public who viewed it with some cynicism. Like everything in politics, timing matters for packages like this. People need to see the impact of changes before they can really believe they'll make a difference. There was no time for that just a couple of months out from the election.

Meanwhile, we needed to do something in the tax space with the death of both CGT and the wealth tax. By this point I was resigned to accepting whatever was decided. Polling revealed that taking GST off fruit and vegetables was a popular policy. I had long suspected that the words 'taking GST off' were the stand-out ones in that particular sentence. But the idea was consistently raised as a practical measure we could put in place to reduce household bills, and the decision was made to make it part of our manifesto.

The problem with the policy was that what sounded good in a focus group translated to just a few dollars a week in the hand. And it was complicated to administer. GST is a comprehensive tax and making exemptions is a slippery slope. A further issue for me was that over the years I had publicly rejected the idea of scrapping GST on fruit and vegetables. Memorably, I had described it as a 'boondoggle', one of my favourite words. I had no doubt that this phrase and my longstanding opposition to the change would be raised immediately.

We launched the policy in Lower Hutt, Ginny Andersen's electorate. A good crew of Labour faithful showed up to the venue, St Paul's Church. Aware that I needed to proactively head off the obvious issue, I said in my speech:

> *I also want to acknowledge Ginny, all the other candidates and you, our supporters. It's your hard work that will get us over the line on the 14th of October. I want to thank St Paul's for allowing us to use the venue today for this announcement. I don't present myself as any kind of saint, but being here today does represent somewhat of a road to Damascus for me when it comes to the announcements we are making today!*

To be frank, I don't think I was very convincing. And in any case the policy did not have a big impact. Whatever its popularity, it was nowhere near significant enough to overcome the impact of the rising cost of everything.

On the other side of politics, National were having trouble getting their numbers to add up — again. The core plank of their campaign was a series of tax cuts that would be paid for by removing the ban on foreigners buying homes but taxing them when they did. They claimed this would raise about $740 million per annum. We had immediately raised a red flag about this as well as some other holes in the plan. Eventually three independent economists released a report that showed National were $500 million out per annum — $2 billion over the four-year forecast period. They insisted they had their own calculations but refused to release them.

It was an interesting insight into the role of timing in politics. In a different environment, like the one we had in the 2020 election, this would have been a body blow to National's chances. But in 2023 people wanted some cost-of-living relief, were tiring of us as a government and were not really engaging in detailed policy analysis.

This was also the election that proved to me that the way the public consume news had totally changed. For many, mainstream media were no longer the main trusted source of news. Social media ruled and the post-truth era meant any claim would be countered by another, and no one was taking the time to really analyse what information was correct. To their credit TV3, who were going through their own dramas, did pursue the issue over many nights, highlighting the gaps in National's costings.

I recall trying to get another nationwide media outlet interested in an aspect of the story and the reporter saying to me, 'But the problem, Grant, is that someone from their side is going to come down and tell me that you are wrong, and that they are right, and then what am I going to do?' It is hugely difficult to campaign in these circumstances. As a democracy we need to be better than this.

Other, newer elements of post-truth campaigning played a part too. The Taxpayers' 'Union' produced an advertisement using what appeared to be an AI-generated voice purporting to be me. We considered making a complaint, but in the end decided that as weak as the ad was, it could be seen to be satire. Elsewhere in the world, political opponents have used AI technology to mimic voices in cold calls to voters. Trust will evaporate if such practices become widespread; it will be impossible to know if a voice is real or not. Regulation of AI in campaigning is essential if we are to avoid entering a very difficult world.

Meanwhile, Covid got to have one last laugh. With just over two weeks to go to the election, Chippy was in a hotel in Auckland when he tested positive for the virus. It was no longer obligatory to self-isolate, but it was clear that he would need to do so, as we were asking others to do this if at all possible. We had, in fact, planned for this scenario. Colleagues stepped in for him at various events, and he had as many meetings by Zoom from his room as he could once he was well enough.

I was having my own health issues as well. My troublesome back, which had been relatively settled in the middle part of the year, went out again. It happened on the day of the Pre-election Economic and Fiscal Update (PREFU), and confirmed that stress had a fair bit to do with how it behaved. It was an incredibly busy time. I flew to Auckland and then down to Queenstown, popping pills all the way to keep me going. I tried my best, but in the final couple of weeks of the campaign the pain of sitting on flights was just too much and I had to pull out of a few events. I felt terrible letting colleagues down, but my body was calling time, even if my mind was still going.

I devoted myself to campaigning locally, and in particular for my friend Ibrahim Omer. He had won the Labour nomination for Wellington Central and was mounting an energetic campaign. I went door-knocking with him and saw constituents' positive reaction to him. His remarkable backstory and three years as a list MP were doing him a huge service. But the tide was going out on us as a government.

In Wellington Central this played out differently from in Auckland. There it was the three Cs that did us in — Covid, Crime and Cost of Living. Labour bled votes to National and New Zealand First. In Wellington it was a different C — Climate — that dominated. Ibrahim's Green opponent Tamatha Paul had won two city council elections in the area and was a strong campaigner. The coalition of voters who had backed me over five elections splintered back out, and it became a three-way contest.

In the end, Ibrahim was just running in the wrong election. On election night I was hoping against hope that he could swim against the tide. As Alf drove us to our election-night event in Lower Hutt, I scanned the results as they came in. I was pretty experienced at reading them now, and when Ibrahim fell hundreds of votes behind after counts were in for the first few booths, I knew he would not make it. I was absolutely gutted for him. He is an incredible talent. I have every confidence he will be back — as will several other Labour MPs who lost their seats.

All across the country, the same story was playing out. The hopes of a comeback we had in the last few weeks faded, and we were soundly beaten.

What I had known in my heart for some time was true. Without a doubt we could have run a better campaign, with a stronger position on some issues, including tax, but it would not have made the difference. Along with the cost-of-living issues, we had endured a series of ministerial scandals and resignations. We began looking ragged and unfocused. At most elections, the public vote out a government rather than vote another one in. This was the case in 2023.

Historians will wonder how a government so popular in 2020 could fall so far in just three years. A couple of encounters I had during the campaign explain it for me.

On a plane in the early part of the election campaign I sat behind three women coming to Wellington for the World of Wearable Arts events. As we got up at the end of the flight, one of them looked at me and said, 'Grant, we were just saying to each other how grateful we were for how you and Jacinda looked after us through Covid. We all run small businesses, and we would not have made it without you.' I smiled. She continued, 'But we are not going to vote for you this time, sorry.'

The time-warping effect of Covid meant our six years felt longer to the public. One person I door-knocked in Wellington Central told me that she was not voting for us because she thought nine years was long enough for any government. It took a bit to persuade her that it had been only six years.

We had been so deeply in people's lives during Covid, it felt like we had been around forever. But ultimately this was a cost-of-living election, and we lost because people, however grateful they were, had moved on.

As for Chippy, he had fought hard and remained positive. Whatever I thought of some individual calls he had made, he had stepped up and stood his ground, especially in the debates. What's more, he had found love on the campaign trail. Toni had been around in Chippy's life for a while, but their relationship had blossomed to the point that he decided to acknowledge and thank her in his concession speech. Immediately texts flooded in asking, 'Has Chippy just come out on national TV?' Andrew Campbell sprinted towards the press pack to assure them that Chippy was referring to Toni with an i and not a y. There had been enough drama already.

It was obvious even on election night that National could, and would, form a government with ACT, and in all likelihood need New Zealand First too. We had ruled New Zealand First out in the election campaign, having determined that we could not work with them again.

We accepted our role as caretaker government and started to pack our boxes to leave the Beehive. But as days turned to weeks, the three coalition partners made an absolute meal of getting agreements. It got so bad that the writs (formal results) for the election were declared and there was still no government.

This led me to become the answer to a future quiz question. Minister of Foreign Affairs Nanaia Mahuta had been defeated at the election, so when the writs were issued she was no longer even an MP. So, for two glorious weeks I was the Minister of Foreign Affairs. I am sure my former colleagues in the Ministry were ready for a reign of terror and the settling of two-decade-old scores — but I managed to restrain myself.

More seriously, we were dealing with the emerging crisis in Gaza. Just a week before the election, Hamas had launched attacks on Israel, killing many and taking hundreds of hostages. It was a bloody attack that got the predictable retaliation from Israel: an all-out bombing campaign launched at Gaza. Whatever right of self-defence Israel might have claimed after 7 October, several weeks on their behaviour was totally disproportionate. The term 'genocide' was beginning to be used as thousands of innocent Palestinians were being killed, and hospitals, schools and universities bombed.

Chippy and I were keen for New Zealand to join growing international calls for a ceasefire. MFAT were not so keen, and sadly neither was the incoming National government. As the coalition negotiations dragged on, it became harder and harder to do as caretaker governments have to do and speak to the policy of their successors. Eventually, we'd had enough. We made clear that we would in our official work and correspondence uphold the position of the in-coming government, but we were going to make a statement on behalf of the Labour Party. One Sunday Chippy came down to Parliament and made a statement as Labour leader, calling for a ceasefire. Officials tried to talk him out of it — but he held his ground. It was the right thing to do.

There was a more pleasant task for me as a caretaker minister. The All Blacks had done far better at the Rugby World Cup than our pessimistic election-date planning had assumed. They had made it to the final, which would be played at Stade de France in Paris on 28 October. It was unthinkable that at such a significant occasion New Zealand would not be represented. I asked Sport New Zealand to reach out to Christoper Luxon to facilitate someone from his team attending. Luxon was in the middle of negotiations, so it was not going to be him. I was pleasantly surprised when he suggested that I should be the one to go. I was still, technically, the Minister for Sport and Recreation, and was happy to accept.

It was a whirlwind five-day trip — but, as ever, if there was a chance for something unexpected to happen, it did. My back was still not great, and required regular stretching, especially on a long-haul flight. I found a place to do this towards the back of the section where we were seated — a gap behind the last row of seats. What I did not know was that it was also a shortcut for crew to get from one side of the plane to the other. As I came up in a back arch stretch in the semi-darkness of the cabin, I was kicked in the head by a fast-moving cabin-crew member. He was incredibly apologetic. I was stunned but initially thought I had escaped any injury.

We got to Paris on the Friday night before the game. The All Blacks did almost everything they could to take the game but could not overcome the South Africans. The next day, after too long without proper sleep, the excitement of an incredibly close final and the drowning of sorrows afterwards, I woke up with a very stiff neck. I had whiplash.

A fitting metaphor for the previous six years.

EPILOGUE

Not I, some child born in a marvellous year
Will learn the trick of standing upright here.

Allen Curnow, 'The Skeleton of the Great Moa in the Canterbury Museum, Christchurch', 1943

Most days now I go for a walk along the west side of Otago Harbour, on the magnificent Te Ara Moana, the shared cycle and walkway. I never tire of the view. Every day is different as the interplay of sky, land and sea summons up different hues of greens, blues and browns. Along with the wind, the tides, the boats, they are all characters in what feels like a glorious Colin McCahon or Robin White painting.

A few weeks back, my oldest friend Alex kayaked over from his place in Waverley, pulled his kayak up onto the gravel at the end of the inlet at the bottom of our driveway, and wandered up for a coffee. I love this place.

Ōtepoti Dunedin has been my place to stand ever since my parents made that fateful decision to head down this way. I feel at home within its egalitarian roots, its creative energy, its 'just big enough' vibe. There is a joke in Dunedin that when someone asks you where something is, the answer is always that it's 10 minutes away. As the promotional slogan for Dunedin in the 1980s used to say, 'It's all right here'— a fine line between a tribute to having all that we want on our doorstep, and an anthem to mediocrity if you get the cadence wrong.

It's also where Mum is — 81 and still going strong 47 years after making that shift. Still full of opinions, stories and bucketloads of love. I believe that where your Mum lives is your home.

Alf and I made the decision that we would come home once I stepped down from Wellington Central. I have a great fondness for the city I represented for so long — but truthfully it never felt like home. As we picked our way through the fallout of the 2023 election, we knew it was time to move on. I did not know exactly what would come next, but I knew it would be back down here. At first I imagined I could be a list MP, then after a while would find something else to do. I knew I was done with politics in the Beehive sense of the word. It had all meant so much to me for so long. But I was, as the kids say, cooked.

Alf had an alert for property in Dunedin, and we popped into a few open homes when we came down to visit, fantasising about a quieter life in the hills. Then one day I got a call to say that the University of Otago, my alma mater, was looking for a Vice-Chancellor — the person I had spent so much time telling what to do 30-odd years ago as student president. It did not seem like an option — the university had only ever had academics in that role. Then I heard that the university might be looking for someone different this time, after a difficult few years.

I called the recruiter, a German woman living in Singapore. She did not have a clue who I was. She told me I had only a couple of days to get an application in. I got up early one day and wrote. Five pages on what the university could be — the place where the big challenges of the world are solved, where the next generation shape and mould their and our futures. It was cathartic, if nothing else.

And somehow — multiple interviews and a couple of those awful personality tests later — I got the job. I felt like the 'graduate imposter' in Janet Frame's *The Carpathians*. Not quite as Janet meant it as the imposter at the top of their game, but rather an imposter in the arcane world of academia.

One of the lessons of life that I share with people now is that everyone, to some degree, is faking it, trying to work out how to do what they do every day. I spent a lot of my life believing I had to be perfect at what I did before I even did it. Sometimes I would not even try to do something, because learning it, and god forbid failing, felt like a weakness. But you must push on — fight your demons, find a way, make it work.

Regardless, I am home. Comforted by the cold, surprised by the sun, buoyed up by the beauty — and now with the chance to give back to the place that gave me so much. I'm 53 years old with a bad back, in the city of my six-year-old self's dreams, my tūrangawaewae, but still trying to learn Curnow's trick.

I don't think Curnow meant 1971 as his marvellous year. I have had a marvellous life, no doubt. I did my best to stand upright, to be me, to support others to be their best selves. But sometimes through my own failings, and sometimes through the prejudice of others, I found myself hunched in my Generation X stance.

As we grew, my generation convinced ourselves we would die in a nuclear war. My favourite teacher Harry Kerr let us watch an apocalyptic post-nuclear war series called *Threads*. I lay awake at night wondering how I would survive, frightened by the world around me. Just a few years later we felt proud as New Zealand stood up in the world to be nuclear free, and as we grappled with who we wanted to be as a country. Homosexual law reform, the Waitangi Tribunal, the creation of Ministries for the Environment and Women all pointed to a desire to define ourselves. But we still culturally cringed our way through much of our national life, unable to reconcile our colonial past with our collective future.

Perhaps Curnow meant 1980. In July that year Jacinda was born into a decade of post-Muldoon optimism, shoulder pads and American music. Aotearoa stuttered again as she hit her teens, blighted by the neoliberal experiment that sucked the hope from so many. How someone comes through that to lead with such clarity, compassion and skill I am not sure, but Jacinda did. She stood proud and tall — in our darkest and toughest moments. She was able to make us all stand upright and be clear about who we were when the worst of times arrived. She is our very best. Yet, I know as her friend that she did that despite herself. Fighting each and every day to serve and to do what was right even as her constant companion of doubt tried to drag her back down.

It is more likely the child Curnow imagined was born as we hit the millennium and Aotearoa was becoming a country that slowly, purposefully, understood more of its history and was discovering its soul. Dame Hinewehi Mohi stood up at the 1999 Rugby World Cup and sang our national anthem in te reo Māori, and every one of those millennial babies learned it that way. Some of them went to kōhanga reo, to kura kaupapa Māori, and learned their culture, their language, their place. They still have to battle the racism, the misunderstanding, the fear — but they do it standing tall.

Māori have of course stood upright here — most especially before colonisation. They are rooted in land, sea and rivers. But we have made it hard for so many generations and do so even now.

As we face a moment in history when all that we have done as a nation to right the wrongs of the past, to find a path to equity, to celebrate what makes us unique, is being challenged, I say to those 'kōhanga kids': this is but a blip. The journey to standing upright here will carry on; it will outlast any politician on a supercharged ideological ego trip.

Others born in a marvellous year find their way. Nina Mingya Powles — that little girl who would give her father, my boss, a McDonald's plastic watch to wear at the UN — becomes a poet and writes about what it would be like if Katherine Mansfield were her best friend:

> *then we would move cities / then countries / at the beginning we would write / then we wouldn't anymore / but sometimes I'd get*

an email from an unknown address / (subject line: MAGNOLIA FLOWERS) / and then we'd collide / by a river in Shanghai / or on a crosswalk in New York / and we would spend one sunburst afternoon / running through art galleries / watching dogs at the dog park / taking pictures of each other's / shadows

'Taking pictures of each other's shadows': that is how we carry a legacy forward. Confidently, moving through her worlds — Wellington, Shanghai, New York. The millennial New Zealander exploring from a solid base.

My former parliamentary colleague Aupito William Sio talks about the Generation Six Bs — brown, brainy, beautiful, bicultural, bilingual and bold. They are the carriers of Pacific excellence that I see every day at the University of Otago: acting in the service of their people, knowing they are the beneficiaries of the sacrifice of their parents, willing to be the shapers of the destiny of their yet-to-be-born children.

At the Pacific graduation events I read part of a poem by Albert Wendt. He says if you can read the ocean, you will never be lost; if you write the ocean, you will never be silenced. These graduates are navigating the journey between and among their cultures and finding their voices in Aotearoa. They are standing upright. Living out our values. Not tolerating difference but embracing it. Not mimicking another country or another place but being confident about our place in the Pacific.

I have never been a fan of being the 'Scandinavia' or the 'Singapore' of the South Pacific. Maybe we have what we need here. We might not have fully harnessed it, understood or even found it. But it's already here. Not perfect, by any means. But trying hard as a nation — to be good, to be our brothers' and sisters' keepers, to treat each other how we wish to be treated. My mother's words — a Kiwi creed.

Maybe that is what standing upright here means? The light in the eyes of the United Nations that is a school kapa haka group, the generation who define themselves, not burdened by labels and expectations, but being who they are. They have the chance to remake history, to mend the hurt of a colonial past.

Of course, we have far to go to realise our full and best self. To give the trans community their fair go, rather than turning them into an imagined enemy. To beat back racism and misogyny. But we are on our way. Fifty thousand people marched for Te Tiriti. In its dishonouring, in its honouring, in its imperfect partnership, it's ours — don't fuck with it.

Here at Otago, we are on a journey to be a Te Tiriti-led university. I love the challenge of exploring the possibilities of what that means. How fostering Māori and Pacific excellence will grow all our futures. How making sure that academic and research excellence and integrity are protected in a brave, new, modern world.

This is a reminder to me, the recovering politician, that there are so many ways to make a difference. In a political sense, it is no longer me but some other politicians working in a marvellous year who have that job. I congratulate them. It is a huge sacrifice, it is draining, but it is worth it. Just look after yourself — and your whānau.

The job for me now is to support others, to help grow the confidence of the next generation. To tell them that anything could happen, and it probably will. And to let them know that they will not know all the answers, they will not always get it right, but if you stay true and stand up, if you listen to others, and you take them with you on your journey, then it is all possible.

No longer imposters in their own land but rooted in it and its history, ready to take on the world. They are the ones who will stand upright here.

Kia kaha, kia māia, kia manawanui.
Be brave, be bold, be steadfast.
We've got this.

ACKNOWLEDGEMENTS

I wasn't sure that I wanted to write this book. As I was finishing up in Parliament I had in mind another book — one that allowed me to talk in detail about the Wellbeing Budget approach. Actually, I had one in mind even before that about Dunedin arts icon and top-tier homosexual Rodney Kennedy. I will get to them both in time.

I was worried that I did not have the perspective to write this book now, that I was still too close to it all. But the pace of history is quick nowadays. I could feel the story of my time in politics being written and set in concrete around me. I wanted to write about what happened and, perhaps more importantly, how it felt.

I am pleased I did. I am proud of what we did and how we did it, and I also know we did not get everything right. I hope you will see all of that in this book.

Doing justice to this task has felt daunting. I have been enormously helped by the team at Allen & Unwin. Michelle Hurley convinced me this was worth doing and gently guided me on the way. Jane Parkin has been a digital voice of patience and clarity as an editor. Thanks also to Annie Reed, Abba Renshaw and Leanne McGregor for their help.

Thank you to Holly Donald for her fact-checking skills, and for being the most exceptional of advisors in our time in government. To Stuart McKenzie and Miranda Harcourt, thanks for providing the transcripts of the interviews we did for the *Transmission* project.

To Jacinda. It is somehow fitting that we ended up writing books at the same time. I am so proud to know you as a friend, a leader and a decent human. Thank you.

So much of what is covered in this book is the work of others.

A heartfelt thank you to all those I have worked with over the years, especially those who worked with me as an MP and as a Minister: Sheila, Anna, Sophia, Kurt, Beth, Reed, Seamus, Kasey, Alka and Thomas in the electorate office, and Jen, Ange, Janine, Alex, Craig, Toby, Beth, Charlie, Sam, Chris, Ellen, Patrick, Peter, Katy, Francesca, Hayley, Claire, Ollie, Jack, Harry, and all the terrific Treasury and other public sector secondees, especially Alastair and Jordan.

To my parliamentary colleagues, I am so grateful to have worked alongside you. The life of an MP is an extraordinary one — so public yet truly known only to a few. I want to acknowledge the many friendships that have flourished amid that craziest of lives, especially with Megan, Chippy, Annette, Trevor, Dazza, Clare, David Clark, Kris, James, Tracey, Barb, Ayesha, Ruth and my brother Ibrahim.

In this book you will get a flavour of the importance to me of friends and friendship. In our world I don't think we talk enough about this. I love my family — and I also love my friends. A special thanks to Alex, Phil, Nick, Andrew, Nige, John S, John H, Rebecca, Nicole, Beth, Michael, Ant, David, Sean, Stephanie, Harp, Fraser, Raj, Mike, Heather, GJ, Davey and countless others for support in good times and in bad.

To the New Zealand Labour Party, my heartfelt thanks. As MPs we're nothing without the party and its people. Thanks to the once Young Labour, now 'middle-aged Labour' crew who helped me through my early campaigns: Reed, Patrick, Bridie, Sophie, Morehu, Kurt, Arena, Max, Ella, Mitch, Nevada, Seamus, Rory, Beth, Jessie, Katie, Luke, Sonny and Melissa — I love you guys.

I am especially grateful to the Wellington Central Labour Party, a wonderful collection of people. You worked so hard, you challenged me and supported me. Special thanks to Dinah V, Dinah H, Alan, Sheila and Andy, Philippa and Ralph, Hugh, Bev and Susan, Geoffrey and Margaret, Dolores and Barry, Rachel, Dorothy, Alana, Hilary, Tolly, Clare, Roger, Kate, Margaret, Fleur, Rebecca, Michael, Josh,

James, Alex, Andrea, Joey, Mohan, Jeremy, Jordan, Sam, Sara, Todd, Angus, Michael, Kathy, Freddie, Mara, Selvi and Stu.

To my brothers Stephen and Craig. Writing this book reminded me again what it is to be the youngest child. You are both inspirations to me and I love you dearly. I am still the academic failure of the family, but at least now I have a book to my name! To Delwyn, Erin, Cleo and Felix, thanks for being a part of the loving shambles that is the Robertson clan. And a special thank you to Craig for the suggestion of the title of this book.

On that subject I am especially grateful to David Kilgour and Bob Scott for agreeing to the use of the lyrics of 'Anything Could Happen'. I sometimes wonder what my life would have been like if I had not discovered your music and that of your Flying Nun contemporaries. Still the greatest sounds I have ever heard. Thanks also to Tim Finn for agreeing to the use of the 'Couldn't Be Done' lyrics, and to Nina Mingya Powles for her poem.

Mum and Dad gave us the best upbringing they could, and we always knew we were loved. As I said in my valedictory speech in Parliament: Mum, I have spent a lifetime trying to live up to your values, courage and wisdom; you are genuinely my hero. I am loving getting the chance to spend more time together. To Lisa, Campbell and Jess, thank you for your support of me, and especially of Mum. I ended up saying more about my dad in this book than I expected to. I miss you, Dad, and I love you very much.

To Hayley, Abe, Keira, Khloe, Miley and Kenny, and the Nolans, I love you guys. Thanks for all the hugs and support.

And to Alf. I know you hate being the centre of attention, and that your support and love for me is only matched by your dislike of politics. I think your distaste for the game of politics masks a set of values that are actually very political. I love your strong sense of right and wrong, your whanaungatanga, your humbleness and your lust for life. Thank you, my baby — let's keep having fun.

INDEX

Women Mean Business

Colonial businesswomen in New Zealand

CATHERINE BISHOP

OTAGO UNIVERSITY PRESS
Te Whare Tā o Te Wānanga o Ōtākou

For my mother Janet, who, I have learned,
should never be underestimated.

Published by Otago University Press
Te Whare Tā o Te Wānanga o Ōtākou
Level 1, 398 Cumberland Street
Dunedin, New Zealand
university.press@otago.ac.nz
www.otago.ac.nz/press

First published 2019

ISBN 978-1-98-853176-2

A catalogue record for this book is available from the National Library of New Zealand.

Published with the assistance of Creative New Zealand

creative nz
ARTS COUNCIL OF NEW ZEALAND *TOI AOTEAROA*

Editor: Anna Rogers
Index: Barbara Frame
Design/layout: Fiona Moffat
Author photograph: Jesse Taylor

Front cover: Mima Pitto probably wore a simpler hairstyle when working in her business. A straw-bonnet maker and dressmaker in Whanganui from the age of 17, she invested in business and property in Wellington after her marriage to John Pollock. *Miss Mima (Jemima) Potto. Harding, William James, 1826–1899: Negatives of Whanganui district, Alexander Turnbull Library, 1/4-008879-G.* Back cover: From left: Josephine Liardet; Makareti Papakura, 'Guide Maggie'; one of the Misses Jay. *Michelle Park Private Collection, Alexander Turnbull Library, PA1-q-012-39-2, Nelson Provincial Museum 10610*

Printed in China through Asia Pacific Offset

FSC www.fsc.org MIX Paper from responsible sources FSC® C136333

Contents

Acknowledgements

This book started life as one half of a PhD at the Australian National University, and would never have made it into print without the assistance of numerous people and institutions. I would like to thank my PhD supervisory panel led by the incomparable Angela Woollacott, and including Desley Deacon and Melanie Nolan. Thanks too to my thesis examiners Grace Karskens, Patricia Grimshaw and Barbara Brookes, who encouraged me to publish. My project was made possible by an ANU College of Arts and Social Sciences PhD scholarship and a New Zealand History Research Trust award from the Ministry for Culture and Heritage.

I also wish to thank Phillipa McGuinness of NewSouth Publishing who selected the other half of my PhD, on Sydney, for my first book. That allowed me to expand my scope to the whole of New Zealand and add considerable new research for *Women Mean Business*.

Staff at numerous archives and libraries in New Zealand and overseas are often the unsung heroes of historical research, and my debt to them is great. Historians around New Zealand and beyond also responded generously to my queries, providing information, copying archives and reading chapters. I am grateful to Pauline Weeks who promoted my project in the *New Zealand Genealogist*. As a result a number of family historians, whose work is so often underappreciated, kindly shared their research with me. Many of them, and others to whom I appealed, are acknowledged in the endnotes associated with particular stories.

I would also like to thank the following, with apologies to any I have inevitably left off this list, which spans 10 years since the start of my PhD project: Barbara Allen, Heather and Dave Arnold, Trevor Bentley, Sandi Black, Simon Bloor, Bettina Bradbury, Carol Byfield, Lloyd Carpenter, Jocelyn Chalmers, Nick Chin, Alison Clarke, Jenny Coleman, Martin Collett, Janice Cook, Kyle Dalton, Raewyn Dalziel, Gary Danvers, Kate DeCourcy, Raeone Dellaca, Stephen Donaldson, Rachel Fenton, Lynley Fowler, Lyndon Fraser, Darryl Gallagher, Keith Giles, Robyn Gosset, Martyn Goundry, Charlotte Greenhalgh, Adrian Humphris, Kate Hunter, Susan Ingalls-Lewis, Chris Johansen, Jenny Robin Jones, Ellen Jordan, Chris Maclean, Sarah Maclean, Jim McAloon, Linda McGregor, Russell McGregor, Jane Malthus, Kate Matthews, Hugo Manson, Tricia Meehan, Anna Monsoon, Clare Natoli,

Heather Newby, Maureen O'Connor, the late Gordon Ogilvie, Helen Pannett, Hazel Petrie, Katie Pickles, Ian Pool, Sandra Quick, Rebecca Reid, Ben Schrader, Jessie Bray Sharpin, Laurel Stowell, Lisa Truttman, Susan Upton, Angela Wanhalla, Jeanette Ware, Peter Warnock, Lydia Weaver, Alexa Whaley, Cynthia White, Gareth Winter and Stephanie Wyse. I am also grateful to the anonymous reviewers of the manuscript who engaged so helpfully with various drafts. Clearly history is always a collaborative enterprise, and much more rewarding as a result.

I have thoroughly enjoyed working with the fabulous team at Otago University Press. I would like to thank Vanessa Manhire, Rachel Scott, Anna Rogers, Imogen Coxhead, Barbara Frame, Fiona Moffat and Victor Billot. Together they formed a 'Department of Magic' and transformed my manuscript into a real live book.

Finally, I would like to thank my mother Janet Bishop, who has been an excellent research assistant and publicist; my daughters, who were forbearing of my unaccountable fascination with long-dead businesswomen; and my partner Richard White, who once again read, commented, encouraged and cared.

BILLIARDS.

S. P. JAMES AND SON

BEG to announce that, with a view to meet the wishes of a large number of their Constituents, they have FITTED UP the UPPER ROOM of their ESTABLISHMENT in Shortland-street, so well known as

THE Q. C. E.,

AS A

PUBLIC BILLIARD ROOM.

The TABLE, by Messrs. BURROUGHS & WATTS, is of the most modern and improved construction, with every appliance for the use of players; and the ROOM, for ventilation, light, and superior accommodation, both for players and those who may choose o be spectators, has, in Auckland,

NO EQUAL.

S. P. JAMES & SON,

WINE AND SPIRIT MERCHANTS, AND IMPORTERS,

SHORTLAND-STREET, AUCKLAND.

FAMILIES supplied with BASS'S PALE ALE, in 3, 5, 10 and 15 gallon casks
Whitbread's Double Stout, do., do.

The above can be had bottled by S. P. James and Son, either in pints or quarts.

☞ Goods delivered by S. P. J. and Son's light cart in all parts of the City and suburbs of Auckland, free of charge.

S.P. James and Son at the Q.C.E., all five initials confusing the public.

Daily Southern Cross, 16 March 1863

Chapter 1

Don't Assume It's a Man: Finding colonial businesswomen

What's in a name? In May 1859 Auckland's *Daily Southern Cross* published a letter purporting to be from an anonymous woman confused by 'those three large capital letters, Q C E, which have presented themselves in every part of the town'. What could they mean? A 'Quorum of Cabalistic Editors'? A 'Qualified and Competent Esculapius'? A 'Quiet Congregation of the Elect'? It was, she concluded, a 'Queer Concern Entirely'.[1]

Auckland would soon become familiar with the letters Q.C.E. By 1863 'S.P. James & Son', wine and spirit merchants and proprietors of the Q.C.E. Auckland Luncheon Larder, were well known.[2] They promised 'Quality, Cleanliness and Economy', with 'hot and cold luncheons' served 'in the style so eminently popular in London'. Locals continued to smile at the epithet, speculating that it really meant 'Questionable Company Encouraged', but it caught on. Q.C.E. hotels appeared elsewhere in New Zealand and New South Wales. It became a recognised shorthand used by catering businesses, although, oddly, when it reached the Northern Territory's Adelaide River, it became 'Quiet, Comfort and Ease'.[3]

What's in a name? The letters Q.C.E. might have caused consternation in 1859 but what about 'S.P. James'? Behind the anonymity of seemingly masculine initials was the exotically named Sophia Paris James. She inherited the enterprise from her husband, Lewis, when he died unexpectedly in 1861, aged 47. Instead of handing it to her sons, Sophia took the helm and the business expanded. With her oldest son, Lewis Rose James, she opened a wholesale liquor store on the other side of Shortland Street, while her second son, Duncan, managed another business in Mangapai, Northland. Sophia bought a large house on the Auckland foreshore and the trio took out second mortgages on all their properties to build a new hotel further up

Shortland Street.[4] But in February 1865 a fire swept through the street, destroying the almost complete hotel and bankrupting the James family. Sophia retired from business and moved to Wellington to live with her widowed daughter, who ran a boarding house popular with members of parliament. Lewis junior struggled on, opening another hotel, also called Q.C.E., but was again insolvent in 1871, perhaps missing his mother's guiding hand.

Although the use of her initials obscures Sophia James' activity as a business-*woman* in the historical record, everyone in 1860s Auckland would have known her business and her sex. And few eyebrows would have been raised, for she was not alone. Strolling through the streets of any town in New Zealand in these years one would have been hard pressed to *avoid* encountering businesswomen. There were all types, including milliners, dressmakers and drapers; women running schools

Although men dominate this picture of Shortland Street, women are busy in businesses. Sophia Paris James' Q.C.E. Hotel is fourth from the corner, and Mary Sims' Commercial Inn is on the next corner. Auckland Libraries 4-183

and keeping boarding houses, pubs and refreshment rooms; midwives, registry office managers, grocers, butchers, even a tinsmith.

Active female participation in business sits awkwardly with traditional images of colonial women. Raewyn Dalziel has described their role as 'colonial helpmeets'.[5] Nineteenth-century New Zealand was advertised as a land of opportunity for enterprising young men, ideally with families or a fecund wife. According to conventional wisdom, the development of a new economy of agriculture, manufacturing and mercantilism was men's business. Women were to add the civilising glue of social nicety and domestic comforts, produce the next generation of sons and heirs, and assist with whatever enterprise their husbands might decide upon.

The popular idea that 'traditionally' a woman's place was 'in the home' has coloured our understanding so completely that the 'businesswoman' is often considered to be a late twentieth-century phenomenon. Nineteenth-century women are usually imagined confined to the private sphere, constrained by broods of offspring, with their twentieth-century descendants gradually fighting their way into the marketplace. Historians, therefore, have not particularly looked for businesswomen in this period, and when we do stumble across them, in apparently small numbers in small concerns, they seem insignificant in the broader story of domesticated wives and mothers and entrepreneurial male pioneers. General New Zealand histories, even very recently, have been known to omit businesswomen, and often women generally, from any consideration in the context of the nineteenth-century economy.[6] This is despite the presence of such local histories as the *Women of Westland* series, in which entrepreneurial, economically active and self-reliant women proliferate.[7]

Although feminist historians have included some nineteenth-century businesswomen in broader studies, especially those discussing female participation in the labour market, Australasian business historians have had trouble seeing them at all.[8] Fairly typical is Ian Hunter's 2007 study of late nineteenth-century New Zealand entrepreneurs, which includes 125 men and eight women but does not recognise gender as a category of analysis. Hunter announces blithely that 'for the sake of style, where *he* appears in the text ... it should also be taken to mean she', and clearly considers a business owner's sex irrelevant.[9] As we shall see, it is extremely relevant, particularly in the nineteenth century, when legal, social, political and economic restrictions and expectations were highly gendered. Elsewhere in the world, business historians have treated gender more seriously. In 2005 British historian Margaret Walsh observed that 'it has become unacceptable to write business history which reports only male activities'.[10] Beatrice Craig's 2016 survey of trans-Atlantic businesswomen since 1500 is part of a new wave in global scholarship that analyses the roles of businesswomen and challenges the notion of a nineteenth-century 'retreat into domesticity'.[11]

This book turns the spotlight fully on New Zealand's nineteenth-century urban businesswomen to reveal that they were more numerous than usually imagined and were engaged in an extraordinary variety of enterprises.[12] It argues that, despite the rhetoric of female domesticity, running a business was neither unusual nor unacceptable for most women, and that in facing and overcoming – or not – the barriers in their way, they helped to shape the society in which we live today.

Businesswomen and/or entrepreneurs?

But what are businesswomen? Are they, for example, entrepreneurs? Definitions of this term vary. For Joseph Schumpeter, innovation is key: entrepreneurs 'revolutionise the pattern of production' through 'exploiting an invention' or new technology to make new commodities, find new suppliers or identify new outlets.[13] Ian Hunter's definition adds 'wealth creation' to 'risk, and judgemental decision-making, and proprietorship, and innovation, and newness, and coordination, and generating one's own income'.[14] Such definitions imply success, the desire for expansion and the world of big business. The frisson of excitement in moneymaking is palpable. Entrepreneurs are the heroes of economic development: they 'shape our world' as 'pioneers, profiteers and racketeers', in the words of Joe Carlin.[15] Business historians Frank Knight and Mark Casson, on the other hand, emphasise risk and responsibility more than innovation: entrepreneurs 'assume the risk of a business in return for the profits', making and accepting consequences of business decisions.[16] This is a more inclusive definition. Size, success and innovation are secondary characteristics. Innovation could be as little as, for example, recognising an opportunity for a laundry business in a raw settlement.

The businesswomen in this book were certainly entrepreneurial in that they owned businesses (sometimes with their husbands), took risks and bore the consequences of their decisions. They often risked everything, not because they put vast sums into untried fields of enterprise, using new technology or inventing products, but because failure meant that they and their often numerous children would be without a roof over their heads, clothes on their backs or food on their table.

Most were in business through necessity, but several had innovative business strategies and delighted in them. Mary Taylor's letters to her friend Charlotte Brontë exude excitement and pride in her Wellington haberdashery business.[17] Blessington Flood's numerous ventures, from wax flower lessons to importing servants, reveal her entrepreneurial nous. Eliza Tye took her Thames drapery 'on the road' through Māori villages in the 1870s, making her one of the country's earliest travelling saleswomen. Later she exploited the mania for alternative medicine, opening a hydropathic hospital in Takapuna. Drapery entrepreneurs, the Milne sisters as well as Marianne Smith, were alert to opportunities to buy up stock from failed businesses – the Milnes targeted Berry Cass in 1874 and Marianne bought out Jane Smith 10 years later.[18] Mary Ann Simpson reinvented her Thames millinery business in the 1880s, rebadging herself as 'Mrs Ah Mow' and importing tea, tea caddies, fancy goods, curios and fireworks from China.[19] Auckland stallholder Margaret Matheson Motion cornered the market with her 'Woodside strawberries, fine shrimps and oysters, eggs from Otahuhu, cabbage and cauliflower from Onehunga, and fresh butter from the Taranaki', which were 'as familiar as "household words"', according to the *Auckland Star* in 1876.[20] Margaret created an air of excitement around her stall. Her oyster sale in 1878 caused such a commotion that when a stranger was told there was a giant sea serpent on display, he believed it.[21] Surely entrepreneurial, too, was Napier laundress Mrs Baldwin, who not only promised 'neatness and despatch' when doing laundry herself, but diversified, begging to 'intimate to the Ladies of Napier, that she has a good MANGLE for hire'.[22]

A focus on entrepreneurship, however, can privilege overall 'success' rather than just muddling through, and big business rather than small. Most businesswomen, like most business*men*, ran small businesses with the aim of simply providing secure livelihoods for their families. Such concerns, often ignored in business histories, were the backbone of urban economies.

This book's definition of businesswomen includes both the spectacularly entrepreneurial and those who lived hand to mouth, running businesses out of sheer desperation. Businesswomen are those who, for varied reasons, earned money to support or help support themselves and their families, not as employees, but through their own enterprises. Their businesses might be part time or temporary, they might be self-employed or employers, but all were responsible, either alone or in partnership, for the multifarious decisions involved in their enterprises, and bore the risk of failure. Some had business nous, recognised opportunities in the market and sought to expand enterprises; others were happy simply to survive. Many did not even manage that. Women who hosted paying lodgers in their homes, took in laundry, delivered babies, cared for children, received a few 'young ladies ... to educate with [their] own daughters', or sold fruit and vegetables at the market or door to door were all businesswomen.[23] So too, as long as they worked for themselves, were tradeswomen such as milliners and dressmakers, feather cleaners and taxidermists, retailers who sold haberdashery, groceries, books, stationery, tobacco or any manner of goods, and entertainers who travelled around as professional singers, had their own theatrical troupes, ran tourist operations or earned a living by their pen or paintbrush. Brothel-keeping was a business, as was prostitution itself, when the prostitute was not an employee. And women in partnership with husbands, running shops, hotels or boarding houses, were all businesswomen, just as their husbands were businessmen. Even if the name above the door or on the hotel licence was

Midwife Catherine Holland's daughter Eliza opened the New Zealand Hydropathic and Fruit Hospital at Sunny Brae in Glenfield in 1890 with her second husband John Warmoll, exploiting the popularity of alternative medicine. North Shore Libraries, T2734

male, there is ample evidence that wives played significant, and often primary, roles in running family enterprises.

This book concerns businesswomen in towns, many of which were service centres for the rural hinterland, where women were equally involved in earning money, often as the suppliers for urban businesswomen. Many women ran farms, usually with husbands. They contributed to farm labour: keeping chickens, milking cows, making cheese and butter and jam and pickles to sell, raising pigs, growing vegetables or planting and harvesting crops. Often they were also the brains behind the operation, doing the books, marketing produce, spotting opportunities and making contracts with buyers and suppliers. Their contributions were critical. Much of the money made on the Campbell farm outside Whanganui in 1843, for example, came from Jessie Campbell's sales of eggs, milk and cheese, which, as she wrote in 1845, paid the shoemaker, tailor and washerwoman. French-born Hermanze Beetham was instrumental with her husband William in 1883 in the establishment of Wairarapa's first vineyard.[24]

The women in these pages generally began businesses between 1840 and 1880, when New Zealand's towns were emerging. The period after 1880 saw substantial changes, especially for women.[25] The Married Women's Property Act of 1880 gave married businesswomen living with their husbands significantly more rights to be treated as legally independent. Education become more available and opportunities for women's employment opened up, including in the professions by the end of the century. And some opportunities narrowed. Department stores expanded and began to replace small drapery shops and independent milliners; public schools multiplied, displacing small educational enterprises. These schools increasingly, however, employed female teachers, just as department stores employed shop assistants and craftswomen, and earning a wage could be more secure than running an independent business. Although a few later nineteenth-century businesswomen have sneaked into these pages, the main focus is to trace the experiences of those who, alone or alongside husbands, fathers, brothers, sons, sisters, daughters and mothers, negotiated New Zealand's mid-century economic booms and busts.

Needles and threads: Sources

The historical record is coy about revealing nineteenth-century businesswomen. Finding them has been akin to seeking needles in haystacks or pulling, very gently, on threads, to unravel stories of trade and enterprise.

Censuses provide an incomplete picture, particularly as New Zealand's census-takers, unlike those in Britain, destroyed individual returns, leaving only statistical tables. This means historians cannot see who was living with whom and doing what on a single night every 10 years.[26] New Zealand held censuses from 1851 but only in 1874 did the 'question of the employment of women' pique statisticians' interest and occupations begin to be coded by sex.[27] Before this, the category 'domestic duties or no occupation stated' was helpfully tagged as 'principally women and children'.[28] Even after 1874, statisticians noted that 122,216 out of 128,533 females were in the 'Domestic Class', leaving 'only 6,317 who were employed in occupations of other than a domestic character'.[29] Significantly, however, this 'Domestic Class' included 'those persons engaged in personal offices to man', which encompassed hotel and boarding-house keepers.[30] The relegation of such businesses to 'domestic' rather than 'commercial' categories undervalued the importance of female enterprise. They provided food to eat and places to sleep, along with rooms and bars in which to chat with friends, argue with neighbours, share a drink with old acquaintances – and perhaps do business. New Zealand statisticians, however, like their New South Wales counterparts, considered that a nation's prosperity was built on households of breadwinning husbands supporting domesticated wives and children.[31] This was entrenched in 1892 when Registrar-General Edward John von Dadelszen, who perhaps should have known better as two of his sisters ran private schools in the 1860s, separated occupation categories into 'Breadwinners' and 'Dependants: Non-Breadwinners'.[32] Wives were automatically categorised as dependants unless specifically stated otherwise. This downplayed any economic input by them, or their children.[33]

Neither did those 6317 women enumerated in the 1874 census as 'employed' include those who might not have declared an occupation, perhaps because it was part time, seasonal or temporary. As early as 1871 statisticians recognised that men often had multiple occupations and might prefer to declare some, 'perhaps from a notion of their superior "respectability"', rather than those in which they were 'most habitually engaged'.[34] But this logic was not applied to women, who were also engaged in numerous small-scale enterprises. Did they, or the husbands answering for them, find it more socially acceptable to put 'housewife', reluctant to declare their lodgers, or the laundry they took in, or the produce they sold? Or did they see such activities simply as part of being a useful wife? Similarly, when the category of 'wives helping' in family businesses was introduced in 1874, initial numbers were small. Defining exactly where domestic work ended and 'help in the business' started could be unclear, especially in a hotel or boarding house. Did making beds, cleaning and cooking, or supervising servants doing those tasks, count as business or domestic work?

It is necessary to look beyond the census. Trade directories are a useful starting point, although no more than that. Some include only paid subscribers, others only certain trades. The 1853 directory in the *Wellington Almanack* contains no grocers, midwives or boarding-house keepers, all common female businesses, and women in partnership with husbands are unnamed.[35] I soon developed a mantra: 'Don't assume it's a man.' The 1860 Auckland trade directory, for instance, lists tradespeople by initial, with only 14 out of the 374 listings, less than 4 per cent, identified as female with the title of 'Mrs' or 'Miss'. Adding in listings for private schools, which were also small commercial establishments, redresses the balance slightly. Of the 15 listed, 10 had identifiably female proprietors; three of these concerns were run by two female partners. This bumps the figure up to just under 7 per cent. But the picture changes more dramatically still when those 374 trade listings are checked

Businesswomen's row on Wellington's Lambton Quay. From the left, next to draper J.T. Steele (who sold his stock to Warnock, Kelly & Adkin) and grocer, H.F. Logan, was hairdresser Mary M. Price. John Cook's daughter-in-law Jane worked with draper Elizabeth Cowles next door, and his daughter Wilhelmina bought the Cowles business. Watchmaker Emily Woodford was next, with Fanny Hill's registry office on the corner.

Frank Arnold Coxhead (1851–1908), Businesses on Lambton Quay and Government House, Wellington. J.H. Christie Collection, Alexander Turnbull Library, 1/2-C-002259-F

GOVERNMENT HOUSE
WELLINGTON
COOK & SON.
COWLES.
HILL
REGISTRY
OFFICE

against newspaper advertisements. This reveals that another 46 of those initials actually hide a woman in business, either alone or with a husband. There were really 73 businesswomen involved in the 389 businesses and schools – nearly 19 per cent of the directory.[36] The same is true for other towns and cities: I estimate that around 20 per cent of businesses were run by women, alone or as partners.[37] And although they were neither the majority of women nor the majority of businesses, and obscured in the archive, these businesswomen were visible in the city streets.

I have used multiple sources to find businesswomen – like piecing together a large jigsaw puzzle without the benefit of the guiding picture on the lid. Trade directories, rates books and other lists gave me names to search, some leading to dead ends. Many, however – with the benefit of the international proliferation of digital data, including *Papers Past*, New Zealand's digitised historical newspaper resource – led to other names and bigger stories, taking me from Nelson or Wellington to Sydney to London to San Francisco and beyond. I found tantalising fragments of lives in letters, diaries and memoirs, in court reports, obituaries and newspaper advertisements. I have accumulated information from passenger lists, births, deaths and marriage records, probates, insolvency records and British census data, and have enjoyed fruitful exchanges with local and family historians, sharing those 'gold-dust' moments when one stumbles upon the missing cousin or sister or aunt and suddenly the whole jigsaw puzzle makes sense.[38]

Using all these sources, and adhering to my 'don't assume it's a man' mantra, allowed Sophia Paris James to emerge from behind 'Messrs S.P. James & Sons'. In Auckland at the same time, 'Powley and Johnson, milliners and drapers' were Harriett Powley and her son-in-law Edward Johnson, and it was Edward's wife who did the millinery with her mother. Widow Mary Bruce owned 'M. Bruce's' clothing store in Queen Street. M.A. Cox, milliner, was Mary Ann, as so many 'M.A.s' were. Alexander Pollock's butcher's shop was run by his wife Christina, with help from son Andrew: Alexander was at their farm at Drury, producing the meat. Elizabeth Holloway helped her husband Francis to run their Shortland Street coffee and luncheon rooms and later their Coromandel store, and Bryant Vercoe's wife Elizabeth was essential to the family hotel business. John Cavanagh was both a boot and shoemaker and a publican, so we can imagine who really ran the pub. After he died in 1863 his wife Catherine switched to boarding-house keeping. Andrew Otto's mother Eliza Rampling was the force in the grocer's shop they ran together. When Alfred Spalding died, his wife Anne took over the tinsmith, plumbing and zinc-working business, still advertising as 'A. Spalding', and Patrick Lorigan's widow

Ellen continued his timber yard, although she advertised as Mrs Lorigan. The cloth cap maker, J. Edwards, was really Ann, his wife, and Mrs Alfred Jones (Sarah) was the real linen draper in the Jones family business. And while George Chapman was busy publishing the trade directory itself from his premises in Queen Street, his wife Margaret was there too, running a servants' registry office.[39]

Many businesswomen's lives have, however, been frustratingly difficult to trace. Not everyone advertised in newspapers or had directory listings; few left business or personal records. Even Mary Taylor, proprietor of one of Wellington's 'principal stores' in the 1850s, relied not on newspapers to attract custom but, like others, on word of mouth or ephemeral handbills and posters.[40] Sometimes a woman's business life is visible in a fleeting mention in a diary, letter, memoir or family history. We know about Sophia Thomas's exploits, for example, only because a descendant recorded family stories passed down through the generations. Sophia, who arrived with her family in 1840, could read, though scarcely write, but was remarkably entrepreneurial. She ran multiple small businesses at various times to help make ends meet. She never had a shopfront, or advertised in newspapers, but she was constantly seeking ways to add to her husband William's income as a builder. In Wellington she put a sign in her window advising she could sew dresses, having taught herself by unpicking and making a pattern from one of her own. She told her grandchildren that she also made surplices, and even ran a dame school for a while. Later the family settled in Napier, where family history records that Sophia 'saw to it that [William] built a large substantial house in Emerson Street, where, by taking in lodgers, she could add to the family income'. Throughout all this she brought up several children, offered her services as nurse and midwife, especially in difficult cases, and was a popular and well-regarded member of the community. Sophia was a frequent visitor to Bishop William Williams and his daughters, 'the Hukarere Aunts'. Yet none of her business activities appear in the public record.[41]

Similarly, it is only through Grace Hirst's surviving correspondence that we know about the importing business she ran in New Plymouth. Her business was fairly discreet, as befitted her social status: the Hirsts were a prominent colonial family. Both well educated, Grace and her husband Thomas had spent the first 20 years of their married life in England, where Thomas tried and failed at numerous business enterprises and Grace gave birth to 11 children. Desperately seeking prosperity, they emigrated in 1851 to New Plymouth. Grace was the breadwinner. She lent money, traded goods supplied by her family back in Yorkshire, exported butter to Auckland and Sydney and produced candles and soap.[42]

Other women appeared momentarily in advertisements or were listed once in a directory but then vanished, the details of their lives and even their first names frustratingly obscure. As would be expected, women with common names, such as Wellington schoolteachers 'Miss Patrick' and 'Miss Hunt', proved impossible to trace. Equally, despite owning property in Wellington, milliner 'Miss E. Campbell' was sufficiently indistinguishable to be invisible. Surely, however, in this age of the searchable digital archive, the delightfully named Miss Peachy (or Peachey?), who had an Auckland boarding house for at least a decade, would be stalkable. She remains elusive. The equally exquisitely monikered 'Miss Plumb' advertised her services as milliner, dressmaker and mantle maker in Princes Street in Auckland in 1856: she also taught 'the elegant and fashionable employment of Wax Flower work' and offered for rent 'an apartment … for a respectable childless couple'. Notwithstanding this array of talents, she has been impossible to positively identify. She was possibly Emma Plumb, who was born in London in 1838 and arrived from Sydney on the *William Denny* in March 1856, before returning there early in 1857 and marrying Joseph Painter. Emma moved to Melbourne and eventually died in Arrowtown, New Zealand, in 1900 with a considerable estate; her executor was one Henry Plumb. But my dressmaker 'Miss Plumb' may have been someone else entirely.[43]

Other women are less obscure. A stroll through *Papers Past*, a serendipitous Google, a gossipy letter in the archives, and suddenly, out of the corner of your eye, you catch a glimpse of an entrepreneurial woman. Connecting the dots is easier when there are more records. When a woman married, or had children, when she moved about, or when she was involved in a court case or had dealings with someone whose letters or diaries survive, a richer story emerges.

Don't assume she's Pākehā

The sources, which also include shipping records and births, deaths and marriage records, were biased towards Pākehā. Nevertheless, the maxim 'don't assume she's Pākehā' also informed my research, and some of those women I could not trace to an immigrant ship were possibly Māori, with Pākehā fathers or husbands or anglicised names. I could not identify as Māori any businesswomen listed in directories or advertising in English newspapers, although I could not check every name in every town. Searching *Papers Past* yields, distressingly, thousands of entries for Māori women being raped, assaulted and murdered, but occasionally an entrepreneurial woman turns up in court: Pia, a 'woman of noted character' (a phrase often used for women who were prostitutes) was fined for drunkenness in Taranaki in 1864; 'Pete' (possibly Erepete/Elizabeth) was fined for sly grog selling in New Plymouth in 1887, as was 'Wiki' (Wikitoria?) at the 'native store' at Paemaka in the Waikato in 1899. Meanwhile, another Māori woman died while she was employed clearing bush at Rotorua in 1888, illustrating that such physical labour was not restricted to men.[44] I did find one advertisement in 1855 from a 'respectable hardworking native woman' seeking 'employment, such as washing, or to make herself generally useful about a house', surely appealing to Pākehā employers.[45] Several Māori language newspapers produced at various times contain advertisements from Pākehā businessmen and women, indicating an integrated market. Other advertisements might be from Māori entrepreneurs, although this area requires more research.

Although they seem not to have advertised, Māori businesswomen were certainly active. The first businesswomen in New Zealand to deal with Pākehā men were Māori. Women in Hauraki traded mats with visiting sailors, and in 1826 Mata Rawa, a Te Arawa woman, ran her own laundry business at Kerikeri, with customers among local Pākehā and from visiting ships.[46] Hazel Petrie has identified entrepreneurial Māori *Chiefs of Industry*, alongside whom Māori women actively participated in the colonial economy as traders, land negotiators, partners in family businesses – notably stores and accommodation houses – and independent businesswomen, often exploiting their cross-cultural connections.[47] Kahe Te-Rau-o-te-rangi, who married Jock Nicoll in 1841, owned and ran a Paekakariki inn patronised by Governor George Grey. She also signed the Treaty of Waitangi, was the grandmother of politician Māui Pōmare, crewed the boat on trading trips with her husband and was famous for swimming 11 kilometres from Kāpiti Island to the mainland with a child strapped to her back to raise the alarm about an approaching war party. Her innkeeping, while important in the context of this book, was perhaps one of her lesser achievements.[48] Huria Matenga of Te Āti Awa, more famous as 'the Grace Darling of New Zealand' for her part in a dramatic sea rescue, is one of several 'business-minded' Māori women who were instrumental in dealings over land, clearly wielding economic and political power. Huria refused to part with her substantial land holdings, instead leasing land to Pākehā farmers and thus becoming prosperous.[49]

Māori women exploited their local knowledge and access to land and networks. Ngawini and Samuel Yates built a large homestead and trading post on Parengarenga Harbour on the west coast south of Cape Reinga, using Ngawini's links with local iwi to facilitate the leasing and purchasing of land. She was an equal partner in the enterprise, which included forays into the local kauri gum trade and breeding bullocks.[50] Similarly, John Faulkner's wife Ruawahine, of Ngāi Te Rangi, was critical in their 1840s trading enterprise in the Tauranga area, while Piipi Raumati Cummins from Hokianga established a kauri gum store with husband Samuel at Waipoua in the 1880s.[51]

Selling fresh food was also a common business for Māori, although few Pākehā diarists and letter writers mentioned the sex of the seller.[52] One Motueka settler recorded that Māori women 'would arrive at the door, bent and stooping under the loads of potatoes for sale carried in flax baskets', and Māori women and men also gathered at the market and in Auckland's Queen Street to sell fruit and vegetables.[53] Susannah Wall, living near Wellington, told her sisters in 1842 that she 'can talk the native language pretty well so as I can be able to understand them and make a bargain with them'; she had 'a good deal of trade', getting blankets and clothing in exchange for pigs. She was proud that she could 'some times make pretty good bargins [sic]', but commented that it was becoming more difficult, as they were 'getting every day more knowing'.[54]

Elizabeth Caldwell, living on a farm near Nelson, remembered a particularly astute Māori businesswoman. Unable to cope with heavy laundry, Elizabeth was pleased when 'Mark's wife Amelia', a local Māori woman 'who had been in service in Town', agreed to take on the task. But Elizabeth was 'forced to agree to her terms': the washing would take 'a whole week' and cost £1.[55] Later, as the New Zealand tourism trade began to prosper from the 1870s, Māori women exploited their exoticism and local knowledge by running businesses as tourist guides.

Of course, not all immigrants were white. Agnes Grieve was born in Canada, the daughter of a Swampy Cree mother and a fur-trader father from the Orkney Islands. She married Orkney fisherman James Harrold in Hudson Bay in 1847 and moved via the Orkney Islands to Dunedin. After first running a store and the ferry at Taieri, the Harrolds moved to Stewart Island in 1861, where 'Granny' Harrold ran the Travellers' Rest, fostered numerous children and was doctor, nurse and midwife.[56] So, although the majority of the businesswomen in this book are Pākehā, women from other backgrounds also ran successful businesses as respected members of the community.

The impact of sex

Were women's businesses any different from men's? They were of similar size and longevity, family networks were important for both, and women could be as business-minded (or not) as men. But there were significant differences when it came to intergenerational transfer, access to credit and education, types of enterprise and the responsibility for children and household management.

Women's businesses, like men's, were, overwhelmingly, small-scale enterprises. Some started modestly and expanded, like the Milne sisters' drapery that became the major Auckland department store Milne & Choyce, or the competition, Smith & Caughey's, founded by Marianne Smith. But New Zealand's economy was, and still is, dominated by small businesses. Individually these may seem insignificant, but collectively they were critical, providing the essentials and luxuries of colonial life.

Women's businesses were almost as long-lived as similar-sized enterprises run by men. A very rough survey of Nelson's trade directories, from 1853 to 1883, reveals that both male and female businesses lasted eight years on average for those first appearing in 1856 and about seven and a half for those first listed in 1863.[57] Given that women did not tend to pass their businesses on to their children, several lasted a remarkably long time. In fact, of all the female businesses started between 1853 and 1856 just under 23 per cent survived longer than 17 years, compared with 30 per cent of male concerns. At the other end of the scale, 40 per cent of women were listed in only one directory before disappearing, while 30 per cent of men suffered the same fate. Although 60 per cent of female businesses lasted fewer than five years, so did 50 per cent of men's. It is notable, however, that most of the 14 female businesses that survived longer than 17 years were founded and continued by women; they were *not* male enterprises inherited by widows. Kezia, Winifred and Eliza Jay's dressmaking business appeared in the 1859 directory and was still listed in 1883. Fanny Drew's millinery business was there in 1856 and still there in 1876. Mary Ann Scaife was a music teacher between 1859 and 1883, after 13 years in the business in Britain, and Mary Ann Nalder ran a boarding house from 1863 until the mid-1880s. Harriet Green's drapery business survived from 1852 until at least 1876. Elizabeth Betts ran a seed store, with intermittent help from her husband, from 1856 until at least 1883. Elizabeth Taylor was variously publican, boarding-house keeper and confectioner between 1842 and 1878, surviving her husband's desertion in 1851.

It is difficult to establish why businesses ended. Sometimes they outlived their usefulness, or the owners moved away or died. Women sometimes, but by no means always, gave up business when they married or had children. Often businesses failed.

This should not be surprising. Even in the twenty-first century around 55 per cent of New Zealand's small businesses still fail within five years.[58] There were many reasons for failure: inadequate capital, cashflow problems, mismanagement, ill health, lack of family support or simply bad luck in New Zealand's boom–bust economy.

Business and family have always been closely connected, especially in the nineteenth century. Families were inclined to settle together, as Raewyn Dalziel's work on New Plymouth shows.[59] Successful businesses tended to be run by those with effective and affective kinship networks. A businesswoman with a supportive husband was likely to be more successful than one on her own, as was a businessman with a wife who was either a strong business partner or an efficient domestic helpmeet. In Auckland the business and kin network of the Hannken, Otto and Rampling families encompassed Queen and Wyndham streets. Elizabeth and Frederick Hannken had a drapery and general store in Queen Street. Later Elizabeth Hannken had a servants' registry office in Shortland Street. Her mother Eliza Rampling ran a grocery store in Wyndham Street with her son Andrew Otto. Another Otto brother ran a bakery around the corner.[60] Also in Auckland were the extended Henderson and Macfarlane families. Widow Ann Taylor (née Macfarlane), 'a really beautiful woman, with exquisite manners and address', emigrated in 1850 to join her siblings. '[D]etermined to win the daily bread for herself and her children', according to her daughter Mary Ann, she initially took over the management of the store at the family business, Henderson's Mill. Her brother-in-law Thomas Henderson thought her 'an excellent businesswoman'. Ann soon informed him that the store was 'too small', that she 'required scope', and she moved to a large shop next to Smeeton's buildings at the lower end of Queen Street, conveniently near the wharf. 'She sold silks, satins, cigars, in fact all that [her brother-in-law's] ships brought in from uttermost parts of the earth.' Mary Ann remembered that her mother 'made a great success' of her business.[61] That success was due to her own skill, but helped by the wider family business network.

Contrasting with these stories of mutually supportive kin is the sad story of Mary Frances Pittock, who arrived in Auckland in 1857 with her husband of three years, Charles, and baby daughter Sarah. She and Charles ran parallel schools for girls and boys first in the city and then, from 1860, in Otahuhu. Mary had four more children, all of whom died as infants. Then Charles died in 1865, aged 52, leaving 44-year-old Mary pregnant with another daughter, who died 11 weeks after birth. Mary could not sustain the business and closed the school. Her last remaining child, 14-year-old Sarah, died in 1870 and Mary, aged 50, was alone in the colony.[62] She worked for

Alice Glover at her Symonds Street school, the pair perhaps bonding over Alice's own loss of two toddler daughters. When Alice died in 1888 Mary moved to the Bay of Plenty. She ran 'morning classes' at her poignantly named Hope Cottage School until 1900 but also repeatedly applied for assistance from the Charitable Aid Board. Unusually for a lone woman without immediate family in the colony, her death in 1906 was recorded in the *Bay of Plenty Times*, suggesting that she was well respected in spite of her poverty. One can only imagine how much better she, and her business, might have fared, had her husband lived longer and their daughter Sarah survived to join the school business.[63] As we shall see, over and over again, personal and family connections were often critical to success.

One big difference between men's and women's businesses was that the latter tended to be single-generational. While men's businesses were handed down to sons and grandsons and occasionally became large corporate or even multinational enterprises lasting into the next centuries, women's businesses tended to remain small and were seldom passed on to daughters. The latter often married and began their own businesses, went into partnership with their husbands, or took charge of home and children. Female-founded businesses that survived into the twentieth century and into the next generation, sometimes becoming companies, were usually those joined by male partners, generally husbands or sons.

This does not necessarily mean that all businessmen were innately entrepreneurial or all businesswomen entirely unambitious, despite much rhetoric about women's and men's different natures. Most businesses, no matter who ran them, were small, suggesting that both men and women were working to achieve a comfortable lifestyle rather than from an all-consuming passion. In *Testosterone Rex,* Cordelia Fine shows how women's assumed aversion to entrepreneurial risk is a social rather than biological construct.[64] Some businesswomen, like some businessmen, were hard-nosed, as Catherine Ralfe discovered when she sought sewing work in Christchurch in 1866. Draper Mrs Black asked if she could sew a silk mantle similar to one in the shop. When Catherine said she 'would try', Mrs Black said that was not good enough – it was either yes or no. Catherine very sensibly gave a firm yes and did well enough to get further commissions.[65] Such 'unfeminine' decisiveness was necessary for a business to prosper.

Finding finance was an issue for anyone in business, but perhaps more so for women. Coverture laws meant married women had to operate through their husbands (see Chapter 4). Single women and widows could legally access business loans and capital on their own behalf from merchants or later from banks and other financial institutions.[66] But did they in reality? Women certainly took out insurance policies, operated savings accounts and were shareholders of companies. Convincing a merchant or bank to lend money, however, was another thing entirely.

There has been very little research on women and banks in New Zealand in this period. Anecdotal evidence suggests that much later, after World War II, banks discriminated against women, whether married or single. This does not mean the same was true of the nineteenth century. Until the 1890s, providing loans for property or business was the province of merchants rather than formal banks. Although much public rhetoric framed women as dependent and financially incapable, most businesswomen would have obtained their supplies on credit, as was customary. There are also a few examples of women both obtaining loans and mortgages and lending money themselves. Both draper Mary Bruce and schoolmistress Alice Glover had mortgages in Auckland.[67] Grace Hirst lent money at 15 per cent in New Plymouth.[68] Widowed Maria Thomson, Christchurch school proprietor, was embedded in the local financial elite. She owned shares in companies, had mortgages and lent money to working-class residents, while strategically mortgaging her own properties when necessary. Some of her pupils were from the upper echelons of Canterbury society and their merchant fathers did business with her. She was a good credit risk; success bred success, and once Maria had established herself as competent in business, her sex did not appear to be an issue.[69] Frances Townsend was variously a boarding-house keeper, publican, coffee-house proprietor and greengrocer in Nelson and then Wellington between 1865 and her death in 1894. In what the *Colonist* described as a 'novel incident', in 1879 she was appointed 'chairman' of a creditors' meeting, because she was the largest creditor. The newspaper reported that 'the remaining proceedings were in regular form', and a male creditor was appointed trustee.[70] Women, like many men, also looked to family for business loans. Mary Taylor and her cousin Ellen Taylor received funding of about £500 in loans and gifts from their brothers in order to open their shop. Mary felt entitled to their support, memorably advising her friend Ellen Nussey: 'Is it that your brothers won't give you money that prevents you coming out? – You should *plague* them till they are glad to be rid of you.'[71] It is telling, however, that it was the businesses in which men were also involved that really expanded, suggesting that men had greater access to capital, and greater persuasive power with other male investors. While women advanced all-important social connections, men could more readily exploit political and economic connections, especially through fraternal organisations such as Masonic lodges and chambers of commerce. Society also expected that men, but not women, would be ambitious in business.

As we shall see in Chapter 5, girls had scant access to secondary or tertiary education or to business training until the last quarter of the century. Professions and trades were gendered. There were no women lawyers or doctors. The first female medical graduate was Emily Siedeberg, in 1896, and a year later Ethel Benjamin was the first woman to graduate from law. There were not even female clerks until the 1890s. Young women could be apprenticed to dressmakers and milliners but not to carpenters, butchers or plumbers, although later in life they might well find themselves running such businesses, having inherited them from a husband or working in partnership with him.

A female economy

On the other hand, some businesses lent themselves to female management, potentially giving women a commercial advantage over male competitors. Who better than a woman to vet servants at a registry office, teach young ladies their manners and accomplishments, or understand the groceries, household goods and baby linen that a housewife required? Who more appropriate to deliver babies, sell corsetry and underwear, or more knowledgeable about the latest fashions in hats and dresses? Small general stores also catered to predominantly female customers because women were often responsible for buying food and household goods. Unsurprisingly, most businesswomen were found in needlework trades, followed closely by schools and hospitality, either because these were skills taught to and considered appropriate for girls, or because their clientele was mainly female.[72]

Few women owned large-scale manufacturing or import/export businesses or engaged in the staples economy, but New Zealand was built on more than banks and butter. In his timely study of New Zealand cities, *The Big Smoke*, Ben Schrader has described the colony's urban cultural milieu and its middle-class hegemony of taste.[73] One does not have to dig too far to find women running businesses essential to the development of that taste – producing the most fashionable hats, or the sweetest baby bonnets, supplying the best servants, playing or teaching music. These niceties of life turned an economy into a society. As we shall see, genteel society relied not just on domestic servants, but on an army of milliners and dressmakers, music teachers and providores (and brothel keepers). Working-class culture also relied on female businesses: pubs and boarding houses, market vegetable stalls and second-hand dealers.

Unlike most of their male counterparts, nineteenth-century businesswomen had no wives at home bearing and rearing their children. Married women running businesses often did so through a physically exhausting 20- or 30-year biennial cycle of pregnancy, birth, breastfeeding and sometimes miscarriage, along with the not uncommon deaths of children. They also had the primary responsibility for childcare and housework. New Plymouth school proprietor Sarah Pratt explained to her sister why she had no time to take music pupils after a morning's teaching: 'I put on the potatoes, sweep out the room, get baby's dinner and give Edith and Ellen theirs and take my own. By this time it is nearly three o'clock. I then wash up the dinner things and twice a week I make bread … and every day wash a couple of roundabout pinafores for baby. By that time it will be nearly five. I bake bread in the evening … my head is weak and my eyesight exceedingly so.'[74] She had 'no girl' at the time, but many women would have employed domestic servants, if their business or other income allowed. Older siblings would also be roped in to help. Nevertheless the dual responsibility for domestic and productive labour was borne by businesswomen but rarely by businessmen, affecting the way they conducted businesses.

Poverty and charity: A first cautionary tale

For many immigrants, the hope for a better life in New Zealand was realised. For others, the journey to a new world did not fulfil its promise. Reading the plethora of advertisements for women's businesses, it is easy to imagine them as respectable, profitable concerns, fulfilling a niche in the colonial economy and bringing their proprietors prosperity and property ownership. But an elegant advertisement could be a smokescreen for a shaky business. Poverty was one small misstep away.

Rather naively, the comfortably well-off Charlotte Godley, whose husband John Godley was a leading light in founding the Canterbury settlement, wrote that 'the pleasantest thing' about Wellington in 1850 was 'the total absence of poverty, or anything like it, among the people':

> They all eat meat, etc., as much, and as often, as we do. Meat to be sure is cheap enough, 5*d.* a pound for the best joints, butter 14*d.* and very good, milk 4*d.* a quart, cream sold by weight the same price as butter, the 2lb loaf 5*d.*, and we get excellent bread; beer bad, and 2*s.* a gallon. Bottled ale from England, 2*s* a bottle. Coals from Sydney 45*s.* a ton, but wood cheaper. You never see anyone who does not look comfortably off.[75]

Despite this picture of a working man's paradise, poverty was a feature of colonial New Zealand. Most susceptible were women, especially those whose husbands had died or deserted, leaving them with young children. Without family protection or financial means, their situation was dire. There was no state welfare: no aged pensions, no illness benefits, no safety net.[76] The precariousness of survival was even more profound for those suffering mental or physical disability. Rosina 'Rosie' Stafford, whose 'weakness of mind' prevented her from earning a living or even looking after her own clothes, was lucky. She found lodgings in Wellington with childless Ruth Bentham, herself the struggling widow of piano maker William. Ruth let rooms and business space to make ends meet, and when she died left her property in trust for Rosie, enabling her to survive.[77]

Friendly or mutual aid societies, including Masonic lodges, also provided assistance for those who could afford to join.[78] Churches gave charitable support at the parish level. The first Ladies' Benevolent Society in New Zealand was founded in Auckland in 1857, followed by Onehunga in 1863, with similar groups in Christchurch, Dunedin and Wellington in the 1860s. The first rescue home for 'fallen women' appeared in Christchurch in 1864. From 1867, the few church-run children's homes were added to by government homes for 'neglected 'or 'criminal' children. All charities were overwhelmed by the extent of female poverty. In 1860 the Auckland Benevolent Society identified drunken husbands as a principal cause of distress. Many women in this book bear testament to the impact of insobriety – their husbands' or their own. It is unsurprising that temperance became popular among women in particular.

Private, neighbourly charity was therefore essential in an era before the welfare state. It might be tempting to romanticise it as more effective than modern bureaucracy and indicative of a more compassionate community. On the face of it, for example, the story of Elizabeth Darby in Christchurch seems to be 'a cautionary tale from which modern society may well learn a lesson'.[79] In 1867 Elizabeth, the destitute widow of Sergeant Major Darby, a fencing instructor and publican, was able, thanks to a benefit concert arranged by friends, to take over a local delicatessen, 'set herself up in business' and 'become financially self-sufficient' until her remarriage four years later to William Price. Thus, it might seem, did Elizabeth become 'once more a self-supporting and self-confident member of the community, without having to go cap in hand to a government agency or a professional charitable organisation', as she would have done in the age of state welfare.

Unfortunately, there is more to Elizabeth's story. She did indeed become 'self-supporting' but not as a restaurant keeper. She advertised 'Darby's Restaurant' in Cashel Street in 1867, but was soon better known as a brothel keeper. She appeared frequently in court charged with drunkenness and keeping a particularly disreputable house and by 1870 was 'an old offender'.[80] She remarried in 1871 but not happily. Within months of the wedding William Price was charged with assaulting Elizabeth, and a year later a neighbour witnessed another attack: William 'struck her in the face with his clenched fist, knocked her down, kicked her when down, and altogether went on in a most disgraceful manner … Mrs Price's face was all covered with blood.' Elizabeth herself gave evidence that 'her husband came home drunk, and, without provocation, used her in a brutal manner: He struck her in the face, kicked her, and knocked her about, until her body was one mass of bruises, and she was scarcely able to stand. He also tore nearly all the hair off her head.' Inspector Peter Pender agreed that 'this was no exaggeration of the truth': she was 'in a frightful state'. Noting that Elizabeth was lucky not to have died, the judge sentenced William Price, who had seven previous assault convictions, to six months' hard labour.[81]

One of the saddest aspects of this story is that William had been beating Elizabeth *before* they were married. In 1870 he had been sentenced to one month's hard labour, after Elizabeth's son called the police. Detective Harry Feast found Elizabeth in her garden 'almost in a state of nudity, and covered with mud and blood'. She said this was not the first attack and that she was 'seriously afraid' of William.[82] Nevertheless, within the year she married him. She may have been desperate, with few other options.

Elizabeth Price continued to drink and made regular court appearances until 1890. In 1879 she applied for a protection order against William because of his 'continual drunkenness and misconduct'. Although the judge recognised William was 'such a weak-minded fellow that he could not refuse drink', he could grant the order only if they lived apart. Elizabeth explained that 'having no other home to go to she had no alternative but to remain' with her husband.[83]

Elizabeth Price's descent from apparently decent wife of a colourful but respected army man to drunk, destitute brothel keeper, shackled to a violent wife-beater, is indeed a cautionary tale. It highlights the precarious nature of life for women in colonial New Zealand and illustrates not only some of the advantages of the modern welfare state, but exactly why running a successful business, and choosing a reliable spouse, could be the difference between prosperity and penury.

Women mean business

The businesswomen in this book range from Elizabeth Price, who found the barriers to business success impossible to overcome, to Mary Taylor, who spent 10 years in the colony making enough money to return to England and support herself as a lady of letters.

Over 500 businesswomen appear within these pages, but not all businesswomen in New Zealand are here. There were just too many. Some colonial businesswomen are well known; they have appeared in print or in *Te Ara – The Encyclopedia of New Zealand*.[84] Many more have been lost in the sweep of history. Some are almost unrecoverable, while others, thanks to the digital archive, can be restored to the stories of New Zealand's colonial towns. Some women, whose stories are barely knowable, are mentioned in the hope that a reader will fill in the gaps, recognising a great-grandmother or great-great-aunt. By including both familiar and more obscure examples, I have sought to give a sense of the range of businesswomen's experiences, and to rescue them, in E.P. Thompson's memorable phrase, 'from the enormous condescension of posterity'.[85]

One of the most compelling findings in this study has been the diversity of businesswomen's experiences: no one was typical. They were young, middle-aged and even elderly; they were single, married, deserted and widowed; they included women born in New Zealand as well as immigrants from multiple countries. Although their families were predominantly working class or tradespeople, they engaged in a variety of businesses. As might be expected, many exploited 'feminine' skills, but others took up more 'masculine' businesses: butchery, bakery and bootmaking, taxidermy, pharmacy and hairdressing. In the nineteenth century hairdressing was a male business, its feminisation a twentieth-century phenomenon.

The following chapters bring these businesswomen to the fore, replacing them in their shops, hotels, workshops, boarding houses and brothels, and back out on the street for all to see. The following chapters set the scene, investigating ideas about 'woman's place' in the colony, outlining the nature of New Zealand's towns and economy, and delving into the legal niceties of coverture, separation, bigamy and divorce. The next six are devoted to different types of businesses run by women. The penultimate chapter looks at mobile women who flitted from one town or colony to another, and the final chapter considers our remembering and forgetting of these often remarkable entrepreneurs.

Illustrating the interconnectedness of business communities in colonial New Zealand, a young George Leslie Adkin, son of William Adkin of Warnock, Kelly & Adkin, poses with his grandmother, Eliza Ann (Lizzie) Denton, and an elderly Susan Waters, erstwhile shopkeeper, whose letters in 1842 were used by emigration boosters to illustrate the opportunities offered by colonial life. The photo was taken by George's uncle, Frank Denton. According to some sources, George's mother Anne (née Denton) was also a photographer. Frank Denton, Alexander Turnbull Library PA1-0-132-20-2a

CHAPTER 2

Women's Place and Men's Responsibility

'It is a truth universally acknowledged, that a single man in possession of a good fortune, must be in want of a wife,' wrote Jane Austen, famously, in 1796. Equally in want of wives were young male emigrants to New Zealand, half a century later. They may not yet have possessed a good fortune, but they were nevertheless exhorted to find 'useful wives' before embarking. Young, single, working-class girls were also encouraged to head to the colonies, to work as domestic servants and provide conjugal options for those male emigrants who foolishly forgot to pack a wife. How then did the phenomenon of a businesswoman, making autonomous financial decisions, fit into this domestic plan?

Family migration was key to New Zealand's early settlement. Edward Gibbon Wakefield's scheme of systematic colonisation, according to which several towns were originally settled, sought families rather than single men. Its advocates hoped to transplant a cross-section of British society and create a new, improved version of it at the other end of the world, built around family groups headed by a male breadwinner, with a useful wife and children as desirable accoutrements.[1] So, while a huge nineteenth-century publicity machine painted New Zealand as a land of economic opportunity for enterprising and hard-working young men, the ultimate aim for female emigrants was marriage, raising children, keeping house and providing havens of tranquillity for their breadwinning spouses. In one of the few advice books written specifically for the Australasian market, *Woman's Work in Australia* (1862), New Zealander Susan Nugent Wood exhorted women to live not for themselves but for their families: 'Woman is the helpmeet, the beauty, the glory of man … Woman's work must begin at home.'[2]

From 1854 until 1870 New Zealand's provincial governments had independent immigration policies. These varied according to perceived gaps in the population, but single women were generally on the list of desirables, particularly in provinces where hosts of single men were seeking gold. In that period around 12,000 single women arrived as assisted immigrants, some alone, many as part of family groups. Two-thirds of them went to Canterbury. After 1870, Premier Julius Vogel developed a New Zealand-wide immigration programme importing about 100,000 assisted immigrants in a decade, about 20,000 of them single women.[3]

The male breadwinner and the masculine ideal

Sole breadwinning, promoted in emigration propaganda, became an important marker of status for white married men, as Annabel Cooper has described. It was achievable, she argued, in the New Zealand of the 1850s and 1860s, but not in the Long Depression of the 1880s and 1890s, when men's masculinity was threatened.[4]

This ideal could be as burdensome for men as domestic expectations could be for women. Some husbands found an independent wife hard to endure. Sarah Wood was in business as a midwife and monthly nurse in Auckland. In 1866 her husband Edward, a house painter aged 60, showed 'great determination' in cutting his throat with a razor, 'a piece of rag having been bound round the joint to prevent it slipping back'. Sarah told the inquest of his past 'fits of melancholy' and suicide attempts, brought on because 'he could not bear to be supported by his wife'.[5] At the other extreme were men who were only too pleased to find a moneymaking wife and took full advantage, drinking and gambling the proceeds of their spouse's business. Or perhaps they were just incapable, like George Rich, husband of mission schoolteacher Elizabeth: Bishop William Williams described him scathingly as 'not a man of much energy, but he can mind the household staff while Mrs Rich attends to the more important part'.[6] In between were the majority of men who had a pragmatic approach, appreciating a useful colonial helpmeet who might have her own business when necessary but relinquish it when no longer required.

The *idea* that Pākehā men should be providers was ubiquitous. James Rollason was blamed when his wife Amelia, a Wellington boarding-house keeper, went bankrupt in 1893, well after the law recognised women's property was their own. The official assignee stated, rather hopefully, that 'her husband is an artist and should be able to support her', and blamed Amelia for a 'foolish' business transaction made 'on the advice of her husband', as if she had no mind of her own. Her bankruptcy apparently had nothing to do with her being a 'bad, bold woman [who had been] well known in Nelson ... for keeping a house of ill fame and sly grog selling'. (Both Amelia and James had had spouses already when they married, but that is another story.)[7]

The ideal colonial helpmeet

The counterpart of a male breadwinner was a domestic 'colonial helpmeet' wife. Most New Zealand women got married, for a multitude of reasons, including societal and family expectations, affection and financial security. Life as a spinster or widow could be lonely, socially precarious and physically unsafe. Widowed dressmaker Maria Forrest, who lived on her own in Napier in 1860, suffered 'the greatest annoyance and alarm from the frequent and cowardly attacks made upon my house by ruffianly persons at unseasonable hours of the night'. Clearly at the end of her tether, she promised in the *Hawke's Bay Herald* to 'most certainly shoot the very next aggressor who disturbs my repose'.[8] She remarried within a year. Rebecca Sharp was a single dressmaker in Nelson, also living alone. In November 1860 she accidentally left her bedroom door unlocked and was attacked by the local constable, William Barry. Recently separated from his wife and prone to overindulgence in drink, he brandished a sword and grabbed her by the throat, later telling the court that it was all in jest. He was not imprisoned but bound over to keep the peace and had to find £40 in sureties. Two months later Rebecca, perhaps seeking protection, married Sergeant John Barton of the 65th Royal Tigers, 28 years her senior.[9]

Married life for women was often a full-time job in itself and, as feminist historians have shown, women's reproductive and domestic work had significant economic value. Through their management of hearth and home, argued Heidi Whiteside, busy wives and mothers contributed to 'the independence of the self-supporting household'.[10] Colonial wives produced and reared the labour force. Not all children survived – sometimes a family would lose half of their offspring, either at birth, soon after, or to typhus, diphtheria and other diseases. Occasionally, as in the case of Mary Pittock, none survived. But it was common to see families with 10 or 15 children raised to adulthood.

A wife was also responsible for housework, shopping and producing meals. This was labour-intensive for working- and middle-class women alike, as domestic servants were scarce. Wives and daughters, who in England might have imagined they would be directing others to do household chores, found themselves sweeping floors, making beds, laying fires, churning butter, baking bread, butchering chickens and repairing the family's clothes. Frances Shayle George, a lawyer's wife, school proprietor and writer, warned migrants they would need to work – 'and work hard' – or they 'had better stay at home'.[11] Teacher Elizabeth Caldwell learned new domestic skills, such as bread-baking and butter-making, all of which were time consuming. Her rose-tinted memoirs tell that she 'greatly enjoyed the easy way of life then the fashion in New Zealand [with] scarcely any furniture'.[12] Because colonial middle-class women did so much more than their English counterparts, Elizabeth was convinced that the climate imparted 'supernatural strength'. Mary Taylor also observed, in 1851, that colonial women had 'more energy' than their English counterparts, who were 'never called upon to stand alone or allowed to act for themselves, [so] of course they lose their wits in time'.[13]

Middle-class women may have swept more floors than they would have liked, but they endeavoured to preserve social distinctions, notwithstanding Mary Taylor's observation that 'classes are forced to mix more here, or there wd be no society at all'.[14] Sarah Pratt, proprietor of a New Plymouth ladies' school, appreciated middle-class niceties and was in awe of Martha and Maria King who ran the 'top school' in town. She wrote to her sister, 'I do not suppose I shall ever know them as they live very comfortably and genteely as we should say.'[15] Elizabeth Caldwell seemed disappointed by colonial insistence on keeping up appearances: 'I thought before I left England that having to do everything yourself would induce people to relax a little in matters of display, but it is only as little as possible.'[16] Nelson's Martha Adams was amused by the unspoken rule that no one went calling until the afternoon so middle-class wives and daughters would not be caught doing household and farm chores.[17]

After lunch these hard-working housewives transformed themselves into visiting ladies, producing the social lubricant to facilitate their husbands' careers and, equally importantly, gossiping about New Zealand society. They formed church committees and ladies' benevolent societies; they raised money for church buildings and other charitable concerns; they took tea with one other, policed societal hierarchies and, through dinners, balls and parties, forged social networks that complemented their husbands' professional ones. These women were from or aspiring to be part of the articulate educated middle class, the leaders of New Zealand society. Their opinions dominated public rhetoric in newspapers and parliamentary debates, and their voices resound in the surviving documentary archive. Their understandings of female respectability – the domestic sphere of marriage and motherhood, female accomplishments and sociability, unimpeachable morality and quiet character – have been well articulated by historians.[18] The men of this class in New Zealand, meanwhile, wielded economic and political power in the rough and tumble of the 'public sphere'.

Ben Schrader credits this class with making modern urban New Zealand society.[19] He paints a rich picture of the 'cultural and social life of cities', focusing on 'the lived experience' of townspeople's existence outside work.[20] But as he surveys New Zealand's five main towns – Auckland, Wellington, Christchurch, Dunedin and Nelson – the lives of tradespeople and businesswomen, shopkeepers, servants, publicans and labourers are largely invisible. When it comes to gendered public spaces his focus is on middle-class leisured women. Their social lives, he writes, were primarily conducted inside. Only in their shopping and philanthropic work, important exceptions, were they 'permitted on the streets'.

But most colonial families were not middle-class. Schrader acknowledges that 'working-class women and prostitutes' – an unfortunate elision – 'occupied city space as public women', and that for them 'the street itself was an important site of sociability'.[21] Working-class women were also visible because they contributed economically to the making of urban New Zealand. Many may have had middle-class aspirations to a domesticated life, but these were not necessarily attainable. Much as in Britain, a wife needed to produce an annual income along with the biennial baby. The 'sole male breadwinner' ideal relied heavily on the contribution of wife and family. In the country, farming was about teamwork. As colonial propagandist Charles Terry enthused in 1842, 'If a settler occupies a small farm – and he and his sons cultivate the land, while his wife and daughters rear poultry, attend the dairy, &c. without any expense of other assistance – they are creating an active capital, and increasing property, not only for themselves, but for the Colony at large.'[22] William Dawson and his wife, for example, ploughed together in Clutha in the 1850s, using 'a horse, which Mr Dawson led while Mrs Dawson held the plough handles'.[23]

Teamwork was also necessary in urban families. The work of a 'useful wife' spilled out of the domestic sphere. Charles Hursthouse's picture of the opportunities for emigrants was explicit: 'Any active tradesman or brisk shopkeeper … would succeed in creating his little landed estate … he could keep both shop and farm – wife and daughter looking to the one, son and self to the other.'[24] Although Hursthouse ascribed ownership of the shop to the husband and father, which was legally correct, the wife was the active tradesperson and shopkeeper. Frederick and Eleanor Olson epitomised this partnership in Christchurch in 1859: Frederick and their son ran a bootmaking business, while Eleanor and their daughter had a boarding house.[25] Acknowledging that 'colonial helpmeets' sometimes also contributed to family economies as assistants in family businesses or in their own enterprises, Raewyn Dalziel mused in 1976, 'It would be interesting to know more details about the contribution women in New Zealand made to family budgets'.[26] Forty years later, with technological developments in archives enhancing the visibility of colonial businesswomen, we can see that being in business was an acceptable and natural extension of the colonial helpmeet role, for both middle- and working-class women.

Middle-class Sarah Greenwood epitomised the colonial helpmeet, and was far more than 'the dearest little old lady' described by one of her school pupils. Her surviving letters show she had a razor-sharp mind, a sense of humour and was an astute businesswoman. She arrived in Nelson in 1842 aged 33, with her doctor husband and eight of their nine children. The Greenwoods were among Nelson's leading families: Dr Danforth Greenwood held a number of public roles. As well as raising and educating her 13 children, with whom she provided the backbone of local musical entertainment, she hosted visiting dignitaries and other travellers and – her principal claim to fame today – was also an accomplished artist. She threw herself into colonial farm life, proudly listing her many daily tasks in a letter to her grandmother: 'I sell milk … And (now for the grand triumph) I sell and make butter: and delicious butter I would have you know … Then I sell pork of my own feeding and salting, we sell our potatoes, and, sometimes a few cabbages'.[27] Later she ran a respected school with her daughters. Her praises were sung far and wide by many male visitors; her female neighbours must have found her perfection intimidating. Eminently respectable, she was the lynchpin holding her family together, both economically and emotionally, a typical 'colonial helpmeet' whose role encompassed business as well as domesticity.[28]

Further down the social scale business was also respectable. Robert Boddington, writing to his family from Nelson in 1842, was pleased with his new house, in which 'one window is occupied by my wife's shop, and the other by watches which I have for sale, and to be repaired and cleaned'. Ann's grocery shop had 'every prospect of doing well'.[29] Also in 1842, John Philps, a Wellington brickmaker, commented that his wife Catherine was doing nursing, and David Harris wrote to his mother suggesting his 'dear sister Jane would do well here, with needle-work for men or her own sex'.[30] William Henwood, an early New Plymouth settler, told his relatives: 'I have got the first cow in the country … one nanny goat, and two cats;

and the best of all, I have got a nice little wife; she is a merry one, and a clever one too.'[31] The inclusion of his wife, Ann Putt, in a list of livestock is a little concerning, but as William went on to run several hotels, he doubtless valued his clever, merry wife even more: a woman was a welcome, profitable, even necessary addition to the trade of a public house. These letters were all published in 1843 to promote emigration, suggesting that for those seeking to shape the new world, the ideal colonial helpmeet could be a businesswoman.

'To get an honest living for my familey'

There is little evidence about the motivations of nineteenth-century New Zealand women who entered the sometimes murky world of commerce. Running a business was usually a means of financial survival or economic advancement, just as it was for men. For single women it could provide a way to avoid marriage, or survive without it; for wives it contributed to a family income; for deserted wives and widows it could provide independence from charity. For the spouses of men like Dr Frederick Knox, who, Mary Taylor scornfully observed, would 'neither do any work nor follow his profession but will live on his wife', cobbling together a living was essential: Mary Knox, she said, 'maintains herself and the children principally with my lodging and a little sewing and some charity'.[32] Susannah Wall, who settled with her family between Wellington and Porirua in 1842, combined an accommodation house with keeping pigs, poultry and cows and a vegetable garden, telling her sisters 'the greatest comefort to me is to get an honest living for my familey'.[33] In the 1860s, Elizabeth Garland, feeling 'that she too should be doing something to help the purse', went out as a midwife and monthly nurse to local women. Her daughter Emma Adams recorded this small business in a 1937 memoir, but by the end claimed the story showed 'how women helped each other in those early days'.[34] This is a stark illustration of a subtle shift in representations of colonial women in middle-class memoirs. A contribution to the family economy was turned into a respectably feminine service to community. There was no discussion of whether Elizabeth Garland enjoyed her enterprise, either through earning her own money or escaping from family duties. By the twentieth century the middle-class rhetoric of female domesticity had triumphed over the pragmatism of the nineteenth century, when being a businesswoman was a respectable female activity, although it was not done to admit to pleasure or ambition in this role. It was a fallback position if marriage did not eventuate, or was undertaken in service of the family economy.

Women sometimes complained of the added burden of business. Wellington school proprietor Jane Spinks wrote in her diary of being 'very angry this morning with M Smith about her … lesson', admitting that she was 'too often irritable with the children'. Jane blamed her shortness of temper on 'a slight cold', but she may not have enjoyed teaching and been relieved to give it up when she married. Her spinster sister Florence was left to cope with the sometimes inattentive pupils for another 10 years.[35]

Necessity, then, motivated many. But there could be more to it. In 1852 that paragon of Nelson, Sarah Greenwood, gave one of her seven daughters some sound advice: 'Independently of all other considerations I honestly think that a life with a specific object to look to is a far happier one than when passed simply doing one's share of sweeping and stocking mending. This belief makes me feel that if a woman has no object she is wise in making one for herself.'[36] That object could be making money, and a successful business could also bring satisfaction and pride. Elizabeth Caldwell, for example, claimed she started giving piano lessons to serve her community, but as these developed into a school, she also, unusually, expressed her pleasure in a job well done.[37]

Single women showed initiative, using business and migration to survive without a husband. Despite the imagined hordes of bachelors desperately seeking wives, some migrants remained lifelong spinsters, whether through choice or circumstance; others bided their time and supported themselves until the right spouse came along. Some ran a business until marriage, to escape marriage or because marriage never eventuated. For many, economic survival was precarious; for others, their self-reliance guaranteed respectability.[38] Some women even emigrated as confirmed spinsters or as widows with children, often leaving behind family and friends as well as established businesses. The image of the typical nineteenth-century migrant is of a man, sometimes accompanied by wife and children, or a young, husband-seeking woman. Some women, though, migrated independently or at the head of their family and they did so for a variety of reasons.

Widow Martha King may have left England for health reasons or perhaps seeking advantages for her children. She arrived aged 36 with three daughters and a nine-year-old son, all cabin passengers on the *Cressy*, one of the first four Canterbury Association ships to reach Lyttelton in 1850. She came from Earl Spencer's estate at Harleston in Northamptonshire, where her husband had been a huntsman and where the rest of her family were employed. She must have had capital: she built a house on the Esplanade in Lyttelton and opened 'Commercial Dining Rooms', cashing in on newly arrived immigrants' need for refreshments. Initially in business with a Mr Beresford (possibly *Cressy* crew member William), she was soon on her own when her partner started a carting business. Although she did not advertise for long in the newspapers, she seems to have been in business until her son grew up. He was successful and her daughters married well; Martha lived until 1884, perhaps longer than she might have done in England.[39]

Annie Whiteley Nowell's motivations for emigration are less clear. She disembarked in Auckland in 1854 with 10 years' experience in the millinery and cloak-making business. She had been in partnership with Sarah Hervey (as Hervey & Nowell) until 1845 and then had her own shop and boarding house in Halifax, Yorkshire. When she migrated she left behind at least two sisters, one a spinster dressmaker in Leeds, the other recently married in Liverpool. Another sister had died two years earlier in London. Their scattered locations suggest that either the family was not especially close or that economic reasons had forced their dispersal. Annie's dual businesses of boarding house and shop in Halifax may have meant neither was viable. She may also have heard positive stories about other emigrants from the local area. By 1854 Mary Taylor, from Gomersal, just 1.6 kilometres from Birstall, where Annie grew up, was already a success in New Zealand. Annie, however, was in business for only seven years before she died in Auckland's Provincial Hospital, aged 40.[40]

The persuasive power of word of mouth (or letters) from successful emigrants cannot be underestimated. Annie Nowell's knowledge of Mary Taylor's experience is speculation, but the connection between the Jay sisters and earlier emigrants is explicit. They are a key example of chain migration, in which people from the same family or area followed one another to other countries over a number of years. This was facilitated by early emigrants sponsoring later ones. Eliza and Kezia Jay ran a shop selling Berlin wool, a specialist embroidery material, in posh Rowcroft in Stroud, Gloucestershire, before migrating to Nelson in 1858. Four years later their older sister Winifred joined them.[41] Why did three spinster sisters, all in their forties, emigrate from Stroud, where their business in an upmarket parade of shops had survived for several years? Their parents had died, but they still had other family in the area, including a married sister, schoolteacher Sophia Coley, and nieces and nephews.

Emigration was common in the region, which had been hit hard in the late 1830s when the East India Company lost its export charter to China for the particular cloth 'stripes' woven in Stroud and many found themselves unemployed.

Local families had been leaving for the United States, Canada and Australia since the 1830s and Stroud citizens were some of the first to settle in New Zealand in 1839.[42] George Hooper and his family, good friends of the Jays, had emigrated to Nelson in 1842 after his butcher's business failed. Hooper did well, establishing a brewery that became a local landmark. When he visited England on holiday in 1857 he was a living, breathing exemplar of a successful emigrant.[43] On the same ship back to Nelson a year later were Kezia and Eliza Jay. Perhaps the competition from Miss Eliza Rosetta Humphries' new Berlin wool shop, which had opened up right next door, was too strong. Perhaps they had read the 1856 feature on 'The Progress of Nelson' in the local *Cheltenham Examiner*.[44] They also had the support of the Hoopers, who belonged to the same Baptist church; George Hooper later offered to co-sponsor Winifred's migration. Armed with the confidence that they could run a successful business, comforted by the presence of friends already in Nelson and of each other, also perhaps eager for adventure, Kezia, Eliza and Winifred defied notions of safe, sensible spinsterhood and shifted their business to the other side of the world.

'A radical step away from convention?'

In its conception and execution, Wellington haberdasher Mary Taylor's colonial adventure was not what might be expected of a woman. Her sojourn was temporary, her aim to make money. Unusually, she recorded her motivations for both emigration and business in deliciously frank letters to Charlotte Brontë and Ellen Nussey in England. These survive principally because of the connection with her rather more famous literary friend.[45]

Mary was a feminist, with strong ideas about women and work that she expressed in private correspondence and in her later publications: 'A woman who works is by that alone better than one who does not and a woman who does not happen to be rich and who *still* earns no money and does not wish to do so is guilty of a great fault – a dereliction of duty.'[46] Some historians have described her as a 'novelty' in New Zealand because she was a woman 'working for a living' – taking 'a radical step away from convention'.[47] Despite her radical ideas, however, and her cultivation of an eccentric intellectual persona in Wellington, she is not mentioned in fellow settlers' letters and memoirs. Perhaps she did not stand out quite so much as she imagined. Running a business was, after all, not uncommon. Mary's point of difference was her explicit expression of a sense of achievement and independence.

She felt stultified by convention in her small Yorkshire village in the 1840s. 'Did you ever notice,' she asked Charlotte, 'that the women of the middle classes are generally too ignorant to talk to, and you are thrown entirely on the men for conversation?' Only Ellen Nussey was worth talking to, 'that I know of at least'.[48] In 1848 Mary Taylor escaped to New Zealand. Initially she taught piano and invested in cattle and property, building shops in Wellington's Cuba Street and living with her brother Waring Taylor, who acted as her agent.[49] When her cousin Ellen Taylor, who had 'just the same wish to earn her living as I have and just the same objection to sedentary empl[oy]ment', arrived in 1850, the two women set up a new business.[50] After considering a school or a shop, they decided that the 'most healthy' choice, although 'the most difficult of accomplishment', was a drapery and haberdashery shop, selling such wares as socks, muslin, ribbon, hats, gloves, cotton and needles. It was a serious moneymaking enterprise: Mary calculated they could make profits of about £300 on an initial investment of £600.[51] Nevertheless, Ellen recorded that 'our keeping shop astonishes every body here, I believe they think we do it for fun'.[52] And there was a sense in their letters that it *was* all an adventure, a grand lark, albeit with profits in mind. The cousins divided home and shop duties between them, taking turns as housekeeper and shop assistant. As Mary wrote to Charlotte, they 'enter[ed] heart and soul into the *project* of keeping a shop'.[53] 'How eagerly we open the packages … How we work! and lift and carry … and sit in the midst of the mess when we're quite tired … and find it is the middle of the afternoon and we've forgotten our dinner!'[54] When Ellen died of tuberculosis in December 1851, Mary, who had nursed her cousin, soldiered on alone, though some of the 'fun' had gone out of her enterprise. And she missed her companion. 'I began a letter to you one bitter cold evening last week,' she told Charlotte in 1852, 'but it turned out to be such a sad one that I have left it and begun again. I am sitting all alone in my own house, or rather what is to be mine when I've paid for it. I bought it of Henry [her cousin] when Ellen died, shop and all, and carry on by myself.'

Although she had decided not to get any help – 'the annoyance of having an unsuitable companion was too great to put up with without necessity' – in the end she found a sufficiently suitable assistant in Margaret Smith.[55] And her shop continued to be successful, listed as one of the 'principal stores' in the 1853 *Wellington Almanack*. As she told Ellen Nussey in 1857, with some pride, 'I look after my shopwoman; make out bills; decide who shall have "trust" [credit] and who not. Then I go buying; not near such an anxious piece of business now that I understand my trade and have moreover a good "credit".'[56]

Mary Taylor sold her business to Margaret Smith and her sister Susan in 1859 and returned to England with enough money to buy her own house and live independently. She also had income from New Zealand property. She wrote feminist articles for the *Victoria Magazine*, later collected as the *First Duty of Women*, and published the novel, *Miss Miles*, that she had written in New Zealand. Although less well received and remembered than those of the Brontë sisters, her books were important articulations of her feminist agenda.

Despite her comments about the English middle classes, Mary felt isolated in Wellington. 'The best part of my life is the excitement of arrivals from England,' she wrote. I have 'the queer feeling of living as I do in 2 places at once. One world containing books England and all the people with whom I can exchange an idea; the other all that I actually see and hear and speak to.' She was disparaging of her fellow New Zealand colonists, particularly middle-class women, whose interests revolved around dressing, eating and their children. 'A book is worth any of them and a good book worth them put together,' she concluded. She also dismissed the intellectual life of Wellington, where 'the women are all ignorant and narrow and the men selfish'. Women of the working classes, on the other hand, had far more equality with their men. She could 'talk very well to a joiner's wife, but seldom to a merchant's'.[57]

But Mary enjoyed being different, reporting proudly that her sister-in-law, Waring's wife, 'thinks I am astonishingly learned but rather wicked'. With great glee she described to Charlotte Brontë in 1848 how she had 'astonished *this* world' soon after arriving, when she went to teach music to Elizabeth Couper, the 16-year-old daughter of the recently widowed 47-year-old William Couper, particularly because she asked 'too high a price' of £70 a year. 'Now that I have begun the same people can't conceive why I don't go on and marry the man at once which they imagine must have been my original intention.' She clearly enjoyed the notoriety: 'I shall probably astonish them a little more for I feel a great inclination to make use of his interested civilities to visit his daughter and see the district.'[58]

In reality, she thought William 'coarse, ugly, selfish, ignorant, cunning and dishonest', although 'very civil' to her because 'he has the idea that he gets his daughter taught music very cheap when he gives me board and lodging for teaching her, *when she has time*, which is only half an hour every now and then'.[59] One wonders what William Couper thought of the forthright 30-year-old Miss Taylor. If there had been any 'interested civilities', he quickly turned them elsewhere, marrying 19-year-old Margaret Knox in 1848.

Mary's sense of ostracism, her New Plymouth friend Grace Hirst noted, may well have been self-imposed: she was 'always considered reticent but I always fancy that she thought she had lost caste by keeping shop and held herself aloof on this account'.[60] Grace, a middle-class businesswoman herself, saw no contradiction between business and respectable gentility. When the Smith sisters took over Mary's business, Grace, while visiting Wellington, would 'make some trifling purchase at their shop on purpose to have a talk'. Margaret Smith was 'such a nice gentlewoman' and Susan 'very strong-minded, a great politician and rather masculine ... fond of discussing Taranaki affairs during wartime'.[61] And when the Smith sisters retired to Melrose in Scotland the *Wellington Independent* wished for them 'that ease and comfort which have been fairly earned by a long course of persevering industry'. James Smith, who bought the business (and ran it with his wife Anne), was no relation, but the newspaper was pleased it would still be 'Smith's' and hoped that the 'new proprietor will more than maintain its reputation'.[62] When Susan Smith died in 1892, the sisters were remembered in Wellington's *Evening Post* as 'excellent businesswomen ... much respected'.[63]

The 'parochial' sphere?

For many New Zealand women, whether middle or working class, the boundary between public and private was not rigid. Private domestic spaces became public as they invited customers in to browse, buy, eat or drink, turning front rooms into shops, classrooms or bars, kitchens into workshops and bedrooms into lodgings. Their wares could spill out onto the street and they traversed the thoroughfares daily, to order, collect and deliver goods, or to commute to a market stall or a business successful enough to have its own premises. Most businesswomen's clientele would have been local and known to them. They operated in a neighbourhood and community space that sociologist Lyn Lofland has usefully described as the 'parochial' realm, part of a continuum between private and public, where the domestic and the commercial merged.[64] A woman's place might be in the home but she could also be at home in business.

The business hub of Whanganui, where a dozen businesswomen could be found at any one time as publicans, drapers, grocers and boarding-house keepers.

View of Whanganui from Durie Hill showing boat sheds on Taupo Quay opposite Market Place. Harding, William James, 1826–1899, Alexander Turnbull Library, 1/2-011819-F

CHAPTER 3

'This Outlandish Place at the End of the Earth'

'Oh it is a sad thing, my dear sister, to be banished to this outlandish place at the end of the earth! I shall never make up my mind to stay here. My heart is not in my own bosom, but at home with you in my native land.'[1] Susan Waters' reaction to her new home in 1842 was hardly surprising. Far from everything that was familiar, New Zealand must indeed have seemed 'outlandish'. Like many other settler colonies around the world, however, it quickly became more recognisable. Towns developed alongside the significant agricultural and pastoral industries. They expanded at varying times and rates, reflecting contrasting economic bases, founding ideals and local environments, as well as external factors such as war or economic depression.[2]

Businesswomen's opportunities and their need to earn a living depended not just on personal circumstances of class and marital status, but also on where and when they were living. The first settlers in Wellington and Nelson in the 1840s, surviving in tents and shacks, or those landing at Lyttelton in 1850 and facing a long walk over the hills to claim a patch of land in what would become Christchurch, had very different experiences from those who arrived later in the mad scramble for gold, or in shiploads of assisted immigrants. These arrivals found established buildings and businesses, albeit still on muddy streets. Māori women, whose families had lived in Aotearoa for generations, recalibrated their lives and expectations in different ways from Pākehā.[3]

Many New Zealand towns were service centres and trading depots for the developing pastoral industry or the goldfields. Local manufacturing industries could grow quite large by adding value to the big primary industries of wool and wood. Other urban businesses, whether run by men or women, were small but provided critical support and infrastructure, along with the necessities and little luxuries of life. Real economic expansion did not occur until the 1870s, when an exponential increase in state-led immigration created a larger internal market and a more complex economy.[4]

The early years of organised Pākehā settlement were characterised by a youthful migrant population, providing a labour force and creating particular business opportunities in education and midwifery. Charlotte Godley noted in 1850 'the almost total absence of *old* people. To be sure, old women are to be found almost everywhere, and I had seen a *very* few of them ... but I never saw an old man here till yesterday, and even he was a very *verdant* one, coming home apparently from work; but his hair was very white, and he was really an *old* man anywhere.'[5] Charlotte Godley was clearly talking only about Pākehā settlers, even though she occasionally socialised with Māori, albeit the carefully selected friends of missionary Octavius Hadfield. Other contemporary accounts tell of Māori of all ages as a visible presence in Wellington streets.

Towns across New Zealand developed individual reputations. Auckland, the capital from 1840 until 1865, always had what Russell Stone called a 'whiff of disrepute', owing to its relentless entrepreneurialism, restless opportunism and constant hum of commerce.[6] Early settler John Logan Campbell observed in 1841: 'The whole & entire object of every one here is making money, the big fishes eating the little ones.'[7] It was a government and garrison town, isolated from the rest of New Zealand both geographically and as the seat of government. Elizabeth Bartley recalled early Auckland as rough and ready, filled with drunken men. Shortland Street saw 'many dreadful riots between sailors and soldiers' outside Mrs Henderson's corner hotel.[8] In 1853 Attorney-General William Swainson wrote that most of Auckland's population, 'being, and feeling themselves to be, but temporary residents', were 'living in comparatively small and inconvenient houses'. Given most were 'government officials and military men', single men predominated, opening up a range of respectable and disreputable business opportunities for women. More positively, Swainson likened the town to 'an English watering place', with 'almost everything necessary to comfort and convenience', although 'not always of the best quality'.[9] The more centrally located Wellington became the capital in 1865, but Auckland remained New Zealand's largest city, except when twice overtaken by gold-fuelled Dunedin. Auckland experienced economic downturns in the 1860s after the departure of government and soldiers, and in the 1880s and early 1890s.

In its organic development, Auckland differed from those southern settlements planned as socially engineered communities to encourage respectable family life.

Wellington, or Port Nicholson as it was first known, was settled in 1840 under a plan of 'systematic colonisation' run by Edward Gibbon Wakefield's New Zealand Company. Seeking to create a cross-section of English society, the company sold land at a 'sufficient price', low enough to be attainable by worthy settlers, but too high for labouring men to purchase immediately, thus ensuring the 'proper' balance of classes. Middle-class, evangelical values were central to Wakefield's concept of ideal families, in which men worked hard at pioneering and women were good helpmeets, wives and mothers.[10] Wellington was soon 'well supplied with places of worship', along with newspapers and a cricket club.[11] Education was valued in a town of growing families, spawning a plethora of schools, many run by women.

When Charlotte Godley arrived in 1850, Wellington 'surpassed her expectations in every way'. The town was 'really uncommonly pretty, and with very good comfortable houses, although certainly no fine buildings, but they are generally built with a gable on to the street, which looks very picturesque'. The 'almost continuous row along the beach for about two miles' reminded her of Hastings in England. She enjoyed 'such nice walks in every direction, whenever it is dry', although 'after much rain the Hutt road is the only tolerable place'. It was 'always the fashionable lounge'; on Sunday afternoons 'everyone walks there, from the Governor and his wife down to all the shop people in their best clothes'.[12] Civilised life, then, was possible, and all those 'best clothes' promised golden opportunities for businesswomen.

Although Wellington's inhabitants lived in 'agreeable residences', its development was limited by 'many difficulties', according to visiting Quaker educationalist, Frederick Mackie, in 1853. He, like generations after him, was obsessed with its windiness.[13] Charlotte Godley, too, felt the wind changed so suddenly that 'you would think it blew from two places at once. The saying is in N.Z. that you may know a Wellington man by his having always his hand on his hat.'[14] Straw-bonnet makers and repairers and haberdashers importing and stocking hatpins found a ready market. Once it became the capital, Wellington's population surged, Europeans numbering 7908 in 1871 and 43,638 by 1901.[15]

Whanganui, originally known as Petre, was founded by the New Zealand Company in 1840 as an adjunct to Wellington at the mouth of the Whanganui River. Like many other towns, including New Plymouth, Nelson, Napier, Timaru, Oamaru and Invercargill, it was a service centre and port for the surrounding countryside. These towns were connected with smaller settlements and with each other, providing clothing and household goods, entertainment, education and postal services. Because travel by sea, or on the Whanganui River, the 'Rhine of New Zealand',[16] was more efficient than any land transport, and roads were poor or non-existent, it is no surprise that such coastal provincial centres proliferated, linked closely with one another and with Melbourne and Sydney.

Several shiploads of hopeful respectable immigrants established Nelson as the first New Zealand Company settlement in the South Island in 1841. Events at Wairau, near Blenheim, in 1843 threatened to set things back.[17] Twenty-two Pākehā and four Māori were killed when a New Zealand Company survey party attempted to illegally annex the Wairau Valley. Nelson recovered quickly and built cultural and educational institutions. Early gold rushes around Golden Bay, followed by Pākehā refugees from war-torn Taranaki in the early 1860s, boosted Nelson's population, which kept pace with Wellington's until about 1865. But then its geographical isolation, the poor harbour and insufficient productive land slowed its development.[18] Nevertheless, it was home to many businesswomen – proprietors of numerous drapery establishments, hotels and schools, as well as a chemist and butcher.

Christchurch, like Wellington, was a planned settlement, the brainchild of Wakefield and John Godley. Dreamed up in 1848 with the foundation of the Canterbury Association, it came to life in December 1850 with the arrival of what became known as the First Four Ships, carrying around 750 'pilgrims'. They included both 'colonists', with money to buy land and destined to be leaders, and 'emigrants', who would be the tradespeople and labourers. Descent from a passenger on the First Four Ships became a mark of some status among Cantabrians. In 1856 Christchurch was named New Zealand's first official city, not through population but because it had an Anglican bishop. Despite this veneer of respectability, in 1869 there were 28 known brothels and drunkenness was just as rife as elsewhere. The combination of respectability and drunkenness meant Christchurch became a stronghold of the temperance movement in later years, under the energetic leadership of suffragist Kate Sheppard.[19]

Dunedin also began as a planned settlement, of upright God-fearing inhabitants, founded in 1848 by the Otago Association, members of the Free Church of Scotland. The town grew slowly, reaching just over 1700 residents in 1858. But from 1861, thanks to gold fever, its respectable and sober growth ballooned. By 1865 it was New Zealand's largest city; its 1870 population was nearly 15,000 and this tripled again by 1881.[20] Like Christchurch, it prided itself on its educational and cultural institutions but also acquired a seedier side. Businesswomen took advantage of the full gamut of opportunities that a boom town offered, despite sometimes prohibitive property prices and rent.

West Coast towns like Hokitika in the mid-1860s, and Thames in the Coromandel from 1867, were also fuelled by gold, but they had none of Dunedin's respectable institutions to temper their boisterousness. In 1865 explorer and future Canterbury Museum director Julius Haast found Hokitika 'a scene of almost indescribable bustle and activity'.[21] William F. Crawford, later mayor of Gisborne, was among the thousands of hopeful prospectors who rushed to the West Coast. He, too, thought Hokitika 'a lively place', in which 'lucky strikers were painting the town red', drinking bucketloads of champagne out of pannikins and 'holding sports and races down Revell Street'.[22] Full of single men, or, at least, men unaccompanied by wives, such towns offered different opportunities for businesswomen: fewer milliners and midwives, more publicans and brothel keepers.[23]

All these developing towns and cities, from Auckland in the north to Invercargill in the south, shared some common features but also had their own characteristics and their own trajectories. Their businessmen and women rode the rollercoaster of economic booms and busts, political caprice and environmental catastrophe, much of it beyond their control.

Earthquake, fire and war

Settlers promised a land of opportunity found that although servants' wages, house rents and the price of imported clothing were high, food and wine were generally cheaper than in Britain and there was an abundance of vegetables and fruit, either grown by settlers or procured from Māori traders, some of them women.[24] For Māori, at whose expense the migrants' opportunities came, there were trading possibilities, new technologies and potential new allies in their internecine warfare. However, New Zealand also presented its own particular problems, quite apart from the ups and downs of the economy.

Most frightening were the 'appalling convulsions of nature' that shook the country at fairly regular intervals.[25] The 7.5 magnitude tremor that struck the lower North Island and upper South Island in October 1848 caused severe damage in Wellington; three people died in one of the many severe aftershocks.[26] The *Wellington Independent* described its effects, 'producing a chill in the heart and dreadful feeling of sickness ... more than sufficient to appal the stoutest minded in the place'.[27] Earthquakes continue to be an unpredictable, destructive and frightening part of New Zealand life.

Fire was also a problem shared by all towns, exacerbated by the preference for building with timber, both readily available and less catastrophic in earthquakes. Fires regularly destroyed homes, businesses and sometimes lives. Buildings were often close together and whole streets could be devastated, such as in the conflagration that annihilated much of Auckland's Shortland Street in 1865, including Sophia James' hotel. The risk was well understood, with regular prosecutions of householders and business owners who neglected to clean their chimneys. Wise businesswomen took out insurance if they could afford it, although it was often inadequate. However devastating, both earthquakes and fire offered business opportunities – there were clothes to make, food to supply and commercial premises and houses to rebuild.

For Pākehā immigrants, particularly those living outside larger towns, the perplexing locals could be even more frightening than fire or earthquake – they had an uncomfortable tendency to assert their authority and a disconcerting capacity to wage war. For Māori, Pākehā intruders were similarly problematic. With their inexplicable assumptions of authority, strange understandings of property ownership and ever-increasing numbers, they posed a threat that came to outweigh any immediate economic or strategic benefits.

Many of the 40 years after the 1840 signing of the Treaty of Waitangi were marked by conflict between Māori and Pākehā, particularly in the North Island, complicated by the fact that some iwi fought with Pākehā against other iwi. Whether justified or not, the fear of a Māori attack dominated European letters and diaries, particularly after the Wairau affray. In the 1860s, war broke out in Taranaki, Waikato and other areas of the North Island, slowing the development of affected settlements. New Plymouth, in particular, suffered an exodus of the Pākehā population to the comparative safety of Nelson in 1860, and though the population recovered, tensions simmered for a decade. Warfare also introduced military personnel into the Pākehā population: some of their wives supported themselves with small businesses while their spouses were otherwise engaged. Louisa Darby was 'mess-woman' for the 65th Regiment in Auckland for about three years while her husband Stephen was on duty with the Royal Artillery in Taranaki and Waikato. 'The excellence and *recherché* character of the viands and wines' she supplied to the Race Ball in 1864 were highly praised but she was already in financial trouble. In July 1863 the captain of the regiment was forced to advertise that none of the officers would be responsible for her debts. Stephen found himself imprisoned for bankruptcy in 1865. Perhaps fortunately for Louisa's solvency, the regiment left Auckland the same year.[28]

Māori and Pākehā

War was just one aspect of Māori–Pākehā relations. Māori were ubiquitous in the early towns of New Zealand, although increasingly marginalised as the century progressed. In 1853 Frederick Mackie was 'forcibly reminded that [he was] in a foreign land ... seeing and hearing the natives who are numerous'.[29] James Adams, an early Dunedin settler, took pains to reassure his parents in a letter home in 1848: 'On our landing we were most kindly received by the natives' who 'are quiet, inoffensive people, and love the whites'. He added, not allaying parental concerns, that 'You cannot give them greater offence than speak of their eating human flesh.' Adams also recorded Māori participation in the local economy: 'They are very useful in cutting wood, and bringing it for fuel, on the easiest terms, either money or food will please them.'[30] In Auckland, however, settlers commented on the business nous of Māori men and women, who quickly realised the value of their labour, services and produce. Māori used the Pākehā court systems and Māori women contributed to family or iwi businesses and land negotiations.[31]

Māori women, particularly those who were the wives and daughters of Pākehā men or of Māori men integrated into Pākehā society, could slot into the working or middle classes, depending upon their circumstances. There were examples of high-ranking Māori women marrying Pākehā whalers and settlers, who educated their daughters well. They could then be married to colleagues of their fathers. Emily, daughter of trading station owner George Russell and Hautonga Haira, of Ngāti Hao, married her father's merchant friend, John Webster.[32] Jane Cochrane, daughter of Northland merchant Dennis Cochrane and Takotowi Te Whata, was both well educated and well connected. Like Emily Russell, she was related to Ngāpuhi leader Tāmati Wāka Nene. At 17 she became the second wife of local resident magistrate James Reddy Clendon, 28 years her senior, six months after the death of his first wife, Sarah, in 1855. The Clendon children shared a governess, Mrs Alice Bennett, with the neighbouring von Sturmer children.[33] Sarah von Sturmer, wife of a Native Land Court judge, was similarly well connected: she was the daughter of Te Rauparaha's niece Te Kahumahinga Reed, and James Reed, rumoured to be French aristocracy.[34]

Māori and Pākehā women played important roles in cross-cultural interactions. In 1842 Wellingtonian Susan Waters learned to speak te reo because Māori 'formed our principal society for the time we have been here'.[35] Elizabeth Caldwell shared meals and conversation with her Māori neighbours on her farm outside Nelson; her sons became proficient in the language. Charlotte Parkinson recalled close friendships between her mother and three Māori sisters in Opotiki in the 1870s.[36] Elizabeth Hannken and her siblings became 'good native scholars' after her family's move from New South Wales to the Coromandel in 1840, because Māori were both neighbours and the 'only customers' of their father's store. Later, in Auckland, the Hannkens employed soldiers' wives to make dresses for Māori women customers. At one Auckland harbourside picnic, however, Elizabeth's father had to 'spin out' the apple pie at lunch after 'that clumsy Maori there put his foot in it'. Was he an interloper or a guest?[37]

Māori were also an important market that savvy businesswomen could not ignore. Susan Waters' general store in Wellington had a predominantly Māori customer base in the 1840s. Hori Grey, a 'native orderly', had an account at Susan and John 'Old' Smith's shop in Wellington in the 1860s.[38] Sarah Hogg in Whanganui prosecuted Māori customers in the courts when they failed to pay their debts.[39] In Tauranga in 1867 Julia Wrigley apprehended a Māori woman who was calmly shoplifting material from her shop.[40] Elizabeth Hannken's sons opened a drapery store branch at Ohinemutu and advertised in Māori newspapers in the 1880s.[41] In 1884 Marianne Smith, later of Smith & Caughey, advertised Smith's Cheap Drapery Warehouse in the Māori language newspaper *Te Korimako*.[42]

A land of opportunity

New Zealand, then, was a complex, multilayered society, with urban settlements ranging from small villages to growing cities. As the economies of the modern larger cities became more complex, a range of specialised niches provided livelihoods for men and women alike, while in smaller settlements there were always opportunities for storekeepers, midwives and schoolteachers. Hundreds of entrepreneurial women were able to find a market and exploit it. As they negotiated their way around men, these spinsters, wives and widows made business their own.

Chapter 4

One Ring to Bind Them All: Marriage and the law

'By marriage the husband and wife are one person in the law, and that one is the husband.' This summary of the legal situation of married women in England, and therefore for Pākehā women in New Zealand after 1840, was attributed to renowned English legal authority William Blackstone.[1] For much of the nineteenth century the law of coverture meant that if a woman married, she disappeared as a legal individual; she and her property became her husband's. On marriage, a man gained financial responsibilities as breadwinner for a family but his business life was otherwise unaffected. For Pākehā businesswomen, however, being a wife and mother often determined the nature of their business and how they pursued it, not only because of social expectations and numbers of children, but also because of the particular legal problems they faced. Whether they had good marriages, bad marriages or marriages that ended through desertion or divorce, they often required creative legal manoeuvring to pursue their businesses, as nineteenth-century legislation endeavoured to keep up.[2]

Māori women's legal position was more uncertain. Those who married Pākehā men were caught in the clash of competing systems of law, property ownership and inheritance.[3] A few managed to exploit Pākehā law to their advantage, using the English law of equity to establish trusts. 'Deserted wives' legislation made special provisions for the children of Pākehā men and Māori women. Māori women's property rights took a step backwards in 1881 when the Native Succession Act removed their right to bequeath their property without their husband's consent. This brought them into line with Pākehā married women, whose property rights had always been restricted by the law of coverture.[4]

Negotiating coverture

Under coverture, a wife became a feme covert – under the 'cover' of her husband – rather than a feme sole. Husband and wife could not sue or make contracts with each other, nor give evidence in court against each other. A wife's property became her husband's; any money she earned was his; she could not enter into any contract without him; she could not sue in court without him. Her husband, legally, had to counter-sign contracts and join her in person to sue a defaulting debtor in court. In any financial transactions, a wife was regarded as acting as her husband's agent.

Coverture had some advantages, which women occasionally exploited. A wife who committed a crime or got into other difficulties could possibly escape punishment by claiming to be acting for her husband. Nor could she be imprisoned for her debts; her husband could be sued and imprisoned instead. She could not be sued in court without her husband present, so creditors found it difficult to pursue her. A husband was required to maintain his wife, so she could run up debts in his name as long as they were for 'necessaries' (and good lawyers argued long and hard about the definition of these).

The law of coverture was a particular burden for deserted wives or for women with hopeless or uncooperative husbands. Even when a woman was supporting herself and her children through her own industry, her husband or his creditors could claim any of her earnings. In 1860 legislation ameliorated the position of deserted wives, but not until 1870 did the law allow a woman cohabiting with her husband to make a case for feme sole status if he was drunk, cruel, openly adulterous or incapable (through incompetence rather than illness) of maintaining her and his children.[5] In 1884, 14 years after England and five years after New South Wales, the Married Women's Property Act finally allowed all married women to be treated as femes soles in their property and business dealings.[6]

Despite the obstacles, wives carried on businesses throughout the century. For those with supportive husbands who were happy for their wives to be ostensibly acting as their 'agents', the issue of coverture did not arise – unless challenged in a legal dispute. If a wife was chasing or being chased for debts, or if a contract she had signed was challenged, technically a husband had to appear in court alongside her, to assure the court that she had been acting on his behalf. However, the law's application varied across the country, coverture being invoked in some cases and not in others.

In 1867 Mrs Goodbraid tried to recover a debt of £3 9s in the Papakura resident magistrate's court, but the summons was dismissed because she 'admitted she was a married woman' whose husband was away. She could not pursue the case until her absent husband returned.[7] In the same year, Mrs S. Frost's case against a boarder who absconded without paying was dismissed. The boarder's lawyer successfully challenged her lawyer's right to appear because Mrs Frost could not prove she had her husband's permission to appoint him.[8]

On the other hand, the redoubtable Whanganui draper Mrs Sarah Hogg made regular appearances in court on business matters, suing and being sued in her own name from 1865 into the 1870s. Although he lived with her, her husband never seemed to appear and the issue of coverture was not raised. Sarah, then 36 years old, opened her business in 1865 when her husband, the Reverend David Hogg, founding minister of St Paul's Presbyterian church in Whanganui, retired aged 53, owing to ill health. Already the mother of eight children and stepmother to three more, she had another six after her husband's retirement. Clearly David was not entirely incapacitated, even if too unwell to work or attend court. In this small town, both lawyers and judges took a pragmatic approach. They knew that challenging Sarah's legal status was a waste of time: her husband would certainly have prosecuted the case on her behalf if necessary. The Hoggs were a 'universally esteemed' Whanganui family, and Sarah was a strong woman, not to be crossed lightly.[9]

More commonly, courts expected men to front up and take responsibility for their wives' debts or dodgy behaviour, even when they were 320 kilometres away, as Charles Crawford discovered in 1844. He was fined £50 for selling spirits without a licence at a coffee shop in Nelson when he was in Akaroa. His wife Sarah, who ran the business, served brandy illegally to Constables Pinock and Jennings and to a Mr Scott. Scott lamely tried to suggest he had bought the brandy elsewhere, but convinced no one. It did not help that in the same issue of the *Nelson Examiner* reporting the case, William Murray was advertising for information about the person who had reported him for apparently supplying spirits to Crawford's Coffee Shop.[10] Charles, who had discovered what happened by reading the newspaper, admitted responsibility for his wife's conduct, but suggested that other married men would understand, 'since some of them could not control their wife [even when they were] at home'. He had taken the added precaution of 'earnestly requesting one of the police force to call at my house every day during my absence', thus proving his 'desire that nothing unlawful should be transacted during my absence'.[11] This extreme precaution seems to have backfired.

Elizabeth Denne's neat storefront next to her husband John's business in Nelson obscured a difficult life. This may be Elizabeth and her daughter Emily, who worked with her. Younger daughter Elizabeth, who had 'acute mania', was incarcerated in Nelson Mental Hospital from 1889 to 1937.

Elizabeth Denne, Dress and Mantle maker, Collingwood Street, Nelson Provincial Museum, Maguire Collection, 47913

Cabinetmaker John Denne may have rued the day he married widow Elizabeth Dinely Estcourt. Widowed immediately upon her arrival in Nelson in 1856, Elizabeth opened a dressmaking business, overextended and hit financial difficulties in 1859. Unable to pay builder James Hargreaves, she was imprisoned for six months. On her release in 1860 she married John Denne and continued her millinery business. But her imprisonment had not discharged her debt, so her new husband was gaoled instead and became insolvent. The case caused a furore in the local papers, but despite support for John, the law of coverture meant that by marrying Elizabeth, he had also married her debts.[12]

Creative lawyers and their clients were often adept at bending the coverture laws: consider Catherine Mason and her lawyer Henry Smythies in Dunedin in the 1860s. When Kate McDonald sued Catherine in 1866 for illegal detention of her property, a usual practice in lieu of rent, the case was thrown out: being married women, neither had legal standing in court.[13] In December 1867, when Catherine was charged with 'being the owner and occupier of a "house of ill fame"', Smythies argued that, as a married woman, she could not legally fulfil such a role.[14] Catherine was well known to the courts, described variously as 'a notoriously bad character' and 'one of the most abandoned women in the Colony', having 'for some time' employed her own daughter, 16-year-old Christina.[15] Despite the magistrate agreeing with the prosecuting counsel, who showed she had 'had control of the house for five years' and could thus be liable, Smythies found various legal technicalities allowing Catherine to avoid prosecution.[16]

The coverture defence was particularly effective when a wife committed a crime while with her husband. In 1863 Isabella Morgan was charged with having stolen two pairs of trousers, 14 tins of coffee and one bar of soap from John Palmer's Waimea West hotel while with her husband George. Palmer recovered the goods and George offered payment of £5. Isabella still ended up in court, but the judge agreed with her lawyer that 'when an offence of this kind was committed by a married woman in the presence of her husband, it was supposed that she was acting under coercion, and was not punishable'. Although this was 'no bar to her husband being tried', there is no record of a later trial. Given the rather odd collection of stolen items, perhaps there were extenuating circumstances not reported in the newspaper.[17]

Surviving a separation

Coverture was problematic for both parties when marriages broke down. Some marriages disintegrated after many years, others when the ink was barely dry on the licence.[18] Separated husbands were quick to disclaim responsibility for their wives' debts, although the legal status of such advertising was uncertain.[19] In 1865 James Mitchell announced in two Wellington newspapers that he would not support his estranged wife Eliza. The next year local butcher James Gear sued him for meat deliveries to Eliza and their several children but James was not required to pay. Six months later, however, when he was sued by another butcher, a different judge declared that James' announcement 'was not binding in the case of the necessaries of life'.[20]

Those 'necessaries' were nowhere legally defined.[21] Selina Taprell, who lived apart from her husband William in Onehunga in the 1860s, attempted unsuccessfully to claim that necessaries included the expenses she needed to establish a shop and bakery to support her children. When she employed Mr Barrie to build a baker's oven and sent the bill to William, he refused to pay, having advertised in the *Daily Southern Cross* in November 1863 that he would no longer be responsible for his wife's debts. Barrie sued him on the grounds that he 'was liable … even for such things as were necessary to enable [his wife] to earn her livelihood'. The judge disagreed because Selina was not carrying on the business under the 'express authority' of her husband, making a distinction between 'necessary' goods and those required for a business. Selina persevered in business, running a small shop and then a hotel.[22]

Women had a small number of options when marriages broke down. Some women moved on to other men;[23] others reconciled with their spouses.[24] But for those who remained alone, running a business could be the best option despite the obstacles involved. Local communities often colluded in the fiction that a deserted wife was a feme sole so that her business survived. Elizabeth Taylor and her husband Joseph had run the Wakatu Hotel and then livery stables in Nelson until Joseph absconded to Sydney in 1851, leaving Elizabeth to fend for herself for the next 27 years. She ran a boarding house, followed by a bakery and confectionery business, until her death in 1878. She rented her Selwyn Place premises, reputedly the first brick building in Nelson, from local politician David Monro. As his diary recorded, because Elizabeth was 'a married woman, altho' separated from her husband, I can enter into no legal agreement' with her, but they got around this by treating her 'as it were as a servant of mine'. In 1857 she paid rent of £30, although Monro felt it was 'much too low', planning to increase it 'to £50 at least'.[25]

Elizabeth could probably afford it. Her boarding house was 'patronised by many of the old colonists', including Monro himself. Despite being separated from her husband, she was a liked and respected businesswoman. Her obituary in the *Nelson Evening Mail* was in no doubt where the blame lay, describing Joseph, still living in Australia, as 'not possessed of the best of tempers'. Meanwhile, Elizabeth, although 'a thorough cripple from rheumatism' and housebound for her last six years of life, had continued to supervise her confectionery business, employing two young women as assistants.[26]

Dealing with deserted wives: Legislation

Colonial legislators and social commentators recognised that deserted wives – or more accurately, the deserting husbands who found it easy to simply disappear – were a problem. The primary aim of the resulting legislation was to ensure that deserted women and children did not become a burden on the public purse. Unlike the 1840 New South Wales legislation on which it was modelled, the 1846 New Zealand Ordinance for the Support of Destitute Families and Illegitimate Children focused on the destitute, not merely deserted families, and held not only a husband and father responsible for their maintenance, but 'the father and grandfather, mother and grandmother, and the children'. Significantly, despite coverture, this implied that women were also responsible for their own and their children's support when required. The legislation also made special provision for the children of Pākehā men and Māori women, imposing an extra levy on the absconding father to cover the children's education. Although this seems unappealingly assimilationist to modern eyes, it was at least an overt acknowledgement of the prevalence of interracial relationships, and of Pākehā fathers' responsibility.[27] The 1846 act did nothing to help a deserted wife who was running a business, however: her husband could resurface at any time and claim any profits or property she had accrued. Furthermore, his creditors could take her money and goods to pay his debts, a wife often being easier to trace than an errant husband. And she could not chase her own debtors in court.

In 1860 New Zealand legislators passed the Married Women's Property Protection Act, two years after New South Wales and England had enacted similar laws. This essentially gave a deserted wife feme sole status in the eyes of the law, effectively protecting any income acquired 'by her own lawful industry' from her husband and his creditors.[28] She could enter into contracts and chase debtors (and be chased by creditors) in court. New Zealand's law gave women both more responsibility and more independence than its New South Wales counterpart. As long as a couple was separated, a husband was not liable for his wife's contracts 'or for any wrongful act or omission by her, or for any costs she may incur as plaintiff or defendant'. He remained responsible for necessaries if he had been ordered to pay alimony at the time of desertion. If a couple later reunited, the wife retained separate control of the property she had gained in the interim, 'subject to any agreement in writing made between herself and her husband before such renewed cohabitation'.[29] Women soon began taking out protection orders. Typical was Auckland's Mary Ann Watson, who applied successfully in 1867. Left with seven children aged from two to 15 when her husband John departed, she was 'obliged to support herself and children by her own industry'.[30]

Some women were able to exploit their situation. In November 1870 Mary Ann Reilly avoided paying a debt of £12 for her Greymouth millinery and dressmaking business because she had taken out a protection order against her husband James the previous August. Prichard & Co. sued James for goods they said were supplied before the protection order, but he was nowhere to be found and Mary Ann claimed that the goods in her shop were acquired after the order. Prichard & Co. was not at all convinced, but could not prove otherwise. Like many other deserted wives, Mary Ann continued to support herself and her children with a variety of successful and not-so-successful entrepreneurial endeavours, including a grocery shop and servants' registry office, on the West Coast and in Wellington.[31]

When sued for the cost of a wrongly delivered bag of sugar, Southland shopkeeper Hannah Ward Barron, whose son Joseph Ward later became prime minister, pleaded coverture: 'She was a married woman, and … her husband should have been sued and not her.' The magistrate was unimpressed, commenting that 'it appeared that she was carrying on a business independent of her husband who was on the West Coast; her plea would render people cautious in trusting her'. He would have been even more disgruntled if he had known that Hannah had cleverly concealed her 1860 deserted wives order, so was legally a feme sole and responsible for her debt. She continued to run businesses in Melbourne and Bluff for decades.[32]

Eliza Jenkins took advantage of the deserted wives legislation. She and her husband William had several children and were practised colonists, having lived in New South Wales and Victoria before ending up in New Zealand around 1861. Initially it seemed to be a good marriage. Entrepreneurial William had a partnership with

Crafty Eliza Jenkins ran hotels in Queenstown from 1866. She expanded in 1871, snapping up the British Lion Theatre for a mere £100. From 1875, family problems, a broken leg and eventually bankruptcy in 1882 spelled the end of her public business career.

Lakes District Museum, Arrowtown, EP0234

Henry Pulford in a successful Dunedin upholstery business. Later, his store on the Dunstan and Lake Wakatipu goldfields flourished 'beyond his most sanguine expectations', according to a later newspaper report. But when William was employed as a gold buyer, in a situation where there was 'little or no police protection, rowdyism was rampant and several robberies had been openly perpetrated in broad daylight', his 'intense anxiety and the fear of being attacked' led to a breakdown. He ended up in the Dunedin lunatic asylum.[33]

Eliza and his business partner liquidated his property and Eliza bought the Melbourne Hotel in Queenstown in her son-in-law's name, becoming a 'respected' hotelier. Upon William's release in 1865, his wife kindly suggested he take a holiday with their son, also William, to recover his health. For years the pair travelled around New Zealand and Australia, opening a furniture business in Brisbane along the way. When William returned to Queenstown in 1874, Eliza immediately applied for a deserted wives order. William sued Eliza and his son-in-law Josiah Mitchison for stealing his property, arguing the order was obtained fraudulently. Eliza won the court case – the only reason she is visible to history – but may not have deserved to. The convoluted evidence included information, prompting much spluttering from the court, that at one point Eliza had charged her husband board and lodging, presumably to demonstrate that they were not 'cohabiting' although living on the same premises. Outplayed, William's lawyer George Elliot Barton deplored the way colonial magistrates dealt with such cases, which, 'at home' were heard in 'the Superior Court'. In New Zealand, however, he complained, it seemed 'a woman could get almost anything from a Magistrate if she complained of ill usage by her husband'. 'It was never intended for one moment that women should use the machinery of the Act for the purpose of getting rid of husbands they did not like,' he concluded.[34] Despite Eliza's success, however, deserted women were generally vulnerable in a court case, and even with a protection order they were still legally tied to their husbands, unable to remarry.

Divorce

For much of the century, divorce was difficult, if not impossible. The 1867 Divorce and Matrimonial Causes Act, following the 1857 English example, imposed a gendered double standard. Men could divorce their wives for adultery alone, whereas for a wife to file for divorce, her husband had to aggravate his adultery with bigamy, sodomy, incest, rape, cruelty or desertion for five years, a disparity that remained until 1898.[35]

Unsurprisingly, few women made the effort. Maria Neill was one who succeeded, although the final paperwork came through just after her thoroughly awful husband had died in Australia. Before then the sordid details of her life were aired in public, even though her husband had not opposed the petition for divorce. Maria was born in Wellington in 1844, the daughter of Wellington's provincial surgeon George Dalrymple Monteith and his wife Elizabeth.[36] Maria lost both parents as a child and was just 20 when she married 34-year-old widower Captain George James Neill, who was the deputy assistant commissary general.[37] Nine months later Maria gave birth to a baby daughter, who lived just eight weeks. George had already begun abusing his wife, who was forced to seek shelter with neighbours. He regaled Maria with details of extramarital sexual adventures 'to annoy her', and her servants 'appealed to her for protection' as he 'was in the habit of taking liberties with them'. Transferred to England, George continued to abuse Maria en route. She said that 'his conduct was so bad' that, on reaching their destination, even 'his brother Officers expostulated with him on his treatment'. Maria had another daughter and a son, but then, upon medical advice, 'she ran away from her husband. After living in London for some time, she returned to Wellington' with the children. George followed 'almost at the same time' and, at her brother's request, Maria 'resumed cohabitation with him; but his conduct again became very bad, and almost daily she received a thrashing from him'. Her brother intervened again, this time removing her from the house.[38]

Eager to build a new life, Maria went to Napier, where two of her married sisters had settled, taking her children and her talking pet Western Australian cockatoo. In 1874 she purchased the goodwill of Tennyson House, a ladies' school, from the Batham sisters.[39] An accomplished musician, she had been a leading light of Wellington's St Peter's Church choir. She combined running her school, renamed Lilian House after her daughter, with regular concerts. Napier audiences admired the 'power and sweetness' of her voice and the 'brilliancy of execution, not often found in unprofessional circles'. She also composed music; her song 'My Spirit King' was published in 1880 and sold in Hawke's Bay and Wellington.[40]

In 1882 Maria returned to Wellington, advertised for pupils and gave a well-received concert with her two children.[41] She also began proceedings for divorce, having finally managed to save enough money. To bring any prosecution in court required funding.[42] She was granted a decree nisi in August 1883. By the time the decree absolute came through a few months later, George Neill had died in Melbourne. His estate of less than £100 was settled on Miss Eliza White, to whom he owed wages.[43]

Maria, now 40, returned to Napier and remarried almost immediately, to Walter Duncan, a 26-year-old auctioneer. Given that she was not a wealthy woman, her marriage to this much younger man was unusual. She continued to offer singing lessons alongside her daughter Lilian, who gave violin lessons. In 1893 Maria and Walter moved to Feilding, where Maria taught music until 1897. They adopted a baby girl, Gladys, in 1894, a rather surprising decision perhaps since Maria was already 50. The child's natural parentage is not recorded, although families often adopted the illegitimate offspring of a husband or relative. When Maria died in 1918 she left her £600 estate to her son and granddaughter; Walter provided for Gladys in his will many years later.[44]

Reputation was critical for a woman in business. Maria Neill was able to maintain her respectability despite her disastrous marriage and humiliating divorce. Her brother's initial instinct to return her to a violent husband shows the social stigma and economic uncertainty for women leaving a marriage. Her ability to earn a living was critical to Maria's survival and eventual recovery.

One spouse too many

Those unable to divorce could still get a protection order, go into business and remain respectable. They could not, however, legally remarry. The simplest solution to an unhappy marriage was to quietly forget that it had ever happened. Identities were easily massaged in the colonies and, as Raewyn Dalziel has shown, bigamy was a common recourse. When bigamy cases came to court, as we shall see in Harriet Corston's case in Chapter 12, they caused a stir, and the rhetoric emanating from the judicial bench was unbendingly disapproving. In practice, however, bigamists were often not pursued unless someone complained – usually the displaced spouse. The burden of proof then lay with the prosecution, which had to prove the identity of the marriage partners and document the marriage. If marriages had occurred overseas, this could prove almost impossible. A person could legally remarry after their spouse had been 'continuously absent' for seven years, although if the spouse then turned up the second marriage was annulled. Technically, any contact in that period would mean they were not 'continuously absent', but this was interpreted flexibly. It was popularly but wrongly believed that a spouse could remarry if their erstwhile partner themselves remarried, but again, those cases of bigamy were not pursued with any great vigour. Thus, throughout the century some women collected simultaneous spouses while others were duped or entered willingly into marriage with men already lawfully wed. But as long as everyone turned a blind eye, they could remain respectable.[45]

The wife of Alfred Domett, New Zealand's fourth premier, was almost certainly a bigamist. Mary George had run her own school in Wellington for about 10 years when she married the 45-year-old, poetry-writing Domett in 1856. The legend was that romance had blossomed when he rescued her from a fire. Mary, however, was no blushing young ingénue. She called herself a widow, but was actually the deserted wife of Edward Tobias George. They had married in Adelaide three weeks after arriving in January 1839 and produced several children in the next three years. They later settled in Wellington, where Edward was an accountant, and Mary started a school and had another daughter, Sarah, in 1847 and a son, Alfred, in 1850. Both were registered as Edward's children, although Alfred was later known as Alfred Domett. It is unclear when Edward actually left but, despite Mary's supposed widowhood, he was sufficiently animate to work the Otago goldfields in 1862 and remarry himself to Winifred Jolly in 1868. He became a publican and the first mayor of Naseby, and died in 1884. Winifred continued running the hotel into the twentieth century.[46] Mary's marriage to Alfred Domett caused quite a scandal in Wellington: they had been cohabiting for some years and young Alfred was likely evidence of some intimacy. In 1851 the Reverend Robert Cole had grumbled in a letter to Governor George Grey that 'Domett publicly keeps his woman (& that woman "a neighbour's wife")'.[47] The marriage may have been delayed until 1856 so that Mary could claim not to have heard from Edward George for the required seven years. Despite the gossip, Alfred held respectable government positions before eventually becoming premier.

Jessie Ann Campbell, on the other end of a bigamous marriage, used business to survive. After she was widowed in 1867 she married Alexander Milne the following year, but soon discovered he already had a wife. She obtained a deed of separation. To support herself, she ran a greengrocer's in Whanganui, finding a ready market for her fruit, vegetables, poultry and oysters, and also offering lunch and importing some fancy goods to sell. She continued her business until 1876 when she married John Campbell McKenzie, a policeman; they moved to Southland and had six children.[48]

Mary Lechner tried to avoid bigamy. When her husband John deserted her in Nelson in the late 1860s, she moved in with Thomas Menary and they had a son but did not marry. (She also apparently shipped her other five children off to John in Thames.) Her domestic arrangements became problematic when Thomas applied for a hotel licence in 1876. The licensing board felt unable to grant this, having been officially told he was living 'in open immorality' with another man's wife. Thomas's lawyer tried to argue that 'there was something to be said for him', since he had come to the rescue of a deserted spouse. Thomas and Mary, he said, had asked him whether they could marry, given that John Lechner had been absent for more than seven years, but he had advised them that, although not liable for a charge of bigamy, if John reappeared their marriage would be invalid. In the end, a month later, the board granted Thomas his licence, although not unanimously, on the grounds that he and Mary had conducted their business respectably thus far. They were persuaded by the lawyer's argument that the private lives of publicans should remain so.[49]

The law

Given the restrictions caused by the law of coverture, one might expect not to find married women running businesses. Yet many did. Courts could be pragmatic, and lawyers befittingly devious, in applying the law. Equally, for successful businesswomen, local communities could turn a blind eye to bigamy or to the absence of a husband. Legislation ameliorated the position of deserted wives as the century progressed. Nevertheless, it remained true that a businesswoman's marital status was an issue for her in ways it seldom was for a businessman.

Chapter 5

'Good Morning, Miss': The business of education

In the nineteenth-century education market, wedded to Victorian ideals of domestic maternalism, women were ideally placed as providers – at least for young girls and boys, and for older young ladies. Even upper-middle-class women who required an income could run a school and retain some social status. And in the colonies, according to Mary Taylor, always observant about business openings, it was possible to 'get your living' at teaching, when you 'would only die of [it] in England'.[1] This chapter considers education as a business opportunity for women, opening with the experiences of school proprietor Isabella Cary.

'A life of trial and much suffering'

Isabella Cary was in the first batch of some 30 governesses shipped off to New Zealand by the Female Middle Class Emigration Society (FMCES) between 1861 and 1885. The society was the brainchild of the indomitable Maria Rye, who also sent governesses to Australia and South Africa, convinced they would solve both Britain's problem of 'surplus women' and the colonies' deficit of respectable educated females. Governesses wrote letters back to the FMCES, repaying passage money loaned by the society, or making excuses for not repaying it, but also describing their successes and disappointments, and holding forth about opportunities for single, middle-class women in New Zealand.[2]

Isabella arrived in Auckland as a 24-year-old in 1861. For the next 15 years, until she died at the age of 39, she advertised schools in Dunedin, Whanganui and Thames. She did not marry. Isabella's four surviving letters are depressing reading: she immediately regretted her decision to emigrate to such a godforsaken place.

She begged the FMCES not to send any more 'first class Governesses', because pay and conditions were even worse than in Britain. She thought it a 'sad mistake for a Lady to come here as a teacher'; schools were plentiful but positions for governesses were rare – 'the houses are too small'. The only options were to 'keep a School or be a Servant'. She lacked the strength to be a servant, she wrote, but keeping a school required paying rent, which could be prohibitive, and there was competition.[3] 'There is much to be done for youth in this place, it is my only comfort that perhaps I may be of some little use,' she wrote piously: 'I have a few Christian friends.'[4]

Isabella initially settled in gold-rich Dunedin where things went well to begin with. She took charge of a ladies' school and after a month's trial, her 'attractive manner of teaching' increased student numbers, the school moved to larger premises and she was promised £100 a year in salary. A year later she was in business for herself, opening a Select School for Young Ladies at Ellerslie House. She employed a teacher trained in the latest 'Pestalozzian system' for younger pupils and offered extras, a dancing master and a 'finishing class in music' with Mr James T. May.[5] (The Pestalozzian system of elementary education was devised by Swiss educational reformer Johann Heinrich Pestalozzi and popularised in the 1840s. At its core was the idea that children should be taught through activity, not abstract ideas, and should be free to pursue their own interests.)

It should have been a sound business decision. She had experience, 'having for some years been at head of a first-class school in Belfast, Ireland', and good references from persons of 'well-known standing' in both Belfast and Dunedin.[6] Located in Dunedin's main street, Ellerslie House had been a ladies' academy for two years, run by the unimpeachable Madame Laura Lubecki, wife of Polish Prince Alois Konstantin Lubecki.[7]

But Isabella's business was doomed by her ill health, lack of capital and Dunedin's high rents. Her enrolments shrank to three in the winter of 1865, and she became sick and fell behind on her rent of £200 per annum. When Miss Lewin from the FMCES in London expressed surprise at this amount, Isabella reaffirmed it.[8] Wages were also high: Isabella paid her servant £36 per year, and later, to make ends meet, she had to forgo the privilege and status of employing one. Her school closed and Isabella apologised to the FCMES for her inability to repay her debt: 'I was nicely established there but when the crash came I lost nearly all my pupils in one month. I tried to struggle and might have got on but my health broke down. I got a little behind in my rent and without getting time or notice I lost everything I possessed and was left without a pound.' And competition was fierce: there were 'quite too

BOARDING SCHOOL AT WANGANUI.

MISS CARY'S BOARDING SCHOOL at Wanganui, combines the advantages of town and country; having, in addition to a large and commodious dwelling house, an extensive and beautiful garden attached.

All the branches of an accomplished education usual in ladies' schools are taught, together with such training as is suitable for colonial life.

Terms: Board and residence, £10 10s per quarter; English, £2 2s per quarter; French, £1 10s per quarter; Music, £2 2s per quarter; Dancing, £1 10s per quarter.

References are kindly permitted to the Right Rev. the Bishop of Wellington; W. H. Watt, Esq., M.G.A.; and D. S. Durie, Esq., R.M., Wanganui.

MISS CARY begs to intimate that she will receive children by the week as boarders in case the out-settlers should wish to place their girls at school during the present unsettled state of the times.

St Hill-street, Wanganui,
July 13, 1868.

The conflict offered Isabella an entrepreneurial opportunity.

Wanganui Herald, 14 July 1868 (above); *Wellington Independent*, 16 August 1867

many persons engaged in teaching, if any other thing turns up, I shall give it up'. Those others included her own music teacher, James May, whose wife Caroline had a 'select boarding and day school' at Manor Lodge in Cargill Street.[9] Isabella advised the FMCES to 'tell the young women to work hard at home and remain there'.[10]

By 1867, through 'the kindness of friends', Isabella Cary had moved north to Whanganui, where she opened a boarding school and offered 'evening classes for girls' for two hours from 7 to 9pm, for £1 1s per quarter, paid in advance.[11] By now she did not regret emigrating. Despite her difficulties and the cost of living being 'three times' that of Belfast, she had broken ties with her home and found it easy to make friends in the colony. But still she found it 'a hard struggle for a lady to succeed' in New Zealand. The 'lower classes' managed, despite difficulties, but it was 'no use' for a 'well educated lady over thirty years of age' to emigrate, she told the FMCES firmly. The 'settlers' able to afford a governess did not want her sort, with refinements of drawing and music; they preferred a 'young strong middle class sort of person that can be helpful to them and teach their children to read and write'. And by 1867 there were 'a great many in New Zealand of this class'.[12] As she wrote at one point, 'the person you sent by the other Ship called upon me, she is the Class that suits'. This woman, Jane Merritt, worked at the St Paul's Anglican Church poor school in Auckland, employment Isabella felt beneath her.[13]

One might wonder why Isabella did not marry, given the purported preponderance of men in New Zealand. But, she explained in 1867, the education market was not the only one facing increasing competition: now 'a great many girls are left unmarried'. Male emigrants she found unsatisfactory. The 'younger sons of poor families, many are very much addicted to drink, just such men as no girl would marry'. Of course, if Isabella found the local offerings not to her taste, perhaps she was not to theirs either. She commented rather acidly, 'I fancy about 5 years back all eligible men were picked up by the servant girls, however their day has passed – there are young ladies enough now.'[14] Significantly, however, Isabella generally couched opportunities in New Zealand in terms of 'making money' rather than 'marrying well', indicating that both she and the FMCES saw the colonies as offering not only prospective husbands but also financial independence for women.

Isabella, who suffered from rheumatism, moved in 1869 to the warmer climate of Thames, where gold discoveries were boosting the economy. She advertised lessons at her home, Emerald Cottage, where a local minister also held divine service, suggesting Isabella found comfort and friendship in the church community. After nine years in Thames, she died in 1878 leaving her estate, valued at less than £100, to her sister in Ireland.[15]

Other FMCES immigrants, including Jane Merritt, about whom Isabella had been so disparaging, had more positive experiences. A 32-year-old governess who had worked in Staffordshire before migrating, Jane was full of enthusiasm for New Zealand. She declared herself 'so charmed with beauties of this exquisite country that I should quite grieve to leave'. Crucially, she was not alone, having emigrated with her brother, and she found eminently respectable friends. She worked for a cousin of Wellington's Bishop Charles Abraham, before teaching at the poor school.[16] Eliza Brook was equally 'charmed with colonial life' in Dunedin in 1869. She notably recognised that education was a business, one in which 'a thoroughly competent business woman would command a far higher salary than one unaccustomed to its details'.[17] Ten years later another FMCES governess, Marian Hett, went into partnership with the Caldwell sisters in a school in Gisborne, before moving to Palmerston North and opening her own establishment.[18] Harriet Herbert, ex-English governess and a one-woman welcoming committee and governess agency in Napier, reported to the FMCES that one Caldwell sister 'hopes soon to retire on an income mostly derived from her own savings'.[19] Other FMCES governesses found New Zealand men more to their taste than did Isabella Cary. Caroline Fox, who thought her charges in Timaru 'very backward', requiring 'more patience than brains to be exercised over their studies', blithely announced in 1880 that she was 'going to try matrimony for a change'.[20]

Demand for governesses varied across New Zealand and changed rapidly. In 1879 Harriet Herbert wrote of the 'great dearth all over New Zealand', asking the FMCES, 'Are you sending out any Governesses now?' Just seven months later, she was crying 'Hold, enough … I hope you will send no more just yet. I cannot place them.'[21] In 1878 Harriet had been the first woman elected to the Hawke's Bay Education Board. The local newspaper hoped her presence would encourage more women to attend the meetings.[22] While teaching itself was becoming increasingly feminised as the century progressed, governing bodies were slower to change.

A respectable business for a woman

It was not just FMCES governesses who entered the education business. Early on in the 1820s, missionary wives, including my own antecedents Jane and Marianne Williams, educated young Māori girls, predominantly training them as domestic servants but also teaching them basic literacy and numeracy. They were in the business of saving souls rather than making money. From 1840, however, with Pākehā emigration schemes based on growing families, businesswomen and men recognised a market, and schools of varying size, quality and longevity appeared. They taught working-class children basic literacy, gave up-and-coming young men a grounding in Latin and economics, and equipped middle-class young ladies with the requisite feminine accomplishments. In 1840s Wellington, alongside schools run by men were at least 11 run by women.[23] Some were 'dame schools', offering a meagre '3 Rs' for young working-class children. According to legend, Mrs Ann Mudgway pinned little ones to her apron to prevent them wandering.[24] Mary Ann Buxton's school was better, lasting from 1841, when she arrived with her gardener husband Harry and several children, until 1878, 30 years past her widowhood. In later years she and her daughter taught 'reading, writing, spelling and manners', with French, sewing, embroidery and deportment also available. Generations of Wellington schoolchildren remembered her as a no-nonsense but kind teacher.[25]

Memories of Sarah 'Granny' Cooper were more varied. From 1867 to 1888 she ran a school at her home in Ascot Street, Thorndon, after her watchman husband, William, died at the age of 50. Historian Fanny Irvine-Smith described 'a tiny little teacher, spectacled and rosycheeked, in print bonnet and voluminous skirts' teaching in a 'tiny little house' with a 'tiny little playground'. Her informant remembered her brother learning, besides reading and writing, the mysteries of knitting. Another pupil, Marcus Marks, recalled a 'tall, thin grey-haired lady with "specs"', a 'martinet'

Tucked away in Thorndon is the little cottage of Sarah 'Granny' or 'Governess' Cooper, dame school proprietor. It was restored by the Thorndon Society in 1972. Photo: Brett Mackay

who 'rapped us hard over the knuckles with a lead pencil'. Whether she was tiny or tall, both accounts remembered her Friday treats of fresh coconut.[26]

Women in the school business were often middle class, exploiting their education, social standing and cultural capital, sometimes becoming pillars of the community. They might be single, married or widowed. For some it was a lifelong career, for others an interlude. Young ladies straight off the ship exploited, or embroidered, their British or continental education and experience and advertised for pupils; wives of lawyers and businessmen capitalised on their social connections and opened select academies; middle-class widows, left penurious by erstwhile spouses, took in boarding pupils to make ends meet. Some schools announced with great fanfare were short-lived, disappearing when their proprietors married, moved elsewhere or went bust. Others became established and respected institutions, supporting their owners for a lifetime. A few were multigenerational, with a succession of female proprietors.

These schools were not necessarily large. Some women advertised for 'a few young ladies to educate with [their] own daughter[s]', suggesting a class of perhaps three or four. In Nelson Elizabeth Caldwell started modestly but had about 20 pupils in the 1850s, including several boarders, although this would prove more than she could handle.[27] Some larger schools had assistants and employed peripatetic teachers, often called, rather grandly, 'professors', for specialist subjects. Advertisements rarely boasted about size – after all, exclusivity was a virtue for a 'select' ladies' academy – favouring instead longevity, curriculum and reputation.

Public vs private

Dame schools and ladies' academies operated alongside church schools and, increasingly, public schools. From the 1850s provincial governments began to establish their own schools and assist others. These could be large, with classes of 50 to 80 children and a single teacher. In 1858 private schools catered for nearly 52 per cent of the school-going population throughout New Zealand and around 47 per cent in 1861, but by 1874, they accounted for only 28 per cent.[28] There were marked differences between provinces. In 1858 in Wellington private schools catered for 78 per cent of children, but in Nelson, with its strong public school sector, only 15 per cent. Nelson was the first province to introduce free public education, passing an Education Act in 1856. It was not universally popular. One *Colonist* correspondent objected to the 'Education Rate', which, he said, gave 'charity to those who do not require it'. James Cazaly, who sent his children to public school, replied. He considered free education 'a neutral ground on which children of all classes should be permitted to meet on an equality', and that the only distinction 'should be that obtained in the school by superior talents and diligence'. He thereby neatly articulated the archetypal meritocratic colonial dream.[29]

The 1877 Education Act established free, national, compulsory, secular primary school education throughout New Zealand for all Pākehā children aged seven to 13, along with quality benchmarks for both public and private schools. Small private schools for young children became less viable, and by 1888 private schools represented only 12 per cent of enrolments.[30] To survive, a private primary school had to provide something extra, often an imagined exclusivity and smaller classes.

Because girls' public high schools were not established until the 1870s, business opportunities in this sphere survived longer. Dunedin's Otago Girls' High School was the first in the Southern Hemisphere in 1871. Christchurch and Auckland followed in 1877. While Nelson College (for boys) was founded in 1856, girls had to wait until 1883, at which time Wellington also established a girls' high school. Although public education reduced business opportunities for private schools, public schools became increasingly feminised, and women who had been in business for themselves could swap independence for the security of a regular wage.[31]

Māori children

Most schools catered specifically for Pākehā children and 'young ladies'. Māori children were generally educated separately, initially by mission schools, with some government support after 1847. From 1867 a more formalised system of 'native schools' was established. Church-run boarding schools provided secondary education, initially for boys. There were few prospects for business ventures, although Wellington's Jane Boughton, wife of a public servant, saw an opportunity in 1868, successfully approaching politician Donald McLean for government financial support over about four years to board and educate selected sons of Māori chiefs.[32] In 1875 Napier's Hukarere Māori Girls' School provided the first secondary education for Māori girls. The fabled 'Hukarere Aunts', Bishop William Williams' spinster daughters, 'Miss Maria', 'Miss Kate' and 'Miss Mary Anne' – my own business-minded great-great-great-aunts – were in charge.[33]

There were exceptions to segregated education. In rural locations, some Pākehā settlers sent their children to 'native schools'.[34] Conversely, higher ranking Māori, particularly those with Pākehā fathers, could be accepted into nineteenth-century New Zealand Pākehā middle-class society – and their schools. Among the pupils at Mary Ann Woolly's Auckland ladies' academy around 1850 was Caroline Russell, half-sister of Emily (see Chapter 3) and daughter of George Russell and his second Māori wife, Herina Tuku.[35] George sent all his children to Auckland and Melbourne to receive an 'English' education.

The 1877 Education Act did not make it compulsory for Māori children to attend school but stipulated that 'any Māori shall be at liberty to send his children to a public school'. Significantly, the definition of Māori specifically excluded 'half-castes', unless they were living in Māori communities. Of course, even if Māori parents had the legal right to send their children to school, that did not mean that they were always welcomed by Pākehā parents.[36] Acceptance had its limits, whether in the public or private sector. When Elizabeth, the unfortunate Pākehā wife of missionary William Colenso, visited Auckland with Wiremu, the young son of her husband

and her servant Rīpeka Meretene, Elizabeth's father refused to allow the boy in his house. Emily Tucker, who ran a school at Woodlands Villa, came to the rescue. She 'kindly took charge of him for a fortnight or so', Elizabeth reported, but 'lost some of her scholars in consequence – the parents being highly indignant, considering it an insult to themselves'.[37] The daughter of a wealthy Hokianga merchant and his Māori wife was tolerable; the illegitimate son of a philandering missionary and his wife's Māori servant was not.

'We can keep ourselves'

The education business was a respectable option for middle-class women, especially if they needed an income while awaiting a husband, to avoid having to marry one, after losing one, or because a lacklustre one failed to provide. A really successful school could be lucrative, but equally, teaching students in small, home-based enterprises required little initial finance, merely an educated woman's cultural capital.

Many eager young single schoolmistresses did not last long, but not necessarily because they lacked pupils. Bright young women with some education and business nous may have relished their new independence but they were good catches in the marriage market. Of the 11 female-run schools in Wellington in the 1840s, at least four proprietors married and departed. Emily Wakefield and Mary George both married future premiers, although the former died in 1857, too early to enjoy her husband Edward Stafford's rise to power. Thirty-year-old Wilmott (Ann) Huxtable Tilke ran the 'earliest school in Wellington' for just a year in 1840 before marrying 21-year-old Joseph Lawrance who, like her, had sailed on the *Adelaide* from Ireland.[38] Another early school proprietor, Anna Maria Smith, married butcher George Luxford in 1847.[39] Elsewhere, Mary Ann Hilton advertised lessons for 18 months in Nelson, then married in 1846.[40] The three delightfully named Misses Crispe and Fussell, who offered a 'sound English education, with the comforts of home' in Auckland in 1857, by 1860 had all married and traded teaching for farming.[41]

Some schoolmistresses reappeared in business after being widowed, or when an extra income was required. Eighteen-year-old Frances Taylor arrived as a cabin passenger on the *Randolph*, one of the Canterbury Association's First Four Ships, in 1850. Listed on the passenger manifest as a schoolmistress, she immediately opened a school in Lyttelton and did not rush into matrimony. Eleven years later she married 32-year-old merchant Thomas Bygrave Trew and closed her school, but reopened it, in Cliff House in Sumner, after her husband died suddenly in 1866. It closed again when she wed likely bigamist Edward Roper in 1875.[42] Mary Ann Trotman ran a school in Wellington as a single woman from her emigration in 1862 to 1869, when, aged 37, she married widower Stephen Fagan. She reopened it two years later when her husband left, but they reconciled in 1873 and moved to Feilding. Stephen's shoe shop there was referred to as 'Mrs Fagan's', suggesting she swapped teaching for shoe selling. When she died in Bulls in 1893 the *Wanganui Herald* recorded that 'quite a gloom has been cast over the town'. Her husband's death two years later caused little comment.[43]

Mary Harvey migrated from Hobart to Wellington in 1840 with her publican husband, who died six years later at the age of 33. He had overindulged in his own wares and become mentally ill. Mary then advertised 'an excellent day school for children' on Lambton Quay. Although she was only in her forties, former pupils described her as an 'elderly Scotch woman' who had a habit of 'so "glowering" through her spectacles' at miscreants that no other discipline was necessary. She also diversified, importing a 'patent goffering machine' used to crimp fabric on ladies' dresses. After marrying John Waterson in 1849 she continued her school for at least four years, whether from a love of teaching or necessity or something in between.[44]

Emily Tucker's motivation was probably necessity. She was in the education business in Auckland from the 1840s to the 1880s, through a succession of husbands. Despite an apparent propensity for choosing unreliable, or perhaps just incompatible, husbands, she seemed undeterred by her matrimonial disappointments. Already widowed when a governess at Paihia's Church Missionary Society mission, she married Henry Tucker of the Royal Navy in 1846 and moved to Auckland. Henry was away frequently and Emily probably opened her school, Woodlands Villa, to support herself. Her husband's absences may have been a relief. When Bishop William Williams visited in 1848, he commented that Emily's 'language plainly intimates that she would be more happy without a husband'. After Henry's death in 1850 Emily continued her school but gave it up after marrying for a third time in 1857. Her new husband, assistant commissary general Frederick Brathwaite, decamped to England in the late 1860s, leaving Emily to fend for herself. Her school business reappeared for a short period, replaced by a boarding house in the 1870s. When she died in 1883 the *Auckland Star* described her as 'a very eccentric person'. Given her marital misfortunes, Emily's ability to run a business was essential to her survival.[45]

Having useless or unlucky husbands propelled several women into the schoolroom. Sarah Pratt opened her New Plymouth school because her husband had no full-time employment. Although she was successful, she confided in her sister in 1858 that she would 'like to drop my school and have music pupils instead', because they were both 'more lucrative viz two guineas per quarter' and would occupy only two days of the week. She achieved this in the 1870s, when advertisements for her music lessons appeared in the *Taranaki Herald*.[46] According to her biographer, Mary Anne Swainson's husband George was 'a likeable man', but he drank. Mary Anne was accustomed to being disappointed by men. Her own father, schoolteacher Henry Arrowsmith, deserted the family in England while his daughters were teenagers. In 1857, with her mother and sister, Mary Anne emigrated to Wellington, where she married George two years later. The school she started in 1869, just before his death in 1870, survives today as Samuel Marsden Collegiate School.[47] Alice Glover ran a school in Auckland from 1865 to 1888, obtaining a protection order against her husband Thomas, who 'followed no occupation', in 1882. They continued to cohabit, with Alice supporting her husband, having carefully arranged her property so it was not susceptible to his imprudent habits.[48]

In 1865 teacher Mary Ann Brassey was so frustrated by her husband's behaviour that she appealed to family friend, politician and later premier, John Hall. Her letter reveals the struggles faced by wives with unsatisfactory spouses. She had married in Sydney in 1846 at the age of 23 but was 'unfortunate in my choice [and] wished now I had married otherwise'. George Brassey, 13 years her senior, had been a lieutenant in the Bombay Native Infantry but was dishonourably discharged for being drunk on duty. Mary Ann bore five children in Sydney between 1849 and 1855, as well as establishing a ladies' seminary in Pyrmont by 1851; her husband was listed in directories as a 'gentleman'.[49] After 'ten years of patient endurance', she told John Hall, she 'determined on leaving' her husband. She escaped to England in 1855 but 'was compelled' to return to the colonies because George threatened to come to England. She implied she acted to protect his reputation, although perhaps she did not want her English friends and family to meet her embarrassing spouse. She brought her five children to Auckland in 1857 and 'made the best' of it, providing for her family by starting a boarding school in Grafton Road.[50] It was successful, notwithstanding competition from at least 20 other ladies' academies and public schools, and in 1867 she marketed her school as 'the oldest-established in Auckland'.[51] Mrs Brassey's academy continued until 1873. She told Hall that she was 'looked on by most as a widow', although George was not dead. Mary Ann, who

Pupils are just visible at the windows of Isabella Lewis's young ladies' seminary above her husband John's fancy repository in Shortland Street, Auckland. On Saturdays she taught dancing. Her school lasted from 1857 to 1869. Auckland Libraries, 7-A11702

sustained the family, did not rate an obituary when she died in 1882, but George, on his death a decade later, was remembered as 'an old identity … highly respected by all who knew him'.[52]

Other women may have had more than financial necessity as a motivation. Isabella Lewis perhaps wanted something to do. She was already 47 when she arrived in Auckland in 1857 with her husband John and stepson Henry. Her husband ran his own jewellery and fancy goods business but the couple had no children of their own. Isabella started a ladies' school that conveniently shared premises with her husband's shop at Cliff House and then Shortland House in Shortland Street from 1860. She continued in business after John's death in 1876 until, following a bus accident in 1881, she retired. By then she had relinquished Shortland House to Frances Haselden and her sister Mary Sabin Harden and moved to the smaller Epsom House. Isabella's 1888 obituary described her as an 'accomplished and successful teacher', and Epsom House as 'one of the best and most satisfactory ladies' boarding schools in Auckland'. She left her small estate of under £100 to her 'adopted' daughter Caroline Butcher Lewis, who had been her student.[53]

Barbara Macdonald may have had religious and evangelical motives, alongside a desire to make money. Widowed in Scotland in her mid-forties, she arrived in Whanganui in 1864 with several children and her sister. She must have had some capital because her long-lived school, St Helen's, was purpose-built on her own property. After her retirement in 1885, her assistant Harriet Stedman took over. When Barbara died three months after retiring, her obituary ignored her 20-year education business. She was remembered as 'well-known and much respected throughout the

Young lady boarders from St Helen's in Whanganui in the 1880s, typical of the pupils of ladies' academies throughout New Zealand. Whanganui Museum, SCS-MISC-043

district, aunt to the present member [of parliament, Robert Cunningham Bruce] for Rangitikei … and ever most active and zealous in the promotion of true religion'.[54]

Many of these women, particularly those with long-lived schools, probably found satisfaction in their work or had a vocation for teaching, but their primary aim was to make a living. Sarah Greenwood ran Woodland House, a boarding school for girls, in Nelson's Bridge Street between 1866 and 1872 with four of her seven daughters. Although Danforth Greenwood contributed £100, which covered the rent, from his salary of £250 as a member of the Legislative Council, the school was the mainstay of the family income, bringing in £750. Mother and daughters rose at six and worked through the day teaching and supervising boarders, while Danforth taught two local boys for two hours and gave a weekly history lesson to the girls, leaving the afternoons free to 'take his ease at his Club … happy and at rest in the knowledge' that his womenfolk were self-sufficient. Sarah's school was deliberately designed for her own and her daughters' independence. Three of the seven daughters remained single, supporting themselves with their own schools in Wellington. Sarah wrote that she was determined to show her husband that 'Come what may, *we* can keep ourselves … This same feeling of <u>our</u> capabilities is also very comforting to our sons.'[55]

Show me the money

As Isabella Cary discovered, running a school involved a delicate balancing act between paying rent and expenses and charging enough, but not too much. Cash-flow was critical, with charges generally levied per quarter and payable in advance to ensure money was on hand during the term. There were no refunds if a pupil was withdrawn, and sometimes a term's notice was specified. Fees varied according to the offerings, the target market and the cost of living. Some school proprietors, discreetly, did not advertise their fees in newspapers; others laid out a schedule that could be compared with those of competitors. At her Auckland school in 1863 Sarah Stothard saw a marketing opportunity and offered 'reduced terms' for 'daughters of settlers compelled to leave their homes' during the wars in the Waikato.[56]

In Wellington in 1841, Mrs and Miss Wakefield charged £8 8s per quarter for boarders, £2 2s for day pupils and extra for French, Italian and drawing.[57] Two years later Constantia Davison eschewed the usual practice of quarterly charges, and instead charged by the week: 1s 6d for reading, English and needlework, plus 1s for writing and arithmetic, and extra for geography, history, French and music.

Sarah Greenwood, who ran Woodland House school in Nelson, was also an artist. She painted this picture of the family's home and school, which attracted pupils despite its distance from the town centre.

Sarah Greenwood (1809–1899), *Woodland House, 5 July 1868*, watercolour, Nelson Provincial Museum, A4133.11

This was cheaper than the Wakefields, at £1 12s 6d per quarter for the basics, but neither her moderate fees nor her gentility guaranteed pupils: her advertisements disappeared within six months.[58] In 1842 a Wellington labourer earned between 30s and 40s a week, around £20 a quarter.[59] It is unlikely such a man, with a large family, could afford to send his daughters to these schools, unless his wife also had a business, but they might have attended Mrs Buxton's school, or been pinned firmly to Mrs Mudgway's apron.

Businesswomen needed to keep an eye on what the market would stand as far as fees were concerned. Miss Mary Ann Hilton miscalculated. She offered 'a useful and elegant education' in Nelson in June 1844 but had to 're-arrange' her charges six months after opening 'in order that they may meet as nearly as possible the present financial state of the colony'. She may not have been able to do so; in any case by the end of 1845 she was married and her business had disappeared.[60] Kawau Island's 23-year-old Emma Evans wrote to her father proudly that her school brought in £2

NEW SCHOOL.

A GIRLS' DAY SCHOOL to be conducted by Mrs. J. Morley, will be opened on Monday, Jan. 10th, in the building on the premises recently purchased by the Congregational Independents in connexion with the Rev. T. Hamer, for Chapel and Educational purposes, at the corner of Albert and Victoria streets, Auckland.

TERMS PER WEEK,

	s.	d.
Reading, English Grammar & Plain Work	0	6
Ditto, with Writing and Arithmetic	0	9
Ditto, with Geography, English History and Fancy Work	1	0

Mrs Morley's charges in Auckland worked out at £3 5s a quarter.

Daily Southern Cross, 7 January 1853

10s per month, adding to the £8–£15 her husband earned. (One might wonder about the quality of the education she offered, however. She apologised to her family for not writing sooner, explaining 'I wrote so bad my Dear Husband would not show me til I was taught to write better'.)[61]

Bigger towns allowed for higher fees, but there was more competition. Auckland's Mary Ann Christopher charged day pupils at 'Russel House' in Upper Queen Street £2 12s 6d with additional charges for music and singing, French and drawing. Her school ran from her arrival in 1855 until her marriage to Samuel Clarke in 1857. She also had boarders, charging per quarter £10 19s for younger children and £12 12s for pupils over 12 for a 'complete course of English education, boarding &c'.[62] In 1857 Mary Jane and Emma Crispe and Ellen Fussell in Epsom Road charged girls under nine a mere £8 per quarter, with £1 extra for young ladies. This provided 'board and instruction in Grammar, Geography, History, Writing, Arithmetic, Crochet, Plain and Ornamental Needlework'. Laundry was extra, as were French, music, singing, drawing and dancing. Their address in Epsom Road was less desirable than Miss Christopher's but it was strategically 'opposite the new Grammar School', ideal for boys' sisters.[63]

Mary Ann Woolly's Auckland school lasted from 1847 into the early 1860s. Although initially coy about advertising her terms, by 1852 she was printing them in full and quoting them in guineas to emphasise the class of her establishment. In 1852 she charged boarders 22 guineas a year (£23 2s) for 'all essential branches of a solid English education', with day pupils paying £1s 5s per quarter. By 1858 she had increased this to 30 guineas, which was the equivalent of about £7 17s 5d per quarter. Weekly boarders were charged 25 guineas and morning pupils 8 guineas a year. French, dancing and music were extra.[64] Frances Shayle George was also in business for a long time, from 1852 until the 1880s. Her charges in 1852 were similar to Mary Ann Woolly's, but she added boarders in 1858 at a flat fee of £50 per annum. This was decidedly more expensive than Mrs Woolly, but cheaper than Mrs Brassey, who charged £55 a year in Parnell.[65] It was also in line with other schools throughout the country at this time.[66] Her charges remained at that level for the next 10 years.

Standing out from the crowd

Marketing was critical in a school business and advertisements proliferated in newspaper columns at the beginning of each quarter. Some were brief, announcing a resumption of lessons, suggesting that the school was going well and elaborate publicity was unnecessary. Others were more detailed, emphasising whatever desirable quality in the curriculum or schoolmistress's experience made the school stand out. References were important. In smaller settlements businesswomen could rely on word of mouth, or distributed printed prospectuses. In more competitive markets there was a pressing need to attract and keep pupils.

A 'sound English education'

Competition was fiercest in the 'ladies' academies', where gentility was on the line. Stock offerings included 'all the usual branches' of a 'sound English education', sufficiently vague terms, one suspects, to allow for some leeway in the quality and exact subjects offered. Science was nowhere in evidence and mathematics limited to arithmetic and, very occasionally, geometry. In 1852 Frances Shayle George appealed to parents who felt isolated in the colonies, bereft of quality educational opportunities. She offered 'Every branch of Education … taught on the improved and simple system now adopted in many of the public [i.e. private] schools in England' at her Wye Cottage Seminary in Auckland.[67] Sarah Stothard also showed she was up with the latest educational practices, offering 'Pestalozzian Arithmetical Classes' and later opening the 'Pestalozzian Collegiate School for Young Ladies'. She also trained other teachers and governesses.[68]

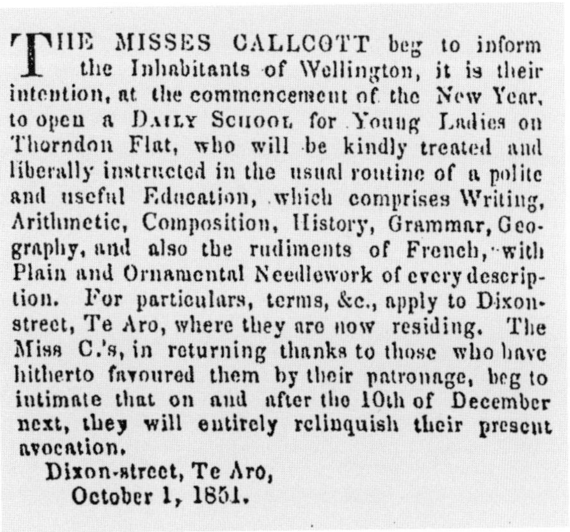
THE MISSES CALLCOTT beg to inform the Inhabitants of Wellington, it is their intention, at the commencement of the New Year, to open a DAILY SCHOOL for Young Ladies on Thorndon Flat, who will be kindly treated and liberally instructed in the usual routine of a polite and useful Education, which comprises Writing, Arithmetic, Composition, History, Grammar, Geography, and also the rudiments of French, with Plain and Ornamental Needlework of every description. For particulars, terms, &c., apply to Dixon-street, Te Aro, where they are now residing. The Miss C.'s, in returning thanks to those who have hitherto favoured them by their patronage, beg to intimate that on and after the 10th of December next, they will entirely relinquish their present avocation.

Dixon-street, Te Aro,
October 1, 1851.

The Misses Callcott helpfully defined the 'usual routine of a polite and useful Education'.

Wellington Independent, 4 October 1851

Offerings expanded later in the century. In 1883, Sophia Tate in Timaru offered 'all Branches of Modern Study':

Latin and calisthenics as well as modern languages, drawing, painting, classical and elementary music.[69] Growing sophistication in curricula required specialist teachers. French, music and drawing, which had been extras, were increasingly included, particularly in the upmarket ladies' schools in larger towns. Specialist masters and mistresses were recruited. As early as 1857 Mary Pittock in Auckland advertised that she employed 'experienced Masters' to teach music, singing, drawing and dancing.[70] Nearby, the Misses Crispe and Fussell were reminding would-be pupils that French would be taught 'by a Parisian'.[71] Alice Glover in 1869 promised that 'Masters will attend for French twice and for Dancing once a week' and she would offer 'Senior classes' for any 'branch of a sound education, arranged to suit the pupil'.[72]

One ladies' school in Auckland may have stepped outside the usual realm of needlework and French. In 1860 Alicia Ormsby Willcocks, a lawyer's wife, took over Hanover House, Mary Ann Woolly's established ladies' school. Her 'efficient staff of teachers' included Miss von Dadelszen, sister of the registrar general; she taught 'young gentlemen' as well as young ladies, and offered places for a 'limited number' of boarders.[73] When Alicia's husband Edward was transferred to New Plymouth under a year later, 'Commercial Parents' wrote to the newspaper deploring the departure from Auckland of 'this accomplished and amiable lady', who had 'by steady perseverance through many difficulties, succeeded in establishing a good Commercial school' catering for the 'rising branches of the commercial community in our City'.[74] Was she offering a genteel education for a new class? Or did she offer a radically new curriculum for girls, including accounting and bookkeeping? Her advertisements did not specify.

Some women eschewed the ladies' academic market and focused instead on boys' preparatory schools. Ann Alabaster ran the highly respected Lincoln Cottage school in Christchurch's Cranmer Square, preparing the scions of Canterbury's elite to attend nearby prestigious Christ's College. Already an experienced teacher, she began the school in 1862 after her vicar husband Charles had to give up his parish owing to ill health. He assisted her in the school, when his health permitted, until his death in 1865. Ann retired in 1882 and took in lady boarders until her remarriage in 1891 aged 49.[75] She had competition in the preparatory school business from 1869. Sibella Ross was the wife of amiable but unbusinesslike George A.E. Ross, who provided her with seven children but lost all their money and then became ill. She started her own boys' preparatory school, charging 10 guineas for day pupils and 45 guineas for boarders. As Canterbury biographer G.R. Macdonald noted admiringly, 'Mrs Ross was … a woman of 29 with a sick husband and 7 children under 10 to

FROM LEFT: Sibella Wilson with her daughters Kate and Sibella, c. 1864. The younger Sibella became Sibella Ross and, like her competitor Ann Alabaster, ran a boys' preparatory school and later a boarding house in Christchurch. Kate lived and worked with Johanna Lohse.

Private collection: Geoffrey Bremner, London

support … the whole burden fell on her and she showed herself well able to support it'.[76] The school moved in 1871 to a large, distinctive corrugated-iron house with a three-storey tower on the corner of Montreal and Gloucester streets built by Sibella's father, Archdeacon James Wilson. Her pupils also came from Christchurch's best families and many went on to Christ's College after leaving her establishment. 'All decent boys loved her,' remembered one ex-pupil, presumably a decent boy himself. Sibella also took in boarders attending other schools, charging £35 per annum. Social

ABOVE: Sibella Ross with two of her grandsons, John William Turton Ross (1891–1915) and Hugh Macpherson Ross (1890–1918). Both boys died in World War I.

Private collection: Geoffrey Bremner, London

LEFT: Sibella Ross in 1929, having seen four of her daughters follow her into the education business.

Private collection: Geoffrey Bremner, London

This distinctive house was home to Sibella Ross's school. Her daughter Rachel taught music here into the twentieth century. Private collection: Geoffrey Bremner, London

connection counted for much in Christchurch, so being the archdeacon's daughter was helpful. From 1875 until her retirement in 1883 her school was included, at her request, on the list of schools 'examined by the Government examiners'.[77] Like Ann Alabaster she then ran a boarding house.

Other women exploited the market for speciality subjects. As early as 1843 Caroline Young diversified at her regular school in Wellington to open a 'dancing academy' on Saturday evenings, charging 10s per quarter.[78] Emma Bessie Knyvett, who advertised piano lessons for seven years from her arrival at the age of 17 until her marriage to Provincial Secretary Alfred Greenfield in 1857, was, with her father, credited by the *Nelson Evening Mail* with 'the foundation of that sound musical taste for which in its early days, and for many years, [the town] was so favourably known'.[79] Mary Ann Scaife offered lessons on 'piano-forte, guitar, concertina, harmonium and in singing &c &c' in Nelson for 28 years from 1856.[80] Widowed in 1839 with a small son, she was in Leicester County Gaol, probably for debt, in 1841, but recovered to run a 16-year business as a music teacher in Leicester, before emigrating with her son and his wife. She became a stalwart of the Nelson Philharmonic Society, where her abilities on the piano were appreciated. In 1862 she lost her house and £500 worth of musical instruments in a fire. A public subscription raised funds to assist her. Twenty-two years later, in 1884, she lost her life in another house fire and was greatly missed in the community. Within a month 'Mrs W. Shannon' was advertising piano lessons from 'the Cottage recently occupied by the late Mrs Scaife', cashing in on the 'old esteemed resident's' reputation.[81]

Caroline Fleetwood, whose husband John was a popular piano teacher and performer, provided dancing lessons in Parnell in Auckland from 1856. She also ran subscription balls, catering variously for tradesmen and for ladies and gentlemen, until her early death, aged 32, in 1858.[82] Isabella Lewis added Friday dancing classes and Saturday 'Tonic Sol-Fa Singing Classes' for children to her ladies' academy at Shortland House in the 1860s.[83] In 1868 Emma Laman offered dancing classes for 1 guinea in Epsom. She began with two classes on Wednesday afternoons, an earlier one 'for the convenience of Children' and another in the evening for adults. Finding herself immediately oversubscribed, she started a second evening class within the month. As the wife of a cowkeeper, Emma probably attracted working-class pupils, although it is tempting to imagine that at least one labourer's son was tripping the light fantastic with a doctor's daughter. By the 1870s she ran balls in her schoolroom and diversified, adding wax flower-making lessons on Thursday afternoons. She remained in business after her husband John's death

MRS. ASKIN'S SCHOOL, WELLINGTON.

THE NOTICE OF PARENTS is called to this Establishment as furnishing all the requisites of a LADY'S EDUCATION. The system pursued is of the most comprehensive kind, embracing English in all its branches, French, Music, Dancing, and Drawing; whilst Religious teaching in conformity with the principles of the Church of England occupies its own proper and prominent position.

TERMS.—Board & Education, 50 guineas per ann.

The above terms are as moderate as is consistent with the character of the School, which, perhaps, is second to no other in the attention bestowed on the Education of its Pupils, and the liberality adopted to secure their health and domestic comfort.

Each pupil is expected to bring two pairs of sheets and four towels.

Kummitoto St.
July 20, 1858.

in 1878 until her remarriage, at 56, to engineer Francis Hewson.[84]

Alongside a variety of subjects, ladies' schools also offered a moral education. In 1860 Annie Willshire promised 'strict attention to the Moral and Mental Training of her Pupils', reflecting parents' concerns in booming Dunedin.[85] Frances Taylor in Christchurch also promised 'the strictest attention … to the religious and moral training of the pupils'.[86] Wellington's Sophia Askin made sure to emphasise that 'Religious teaching in conformity with the principles of the Church of England occupies its own proper and prominent position', importantly signalling that she was not Catholic.[87]

Others had a softer approach. Schoolmistresses, especially those offering boarding, were in loco parentis, often emphasising 'parental care' in their marketing.[88] Auckland's Mary Ann Woolly headed her initial advertisements 'Home Education' in 1852.[89] Margaret and Caroline Callcott in Wellington in 1851 reassured parents that their pupils would be 'kindly treated'.[90] In Auckland in the 1860s Alicia Willcocks offered places for boarders 'to whose comfort and happiness particular attention will be devoted', without forgetting that 'their religious and moral training [would be] carefully attended to'.[91]

Although advertising the comforts of home was a marketing ploy, those comforts were also memorable parts of a boarding school education. The Barr family in Whanganui remembered housekeeper Aggie McGregor's cakes at Barbara Macdonald's school as a major incentive for attendance (and for boys to visit their sisters), and boarders at Mary Anne Swainson's school in Wellington were particularly fond of her elderly mother Isabella, because of her 'special delectable teas'.[92]

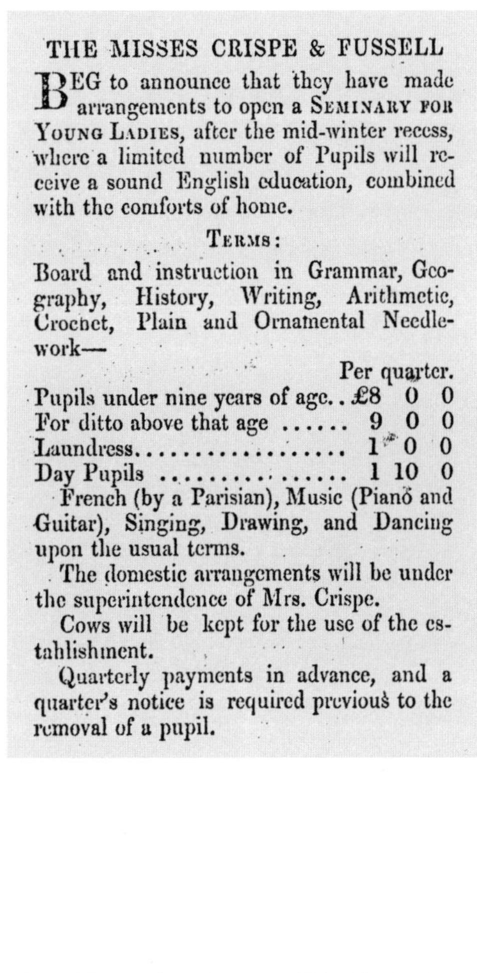
THE MISSES CRISPE & FUSSELL

BEG to announce that they have made arrangements to open a SEMINARY FOR YOUNG LADIES, after the mid-winter recess, where a limited number of Pupils will receive a sound English education, combined with the comforts of home.

TERMS:

Board and instruction in Grammar, Geography, History, Writing, Arithmetic, Crochet, Plain and Ornamental Needlework—

	Per quarter.		
Pupils under nine years of age..	£8	0	0
For ditto above that age	9	0	0
Laundress..................	1	0	0
Day Pupils	1	10	0

French (by a Parisian), Music (Piano and Guitar), Singing, Drawing, and Dancing upon the usual terms.

The domestic arrangements will be under the superintendence of Mrs. Crispe.

Cows will be kept for the use of the establishment.

Quarterly payments in advance, and a quarter's notice is required previous to the removal of a pupil.

LEFT: Sophia Askin justified her high fees with reference to her attention to her students' health and domestic comfort. *Hawke's Bay Herald*, 31 July 1858

RIGHT: In 1857 Mary Jane and Emma Crispe and Ellen Fussell emphasised the comforts of home.

New Zealander, 9 July 1856

With 'considerable experience'

Establishing oneself in a new business in a new town was never easy. Citing experience, whether real, exaggerated or imagined, was important. When she opened her Auckland school in 1863, Miss Mary Grace Anstie announced she was 'a lady who has had considerable experience in the work of Tuition in the neighbourhood of London'. This was so vague that she might have been a governess with a single pupil, but she had in fact run a school in England with her sister Sarah for at least 12 years.[93] Margaret Fleetwood was equally imprecise about her 'experience in the tuition of children' when she opened a Young Ladies' Seminary in Ghuznee Street, Wellington.[94] Later, in Napier, she traded on her husband's expertise, as 'the Widow of the late Mr Fleetwood, Professor of Music'.[95] When Mary Ann Fagan resumed teaching in Wellington after her marriage, she hoped her 'management of children both mentally and physically [was] known and appreciated too long to require comment'.[96] Mrs Garland, assisted by Miss Susan Seaman, opened her school in Auckland in 1872, claiming 'English and colonial experience in teaching', although her experience has been impossible to verify.[97]

The advantage of experience and connections in Britain was undeniable. England was the benchmark of gentility in ladies' education. In 1849, Auckland school proprietor Mrs Thomas advertised that she had 'for many years kept a similar establishment in Cheltenham, well known as one of the most fashionable watering places in England'.[98] In 1873 and again in 1875, FMCES governess Kate Brind wrote of the 'great demand' for English governesses by employers 'thinking nothing of colonial girls'. 'The very fact of their coming out from England is a recommendation,' she declared.[99] In Whanganui in 1868, Barbara Macdonald advertised the assistance of both her sister and 'a most accomplished lady from the Home Land' (Miss Spalding). She could therefore 'offer an education second to none in New Zealand'.[100] The European continent was also an advantage in the right circles. Mademoiselle Anne Lempriere's name may have gained her some exotic cachet when she advertised her school in Rozel Cottage in Union Street, Auckland, in 1865, although she was from Jersey, not Paris.[101]

Those without experience used their own education and social background. Wellington's Constantia Davison, running a 'respectable day school for little girls' in 1843, emphasised she had 'received the education of a gentlewoman' and was 'the widow of a gentleman, who for several years held a responsible situation in the government'.[102] Music teachers claimed to have studied with great masters. In the *Otago Daily Times* on 26 May 1863, 'A LADY (Pupil of Stephen Glover and

EDUCATION!

SUPERIOR ADVANTAGES!

MRS. PITTOCK, from London, who has been engaged for many years in the instruction of young Ladies in the English and French languages, has Vacancies for a few Pupils. Experienced Masters attend for Music, Singing, Dancing, and Drawing.

Prospectus can be obtained at Mr. Wayte's, Queen-street, Mrs. Law's, Parnell, or at the Office of this paper.

*** The ensuing term commences on the 29th September.

Thalberg)' offered 'Finishing Lessons' on pianoforte, singing and instruction in drawing and French. She signed herself 'Marguerite', perhaps also hoping to sound continental. On the same page, 'a pupil of Franz Liszt' offered music lessons.[103] Well-travelled Eliza Reynolds, who had lived in China, Canada, the Caribbean and the United States before arriving in Nelson in 1858, advertised not only as 'late Organist at the Roman Catholic Cathedral, Georgetown', with 'considerable experience in tuition as resident finishing Instructress in noble and distinguished families in Europe', but also claimed to have been 'for eight years pupil of the celebrated Henri Herz, pianist to the Royal Family of France'.[104] This was a popular assertion, according to Herz's contemporary, composer and music critic Oscar Commettant. 'To be a student of Herz conveys a title: it is almost a license,' he commented, wondering 'how many women professors have had nothing to recommend them to their clients except that they were pupils of Henri Herz'. He observed cynically that 'If all the students of Herz had taken lessons with that master it would be perfect but

Mary Pittock promised 'Superior Advantages' because of her experience. Unfortunately she also later advertised lessons in 'wax flour making', casting doubts in parents' minds about her spelling, if nothing else. *Daily Southern Cross*, 22 September 1857 and 24 September 1858

EDUCATION.

MRS. PITTOCK'S Young 'Ladies Establishment, for Boarders and Day Pupils. The course of Instruction comprises English in all its branches, with French, Music, Drawing, Plain and Fancy Needlework.

Lessons can also be had in Wax Flour Making

The ensuing quarter will commence on the 29th inst. Prospectuses on application.

Upper Queen-street,
September 18th, 1858.

Mr. Pittock's

PREPARATORY School for Young Gentlemen. The ensuing quarter will commence on 29th instant.

Terms .... £1 11 6 per qr.
Under six years of age 1 1 0 " "

September 18, 1858

if you look carefully you will find many that do not even know him.'[105] Qualifications were difficult to check in the far-flung colonies of the British Empire.

The right references

Alongside the right fees, the perfect curriculum and some experience, it was important to have references, ideally local and checkable. These established one's community connections, which could be the making or breaking of a school business, and reinforced one's respectability and gentility. Mary Ann Christopher, 'lately arrived from England', offered references from 'Ministers and influential gentlemen' when she opened her school in Auckland in 1855.[106] The Wakefields in Wellington in 1841 were more specific, directing interested parents to three local gentlemen: the surveyor general Captain William Mein Smith, prominent businessman Thomas Mitchell Partridge and *Gazette* newspaper proprietor Samuel Revans.[107] In February 1866 Mary Stedman, reportedly 'not quite 7 ft high but positively taller than almost any man in Christchurch', provided as referees 'Rev. Archdeacon Jacobs, Dr Turnbull, Mrs Bealey and Mrs Macfarlan', all well-known residents.[108] In 1869 Mrs Mary Ann Graves in Upper Symonds Street in Auckland offered two Wesleyan pastors, indicating her religious affiliation, and a local surgeon. She also emphasised her school was 'lately the residence of J.H. Burnside, Esq', a local businessman, illustrating it was a suitably elegant location for young ladies' education.[109]

Some traded off the reputation of previous school proprietors. Frances Taylor advertised in 1858 that she had taken over the Gloucester Street premises of Mrs Beechey, who was one of the few trained singers in Christchurch (see Chapter 11). From 1860 Frances also cheekily advertised as 'Christchurch Ladies School', a title already in use by the redoubtable Maria Thomson, who had been in business since 1853.[110] In 1869, Auckland's Alice Glover outlined the

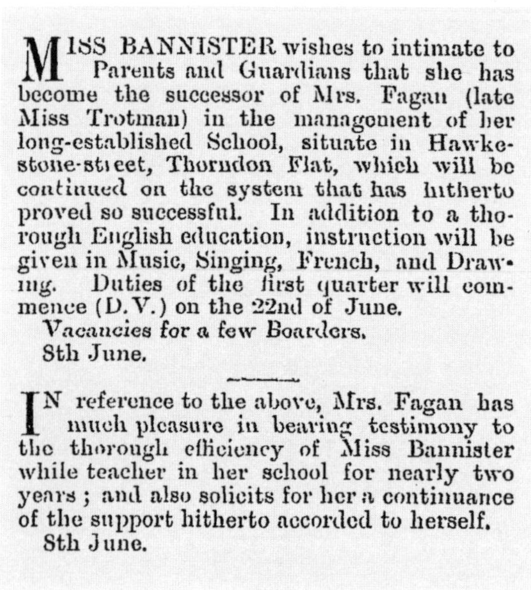
MISS BANNISTER wishes to intimate to Parents and Guardians that she has become the successor of Mrs. Fagan (late Miss Trotman) in the management of her long-established School, situate in Hawkestone-street, Thorndon Flat, which will be continued on the system that has hitherto proved so successful. In addition to a thorough English education, instruction will be given in Music, Singing, French, and Drawing. Duties of the first quarter will commence (D.V.) on the 22nd of June.
Vacancies for a few Boarders.
8th June.

IN reference to the above, Mrs. Fagan has much pleasure in bearing testimony to the thorough efficiency of Miss Bannister while teacher in her school for nearly two years; and also solicits for her a continuance of the support hitherto accorded to herself.
8th June.

A new proprietor was especially blessed when her predecessor vouched for her.
Evening Post, 9 June 1869

'ample advantages' of her newly leased 'Large House and Extensive Premises lately occupied by Mrs Brathwaite, in Symonds Street, and known as Woodlands Villa'. Acknowledging Emily Brathwaite (previously Tucker) was a smart business move, since she had been teaching at Woodlands Villa on and off for at least 25 years.[111]

The right connections

Having friends and, even better, family around you, not only meant a happier life, but also a more successful business. FMCES governess Fanny Cross, like Isabella Cary, felt that although New Zealand's climate was agreeable and the people generally 'hospitable', 'this is a very Monstrous life, and I should not advise any single woman to come out to the Colonies without having some friends'.[112] Community connections were vital. In 1855 Sarah Pratt in New Plymouth told her sister that she had six students in her fledgling school and 'wanted more but being a stranger, I am told is a drawback so I must wait'. Three years later she had 14, which she found more than enough.[113]

Mary Ann Woolly started her school in Auckland after being widowed in 1847, her husband leaving her little but his good name. She had, however, experience and a network of family support. With her sisters Rebecca and Sarah Ann Cuttell she had run a school at Hanover House in Highgate, London, in the 1830s, and by the 1850s all three sisters were in New Zealand. Rebecca married George Reynolds and ran a Wellington boarding house but then joined Mary Ann in her Auckland school in 1848. Sarah Ann married Thomas Cleghorn and after his death in 1854 also joined the school business. Although both sisters moved to Melbourne two years later, Mary Ann had built her reputation: when she moved to Remuera in 1860, she advertised her school as the 'old and select establishment for the education of young ladies'.[114]

In 1863 50-year-old Mary Grace Anstie relied on the assumed unimpeachability of the church when she advertised her school from the home of her sister Anna and brother-in-law, Baptist minister Philip H. Cornford, in Newton, Auckland.[115] The arrival in 1874 of her younger sister Sarah, with whom she had taught in London, provided added support. The Misses Anstie were back in business together by mid-1875.[116]

In Christchurch, connections to the Anglican establishment were most beneficial. Both Ann Alabaster and Sibella Ross benefited from this. In Sibella's case education was also a family business: four of her daughters, Dolly (Cecilia), Margaret,

Tibe (Sibella) and Rachel, were teachers. Rachel advertised music lessons from the tower house into the twentieth century. Meanwhile Sibella's sister Kate Wilson lived and worked with Johanna Lohse, who ran girls' schools in Riccarton and then central Christchurch between 1873 and 1890. Although German, Johanna Lohse also made herself part of the Christchurch establishment through the Anglican Church, funding scholarships for daughters of clergymen. As a native speaker, she offered German lessons, which gave her school a point of difference. She also published *Mistaken Views on the Education of Girls* in 1885, once again propelling her business into the public eye.[117] Johanna's pupils were taken over by her neighbour, Annette Bowen, after the death in 1890 of her husband Archdeacon Croasdaile Bowen. She ran the school until 1909, retiring upon the establishment of an Anglican girls' school, St Margaret's, which survives today. Her staff included Sibella's daughter Tibe, who 'overworked herself at Mrs Bowen's', according to her nephew Philip Hedgeland.[118]

Sarah Greenwood's school Woodland House in Nelson was not advertised in the newspapers – it did not need to be. Although their school was not central, but near the river on Bridge Street in the 'Wood', their public reputation ensured a stream of students. The importance of community connections was evident when Elise Pickett took over Woodland House in 1871. Having had a successful store in Wellington, and then a failed partnership with her brother on a property at Lake Wakatipu that ruined both families, Elise and her husband Gilbert moved to Nelson, where Elise's sister lived. Elise had Woodland House for two years before moving to larger, more central premises in Hardy Street. Her school failed to thrive, despite repeated advertisements for five years.[119] Gilbert, an accountant by training, wrote in desperation to politician Donald McLean seeking employment because 'the school does not bring in enough to keep us in food and clothing'.[120] Competition in Hardy Street from the thriving public school was a possible reason for its failure. Another was Elise's lack of community connections, in contrast to the Greenwoods. She was often in court chasing parents' fees. When she tried to air her grievances in the local newspaper, it published a polite but firm refusal to engage in a private dispute. After the demise of the school she and Gilbert ran a boarding house before Elise discovered a different sort of life and community. In 1889 she moved to Melbourne without her husband and, at the age of 63, reinvented herself entirely, not as a businesswoman but as a theosophist. The 'Indefatigable Pickett', as she became known, founded societies in Melbourne, Adelaide and Sri Lanka, living what she called 'the most momentous and important part of her life'.[121]

Elise Pickett escaped her husband and an unsuccessful Nelson business to become a theosophist in later life. The 'Indefatigable Pickett', as she was known, was founder of the Melbourne Theosophical Society and headmistress of a school in Colombo, Sri Lanka.

Photo: Anne Coombs

Location, location, location

Location was almost always critical to a successful school and wise businesswomen advertised the particular benefits of their situations. In 1849 Mary Ann Woolly achieved the desirable trifecta of size, centrality and health, when she moved to Prospect House in Auckland's Hobson Street. It was a 'commodious and delightfully situated house in a most healthy, and at the same time most convenient, part of town'.[122] Her emphasis on its wholesome atmosphere counteracted memories of the previous year's evacuation from her old school when her daughter had scarlet fever, but a healthy location also denoted a good part of town.[123] Her competition, Mrs Thomas, likewise suggested that her Queen Street house, 'being large and commodious, and in a most healthful situation, is particularly adapted to promote the comfort and health of the pupils'.[124]

At the other end of the country in Southland in 1867, chemist's wife Louisa Rocke, 'late of Carlton, Melbourne', enthused about the benefits of her new 'first-class' boarding and day school in Riverton, which was 'well-known as the most healthy and picturesque district in the Province', offering children 'a healthy and cheerful seminary'. Whether she managed to convince any parents is unknown: her advertisements disappeared within six months. By 1875 she was employing a governess herself: perhaps her husband Richard's business had profited sufficiently for Louisa's income to be unnecessary.[125]

An air of gentility

Ladies' academies clustered in the better streets: Alice Glover, Mary Ann Graves and Mary Grace Anstie were within a stone's throw of one another in Auckland, creating a zone of genteel refinement.[126] Gentility was critical because most teachers, and their potential pupils, were middle class. Their ideal of feminine behaviour proscribed engagement in the grubby world of commerce and advocated modesty, self-sacrifice and a quiet life revolving around the drawing room, kitchen and garden. Teachers needed to present themselves as appropriate role models. Advertising in public spaces and teaching pupils for money was, by definition, the antithesis of such behaviour. Schoolteachers navigated this contradiction in various ways.

Some advertisements were particularly coy, obscuring name, address and charges, underscoring the well-bred nature of the demure advertiser. In Wellington in 1853, for example, 'A YOUNG LADY having a few leisure hours each day' advertised that she 'would be happy to give Lessons in Music. For particulars apply at the Office of this Paper.'[127] Not only was she careful to describe herself as a lady, and a young one at that, but there was no suggestion of anything so vulgar as running a business. This was a mutually beneficial activity to be conducted in leisure hours. Concealing her identity and address kept her at one remove from the commercial nature of the transaction and allowed her to retain a degree of privacy. Her advertisements appeared regularly. In September 1853 she revealed she was based in Te Aro and 'will also be happy in arranging to go to the Hutt once every week' as she 'wishes to add a few more to the number of her Pupils': she was touting for trade but as discreetly as possible.[128]

Elizabeth Caldwell adhered to the middle-class female script of modest gentility, downplaying her initiative, when she described her business in her memoirs. She claimed she 'was *beset* to give lessons' on her piano as there were no music teachers in Nelson in the 1850s – and indeed few pianos. Then, because there was no 'select school', she 'consented to take a few pupils for other subjects', implying that service to community was her motivation. Her 'few pupils' expanded until she had about 20, including six girl boarders. Despite her modesty, she could not help admitting satisfaction in her enterprise: 'having been educated at the best schools in Edinburgh and pursuing a well-directed system the teaching was a great enjoyment to me'. Although she had difficulties, her boarders 'did well with their studies and were happy with us – [and] afterwards filled good positions in Society'. One, she noted piously, 'became an eminent missionary so that the fruit of my labour was not lost'.[129]

Middle-class women trod a careful line between being capable individuals and retaining an appropriately feminine vulnerability. This façade of helplessness has sometimes deceived later chroniclers, unable to imagine that a young gently bred woman could fend for herself. Such was the case with Sophia Askin. She lost her husband of two years, Walter, within a week of reaching Wellington from Ireland in 1857. At just 23, Sophia was left in an unfamiliar country with a stepdaughter and baby to support and property worth less than £200. Fortunately her 21-year-old sister Catherine Hannon had accompanied them. A 1992 family history suggested rather dismissively that 'neither woman had any idea how to earn a living, but somehow managed to set up a small private school in Wellington'. In fact, Sophia had quite a good idea of business. Her school in Wellington's Kumutoto Street (now Bowen Street) was advertised as far away as Hawke's Bay and Nelson and her pupils included George Clifford, son of the speaker of the House of Representatives.

She could afford, and was astute enough, to take out life insurance, aware that she was her daughters' only means of support, particularly once her sister married in 1859.[130] Sophia herself remarried in 1863, to bank employee Edward Tate, and the family relocated to Timaru in 1868. In 1882 53-year-old Edward died of apoplexy when their youngest child was barely two. Sophia, his executor, estimated his estate to be worth 'under £3000'; subsequent court cases with creditors suggest it may have been substantially less. Sophia went back into business, opening Baltrasna School at her home in Elizabeth Street with a Miss Kemp. It continued for at least five years.[131] Sophia was obviously capable of supporting herself and her family when required.

A whiff of scandal

For a woman making a living educating respectable young ladies, personal reputation was critical. Elizabeth Burbidge, proprietor of a ladies' school in Mulgrave Street, Wellington, hit the headlines in 1858 and was lucky to salvage anything from the ensuing scandal.

Among Elizabeth's pupils were three daughters of Nelson businessman George William Schroder, who was taken to court by local Anglican vicar, the Reverend Arthur Baker, for publicly horse-whipping him. Schroder countered by accusing Baker of sexually assaulting his youngest daughter, 12-year-old Mary. The three Schroder sisters had been staying with Reverend Baker, presumably a family friend, while attending Miss Burbidge's school. One day Mary was ill and remained behind while her sisters went to school, and Baker apparently assaulted her. Mary told her sisters and Elizabeth Burbidge of the attack.

The court case excited much public interest. Elizabeth was undone when her letters to Baker were published: they revealed she had thought she, rather than Mary, was the object of his attentions. Inevitably, Elizabeth's position as a suitable carer, educator and guiding force in the lives of respectable young girls of Wellington seemed untenable. She appeared ridiculous at best – a gullible middle-aged spinster – or at worst, negligent, oblivious to an assault on a girl in her charge. Nevertheless, she remained at the same address for another seven years and was purchasing school stationery from Old Smith's store in Te Aro in 1867, suggesting that she still had pupils, although perhaps not of the same social class. She died a year later aged 50 in the less salubrious area of Pipitea Point, leaving an estate of about £50.[132] Gentility, once lost, was seldom regained.

Behind the hype

Newspaper advertisements were not designed to tell the truth about a school. Even repeated advertising did not necessarily denote a successful enterprise. Fortunately we have tantalising glimpses of actual life behind schoolroom doors in memoirs and letters of pupils, parents and visitors. Some endorsed the advertisements. Caroline Newman, wife of Auckland Provincial Council member Joseph, sent her daughters Hannah and Carrie to Mary Ann Christopher's school in Auckland and wrote home in 1855, 'we like Miss Christopher very much'. They were surely disappointed when she married in 1857 and moved away.[133]

Others do not tally with the marketing hype. Emily Tucker's advertisements in 1848 suggest she ran a well-regarded, excellent school: she promised to 'continue to bestow the same attention to the health and Education of her pupils which has long characterised her Establishment at New Zealand'. Her previous employer Bishop William Williams was unimpressed, however, commenting that her replacement at Paihia mission, Elizabeth Rich, was 'as much superior in manner and attainment to Mrs Tucker as possible'.[134]

The diary of one of Mrs Caroline Barnes' pupils exposes the harsh reality of her Auckland 'ladies' academy' in the 1860s. Emma Garland's family emigrated in steerage on the same ship as Caroline and John Barnes, who were cabin passengers. After settling in remote Awhitū, the Garlands sent young Emma to board with the Barnes family, understanding she would be educated while helping with Caroline's new baby, Annie. In fact, as Emma later remembered, her lessons were 'a farce ... all that Mrs B wanted was a little nurse girl, who could give no trouble, and could run all the messages'. She was dispatched daily to the local Thistle Hotel for Mrs Barnes' lunchtime half-pint of beer, and was ousted from her tiny bedroom during a long period of the Barnes' marital discord and made to sleep on the schoolroom floor. That was about the only time she saw the inside of the schoolroom – the promised afternoon classes with the other pupils rarely eventuated. Although 'not an unhappy child', Emma always had 'that lonely feeling' while she was living with Mrs Barnes, who was 'a hard woman'. Despite visits from her family, it was a year before her father fetched Emma home. In 1872 young Annie Barnes was sent by the magistrate to the Auckland Industrial School as a neglected child. Caroline had left her with a neighbour, a 'bad character', while John Barnes was in gaol for assaulting his wife. Nevertheless, Mrs Barnes advertised her 'seminary for young ladies' until 1875.[135]

Henry Daniell's educational problem

Nelson's early obsession with education was no guarantee of quality, at least according to accountant and New Zealand Company employee Henry Cooper Daniell. Blessed with four daughters and two sons, he complained vociferously to his sister in England about the quality of Nelson's schoolteachers in the 1840s and 1850s.[136] One school, run by a 'young person from Launceston' in early 1846, 'might have succeeded tolerably well', but the teacher 'unfortunately had acquired a love for drink' and was 'obliged to leave'. A month later he reported that 'a Lady who had the necessary qualifications' was to open a school. She retired within six months because of ill health, and the only available option was a 'very mixed affair' run by a surgeon's wife.

In 1847 Henry Daniell more happily sent his daughters to be educated by the newly arrived Dorothy Tomkies (see Chapter 12) and, after she left in 1851, to Elizabeth Caldwell, who took some pride in her achievements. Henry was not so impressed. He described it as a 'most unsatisfactory' school with '18 to 20 girls all ages, sizes and capabilities to whom she was supposed to communicate in addition to the ordinary branches of education, Music, drawing &c'. It was probably typical of many. Elizabeth had also 'two or three small children continually about her (one an infant) besides two or three great boys, as often without a servant girl as with one – and her husband fully occupied in other pursuits'. Henry conceded Elizabeth was an able teacher, but 'under such difficulties and disadvantages, what education or instruction could be expected?'[137] Even Elizabeth admitted that the servant problem and an absent husband meant teaching on top of 'the cares of an increasing family … seemed more than I was equal to'.[138]

Fortunately for Henry Daniell's piece of mind, his estimable spinster sister, 45-year-old Sarah, appeared in Nelson in 1856 to save the day. Although she arrived in the same year that the province introduced free public education, she ran a school in Nelson for 23 years until her death, when her niece, Ann Randall Daniell, took over. We know little about the school other than of its existence. Sarah advertised for boarding pupils in Hokitika newspapers, and later also taught boys. 'Miss Daniell's School' was still advertised half a century later in 1909, by which time Ann was nearly 70.[139]

Parental dissatisfaction and the ephemeral nature of individual schools gave rise to much shopping around. William Charles Hodgson, himself a teacher and then Nelson's inspector of schools (recommended as his successor by Danforth

Greenwood), sent his daughters to three schools. Rebecca and Agnes went first to Sarah Daniell with their cousins. Then they went to widow Catherine Rentoul, who ran a school in Trafalgar Street for at least nine years from 1860. She did not advertise details of her curriculum and Rebecca remembered her merely as 'a fine old lady', who taught with her daughter.[140] Rebecca left Mrs Rentoul when Sarah Greenwood's school opened in 1866. Rebecca recalled the Greenwoods as a 'most accomplished family', her favourite teacher being daughter Jane, who taught drawing and later exhibited successfully as Jane Stowe. Sarah Greenwood spoke and taught French well, was 'an Italian scholar, a good musician' and 'the dearest little old lady with a great sense of humour'. She was, of course, as we have seen, much more than that.[141]

There were no official reports on individual private schools and their teachers, but public schools were regularly inspected, with details and examination results published in local papers. These include reports about one teacher who switched from private enterprise to paid employment when Nelson introduced free public education, illustrating the qualities expected of a female school proprietor.

Elizabeth Smith ran a private school in Collingwood Street in Nelson from 1852 after arriving in 1850 as a 25-year-old with her parents, Richard and Elizabeth Smith, and an abundance of younger siblings. Her father died shortly after their arrival and her mother opened a popular general store (see Chapter 9).[142] Elizabeth's school continued past her marriage in 1855, aged 30, to 50-year-old Francis Sait. The following year, with an established business, a schoolroom ready and waiting and good community connections, Elizabeth was appointed as an ideal 'duly qualified' teacher to run Nelson's new girls' public school. All that was required was to rename Mrs Sait's private academy. Elizabeth remained a public school teacher in Nelson for 26 years.[143]

Early reports of the new school were positive. In 1857 she had 90 pupils, testimony, said the *Nelson Examiner*, to 'the confidence shown by the public in [her] ability'. At the end of the year examiners pronounced themselves 'well satisfied' with the now 118 girls, particularly considering that they were crowded into a schoolroom 'adapted to accommodate comfortably' just half that number.[144] In 1864 the school was split in two, with 50 girls in Mrs Sait's care. Inspector William Hodgson was impressed that they were 'well-grounded' in their subjects, but also that 'great attention is paid to keeping the schoolroom neat and tidy', adding somewhat fastidiously, 'It is beginning to be understood that these apparently trifling matters go far to make up the sum of what is meant by a good school.'[145] He did not, however, send his own daughters there.

By 1868 Elizabeth had a pupil teacher and the school was considered second only to the first division boys' school in the town. This, impressively, placed her 60 pupils near the top of the 2768 pupils in the Nelson public school system. In 1874 her students presented her with a 'silver mounted butter dish and two preserve dishes' as a 'small offering of love and respect' in appreciation for the 'care, attention and great kindness bestowed on us by you, our worthy teacher'.[146] Two years later the *Colonist* commented that her school 'had not lost a tittle of the high character it had hitherto enjoyed; the writing of her pupils was excellent, and they showed a superior knowledge of New Zealand geography'.[147]

By 1879, however, pernickety Inspector Hodgson had revised his favourable opinion of 15 years before, concerned about the cramped conditions – 80 students in one class supervised by Elizabeth Sait and a monitor – and outdated teaching methods.[148] 'History is taught in a fashion that is, I hope, unique – the text-book, Collier's History, being committed to memory, word for word and chapter by chapter.' He did acknowledge, however, that 'the extraordinary energy of the teacher goes far towards compensating for any deficiencies in system and organisation'.[149]

Education standards and expectations had moved on, but Elizabeth's methods had not. In 1883, aged 53, she resigned to take up a position at Opaki School in Wairarapa. When she died in 1910 she left an estate of £2391, nearly eight times her husband's 1872 legacy of £300, suggesting she had invested astutely.[150] Her brief obituary ignored her long-term teaching career, but she was celebrated in Nelson. Former pupils organised a memorial, asking for subscriptions of a shilling.[151]

Although Elizabeth was primarily a public school teacher, the annual inspector's reports indicate something of the nature of her earlier ladies' academy. Her career also illustrates the changes in girls' education. It was certainly improving, thanks to some outspoken women (see Chapter 11). Frances Shayle George published a pamphlet, *Education of Girls*, in 1874 and the following year named her Auckland school a 'High School'. The *New Zealand Herald* recorded hers as the only private Auckland girls' school whose scholars obtained certificates of proficiency in the provincial scholarships, which was particularly 'creditable'. She was frustrated, however, that her pupils could only achieve certificates while boys obtained scholarships to further their education. When she removed to prestigious Ponsonby in 1879, she used former students' achievements as evidence of her establishment's 'high-class character'.[152] In 1877 Marion Baird Martin, one of Ellen Greenwood's pupils in Wellington, was the only girl to pass the Cambridge local examinations; in 1876 another had been one of only 24 successful candidates in the British colonies.[153]

The quality of the education provided by these ladies' academies clearly varied greatly. The more successful schools were run by very able women demonstrating business nous, but even the smallest part-time school required an understanding of marketing and economic management. Generally speaking, family and community connections and experience were critical to success, although there were exceptions, such as Maria Thomson, who succeeded although she had neither family nor, apparently, experience.

'The great moral engine'

Maria Thomson of Christchurch was all about business. She ran a highly successful school, invested in property, dabbled in finance, wrote a travelogue and moved in extremely respectable social circles. Unusually, she did this without the support of husband or family. Within a year of arriving in Canterbury in 1852 she purchased a large section on Oxford Terrace and opened Christchurch Ladies' School. She advertised as Mrs Charles Thomson, suggesting she was a widow, although the whereabouts and fate of her husband are unknown. Despite her solitary status,

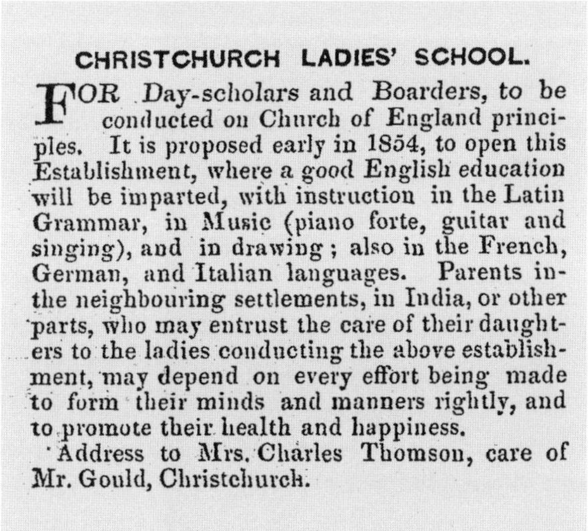

CHRISTCHURCH LADIES' SCHOOL.

FOR Day-scholars and Boarders, to be conducted on Church of England principles. It is proposed early in 1854, to open this Establishment, where a good English education will be imparted, with instruction in the Latin Grammar, in Music (piano forte, guitar and singing), and in drawing; also in the French, German, and Italian languages. Parents in the neighbouring settlements, in India, or other parts, who may entrust the care of their daughters to the ladies conducting the above establishment, may depend on every effort being made to form their minds and manners rightly, and to promote their health and happiness.

Address to Mrs. Charles Thomson, care of Mr. Gould, Christchurch.

Mrs Charles Thomson appealed to the local elite with her school 'conducted on Church of England principles', but also set her sights further afield to Australia, India and beyond. *Lyttelton Times*, 8 October 1853

Maria had enough money, class and respectability to satisfy the Canterbury elite, many of whom sent their daughters to be educated by 'the great moral engine', as she became known. Her pupils included Sibella Ross's sister, Kate Wilson, who later taught and lived with Johanna Lohse.[154]

Between 1854 and 1865 Maria's school moved about, although not through a lack of pupils or finance. She bought more town sections in 1858 and in 1862 built 'a very large and handsome house … decidedly the largest private house in or about Christchurch' in Papanui Road.[155] She closed the school in 1863 while she took an extended tour to England, during which she kept a journal, published in 1867 as *Twelve Years in Canterbury*. The book was less about Canterbury than her travels, but one chapter was essentially a guide for prospective settlers. She also included, as an appendix, some embarrassingly bad poetry, composed on board ship.[156]

Maria returned to Christchurch in 1868 and reopened her school in Avon House on Oxford Terrace.[157] By the end of the 1860s there was plenty of competition: Diane Willesford, Sibella Ross, Mrs Clark, Mrs Haughton, Ann Alabaster, Mrs Cole, Ellen Deighton, the Misses Sheath, Miss Cameron, Miss Thompson, Miss Paynter, Miss Ashwin, Miss Thornton, the Misses Campbell and Miss Neilson (of Richmond House). Maria Thomson's advertisements, however, often appeared alongside those for elite boys' schools, rather than among the ladies' academies, a sure sign of her sense of superiority.[158]

She devoted time and money to the Anglican church – for a short time in the 1860s, she taught working-class children at a partially government-funded Anglican school – but she was primarily an active businesswoman. She had both mortgages and investments and was well connected and prosperous. G.R. Macdonald suggested she was 'probably rather an alarming person', although this may say more about his response to such a successful woman than about Maria herself. It is surprising, then, that Maria's sudden death from a stroke at the age of 67 in 1875 received only a simple death notice but no obituary. Was this her wish, as one historian suggested, or was it that as a childless woman, however worthy, she was just buried and forgotten, at least for the next century? She was resurrected as the only woman of eight 'Canterbury personalities' in Richard Greenaway's book celebrating the 150th anniversary of the founding of the province.[159]

This substantial house on The Terrace in Wellington was the school of Miss Mary Greenwood, the eldest of several schoolteacher daughters of Sarah Greenwood of Nelson. The area is now a forest of high-rise buildings.

The Terrace School, Wellington, Alexander Turnbull Library, 1/2-092320-F

A middle-class business

Education was one of the few businesses available to middle-class women wishing to retain some gentility. For most, the business arose out of necessity, but some were passionate about girls' education. Others vented their frustration about settlers' expectations for their daughters in private letters. Mary Greenwood, one of Sarah's spinster teacher daughters, wrote to a friend in 1870 bemoaning that New Zealand parents had no 'tolerable idea of the time required for a girl's education';

> but it generally happens that by the time they can parse a sentence in English and have learnt that such countries as Greece and Rome did once exist, they are considered finished and taken away. I have now got a class of girls who are beginning to be capable of receiving ideas, but I am afraid that chances are ten to one against them remaining much longer with me.

More positively, she described her students as 'hungry readers'.[160] They usually graduated to become the wives and mothers of proper middle-class men, but some may have run businesses, enabled and inspired by the teaching and example of their female schoolteachers.

Chapter 6

A Stitch in Time: Dresses and drapery

For ladies in search of fashionable bonnets, new frocks, galoshes, parasols, or just some Berlin wool or embroidery threads, a stroll through the centre of Dunedin in the early 1850s would have produced a variety of establishments willing to serve them. The fledgling settlement already had a growing garment trade. Every immigrant ship brought more women who were clever with their needle, more crates of 'the latest Paris fashions' and more settlers who needed to be clothed. Male drapers and general storekeepers, including James Macandrew and John Mollison, supplied a wide range of stock in large stores, supported by female employees as shop assistants, needlewomen and seamstresses, some of whom were outworkers. Shopwork was even considered a specifically female occupation by some. In 1869 the *Westport Times* criticised men who 'usurp women's functions by serving behind drapers' counters as shopmen'.[1] Women also ran drapery businesses. Plain sewers, needlewomen, seamstresses and shirt makers worked from home, both for private individuals and for larger drapers. Other women had shopfronts and advertised as dressmakers, milliners (who did more than just hats), straw-bonnet makers or sometimes as drapers. They sold millinery, fabric and haberdashery and offered dressmaking services, employing other women as 'first hands', shop women, skilled needlewomen and apprentices.[2]

In the 1850s in Dunedin, Miss Alison Hunter Bell, 'milliner and dressmaker', was in Moray Place just off Princes Street. She sold ladies' and girls' boots, slippers and galoshes, stays, bonnet wire, cotton reels, Berlin wool, prints, ginghams and checked muslins, socks, hose, veils, combs, hairbrushes, toothbrushes and cambric handkerchiefs.[3] Carpenter William Young's wife Jenny advertised as milliner, dressmaker and straw-bonnet maker on the corner of Princes and Walker (now

Carroll) streets.[4] Miss Grace Sinclair and her apparently widowed sister Mrs Georgina Gilroy also set up shop in Princes Street, selling, among other things, straw bonnets, artificial flowers and children's stays. They married two brothers, Robert and William Millar, in 1857 and moved to Invercargill, leaving their business in the capable hands of older sister Mary, who had joined them in 1854. Mary herself did not marry but continued the business until 1861 before taking on a partner, Walter Hislop, and retiring a year later.[5] Further down Princes Street, Christian Sprott Bain, with three young children including a three-week-old baby, stepped into her deceased husband Thomas's shoes in 1853 and ran 'Mrs Bain's' drapery store. She married merchant James Paterson in 1856, but only the name changed on the store. 'Mrs Paterson's' lasted until 1861, when the new owners, William Hall & Co., made sure to advertise as 'late Mrs Paterson's'. So, too, did Robert Leith Begg and James Christie, who bought the business two years after that. The store later became Brown, Ewing & Co.[6] Reversing the usual pattern of forgetting female entrepreneurship, the later firm's contributor to the 1905 *Cyclopedia of New Zealand* mistakenly credited Christian with founding the store as 'a widow' in 1849, enthusing, 'This enterprising lady was rewarded for her plucky attempt to establish the soft goods trade in this part of the Colony.'[7]

Just off Princes Street, in Maclaggan Street, Matilda Baker, a milliner who had run her own shop in London, imported an exciting range of goods including 'Ladies' Habit Shirts (new style)', chemises, muslin sleeves, stockings, calicos and flannels and 'a large variety of Infants' French Merino Braided Cloaks and Pelises'.[8] In 1855, departing from her normal offerings, she advertised that orders for 'several thousand Shingles' might be left with her.[9] This was probably her husband Andrew's entrepreneurial venture. Matilda closed her store at the end of 1856, instead offering millinery services from her home, Alma Cottage in Upper Harbour, and using her neighbour in Maclaggan Street, Agnes Campbell, as a conduit for orders.[10] The reduction in scale may have indicated that she was not doing well or, conversely, that she no longer needed a shopfront. Perhaps, too, a growing family made working from home more convenient. The following year, however, Matilda moved back into Princes Street, advertising an extensive array of millinery.[11]

By the end of 1860 Matilda had traded millinery for hotelkeeping at the Northern Hotel in the newly established town of Oamaru, where she and Andrew joined her sister's family.[12] In 1866 Andrew Baker gave up the hotel, apparently due to ill health, but rather than return to millinery, Matilda let out rooms and farmed in the area. Perhaps the competition of Miss Sewell and Jane Falconer, along with the 'first-class milliner and dressmaker … constantly on the premises' at Shrimski & Moss, established drapers in Oamaru, was too intimidating.[13] Matilda died in 1900, unnoticed by any obituary. This was a little surprising, not so much because of her business achievements but because her son, Charles Alma Baker, had acquired both distinction and notoriety in Malaya and New Zealand after marrying politician Frederick Whitaker's daughter. (His philandering provided Matilda's best modern claim to fame: as great-grandmother of the late New Zealand novelist, Pat Heretaunga Baker.)[14]

Matilda's neighbour in Maclaggan Street, Agnes Campbell, whose printer husband Daniel rose to be manager of the *Otago Witness*, had a thriving drapery business, importing her stock from Glasgow and Melbourne. Her first advertisement did not appear until 1857, but she had certainly been in business earlier and only began advertising, always in the *Otago Witness* and no doubt with a discount, once Daniel was working for the newspaper. Her business expanded. Early in 1858 her daughter Jessie joined her, making straw bonnets.[15] By 1861 the Campbells' store was called Dunedin House and in October, Mrs Campbell advertised for a milliner: 'highest rate of wages given. None but a first-rate hand need apply.'[16] A month later she sought an experienced 'RESPECTABLE FEMALE' for what she now called 'a Drapery Business'.[17] Given the hierarchies in the fashion business, the renaming suggests Agnes was aiming to compete with larger stores.

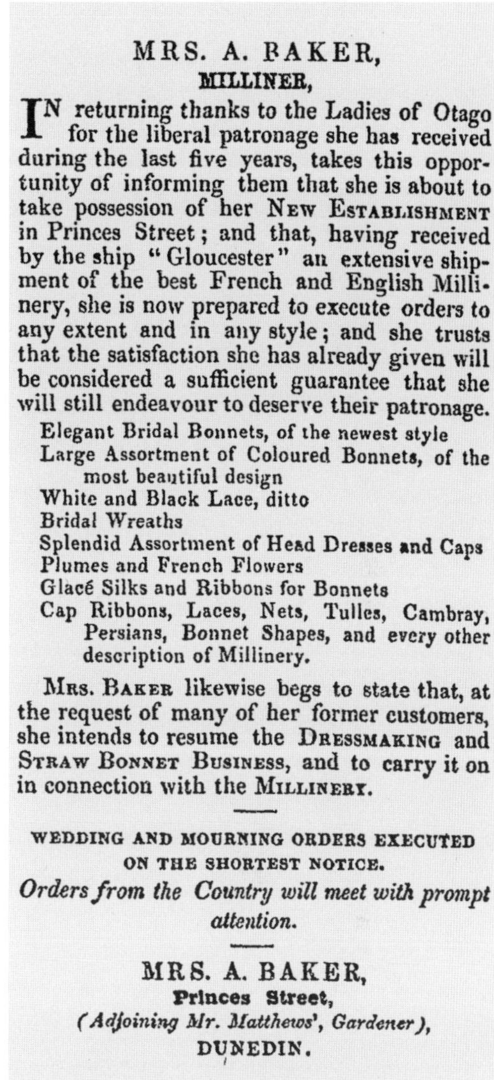

MRS. A. BAKER,

MILLINER,

IN returning thanks to the Ladies of Otago for the liberal patronage she has received during the last five years, takes this opportunity of informing them that she is about to take possession of her NEW ESTABLISHMENT in Princes Street; and that, having received by the ship "Gloucester" an extensive shipment of the best French and English Millinery, she is now prepared to execute orders to any extent and in any style; and she trusts that the satisfaction she has already given will be considered a sufficient guarantee that she will still endeavour to deserve their patronage.

Elegant Bridal Bonnets, of the newest style
Large Assortment of Coloured Bonnets, of the most beautiful design
White and Black Lace, ditto
Bridal Wreaths
Splendid Assortment of Head Dresses and Caps
Plumes and French Flowers
Glacé Silks and Ribbons for Bonnets
Cap Ribbons, Laces, Nets, Tulles, Cambray, Persians, Bonnet Shapes, and every other description of Millinery.

MRS. BAKER likewise begs to state that, at the request of many of her former customers, she intends to resume the DRESSMAKING and STRAW BONNET BUSINESS, and to carry it on in connection with the MILLINERY.

WEDDING AND MOURNING ORDERS EXECUTED ON THE SHORTEST NOTICE.

Orders from the Country will meet with prompt attention.

MRS. A. BAKER,
Princes Street,
(Adjoining Mr. Matthews', Gardener),
DUNEDIN.

Matilda Baker's advertisement shows a range of millinery, imported on the most recently arrived ship from England.

Otago Witness, 1 January 1859

Oddly enough, just below Agnes Campbell's advertisement, a Miss Doran, who had 'first class experience in Melbourne', was seeking just such a position 'as a milliner or shopwoman, in a drapery store'. Did she apply? If so, she was unsuccessful. Barely two months later, Agnes announced she was 'retiring' from the business, leaving in charge of the dressmaking department at Dunedin House a Miss Reville, who had previously been in business on her own account and hailed 'from Madame Devy of Gloucester Street London'.[18]

Agnes's business made a significant contribution to the family's financial well-being. This became apparent in 1883 when Daniel, embroiled in some dubious property deals to avoid his creditors, found himself bankrupt. One of those deals assigned High Street properties, including the shop she had once run, to Agnes. She later explained in court that 'the land had been acquired out of moneys belonging to her and it had always been agreed between them that the same should be considered as her separate property'. Unfortunately, to avoid her husband's creditors, Agnes signed over the property deeds to 'friends' for a sum half the property's worth and was duped. She tried to sue but failed.[19] The Campbells beat a strategic retreat to San Francisco, returning to Dunedin a few years later once the dust had settled.[20]

Unusually, Agnes's obituary in 1908 acknowledged her entrepreneurship, although her husband was accorded the true 'breadwinner' role: 'Mrs Campbell supplemented her husband's earnings by entering into business, and by the exercise of thrift and frugality, the couple saved a sufficient sum to buy land in and around Dunedin.' She had been 'an active woman in business and private life, and … an ideal wife and mother, commanding the respect of all with whom she came into contact'.[21]

Women's business

If education was essential for the new colony, clothing the growing population was equally so. Even if every young girl and woman in the colony was taught to sew, she rarely produced the entire family's wardrobe, which included undergarments, shirts, dresses, trousers and coats, along with household needs, such as table and bed linen, towels, curtains and furnishings. Someone had to supply these goods, and alongside importers of ready-made items, there were opportunities in every town and community for capable seamstresses to set up in business. It was hard work, particularly for a woman working on her own. Foxton dressmaker Lydia Burr's children remembered her sewing until 2am to complete orders in the 1870s.[22] Running a successful business, however, as Wendy Gamber has pointed out, required more than just being clever with your needle. You needed a good head for business and many served a formal apprenticeship.[23]

Proficiency in sewing was important for nineteenth-century women of all classes. For the upper and middle classes decorative embroidery was an 'accomplishment'; for others, needlework was an essential domestic skill, enabling them at the very least to mend, darn and make simple items, to retrim a bonnet or take up a hem. Others made it a livelihood. Jane Malthus's detailed analysis of nineteenth-century New Zealand needlework trades showed they were 'second only to domestic service as a form of paid employment' for women, as employees or as businesswomen.[24] Whether needlework was 'a source of pecuniary advantage' or 'a pleasant pastime', as American etiquette expert Florence Hartley wrote in 1860, it was, she enthused, 'an amusement for otherwise idle fingers, from the cottage to the palace'.[25] Lydia Burr may not have agreed.

Millinery, dressmaking and drapery businesses were run by single, married and widowed women at all stages of their lives. Harriet Reed (see Chapter 12) was 19 when she started her millinery shop in Auckland around 1860.[26] Mary Ann Coe was just 18 but already a wife when she opened her drapery store, Albion House, in Lyttelton in 1855; she moved to Christchurch a few years later and was in business until 1865. By this time she had nine children, including two sets of twins.[27] At the other extreme, the unmarried McLaughlin sisters, whose story appears later in this chapter, were in their seventies by the time they retired from their Auckland emporium. Some, like Dunedin's Matilda Baker, transferred businesses from England; others used previous experience as employees either at 'Home' or in the colonies to attract customers. Some established long-lived businesses that sustained them throughout long spinsterhoods, or were revived at different stages of their lives when required. Several businesses passed through generations of unrelated single women; others became family concerns and then twentieth-century department stores. Needlework businesses included retail outlets as well as manufactories, selling haberdashery, materials and ready-made goods as well as offering the sewing of dresses, trimming of bonnets and making of stays. Businesses in small towns tended to be less specialised, but as the century progressed the offerings of all became more sophisticated, particularly in those catering to the upper end of the market. Mass production, new technologies, competition from department stores and the increasing regulation of female labour all had an impact on women's needlework businesses. The arrival of sewing machines and patterns, notably those of the entrepreneurial Madame Weigel across the Tasman, altered the market.[28] As with developments in teaching, these changes tended to shrink opportunities for women operating independent businesses by the end of the century, although also opening up more, but not necessarily well-paid, employment.

Importing, making and marketing

The Dunedin businesses of the 1850s that opened this chapter were typical of the rest of the country. They show not only the remarkable range of goods for sale, but also how important it was to be up with the latest European fashions. They also reveal both the sources of goods and the marketing strategies used to sell them. Fashion was at the forefront of the new consumer economy and a business needed not only to offer the same or better quality, fashion and value as everyone else, but to stand out from the crowd by promising something special, especially in larger towns. When Harriet Langford started business in 1847 as a straw-bonnet maker in Queen Street, Auckland, she announced that she had 'lately received' her materials 'direct from England', and was able to provide orders 'favored with neatness, and according to the latest and most approved fashions'.[29] In 1852 Ann Hamer, also in Queen Street, announced the arrival 'of the latest Parisian fashions': 'for goodness of quality, elegance of style and cheapness they cannot be surpassed.' She also sold 'Several Hundred Muslin Collars, Habit Shirts [for riding], Lace Sleeves, French and English Flowers, &c &c'.[30] Her inclusion of collars, sleeves and flowers reminds us of the ways in which garments were made over; those parts that became worn quickly – collars and sleeves – could be replaced, or an outfit updated to 'the latest Parisian fashion', just as bonnets and hats could be redressed with the latest trimmings.[31] Such fashions were always significantly out of date because of shipping times, but as the Misses McLaughlin cleverly pointed out in 1856, being six months behind Europe, their 'large variety of fashionable MILLINERY' was exactly 'suitable for the present season'.[32]

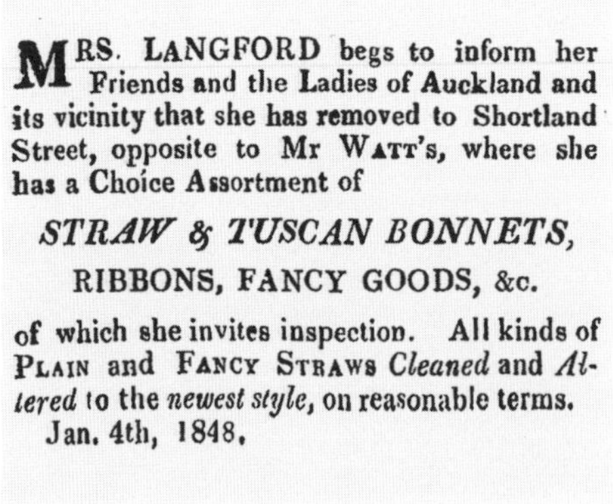
MRS. LANGFORD begs to inform her Friends and the Ladies of Auckland and its vicinity that she has removed to Shortland Street, opposite to Mr WATT's, where she has a Choice Assortment of

STRAW & TUSCAN BONNETS,

RIBBONS, FANCY GOODS, &c.

of which she invites inspection. All kinds of PLAIN and FANCY STRAWS *Cleaned* and *Altered* to the *newest style*, on reasonable terms.
Jan. 4th, 1848.

In her advertising Harriet Langford emphasised both reasonable terms and 'newest style'. *New Zealander*, 5 January 1848

TO TOWN AND COUNTRY SETTLERS.

NEW WINTER GOODS,

Direct from the Houses of Campbell & Co., and Stewart & M'Donald, Glasgow.

Ladies' Dresses of an entirely New Style.

MRS. CAMPBELL respectfully intimates that she has now received by the "Storm Cloud," direct from the above Houses, the following GOODS, all selected to her order, which she can confidently recommend as good and cheap:—

Plain and Coloured Silk Dresses
Black Silk—Checked Challies
Flounced Dresses—Cashmerians
Flounced Winsey Dresses
Black and Coloured French Merinoes
Aberdeen Light and Heavy Winseys
Coburgs—Lustres—Cross-overs—Circassians, Mohairs, and Poplins
Plain and Striped Winseys
All-wool and Gala Tartans
French and Checked Baize and De Laines
Gingham, Derry, Drugget, and Regatta
Hoyle's Prints—Alloa Worsted
White and Coloured Stays, all sizes
Ladies' Sewed Collars and Sleeves, new style
" Silk Ties and Scarfs
Calicoes, Holland, and Diaper
Ladies' and Children's Hose
White and Blue Flannels, all prices
Trimmings of all kinds

ALSO,

A large assortment of Patent TERRY COUNTERPANES, QUILTS, and TOILET COVERS.
&c. &c. &c.

Marriage, Mourning, and Country Orders promptly attended to.

☞ HIGH STREET, DUNEDIN.
(*Opposite Manse-street.*)

ARRIVED BY THE "PIRATE,"

A CHOICE ASSORTMENT OF **DRAPERY GOODS,**
&c. &c.,

Including Muslin and Fancy Dresses, Silk and Cloth Mantles, Ladies' Hats and Bonnets, Flowers, Trimmings, Blonds,
And a great variety of other Articles in the Ladies' Department,
Of the Newest Style, and durable material,
Selected in Melbourne by
MRS. CAMPBELL.

Also shortly to Arrive from Glasgow, a Large and Varied Assortment of Drapery Goods, selected to Order.

WANTED, A MILLINER.
Apply to Mrs. CAMPBELL, High-street.

LEFT: Agnes Campbell made a point of advertising that she imported her varied stock from well-known shops in Glasgow.

Otago Witness, 12 May 1860

ABOVE: Agnes selected stock on buying trips to Melbourne which, like Sydney, was an important point of reference and source of supplies for New Zealand businesses.

Otago Witness, 1 December 1860

So where did this tempting array of fabrics and fripperies come from? The three Jay sisters in Nelson in 1859 chose and ordered their range of goods 'direct from London', bypassing other importers.[33] The newly married Betsey Inglis in Wellington in 1841 advertised that she received 'fashions regularly from Paris'.[34] Agnes Campbell shunned the cachet of London or Paris to order 'from a Glasgow House', which might well have had more appeal in strongly Scottish Dunedin.[35] Customers were cajoled into trusting proprietors' taste in choosing fabrics and clothing for sale. Some businesswomen prevailed upon friends in England to dispatch boxes of selected goods. In the 1850s Mary Taylor asked her friend Ellen Nussey to send over ribbons and lace for her Wellington haberdashery and drapery shop.[36]

Mary also bought stock locally from wholesale importers. She 'gets as fierce as a dragon', Ellen Taylor told Charlotte Brontë, 'and goes to all the wholesale stores and looks at things, gets patterns, samples, etc. and asks prices, and then comes home and we talk it over and then she goes again and buys what we want'.[37] It was daunting initially, knowing what and how many of each item to stock, and how much to pay and to charge. To succeed, women needed a good eye for what would sell. Both family members and business partners could help. Mary Taylor paid close attention to her brother's dealings, noting 'the extent to which Waring sells on credit and how glad my [many] of these people would be to sell for money'. She felt confident that she knew 'pretty well the prices I can get … and what I ought to give'.[38]

Mary, who found people 'always very civil' when she visited local warehouses to buy stock, was just one of many businesswomen who did so.[39] Although some imported individual crates of selected items, others bought stock from importers and inspected it personally. They headed their advertisements with the name of the ship on which it had arrived. With settlers keenly aware of shipping arrivals and departures, this was essential: the most recently arrived vessel guaranteed freshness, novelty and the latest possible European fashions.

Successful business also involved being aware of the market, seeking niche opportunities, diversifying when necessary, moving with the times and keeping up with technology. Sarah Brown, 'fashionable dress and mantle maker', moved from Dunedin to Wellington in 1865 with her upholsterer husband Thomas and advertised as the 'inventor and manufacturer of the horse-hair crinoline skirt'. Given that horsehair (crin) fabric used for crinoline petticoats dated from much earlier, what did she mean by 'inventor'? Had she developed a new style or shape or was this just inventive marketing? Her advertisements disappeared quickly so perhaps it did not catch on.[40] 'A.R. Logan' described her new business in Dunedin's Princes Street, less

Could these three photographs, all labelled 'Miss Jay', be the three Jay sisters, Eliza, Kezia and Winifred? Their tenant, photographer George Hoby, was in partnership with William Davis, in whose collection these photographs are, so it is likely that he took these portraits.

Nelson Provincial Museum, Davis Collection, 10610, 10611, 10612 than a year after she arrived with her sister Mary, as 'a new furnishing shop'. Agnes Logan was trying to provide a point of difference, although she also sold a wide range of drapery, clothes and novelty items. She was in business until 1864 before marrying fellow Scot, furniture dealer Henry Berwick, in 1865.[41]

Jane Levy focused on baby linen in Lambton Quay in Wellington in the 1850s. Married at the tender age of 14 to 27-year-old Solomon Levy, she was producing children herself at regular intervals (although at least one, apparently, was not her husband's) and recognised a gap in the market. Larger drapery stores included baby linen in their ranges, but she was the only specialist in Wellington. (Widow Ann Mary Pearce, who had run a similar business in 1855, remarried in 1856 and moved to the Hutt.[42]) Jane Levy had a good head for business. She sold other items that might appeal to her customers, including 'a choice selection of ladies and children's hats in great variety and of the very latest fashion', along with an array of underclothing, baby baskets, trimmed bassinets, 'Parisian Jupons [underskirts], Skeletons [metal cages for skirts], gloves, hairnets, feathers' and 'Winsey and Royal Repp Petticoats'. Aware of her market, she offered discounts for cash in 1858 and in 1861 sold at 'reduced prices to meet the times'. She ensured her store was a landmark by selling tickets to local events, such as a steam excursion to Lowry Bay on Wellington Anniversary Day 1863 in aid of the Lancashire Relief Fund, and in 1865, along with other drapers, she adopted early closing. After over 20 years in business she retired in 1877, selling out to Hallenstein Brothers.[43]

Nelson's Jay sisters also diversified. In 1859 they sold drapery as well as 'patterns, wools, canvas and floss [embroidery] silks … braids, buttons and every article for fancy work'. They had 'a large assortment of toys and children's books', appealing to Nelson's growing families. A year later they took orders for straw-bonnet maker Mrs Browning, based in the Toi Toi Valley. When 'ladies' felt hats' were all the rage in Nelson in 1862, the Misses Jay had a 'beautiful assortment'. They also let space to local photographer George Hoby, who frequently advertised his location at the 'Misses Jay's' in Bridge Street, thus providing both free publicity and passing trade from those having their portraits taken. No doubt they tried to persuade George's clients that a new bonnet or trimming would improve a photograph.[44]

In Whanganui in 1875 Agnes Cummins added interest to her long-standing drapery shop in Taupo Quay by displaying 'some very neat specimens of Native art … a tea cosey [sic], worked with beads, and a large cushion'. The *Wanganui Herald* praised the 'exquisite … taste and skill' with which the items had been made by Māori girls at the Catholic school on the Whanganui River, suggesting, rather patronisingly, that they could not 'be excelled by Europeans'. Local worthy Henry Churton, who had sent the items to the shop for sale, planned to donate the proceeds to the Rangitikei Cottage Hospital. There was no mention of recompense for the craftswomen.[45]

Some businesswomen embraced modern technology. Mary Taylor is credited with importing New Zealand's first sewing machine, a revolutionary advance powerfully attested by the enthusiastic comments in women's correspondence. Whether she did or not, by the end of Mary's time in New Zealand, the sewing machine was certainly more common in larger towns. By the mid-1860s a new job, that of 'sewing machinist', was advertised, providing another avenue of often badly paid female employment.[46] Even so, Christchurch's Catherine Ralfe remembered being one of the few sewing machine owners in 1865, when supporting herself and her brother's family with her sewing and fancy work, suggesting that they were still comparatively rare.[47]

Victorian technology and innovation were, and are, often presumed to be the province of men, but businesswomen in the needlework trades were well up with the times and made sure their customers knew it.[48] In the 1870s and 1880s Elizabeth Cowles and her successor Wilhelmina Cook in Wellington made the most of being sole agents for famous Madame Weigel's patterns, and Sophia Anstice in 1888 advertised the use of her new lock-stitch machine in her Nelson drapery.[49] Miss F.M. Brown offered lessons in 'scientific dress cutting' in Rutland Street in Auckland in 1894. She was competing with Miss E. Forbes of the 'School of the Improved Excelsior System of Cutting Dress and Habit', who promised her system was 'easily learned in six or seven lessons', giving 'numerous testimonials from Auckland pupils' as proof.[50] In 1892, however, 'Madame Alice (late of London and Paris)' offered lessons in 'Artistic Dressmaking and Millinery', specifically 'not scientific system', promising pupils the ability to 'secure lucrative positions in any first-class establishment of London or the Colonies', suggesting that traditional craftswomanship was also still valued.[51]

A modern workplace: Sweatshops and outwork

New technology was accompanied by mass production and the development of larger workshops and factories, providing employment for an army of seamstresses and other female workers. Concern over female working conditions led to the Employment of Females Act in 1873, specifically 'to provide for Employment of

Females in Workrooms and Factories'. It was fairly brief. It regulated an eight-hour working day, banned employment between 6pm and 9am and stipulated Saturday half-days along with holidays on Sunday and public holidays. Workrooms were to be 'properly ventilated'. The act was amended in 1875, introducing a lower age limit for employment and adjusting hours for some industries; saleswomen could be employed whenever a shop was open; some factory workers could start work at 6am and printers' offices could employ women until 4.30pm on Saturdays. In addition, 'Notices shall be posted in conspicuous places in each factory, and shall specify … hours', copies being sent to resident magistrates and inspections to be undertaken to ensure compliance.[52]

These regulations applied to both small workrooms and large factories, as Sarah Wilson found out to her cost in Dunedin in 1879. In spite of being a married woman, she was fined 5s plus costs for employing two girls after hours. She tried to plead that her establishment in Ross's Buildings in the Octagon was not a factory since she employed only two girls, one of whom boarded in the house. The pair could be seen 'by any one passing along the street'. She was surely being disingenuous. Her husband Robert, a well-travelled Irishman 19 years her senior, was an editor at the *Otago Witness* and Sarah also ran a servants' registry office; it is unlikely that she would have been unaware of the legislation. We do not know if she improved her workplace practices. Six months later Sarah was dead at 41, along with her husband, four of her children and their servant, burned as a fire swept through Ross's Buildings. Daughters Lily and Louisa survived, as did two young women who had been boarding with Sarah while awaiting servants' positions.[53]

The Employment of Females Act proved difficult to enforce and resulting prosecutions were not always effective. In 1881 Jane McLaughlin was charged for breaching the 1875 legislation by not conspicuously displaying signs specifying hours of employment in her Auckland workshop. Her lawyer, Richard Laishley, argued that since Sergeant Richard Gamble had failed to physically enter the workshop during his inspection, he could not prove women were actually employed there – and if there were no employees, there was no need for signs. The lawyer concluded eloquently that 'it was his duty to have gone into the room and not to stand in the shop, take a lady's word, and subsequently use it to catch and prosecute her'. Jane had obviously told Gamble she had employees but the judge was convinced by, or admired the slipperiness of, her lawyer's argument and dismissed the case.[54]

In 1883 Nelson's Elizabeth Ann Pamely, of Mrs Pamely's Mode de Paris, avoided prosecution for 'employing certain females after 6 o'clock' because, as her lawyer

Demure Mrs Elizabeth Ann Pamely, proprietor of Mode de Paris in Nelson, did not really need her husband George's protection. By 1893 she was in Australia, reinventing herself as licensee of Perth's Leisure Hour Club in 1910, living with her 'good friend' Emily Dawson.

Pamely, Nelson Provincial Museum, Tyree Studio, 176230

pointed out, 'being a married woman [she] could not lawfully employ these young women, and if she could not lawfully employ them she could not unlawfully employ them' after the stipulated time. The judge's solution was to 'direct the police to lodge an information against *Mr* Pamely for not complying with Section 9 of the Act, by posting up in his workroom a notice specifying the hours of labor'. Two years later George Pamely was prosecuted for having three women sewing on the declared half-day, Thursday. He claimed they were saleswomen and all three women backed him up, undermining Inspector Sergeant John Nash, who, it was implied, had been victimising the Pamely establishment.[55]

The Employment of Females Act may have gone some way towards ameliorating conditions for factory workers, but it did nothing to assist outworkers who completed garments in their own homes for piece rates. In 1888 Nelson draper Sophia Anstice took care to advertise 'all Goods made on the premises', not only implying better quality under constant supervision, but distancing herself from the practice of outworking, which was becoming notorious.[56] In Dunedin in 1889 an Anti-Sweating Committee, established to investigate the exploitation of factory employees and outworkers, met with an all-male group of warehousemen and manufacturers to consider establishing a system of fixed prices to be paid to workers for particular items. In the course of the discussion it emerged that Elizabeth Keates, who had been running a drapery, dressmaking and shirt manufactory business in Castle and then Hanover Street since about 1870, was paying different prices from other manufacturers. Mr Ross of Sargood, Son & Ewen complained that she had been paying higher prices for some time 'for the purpose of drawing the best labor from the other factories', thus 'raising wages falsely'. Mr Wilson of Bing, Harris & Co. replied smugly that 'his firm were paying higher wages than some others; and why should they not do so if they felt inclined?' He, like Elizabeth, 'wanted good workers and good work' and was prepared to pay for it. She may have paid better wages but Elizabeth had other problems. Less than a year later her husband Timothy had her committed to Dunedin's private mental hospital, Ashburn Hall, for 12 months on the grounds that 'through habitual drunkenness you have recently been wasting my means'. Elizabeth did not appear in business again and in 1897 her daughter had a prohibition order taken out against her, meaning no one could supply her with alcohol.[57]

Balancing the books was always a problem for small businesses and the temptation to exploit workers was powerful. In 1890 a Sweating Commission found that sweating did not exist in New Zealand, although the dissenting opinion of three of its members, including the Reverend Rutherford Waddell, who had led the

Elizabeth Keates' Kent House in Dunedin, probably with Miss Griffiths and Alice Hanlon outside. Elizabeth, who was in business from about 1870, was an alcoholic and was committed to the lunatic asylum in 1890.

Mrs T. Keates, Hanover Street, c. 1890, photographer unknown, Hocken P1997-155/04-1783 anti-sweating campaign, suggested otherwise. 'There are,' they wrote, 'numerous overcrowded and insanitary workrooms, great numbers of workers labour long and irregular hours, and wages in many trades are at the lowest possible ebb.' Many of those workers were women, as were some of their employers.[58]

Beyond the big smoke

Unlike in larger centres, where specialisation was more common, in provincial towns women were likely to be both dressmakers and milliners, also selling drapery and haberdashery. Corset making, feather cleaning (for hats) and straw-bonnet making were sometimes advertised as separate businesses, but few lasted long, suggesting markets were not big enough. Even in Wellington, Jane Levy sold other lines compatible with her core business of baby linen. More niche businesses appeared later, but were in competition with the mushrooming urban department stores.

Most businesses catered for locals. They might, like Agnes Campbell, take buying jaunts across to Melbourne or occasionally to London, or import stock from Europe, but generally they advertised to sell to their immediate neighbours.[59] Country customers used mail order, although larger department stores and draperies with more resources came to dominate this market. A few women travelled to different places with goods, including Eliza Tye (Chapter 1), who sold drapery in Māori villages on the Coromandel Peninsula, and Miss Forbes, who took her Excelsior System of dressmaking on the road in the late 1890s and into the twentieth century. Earlier, Eliza Wrigley, who ran a millinery and drapery business with her husband Henry in Wellington's Cuba Street, imported goods from London and set her sights on a broader market. She visited Napier for three weeks in 1864, announcing her arrival as a 'Milliner of Wellington' with 'a choice selection' of goods. When Eliza died suddenly in 1867, Henry immediately sold up, telling potential buyers that 'the connection already established is very extensive', underscoring both his wife's centrality to the family business and her marketing ability.[60]

Eliza Wrigley's foray into the provinces in 1864 was recognition of a gap in the market. Hawke's Bay, with a population of about 1063 Europeans in 1859 and 3770 in 1864 (and 2450 of those were men), was not exactly awash with milliners and dressmakers: only a few advertised in the newspapers and their businesses were short-lived.[61] Dressmaker Maria Forrest appeared briefly in 1859, and Agnes Smith, whose husband William was variously schoolteacher and photographer, offered dressmaking services from her house in Carlyle Street between 1859 and 1862, until they moved to a general store in Havelock.[62] Eliza Richards, another photographer's wife, was in the millinery business for three years before moving to Wellington with her husband Edward in 1862.[63] All three were gone by 1864. Messrs William R. Robinson & Co., general drapers, advertised their employment of a 'first-class milliner' to provide for the needs of the ladies of Napier in September 1864, just a few weeks before Eliza Wrigley's visit.[64] A few months later Mrs Sarah Williams and Miss Lambert opened up shop in Hastings Street. The business was taken over by Ellen Caulton in 1867. The latter, however, was also advertising for boarders by the following year.[65] Perhaps by then the new competition, in the form of Susannah Kemp, was too much.

Susannah saw the potential of the provinces. A 'professional theatrical costumier', she had a millinery and dressmaking business in Auckland after arriving with her son in 1862, then moved to Napier in 1867. There she remained in business until her death 20 years later. She initially used the cachet of Auckland and was the only milliner and dressmaker advertising for any length of time in Napier in the late 1860s and 1870s. Her main competition, until the mid-1870s, was from W.R. Robinson & Co., but they catered primarily for the ready-made market, whereas Susannah promised a more personal service that included making ladies' riding habits to order.[66]

Other provincial towns also had milliners and dressmakers, some of whom could build up impressive businesses. In New Plymouth Mrs Tapp and Kate Savery advertised briefly, but Mary Ross and Mary Hood became institutions.[67] Mary Ross's business was essential for her economic survival, enabling her to cope with widowhood and scandal. Her first husband was Robert Ross, with whom the newly married Mary emigrated to Nelson in 1842. Robert's letter home in November, which enthused that he had 'got on amazingly … being able to build property to the amount of £500', was included in a collection published to promote emigration, as he exemplified the ideal hard-working, go-getting immigrant. Unfortunately, however, Robert liked to drink. He was stout, although 'not so fat as to be unwieldy', and, although he 'was always very kind' when sober, while drunk would become 'quarrelsome' and sometimes violent. In 1858 he threatened to murder his wife and daughter, Annie, both of whom sought refuge with a neighbour, William Harley. The belligerent and suspicious Robert Ross went looking for them. After William had hit him with a paling, Robert stumbled home, where he was later found with his head bashed in. William was found guilty of manslaughter and sentenced to two years' hard labour, ending his courtship of Annie Ross.[68]

M. ROSS
DEVON
HOUS

Despite the proprietorial gentleman in the doorway, Mary Ross owned and ran New Plymouth's Devon House, in premises newly built in 1872 next to her old shop. Opposite was Alice Townsend's first tobacco business.

Puke Ariki, PHO2008-101

Mary Ross looked to her own resources, starting a grocery store in Bridge Street by 1862. Although her father, John Street, had also emigrated to Nelson in 1855, Mary moved to New Plymouth at the end of 1864 when many Pākehā settlers were returning to the area, having sought refuge in Nelson. As 'M. Ross', she announced the arrival of a 'New Drapery Establishment', selling fashionable and exotic sounding (but 'very cheap') goods 'of most recent manufacture'. Her stock included 'the new Princess Alexandra Shawl' and 'real lace Mantles … in Maltese, Chantilly, Pucher, Spanish, and Guipsure [sic] lace'; her fabric colours were 'exquisitely delicate' but 'perfectly fast', owing to 'recent chemical discoveries'. She was technologically up-to-date, advertising for sewing machine hands in 1866, and recognised the cachet of Europe, employing a 'first-class milliner, recently arrived from London'.[69]

In 1873 Mary Ross married Robert Powell, but continued to trade as M. Ross. Her store, Devon House, was used as a landmark by other storekeepers.[70] Mary sold her business in 1878 but had a small general store on the corner of Devon and Watson streets until 1882, when she retired, aged 66, selling it to Lucinda Grey.[71] Her retirement may have been precipitated by the death that year of her second husband: Mary found him hanging in the shop storeroom. The second Robert, too, was remembered as a heavy drinker, putting away 'about twenty half-pints a day', although he was well liked, noted for 'his inoffensive and kindly disposition – especially towards children'.[72]

Endeavouring to ensure that her lifetime of hard work did not go to waste, in 1884, on her lawyer's advice, Mary established a trust for the benefit of herself and her grandchildren. This was a mistake. In 1891 she was forced into formal bankruptcy because she was unable to access funds. Her creditors 'warmly sympathised' with the 71-year-old widow, who was 'too old to work' and reliant upon the income from the trust. One creditor noted she had always been 'very straightforward in all her dealings'.[73]

Victoria House was an equally long-lasting enterprise. Among the first settlers in New Plymouth, Mary Lye married a fellow passenger, Peter Hoskin, and together they established a thriving multifaceted business, including a general store specialising in drapery and fancy goods and managed by Mary. Unlike many other Pākehā wives, Mary remained in New Plymouth when war broke out. Peter Hoskin died in 1860 at the age of 47, leaving her pregnant and with several children, two of whom died the following year. The drapery business, Victoria House, continued through Mary's widowhood and remarriage two years later to soldier Archibald Hood. It was variously referred to as 'Mr Hood's' and 'Mrs Hood's', suggesting both were

Sarah Hogg, proprietor of Whanganui drapery, Ayrshire House, and the family breadwinner, places a protective arm around the shoulders of her invalid husband, a patriarch perhaps in name only. Whanganui Museum, IP-WF-052

involved.[74] Family history tells that Mary also had business interests in Thames, with a part share in a grog shop. The New Plymouth store survived until 1892 when, like Mary Ross, she struck financial difficulties, doubtless affected by the Long Depression. She salvaged something, however, since she left an estate of £600 when she died in 1902. Her 50-year-long business supported a family of 13 children.[75]

Redoubtable Whanganui draper Sarah Hogg (see Chapter 4) went into business in 1866 in Campbell Street, calling her drapery Ayrshire House after her Scottish home. The business went from strength to strength and she prospered sufficiently to send three of her boys to the fee-paying Collegiate School, regarded by one local critic as catering to 'the sons of the snobocracy to the exclusion of the poor man's children'.[76] She employed John Brechin as bookkeeper. One local historian suggested he 'soon was managing the business in her absence while she gave birth to five children', but other evidence suggests she remained at the helm: she pursued debtors in court and imported goods and advertised in her name.[77] Her husband David Hogg died in 1880 and Sarah retired six years later, transferring the business to two sons

The Whanganui Christ Church choir, photographed about 1874, included dressmaker Emily Neville, aka Croucher, reinventing herself after an unhappy marriage.
BACK ROW, LEFT TO RIGHT: Mr Webb, Mrs Lyall, Dr Ebbs, G.F. Allan-Willmot, Mr Powell, Mr Oakley, G.J. Woon, William Hudson Davis, Robert Taylor Davis, Sheriff.
FRONT ROW: Miss M. Gordon (Mrs MacLean), Miss A.A. Gower, (Mrs Pinches), Mrs Webb, Miss A.A. Gower (Mrs Rockell), Miss Neville (Mrs McWilliam), Miss Harding (organist), Mrs Dr Ebbs, Miss Gilbert (Mrs Fleetwood), Miss A. Gordon (Mrs Thorpe), Miss Beatrice Davis (Mrs John Spencer Russell). (The two Misses A.A. Gowers were sisters and had three brothers and two other sisters. All the siblings had 'A.A.' initials, such as Agnes Ada and Albert Augustine.) Alexander Turnbull Library, 1/1-000057-G

in partnership with John Brechin. When she died in 1901 she left a considerable estate of over £4000, which she distributed very precisely in a detailed will.[78]

Sarah was not the only draper or dressmaker in Whanganui. In the late 1860s the directories listed several needlework businesses. 'Miss Nevill' was escaping an unfortunate marriage. Married in her teens in 1860 to her brother's business partner, 29-year-old Elijah Croucher, in Wellington, Emily Croucher (née Canty) soon ran away to Whanganui. Three years later her husband bigamously married her brother's widow. Emily meanwhile set about reinventing herself, taking the name Nevill(e) and working as a dressmaker. She became a stalwart of the Christ Church choir and was presented with some books when she left the area 'as a slight token of esteem and respect'. She had her first marriage annulled in 1869 and in 1873 became the wife of Otaki missionary James McWilliam. Shortly after their marriage local worthies congratulated James for having chosen 'a lady who could bring with her a public testimonial of merit and regard'. Emily became one of the few colonial women to be given a public memorial: grateful Pākehā and Māori residents purchased a clock in her memory, initially set on a pedestal in the main street and later installed in the Otaki Post Office. Her youthful indiscretion was well and truly forgotten.[79]

Jessie Aikman used a drapery business in Taupo Quay to survive her estranged publican husband's various drunken returns between 1867 and 1877.[80] In this period Whanganui was also home to, and possibly oversupplied with, dressmakers, most of whom had less obviously dramatic personal lives: Miss Gaites and Mesdames Craig, Green, Nash, Potto, Rankin, Reilly, Thorpe, Tingey, Wilton and Goodfellow, who was 'late of Regent Street London'.[81] Only half advertised in newspapers, others appeared in one trade directory and never again, but in provincial towns serving rural hinterlands such small businesses often relied more on word of mouth to establish their reputations.

'Late of London or Paris'

Businesswomen emphasised their experience, sometimes dressing it up with a ribbon or two. Richard Balmer's wife Emma Eugene of Christchurch in 1851 claimed 'long experience in some of the most fashionable houses in London's Oxford Street'.[82] Anna Cole Thick and her sister Elizabeth, 'Milliners, Dress and Mantle Makers' in Vaile's Buildings in Queen Street, Auckland, in 1856, said they were 'from London', but were in fact from provincial Bath.[83] Miss Elise Godfrey, who was making 'Morning, Walking, Evening and Ball dresses in the most modern fashions and correct taste' at Brynn Morwood Cottage in Stuart Street in Dunedin in 1863, had impressive (and uncheckable) credentials as a 'Court Milliner and Dressmaker, having recently arrived from Paris'. She advertised briefly and disappeared from the records, as did another 'Court Dress Maker' in Christchurch, 'Madame Eleonore Pearl' in 1868.[84] Sarah Williams and Miss Lambert arrived in Napier in 1864, claiming long experience in 'the most fashionable town in England', although they did not specify exactly which one.[85]

Women who had been employees in Britain or elsewhere became businesswomen in New Zealand, where there were more entrepreneurial opportunities. Ellen Caulton cited her Melbourne experience with 'Bank Bros, Bell & Co.' when setting up on her own account in Napier in 1867.[86] Elizabeth Ann Buller was an apprentice dressmaker in Liskeard, Cornwall, before emigrating to Auckland in 1855. She ran a 'fancy baby linen and children's clothing establishment' next to her brother Edward's tailoring business in 1856, before selling off her stock in April the following year and disappearing into the bonds of matrimony and then across the Tasman with William Jones in 1859.[87]

Experience did not guarantee success. Forty-year-old milliner Harriet Green emigrated to Nelson in 1851 with her daughter, also Harriet, and 28-year-old sister Naomi Wing. She established the Nelson Millinery and Drapery Establishment in Trafalgar Street, touting her sister's 'great experience in some of the leading West End houses'. Harriet, too, had been in business in London. Whether they made money is unclear: she was bankrupt in 1860. She thanked her customers 'for their kind support during the past nine years and most especially through a period of protracted personal suffering and unusually painful events'. Her newly married daughter Harriet Walcot officially took over the business but her mother remained involved 'in the execution of all orders so far as her health will permit'.[88]

Harriet Walcot should have been more successful than her mother. Her new husband, Robson, was an accountant. They were advertising for boarders by 1865, however, the drapery business perhaps unable to support four adults and the babies that appeared every two years. Robson was actually more involved in performing in local theatre, teaching music and tuning pianos than in accountancy. He also advertised Harper Twelvetrees soap powder and Brigg's Australian Satin Day Starch for sale from his wife's drapery store.[89]

Harriet Green resumed advertising the business in 1866 and was in Trafalgar Street until 1872, but then the family scattered, exemplifying the geographical mobility of quite ordinary nineteenth-century people. She died in Timaru in 1889. The Walcots moved to Christchurch, where Robson was appointed choirmaster of St John's Church in 1874, before going to Sydney and then Fiji. Naomi Wing resurfaced in the records in rural New South Wales in the 1880s, as a widow, probably of Samuel Cherry, running a small store near Young.[90] None of the family appear to have made their fortunes, but their lives were arguably more interesting than if they had stayed in London.

Moneymaking ambitions?

Rarely is there explicit evidence for why women went into business. The frank letters of Mary Taylor are exceptional in this regard. Other women were more reticent about any ambition or enjoyment, and for most sheer financial necessity was a primary motivator.

It was certainly necessary for Isabella Williams, who sailed into Lyttelton in 1850 with her husband John, a baker, and seven children. Leaving his family at the immigration barracks, John, like many others, walked over the Port Hills to stake a claim for his family in the new settlement of Christchurch. But he never made it: on the way he suffered a stroke and died. An appeal was launched for his widow, who initially sold her husband's yeast supply to needy settlers, and then arranged to import drapery from Scottish relations. In 1852 she opened Glasgow House in Christchurch's Colombo Street opposite Market Place (later Victoria Square). As well as fashionable hats and bonnets 'of the newest shapes and the most fashionable material', her stock included sensible Scotch tweeds and knitted socks for winter.[91]

Glasgow House was successful. Isabella retired in her sixties, in 1871, and sold the business as a going concern. It eventually became part of well-known Christchurch department store T.J. Armstrong's. Her daughters worked in the shop and one, Marjory, married John Campbell Aikman, going into business with him and continuing their drapery two years after his death. Another became the mayoress of Christchurch, although the mayor was unmasked as a wife beater and embezzler. Isabella did not remarry. Although she was surely a good catch, her thriving business gave her financial independence. Isabella left an impressive estate of £4000 when she died in 1882. Her obituary made much of her misfortune at being 'left alone with a young family and but slender means, to maintain the battle of life', and recorded that she had 'resolutely and courageously ... set about the discharge of her duty', but failed to mention her 20-year-long business. Instead, her success was measured 'by the fact that she has lived to see each of the members of her family occupying good and honorable positions in the community, while she has … spent the last few years of her life in quiet and comfortable retirement'.[92]

Margaret Holland's Christchurch business was also born of necessity, but despite lasting over two decades, it was more of a hand-to-mouth affair. Margaret emigrated as a single woman with her parents and sisters in 1867 and, although listed as a domestic servant on the ship's passenger list, she opened a millinery shop.[93] She had competition: as well as Glasgow House, there were at least 13 milliners and dressmakers in Christchurch and six more in Lyttelton in 1868.[94] By 1871 Margaret had married butcher and perennial insolvent John Bean, and had diversified. She sewed dresses, made hats and straw bonnets and cleaned them, 'cleaned and curled feathers' and ran a registry office for female servants. Over the next 20 years she cared for three stepchildren, gave birth to 10 babies and lost four of them, was widowed in 1884 and moved her business around central Christchurch almost annually. She added the cleaning of gentlemen's hats, 'made equal to new', and advertised on one occasion under the heading 'Economy'. By 1893 she was in Armagh Street and had moved with the times, advertising for a knitting machine operator. The fact that her business moved frequently, combined with the multiplicity of her offerings and emphasis on 'economy', suggests that her enterprise was not as large or as successful as that of Isabella Williams, but it provided a livelihood.[95] She married John Sumner in 1902 and died aged 65 in 1912.

'A lady not unknown to fame in Wanganui'[96]

Necessity sometimes called for more desperate measures. Clara Rankin survived for 15 years as a milliner and dressmaker in Whanganui, but longevity did not mean success. She made dresses and sold drapery along with a range of fancy goods, toys and fripperies, from 1869 to 1883 in Wicksteed Place and then in Ridgeway Street.[97] The business took on greater significance when she was widowed in 1871, at the age of 30, and left with five young children and another on the way. Evidence suggests, however, that her core business was insurance fraud. Like many other businesswomen, she insured her stock against fire. Her premises were burned in 1870, 1877, 1878 and yet again in 1882. Each time she made claims. In 1877 the local policeman suspected she was responsible for the fire, but made the mistake of accusing her and grabbing her arm in front of witnesses while he was, allegedly, intoxicated, and Clara successfully took him to court for assault.[98] An inquest into the 1882 fire was inconclusive, but it had started under the stairs next to Clara's shop. The Colonial Insurance Company considered her claim for £750 inflated and refused to pay.

A year later, Whanganui was in a state of 'considerable excitement' when Clara accused a respectable insurance agent, 31-year-old John Notman, who had been investigating her claim on behalf of the Colonial Insurance Company, of stealing a £5 note and a gold locket. The ensuing case cleared him of all wrongdoing, exposing instead a 'diabolical plot' hatched by Clara as revenge for having been bankrupted in the interim. The *Observer* took great delight in the story of 'the comely matron' who had 'entrapped' the respectable citizen 'under the guise of friendship, if not a less platonic relationship'. She had apparently invited him into her house, relieved him of his coat and boots, laid him on the sofa and then called a policeman and accused John of theft. The sage advice offered by the newspaper was that respectable men 'should not pay clandestine visits to the houses of handsome ladies (more particularly buxom widows) in which category, in the absence of any reference to a husband we place Mrs Rankin'. John Notman may have been made to look a fool but he recovered, remaining a respected public figure. Clara's business failed to survive this latest debacle; in 1883 she was insolvent, with liabilities of £200 and assets of just £25. She did not appear again in the newspapers or in business, but must have had some resources: when she died in Whanganui in 1924 she left an estate of over £1500.[99]

Here today, gone tomorrow

Many dressmaking businesses were short-lived and others disappeared from the records, possibly continuing but relying on word of mouth, invisible to historians. Even in Auckland where, from the beginning, the wives and daughters of government officials and wealthy entrepreneurs wanted to dress the part, needlework businesses came and went with remarkable rapidity. Elizabeth Kitchen, Ellen Lewis and Marie Hemmings were listed as dressmakers in the 1845 census, then vanished.[100] Perhaps they just took in sewing for neighbours, or were employees rather than businesswomen. Miss Meaker had a large enough business to hire apprentices between 1848 and 1855, but then packed up and left the colony.[101] Mrs Hurry advertised dressmaking briefly but gave it up to join her husband in the Wesleyan Day School, with more secure employment teaching needlework and 'other branches of female education'.[102] Harriet Langford, who advertised 'newest and most favoured styles', was only in the straw-bonnet making business for a year before her husband took it over in 1848, selling to draper Henry Ellis in 1851.[103]

But if these businesses did not last long, by 1851 there were nine more businesses along similar lines in Auckland to replace them.[104] Seven were relatively fleeting. Once again, some women left the colony, others married. Ann Hamer was in the millinery and straw-bonnet business for two years after arriving with her brother, the Reverend Thomas Hamer, and his family in 1851. In April 1854 she married Onehunga timber merchant Samuel Fleming and left her business.[105] It had, however, been sound enough for one of her erstwhile employees, Mary Ann Neale, to boast she was 'late of Miss Hamer's Establishment' when setting up on her own account. In 1856 Mary Ann married builder and publican Ephraim Mills and, probably busy in the hotel, did not appear in business in her own name again.[106] Elizabeth Webster then took over Ann Hamer's premises, again making sure to advertise the connection. Elizabeth became embroiled in her irrepressible husband Hartley's entrepreneurial endeavours, but her millinery business may well have been the stable one in the family. Hartley set up as a chemist, tried his hand at photography, sharing premises with his wife's hats, and also opened public baths.[107] When he resurfaced in New Plymouth in 1859, the milliner sharing his premises was not his wife but 'Miss J. Kirk from Auckland', who had arrived in New Plymouth with the Websters. Elizabeth did not appear in business again, perhaps because Hartley was becoming successful and her income was no longer required.[108]

For some women, the security of a paid position could prove more attractive than the vicissitudes of independent business, particularly if they lacked family support or faced fierce competition. This was the case for Ann Forsyth in Dunedin. She and her sister Jane took advantage of family networks, opening their dressmaking and millinery business above their brother-in-law Alexander Mollison's shop in 1858. Ann's business began to unravel after sister Jane married and then Alexander sold his business to Hugh Kirkpatrick & Co. in 1861. Within three years Ann's independent business was subsumed within the larger store, Kirkpatrick's advertising their mantle department 'under the supervision of Miss Forsyth'. Without the cocoon of intertwined family businesses, this change offered security. On the 1893 electoral roll Ann Forsyth listed her occupation as 'managing dressmaker' – she may have been an employee but she was no mere needlewoman. Such positions in department stores became increasingly available in the larger towns.[109]

Creating family networks and partnerships

Family networks were integral to the Forsyth/Mollison siblings' business success and the same was true for 27-year-old Emma Marriott. She opened a millinery and dressmaking store on Lambton Quay in Wellington in 1853, in premises owned by her father, James Henry Marriott, and next door to his optician's shop. Emma remained there for nearly 20 years. She had the support of her mother Sarah, who was also a milliner, and a businesswoman role model in her aunt, widow of James' brother William, who had carried on his London optician's business after 1846.[110] Emma's business benefited from her father's active engagement in Wellington society. He was not only an optician, but also an instrument maker, engraver and bookseller, and a leading light in the Oddfellows, the Wellington Athenaeum and Mechanics' Institute and provincial affairs generally, responsible for building the first Wellington theatre.[111] Emma merely announced her presence periodically as 'Miss E. Marriott, Milliner and Dressmaker, Lambton Quay', generally following a more elaborate advertisement for 'J.H. Marriott, Telescope Manufacturer, Telescopes made and repaired, spectacles to suit all sights, compasses etc repaired, engravings &c &c'.[112] Family connections worked both ways, however. Emma was only 47 when her business disappeared from advertising columns and trade directories in 1872. It is possible that her brother Edward's insolvency that year affected her business: when he became bankrupt again several years later she was one of his main creditors.[113] Or perhaps she stopped work to help care for her parents, both then in their seventies.[114]

The most common form of family support for women's businesses came through marriage. Some were propelled into business by incompetent spouses, but others were able to start or expand their own enterprises by sharing a new husband's premises or gaining access to capital. When recently arrived migrant Maria Page married Gilbert Butler in Christchurch in 1859 he provided £400 to start her drapery business, which she operated until 1880. Maria advertised the business, did the millinery and fronted the shop, but Gilbert both provided the initial capital and was a partner, for all that his wife later argued in a dispute in court that 'she had conducted a business entirely by herself'. Although he was 'never seen with a needle in his hand', as one witness put it, he carried parcels and generally helped out, keeping the books, doing the banking and sending stock orders to England.[115]

Running parallel businesses could also be mutually beneficial. In 1859 Amelia Usher was a milliner and straw-bonnet maker and her husband Thomas a boot and shoemaker in Nelson's Trafalgar Street.[116] Tailor David Wagg and his milliner wife Eleanor were also both in business in Nelson after arriving in 1851. Her advertisements disappeared in 1862, but David's continued as a tailor 'and draper', the addition suggesting Eleanor's continued involvement. When she died, her marital replacement, Julia, was also entrepreneurial, running a restaurant in Richmond, near Nelson, in the 1880s.[117]

Sometimes husbands gained the advantage by marrying an established businesswoman. Bookbinder William Valentine Salter married Theresa Manning, 15 years his senior, in Nelson in 1862. Theresa had emigrated in 1860, aged 37, on the same ship as William. Within a month of disembarking, accompanied by crates of 'a choice selection' of drapery, 'T. Manning (late of London)' was in business in Bridge Street. Two years later, just before her marriage, she moved to new premises, Silvertown House, in Hardy Street. The marriage was prudent financially, particularly for young William, who set up on his own account in September 1864, operating out of his wife's premises. Their parallel businesses continued into the 1890s.[118]

Dual businesses were one thing; other couples, such as Maria and Gilbert Butler, were business partners. Draperies, like hotels, were particularly suitable joint ventures. James and Fanny Drew were in and out of the drapery business in Trafalgar Street in Nelson between 1855 and 1877. Family member John M. Drew rescued them after James' insolvency in 1860, buying stock and shop. He employed Fanny and not her husband as manager, suggesting she had the better business head of the couple.[119]

Emma and Charles Bartlett were also business partners in Nelson in 1858. Both had experience: Charles had owned a draper's shop in London and milliner Emma had 'for many years been in the business in the West-end'.[120] Two years later, however, Charles was an early victim of drink driving when William Watts, in charge of the local hackney cab, collided with his cart at night, fatally injuring him. The jury in the inquest suggested that 'a man of such intemperate habits such as Watts should not be allowed to drive any public vehicle for hire'.[121] Within a week of her husband's death, Emma was thanking Nelson 'for the favours conferred on her late husband', announcing she would 'continue the business' and promising 'moderate charges, care and punctuality in the execution of orders entrusted to her, and every possible attention to the general requirements of her customers'. Running a business alone was not easy. Very quickly Emma was forced to assert her authority by sacking a difficult employee. She used various strategies to attract customers. Her stock was 'selected with the utmost care from the best London Houses' and she advertised

William Salter married well, moving into his wife Theresa's existing business premises in Nelson in 1862. Although she remained in business until the 1890s, Theresa's obituary remembered her community involvement, especially her 'attachment to dumb animals'.

W.V. Salter, Bookbinder, and Mrs Salter's Baby Linen Warehouse, Nelson Provincial Museum, Maguire Collection, 57257

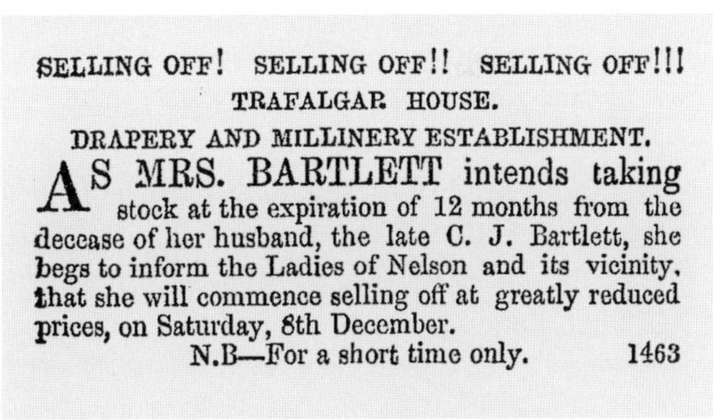

SELLING OFF! SELLING OFF!! SELLING OFF!!!

TRAFALGAR HOUSE.

DRAPERY AND MILLINERY ESTABLISHMENT.

AS MRS. BARTLETT intends taking stock at the expiration of 12 months from the decease of her husband, the late C. J. Bartlett, she begs to inform the Ladies of Nelson and its vicinity, that she will commence selling off at greatly reduced prices, on Saturday, 8th December.

N.B—For a short time only. 1463

Was Mrs Bartlett subtly reminding her customers of her recent bereavement as a clever appeal for sympathy?

Colonist, 14 December 1860

that because it was 'to MRS BARTLETT'S own order, she [could] confidently recommend [it] to the public as being especially worthy of attention'. She widened her market, promising country orders would be 'punctually attended to'. Within a year, however, she was selling stock off at half price, ostensibly to do a stocktake. She remained in business for another four years before moving to Grove Street in 1866 and opening a small general store, which she ran until her death, aged only 48, in 1869.[122]

Will the real draper please stand up?

Some husbands were much less directly involved in the business than their name above the door might suggest. 'Wardell and Jennings', who opened their doors in Auckland in 1848, were business partners Edward Wardell and his sister-in-law Jane Jennings, who had both moved from Sydney. There, however, it had been sisters Jane and Maria Jennings who started a business in 1841, claiming to be from 'Mademoiselle Laurie's of London'. Maria's marriage to Edward in 1844 rendered her participation in the business invisible. She reappeared in Auckland after Jane married and Edward became insolvent in 1851, announcing she would 'carry on the Millinery business', suggesting she had been involved all along.[123]

The Auckland jury list in 1859 described Thomas Elvin Powley and his new son-in-law Edward Johnson as drapers.[124] 'Powley & Johnson' advertised from Shortland Street. Thomas Powley was not a draper, however, but a policeman. He and wife Harriett had arrived in Auckland from Norwich via New South Wales and Tasmania in about 1848. Thomas was an active policeman, although it was suggested that while his wife was busy with their 11 offspring, as well as running her own dressmaking business, he visited brothels in other than a professional capacity.[125] He retired from the police in 1860 and by 1869 'had no occupation'. His son-in-law was more entitled to the epithet of draper. He occasionally appeared in the shop and was the official business partner with his long-suffering mother-in-law Harriett,[126] who actually ran the drapery with her milliner daughter Eliza Jane Johnson.[127]

Powley & Johnson was a feature of Auckland for 10 years, surviving a fire that started next door in 1863 and the subsequent inquiry, but in 1869 42-year-old Edward Johnson died suddenly from poisoning, having accidentally drunk medicine that was meant to be applied externally. His death threw the business into disarray. Within eight months his widow, with four young children, had remarried and moved to Melbourne. The partnership was dissolved and Thomas Powley was declared bankrupt. Harriett resumed business on her own account in 1871 and, like many other Aucklanders, dabbled in mining company shares.[128] In 1873 there was another fire in Queen Street. The 1863 blaze had started accidentally next door to Harriett's shop, but this one definitely ignited in her store. Over 50 buildings were destroyed. No lives were lost, other than that of Harriett's dog, chained up in the shop. Her stock was insured for £400, although it was reported to be worth double that. This was the end of Harriett's business: her son George took over the family business mantle as a draper and shirt manufacturer in the 1880s.[129]

Sisters could also be obscured behind brothers, despite their legal right to act independently. In the 1860s, Herbert Ernest Lowther was a Christchurch shop-keeper with a grocery in Montreal Street. But gossipy Christchurch diarist William Ellison Burke also described 'a sort of drapery' kept by 'one Henry Lowther and his sisters' in Cathedral Square. The H.E. and M.S. Lowther who advertised drapery, however, were in fact his older sisters, Harriett Ellen and Mary Selina. Unlike Burke, other Christchurch residents knew exactly who ran the shop. J. Pepperill advertised his business's proximity to 'Miss Lowther's', and when milliner Miss Hicks, 'having had the honour of supplying the Princesses of England and the nobility', set up shop, it was in 'Miss Lowther's' premises. When the family returned to Wales, the sisters to live with their mother in Cardigan, the 'Misses Lowther' announced the clearing out sale. Mary's considerable estate of over £1000 on her death in 1910 included property in New Zealand.[130] Such familial partnerships dominated female needlework businesses. Daughters were more often partners than sons, although the partnership frequently dissolved when the daughter married and set up alone or with her new husband. A few partnerships brought younger generations of males on board, as with Powley & Johnson. Mary Ann Warmoll advertised drapery from her son John's mattress manufactory on Lambton Quay, Wellington, from 1858. She and her daughter had had a shop in 1857 in Sydney where they exploited the rush for gold in Victoria by selling 'modern and very cheap' theodolites, among other items.[131]

Kate and her boys

A more unusual partnership was that formed in 1885 by the unrelated Kate Kelly, Thomas Warnock and William Adkin. The partnership of these three entrepreneurs was a business relationship based solely on each person's professional skills. William Adkin's journals provide an insight into the business.[132] In the 1870s Kate Kelly was

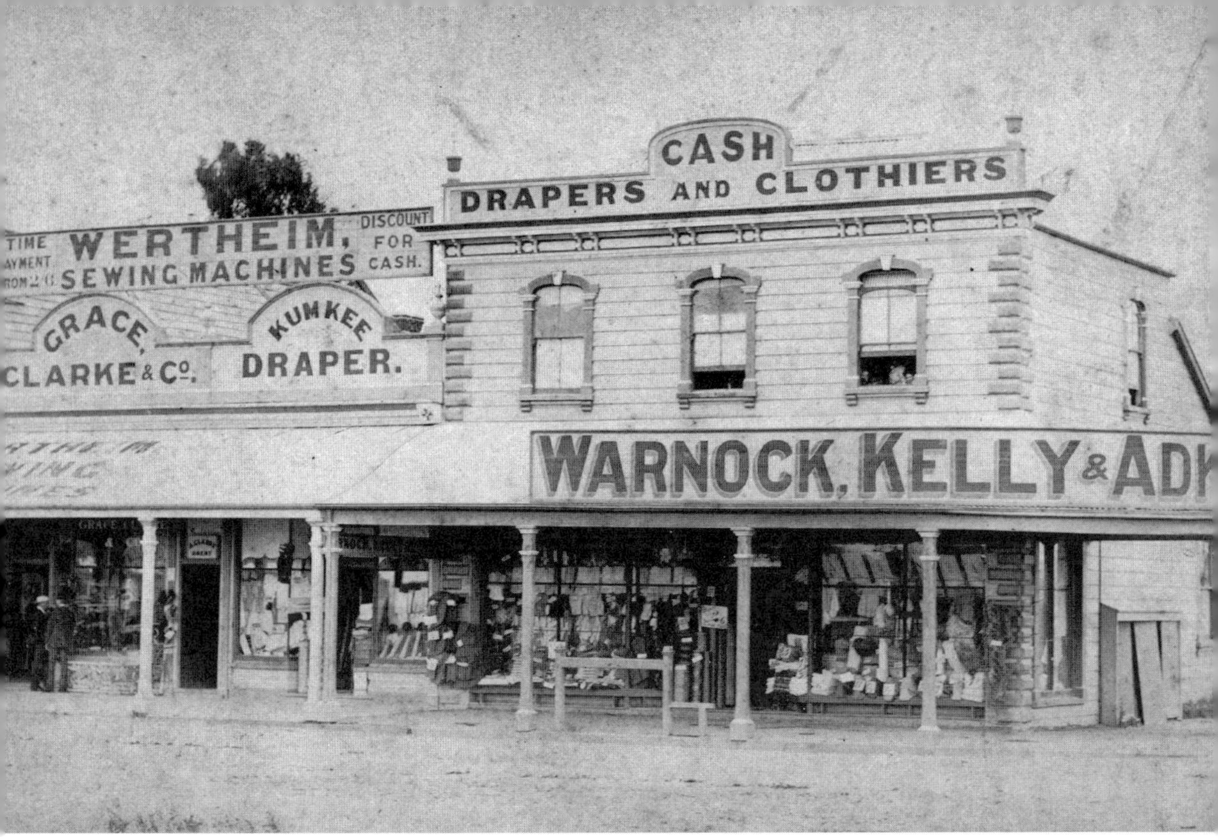

Warnock, Kelly & Adkin opened branches, including this one in Palmerston North, when other businesses were folding in the Long Depression.

Palmerston North City Library – Manawatū Heritage

imported from Melbourne by Wellington department store Kirkcaldie & Stains to run their showroom at a handsome salary of £195. She must have had experience but we know only that she had emigrated to Victoria from England with her aunt as a 12-year-old and married 44-year-old John Forward Kelly in 1864, when she was 22. There seems to be no record of her subsequent life in Australia.[133] Kate worked at 'Kirks' for a number of years, but in 1886, aged 43, she joined forces with fellow employees, 35-year-old Thomas Warnock and 30-year-old William Adkin. Having bought the stock of draper James Thomas Steele, 'Warnock, Kelly & Adkin' were in business. Kirkcaldie & Stains immediately sued them for a month's wages because they had departed without notice, but had limited success. According to William Adkin, the action merely inspired public sympathy for the three renegades.

Their foray into independent enterprise was a brave move in depressed economic times.[134] Advertising as 'late of Kirkcaldie and Stains', they attracted some of their old customers. Kate was in charge of the mantle, millinery and ladies' departments, Thomas oversaw the 'fancy part of the trade … laces ribbons sunshades hosiery &c'

Capable-looking Kate Kelly, 'the most successful saleswoman in Wellington', according to her business partner, William Adkin.

Private collection: Carol Byfield

and William had the dress department, silks, manchester and furnishing.[135] They survived with some bold decisions: in 1888, for example, undeterred by cashflow and staffing problems, Warnock, Kelly & Adkin expanded, opening a branch in Palmerston North right when other businesses were folding.[136]

The impetus for the partnership came from Thomas and William, according to the latter. Dissatisfied with management at Kirkcaldie & Stains, they 'promenade[d along] the Quay talking about starting in business' in 1885. The addition of Kate to the team was Adkin's idea, he recorded, and her house became the headquarters of their plotting.[137] She was central to the plan because she was 'perhaps the most successful saleswoman in this city' and 'K&S felt her leaving very much'. Of the company name order, he joked to his family, 'We put Kelly in the middle you see with the idea of protecting lovely woman [sic], ahem!!'[138]

We have only William Adkin's account of the business's genesis. Did the two men approach her initially as a partner or as an employee? Did she insist on the partnership or was her name an obvious coup? Or did she in fact put the idea of a business into their heads and ensure she was a part of it? However it happened, Kate was integral and difficult to replace. She officially left the partnership after seven years in 1893 but, having announced her retirement, then stayed on to run the millinery department for another six months. William Adkin departed in 1900 and a decade later Thomas Warnock moved his primary store to Whanganui, where Warnock's remained a landmark into the late twentieth century.[139]

Multigenerational businesses

Daughters seldom inherited their mother's enterprises, but Sarah Potto's three daughters were an exception. After her sudden early death in 1871 they maintained her straw-bonnet business in Whanganui until 1891, adding millinery and dress-making to their services.[140] Some long-standing businesses were, however, passed through multiple generations of unrelated female owners.

The business started by Elizabeth Willcox in 1857 lasted for 31 years and supported several female proprietors. Birmingham-born Elizabeth was already 39 when she reached Wellington in 1853 with three brothers, a married sister and a brother-in-law. Her brothers were much younger: 18, 20 and 26. In 1851 Elizabeth and brother Henry had been lodging in a household in Everton, near Liverpool, where she was a daily governess and he a stationer's assistant. Brother Joseph was an apprentice druggist in West Derby. An older brother, John, emigrated to Christchurch that year.[141]

Elizabeth saw new opportunities in a new land – not as a governess or in keeping house for her bachelor brothers, but in business. Henry and his brother-in-law, Benjamin Smith, had established a stationery and fancy goods firm, Smith & Willcox, in which Elizabeth may have assisted. By 1857, however, she had her own drapery and millinery business in Willis Street; she later moved to Lambton Quay, where she rented premises from Mary Taylor. She was astute enough to take out fire insurance, valuing her household goods and furniture at £20 and her stock at £30. Given that she appears to have had no similar experience in England, it is reasonable to assume that, like Mary Taylor, she received advice and possibly initial capital from her brothers. Nevertheless she was independent, corresponding with the insurance company when required. In 1858 she added to her stock the drapery part of Thomas Barlow & Co., who sold 'Millinery, Haberdashery, Music, Pianofortes, and Perfumery', initially acting as their agent but then assuming full responsibility. 'E. Willcox', as she preferred to advertise, continued in business for another 16 years. She retired

Mima Potto meant business. The marital property was in her name, and she bequeathed her husband John Pollock the 'use and enjoyment during his lifetime' of a house, after which it passed to her children.

Miss Mima (Jemima) Potto. Harding, William James, 1826–1899: Negatives of Whanganui district, Alexander Turnbull Library, 1/4-008879-G

Is this draper Miss Elizabeth Cowles herself, posing on her Lambton Quay doorstep with a satisfied customer in the early 1880s? The window display shows the array of items sold by such shops. Cowles shopfront, Lambton Quay, Wellington, Alexander Turnbull Library, 1/2-056053-F at the end of 1872, selling the remaining stock to Elizabeth Cowles.[142] Having supported herself for 20 years in retirement, she left a fair estate of more than £250 when she died in 1893. Her 11-line obituary in the *Evening Post* celebrated her devotion 'to philanthropic and benevolent objects until the infirmity of old age prevented her from pursuing an active life' and added, almost as an afterthought, 'For many years deceased carried on a drapery business on Lambton Quay.' Emigration had improved her fortunes substantially, from the hand-to-mouth existence of a daily governess to a respected, comfortably off businesswoman. Her involvement in philanthropy exemplified the avenues for public service then open to women. In contrast, one of her brothers served as a Justice of the Peace while another, John Smith Willcox, was mayor of Lyttelton.[143]

Elizabeth Willcox's successor in the drapery business, Elizabeth Cowles, was a milliner who lived with her mother in Devon until, at 33, she emigrated as matron in charge of the single female immigrants on the *Celaeno*, arriving in Lyttelton in 1870.[144] She disappeared from the records until 1872, when she resurfaced in Wellington purchasing Elizabeth Willcox's stock, though not her premises. She initially advertised from her lodgings at Ruth Bentham's house in Willis Street.[145] In December 1872, Elizabeth moved to Thorndon House, next to tailors John Herman Cook & Sons in Lambton Quay. She imported goods from England, including children's toys and baby items, ladies' underclothing and crinolines, as well as linen and flowers. She took on a partner, newly widowed milliner and dressmaker Jane Stoddart. They were in business together as Cowles & Stoddart until 1874, when Jane married farmer Henry Cook, one of the sons of Cook & Sons next door.[146]

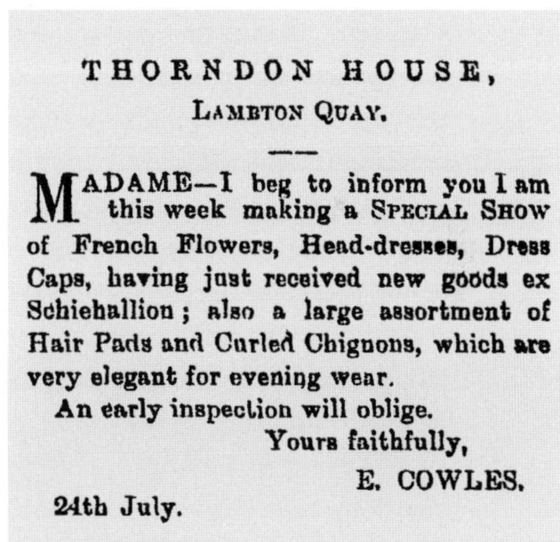
THORNDON HOUSE,
LAMBTON QUAY.

MADAME—I beg to inform you I am this week making a SPECIAL SHOW of French Flowers, Head-dresses, Dress Caps, having just received new goods ex Schiehallion; also a large assortment of Hair Pads and Curled Chignons, which are very elegant for evening wear.

An early inspection will oblige.

Yours faithfully,

E. COWLES.

24th July.

Framing an advertisement as a personal letter emphasising a 'special show' was one inventive strategy of Elizabeth Cowles in Wellington. *Evening Post*, 31 July 1873

Elizabeth continued alone and by 1879 was the sole Wellington agent for Madame Weigel's famous paper patterns. Like others in Wellington she suffered from periodic economic downturns, in 1879 advertising 'Great Bargains for ONE SHILLING in consequence of depressed trade, which are displayed in the Window for three weeks only'. To pull in 'those at a distance', she also offered two free tram tickets to anyone spending more than 5s in the sale. Thanks to her entrepreneurial flair, she prospered sufficiently to buy property in Petone. Yarnacombe in Britannia Street was a seven-room house in half an acre of gardens and orchards, with a section next door used as a tennis court and bowling green.[147]

In 1883 Elizabeth sold her business to Wilhelmina Cook. She popped up in Masterton in the Wairarapa for two weeks in May 1886, taking George Sage's shop and selling off an eclectic range apparently left over from a Wellington bazaar, including tennis balls, ladies' and children's chest expanders and the inevitable Madame Weigel's paper patterns. She was also authorised to take orders for 'Dr Carter Moffat's AMMONIAPHONE', for 'strengthening and enriching the HUMAN VOICE and for the treatment of *Coughs, Bronchitis, Asthma* … considered by some to be the most BENEFICIENT DISCOVERY of the day'.[148]

The following year she renovated Yarnacombe and advertised part of it to let, 'suitable for newly-married couples or ladies'. In 1892 she signed a suffrage petition and, when New Zealand women obtained the vote in 1893, she celebrated her fifty-sixth birthday by becoming involved in politics. She was elected chairwoman of a women's working committee supporting Dr Alfred Kingcome Newman's candidature as member for Wellington Suburbs in the forthcoming election. The following year she stood successfully for the Wellington Licensing Committee on a complete temperance ticket. A strong prohibitionist, she remained on the committee for at least three years. She was also elected to a committee of locals dedicated to fighting for prohibition in Petone in 1899.[149] When she died in 1903 there was no newspaper obituary, despite her 30-year residence in Wellington and Petone, in business and as a local public figure and landowner. She left most of her very respectable £2610 estate to her widowed sister and three nieces, who had followed her to New Zealand with their mother.[150]

Wilhelmina Cook, who took over Elizabeth Cowles's shop in 1883, was neighbour John Cook's daughter. In 1885 she was joined by surgical belt maker Josephine Macdonald (see Chapter 12). The last mention of Wilhelmina's business was in 1888; she married Charles Bray of Feilding the following year.[151] The drapery business that had provided a living for five women for over 30 years finally closed its doors and was, it seems, instantly forgotten.

'Ground floor, going up'

The modern department store emerged in the nineteenth century and expanded in the twentieth, symbolising the bourgeois culture of the modern city. Le Bon Marché in Paris set the trend in 1852 and soon every growing city boasted a department store or two, generally targeting female customers.[152] New Zealand was no exception. Anyone growing up in Christchurch would know Armstrong's, Ballantynes and Mrs Pope's, just as Aucklanders were familiar with Smith & Caughey's and Milne & Choyce. In Wellington were Kirkcaldie & Stains and James Smith's; in Dunedin Brown, Ewing & Co. (later swallowed by Hays); and in Nelson, S. Anstice, Son & Co.

All of these stores, except Kirkcaldie & Stains, had their origins in female entrepreneurship, often growing out of millinery and dressmaking businesses. Armstrong's traced its origins not only to Isabella Williams' store, as we have seen, but also to Thomas Armstrong's wife, Mary Maria, who actually started the business that became T.J. Armstrong & Co. and lasted until the 1960s.[153] James Smith in Wellington ran his store with his wife Anne after he bought the business from Margaret and Susan Smith who, in turn, had bought the shop from their employer, Mary Taylor.

New Zealand was not unique in this; nineteenth-century female entrepreneurship was a global phenomenon. Across the Tasman some of Sydney's best-known department stores had their origins in businesses run by women whose contributions were often quickly written out of the store histories, as were those of many New Zealand businesswomen.[154] Smith & Caughey's in Auckland was founded by Marianne Smith in 1880, but an 1898 history of the store omitted her entirely.[155] She was also officially sidelined in the business, being a shareholder but not a director of the expanding company until her husband died. Then, as a director, she reputedly never missed a board meeting and was by all accounts a force to be reckoned with. Her rightful place as the store's founder has been resurrected in recent years on the store's website and elsewhere.[156]

Maria Pope, a 44-year-old widow who emigrated alone from London in 1859, founded what later became Mrs Pope's Variety Stores in 1862. She was joined in 1860 by her delinquent son Fusedale, who had been in reform school for ambitiously stealing £6000 from his employer at the age of 13, and in 1862 by her more responsible daughter, Sarah, who worked in her mother's business.[157] Maria began as a stationer in Market Place, where she was the agent for the *Lyttelton Times* and the *Press*. By 1866 she included haberdashery and fancy goods, appealing to a female market.[158]

Mrs Maria Pope's business lasted well into the twentieth century and retained a tradition of female management for many years.

Robyn Gosset, History of Mrs Pope Ltd

Mrs Pope's store thrived, despite setbacks and unsavoury neighbours. Her premises were damaged in a disastrous fire in 1868, when she was underinsured to the tune of £200. The fire was deliberately lit by Thomas Swale, the next-door grocer, in a dramatic and unsuccessful attempt to hide his murder of business partner John Rankin. Another neighbour, 'confectioner' Eliza Edwards, was charged with brothel-keeping the following year. In the 1870s the Pope family prospered enough to move from above the shop to a house called Olney in Papanui. According to legend, Maria commuted to work on a tricycle. Sarah assumed responsibility for the business in the 1880s and Maria was retired by 1897. In 1902, aged 62, Sarah married William Ensom, 11 years her junior. Unlike many other husbands and sons, William did not join the company. The business remained in the family until the 1920s, became a chain of variety stores in the 1960s and lasted until 1993. The tradition of female management also continued, with Isabella Pringle in charge from 1916 to 1943.[159] Mrs Pope's was one of the few female-headed businesses to survive for so long without male input.

Landmark Christchurch department store Ballantynes began in 1854 when Esther Clarkson, who had emigrated with her carpenter husband David and a young son in 1851, turned the front room of her Cashel Street house into a shop, importing boxes of straw bonnets. The store expanded, literally, thanks to David's skills. His cousin Thomas Atkinson was a partner and they advertised as T. Atkinson & Co. in 1854 while David and Esther were in Sydney purchasing stock. When Thomas left the partnership in 1856, the Clarksons renamed the business Dunstable House and David's sister Elizabeth joined them. The Clarksons sold out to William Pratt in 1864, then spent some time in business in Timaru before returning to England, having made enough money to live comfortably.[160]

David's sister Elizabeth had been in business for herself in Lyttelton, where she took over Margaret Culling's straw-bonnet shop when the Cullings moved to Otago. Elizabeth, who had begun as an apprentice for Margaret in 1853, came to Dunstable House as 'first assistant' in 1856. In 1860 Elizabeth married Prebbleton farmer George Taylor but remained at Dunstable House, retiring only after it was bought by John Ballantyne in 1872. She reputedly 'taught Ballantynes' milliner how to trim a hat' properly.[161]

Women founded Auckland's two most famous department stores – Smith & Caughey's and Milne & Choyce. The latter is also an example of a multigenerational business of unrelated women. Mary Jane and Charlotte Milne emigrated from Ireland with their parents and younger brothers in 1863. After working for draper David Graham for four years, 23-year-old Mary Jane took over an established business on the corner of Wyndham and Albert streets with her younger sister.

They bought the business from Mr and Mrs Wilson but it was better known as 'Mrs C. Lowson's'. Elizabeth Lowson was a straw-bonnet maker and milliner from before 1849. Like a number of wives in business, she always advertised under her married name, often with her husband Charles's initial, making her first name almost impossible to identify, even with the benefit of the digital archive. By the 1860s she was advertising a 'Millinery and Drapery Establishment', offering a 'most elegant' selection of goods, and her shop was a local landmark. In 1855, for example, new dressmaker Madame Nakin advertised her position next to Mrs Lowson's shop. Elizabeth retired in 1864 after fire damaged her stock and premises. Her shop was so renowned that *both* of the subsequent owners – the Wilsons and the Milnes – referred to their business as 'late Mrs Lowson's' for some years. When Elizabeth died in 1873 aged only 53, her obituary, unusually, eulogised her as 'at one time one of the best known persons in Auckland, having been engaged in business in Wyndham Street for nearly twenty-five years'.[162]

According to Milne & Choyce historian Ken Tucker, the shop suffered from being at the top of Wyndham Street, away from the main shopping district on

Shortland and Queen streets, but the ladies of Auckland were made of sterner stuff than he imagined, at least when in pursuit of a matching button or a new ribbon. An 1860 advertisement requested the return of a 'red velvet purse' lost on 4 December, 'between Miss McLaughlin's shop, Shortland Crescent, and Mrs Lowson's shop, Wyndham-street', suggesting that at least one person braved the 10-minute walk between the two well-regarded establishments. (Coincidentally, the purse's owner asked for it to be returned to Gloucester House in Parnell, run by yet another businesswoman, Sarah Steele.)[163]

Unlike many businesswomen, the Milne sisters did not live on their shop premises but with their parents. Significantly, however, for the 40 years of their tenancy, the lease of the family home was in Mary Jane's name, not her father's, a sign of where the family's entrepreneurial initiative lay.[164] Seven years after it opened, the Milnes' business expanded, moving to the larger premises of Cheapside House on the corner of Queen and Wellesley streets in 1874. Later that year Charlotte married Henry Choyce, a buyer for clothing company Archibald Clark & Son, one of the Milnes' main suppliers.[165]

The old Wyndham Street premises reverted to the Lowson family. Elizabeth's nieces Christina Clayton and Agnes Cook advertised as 'Cook and Clayton', running the business 'which has for so many years been successfully carried on by their Aunt (the late Mrs Charles Lowson)'. They lasted a year before asset strippers George Hemus and Walter Trigg took over the stock in 1876 and sold off the remaining goods, ending a 30-year business run by successive female entrepreneurs.[166]

Meanwhile the Milne sisters moved onwards and upwards. Cheapside House was a better location and they took over the stock, and presumably goodwill, of draper Berry Cass, who relocated to Christchurch. Previously they had focused on high-quality specialised lines, but now they expanded their range. In 1876 Henry Choyce joined the firm and it became Milne & Choyce. Mary Jane's legal partner was now Henry, not Charlotte, and the latter's involvement became invisible. A new store opened in 1885 and the business continued to grow.[167] Although the business expanded into a fully fledged department store when Henry Choyce arrived, it is worth remembering that it was the entrepreneurial Mary Jane and Charlotte who had made that initial and important expansion to Cheapside House and a broader market.

As with so many others, however, in the shift from successful shop to big business the female founders slid out of the picture. When Milne & Choyce became a public company in 1901 Mary Jane Milne was not on the board. Although she had

Queen Street from Wellesley Street: Mary Jane Milne and Charlotte Choyce's Cheapside House; opposite were taxidermist Jane Yandle and tobacconist Mary Haines. Grace Chapman's Pacific Hotel and milliner Matilda Butterworth were further on.

Creator unknown: Photograph looking up Queen Street, Auckland, Alexander Turnbull Library, PAColl-8475

founded the store, Henry Choyce became managing director. One might argue that, at 60, Mary Jane was ready to retire, but Henry was exactly the same age, and it was not until 1920, when he was 80, that he 'indicated he would like a less active part in the company and accepted an advisory role, paid £350 a year'.[168] Mary Jane nevertheless remained influential, not least because she was a principal shareholder. She was well equipped to deal with changing business environments, and she certainly embraced modernity in other aspects of her life. In 1903, aged 62, she traded in her horse and gig for a brand-new twin-cylinder Darracq car.[169]

Her nephew and ward, John Stewart Milne, who had joined the business at the age of 17 in 1897, became secretary in 1901 and a member of the board in 1909. Mary Jane had raised John and his sisters, Ethel and Mary, the orphaned children of her brother. Her nieces also worked in the business, tellingly not in management but as saleswomen and sales representatives.[170]

The firm's fiftieth jubilee celebrations in 1916 reinforced Mary Jane's invisibility, as did her later obituary celebrating her as a 'first-rate milliner', rather than as a first-rate businesswoman. She was acknowledged in 1916 as 'one of the founders' of a business that 'even in those early days, [was] looked upon as the exclusive ladies' emporium of the city'. However, the Wyndham Street premises was described as 'a little shop' dealing in millinery and ladies' outfitting. The expansion to Cheapside was wrongly dated to well after Henry Choyce joined the firm, ignoring the entrepreneurial initiative taken by Mary Jane Milne and Charlotte, before the latter married Henry.[171] Similarly, in 1926, when the *Auckland Star* celebrated the store's sixtieth anniversary, it eulogised the 'keen, solid men at the head of the firm', forgetting the two sisters who founded it.[172] Milne & Choyce closed its doors in the 1990s, although the 1924 flagship building still stands in Queen Street. Recognition finally arrived in 2012, when Mary Jane Milne (but not Henry Choyce) was made a laureate of the New Zealand Business Hall of Fame, joining Marianne Smith, who had been inducted in 2009. Brewer Mary Innes would follow in 2013. Charlotte Choyce, however, remains in the shadows.[173]

Nelson's S. Anstice & Co. survived into the twentieth century under the management of its founder, but was apparently swallowed up in a family inheritance dispute after she died. Sophia King started a dressmaking business in Karamea on the West Coast in 1876. After her husband Edwin became ill two years later, the couple and their two children moved to Nelson, where Sophia continued her business and had another daughter, Harriet, in 1879. Edwin died in 1880, followed just months later by Harriet. Sophia carried on. She made the most of her 'very extensive experience in all the leading West-end Houses': her ladies' undergarments were 'in a very superior style, at very low prices'. By 1885 Sophia had moved to the 'Commodious and Convenient' premises 'lately occupied by Mrs Pamely, Mode de Paris'. She became 'MRS KING, Mode De Paris', and may also have employed Mrs Pamely's five young saleswomen and her needle workers, although it is to be hoped she treated them rather better. In 1886 Sophia, then 37, married the recently widowed John Snook Anstice, a 60-year-old baker, and created a formidable business partnership. Along with a new husband, Sophia gained 12 stepchildren ranging in age from seven to 34, and several grandchildren. She had two more children herself, but only one, Herbert, survived infancy.

Sophia advertised an 'Economic Drapery Establishment', a 'Small Shop with a Large Stock'. She embraced modern techniques, advertising her lock-stitch machine. In 1891 she invested in a section on the corner of Hardy and Hope streets and in

Sophia Anstice's model, Miss Dement, imitating an election campaign – 'Mrs Anstice for Draper!' – in the Nelson Rowing Club Fancy Fair's Poster March, was clever advertising in July 1905. Miss Dement, Nelson Provincial Museum, Tyree Studio, 68255

Perhaps taken in 1891 to celebrate the grand opening of Sophia Anstice's new purpose-built St Alban's House in Hardy Street, Nelson, this photo reveals a usually hidden female workforce. Sophia Anstice, Draper and Dressmaker with group, Hardy Street, Nelson Provincial Museum, Tyree Studio, 46391/4

January 1892, with great fanfare, opened St Albans' House, a purpose-built emporium. This had moved again to Trafalgar Street by 1900 and she continued to expand into the twentieth century, with branches in Takaka, Motueka and Murchison. Sophia kept her finger on the pulse of the business, visiting her branches frequently, travelling by public passenger coach. When the Anstices toured Europe, Sophia did business with Catesby's, her brother Edward's Tottenham Court Road department store. John Anstice was 91 when he died nine years before Sophia. As she grew older their son Herbert Anstice took more responsibility. He and his half-sister Lilian inherited the business but it was Herbert and his family who continued it, until legal disputes with Lilian appear to have caused its demise. The Anstice name survives, however, in two heritage buildings in Nelson.[174]

As a postscript, it is worth noting that Sophia was not the first Mrs Anstice to advertise millinery in Nelson. While she was struggling to establish a foothold in Karamea, John Anstice's first wife Emily was advertising 'Splendid Value in Fashionable Ladies' Costumes', from Hardy Street in Nelson. She assured customers that 'we do more than give mere value. Incessantly we are offering goods the value of which exceeds the selling price.'[175] She advertised only once: 'incessant' selling of goods for less than they were worth was probably not an effective business strategy.

Gone and forgotten

If the female founders of modern department stores have often been sidelined, unmarried women who ran long-lived dressmaking businesses, but lacked a second generation to commemorate them, have been completely forgotten. This was true of Elizabeth Willcox and her successors in Wellington, as well as Auckland's McLaughlin sisters, contemporaries of Mary Jane and Charlotte Milne, although they arrived eight years earlier. They were also from Northern Ireland, from Strabane in County Tyrone.

Jane, Margaret, Marianne and Sarah McLaughlin, aged between 28 and 33, emigrated with their brother John and widowed mother Sarah. In 1856 they established a 'New Millinery and Dressmaking Establishment' in Shortland Street. Like the Milne sisters they lived away from the shop, with their mother and possibly their brother on the corner of Symonds and O'Rourke streets.[176] The shop and manufactory supported the sisters for nearly 40 years. In March 1895 Jane and Marianne retired in their seventies, selling off their stock and shop fittings. Although the McLaughlins were a long-time fixture in Shortland Street, there was no newspaper

WINTER FASHIONS.

EX 'BELGRAVIA.'

THE MISSES McLAUGHLIN respectfully invite the attention of the ladies of Auckland and vicinity to their Stock of Winter Goods, comprising all the latest novelties in material and design.

MILLINERY.

An Elegant Assortment of BONNETS in Velvet and Silk, Trimmed and Untrimmed Straw

The latest styles in Beaver, Plush, and Straw HATS, all sizes]

FEATHERS, FLOWERS, Real Lace FALLS, &c., &c.

MANTLES.

Rich Silk Velvet, Velvet Pile, Plush, Satara, Cloth, Waterproof, &c., in all the Leading Shapes

Paisley and Wool SHAWLS, Long and Square.

DRESSES.

Plain, Check, and Brocaded SILKS
Black Gros and Glace SILKS
Plain, and Embroidered WINCEYS
All Wool Serge, Poplins, and Chene LUSTRES.

Ladies' and Children's Fur BOAS and MUFFS.

EVENING DRESSES

An Elegant Selection of Evening Dresses in White Lace TUNICS
Black Lace TUNICS
Embroidered Tulle, &c.
Grenadine Dresses (very elegant)
Rich White, Maize, Pink, Sky, and New Blue Glace SILKS
TARLETANS in all shades.
HEAD-DRESSES in Beautiful Designs
All Silk HOSE
White Kid and Satin BOOTS and SHOES
Black Satin and Silk BOOTS and SHOES
White and Scarlet SILK CORD and TASSELS.

Cont'd next column.

UNDERCLOTHING.

They would invite particular attention to their Choice Stock of UNDERCLOTHING, which they are confident will well repay inspection.

The Belgravian, and French-wove CORSETS, the most elegant ever imported.]

Ladies' Skeleton and Covered JUPONS
Misses' JUPONS, first-class quality
STEEL BUSKS.

Linen and Muslin sets COLLARS and CUFFS
LACE CHEMISETTES
FANCY BUCKLES, TORTOISESHELL COMBS, &c.

An assortment of Ladies' Winter BOOTS of very superior quality.

Auckland, May 23, 1865.

The Misses McLaughlin invited particular attention to their 'Choice Stock of UNDERCLOTHING', but had a wide variety of stock.

Daily Southern Cross, 25 May 1865

acknowledgement of the shop's closure.[177] Marianne died in 1899, aged 75, and Jane in 1904, aged 82. Their deaths were reported without mention of their many years in Auckland or their long-lasting business. As single, childless women, there was little impetus to memorialise them, and as Irish Catholics, they may not have been well connected to the Auckland establishment.

A stitch in time

Needlework could be notoriously poorly paid, with sweating an increasing problem. On the other hand, a savvy businesswoman, with a bit of luck and family support, could flourish. These milliners and dressmakers, feather cleaners and dyers, haberdashers and drapers, were essential in the developing towns and cities, providing not only clothing and trimmings, but also table and bed linen, curtains and rugs, to an ever-growing market. Some embraced technology and expanded their businesses, becoming the household names of the twentieth century; others' businesses died with them, having fulfilled their purpose of providing a living for their proprietors. And perhaps that is all they ever wanted – a stitch in time indeed.

Matilda and Andrew Baker were the first publicans of the Northern Hotel in Oamaru. Next door was the labour mart, run from 1876 by Robert Whitmarsh, and milliner 'Mrs R.P. Whitmarsh' – actually Mary Ann Masters, not his estranged wife Elizabeth. Waitaki District Archive, 2018/302

CHAPTER 7

'Personal Offices for Man': Beds, booze and bodies

'Persons engaged in entertaining and performing Personal Offices For Man' was one of the more intriguing new categories introduced into the New Zealand census in 1874. This chapter considers some of the businesswomen who officially fell into this category – publicans and boarding-house keepers – and some who did not, namely brothel keepers, who were allocated to the criminal class in the census but certainly supplied offices more personal than most. Running hotels, boarding houses and brothels were all commercial exploitations of what were regarded by many as domestic female tasks: providing food, drink, beds and warm bodies to go in them.

Pulling pints

Hotels abounded across colonial New Zealand, catering for country settlers looking for comfortable town lodgings, for commercial travellers and for thirsty soldiers, workers and miners, celebrating or drowning their sorrows, or seeking gambling, dancing and sex.[1] Hotels were liminal spaces – providing home comforts to strangers, inviting the public into private rooms. Most hotels, particularly early on and in smaller towns, were small, domestic spaces transformed into business premises. Female publicans occupied a similarly ambiguous position. Although many customers would have been locals, meaning that hotels could be situated within the comfort of the parochial realm, some, especially in goldfields or port towns with their fluctuating, ever-changing populations, were not. Drinking was also constituted as a male activity. No 'respectable' middle-class woman would be seen in a hotel, drinking in public, but those lower down the social scale were more likely to drink, albeit mostly in the privacy of their own homes. As we saw in Chapter 5, Caroline Barnes, for instance, sent her 'pupil' Emma Garland to fetch her a lunchtime tipple in Auckland in the 1860s. Hotels were often sites of sexually and socially transgressive behaviour; they were loud, violent and unruly places, where men squandered hard-earned wages on grog, gambling and girls, sometimes leaving distraught wives at home unable to feed their children. They were no place for a lady, and running a pub was no job for the faint-hearted. Take the Commercial Hotel in Shortland Street in Auckland in the 1840s. It advertised the novelty of a ten pin alley 'peculiarly adapted for healthful exercise and innocent recreation during the inclement season of Winter'.[2] The alcohol sold to accompany this recreation, however, made it rather less healthful and innocent. The hotel was close to the harbour and popular with soldiers and sailors on leave. In her memoirs, Elizabeth Bartley remembered a night when Catherine Henderson, wife of Thomas the licensee, 'endeavouring to close the Hotel doors against the drunken crowd … was so severely injured that she almost lost her life'.[3] This was not an isolated incident in a garrison town. Historian Dean Wilson has described colonial Auckland hotels as violent masculinised spaces, where men met to drink, collect debts and settle scores.[4]

Hotels were also centres of more respectable social interaction, however: public meetings were held there, local clubs met there, friends gathered in the hotel's public rooms, which could be more commodious than their own homes. Hotels, alongside churches and Mechanics' Institutes, were some of the early communal spaces. Community engagement also made sound business sense, ensuring that a publican was a respected citizen and the hotel well patronised. Andrew and Matilda Baker hosted local societies' meetings in the assembly rooms of their Northern Hotel in Oamaru in the 1860s, making it central to social and community life.[5] In Nelson the Mechanics' Cricket Club met at Martha and John Lewthwaite's Wakatu Hotel, while the Nelson Artillery Volunteer Corps patronised Catherine and Charles McGee's Nelson Hotel.[6] When Annie Barker took over the Castlecliff Hotel in Whanganui in the 1890s, she not only donated to charities and the church but provided accommodation for local Māori when the river was in flood. They responded with bundles of fresh vegetables. On her retirement in 1897 townspeople presented her with an illuminated address and gold bracelet.[7] George and Elizabeth Compton, who ran Lyttelton's Mitre Hotel, owned by widow Ann Bowen, for eight years until George's suicide in 1859, showed similar business nous. Eminently respectable settler Jane Deans remembered many years later the kindness of Elizabeth Compton, who sent her fresh butter on board the *Minerva* when she arrived as a newly married 20-year-old in 1853. Later, she naturally chose to lunch at the hotel. The reality of the Mitre Hotel was rather different. Sources suggest George's suicide was caused by intemperance and insolvency and Elizabeth was fond of a drink herself: after the hotel was sold she refused to leave until tempted out with a glass of gin.[8]

'A maternal presence'

More reputable hotels were often distinguished by a strong maternal presence. While flirtatious young barmaids who enticed men to drink, dance and debauch were regarded by some as a national menace, a responsible female licensee or licensee's wife was understood to have a moderating effect on excesses of male bad behaviour. Licensing boards looked favourably upon a respectable motherly female presence. In 1874 bachelor Thomas Dodson was granted the licence of the Provincial Hotel in Port Chalmers because his brother and sister also lived on the premises, and a year later Dunedin resident magistrate John Bathgate reportedly refused licences to unmarried male applicants, declaring 'No public house can be well-conducted without a matron.'[9] The 1885 Otago Licensing Committee election candidate, Donald C. Cameron, agreed that 'young unmarried men were not so capable of conducting a hotel as older people.'[10]

Hotel businesses certainly saw benefits in advertising a respectable female presence. William Meech emphasised that both he '*and Mrs Meech*' (my emphasis) would 'use every exertion to make their guests comfortable' at the newly opened Caledonia Hotel in Tinakori Road in Wellington in 1851.[11] Both Mr *and* Mrs G. Taylor advertised their removal from the Anchor Inn to the Trafalgar Hotel in Nelson in 1855, also announcing that 'Mrs Taylor had secured the services of an experienced French Cook' to assist her in producing dinners 'in a superior style.'[12] For publicans and boarding-house keepers on the goldfields and in other locations where women were scarce, no such sophistication was required. A female presence was enough and a meal cooked by a woman a rare and valued commodity.[13]

Being a woman did not guarantee respectability, of course. Andrew Baker advertised that the kitchen of the Northern Hotel 'was under the immediate superintendence of Mrs Baker', albeit 'with the assistance of a good cook'. But Matilda Baker was not an entirely calming presence, having acquired a taste for alcohol. In 1866 she told a waiter to clear away lunch, disputing his claim that a customer was still present. Accusations of insobriety flew thick and fast, with the waiter finally exclaiming that his employer must be 'drunk with stupidity' not to see the guest. Matilda called her husband to evict the waiter, but then she herself 'took [him] by the back of the neck and pushed [him] violently'.[14] Both the Bakers were fined by the court.

A respectable business for a woman?

So long as one had a good head for business, did not become too fond of one's own product and could command respect – and payment – from one's customers, a hotel business was potentially profitable for a woman, either on her own or with a husband. Providing clean bed linen on comfortable beds, home-cooked meals and pints of beer served with a smile could produce sufficient income to keep a family.

Hotels varied in their level of respectability: as today, each town had a hierarchy, and establishments marketed themselves to different types of customers. Widowed Agnes Hossack ran Clontarf House as a boarding house in Christchurch's Cashel Street in the 1860s. When she applied for a wine and beer licence she was warned she would have to serve people other than her boarders, but was undeterred: 'she had fully considered that point and had been legally advised she could charge as much as she liked for nobblers [drinks] and thus keep her hotel select'. She was in business for several years. Her hotel attracted quality customers and was described by the inspector of police in 1865 as 'very quietly and respectably conducted'.[15]

Advertising a respectable hotel did not necessarily produce one. When Elizabeth Bond took over the Criterion in Auckland's Hobson Street after her husband died in 1864, she promised her customers would 'meet with every accommodation and civility, as at a first-class Hotel'. She made her intended market clear: 'Gentlemen and travellers from the country' would appreciate her hotel's location in a 'healthy part' of Hobson Street and 'within a few minutes walk of the mercantile parts of the city'. Despite her good intentions she failed to thrive, perhaps suffering from the departure of many 'gentlemen' when parliament shifted to Wellington the following year. She sold the business, became insolvent and died four years later amidst allegations of drunkenness, destitution and immorality.[16]

There were conflicting ideas about female publicans, as Sandra Quick has shown with regard to the Otago goldfields. Some were derided as 'the most infamous characters', while others were exalted. The 1918 obituary of Jane McBride, a Queenstown publican of 47 years' standing, called her 'a magnificent stamp of a woman … No more public-spirited citizen (as far as it lies in the power of a woman to qualify for that standing) has ever lived amongst us.' Not only would 'her name … ever be held in reverence', she being 'a lady bountiful in all her deeds, and the friend of all those in need', but she was 'particularly capable, wondrously bright, and possessed of very singular charms'. Whether the women of Queenstown appreciated those charms as much as the almost certainly male reporter at the *Lake County Press* is not recorded.[17] Respectability depended upon who was judging it.

The esteem in which publicans could be held, especially in smaller settlements, was illustrated when Whanganui's Mary Maria Blair of the Steam Packet Inn on the corner of Victoria Avenue and Taupo Quay died in 1876, aged 49. She received a glowing obituary, which acknowledged her hospitable management of the hotel. She and her first husband John Davidson had arrived in the hotel in 1858. Mary held the licence in her own name after he died in 1867 until her marriage to Gavin Blair in 1870. Mary Maria Blair's funeral in 1876 included 'a long procession of mourners', shops along the route closed up their shutters and ships flew their flags at half-mast.[18] After her death the next two licensees were her sons-in-law, John Batchelar and then William Paterson, and the hotel finally left the family after the death of Mary Ann Paterson in 1884. Similarly respected was Ann Butler, publican in Ashburton from 1878 until her death in 1895. Her obituary recorded that when her husband became paralysed, 'his courageous wife took the reins in her own hand, and became the breadwinner'. The family of Premier Richard Seddon sent a wreath to her funeral: Louisa Seddon and Ann Butler had been rival publicans at Kumara on the West Coast.[19]

It is doubtful that either Matilda Hubert or Charlotte (aka Nancy) Dawson, both Dunedin publicans, took tea with the city's upper- and middle-class matrons. Those matrons' husbands, however, probably patronised their establishments, which were advertised to appeal to the best possible clientele. Hubert's Café and Club in Princes Street, run from 1862 by Matilda, or 'Madame Hubert', was a 'palatial' café and club, 'a fashionable resort' suited to 'members of professions, merchants and the elite of Dunedin'. She hired 'the chief cook of the *Melbourne Criterion Hotel*'. (Perhaps she had met him while running a cigar and tobacco shop in Bourke Street, Melbourne, in the 1850s.) Her customers included future New Zealand premier Julius Vogel. Matilda annoyed licensing authorities in 1862, however, when she altered her café, which had a wine and beer licence, by fitting 'an open bar' in the shop. Her licence was renewed on condition that she remove this. 'A woman could not manage such a place properly', the licensing committee suggested, although one member felt that Madame Hubert had in fact used 'her womanly ways' very effectively to manage the committee itself: she 'had all along presumed' and had pushed the limits of her licence.[20]

At the end of the year Matilda's estranged husband John, whom she had left in Melbourne after eight years of marriage, reappeared and attempted to take over her business. Matilda took out a ladylike advertisement asking 'the public to suppress their judgment respecting our unhappy family differences' while she went to court. Embarrassing allegations from her own father of Matilda 'throwing herself about in the most voluptuous manner' while at the theatre were vehemently denied by her companion, a storekeeper from the Waitahuna goldfields, J.H. Moses, who appears to have been a regular visitor. Her protection order application failed, meaning John could take her property. Matilda briefly took over the Abbeyleix Hotel in Maclaggan Street, then reappeared in her original premises before disappearing in 1864. Whether she was entirely respectable or successful or not, her establishment was certainly known; subsequent owners advertised it as 'late Madame Hubert's'.[21]

'Nancy Dawson's corner' quickly became a fixture after 'Madam Dawson' announced the opening of her family hotel on the corner of Manse and High streets in Dunedin in 1861. The Melbourne Club Hotel had twenty 'large and lofty rooms ... finished in a style not surpassed in the city', and a five-stall stable. A 'first-class Private Hotel', it catered for permanent boarders at 2½ guineas per week. Charlotte, also widely known as Nancy, must have had some capital, for she owned her hotel, leasing the land on which it stood. She had a mortgage from local solicitors Kenyon and Maddock, indicating that some women at least could get property loans. According to a contemporary, she had an upper-class accent and manners, which doubtless helped convince potential lenders.[22]

Like Matilda Hubert, Charlotte Dawson pushed boundaries. She was fined £50 in 1862 for serving spirits when she had only a wine and beer licence. She was caught, along with several others, in what was later publicly identified as a sting operation, involving two men doing the rounds of local hotels. In the same year she got into a public stoush with the town board over the level of the footpath outside her hotel and a few days later was fined £2 and costs for not having a lighted lamp outside the main door of her house. This was a breach of the licensing ordinance that usually attracted a caution, but Charlotte was a repeat offender. The next time she was fined £3, despite contending that 'the wind was very violent, and broke the glass of the lamp'.[23]

Charlotte's business may have been profitable, but in April 1863 she was, according to the *Otago Daily Times*, seriously 'disfigured' in a carriage accident. This may well have affected her business. By July she was in financial difficulties and the hotel was for sale in October 1863. She disappeared from Dunedin in the middle of

Henry Walter's Occidental Hotel in Dunedin had been Charlotte Dawson's popular Melbourne Club Hotel. Her descent into destitution, drunkenness and eventual suicide epitomised the precariousness of financial survival for women on their own.

Occidental Hotel on the corner of Manse Street and High Street, c. 1865–1870, photographer unknown, Hocken Box-226-002

1864.[24] Her next appearance in the records is in November 1867 when, struggling with alcoholism and living in poverty, she attempted suicide in Westport. The *Colonist* revealed that her small hut opposite the courthouse on the square nevertheless contained 'certain evidences of refined taste' – on her table there was, 'beside a bottle of gin, a volume of Carlyle's Life of Schiller'. She had recently 'parted with a number of expensive dresses, ornaments, and other matters at sums ridiculously below their real value', and had been '"planting" other things in neighbouring tents, where she appeared to think that they would be safe from seizure'. A man found in her tent trying to revive her was subsequently charged with being drunk and 'in a woman's house for an unlawful purpose'. Had Charlotte been reduced from selling beer to selling sex? Two months later she was dead, her second attempt to cut her throat with a 'small dessert knife' more successful than her first. The *Westport Times* reported her 'romantic and melancholy' history: 'She claimed for her progenitor no less a person than George IV, and her education and manners certainly warranted that assumption.' The 'tragic narrative' was reported across the country, although only one newspaper mentioned that she had been a publican in Dunedin.[25]

Charlotte Dawson's decline into drunkenness, insanity and, ultimately, suicide, illustrates the knife-edge on which many businesses and lives operated, particularly for women. As a female publican, Charlotte had both a living and an established, respectable place in society. Without family support she relied on her wits and her business nous, exploiting her education, manners and accent, and probably promoting the rumour of royal connections herself. The carriage accident may have been the catalyst for her loss of business and descent into alcoholism; once on the slippery slope, she struggled to recover.

How many women?

Charlotte Dawson, Matilda Hubert and Jane McBride all held licences in their own right. Licensing boards favoured mature widows, particularly those of publicans. They had a matronly gravitas and experience in the ways of men. Young single women were presumed to be more naïve in the ways of the world and more vulnerable to moral corruption. In the middle of the century, about one in 10 hotels had a female licensee, although this obscures the numerous wives who were business partners, and the proportion varied according to time and location.[26] Licensing lists for towns outside the goldfields show few female names. Nelson, for example, had only one in 1858, Mary Cleaver. Widowed in 1856, she took over the licence of the Plough Inn in Richmond from her husband William, who had held it since 1852. She continued to run the hotel into the 1860s, acting as landlady after she sold the hotel in 1861. She then married her barman, Frederick Reid, 10 years her junior, and moved to Blenheim where Fred worked as a baker.[27]

But she was not really the only woman running a hotel. Of the other 18 licensees in 1858, we know that when John Luck of the Trafalgar Hotel died his widow Lydia took over the licence, later running another hotel with her son; Margaret Beach stepped into her dead husband's shoes at the Stoke Hotel in 1862, and Martha Lewthwaite hired hotel staff from Melbourne for the Wakatu Hotel where the licensee was her husband John.[28] A decade later, however, the Nelson directory still had only one female name. Lucy Kite took over the licence of the Red Horse in Richmond after the death of her husband Thomas in 1860, and was a publican until her death in 1885. It is reasonable to assume that, like other licensees' wives, she had always worked in the business. There were similar examples elsewhere. In Wellington Mary Minifie took over the Queen's Hotel when husband John died in 1868. Mary Barry was the proprietor of the Ship Hotel in the same year after her husband Richard committed suicide while suffering delirium tremens, a common cause of death for a number of hotelkeepers (including Charlotte Dawson) who developed a taste for their own product.[29] Jane Calder continued the Rainbow Inn at Kaiwharawhara after her husband drowned in the Ohau River in 1858. She still owned the hotel in 1895 although she was no longer the licensee.[30]

Census statistics, available from 1874, also suggest that around 10 per cent of all licensees were female. On the goldfields, however, it was nearly 17 per cent; this may be why debates about the suitability of female publicans began here. Censuses from 1874 and 1881 also included wives 'assisting in the business'. In 1874 only 34 wives of the 1356 male licensees in New Zealand declared themselves in this way; by 1881 this figure had jumped to 299 of 1649 male licensees. As Susan Upton suggests, this was indicative of better reporting rather than an actual increase, and still underestimated the real numbers. Nevertheless, even these figures show that in 1881, 22 per cent of those recorded as involved in running hotels were women.[31] They were a visible and significant part of the hotel industry.

Licensing: Laws and loopholes

Licences were granted and renewed annually. Until the 1870s licensing boards were generally made up of local justices; after the 1873 Licensing Act more broadly constituted boards were allowed. They could include women, although this was still sufficiently unusual in 1896 for the *Thames Advertiser* to use the headline 'Lady Appointed to a Licensing Committee' when reporting the appointment of Emily Hill to a committee in Napier. Mrs Hill, like draper Elizabeth Cowles who was elected to the Wellington Licensing Committee in 1894, was a prohibitionist.[32] Licences were expensive, to control the number of hotels and class of publican, but were an important source of revenue for provincial governments.[33] Licensing was also complicated. Rules varied in different provinces but generally demanded that establishments provide both accommodation and drinks, and there were stipulations on the types of alcohol that could be sold. As Charlotte Dawson discovered, a beer and wine licence was different from one that allowed a licensee to peddle spirits.

Licensing boards were responsible for judging the suitability and character of the applicant, as well as assessing the need for yet another hotel in an area, something that became more difficult to justify as the temperance lobby grew louder.

Unlike many other areas, such as education, employment opportunities, married women's property rights and suffrage, the rights of women to hold hotel licences actually went backwards across the nineteenth and twentieth centuries. Significantly, however, this was not because of the legislation itself. Licensing legislation did not actually ban any woman from holding a publican's licence until 1889, with the exception of one year in one location. The first Licensing Act in 1842 made no mention of the sex of the licensee, and an 1847 amendment specifically declared that 'nothing in the said recited Ordinance contained shall be held to prevent a woman from holding a license'. In 1874 women were again referred to as potential licensees and in 1881 unmarried women were specifically included in those allowed to hold licences.[34]

Coverture laws essentially prevented married women from being licensees as they could not legally enter into contracts or sue or be sued in court. The dismantling of those laws in the 1884 Married Women's Property Act removed the easy justification for refusing a wife a licence, prompting changes to the licensing laws. In 1889, while endorsing the legality of existing married female licensees, licensing legislation declared that no married woman could hold a new licence unless she had an order under the 1880 Married Women's Property Protection Act. Single women's and widows' licences would automatically be transferred to new husbands. Finally, in 1893, single women were legally banned from holding licences; this legislation was not repealed until 1952.[35]

Regardless of the actual law, licensing boards often made decisions based solely on local conditions and prejudices. This could work both for and against female applicants. There were ways around the law of coverture, as Amelia Hayne discovered when she applied for the licence of the Royal Oak in Westport in 1871. The judge explained that it 'would have to be granted to the husband', but that she could 'apply for a leave of absence' for him 'for some fixed time'. This strategy succeeded, for when Robert Hayne later appeared in court for beating his wife, having arrived home and found her in bed with another man, Amelia was described as keeping the Royal Oak.[36] When Jane Rapley appeared before the licensing court in Whanganui in 1874 on behalf of her husband James, applying to renew the licence of the Prince of Wales Hotel on Taupo Quay, the bench 'granted the renewal on condition that it be made out in Mrs Rapley's name'.[37] This flew in the face of the law of coverture, but

Jane had proven herself a good publican, running both the hotel and refreshment booths at local race meetings. Her family was also influential: her father, Henry Nathan, was on the town board and would later be mayor.

Thanks to a pragmatic and empathetic decision, Mary Corbett also managed to obtain a hotel licence, despite being a married woman. The Aglionby Arms nearly disappeared into the Hutt River during floods in 1858, and by 1862 licensee William Corbett had moved south, leaving his wife to soldier on in the hotel.[38] She successfully applied for a licence in July 1863, although she only obtained a protection order, legally making her a feme sole, in 1864. She held the licence until 1869, assisted by her son John.[39] In Ashburton, well-respected married woman Ann Butler held the licence of Butler's Family Hotel in the late 1880s in her own name. She, along with a number of others including Jane Ormsbee (previously Rapley), faced problems in 1889 after the Supreme Court, hearing the case of Margaret Roche in Dunedin the previous November, had ruled that married women could not hold licences. Licensing boards around the country bent over backwards to get around the situation. Ann's daughter Esther applied for the licence of Butlers' Family Hotel in her stead, and was eventually granted it. In Wellington, the licensing committee considered the cases of Annie Smith, Annie Barker and Jane Ormsbee, the last of whom was 'not sure she was a married woman at present', and declared that wives living apart from their husbands could hold licences. This prompted the *Evening Star* to comment wryly that 'the vagaries of the licensing committees are becoming quite common', pointing out that licensing committees in Southland had reached the opposite decision.[40]

Widows usually escaped these legal issues, but sometimes they were equally as inexplicably refused licences in spite of the law. Matilda Ritchie, noted by the licensing board as a 'highly respectable widow keeping a baker's and grocer's shop' in Port Chalmers, was initially denied a bottle licence in 1874: 'her being a widow told against her application', although its exact significance was not specified. She reapplied successfully in December.[41] In March 1875 Eliza Searight, previously licensee of the Concord Hotel, applied for the licence of the Court House Hotel in Greymouth. Although there were no objections to her character, she was refused merely because 'a majority' of the three earnest gentlemen on the bench had arbitrarily 'decided as a rule not to grant licenses to females'. This, according to the *Grey River Argus*, was not only 'contrary to the spirit of the law' but went 'beyond the discretionary powers' of the court. Eliza was 'a widow [with] a young family, and who had previously been permitted to exercise a license' and 'complied with all the conditions prescribed by law'. The board was unmoved. She married Moore Ellis Mawhinny in 1876 and they continued in the hotel business.[42]

Hebes behind the bar

More problematic than female publicans were barmaids, whose presence became increasingly controversial, leading to a ban in 1910 (female licensees and licensees' family members were specifically exempted). The ban followed decades of lobbying about the immorality and exploitation of temptresses behind the bar, luring men to spend their money on drinking, dancing and sex.[43] These concerns had their origins in the goldfields, where the abundance of hotels made barmaids and dancing girls more visible amid a predominantly male population.

Dancing girls could apparently earn good money. In Hokitika in 1868, one employment agent suggested that 'smart girls, who can dance well and are willing so to do, and in addition attend a bar, obtain immediate employment at from £2 to £3 per week, according to the distance from town'. Barmaids could garner a significantly lower 30–50s per week, while domestic servants earned 20–30s.[44] All of these were substantially lower than men's wages; a shopman in Greymouth, for example, was paid £6 a week in 1868.[45] In addition, as numerous court cases testified, barmaids and dancing girls were also often exploited, suffered appalling conditions and were forced to work long hours. So while some greeted the arrival of a new barmaid or dancing girl with enthusiasm, others were concerned for their moral welfare. According to Aiden Doyle, a candidate in the 1869 West Coast local election, 'It was a well-known fact, that a single girl could not stand behind a bar, and dispense drink herself, without her modesty having to suffer for it. Her character, self-respect and reputation must suffer.'[46] His Honour Mr Justice Christopher William Richmond agreed, telling a grand jury in Hokitika 'to consider the fate of a woman condemned to a life-long handing of glasses to half-drunken men and what must be the effect on her mind'. The *West Coast Times* felt the judge had a 'somewhat exaggerated view of "barmaid life"', suggesting that 'a respectable female is unquestionably a great preventative to gross impropriety of behavior or language at the bar of an hotel'. It felt 'many very respectable educated women follow the occupation', although, they suspected, 'more from necessity than choice'.[47] Eleven years later, in 1880, when a licensing bill was being debated, the *New Zealand Herald* conceded that 'there is doubtless an advantage in the employment of females in bars. They have an ameliorating tendency, their presence exercises a restraining influence in some respects, but', they concluded ominously, 'on the whole their presence is productive of incalculably more evil than good'.[48]

Arguments used against barmaids were extended to single female licensees, particularly on the goldfields, where there was increasing concern about bad behaviour. Nevertheless, until 1893, there was only one occasion on which single women were legally barred from holding licences and only in one province. The Nelson Goldfields Licensing Ordinance of 1867 specifically stated that licences would not be granted to single women. A year later, when the ordinance was revised, this clause was removed.[49] This may have been because single women were running hotels anyway, with male friends and relatives nominally holding licences. This was certainly true in Charleston, as the *Westport Times* observed disapprovingly: while 'some of these places are quite respectable … the majority are said to be mere brothels in disguise'. The practice had reached such proportions that 'the diggers have given a shameful nickname to a principal street of the town', the newspaper recorded, too conscious of its readers' sensibilities to specify the nickname, unfortunately for the historian.[50]

Regardless of the actual law it became increasingly difficult for single women to obtain licences. Sometimes it would have been better to stay quiet about one's status, as Robert Ellis and Fanny Edwards found to their cost when Robert applied to transfer the licence of Ellis's Family Hotel in Dunedin to Fanny in 1870. There was an objection because Fanny was a single woman, and one 'who would not be likely to conduct the house in a respectable manner'. Fanny and Robert's lawyer argued that Fanny was doing the job already. She had '*de facto*, kept the house in a respectable manner for some considerable time past', having lost her husband 18 months before. Her lawyer, however, admitted that 'there was no mincing matters': his client 'had at one time been a somewhat notorious woman; but she had reformed, and wished to keep the house properly and respectably'. The transfer was refused because 'the house was not well conducted' and was 'a place of resort for a questionable class of women'.[51] Being an existing licensee with a more respectable house helped. Mary Duggan's licence was renewed in 1871, purely on the grounds that she was already the licensee of the Canadian Hotel in Richmond Quay in Greymouth. She was lucky, however. The magistrate commented that, following the recent 'recommendation of the Grand Jury in Hokitika', in future no licence would be issued to a single woman.[52]

'Murder at the Grey'

The Hokitika grand jury's recommendation was not based in any legislation but was sparked by an incident in the goldfields settlement of Nobles in the Grey Valley a few months earlier. The publican concerned was Margaret Quigley. She was very young for such a role – just 20 – and single, with a 'tall slender figure, somewhat prepossessing'. According to her neighbour, storeman Colin Algie, she was 'virtuous and kind', with 'an excellent character', not 'hasty in her temper' but 'would not allow men to be familiar with her in any way'. Neighbour John McCafferty agreed: although never 'hot-tempered', she was firm, able to expel men from her hotel if they 'commenced blackguarding her and using rude language to her'. 'I never heard anybody say anything wrong of her,' he commented, adding that she would 'cook tucker' for anyone who was hungry.[53]

So how did such a paragon of virtue and good manners cause a Hokitika jury to issue a moratorium against single female publicans? On the evening of Tuesday 27 December 1870, Margaret Quigley went to Colin Algie and asked to borrow a knife. She noted it was blunt and asked for it to be sharpened. About 20 minutes later she stuck it, with fatal results, into the side of 35-year-old French Canadian miner George Patenaude, who had been taking liberties with her for some time. She was found guilty of manslaughter and sentenced to four years' penal servitude. A week after her early release in 1873 she was on a boat to Melbourne, where she disappears from the records.[54]

Her crime was instantly attributed to her position as a young single female publican.[55] Even those commentators who pointed out that such murders happened elsewhere, *not* committed by such people, agreed that the practice of licensing young single women was undesirable. The *West Coast Times* lamented in 1871 that it was 'sad and discreditable to the community' that women could not carry on a 'lawful' occupation without 'sufficient respect for their honor to prevent the perpetration of offences against them, or to prevent the perpetration, on their part, of crimes involving the public peace and the lives of others'. It nevertheless suggested that 'young and pretty publicans should be protected even against themselves'. Female publicans, it seemed, could not win. Either they were 'frail' (i.e. immoral) and turned their hotels into 'public nuisances', or their very 'fairness' might 'incite to indiscretion the … licentious admirers of the licensee'. Either way it was their fault, as the *West Coast Times* explained in an impressively long sentence:

> There cannot be a doubt, however, that, by the law permitting young and unprotected females to place themselves in positions of temptation either to themselves or others, and especially by permitting them to have the sole charge and management of such drinking saloons as are generally to be found on the diggings, incidents may and do arise which are calculated to lead to the commission of offences either by them or against them, and that it is highly desirable, by some intervention of the law, to limit, as far as possible, the chances of such incidents occurring.

The newspaper also suggested that any liberties George Patenaude may have taken were 'nothing egregiously out of the common'.[56]

Nevertheless, a *legal* ban on single women publicans was not reinstated on the goldfields or anywhere else until the 1890s. Debate continued over the suitability of both single and married women as licensees. A *New Zealand Herald* editorial in June 1880 claimed sweepingly that 'experience shows that as a rule a landlady cannot manage a licensed house a well as a landlord'.[57] During the parliamentary debate on the new licensing bill a few days later, future premier Richard Seddon went further, apparently forgetting that his own wife Louisa was running their Queen's Hotel in Kumara, on the West Coast, when he first entered politics. He was proud that, in his district, 'the licensing officer carried out the principle that no single woman should have a license'. He ignored the fact that this was legally allowed: 'It is morally an impossibility for a single woman to exercise the supervision which you say must be exercised,' he huffed, kindly adding that 'there is no hardship in refusing to grant a license to a single woman, because she can very easily remedy the fact by getting married'. Significantly, both the *Herald* and Seddon did allow that 'exception might be made in the case of widows'.[58] They were arguably less competitive in the colonial marriage market and no one wanted to be seen to be denying a deserving widow a livelihood.

Publicans in all but name

The automatic transfer of a licence from a dead publican to his bereaved spouse was a recognition that licensees' wives were often already in the business. Many wives, like Louisa Seddon, were actually the 'real' publicans. Twenty-six-year-old Ellen Piezzi carried on the Helvetia Hotel in Hokitika after the death of her husband in 1876; when she married Irishman Dennis Maher in 1883 they continued to run hotels on the West Coast and later in Wellington.[59] Mary Maria Davidson lost her publican husband John in 1867 when he was only 40. She took over the licence of the Steam Packet Inn in Whanganui and continued to run the hotel after her second marriage to ship owner Gavin Blair in 1870, although he was the official licensee.[60]

Like many other publicans on both sides of the Tasman, Mary Ann Ames was part of a hotelkeeping family, the daughter of Sydney whaler-turned-publican John Hull. Mary Ann married another whaler, James Ames, in 1838 and moved to New Zealand in 1841. They lived for a time at the Tokomapuna whaling station just off Kāpiti Island. James was appointed pilot for Wellington Harbour in 1848 and by the time he died suddenly in 1850 was also the licensee of the South Sea Hotel on Lambton Quay. Mary Ann, with six children under 12, including an infant, took over the licence. After the hotel was damaged in the severe 1855 earthquake Mary Ann moved to Johnsonville and opened Ames Hotel on the Porirua Road. In 1857 she married George Ashdown, a Wellington storekeeper and ex-whaler who was separated from his partner Mata Pekamu Tamatuhiata, with whom he had several children.[61] Mary Ann continued to run Ames Hotel at Johnsonville after her second husband died in 1858, reverting to her first married name in the 1860s. She leased the hotel to James Bryant in 1860 and sold the building 10 years later. Several of her sons continued the family tradition of hotelkeeping.

When she died in 1887 she received a number of obituaries. The *Evening Post* identified her as the mother of the city valuer and focused on a legendary and possibly mythological tale of her bravery when Ngāti Toa leaders Te Rauparaha and Te Rangihaeata landed at Tokomapuna in 1843 before the Wairau incident.[62] Her courage would have been useful as a publican, as would the 'hospitality, geniality and general kindness' ascribed to her by the *New Zealand Times*. Both obituaries ignored her business life, however, describing her as 'a fit woman to be a settler's wife, full of untiring energy, blessed with splendid health, and always carrying a high and cheerful heart'.[63]

Ann Macready in Auckland was equally the mainstay of her family's hotel. Although her husband Thomas held the licence of the Duke of Marlborough and then the Star in Auckland between 1859 and 1872, Ann was the real publican. She and her first husband William Dennett had been at the Duke of Marlborough since 1848.[64] When William died in 1856 the licence passed to Ann, who married watchmaker Thomas Macready three years later. The hotel was destroyed in the June 1863 Queen Street fire that started next to Harriett Powley's shop and spread as far as Ann's hotel, but no further, thanks to the quick action of firefighters. Shops between the hotel and Vulcan Lane were spared the fire, but not the overenthusiastic actions of volunteers, who had 'evacuated' their stock. Thomas's watchmaking and jewellery shop and five more, including those of dressmaking sisters Anna and Elizabeth Thick and capmaker Ann Edwards, suffered losses. All were fortunate they had insurance. Ann Macready advertised that she had moved the licence temporarily to 'her own premises' on the corner of Albert and West Queen (now Swanson) streets, until 'new Premises on a large and extensive scale' were built on the Queen Street site. The business survived the fire, as well as Thomas's dabbling in speculation with the Duke of Marlborough Gold Mining Company in 1869. By this time Thomas also held the licence of the Star in Lower Albert Street, also in name only. Unlike Mary Ann Ames, Ann Macready's 1872 obituary made it clear who was really running the hotels: she had resided at the Duke of Marlborough until recently, 'when she devoted her attention entirely to the management of the Star Hotel, one of the best houses in the City'. Mrs Macready 'was generally popular and will be widely regretted'.[65]

As with any business, running a hotel required an ability to respond to changes in the market. In Queenstown, for instance, this meant moving from supplying copious amounts of alcohol and the temptations of barmaids to thirsty, sex-starved miners, to providing high-class comfortable accommodation to increasing numbers of tourists in the 1880s. Jane McBride successfully made the transition, offering five sitting rooms, hot and cold water, and vehicles and 'first class' hacks for tourists wishing to explore the area.[66] Emma Barber of the Union Hotel in the Central Otago settlement of Hamiltons expanded and diversified her business interests after her husband's death in an accident in 1871, recognising that the decline in gold fever would affect the hotel. She increased her husband's bankrupt estate to one worth over £3000 by the time of her own death 16 years later.[67]

Sometimes widows transferred the licence to others, although this did not necessarily mean that they were eschewing independence or entrepreneurialism. Edward and Elizabeth George ran hotels in Auckland and Onehunga after arriving in New Zealand in 1842. They built the Royal Hotel near the beach at Onehunga and, at Elizabeth's suggestion, included a 'Long Room', which was used for meetings, public lectures and the coroners' court. After Edward died in 1855, aged 39, Elizabeth took over the hotel licence, relinquishing it a year later but retaining ownership of the property. She ran a store next to the hotel and advertised a cargo and storage business as far afield as Nelson. She was a force in the local community, and a founding member and first president of the Onehunga Ladies' Benevolent Society. The hotel burned down twice in the 1880s but Elizabeth rebuilt, and it operated for several years after she died in 1902.[68]

Surviving difficult spouses

Running a hotel could be a way to survive a deserting husband, particularly after the 1860 Married Women's Property Protection Act. Mary Ann Kennedy's husband John, a former sergeant of the 65th Regiment, was the licensee of several Wellington hotels in the 1850s. Mary Ann was also involved in the business. By 1858 John was in Nelson and Mary Ann, although a married woman, continued to run hotels. She applied for a protection order in 1862 and, when her watch was stolen in 1863, insisted she had 'purchased the watch ... since my husband left me, out of my own earnings'.[69] On her death aged 48 in 1874 she owned two hotels as well as other property.[70]

Annie Wright moved from Victoria to Hokitika with her brothers in the early 1870s and married Thomas Barker in 1872. They and their several children moved around the West Coast running hotels. By 1884 Annie's name was above the hotel door and Thomas had vanished, perhaps seduced by gold fever: his next appearance in the records is as a miner in Inangahua on the 1893 electoral roll. Annie became a serial licensee in Westport, Wellington and Whanganui. She used her mobility as a selling point, advertising as 'Mrs A.A. Barker late of Westport and formerly of Echuca, Victoria', suggesting experience and competence.[71]

Mary Power followed a similar path. There was no sign of her husband when she appeared as licensee of the Dunedin Hotel in Princes Street, Dunedin, in 1864. She abandoned it a year later for a new hotel, also called the Dunedin, in Hokitika. She was there for 10 years, despite her cook, 'a man of color, named Russell' getting into a fight in 1866 with 'an Irishman', whose friends set upon the cook, causing newspapers to suggest Mary was not conducting her house 'in a quiet orderly manner, as required by the terms of the licence'. 'Mrs Power's Dunedin Hotel' became a point of reference for other businesses. One man remembered her as 'Mother Power', nicknamed 'the Miner', perhaps, suggests Julia Bradshaw, because she made money. The local policeman gave Mary a reference before she moved north in 1875 to Wellington, where she kept first the Commercial and then the Albert Family Hotel. When she applied for this last licence in 1877, Inspector Atcheson questioned whether 'an old lady of sixty years of age is suitable for the landlady of such a hotel'. The licensing board felt she was. Five years later she moved on, apparently having 'neglected to pay any rent whatever for a considerable time past'. She took over the Empire, one of the 'best conducted hostelries' in Whanganui, for a year before passing the licence on to Constance Ballam and returning to Wellington. There, having received 'an

Mary 'Mother' Power, 'the Miner', was the licensee of Hokitika's Dunedin Hotel in the 1860s. A publican for 25 years, she was 'justly esteemed for her many amiable qualities and her open-handed charity'.

Tait Brothers (Firm). Tait Brothers (Hokitika) fl 1867: Photograph of Dunedin Hotel, Alexander Turnbull Library, PA2-1757

excellent character' from members of the licensing committee, she took over Tattersall's Hotel in Cambridge Terrace, where she died in 1886. As with many other publicans, her funeral was well attended, and she was 'justly esteemed for her many amiable qualities and her open handed charity'.[72]

In Nelson Mary Lechner (Leckner), daughter of storekeeper Mary Stanton (see Chapter 9), used hotelkeeping to survive the departure of her husband John. She first teamed up with publican Thomas Menary (see Chapter 4), and although they never married, they ran the Exchange Hotel in Bridge Street from 1876, moving to the Forest Inn in Wakefield in 1881. After Thomas died in May 1883, Mary finally took out a protection order against John Theodore Lechner so that she could be granted the licence of the Forest Inn in her own name. Within a few months she married Samuel Hollister, who assumed the licence. They moved to the Provincial

Hotel in Nelson early in 1885 but Samuel did not live long to enjoy it: he died in May at the age of 38. Mary gave up the licence of the Provincial but was soon in the hotel business again. In 1886, aged 39, she married William Evans Dempsie, nine years her junior, and they moved to the Turf Hotel in Stoke. She ran the hotel, although William held the licence, while he continued his own job as a licensed express driver. But William was a drinker. By 1888 the couple was at the Clarendon Hotel on Haven Road until William's publican's licence was revoked when he was found guilty of stealing hay. Unless she obtained a protection order and banned William from the premises, Mary could no longer run a hotel. They moved to Wellington and opened a boarding house and then went their separate ways. Mary ran a series of boarding houses in the capital before moving north, and died in 1909 in a tiny speck on the map called Manganoho on the Rangitikei River.[73]

Licensing magistrates sometimes refused licences even when a protection order was in place, as Jane Mounce discovered. She obtained an order in March 1867 when her publican husband John departed, leaving her with six children. Although she was the acknowledged landlady of the Odd Fellows Arms in Chancery Street, Auckland, and had been even when her husband was present, her licensing application was refused in May 1867. She was in dispute over rent with hotel owner William Bacon, whose lawyer ignored her protection order and suggested, wrongly, that as a married woman Jane 'had no right to have a license, and no right to have possession of the house'. The court told her, unsympathetically, that if she 'suffered any hardship she was herself to blame in not having come to some arrangement with Mr Bacon', who claimed he had offered her 'fair and liberal terms'. There was clearly more going on: William Bacon himself applied successfully for the licence shortly afterwards.[74]

Legally, Jane should have been treated as a feme sole; instead she lost her home and her livelihood. She relocated to Thames where she ran a boarding house. In 1871 her erstwhile husband John burned to death in his hut on the Grey River, where he worked as a boatman, by all accounts 'very much broken down and broken hearted … in the habit of taking a glass too much' since the disintegration of his marriage.[75] A year later Jane married for the third time.[76] Thomas Ower was not a good choice: in February 1878 she was in hospital and Thomas was in court for putting her there.[77] Eight years later she obtained a protection order against him, telling the court that 'her husband sometimes behaved like a madman, and on one occasion threatened to drown her. He had turned her out of the house on several occasions.' Jane stated firmly that 'she was quite able to support herself'. Thomas countered with the accusation that his wife was 'an habitual drunkard and associated with the worst characters in the town … he would be only too pleased to be separated from her'. The order was granted. Oddly, upon his death in 1893, Thomas was described as Jane's 'dearly beloved husband'.[78]

Another husband possibly better loved in absentia was American George Ormsbee, who died in the United States in 1904 while his wife was living in Wellington. Unlike Jane Mounce, Jane Ormsbee had better luck with obtaining a publican's licence. Not only did her desertion occur later, in 1886, after married women had gained more property rights, but she was an experienced licensee. Her first husband had been James Rapley, over whom Jane had been preferred for a licence in contradiction to the law of coverture in Whanganui in 1874. After James died Jane married George Ormsbee in 1878 and he took over the licence of the Prince of Wales. Initially enthusiastic, George invested in enlarging the hotel, although it was still known as Rapley's. Jane provided food at race meetings and developed a reputation as an excellent caterer. Life and business were going well, and in 1885 Jane's daughter Mary married Charles Chavannes and took on running the Victoria Hotel in Victoria Avenue, in a typical example of the way publicans' families intermarried.[79]

In 1886 George Ormsbee disappeared. Jane had no problem assuming the licence of the hotel, although she quickly passed it to Michael Foley, while retaining ownership. She moved to the Central Hotel in Wellington. Although Jane went bankrupt in 1890, as many did in the economic downturn, she picked herself up and by 1892 was the licensee of the Oriental Hotel. She remained in business until 1910 and died two years later aged 78.[80]

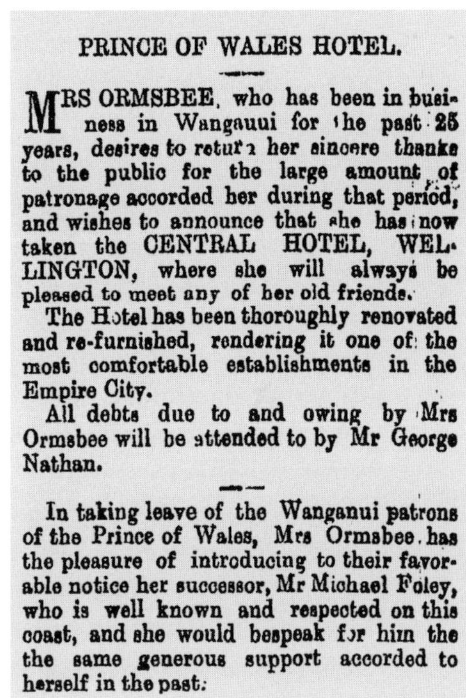

PRINCE OF WALES HOTEL.

MRS ORMSBEE, who has been in business in Wangauui for the past 25 years, desires to return her sincere thanks to the public for the large amount of patronage accorded her during that period, and wishes to announce that she has now taken the CENTRAL HOTEL, WELLINGTON, where she will always be pleased to meet any of her old friends.

The Hotel has been thoroughly renovated and re-furnished, rendering it one of the most comfortable establishments in the Empire City.

All debts due to and owing by Mrs Ormsbee will be attended to by Mr George Nathan.

In taking leave of the Wanganui patrons of the Prince of Wales, Mrs Ormsbee has the pleasure of introducing to their favorable notice her successor, Mr Michael Foley, who is well known and respected on this coast, and she would bespeak for him the same generous support accorded to herself in the past.

Jane Ormsbee introduces her successor and advertises her new business. *Wanganui Chronicle*, 24 November 1886

Fortunately, because Jane's father was the mortgagee for her Prince of Wales Hotel in Whanganui, it remained in the family despite her insolvency, a clear example of the difference broader family support could make. By this time, unusually, it had two unmarried sisters as licensees, Emma and Alice Siddells. They continued to run well-patronised race meeting stalls and the hotel was popular with theatregoers. In 1892, however, they were unable to renew their licence. In what the *Wanganui Herald* described as an 'arbitrary action', the prohibition members of the licensing committee held sway and decided that, as unmarried women, they should not be licensees. The Siddell sisters briefly converted the Prince of Wales into a temperance hotel before turning, like Jane, to family for support. They went into partnership with brother Charles, who was licensee of various hotels. When Emma died in 1940, leaving a substantial estate of around £11,000, she was still recorded as a 'hotel proprietress'.[81]

Lydia Burr (see Chapter 6) was the mainstay of her family's income, using a combination of hotelkeeping and dressmaking to keep herself and her family afloat and earning herself respect in the little Horowhenua town of Foxton. She arrived in the colony with her family as a child and in 1855, at the age of 17, was married off, reluctantly, according to family history, to 33-year-old widower Amos Burr. An ex-seaman, Amos was known as Hookey because of the metal hooks that replaced the hands he lost in an accident just as he reached New Zealand in 1840. His first wife, the daughter of Te Raotea of Ngāti Raukawa, died in 1850, having spent her married life helping her husband to cope with his disability while running an accommodation house in Te Papa Ngaio, a village on the Manawatu River.[82]

Amos was entrepreneurial, purchasing land in the Manawatu area and variously acting as interpreter, ferryman and hotelier and, in the 1860s, as overseer of roads around Palmerston North. He was insolvent in 1863, 1869, 1873 and 1876. The family lived in Wirikino and Petone until about 1865 and then in the fledgling settlement of Foxton. Lydia gave birth to no fewer than 11 children, despite Amos's frequent absences, and also ran several businesses. Although Amos was the licensee of the Adelaide Hotel in Foxton, Lydia ran it and the local ferry from 1866, advertising in her own name after 1867. Her advertisements were brief – just a business card that said 'Adelaide Hotel by Mrs L.H. Burr Foxton, Manawatu'.[83] Either she was sufficiently well known or she could not afford more effusive publicity. In 1876 Lydia applied for a protection order. This may have been a mutual strategy to protect the family property in the latest insolvency, but the couple separated shortly afterwards and Lydia traded hotelkeeping for a 20-year dressmaking business to support her family.[84]

Hotelkeeping, then, could be a viable business for a woman, since a responsible female presence behind the bar was a desirable addition to an establishment. The vagaries of licensing boards, however, particularly as the power of the temperance lobby increased, meant that female publicans could find themselves without a licence through no fault of their own. They had to find different enterprises.

Bed and board

Boarding houses were obvious businesses for women, whether as a first choice or as an alternative when they failed to obtain a publican's licence.[85] Located in the home, they suited women with childcare responsibilities. They required little initial capital. For widows left destitute with no skills other than housekeeping, they were viable moneymaking options. Even middle-class women could take a deep breath and, as the eminently respectable Sarah Miles, wife of the New South Wales police chief, said when she began business in Sydney in 1850, 'put [their] shoulder to the wheel' in a 'new and anxious occupation', that could nevertheless 'be conducted by the female part of creation', hoping for 'respectable steady people' as lodgers.[86] Boarding establishments varied from taking in one or two lodgers, having squeezed one's children into as few rooms as possible, to offering board and lodging in bigger houses to several gentlemen or families, sometimes with private sitting rooms.

Boarding-house keeping can be seen as a deliberate exploitation by women of their femininity. A meal cooked by a woman was particularly valued on the gold-fields or in port towns providing for transient sailors and merchants and newly arrived immigrants.[87] Care is needed, however, with placing too much emphasis on women's supposedly superior cleaning or cooking abilities. Men ran boarding houses too. It seems likely that, to do so, they employed domestic servants, and surely some female boarding-house keepers did the same, particularly in larger establishments.

Boarding-house marketing, however, emphasised the comforts of feminine domesticity, and this made sense. Boarding houses could be lonely and depress-ing; a woman's presence and the food she offered had special value. Canny male proprietors included their wives when they advertised. In July 1860 both Mr *and* Mrs Harrison were named in the advertisement for the new Bellevue Boarding House in Onehunga.[88] When Johannah Rossiter of Sulyard House in Cashel Street, Christchurch, died in 1861, her husband Frederick advertised that he *and his daughters* would continue to run the boarding house and thanked 'the clergy and gentry for their kind patronage so liberally bestowed on his late wife'. He lasted a year before returning to England.[89]

When Sarah Winch died in 1860, her husband Charles, a jeweller, announced he would continue her successful five-year-old boarding-house business at Claremont House, in Auckland's Princes Street, 'with the same attention to the comforts of its inmates for which, under the management of Mrs Winch, it has obtained so high a reputation'. A year later he sold to Benjamin and Mary Hayles and vanished from Auckland. The Hayles also moved on within 18 months to more salubrious Eden Crescent and James and Susanna Courtayne took over Claremont House, where they remained for several years. In the 1870s Susanna also had a side business of a servants' registry office.[90]

'A comfortable home'

Advertisements often offered 'a comfortable home' to single gentlemen. Although some less respectable boarding houses offered more intimate services, the emphasis on comfort appealed to a desire for maternal care. Margaret ('Mrs W.C. Wilson'), the wife of *New Zealander* newspaper proprietor William Chisholm Wilson, advertised 'comfortable entertainment' for 'Country settlers and Strangers visiting Auckland' at her establishment Cliff House in Shortland Street in Auckland in 1846. To modern ears this phrase has a whiff of the disreputable but it probably just meant a nice cup of tea and good conversation for her 'few respectable' boarders.[91]

In 1855 Bridget Dixon offered 'a Snug and Quiet Safe RETREAT' at the Retreat Boarding House next to the Masonic Hotel in Princes Street, within five minutes' walk of the post office and 'business parts of the Town', and 'in a fine healthy' area. She disappeared after six months when William McKelvie took over. Despite experience as a ship's steward and making 'extensive alterations … with well-furnished bedrooms and sitting-rooms', he also sold up after a year.[92]

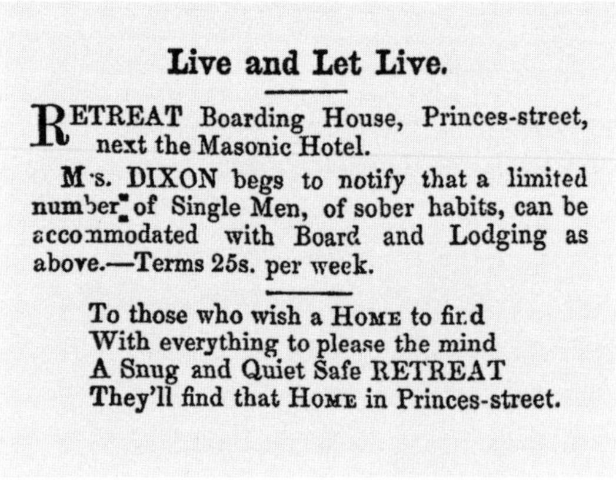

Live and Let Live.

RETREAT Boarding House, Princes-street, next the Masonic Hotel.

M's. DIXON begs to notify that a limited number of Single Men, of sober habits, can be accommodated with Board and Lodging as above.—Terms 25s. per week.

To those who wish a HOME to find
With everything to please the mind
A Snug and Quiet Safe RETREAT
They'll find that HOME in Princes-street.

Bridget Dixon used a catchy ditty offering an alternative to hotel accommodation – a 'HOME' in Auckland.

Daily Southern Cross, 13 November 1855

Some boarding houses advertised themselves as non-drinking establishments, setting them apart from the rowdier accommodation option of a hotel – and from other boarding houses where alcohol was

Men and women, Māori and Pākehā, share Princes Street, Auckland, in 1850. Sarah Winch's Claremont House is on the left. Three doors down beyond the Masonic Hotel with its flagpole is Bridget Dixon's Retreat Boarding House. Hannah Losee and Emily Chevassut sold 'fancy and dunstable bonnets' opposite in 1851. Sketch, Major Cyprian Bridge, 1850, Auckland Libraries 7-A4787

perhaps tolerated and quietly supplied. It was unsurprising that Sarah Dougherty elected to run what became a well-patronised temperance boarding house in central Wellington. Her husband Daniel, originally a whaling captain and then a pilot on Wellington Harbour for eight years, had drowned while intoxicated in 1857. Sarah lost her home and livelihood along with her spouse. She was, however, ideally suited to run a boarding house. She had travelled widely with Daniel and when he set up a whaling station at Port Underwood, she provided hospitality for many visitors.[93] In Christchurch Susannah and John Bligh also chose temperance, running a restaurant and boarding house targeting honeymooning couples and providing 'special bridal chambers'. In an interesting reversal of roles it was John, an ex-steward on the Panama mail boats, who was celebrated as 'one of the best cooks that ever put a pie in the oven', while Susannah was the business head. They did an 'immense trade and made money', according to diarist William Burke. Susannah left an estate of £3400 when she died of cancer in 1888. Her husband remarried quickly, overstretched himself financially and had only £400 when he died eight years later.[94]

Regular boarders, such as commercial travellers, doctors, dentists and theatrical performers, were the lifeblood of many boarding houses, and provided free advertising when they announced their arrival in town and the availability of their varied services. Surgeon dentist Dr T. Trafford always stayed at Cudlipp's Family Boarding House on the corner of Liardet and Devon streets ('Cudlipp's Corner') in New Plymouth when he visited in the 1860s. Frances Cudlipp, who was also a midwife (see Chapter 8), ran the establishment with her husband Edward for many years, and made sure to advertise that their guests included 'the late Governor [George Grey] and Military'.[95]

Boarding houses often had serial landlords/ladies, sometimes because they were unsuccessful businesspeople, or as personal circumstances changed. Blair Cottage in Carlyle Street, Napier, lasted more than 30 years with a series of proprietors. Mary Haswell advertised board and lodging there from January 1867, probably because her husband Robert's greengrocery business was in trouble. When he became insolvent in 1868, Blair Cottage was taken over by Harriet Vaughan, who moved her business from Emerson Street. She was still advertising in 1870 but then she and husband David took on the Meanee Hotel.[96] Five years later Mrs Louisa Brenton was advertising for boarders for the cottage. She had lost her husband and eldest son in a boating accident in 1870. Locals took up a subscription and raised over £80, sympathetic towards 'a very estimable woman and helpless family' left 'without means, or relatives'. She used the money to start her business and stayed at Blair Cottage until 1886, extending to make it 'a commodious boarding house'. Mrs McKeown was in residence in 1886, and in 1889, when the building burned down, Phillippa Terrill, whose musician husband John had deserted her, was in charge.[97]

Even though she was only renting it, Louisa Brenton had extended Blair Cottage, seeing the opportunity to expand her business. Such a gamble did not always pay off, particularly in challenging economic times. Agnes Watson turned to boarding-house keeping after her husband left in 1879 taking with him the £500 he had raised by mortgaging their Kaipara farm. After the mortgagee foreclosed Agnes sold her furniture and moved to Auckland, where she ran a fairly successful boarding house, Jervois House in Wellesley Street, until 1884. She arranged with the landlord to extend and upgrade the premises in May that year, advertising three months later the 'reopening of a First class Boarding Establishment', featuring not only 'spacious rooms' but 'piano, plunge and shower bath'. But in October she was still advertising vacancies in her 'lofty and well-ventilated' bedrooms, on 'moderate' terms of £1 per week. She did have at least two lodgers in December 1884. One was a 'young lady' wishing for 'a Situation in a first-class Hotel as a barmaid', although this could have been a family member, and the other was A.A. Fromm, who was seeking employment as an engrosser (a maker of final copies of legal documents) in a law firm. Mr Fromm was also looking to rent or buy a small suburban cottage and garden, so he was not a long-term resident. The following year Agnes was bankrupt with liabilities of £229 0s 6d, including a loan of £30, rent of £30 12s 8d, a bill of sale of £28 and household necessities of £140 8s; her assets were just £39 4s 6d, including furniture. After her bankruptcy she and her children disappeared from the records.[98]

Lodging-house keeper Sarah Steele, who ran Gloucester House in Parnell in Auckland for 20 years from the 1860s, also got into trouble, although it was as a result of desperation. She and husband William had emigrated from Rodborough, Gloucestershire, in 1837, initially to Sydney, then to the Bay of Islands, before ending up in Auckland. In 1878, however, at the age of 70, Sarah was in court for stealing four £1 notes from a lodger. Fortunately the victim was persuaded to drop the charges, on account of Sarah's 'extreme age' and because she was 'infirm and feeble'. The magistrates felt they would have been placed 'in a most disagreeable position to have to send an old woman like [her] to gaol'. Despite its longevity this was perhaps not a thriving business.[99]

Running a boarding house was hard work – and that included putting up with one's paying guests. In 1877 Dunedin boarding-house keeper Catherine Pledger took lodger Thomas Parker to court for assault. He had a tantrum when she failed to provide him with a hot plate for his lamb dinner, which he then threw at the dog, behaviour he regarded as 'justified'. He vehemently denied then slapping Catherine on the face. She sued him for £23 but the judge awarded her only 40s.[100] Nevertheless, Catherine was still in business 25 years later with an even more idiosyncratic lodger, a bookshop assistant who gave his name as Thomas Parkes. When he died suddenly in 1912, however, he was discovered to be a 20-year-old woman, Annie Read, from Dubbo in New South Wales. Found unconscious in her room with the

Catherine Pledger, Dunedin boarding-house keeper, whose tenants could be idiosyncratic.

Private collection: Margaret Gillingham

body of a newborn baby beside her, she died later in hospital. The tragic story made headlines around New Zealand. When she first arrived in New Zealand Annie had described herself as 'not a boy, nor was she a girl'.[101] Such headline-creating guests were unusual, but Annie's experience shows how boarding houses, if sometimes lonely in their anonymity, could also offer those in need opportunities for reinvention and subterfuge.

Sometimes the boarding house itself, or its location, meant that the business was not viable. Tweed House in Cashel Street in Christchurch was one example. Thomas Atkinson, formerly the partner of the Clarksons at Dunstable House, opened Tweed House as a boarding house in 1859 with his new wife Martha. George Allfrey and his wife Arabella took over in 1862 with a hotel licence. This passed, in 1864, to John Jonas, who was wanted for fraud in Sydney, and then to Noah Edgar, both of whom hit financial difficulties. Noah also had a struggling drapery business and was repeatedly insolvent, leaving his wife Annie to cope with Tweed House and their rapidly increasing family. Arabella Allfrey resumed control, without a liquor licence and in her own name, in 1866, while her husband faced insolvency. She did not last long and Tweed House continued to be passed from one hopeful businessperson to another in quick succession.[102] A report from 1864, when Tweed House had a hotel licence and was subject to annual inspections, provides one possible reason for its lack of profitability – although 'of a fit and proper character', Tweed House was described as small.[103] Undeterred by their failure at Tweed House, the Edgars moved on in 1866 to the more successful Eastern Hotel on the corner of Fitzgerald Avenue and Cashel Street. Serving alcohol was more profitable and the location was better. Noah died in 1870 and Annie Edgar continued the business for another 30 years through widowhood, remarriage and widowhood again until her death in 1900. There is still a hotel on the site today.[104]

'Providing some family income'

For some women, a boarding house was a straightforward way to augment the family income. Taking advantage of her home's location on the main road between Wellington and Porirua, Susannah Wall offered 'beds and refreshment for travellers' at Halfway House, while her husband and older son worked as labourers.[105] Susannah Lloyd used her boarding-house business in Nelson to offset her second husband's lack of prosperity. She had probably never envisaged she would be doing so. When she left London in 1859 she was Susannah Jones, a wife of three years, travelling with her first husband Thomas and two sons, two-year-old Thomas Henry and 14-month-old Charles. But when Susannah arrived in Nelson a few months later, both her husband and Charles had died en route. It is difficult to imagine the shock and despair of such a loss, and the stark contrast between her arrival in Nelson and her hopes on leaving England. She was fortunate that her sister Grace Mitchell and her husband John and three children had emigrated with her and that her parents and brothers were already in Nelson.

Susannah remarried two years later to ex-sailor and coal merchant William Lloyd, who went into business briefly with his wife's brothers, Joseph and Charles Bray. Susannah had 10 more children, including two sets of twins, but only five survived to adulthood. William became embroiled in gold-mining companies and was insolvent in 1869 and 1878, and Susannah took up boarding-house keeping. By the time she died in 1891 aged 53 she had been running a successful establishment for at least 10 years. She left her estate worth 'over £100' to her two youngest children, Lilian (14) and Frank (11). Her husband William was not mentioned. Her eldest son, Thomas Jones, and his wife Florence bought the boarding house.[106]

Making a living and finding a niche

Boarding houses, like hotels, were most often run by widows and wives. It was both risky, and perhaps vaguely disreputable, for a single woman to open the doors of her private house to paying guests, especially if they were lone men and strangers to the community. Like hotels, boarding houses pushed at the limits of the comfortable parochial realm. A full boarding house, particularly with regular or long-term residents, was safer and more respectable than a nearly empty one, so success was important. A few brave single women, however, did venture into the business.

Spinster Jane Barnwell, who had been a kitchen maid in England in 1851, emigrated at the age of 36 with her orphaned nephew, eight-year-old Tom Price.[107] Perhaps she thought New Zealand offered more opportunities for him. (He took full advantage, disappeared from his aunt's life and was last heard of in Waimate.)[108] With a child in tow, live-in domestic service was not a possibility for Jane, but opening a boarding house was feasible. She opened a 'first-class boarding house' offering residents a 'respectable, quiet and comfortable home' at Belgrave House in Princes Street in Dunedin in 1860.[109] She advertised for servants, including a waiter, suggesting it was an upmarket establishment. One of her first tenants was teacher Annie Willshire who had a school in Maclaggan Street.[110] At the end of 1862 she

Nelson boarding-house keeper Susannah Lloyd may be the woman at the door, or in the upstairs window with her children Frank and Lilian.

Mrs Lloyd's Boarding House, Hardy Street, Nelson Provincial Museum, Maguire Collection, 46309 sold off her boarding-house furniture, renamed her house Belgrave Chambers and rented out office space, taking advantage of her property's location in the heart of the town's commercial centre two blocks from the Octagon. Renting out office space was likely more profitable and less time-consuming and intrusive than housing boarders.[111]

By 1866 Jane had moved on, advertising again for boarders in George and then Stuart streets.[112] Whether profitable or otherwise, her business was recognisable in Dunedin. A competing establishment, the Atlas Boarding House, cheekily advertised its position as 'next to Miss Barnwell's Stuart Street'. Jane moved to Clyde Street later that year and Mrs Black took over: she carefully identified it as 'Late Miss Barnwell's'.[113] Jane moved around until 1874 when she publicly announced she was returning to England.[114] A year later, however, she was still in Dunedin. Perhaps meeting 43-year-old Irish shopkeeper William Harvey Simpson had changed her plans, for in July 1875, when she was 41, they were married.[115] The couple ran a grocery store until they died within two weeks of each other in 1889.[116]

Some boarding houses targeted specific clientele. In Auckland in 1886 a Miss Lloyd spotted a gap in the market. She opened 'an establishment for young women in business, school-teachers and others', conveniently located in Turner Street near the girls' high school. She offered 'every home comfort at a most reasonable charge'. She was of unimpeachable respectability. The *Auckland Star* praised her as 'highly spoken of by the members of the Young Women's Christian Association', and lauded her enterprise: 'such a place for young women has been much required in the city'. The business was apparently short-lived. Her advertisements disappeared within a few months: it is likely she was the Jeannette Bruce Lloyd who married Alfred Shalders, son of the founder of the New Zealand branch of the Young Men's Christian Association, in December 1886.[117]

Boarding-house keeping was not the most glamorous or profitable of occupations, but it could, with careful management, provide a living. For some women it was a temporary business, for others it was life-long. One boarding house could serve many successive proprietors, particularly if well located and possessing the right number of good-sized rooms and amenities. Genteel respectability ensured full rooms and a well-regarded establishment. The opposite extreme could also prove profitable. Women who ran less-than-respectable boarding houses, offering more personal services than meals and a room, did not advertise openly. Instead they come to light in court reports.

The oldest profession

According to the 1874 census there were just 17 female prostitutes in New Zealand, all in Westland towns with over 500 inhabitants, and only one, who was clearly very hard-working, on the 'goldfields'. This was obviously an underestimation of the total number of women working in the sex industry. They were unlikely to declare their occupation to census takers. Five years earlier, in 1869, a survey in Dunedin found 65 prostitutes working in 46 brothels, most of which were clustered in particular alleyways and streets, often in neighbouring houses. A Christchurch survey found that this town, too, was generously endowed with women selling sex in brothels of varying sizes run by both men and women.[118]

Prostitution and brothel-keeping were ubiquitous throughout New Zealand across the century. Early encounters between Pākehā and Māori often included transactions involving sex, although, as Angela Wanhalla explains, these are often better understood within a framework of Māori cultural and sexual practices rather than a European dichotomy of prostitution/marriage. This is particularly true when considering relationships before 1840.[119] The general understanding among authorities in colonial New Zealand, in fact, was that prostitutes were recruited from the young single female immigrants.[120] According to William Burke in Christchurch, the first of those he called 'town girls' arrived in 1857 in the *Mystery* and 'soon commenced business … "under the rose" [secretly]'. Before they arrived, he claimed, somewhat disingenuously, that 'there was no recognised institution of the sort'.[121]

There is some evidence of Māori prostitutes working in similar ways to Pākehā women. The behaviour of military troops in Tauranga in 1843 caused the commander of the armed forces to warn officers that if caught 'injuring the native population by destroying the morality of native females' they would face court martial, suggesting that, at the very least, Māori women were being compromised. It could also indicate the presence of a sex trade.[122] Ten years later, in 1854, in a speech advocating stricter alcohol controls in Auckland, the Reverend Thomas Buddle deplored the 'increasing prostitution existing among native females', telling his audience that there were 18 'houses of ill fame occupied by these unfortunate creatures'.[123] Like their Pākehā counterparts, many were catering for the military market. Robyn Anderson, in her study of prostitution, suggests that the number of Māori women in the business decreased in the late 1850s, as indicated by the lack of prosecutions after 1857.[124] In 1874, however, William Wright was murdered in what was called a 'Maori brothel' in Auckland's Queen Street.[125] There were no women identified as Māori in the Christchurch and Dunedin brothel surveillance returns in 1869,[126] but Elizabeth Johnson, alias 'Maori Liz', was charged with disorderly conduct in George Street in Dunedin in 1871, although whether she was soliciting or just enjoying herself too loudly is unclear (and she may not have been Māori).[127] When Wellingtonian Frank Folland was charged with vagrancy in 1881 he was described as living in 'a brothel in the Maori Pah, kept by one of the most degraded women in the city'.[128] Brothel businesses clearly crossed racial boundaries, and could also be run by Māori men, although not necessarily with Māori prostitutes. In 1876 a Māori man identified only as 'George' narrowly escaped prosecution for brothel-keeping after a particularly wild party in Wellington. Three of his female guests, Elizabeth Burke, Hannah Mendoza and Annie Greer, already familiar to police and recently released from prison, did not escape punishment. However, Elizabeth, 'a young woman of twenty-six who could at one time boast of good connections in Melbourne' but 'sinks daily into deeper degradation', Hannah, 'a depraved harridan of the worst type', and Annie, 'better known in the Police Court by her ironical sobriquet "Gentle Annie"', were not identified as Māori.[129]

A business choice?

Female brothel keepers and prostitutes who worked independently were businesswomen with a niche role in the colonial economy, making money by catering to a ready market for sex – and probably more money than if they had run a boarding house or a shop. Nevertheless, framing prostitution and brothel-keeping as a business is problematic because it so often involved exploitation and desperation. The unhealthy combination of alcoholism, homelessness and soliciting was common. Women who featured in court cases frequently had drunkenness added to the descriptions of their behaviour, and prostitutes picked up on the streets were often homeless. Selling sex was often a last resort. There was no safety net for those who found themselves without 'respectable' employment, for those whose breadwinning husbands had deserted them or for those who found themselves ill or in trouble without family support. For a woman without education or a trade, without capital or connections, brothel-keeping or prostitution were two of few choices available.

Brothel-keeping was risky, illegal and placed women beyond the pale in respectable society. In April 1869 Mary Cox sued her husband John, of the 4th Waikato Regiment, for desertion, but her efforts to support herself by going into business

– running a brothel in Tauranga and cohabiting with other men in the regiment – were unappreciated by the court, particularly as she had apparently been training her daughters in the business. Her husband, on the other hand, attracted the court's compassion as a man of great respectability, dragged down by the immoral character of his wife.[130] Significantly, the court assumed that her character, rather than financial desperation, had led Mary into prostitution.

The letter of the law

Prostitutes and brothel keepers were not listed in trade directories or newspaper advertisements. Their encounters with authorities, either in surveys, censuses or in court, brought them into the historical record. Like Catherine Mason, whose legal battles were detailed in Chapter 4, women appeared in court for running 'disorderly houses', or for being drunk and badly behaved on the streets of New Zealand's towns as they touted for business.

Running a disorderly house was a crime but prostitution itself was not technically illegal in New Zealand. It was initially controlled under vagrancy legislation and council by-laws: women were charged with 'having no visible means of support' or with being 'idle and disorderly persons'. In 1874 Lowther Broad, resident magistrate in Nelson, insisted that, under the strict letter of the law, prostitutes were *not* 'idle and disorderly persons'. He was making a technical legal point, but he was also correct: prostitutes were anything but 'idle'. Broad acknowledged, too, the core dilemma for lawmakers and enforcers: 'The law has not declared such a mode of life unlawful, and I am inclined to think it has tacitly acknowledged the existence of an incurable evil by providing means to keep it in as decent bounds as possible.'[131]

The controversial Contagious Diseases Act of 1869 was an additional means of control. This targeted the female prostitutes and brothel keepers rather than their male clients, forcing a woman to undergo a compulsory genital examination by a police surgeon if *suspected* of being a 'common prostitute'. If she refused the examination or was found to be infected, she could be imprisoned.[132]

Not in my backyard

Essentially, prostitutes and brothels were tolerated except when they drew unnecessary attention to themselves and became 'public nuisances'. Authorities targeted noisy houses with many comings and goings, or loud, drunk women wandering the streets at night, but ignored discreet activity. Complaints from local residents also brought action.

When Eliza Edwards (aka Avery) moved in next door to Maria Pope in Colombo Street in Christchurch in August 1869 she may have regretted her choice of location. Eliza had been selling 'wines spirits and cigars' from the 'bar of the Billiard Room at the Dunedin Club Hotel'. In her new premises she offered 'a select stock of confectionery, cordials, &c.', plus 'hot suppers twice a week … coffee always ready'. Coffee, however, was not the only thing that was 'always ready' at Miss Edwards' establishment. In November 1869 Eliza was in court, following 'numerous complaints' from neighbours, on a charge of 'allowing prostitutes and persons of notoriously bad character, to meet together in her house'. Maria Pope gave evidence of 'drunken' men coming and going at all times of the night, 'climb[ing] over the palings at the back and [being] admitted to the house', and loud piano-playing after 11 in the evening. Eliza denied keeping a disorderly house and was given the benefit of the doubt, as this was her first offence. She was fined 20s plus costs and warned not to appear before the judge again. She does not seem to have done so, although she may merely have moved on, kept her piano playing quieter and the comings and goings of customers and 'girls of ill fame' more discreet.[133] Similarly, Catherine Palmer, 'a hardened case', closed her Wellington establishment in 1872 to avoid prosecution when two neighbours complained that her house 'was the resort of disreputable characters, male and female, whose unseemly habits, generally indulged at unseasonable hours, were a source of great annoyance'.[134]

Sometimes public protest came from more than just one or two neighbours. In December 1870, 114 ratepayers petitioned Hokitika's Borough Council, asking 'that some means should be taken to remove the houses of ill-fame from North Revell-street'. They were concerned about the welfare of the 'large number of children' living in the area. Parents' endeavours to raise them properly 'were nugatory, owing to the disgusting scenes and frightful language they were compelled to listen to daily'. The councillors tut-tutted in sympathy and agreed that something needed to be done, although this did not mean closing the establishments. The favoured solution was to move them on to 'some other and less conspicuous part of the town'.[135] A few months later, Hokitika's inspector of nuisances Richard McCormick reported proudly that he had served six 'houses of ill-fame keepers' in the same street with notices to quit. Unfortunately he also admitted that only one had actually moved and a further 'notorious keeper of a house of ill-repute' had escaped being served.[136]

Catherine Mason (see Chapter 4) was also moved on. She was a frequent presence in Dunedin courts, both before and after her lawyer's creativity with coverture, charged variously with using bad language, creating a disturbance and theft.[137] In 1869 her disorderly house was, according to local policeman John Golder, 'large' and 'elegantly furnished', but also 'the worst conducted brothel he was ever in'. Catherine was 'one of the most foul-mouthed women he ever knew' and he had several complaints from men who had been robbed there. Catherine, he said, 'sheltered herself behind the delicacy of those who had been robbed, who did not like their names to be made public'.[138] Eventually, in 1871, the latest charge of keeping a disreputable house was dismissed on condition that Catherine 'in company with a constable, should go on board a steamer leaving the colony'. She agreed to do so. The 'Miss Mason' who left on the *Alhambra* for Melbourne a few days later may have been her. Nothing more was heard of her, no doubt much to the relief of Dunedin magistrates, who, far more effectively than their Hokitika counterparts, had shipped their problem on to another jurisdiction, out of sight and out of mind.[139]

Old offenders

Police, court officials and newspaper reporters got to know the women who appeared in court frequently.[140] Prostitution was an ongoing business and lifestyle. In 1873 the *Wellington Independent* described Catherine Palmer as 'one of the female incorrigibles who flit at regular intervals between the Police Station and her Majesty's Gaol'. Similarly, Margaret Gill was 'an old offender' in Wellington by 1865, having appeared regularly since 1858, charged variously with drunkenness and keeping a disorderly house.[141] Elizabeth Pepper, who lived on Baker's Hill, Karori Road in Wellington, was popularly called 'Old Mother Pepper' in the 1860s and 1870s, suggesting a degree of matriarchal authority, if not respectability. She styled herself 'the lioness of the 65th Regiment'. Some were appalled by the 'unblushing manner in which she carried on her obnoxious trade, even in the presence of her own son not quite seven years old'. Her house 'bore a very bad character as … the common resort of men of pleasure and women of the town, who frequented it for immoral purpose … and annoy the neighbourhood by making noises'. According to one disapproving neighbour, these men even included 'clergymen and gentlemen … men of bad character, sometimes those known as respectable members of society'.[142]

Constable James Edwards gave damning evidence that he had found Elizabeth Pepper 'in bed with two men, one dressed, the other undressed' at two o'clock in the morning, and that she had 'throw[n] her arms round [him], wishing him to have carnal connection with her'. Judge James Johnston, enjoying himself a little too much, asked if he had acceded to her request. Edwards claimed to have declined. Elizabeth Pepper's lawyer argued in her defence that she 'had been a respectable honest and hard-working woman, until she had been ruined by a bad husband'. The judge also found a man to blame, suggesting the landlord of the house was worse than Elizabeth herself by 'knowingly' letting his house 'to a prostitute'. He nevertheless sentenced 'Mother Pepper' to six months' hard labour. She remained a familiar face in Wellington courts until the 1880s.[143]

Like Old Mother Pepper, Mary Ann Mason, 'the vagrant queen', was a character deplored by respectable Wellingtonians but good copy for court reporters. Her 'filthy and dilapidated' house was described in 1874 as 'a most disorderly and disreputable one, frequented by persons of bad character of both sexes whose conduct was disgraceful in the extreme, the noise and bad language being audible all over that end of the town'. Her 'neglected and dirty' children witnessed 'the abominable scenes which always were going on in the house'. Mary Ann, it was said, had 'corrupted a great number of very young girls, and altogether her place was a disgrace to the place and a public nuisance which had been complained of by all the neighbours'. Much to the amusement of the newspaper reporter, Mary Ann 'made a long and a very flowery oration, quite uninterrupted by stops and apparently all in one breath … an indignant repudiation of the charge, a stout protestation of innocence, industry, sobriety, and all virtues'. Like the similarly 'long and eloquent defence' of one of her frequent 'visitors', Elizabeth Griggs, it had little effect on the judge.[144]

'Rather be sent back to gaol'

Old Mother Pepper and Mary Ann Mason had some control of their own destinies, or at least put on a good show. Other women were not so resilient. Eliza Gooden's predicament epitomises the lack of choices available to destitute women. She and husband Henry, who arrived in Wellington in 1856 with their two young children, were 'very respectable people', according to Thomas Braggins, who was on the same ship. Things went downhill for Eliza when her husband left after catching her in bed with another man. By the time she came before the courts in March 1864, Eliza was running a brothel and drinking heavily: she had recently been taken to the local gaol suffering from delirium tremens. She now had five children, four in care and the youngest 'a child at the breast, in a very emaciated state'. Robert Johnston, an officer at the gaol who lived in the same street, reported he had seen 'soldiers, sailors and females of bad character frequent the place'. The judge sentenced Eliza to three months' imprisonment with hard labour and was appalled that she had allowed her 10-year-old daughter to witness her activities.[145]

Upon her release in June Eliza turned up in court again, this time on vagrancy charges. Now, however, she was there at her own request, telling the court that she was 'entirely destitute and had no home … she would rather be sent back to gaol than pursue her former course of life'. The gaoler supported her; she had behaved 'remarkably well' in prison, and upon her departure had 'begged to be allowed to remain'. She was returned to prison for one month, after which she vanishes from the records.[146]

Eliza was not alone in asking to be sent to gaol. In 1867 Mary Ann Weston appeared three times, charged with drunkenness and vagrancy. On both the second and third occasions she begged the police to charge her, 'as she had no home to go to'. She appeared in court looking gaunt and clearly in need of assistance. The magistrate granted her request, remarking that 'this was a very bad way of getting an unfortunate woman a month's lodging, and he thought it a disgrace to the town that there was no place provided to send people to'.[147] These cases, along with the cautionary tale of Elizabeth Darby and her descent from respectable wife to drunken prostitute beaten severely by her new partner (Chapter 1), show the ease with which respectability and relative security could become destitution and disgrace, particularly in an era with little benevolent assistance available.

'And other little delicacies'

Brothels came in many guises. Various businesses could be a cover for prostitution, gambling and illegal drinking. Hotels and boarding houses were arguably the most obvious locations, but also used were coffee and confectionery shops, like that of Eliza Edwards next door to Mrs Pope's.[148] Tobacconists, with mainly male customers, made ideal fronts for brothels. When Mary Haines was charged with selling liquor without a licence in Auckland in 1880, the *Auckland Star* described her as 'the interesting young tobacconist of Queen Street'. Sub-Inspector William Pardy reported that 'some ladies had been stopping with her' at her shop, and 'gentlemen friends were in the habit of calling upon them to indulge in pleasant conversation'.

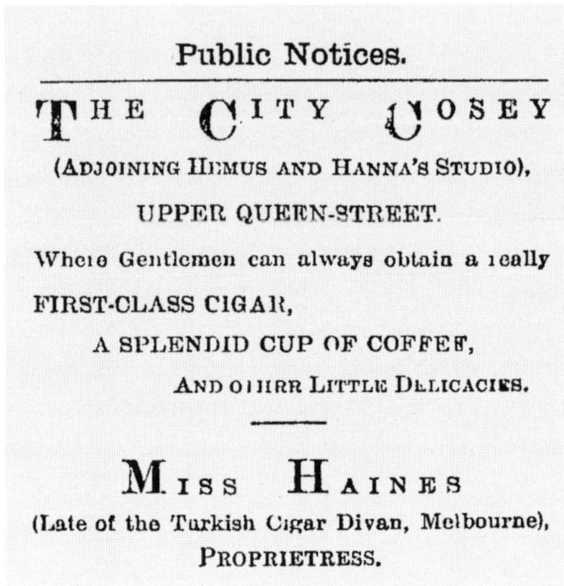

Mary Haines was probably running a brothel: her advertisements were certainly suggestive.

Auckland Star, 9 May 1879

When the magistrate asked him if he was implying the shop 'was a mask for something else', Pardy refused to be drawn. Mary was found not guilty of the charge of supplying liquor to 'her very old friend' Henry Reilly, who testified he had bought cigarettes but that she had 'shouted' him the liquor.[149]

Jane Sinclair of Hokitika appeared only briefly in the public record, respectably in the directories of 1865 and 1867 as a tobacconist in Revell Street, and less respectably in newspaper court reports. In 1866 she was accused of stealing £10 from Claus Japp, a local man drinking at her house. Accounts of the evening's entertainment, which included drinking and card playing, suggest that Jane provided more than tobacco. Witnesses said the pair had announced that Claus 'was going to sleep with' Jane that night. In the morning Claus missed his money. Jane escaped prosecution on this occasion because everyone's level of inebriation led to a garbled version of events.[150] She appeared in court a year later for being drunk and disorderly and using obscene language, as well as for 'destroying the waterproof of the constable who arrested her'.[151] (This was a common fate of arresting constables' raincoats in

Hokitika: peculiarly, at least six people were charged with the same offence between July and September 1867. Perhaps they felt it an effective form of protest in a West Coast winter.[152]) Mrs Sinclair vanished from Hokitika, or at least from the newspapers, in 1869, when her house and furniture were auctioned.[153] As with many such peripatetic working-class women, particularly those who operated on the fringes of respectability, her fate remains unknowable.

Goldfields towns, with their vast populations of single, itinerant men, were ideal breeding grounds for brothels. Hokitika was famous for its hotels, gambling dens, dancing palaces and bawdy houses, run by businessmen and women helping lucky gold diggers to part with their hard-won cash. Businesswomen in gold towns were tough, used to exerting their authority and capable of slinging not only pithy epithets but even, if the situation required it, punches or rocks at policemen, clients or each other, generally loudly and publicly enough to entertain or outrage passers-by.

One such character was Maria Clarke, known more popularly as 'Porpoise Maria', allegedly 'an affectionate nickname bestowed on her in consequence of her obesity'. One of the many female inhabitants of Revell Street in Hokitika, she appeared in court regularly as 'the keeper of a notorious house of ill-fame … frequented by thieves and persons who have no visible lawful means of support'.[154] She was sentenced to two months' imprisonment with hard labour in 1869 for being a 'disorderly prostitute', apprehended while 'enjoying a stand-up fight' – not as a spectator but as a participant.[155]

One might imagine that the likes of Maria would avoid the legal system whenever possible, but she and others also used the courts for redress. In 1868 Maria reported 'two most disreputable characters', her neighbours Margaret Carr and Sarah Dugmore, for assaulting her and threatening 'to have her life'. Like Maria, they were familiar faces in the courtroom. Sarah, under the surname Miller, had been fined £1 that very morning for being drunk and disorderly.[156] In 1873 Maria was herself accused by Mary Sweeney of using threatening language. The case was delayed because the prosecutrix, Mary, was, as the newspaper put it tactfully, 'suffering a recovery'. She 'conducted herself so indecorously while giving her evidence that she was ordered to be locked up until … morning'.[157] Until the mid-1870s Maria appeared in court accused of theft, being drunk and disorderly, using obscene language, smashing 12 panes of glass in Samuel Jacob's window, throwing a stone through the window of the Rainbow Hotel, and assault – the last several times, in company with other women in what appear to have been all-out brawls or ongoing feuds.[158]

Challenging definitions of femininity

Maria's behaviour was not peculiar to prostitutes or brothel keepers. She appeared in court for reasons other than her business, although some of the disputes may well have stemmed from a deal gone wrong. Maria stood up for herself and gave as good as she got. She and her neighbours were performers and the street and the courtroom their stage. These down-to-earth, rough-and-ready publicans, boarding-house keepers and brothel owners, working-class tradeswomen and shopkeepers were all well able to deal with cheeky, mostly male customers in towns where testosterone ran riot. They represent a different version of colonial femininity from genteel schoolteachers and demure dressmakers, but filled important roles in the colonial economy and in the lives of the towns as they provided their 'personal offices for man'.

Chapter 8

'Personal Offices for Woman': A female economy

If prostitution was a 'personal office for man', other businesses catered for women. Men could be involved in some, but many were solely female. Birthing babies, attending to mothers, addressing 'female complaints', making and fitting corsets, vetting servants and attending ladies at public baths were all activities most appropriately done by women.

Intimate women's business

Midwifery and monthly nursing, where women cared for new mothers, babies and families for a period after the birth, were very much female activities, as Alison Clarke has shown. Some medical men promoted their midwifery skills, but others did not expect to attend anything so mundane as a routine confinement.[1] In Dunedin in 1873, Dr Robert Bakewell was most put out when asked to 'a perfectly simple case, which any old woman might have attended just as well as myself'.[2] Doctors would attend when complications arose, but even then there were exceptions. When Patrick Manion, a private in the 14th Regiment, ran for the doctor on the instructions of not one but two midwives during the birth of his wife's eleventh child in Auckland in 1865, William Alstin, the surgeon attached to the Royal Artillery, 'said he was not expected to attend a woman in labour, and declined to come until he had seen one of the midwives'. He resented having to attend to the women and children of the garrison 'in addition to my other duties'. Elizabeth Manion died that evening. The jury at the inquest 'lament[ed] that no provision [was] made for medical attendance to soldier's [sic] wives on their confinement'.[3]

Midwifery was a perennially reliable business: there were always babies to be delivered. Neither nurses nor midwives were registered until the twentieth century and businesswomen, some of whom had small lying-in homes, operated alongside the widespread informal midwifery services of neighbours and friends. These services transcended boundaries between Māori and Pākehā.[4] Sophia Thomas's granddaughter remembered her grandmother's story of her 'great walk' from Wellington to Whanganui in the 1840s. (She refused to board the steamer because she feared it would be wrecked, and she was renowned for second sight.) En route she assisted a Maori woman through a difficult childbirth, allegedly ensuring their safe passage to the new settlement. She continued to provide midwifery services throughout her life.[5] Eliza McDiarmid, who grew up in West Taieri in the 1860s, wrote proudly of her mother Janet's role in her community as a nurse and midwife, a service 'freely given … a labour of love for humanity's sake, [with] no remuneration of any kind given or expected'.[6] Her reminiscences echo those of Emma Adams (Chapter 2) who also emphasised her mother's service to the community, although her mother Elizabeth Garland was paid for her midwifery services.

Janet McDiarmid and her husband were prosperous settlers, so she could afford to provide nursing to her neighbours without asking for payment. Other women's circumstances were not so comfortable and they found a niche market in a specifically female economy, as Patricia Sargison has shown.[7] Some operated by word of mouth. For over 30 years after Bridget Kelly's soldier husband John drowned in 1867, she was midwife and monthly nurse for the women of Opotiki. She delivered babies and nursed the mothers without a doctor in straightforward cases, and did housework and cooking for her patients' families. She later ran a small lying-in hospital, taking women into her own home. She and Mary Capper, who performed similar services in the area, charged a guinea for a nine-day term and used to ride to outlying areas. Neither woman advertised in the newspapers.[8] Catherine Carran, who was of Waikato and Ngāti Pūkeko lineage, ran an accommodation house at the Mataura River near Invercargill in the 1860s with her husband William. After his death in 1871 Catherine remained in the south, remarried and supported herself and her family with farming, nursing, midwifery and an accommodation house in Waikawa. (Her second husband, William Patterson, whom she married about 1872, left her in 1883.)[9] Douglas Mary McKain, who emigrated with grown children as a 51-year-old widow in 1841, was a much sought-after midwife and monthly nurse for 20 years in Wellington; she also dealt in land and rented out property. Her business life is invisible in public records but revealed in a surviving diary and account book, which listed several of Wellington's social and political elite among her customers.[10]

Some midwives and monthly nurses advertised in newspapers in towns, often only once or twice to introduce themselves and afterwards relying on personal recommendations. Elizabeth Hodgson advertised as a monthly nurse from her home in Salts Gully in Canterbury for just one month in 1857.[11] Her advertisements were brief, but others announced their qualifications as a selling point, adding an air of professionalism. As early as 1843, Mrs Marshall of Queen Street, Auckland, offered 'certificates from the Regius Professor of Midwifery of Glasgow College, of her having passed Examination as to ability'.[12] In 1852 Mrs McKenzie in Wellington announced she would continue 'her profession' in Herbert Street alongside her husband John's new general store, promising 'moderate charges', and reminding customers that she had a diploma and had served with 'as great a Medical Professor as Great Britain can boast of', although she did not identify him.[13] In Nelson Mrs Smith advertised as 'Late midwife to the Royal Maternity Charity in London' in 1853.[14]

Frances Jane Tuck felt 'every confidence in coming before the New Plymouth public' in 1855. She had been trained 'by one of the first Physicians in London' and had been 'midwife at the Royal Kent Dispensary for four years' along with a 'very large private practice'.[15] The title 'Mrs' helped her credibility as a midwife, but she was actually single: she married tinplate worker Edward Cudlipp in 1858. She returned to midwifery a decade later, having also run a boarding house (see Chapter 7).[16] In Dunedin Mrs Agnes Callender persuaded a local resident magistrate to certify publicly in 1858 that he had seen her Glasgow diploma and certificates 'testifying to her general good character and conduct'. Mrs Sarah Wood published testimonials when she arrived in Auckland from Cape Town with her second husband in 1865. She was also, comfortingly, 'able, sober and honest'.[17] Sarah, who practised midwifery from 1845 until at least 1878, in Cape Town and then in Auckland, was self-reliant and successful. In 1876, while suing James Johnston for payment of her charges of 30s a week, a typical amount, she said she 'had always been able to keep a home over her head'. She had to be; as noted in Chapter 2, her husband Edward killed himself in 1866.[18]

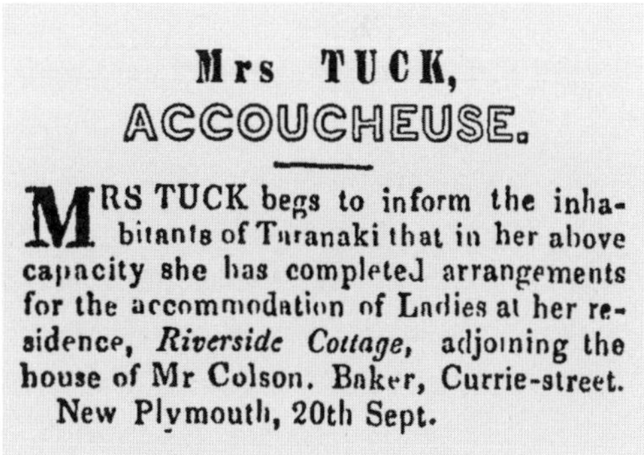

Mrs TUCK,
ACCOUCHEUSE.

MRS TUCK begs to inform the inhabitants of Taranaki that in her above capacity she has completed arrangements for the accommodation of Ladies at her residence, *Riverside Cottage*, adjoining the house of Mr Colson, Baker, Currie-street.
New Plymouth, 20th Sept.

Frances Tuck ran a lying-in home for a year until her marriage.

Taranaki Herald, 20 September 1856

All the qualifications in the world did not help if a patient died. Isabella Stewart, wife of Nelson police constable Alexander, had 'a

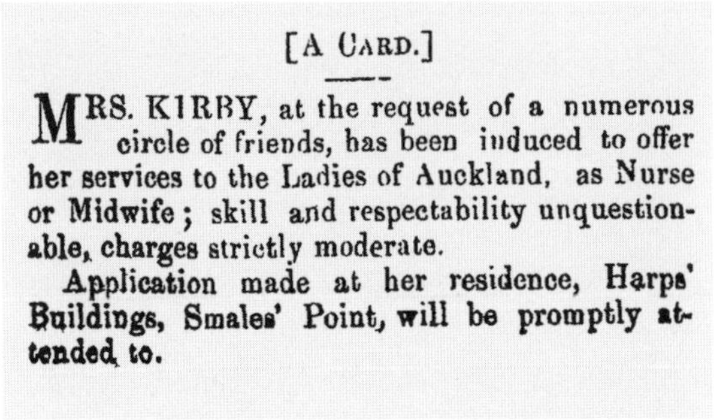

[A CARD.]

MRS. KIRBY, at the request of a numerous circle of friends, has been induced to offer her services to the Ladies of Auckland, as Nurse or Midwife; skill and respectability unquestionable, charges strictly moderate.

Application made at her residence, Harps' Buildings, Smales' Point, will be promptly attended to.

Mary Ann Kirby did not advertise formal qualifications, but offered her 'numerous circle of friends' as referees, also implying modest reticence and service to community. She had previously run a ladies' boot and shoe warehouse.

Daily Southern Cross, 24 March 1857; *Daily Southern Cross*, 16 October 1855, p. 2

first-class certificate from a Professor of Midwifery at the University of Edinburgh'.[19] In September 1862 she delivered 27-year-old Ellen McAllister of twins. Ellen died two weeks later. Although an inquest ultimately found no fault in her care, the evidence was reported in detail in newspapers, which would have caused concern for would-be patients.[20] She was not the only midwife to have a patient die. Reports appeared frequently, with husbands, midwives and doctors all anxious to avoid blame. Nevertheless, as was recognised by frustrated commentators at the time, the costs of qualified medical attention were such that a death did not necessarily mean the end of a business.[21] Ellen Waterhouse was found to be incompetent when Janet King died in Dunedin in May 1870, but she continued to be employed as a midwife, evidenced by a repeat appearance at a coroner's inquest investigating Margaret Cochran's death just seven months later. She was later charged with manslaughter but acquitted.[22]

Some advertisements were discreet, reflecting the personal nature of the service being offered. 'A.R.', a 'respectable Married Woman' seeking employment as a monthly nurse, could be contacted by letter at the *Daily Southern Cross* offices in 1859.[23] Christchurch's 'Mrs B.T.' was equally anonymous, requesting clients to contact her through 'Mrs Dearsley, St Asaph Street'.[24] 'C.J.' of Dunedin identified herself only as 'an ENGLISH PERSON of practical experience' with 'no objection to any part of the country'.[25]

Midwifery businesses were often combined with lying-in homes. Nelson midwife Anne Mary Rush's Bridge Street boarding house was probably for her midwifery clients.[26] In 1865 'Experienced Midwife' Mrs Shaw entrepreneurially offered accommodation in Auckland's Freemans Bay for 'ladies residing in the country and others requiring CARE and ATTENDANCE during their CONFINEMENT', promising moderate terms and a 'Medical Man always in attendance'.[27] Similarly, Dunedin midwife Mrs Anderson stressed that her home in Great King Street was fitted 'with every convenience and comfort for ladies during their confinement'.[28]

Others diversified in different ways. Mrs McLean in Dunedin claimed in 1865 that in addition to midwifery she had 'great experience in curing rheumatism', although she did not specify how or offer references.[29] Mrs Elizabeth Baird Ross, who was a midwife for 39 years, added a registry office for nurses to her midwifery services in Christchurch in 1880.[30] According to her obituary in 1911 she delivered nearly 9000 babies and was the first midwife to be registered in New Zealand in 1904. She was renowned for her 'strong personality, absolute probity, untiring patience and woman's gentle tactfulness', all of which 'eminently fitted' her for 'her profession'.[31]

'Restoring regularity'

Midwives may also have performed abortions, although specific evidence is scant. Chemists and doctors also provided advice on limiting families and sold pills to 'correct all irregularities', but one imagines some women were happier consulting other women. Abortionists were part of New Zealand's business community, albeit clandestinely. A search for the terms 'abortionist' and 'abortion' in New Zealand newspapers for much of the century uncovers only stories of overseas court cases. One reason was that abortion was not illegal until the Offences Against the Person Act of 1867. Even then, abortionists were charged only when a mother died or evidence surfaced that could not be ignored.[32]

Caroline Peyman, who lived with her photographer husband Benjamin in Whanganui from the mid-1860s, was a self-proclaimed 'disciple of Malthus', advocating contraception. She 'practised and taught the water and diet cure', which seems to have been some sort of purgative remedy, and 'gave advice to married women on the generative organs, complaints which they did not care to explain to medical men … and had taught a good many to cure themselves'. She also advised 'poor working men's wives' on 'limiting their families to their incomes and means of support'. She came to attention in 1891 when she was in her mid-fifties, described unflatteringly by the *Wanganui Herald* as a woman 'of medium height and spare figure with a considerable stoop, iron grey hair and heavy, rather square features of decidedly unintellectual type'. She was charged with causing the death of Emily Spicer after a botched abortion. As well as performing some sort of operation she had provided her with Towle's Pills for Females, advertised to 'quickly correct all irregularities, and relieve the distressing symptoms so prevalent with the sex'.[33] (The euphemisms are fairly obvious.) The trial was widely reported and the eventual verdict of not guilty caused a 'sensation' in court. The *Wanganui Herald* was appalled, claiming that the jury had branded the dying girl a 'wilful, corrupt and malicious perjurer' by declaring Caroline Peyman innocent.[34] If nothing else, the case illustrated the desperation felt by women who became pregnant without support, along with the opportunities for unscrupulous or unqualified practitioners.

Quackery?

Caroline Peyman was part of a broader trend. Female 'gynaecologists' appeared alongside increasing numbers of alternative medicine practitioners at the end of the century. In Dunedin in 1893 Madame Burnley, 'Eminent Gynaecologist and Lady Specialist', offered consultation on all diseases, with her own 'corrective pills a specialty'. Patients could be 'treated equally well at a distance', she reassured the ladies of Oamaru in their local paper. She advertised alongside 'Professor Burnley M.E., The Eminent Medical Electrician'.[35]

At the other end of the country in Auckland were 'Mrs Dr Burnaby' and her husband, Dr William Burnaby. They arrived from Sydney, where Helena Burnaby had advertised as 'the only lady physician' in the city.[36] They quickly became known in New Zealand, where they gave 'men only' and 'women only' lectures on medical matters. After her husband died suddenly in 1894, Helena became 'Dr Helen Burnaby, MD DDS', continuing to lecture and advertise as an '"Eclectic" Physician and Surgeon'.[37] In fact, as a 1900 Australian inquiry revealed, she had no formal qualifications, merely having 'studied' with 'Dr Matthew McLarin of Boston'.[38] She was, however, an accomplished performer. Her first appearances on the public platform had been not as a medical lecturer but as a singer in Ballarat, where she also ran a ladies' school in the 1860s. She had also married Henry Cazaly, a marriage conveniently forgotten when she tied the knot with William Burnaby several thousand kilometres away in Boston in 1883. Reinvention was Helen's speciality, and she was well suited to the turn-of-century 'medical' business, which was as much entertainment as science.[39]

Alongside Mrs Dr Burnaby's advertisements were those for Mrs Clucas & Co.'s herbal remedies, for Madame Zenobia (aka Mrs Cowan), 'the greatest palmist in New Zealand', and for clairvoyant, palmist and phrenologist Madame Wine, who claimed to 'read past and future by sight'.[40] Madame Wine attracted the attention of an enterprising young journalist who sought her advice and wrote an exposé in 1889, making the most of her dropped 'h's', several husbands and overall charlatanism.

The reporter remarked disapprovingly that she made a considerable fortune out of gullible servant girls.[41]

By 1894 palmistry and fortune-telling were indictable offences. In that year Lily Hansen, alias Madame Tisher, was taken to court by a policeman for 'telling his fortune' in Wellington. The reporters clearly enjoyed the case, relishing the policeman's discomfiture as his various foibles were revealed in the details of Madame Tisher's predictions. She was found not guilty. Madame Tisher, who had certificates in palmistry, had been traversing the North Island since 1891. She held séances in Whanganui and palm readings in Feilding, Dannevirke and Wellington. By the time she reached New Plymouth in 1892 she was also a herbalist, who could be 'consulted on all complaints and diseases of the Heart and Lungs, Asthma, Indigestion and Consumption'. She claimed the daughter of Parihaka spiritual leader Te Whiti-o-Rongomai as a 'patient', who was 'getting on remarkably well under a course of treatment'. She advertised as a scientific palmist in 1894 and, undeterred by her appearance in court, continued to practise, advertising in the South Island until the turn of the century.[42]

Beneath bodices and skirts

Like the discomforts of pregnancy or 'restoring regularity', the intricacies and intimacies of undergarments were best discussed with a fellow sufferer. There was a market for specialist stay makers, although they often included other needlework services and goods in their businesses.

Nelson's Charlotte Packer combined stay-making with straw-bonnet manufacture in the 1840s, as she had in Middlesex before emigrating in 1841.[43] Mrs Howie, stay maker in Auckland's West Queen Street, possibly the wife of shipwright Robert, advertised twice in 1849 and then vanished.[44] Sarah Legg lasted longer than most. She wasted no time after disembarking in Auckland in January 1861 with her husband Edward and boxes of 'First class Stock … of French Stays, Corsets of every style'. Claiming to be from London's Regent Street, and able to produce 'testimonials from ladies of the highest distinction in England', she opened her business

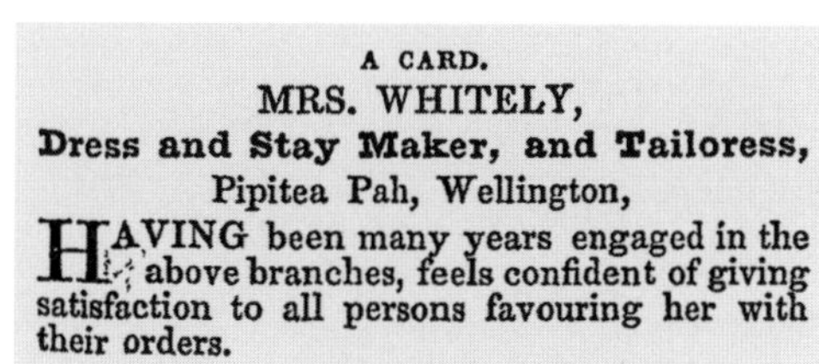

One of the first stay makers to advertise, albeit only once, was Mrs Whitely.

New Zealand Gazette and Wellington Spectator, 26 June 1841

conveniently 'adjoining Mrs Brown's millinery shop' in Victoria Street.[45] As a 'practical Stay-maker', she promised 'perfect fit, ease and comfort'.[46] She did not appear in business for herself either as Mrs Legg or Miss Whitbread in London, but may have worked for someone else, using emigration to make the leap from employee to businesswoman. She was successful, moving within a year to bigger premises on Queen Street, where she advertised as a 'French Corset and Elastic Belt Maker'. Her customers included Lady Mary Ann Martin, wife of Chief Justice Sir William Martin, Barbara Layard, wife of Sir George Grey's private secretary Edgar Leopold Layard, and 'other ladies of distinction'.[47]

Sarah's husband Edward, meanwhile, sold pianos made by his brother in London, John Legg. Sarah and Edward were already in their fifties when they emigrated and it is possible that the family firm dispatched Edward as an agent. After he died in 1865, Sarah continued both the corsetry and piano businesses. She 'retir[ed] from the shop branch' in August of that year but continued to take orders for corsetry and to 'IMPORT (and keep in stock) the same celebrated PIANOFORTES which were so universally admired by patrons of the late EDWARD LEGG'.[48] These were tough times in Auckland, however, and Sarah also advertised a 'comfortable bedroom and sitting-room, with attendance, on reasonable terms' for 'a gentleman'.[49] In 1868 she moved to Upper Chapel Street, now Federal Street, a less salubrious part of Auckland better known for its bawdy houses than its fashionable stay makers. In 1872, in her sixty-fourth year, Sarah Legg died, described in her death notice as 'relict of Edward Legg, pianoforte importer' rather than as a businesswoman in her own right.[50]

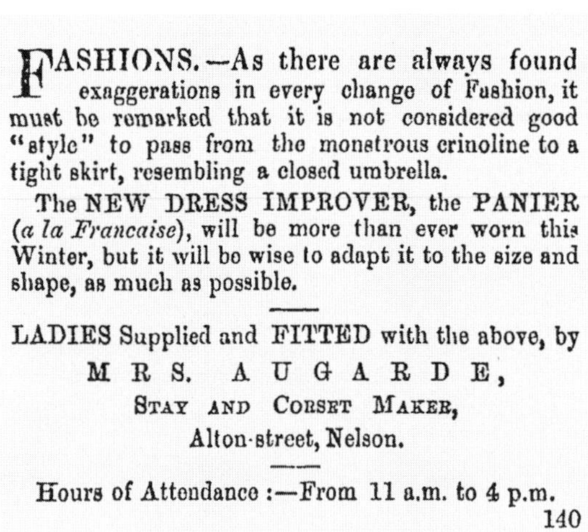
FASHIONS.—As there are always found exaggerations in every change of Fashion, it must be remarked that it is not considered good "style" to pass from the monstrous crinoline to a tight skirt, resembling a closed umbrella.

The NEW DRESS IMPROVER, the PANIER (*a la Francaise*), will be more than ever worn this Winter, but it will be wise to adapt it to the size and shape, as much as possible.

LADIES Supplied and FITTED with the above, by

MRS. AUGARDE,

STAY AND CORSET MAKER,

Alton-street, Nelson.

Hours of Attendance :—From 11 a.m. to 4 p.m.

140

Lucy Ann Augarde set herself up as a fashion expert in Nelson.

Nelson Examiner and New Zealand Chronicle, 23 January 1869

If Sarah Legg took on piano importing as an afterthought, 45-year-old Lucy Ann Augarde did the same with corsetry. She and husband Henry were in Nelson for 18 years, as farmers, hoteliers and regular singers at local concerts, before she appeared in Alton Street in 1869, offering to supply and fit the 'NEW DRESS IMPROVER, the PANIER (*a la Francaise*)', which created a bustle effect. Lucy Ann Augarde (née Unwin) was a Londoner but exploited her French-sounding name, advertising as a 'French and English Stay and Corset Maker'. She was also discreet, offering to attend ladies 'at their residence'. Meanwhile her husband ran multiple enterprises, as auctioneer, commission agent and employment agent. Quite where she gained her stay-making skills is unclear. She had married at 16, given birth to at least 16 children and had been busy in other endeavours. She seems to have failed to convince Nelson women of her expertise: her advertisements disappeared quickly.[51]

One Christchurch stay-making business lasted nearly 40 years with three different proprietors, who diversified when times were tough. Its founder, Henrietta Bowler, followed her husband Frederick to Christchurch in 1866. He had been in the colonies since December 1863 looking unsuccessfully for gold, after leaving Henrietta in Taunton, Somerset, with one child and another on the way. Upon her arrival in Christchurch Henrietta opened the Canterbury Stay and Crinoline Manufactory in High Street.[52] The 1867 *Stevens and Bartholomew Directory* listed it as the business of 'F.C. Bowler', but it was Henrietta who advertised.[53]

Ten years later Henrietta sold the 'stock, materials and patterns', along with the goodwill of the business, to dressmaker Ruth Verrall, who was based in Yeldham House on the corner of Cashel and Montreal streets.[54] Ruth, who had arrived in the colony as a seven-year-old in 1859 with her parents and siblings, possessed, she claimed, 'a thorough knowledge' of the business. She advertised as 'successor to Mrs Bowler', while ensuring customers were aware that she was at a different address. This is an early example of a woman passing on the goodwill but not the premises of a business, as did Elizabeth Willcox (see Chapter 6). Ruth continued dressmaking and millinery, as often advertising children's and ladies' hats as corsetry.[55] She was regarded as 'the crack staymaker' of Christchurch, at least by a *Southland Times* reporter at the 1882 International Christchurch Exhibition who suggested that the 'blue and pink satin corsets, adorned at the necks with expensive Maltese lace, are so showy that I really think the ladies ought to wear them outside their dresses, as I have seen the farmers' wives and daughters doing with their stays at Berne and Solerne, in Switzerland'.[56]

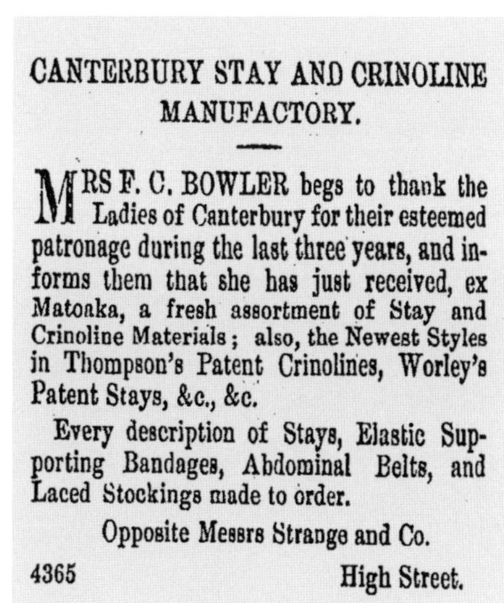
CANTERBURY STAY AND CRINOLINE MANUFACTORY.

MRS F. C. BOWLER begs to thank the Ladies of Canterbury for their esteemed patronage during the last three years, and informs them that she has just received, ex Matoaka, a fresh assortment of Stay and Crinoline Materials; also, the Newest Styles in Thompson's Patent Crinolines, Worley's Patent Stays, &c., &c.

Every description of Stays, Elastic Supporting Bandages, Abdominal Belts, and Laced Stockings made to order.

Opposite Messrs Strange and Co.

4365 High Street.

Lyttelton Times, 12 March 1869

Despite this accolade, Ruth Verrall went bankrupt in 1886. Upon resuming business in 1888 she identified a new fad, becoming the sole agent in Christchurch for Flamwell's Patent Metal-corners Scientific Dress-cutting System. She gave up millinery in 1899 but continued her corsetry until 1905, when she advertised the stay-making business for sale, carefully reminding people that this was 'late Mrs F.C. Bowler's' and the 'Chief Corset Business in the colony'. She offered to teach the new owner all necessary skills.[57] A Mrs Spensley took up the challenge, '2 doors from Miss Verrall's and under her supervision'. Her advertisements did not continue for long, however, in the era of the unbound New Woman. So ended a 37-year-long multigenerational business.[58]

Corsetry businesses were ideal for women, but their longevity was restricted by changing fashions, and by the turn of the century a woman would have been better off designing and making bloomers and bicycle costumes. As with most businesses, those who changed with the times and diversified did best.

'Wanted: good general servants'[59]

The 'servant problem' was much aired in colonial drawing rooms. From Melbourne to Dunedin, Hobart to Auckland, the grumbling of middle-class matrons could be heard, deploring the cheekiness, independence and general lack of ability of the overpaid, uppity madams they were forced to employ for cooking, cleaning and childcare. Nelson settler Martha Adams was taken aback when her servant suggested she be addressed as 'Miss Sarah', and Lady Barker in Canterbury felt threatened by the presumptuousness of her colonial maid's request to borrow her best riding habit so she could copy the pattern.[60] Jemima Martin described servants as 'exceptionally independent' and 'the plague of the colony',[61] while Whanganui's Jessie Campbell complained to her sister in 1845 that her servant had quickly 'found out her own value [and] neither can nor will work'. She had 'two qualifications not often met with here, sobriety and honesty', but 'The best I can say of her is that she is kind to the children.'[62] As William Swainson declared in 1853, 'the only serious drawback to New Zealand as a place of residence for ladies is the difficulty of finding and keeping good servants'.[63]

Employers went across the Tasman to find their servants. In 1859 Nelson publican Martha Lewthwaite hired her hotel cook Hannah Veck and servant Ann Jervis from her friend Jane Bunter of the Barkly Arms in Melbourne. Mr and Mrs Elderton entrepreneurially advertised their Melbourne registry office in the *Otago*

Mrs Harriet Humphrey's Servants' Registry Office in Main Street, Masterton, in the 1890s was, typically, run alongside many other enterprises. Started in 1892, it disappeared after 1901, along with Harriet herself. Wairarapa Archive, 97-151/72

Witness in 1861.[64] There was a crying need, therefore, not only for domestic servants, but for agencies to supply and screen them. Businesswomen and men in New Zealand recognised the opportunity to cash in. For a small commission, registry office proprietors would match servants, mostly female but sometimes male, with employers. Mrs Hungerford in Pitt Street in Auckland charged 1s in advance for this service in 1866.[65]

Registry offices placed all types of servants in private homes: cooks, general domestics, nursemaids, kitchen maids, laundresses and nursery governesses – as well as finding barmaids, dancing girls, waitresses, waiters and billiard markers for hotels. Country servants who knew something of dairying, cheese and butter-making were sought after. Smart registry office proprietors also interacted with their communities in other ways. Mrs Hungerford sold ladies' fancy work on commission.[66] Barbara Allan in Dunedin often carried advertisements for rooms to let and, when James Simpson Read decamped leaving his wife and children to fend for themselves, information was asked for through her office.[67] Margaret Chapman, whose husband George ran a bookshop, stationers and circulating library and produced an Auckland trade directory, did not charge for her employment office service. It was used to project a spirit of community service and as what is now known as a loss leader, attracting customers to their other businesses.[68]

A good registry office proprietor had to inspire confidence in her (or his) ability to judge character, on both sides of the employment equation. In 1867 Mary Dick in Hokitika advertised that she could 'at all time suit employers with good Servants, and Servants may rely upon obtaining respectable situations'. She also promised 'prompt attention to country orders'.[69] Country employers, who paid their servants' fares, trusted the registry office proprietor to provide respectable and good servants quickly. Having connections helped. Dunedin registry office proprietor Caroline Alpenny had been the matron of an immigrant ship and was friendly with Maria Rye of the FMCES. As soon as she arrived in Dunedin in 1863 she propelled herself into the public eye by giving lectures on the benefits of adult education for both sexes.[70] Barbara Allan's connections were more family-orientated. Her brothers had already emigrated – one was an immigration agent, the other a respected schoolteacher, so she moved in the right circles.

Servants' registries could also be added to established businesses, albeit with varying degrees of success. In 1851 the *Otago Witness* added a labourers' and servants' registry office, hours 12–1pm daily. When applicants found the office unattended, the editor admitted a little shamefacedly that the good intentions of the scheme's organisers had been thwarted by the 'cumbrous' 12-member committee. He also explained that the newspaper would happily receive written communications, but that they could not 'attend to verbal applications, as we find it leads to gossiping, and interferes with the business of the office'.[71] Dunedin would have to wait nearly a decade for commission agent G.L. Fleury and Mrs Bowern to open servants' registry offices in 1860 and 1861 respectively.[72] Miss Margaret Maguire opened a shop in Carlyle Street in Napier in July 1864, offering 'juvenile dressmaking, Baby Linen and Ladies Underclothing'. By October she had diversified, 'having been induced by the desire of several Ladies' to open a servants' registry office.[73] This may have been prompted by the advertisements of Josephine Venables from Auckland, who was offering to send servants south to Napier (see Chapter 12).[74] A year later Margaret

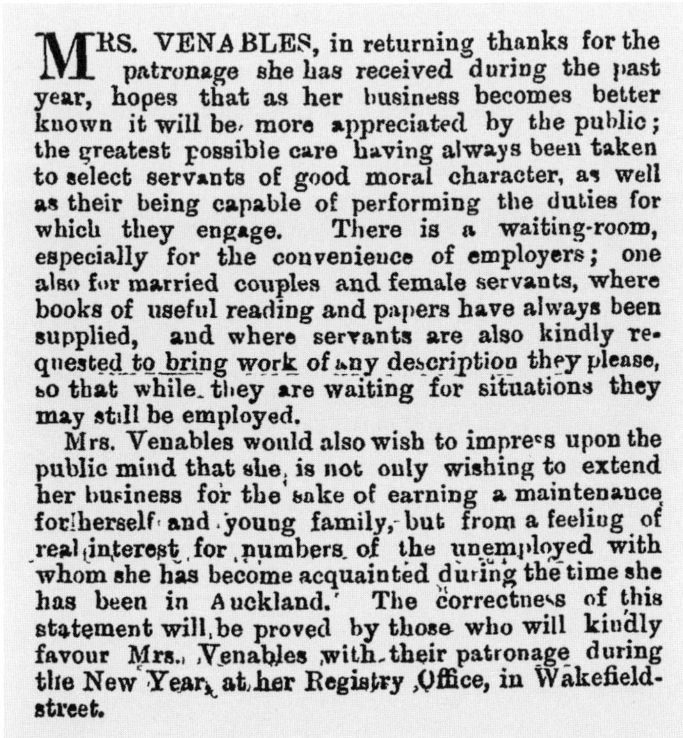

MRS. VENABLES, in returning thanks for the patronage she has received during the past year, hopes that as her business becomes better known it will be more appreciated by the public; the greatest possible care having always been taken to select servants of good moral character, as well as their being capable of performing the duties for which they engage. There is a waiting-room, especially for the convenience of employers; one also for married couples and female servants, where books of useful reading and papers have always been supplied, and where servants are also kindly requested to bring work of any description they please, so that while they are waiting for situations they may still be employed.

Mrs. Venables would also wish to impress upon the public mind that she is not only wishing to extend her business for the sake of earning a maintenance for herself and young family, but from a feeling of real interest for numbers of the unemployed with whom she has become acquainted during the time she has been in Auckland. The correctness of this statement will be proved by those who will kindly favour Mrs. Venables with their patronage during the New Year, at her Registry Office, in Wakefield-street.

Josephine Venables' advertisements, if a little wordy, were models of their kind, emphasising respectability, convenience and comfort, a solid appreciation of the work ethic and sympathy for those worse off than herself. *Daily Southern Cross*, 3 January 1866

Maguire was also taking in boarders and did not continue with the registry office.[75] Her competition by then included both Mrs Venables and a newcomer in the sector, Henry Yates, who started his own business locally in 1865.[76]

Margaret Holland (later Bean), who had a millinery shop in Christchurch from 1868, added a servants' registry office in 1871.[77] Newly married and almost immediately separated, Catherine Stent opened a registry office 'in connection with her [year-old] Green Grocery & Fruit Establishment' in Victoria Avenue in Whanganui in 1879, promising not to send any domestic servants to employers without 'first-class references'. Whether her joint businesses would have blossomed is impossible to tell. She died in 1881 at the age of 40.[78]

Specialising in servants

Two specialist registry offices each lasted four decades in Dunedin. One was simply an employment agency, run for much of its existence by a Scottish emigrant spinster. The other combined a servants' home and registry office for its early existence and had a series of proprietors, including a well-connected English divorcée and an outspoken married woman.

Barbara Allan, from Scotland, started out as a dressmaker. She was based in George Street in 1863 in partnership with Christina Little ('from Miss Metcalf's in Edinburgh and Mrs Russell's, Court Dressmaker, Dublin'). Barbara had emigrated four years earlier from Skye with her sisters and her mother, joining two brothers already in New Zealand.[79] After Christina married Henry Dreixler in 1864 and moved to Invercargill, Barbara went solo and diversified, adding the servants' registry office. Her dressmaking lapsed as the trade in servants boomed: she extended her premises in 1866 because of 'an increase in business'.[80]

Barbara Allan's advertisements were brief – she had no need to blow her own trumpet – merely reminding Dunedin residents of her presence in George Street. In 1878 she added 'Established 1864' to emphasise her longevity. After moving around the corner to St Andrew's Street in the 1880s, she was joined by her younger sister Jessie. Both were listed as registry office keepers on the 1893 electoral roll. When Mrs Stuart (Maria Eleanor) Mackintosh took over the 40-year-old business in 1905, she strategically advertised it as 'late Miss Allan's' for nearly two years and kept it going until the middle of 1909. Jessie Allan died in 1913 and Barbara in 1917 aged 88, her estate worth £669. Barbara's recognition of a market opportunity in 1864, and her courage to change businesses, had paid off. The registry office had supported two spinster sisters for four decades.[81]

Barbara's was not the only show in town – in Belgrave Chambers in Princes Street was English divorcée Caroline Alpenny. As well as having close connections to Maria Rye, she was an experienced businesswoman and a woman with a mission, inspired by well-known promoter of female emigration to Australia, Caroline Chisholm.[82] Caroline Alpenny had already established a flax farm in Ireland to provide work for women and girls, and her servants' registry office was founded in 1863 on similar altruistic – and money-making – principles. She ran the office for eight years, claiming to have averaged 2000 placements per year, gave public lectures, and provided the *Otago Daily Times* with labour market reports. After her second husband, Dunedin Town Board member and local chemist George Howard, died in 1871, Caroline returned to London, where she talked herself into a position recruiting government immigrants for Otago. In 1874 the 37 young Irish Catholic women she sent from the Cork workhouse were subjected to great scrutiny upon arrival in Otago and their moral character found wanting. Caroline was sacked and turned her attention away from New Zealand.[83]

As well as providing a registry office service, Caroline Alpenny offered accommodation for female servants. This was recognition of the much-publicised problem of where to house newly arrived, single, female, domestic-servant immigrants and those between placements. She not only obtained servant clients through her connection with Maria Rye and various emigration schemes, but, by housing them, had a ready supply of employees available at a moment's notice.

Exploiting entrepreneurial opportunities

Caroline's registry office was taken over in 1871 by Marion Cane and then in 1875 by Mary Dick, who was an experienced businesswoman.[84] After migrating in 1860 and marrying Frederick Dick two years later, Mary ran a registry office and servants' home in Weld Street, Hokitika, from 1867 until 1874. Her direct competition was Josephine Venables, now Macdonald, who had remarried and moved from Auckland. Josephine advertised in Hokitika for 'tidy little maids from 12 to 15'.[85]

Mary upped her entrepreneurial game in June 1871, when, apparently 'at the request of several of her constituents', she announced she was going to recruit 'Servants suitable for the Coast' from Melbourne, requesting applications from interested employers. Her foray across the Tasman to recruit domestic servants was unusual, but not unheard of. Perhaps she had been inspired by the exploits of Blessington Flood (see Chapter 12) a few years earlier, or, like Caroline Alpenny, by Caroline Chisholm, who imported servants on a much larger scale from England to Australia in the 1840s and 1850s.[86] Nevertheless, one local paper, the *Evening Star*, was puzzled, wondering how she would succeed when wages for domestic servants were considerably higher in Melbourne, ranging from £28 to £39

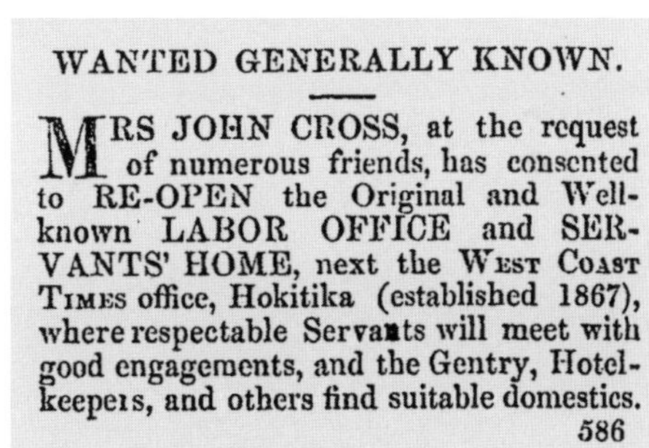

WANTED GENERALLY KNOWN.

MRS JOHN CROSS, at the request of numerous friends, has consented to RE-OPEN the Original and Well-known LABOR OFFICE and SERVANTS' HOME, next the WEST COAST TIMES office, Hokitika (established 1867), where respectable Servants will meet with good engagements, and the Gentry, Hotel-keepers, and others find suitable domestics. 586

Mary Dick had more competition after she moved across Weld Street to Verandah Cottage, when Wilhelmina Cross took over her premises.

West Coast Times, 23 August 1869

per annum. Servants in Nelson could expect from £15 to £20, the same as in Auckland, while Hawke's Bay wages were lower still. The paper did not specify Hokitika wages but they must have dropped since 1868, when the Dicks reported that general servants could earn more than 20s a week (£52 per annum). It is not known whether Mary's Melbourne expedition in August was successful, although her appointment as matron of the local hospital in December 1871 suggests possibly not.[87]

Like her husband Frederick, who was a frequent and often outspoken correspondent to the local newspaper on a number of matters, Mary made her feelings known. In 1871 she wrote an open letter to the *West Coast Times*, 'return[ing] my sincere thanks' to the board of management of the Manchester Unity Hall for 'their kind and considerate behavior to me on Saturday last' but expressing her disappointment that 'their tender feelings would not allow them to pay me the compliment I think due to a female, and ask me in Mr Dick's absence for the large amount of £2 3s 2d, which I *then* owed them (after being eight months their tenant)'.[88] When many women chose to hide behind coverture to avoid paying their debts, Mary wanted to be held accountable.

Mary's time as matron of the local hospital was brief. In May 1872 she was dismissed following complaints about her 'inattention'. Mary was livid, complaining to the *West Coast Times* that she had been 'placed in a false position, and my character injured', by the lack of proper investigation of the complaints. An anonymous letter claiming to be from a former patient declared that 'had Mrs Dick been my nearest relative, she could not have paid more attention, both day and night, than she did to myself and the other patients … a more kind hearted and attentive lady as a matron of a hospital … I never saw'.[89]

In 1874 Mary and Frederick moved to Dunedin, where they became embroiled in a dispute with another registry office and servants' home proprietor, Elizabeth Clayton. A widow supported in part by remittances from her sons in Australia, Elizabeth had seen an opportunity in 1873 to 'supply in Dunedin a much felt want in the shape of a Home for the accommodation of governesses, shopwomen, and female servants'. She promised reasonable rates and, like Caroline Alpenny, combined a registry office with the home in Dowling Street. The *Otago Daily Times* admired her 'praiseworthy exertions' to establish 'a Home of unimpeachable respectability'.[90]

When the home was subject to an arson attack under strange circumstances late in 1874, Elizabeth herself was suspected, because she had insured her furniture, but there were more obvious culprits. Elizabeth's boarders included Frederick and Mary Dick. Mary had begun advertising as the proprietor of the registry office, announcing herself as Elizabeth's successor. Elizabeth immediately declared this to be 'totally unauthorised' and that the registry office was closed. She gave the Dicks notice to quit. They claimed she had broken their agreement, which does appear likely, and Frederick Dick told a witness, perhaps unwisely, that 'he would make it hot for her'. The jury could not decide who had started the subsequent fire.[91]

Mary Dick won the war, continuing to advertise her proprietorship of the registry office and boarding house, while Elizabeth, who was ill, disappeared in April 1875, possibly to Sydney. By June Mary Dick had moved her registry office to the premises previously occupied by Caroline Alpenny and Marion Cane. Frederick died 12 years later but Mary continued the business until 1908, when Mrs Fraser took over. The registry office closed its doors in 1913, half a century after Caroline Alpenny had founded it. When the indomitable Mary Dick died in 1917, aged 85, she was, unlike many others, remembered as a businesswoman, a role she had filled for 41 years.[92]

Splashing out

In addition to the natural hot springs, around which hotels and tourism developed early on, notably involving Māori enterprise, sea bathing, public baths, hydropathy and later Turkish baths were popular in colonial New Zealand. But decorum needed to be preserved. According to the provisions of the Constabulary Act of 1849, bathing 'within view of a public wharf, quay, bridge, street or other place of public resort so as to offend against decency, between the hours of eight in the morning and eight in the evening' risked a fine of 20s.[93] Bathing was also strictly segregated by sex, with different times or different facilities for men and women. There were openings for businesswomen, as proprietors and partners, to provide respectable attendance and supervision for ladies visiting the baths.

Bathing machines protected female modesty at the seaside. In Auckland in January 1857, the *New Zealander* announced with some pleasure the opening of 'Webster's Bathing Machines': 'Mr and Mrs Webster' were 'prepared to supply the want so long felt, of the means of sea-bathing for ladies' at the Auckland Baths on Wynyard Pier. Elizabeth Webster (see Chapter 6) had a millinery business but also sold tickets for the baths and probably also attended the female clients.[94] In 1876 Louisa Oram of Christchurch's New Brighton Hotel advertised her hotel's machine in 'the most approved English style' and 'with efficient attendance and every convenience' on New Brighton Beach.[95]

Public seawater baths were built in many coastal towns, sometimes by public subscription and sometimes through private enterprise. In October 1858, after a flurry of public subscriptions, Nelson opened its baths. A single bath cost 1s while an annual ticket was £1. 'The ladies baths especially received several visitors,' recorded the *Nelson Examiner*.[96] There were even public baths in Invercargill, where the climate was hardly conducive to sea bathing except for the very hardy. Located in Esk Street, they were spring rather than seawater, and both hot and cold baths were available.[97] The Auckland Salt-Water Bath Company opened Ladies' Baths in 1867, charging £2 2s a year, or 6d for a single bath. Women were allocated certain times for bathing, 'during which a Red Flag will be hoisted'. They were permitted in the water from 10am until 1pm on weekdays and 9 until 10.30am on Sundays. This, of course, left the warmest part of the day for men to enjoy the water.[98]

A cure for all ills

Henry Barraclough set himself up as a 'medical herbalist' in Nelson in the late 1860s, opening hydropathic baths in Hardy Street. Hydropathy, one of a plethora of increasingly popular alternative medical systems, used various water treatments to alleviate and cure diseases. Henry had decamped from Castlemaine in Victoria, where he had narrowly escaped conviction on several occasions for administering medication to patients who later died. As one qualified medical practitioner commented, 'I do not recognise Mr Barraclough as a doctor; he evidently thought that the lungs were the liver.'[99] He had better luck in Nelson, where he and his public baths were well received. Henry's wife Mary Ann sold 'warm bath tickets' for £1 6s each. Sometime before 1875 Henry disappeared back across the Tasman, where, as 'Dr Barraclough', he established a pharmacy in Boggabri, New South Wales. The Nelson baths moved to the Toi Toi Valley, where Mary Ann took on son Henry as a partner and also took in 'Lady boarders'. In March 1880 she promised 'a safe Cure' for 'Rheumatism, Dropsy, Indigestion and severe Colds' at 'Mrs Barraclough's Hydropathic Baths'. When Mary Ann died a few months later, aged 49, her son Henry assumed his father's mantle more completely, running the baths, advertising herbal cures and eventually becoming 'Professor' Henry Barraclough.[100]

In Auckland, Eliza and John Warmoll reinvented themselves and opened a hydropathic hospital at Sunny Brae in Takapuna in 1889. A granddaughter remembered particularly the baths 'of various shapes and sizes … on a raised dais'

Entrepreneurial Eliza Warmoll, previously Tye, née Holland, had a storefront in Thames and sold drapery on the road, then went into the hydropathy business.

Private collection: Maureen O'Connor and Heather Matthews

in a large zinc-lined room. 'One was shaped as a big boot for a foot and leg bath [and] there was a sitz bath with a back to it, and some big basin shapes'. The water was heated in a 'big copper cylinder' on a two-oven stove in the kitchen.[101]

Full of hot air

Inspired by similar developments across the Tasman, the first Turkish baths appeared in New Zealand in Dunedin in 1874.[102] These hot air baths were often connected to hydropathic establishments, adding sophistication, and were frequently run by couples. As ever, a female presence was desirable to maintain respectability and, as with other public baths, female clients were allotted specific times. In Dunedin, Wednesdays were set aside 'exclusively for the benefit of ladies, who will be properly attended to by Mrs Burton'. With her husband William, Mary Burton had 'many years' experience in the management of baths in Australia and Great Britain'.[103] Thursdays were ladies' day at Auckland's Turkish Baths in 1875. In attendance was Elizabeth Sykes who, with her husband, later moved to Wellington and introduced the 'Hot Air Bath' to invalids of that city.[104]

Unlike many other wives, Mary Hall had nothing to do with her husband John's hydropathy and Turkish bath business, which spread from Dunedin to Christchurch to Wellington from the 1870s. Instead, Ellen Cox appeared as an assistant in the early 1880s, not so coincidentally at the same time as John Hall was sued for failing to maintain his wife and seven children. The 1882 court case identified Ellen as 'the "lady" who was the cause of this little trouble'. In contrast to the impression given by his frequent advertisements, John claimed to be unable to maintain his family because his Christchurch business was attracting few 'patients'. Business must have improved, for John and Ellen built Turkish baths in Manners Street in Wellington in the 1890s and moved north, leaving Mary in Christchurch, and John's son Robert running the Dunedin and Christchurch businesses. When John died aged 63 in 1900, he was described in the *Star* as 'the husband of Mary Hall, Huxley Street, Sydenham', but he bequeathed Wellington's 'Hall's Turkish Baths' to his 'housekeeper', named as 'Ellen Cox Hall'. 'Mrs Hall' continued to run the business until her death at 80 in 1922.[105]

A feminine presence

Women, whether wives or otherwise, were critical to the bathing business, in order to preserve respectability, discretion and decorum. When Raymond Collins bought the Wellington Swimming Baths in 1868 he reassured customers that his widowed mother Margaret would be on hand to supervise the ladies' baths. Margaret was not an ideal choice. In 1871 she landed her son in court by selling porter, without a licence, to a young sailor at the baths. According to the arresting policeman, Raymond had cursed 'that fool of an old woman', because as the owner he was responsible. A one-time oyster seller in Lambton Quay, Margaret was no stranger to business and accustomed to standing her ground. When she claimed that she had merely left the porter on the table in front of the sailor, and so had not sold it, 'the manner in which [she] gave evidence', according to the newspaper, 'did not improve her son's case'.[106]

When Henry Meech took over the Wellington Swimming Baths from Raymond that year and renovated them, he made a point of mentioning that 'the Ladies Baths will be considerably more private'.[107] He reassured female customers that Mrs Meech would be 'always in attendance to secure their comfort'.[108] Like Margaret Collins, Matilda Meech had business experience. She had arrived in Wellington from Kent with her first husband, John Sancto, and one of their two daughters in 1855. When John drowned in 1859, leaving Matilda with three young children to support, she opened a fruit shop and general store on Lambton Quay.[109] Judging by the number of civil court cases in which she was either suing or being sued, she was a woman to be reckoned with and her willingness to chase debtors was one reason for her success in business.[110] Matilda continued to run the store after her marriage in 1868 to widowed shipwright, Henry Meech. Her shop closed in the 1870s when Henry and Matilda went into business together, taking over the local saltwater baths.

Matilda was a driving force in the success of the enterprise. Initially the respectable female attendant, she continued the business after Henry's death in 1885. In 1891 she took Wellington City Council to court for polluting her baths and won damages of £200.[111] Mrs Meech's Te Aro Baths at Clyde Quay were a local landmark until 1901, when they were closed and new baths erected by the harbour board nearby. Managed by Matilda's youngest daughter Emma and her husband Alfred Wilton, the new establishment appears not to have compared favourably with Mrs Meech's business. Matilda's 1907 obituary regretted the loss of her baths, which had been 'well-kept and managed profitably'. The location and aspect of the new baths meant they were prone to pollution.[112]

A female economy

Women were ideally placed to take full advantage of the 'female economy', not only in the market for hats, frocks and frippery, but also in more personal services. Midwifery and nursing could provide an income and sometimes accommodation, with practitioners living in and taking over the household while the new mother recovered. It could be acceptably framed as a 'service' to the community and was frequently repackaged as such when written into historical narratives. Later in the century, enterprising and sometimes not entirely ethical businesswomen exploited the mania for alternative health and miraculous cures, their sex proving a distinct advantage. Only slightly less intimate than birthing babies was the provision of corsets and stays, while the ever-pressing need for domestic servants meant that a servants' registry office could be a popular business, whether on its own or in conjunction with other small enterprises. The Victorian obsession with decorum and respectability, at least on the surface, also offered a place for businesswomen in the new leisure economy, as chaperones at ladies' baths. All of these enterprises were small but they helped to shape the colony, whether by ensuring healthy population growth or contributing to the development of popular culture.

At Old Smith's Store, on Thorndon Flat,
You'll get the best and cheapest *Hat*,
And when you're there you can also choose
For self, Wife, or Child, the cheapest *Shoes*,
Stays, Stockings, Dresses, Frocks, or Blouses,
Coats, Vests, Shirts, or Trowsers;
Gala Plaids, and Calico for Sheeting,
Flannel, Prints, and *Horse-hair Seating*;
Cheap Slops, and Goods of every kind,
With Books to improve the youthful mind;
Brushes, Brooms, all sorts of trade,
Iron Pots, Pick axe, or Spade.
More useful things than I can tell—
Go, to Old Smith's, he'll use you well.
The Store is plain, and to find it easy,
For over the door is *Vide et Crede*.

June 20, 1851.

OLD SMITH,—the noted by the *Independent* as a Rowdy Leader, which he takes to mean a conservative of public interest, has lately purchased a large quantity of Boots, Shoes, Crockery, Paper hangings, &c., and he purposes his customers shall have the advantage of the depressed and over supplied stock in the market; he has lately found an increased retail trace by the low prices he puts upon his goods, which is very flattering to him; and by the distinction of the *Independent*, he still hopes to increase in the estimation of all the thinking population of the Province.

Thorndon Flat,
28th March, 1859.

LOST! LOST! LOST!

OLD SMITH has lost all his Customers, but he knows not where; any one bringing back the same to his store, shall receive a liberal per centage on whatever Goods they purchase.

N.B.—Politics discarded.

1st April, 1859.

John Sidney's 'Old Smith' advertisements were memorable, as were he and his wife Susan.

Wellington Independent, 21 June 1851; *Wellington Independent*, 8 April 1859

Chapter 9

The Corner Shop: For better or for worse

Before the age of department stores and supermarkets, the corner shop was ubiquitous in New Zealand towns.[1] As his advertisements suggest, Old Smith was eccentric but his stock was typical. In smaller towns such shops also sold groceries. Typical, too, was the involvement of Old Smith's wife. It was appropriate that women should also be choosing and selling stock, since many customers were female – the wives and mothers of large families purchasing essential household items and the odd lolly for their clamouring offspring. In these archetypal family businesses wives, as often as husbands, showed entrepreneurial nous. Their names might not have always been above the shop door, but they were business partners and sometimes the de facto heads of both family and business.

Susan and John Sidney Smith established their small shop, Old Smith's, in 1848 in Molesworth Street, where it quickly became a Wellington landmark. By 1865, when John was 62 and Susan 56, she was the front person – advertising in the newspaper and adding a circulating library, servants' registry office and newsagency. She also sold tickets for community events, donated to the local benevolent society and advertised for boarders, although whether on her own account or on behalf of others is unclear.[2] A surviving shop account book from the late 1860s reveals a large customer base reaching the Wairarapa and Rangitikei. Its catalogue record in the Alexander Turnbull Library notes significant male customers, including Bishop Octavius Hadfield and politicians Julius Vogel, Edward Stafford and Alfred Domett, but there were many businesswomen too: school proprietors Margaret Fleetwood, Elizabeth Burbidge, Helen Welch and the Misses Carroll, milliner Emma Marriott and boarding-house keepers Sarah Dougherty and Carolina Liardet.[3] Sadly, few such account books survive to illustrate the interconnectedness of small business communities. In October 1877, 'Mrs Old Smith' retired, passing the newsagency to her neighbour and requesting library books be returned. Less than a month later she was dead. Her obituary recorded she was 'quite one of the local institutions', 'much liked and respected', and would be 'greatly missed by Wellington ladies'. Her husband benefitted from his own early retirement, outliving his wife by three years.[4]

Running a corner shop required agility and flexibility. As well as being connected to the local community, one had to juggle multiple products, understand what would sell, create clever marketing strategies and exploit all angles to make every penny count. Susan and John Smith were exemplars, with their multiple businesses run from one shop and quirky advertising. Others also used a range of marketing ideas. Mary Ann Bibby exploited her connections within Māori society and the possibilities of mail-order to create new markets for her Waipawa store in the 1860s.[5] Tom and Annie Scott diversified, running multiple businesses including a ferry, accommodation house, store and mail run at Scotts Ferry in Rangitikei. They picked the right location – on the only route from Wellington to Whanganui – but much of their success was due to Annie's reputed ability to create 'a haven of rest', with 'a dish fit for a king's breakfast', along with her renowned and delicious scones.[6]

Although visible to contemporaries, the participation of women as partners in these enterprises is hard to uncover, particularly if they did not advertise the business themselves. Sometimes only in surviving letters, diaries or memoirs of neighbours and customers, or occasionally in obituaries, is a wife's role in the shop recorded. The obituary of 'Mrs W. Harrison' upon her death at Mangapai aged 92 in 1916 is the only record we have of her involvement in the family shop: 'Harrison's store is one of the old land marks of the district, and to her in a great measure the continued success of the business must be attributed.'[7] It also mentions the otherwise unrecorded Auckland millinery business she ran as Jane Donaldson before marrying widower William Harrison in 1868.[8]

'Mrs Waters' store'

Wives' roles as business partners were valued and respected, if seldom publicly remembered. Emigration boosters used letters featuring such women as exemplars of the colonial experience. In 1848, for example, *Chambers Edinburgh Journal* published a selection of Susan Waters' early letters home to England.[9]

Susan and George Waters arrived in New Zealand in 1842 with two small daughters and George's 16-year-old brother, Thomas. George and Thomas were painters and glaziers by trade. Because there was not initially much call for their skills in Wellington, the family rented land and built a store, 'tumbl[ing] everything saleable … [including] linens and wearables' into it. They bought goods to stock their store from other immigrants and wholesalers as well as from local Māori, who were also their principal customers. As Susan told her sister in 1842, 'We sell whatever we can buy, anything or everything; and are getting a tolerable business.' By the end of 1843, George was employed at his trade and had two journeymen, Thomas helped in the shop, while Susan, as well as caring for four lodgers and the shop, had 'as much employment as I choose in dressmaking, mostly for the native women.'[10]

In 1845 Susan celebrated that she was 'far more easily circumstanced' and able to 'devote my whole time to the care of my family', free from both shop responsibilities and housework, since they now had a servant and a 'respectable' housekeeper. She and George sent their daughters to 'a very excellent person who has a seminary near Wellington … truly grateful that we can well afford it', because the house had become 'so much a place of traffic'. Although they were still living on the shop premises and probably had lodgers, this was the colonial dream. Another aspect of that dream was land ownership. As Susan told her sister in 1847, 'It is true we do not save or lay by much money, because we find it more to our advantage here to expend our profits on land. We have bought a lot of land besides that we live on.'[11]

The 1850s were not so prosperous but the shop survived. It was now popularly known as Mrs Waters' store, though the directories recorded her husband as proprietor. Susan's domestic responsibilities had again expanded to include business activities. George's brother Thomas was by now in his own business and had also married a businesswoman, bonnet-cleaner Elizabeth Luxford. In 1865 George was imprisoned for selling guns to Māori during the wars in Taranaki and Waikato, so Susan ran the store while he served his time. Upon his release George resumed nominal management of the store until his death in 1873, although it continued to be known locally as Mrs Waters' shop.[12]

Despite George's imprisonment the family remained highly respected in Wellington, where a petition to mitigate his prison sentence attracted over 650 signatures. His obituary made no mention of the conviction, praising him for playing 'an active but unassuming part in furthering the public interest of the province'.[13] Susan was prominent in the Wesleyan community, serving on the Ladies' Christian Association committee and running stalls at bazaars.[14] When she retired from shopkeeping in 1883, the store was advertised as a continuing business, having 'been conducted for a considerable number of years by the proprietress and … capable of great extension with every prospect of success'.[15] Susan's successor, Mary Durrant, did 'a very nice lucrative trade … [in] Drapery and Groceries'.[16] Susan lived to be 88, dying in December 1899. She did not rate an obituary, although she had been mentioned in her son's obituary the previous January for being 'as widely esteemed as her late son for her benevolence and for her example of a woman's work'.[17]

Head of the household

Hannah Baker and her sickly 54-year-old husband George arrived in Nelson with their children in 1856. She quickly recognised a moneymaking opportunity and started trading goods. While George opened a storefront on Trafalgar Street, Hannah returned to England in 1857 to select stock. Before leaving Nelson she also offered to 'take charge of any commissions entrusted to her care' and advised that she was 'a purchaser of silver plate and New Zealand curiosities for cash'. A year later the entrepreneurial Hannah returned not only with her own stock but with 1500 pairs of boots, personally 'selected by her in England'. Local boot warehouse owner Benjamin Jackson purchased her whole shipment. On the return journey from England she also picked up a 30-year-old husband, James Duff Hewett, for her 14-year-old daughter Ellen. They were married three weeks after her fifteenth birthday. Ellen was widowed five years later when, on 9 February 1865, James was killed in a Hauhau raid on their farm.[18] Meanwhile Hannah and George continued to import millinery and drapery to sell 'at the lowest possible prices'. George died in 1864 and Hannah returned to England a year later with her three daughters, including Ellen and her children.[19]

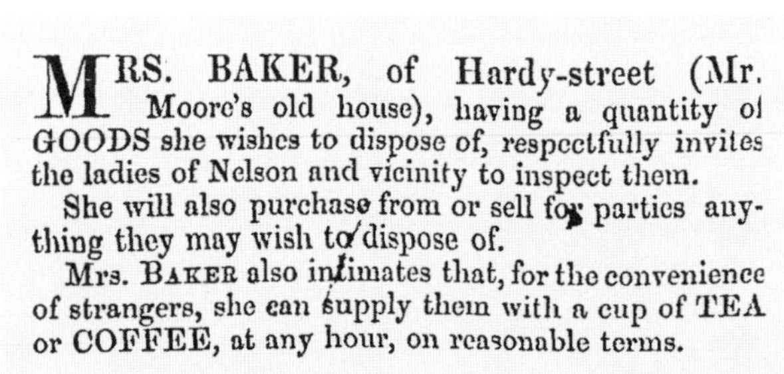
MRS. BAKER, of Hardy-street (Mr. Moore's old house), having a quantity of GOODS she wishes to dispose of, respectfully invites the ladies of Nelson and vicinity to inspect them.

She will also purchase from or sell for parties anything they may wish to dispose of.

Mrs. Baker also intimates that, for the convenience of strangers, she can supply them with a cup of TEA or COFFEE, at any hour, on reasonable terms.

Hannah Baker's address to the 'ladies' of the area imbued her wares with a sense of desirability and class. One might even have inferred that she was not actually a tradeswoman, but a lady discreetly offloading select items surplus to her own requirements.

Nelson Examiner, 6 September 1856

Mary Snow was also the real head of a family enterprise. She and her husband William were 38 and 39 respectively when they arrived in Nelson in 1842 with eight children aged from 14 to just six weeks. William was an agricultural labourer on the passenger list and a tailor three years later, but by 1849 they had a store in Trafalgar Street as well as a farm in Waimea East (later Richmond). Newspapers in 1852 carried proud advertisements for 'William Snow's Victoria House', where he sold 'port and sherry wines of the finest quality'. In 1855 William retired from the shop, thanking his customers for their 13 years of support, and he and Mary moved to a new house on Waimea Road.[20] The 1849 Nelson census and a later sketch map by early resident W.H. Cole, however, both showed Mary as the storekeeper in Trafalgar Street, and in 1853 it was 'Mrs Snow' announcing the arrival of an exciting new array of goods at Victoria House. She also rented out cottages, had an informal servants' registry and sold tickets for local church concerts.[21] The area around the Waimea Road property became known as 'Mrs Snow's Hill'.[22] Evidence in an 1861 court case also pointed to Mary's exercise of authority. Tenant Ninian Lockhart declared he paid rent to her, not her husband, and that she was 'the most prominent person in the transactions' he had with the family. Another witness said that it was 'Mrs Snow who refused to give the bills' as requested. Thomas, her son, who was being sued, would act only 'if his mother would consent'. He was represented legally as Mary's agent, although, technically, he should have been described as his father's agent because, as a married woman, Mary had no property. It was clear to everyone who was really in charge.[23]

When Mary died in 1884, the *Nelson Evening Mail* described her as having 'taken an active part ... in the trade and commerce' of Nelson. She had identified one of the few men 'who understood the art of brick making' and had employed him to erect the substantial brick store and house on the corner of Trafalgar and Hardy streets. In addition, although 'even at that time not a young woman ... she was possessed of an active mind, and keen business instincts', and had often travelled to get stock, sailing 'in the little cockle shells which in those days formed the sole means of communication' between Nelson and Wellington. In time she retired 'having acquired a handsome competency'. William had not attracted attention from the media when he had died a decade earlier.[24] Eighty years later, however, a 1966 *Nelson Historical Society Journal* article recorded that Snow's Hill was named after William.[25]

Such rewriting of history, particularly evident in the mid-twentieth century, was not limited to Mary Snow. In the 1950s local historian Vernon R. Gunn recorded that 'the distinction of opening the first store for the sale and purchase of household goods in Richmond belongs to William Stanton'. William was the local constable and poundkeeper, but the storekeeper was actually his wife, Mary. Also the mother of several children, she ran the store from 1846 until at least 1862. She seldom advertised, although in 1855 she was listed as a stockist of 'a solution of chloride of Zinc, as employed for the Purification of Ships' Holds … and for the treatment of Erysipelatous, Ulcerative, and other diseases', available for 7s 6d per bottle. Her long-lived store was nevertheless well known and she garnered some free publicity in 1856 when William Matthews advertised that his new butcher's shop was 'opposite Mrs Stanton's store'.[26]

Several other corner shops were also run by women in the Nelson area. Grace Smith, wife of schoolteacher Thomas James Smith, started Smith's store in Wakefield in 1846, selling it to musician Louis Drager nearly 20 years later. His wife Ellen ran the shop, locally famous for its sweets, and the couple built an accommodation house.[27] Elizabeth Buckeridge ran a grocery store in the Toi Toi Valley from 1866 to 1868, before passing it over to her printer husband George when he retired owing to ill health. She started again with a toy and fancy repository in Trafalgar Street the same year.[28]

Rebecca Berry spent nearly 30 years struggling to offset her husband Thomas's lack of business acumen, fondness for alcohol and increasing violence, while supporting their 10 children. They began a general store and tea and coffee room in Nelson's Haven Road before moving to Bridge Street. By 1850 they were advertising it as 'the old established store'. In October 1853 Thomas was accused of stealing a gold watch and acquitted only because his alleged victim died before the case came to court.[29] They closed the Bridge Street store in 1854 and moved back to Haven Road, but in 1857 and 1858 auctioneers were selling off their stock, while Thomas became embroiled in gold-mining ventures. The last stock went in 1860 to satisfy creditors.[30] Meanwhile, in 1857, Rebecca had bought a cave on the Slate River near Collingwood, possibly with the intention of creating a tourist attraction: in a newspaper advertisement she promised prosecution for any 'parties visiting the locality' who might 'break or destroy any stalactites or other curiosities within the said cave, which is wanted to be kept in a complete state of preservation'. She also received a Crown land grant in her own name in March 1859.[31]

Rebecca reopened the Haven Road store, 'in the grocery line', in 1862.[32] Thomas was imprisoned several times for stealing – usually while drunk. He had a hackney cab licence for a while but lost it in November 1865 when he was stopped for the third time for driving furiously while drunk, only to be convicted a few months later of charging passengers for a ride without a licence. He was 'an old offender', with the *Nelson Examiner* commenting in December 1865 that 'there would be very little doing in this Court just now, but for the frequent attendance of T.R. Berry, who has a peculiar proclivity for falling into the meshes of the law'. Then he was charged with beating his wife.[33] In the next two years he was charged variously with drunkenness and assault on different victims. His death in 1868 may have been a relief for Rebecca, who died three years later, aged 49, in Westport.[34]

Striking out on her own

A small store could also be a viable business for widows or deserted wives. When Elizabeth Caradus's husband James succumbed to gold fever and disappeared in the 1860s, she supported their numerous children by running a small shop in her front room in Freemans Bay in Auckland. She was no stranger to hard work, having delivered boots for a cobbler before her 1848 marriage, at 16, to James.[35]

A storefront could be basic – a room in a home, wares spilling onto the pavement. Little initial capital was required, particularly if you convinced wholesalers to provide goods on credit, which was an accepted part of colonial business life. It is not clear whether women had more difficulty than men in obtaining credit, but widows and deserted wives at least attracted sympathy. Charitable appeals on their behalf, many explicitly to enable them to start businesses and become self-supporting, were well subscribed.

Corner stores were often hand-to-mouth affairs with not much room for manoeuvre in terms of cashflow. They were also central to their communities, especially in smaller settlements, frequently long-lasting and could provide a living. Although she did not advertise, Elizabeth Smith's general store in Nelson's Bridge Street was well known. Widowed soon after her arrival, and with numerous children, Elizabeth ran the store for nearly 10 years. She is one of the few businesswomen for whom a bank account record has survived. It shows that she was successful. From June 1854 to May 1855 she deposited £1500, maintaining a credit balance and having £44 1s 1d in the bank at the end of May 1855.[36]

Mary Hannah Smart, a 52-year-old spinster who emigrated from Birmingham in 1856, took over the store in 1859.[37] She ran a variety of businesses from the spacious premises, which consisted of a seven-room house, shop, cellar, kitchen, storeroom and 'all necessary offices', set in 'a large and fruitful garden'. She continued Elizabeth's general store, offered board and lodging to students of the nearby grammar school and let space to milliner Lucy Crompton. In 1861 auctioneers sold off her furniture because she was 'declining housekeeping'. This was not a bold abandonment of housework; she was giving up her boarding house. She moved to Trafalgar Street where she ran a Berlin wool and toy business, including a 'fancy trade', leather for leatherwork, women's underclothing, stays and baby linen, appealing to a female market. In 1868, aged 60, she retired and married James Roberts, five years her junior. She lived for another 30 years, her obituary recording her as 'at one time well-known in the district'.[38] Elizabeth Smith, meanwhile, had faded into obscurity.

At least three women ran long-lived New Plymouth general stores with and without their husbands, with varying degrees of success. Mary Ann Wells' husband had absented himself. Her drapery and grocery store in Devon Street lasted from the 1860s until at least 1915, under the management of Mary Ann herself, her son-in-law Samuel Crocker and her married daughter Emma Pearce.[39]

Elizabeth Pote had been living on a farm with her sawyer husband William at Omata until March 1860, when their nine-year-old son James and nephew George Parker were tomahawked to death by Māori and both families' farms were burned. The Potes evacuated to Nelson with their remaining children. Upon their return to New Plymouth they opened a grocery store in Devon Street, which continued past William's death in 1867 and Elizabeth's remarriage to Edmund Dover, at least 15 years her junior, a year later. We might speculate on Edmund's motives in marrying an older woman; widows with businesses were attractive propositions. The shop's proprietor was listed ambiguously as 'E. Dover'. It disappears from the records when Edmund became the licensee of the Red House Hotel in 1873. Edmund did not live long to enjoy his wife, young son or business: he died in 1875 at 41. His will left a third of his estate in trust for the use of Elizabeth, and the remaining two-thirds in the hands of the same trustees for his six-year-old son. Whether or not Elizabeth had been involved in the management of the store or hotel while married to Edmund, she was now thrown once again upon her own resources. The licence of the Red House Hotel was resumed by its owner, Richard Langman, one of Edmund's trustees, and Elizabeth moved to Bell Block where she opened another store. She lived until 1898, remembered in her obituary as a popular wife and mother, with an 'unassuming manner and trustful disposition', who had 'endured with great fortitude the vicissitudes of pioneer life'. Those vicissitudes included the loss of two more sons in 1860 as toddlers and the 1877 trial of her oldest boy for the manslaughter of his lover.[40]

On the same day in March 1860 that Elizabeth Pote lost her son James at Omata, another Elizabeth lost her husband and breadwinner. Māori killed saddler and storekeeper Samuel Ford and three other settlers. Because he had had Māori customers Samuel had not considered himself to be in danger, despite increased local tensions. Elizabeth retreated to Nelson with other Pākehā, and when she went back to New Plymouth she opened a store on the corner of Devon and Brougham streets, while her son Harris took over his father's saddlery. She sold an array of goods, from apples and drapery to tea, butter and camp ovens. She ensured her business on 'Mrs Ford's corner' was a landmark by including such activities as selling tickets for the Taranaki Teetotal and Band of Hope Festival.[41] The store lasted nearly 20 years but provided insufficient income, judging by local efforts on her behalf. In 1864 members of the provincial council presented a petition to the superintendent, requesting she be granted a pension of £40 per year under the Militia Act because her husband had been killed in the wars. The general government rejected their request. Ten years later they tried again. Elizabeth was deserving, having 'struggled on … and had succeeded in rearing her family respectably, unaided', but had 'been treated exceptionally' in being denied a pension earlier. This time the plea was successful but £46 per year was too little too late, for by 1879 Elizabeth was bankrupt. Her children were grown and she did not appear in business again, perhaps managing to live on her pension. She died in 1918.[42]

An ideal family business or sole concern

Corner stores offered opportunities for women to conduct small-scale businesses beyond drapery. They were integral to local communities and small towns, selling a plethora of assorted goods, and were also places where news was exchanged, jobs advertised, rooms rented and gossip flourished. Often run by husband and wife partnerships, they were also carried on by women on their own, with husbands otherwise occupied, incompetent, intemperate or absent. Corner stores were not extremely profitable, but could, with careful management, sustain a woman and her family, sometimes for more than one generation, with potential for diversification and expansion.

Emma Jane Dixon's factory is prominently featured in this 1895 Wellington poster (top left), and is the only female business represented. View of Wellington [c. 1895] from Mt Victoria. F.W. Niven Co., Ballarat, Victoria, Alexander Turnbull Library, D-002-007-001

CHAPTER 10

Butchers and Bakers and Cordial Makers

Alongside drapers, boarding-house keepers, publicans, prostitutes, entertainers and shopkeepers, visitors to colonial New Zealand might also stumble across a female butcher, chemist, bootmaker or hairdresser, dentist, taxidermist, seedswoman or watchmaker. Sometimes widows inherited businesses; sometimes wives took charge when spouses were unsatisfactory. A few women forged careers for themselves. In this chapter we meet some more unusual businesswomen, many of whom carried on bravely, often in the midst of unimaginable grief at unexpected loss.

Stepping up

Mary Ann Coster 'just wanted to die', she told her grandchildren, when her young husband, John, was killed in the Wairau conflict in 1843. Mary Ann was only 22. A year earlier she had run away from her home in Kent to marry John in London; now she was widowed, with a baby, half a world away in Nelson. But, as she said, 'there was little time for self-pity'. Supported by new friends, she opened a small straw-bonnet store. Within 12 months she married Richard Wallis who, according to local stories, was a customer. The couple opened a school in Richmond and ran the post office before moving to Motueka in 1866. There they founded an orphanage for 'fallen women' and street children that lasted until 1887, five years after Richard's death.[1]

Widowhood was a common experience. Husbands dropped dead at all ages, unexpectedly and inconveniently (and occasionally to their spouses' great relief). Quite apart from the dislocating emotional trauma, the loss of a money-earning husband could leave a family in a fragile economic state. For many widows, penury and disrepute were within touching distance, as was graphically illustrated in Chapter 1 in the case of Elizabeth Darby. There was no social welfare net: a widow left little by her dead husband relied on familial support, private charity and, ultimately, on her own resources. A gradual diminution in dower rights had undermined the financial security of widows; by the mid-1870s a widow was no longer entitled to a proportion of her late husband's estate.[2] As she was when he was alive, a woman was at the mercy of her husband's disposal of his property. The luckiest women were those few left independently wealthy by their departed spouses. Often, however, any family property was tied up in trust for children, the widow having a life interest that provided her with an income but did not allow her to sell or expand the property. She was dependent upon the good will of her offspring or of her husband's trustees or executors.

One might think that most widows would remarry quickly, as Mary Ann Coster did, given this was an economically viable and socially acceptable option, ideally also offering emotional support. But this was not the case. In New Zealand, as elsewhere, it was widowers, seeking a replacement household manager and carer for their children, rather than widows, who raced to the altar.[3] Men preferred young single women without encumbrances. A widow with children was less attractive, unless she was custodian of a viable business or wealth. Of course, second husbands were not always desirable for those who had lost their first. Divorcée Mary Ann Griffiths shocked Nelson middle-class matron Martha Adams when she confided that 'as I have no husband to please I can suit my own convenience'. Mary Ann had obviously had an unhappy first marriage, but Martha was surprised that this 'fair gentle-looking woman', whose 'soft blue eyes looked as if fully capable of appreciating a being who would love her', was so 'calm and unmoved' about the prospect of being single. Martha could see no pleasure in such 'a life of misery'.[4] So, while some widows remarried, others found alternative means of support or chose to remain independent, rather than lose control over what resources they enjoyed. And remarriage, as we have seen, did not necessarily mean escape from business.

Finding a respectable means of obtaining an income was key to widows' survival. Many chose business. Waged employment was often not possible because, like many married women, widows often had childcare responsibilities, and female wage rates were not based upon women having financial responsibility for their families.

Those further up the social scale had the additional problem of maintaining gentility. Jane Takotowi Clendon was 35 when her 72-year-old husband died in

1872, leaving her with eight children of her own, several stepchildren and a pile of debts. Jane's home, Clendon House in Rawene, Northland, now a Heritage New Zealand property, celebrates her enterprise and fortitude. Through a variety of business activities, including trading kauri gum and other goods, such as firewood, garden produce and bark, she endeavoured to pay her husband's debts. She used her education to write finely crafted letters to well-placed friends, asking for assistance.[5] Jane's enterprise was essential to maintaining the appearance of genteel living and ensuring her children were educated. The pressure of preserving middle-class niceties was one that many widows in Jane's position felt keenly.

More fortunate were widows who inherited ongoing businesses. Here we often find women in more unusual enterprises. Most curious, however, is Mary Jane Bennett, who inherited her husband's government job – a well-paid position that at least one man felt required masculine skills.

An unusual case

Mary Jane Bennett was the first and is *still* the only female lighthouse keeper in New Zealand's history. She inherited the job from her husband George, who died aged 40 in 1855. He left her with four children and pregnant in a wooden cottage with a light in the front window on isolated Pencarrow Head at the entrance to Wellington Harbour. When a proper lighthouse was built and opened in 1859 Mary Jane was officially appointed keeper. Keeping the light burning was a round-the-clock task. Her assistant William Lyall, 10 years her senior and possibly miffed at not being appointed keeper himself, complained of the difficulties of caring for the lighthouse 'with the help of a woman only'. His 1860 letter to his employers suggested two men could cope well, because they could share the work of 'extra repairs and cleaning and work' that 'a woman cannot even assist in'. He included an exhaustive list of tasks he considered essential but Mary Jane did not: 'It is her idea that such work is extra and not expected of a lighthouse keeper.' Despite this, government officials considered Mary Jane capable, as evidenced by her decade of service, her professional correspondence with the Marine Board, and officials' reports of her as 'orderly and efficient'.[6]

Around 1865 Mary Jane and her family returned to Yorkshire where she lived independently, her lighthouse-keeping days behind her. This may have been a relief. Pencarrow Head on a fine summer's day is beautiful, but in less clement conditions would not be so charming. Living in an isolated, cold, windy place, with five young children, and coping with William Lyall's insistent and pointed diligence, was probably not Mary Jane's colonial dream. On the other hand, her annual salary of £125, one usually paid to breadwinning males, was more than she could have earned in another business and it facilitated her return to England. Her sons later went back to New Zealand, one following in her footsteps and becoming assistant lighthouse keeper at Pencarrow in 1880.[7] William Lyall finally got his own lighthouse in 1866 on Somes Island, where he died in 1871. His wife Lucy, by then in her seventies, did not take over his job. 'Granny Lyall' lived another 15 years in Wellington, supporting herself more conventionally by taking in boarders.[8]

A mail business

Employees' widows were rarely appointed to their husbands' jobs. It remains a mystery why Mary Jane was so privileged, when William Lyall was available. She was a well-educated squire's daughter, so perhaps this was influential. Generally, the only women who held government positions were office caretakers and post office officials. When Sarah Middlemas's husband Joseph died suddenly in a carting accident in 1862, she was appointed Drury postmistress in his stead, paid £20 a year. She continued to run their store, a focal point for the village. Goods were delivered to the Drury Post Office from Auckland, orders taken and property sales advertised, with Mrs Middlemas as a communication point. Sarah was experienced; Joseph had been busy as clerk of the resident magistrate's court, a member of the Forest Rifle Volunteers and on the Auckland Provincial Council from 1857 to 1859. She continued the business after marrying publican George Walter in 1868 and, still as Mrs Middlemas, was listed as postmistress and agent for the *Daily Southern Cross* newspaper until the end of 1870, when William Ashdown took over.[9] Sarah was not the first woman to run a New Zealand post office, however. That honour belongs to spinster schoolteacher Sophia Bates, who was Onehunga's postmistress from 1849 to 1855.[10]

Keep calm and carry it on

Women inherited a variety of businesses. In Wellington, Lucy Houghton managed a shipping business with her sons after her husband Robert's death in 1846.[11] Jane Day was a cowkeeper and dairy farmer in Whanganui after husband John died. She also had an interest in the Jockey Club Hotel, with her two sons.[12] In 1868 New

Plymouth draper Letitia Yems reinvented herself as an auctioneer after her husband James died, and continued to employ William Bennett to run the auctions themselves until her retirement from business in 1875.[13]

Jane Hair carried on the farm surrounding Whanganui's Virginia Lake with aplomb after her husband William died in 1853. When the local council tried to buy rights to the water in the lake for the town's water supply in 1874, Jane rejected the initial offer of £500 and made a counter-offer of the same amount 'to leave the lake alone'. The dispute escalated and in 1876 she rejected £1000 compensation as inadequate and 'began to dip sheep in the lake', thus rendering the water undrinkable. The *Evening Post* was amused by the stand-off, suggesting that she was the 'mistress of the situation'. The battle continued beyond Jane's death, when it was eventually resolved in the courts.[14]

Some widows gave up inherited businesses when they remarried. Auguste Hanneke, widow of Wellington watchmaker Georg, who died in 1861, continued her husband's business for four years but then remarried and no longer required it.[15] Some sold out for a profit after a few years or, like Sophia Paris James, passed the business to grown sons. Harriet Stallard continued her husband William's Nelson painting and plumbing business after his death in 1854 until she remarried in 1857, when her son, also William, took over.[16]

Others found it difficult to make a living. Elizabeth Dew inherited her husband James' Christchurch gardening business after he died in 1862. They had emigrated in 1855, elderly for desirable immigrants at 48 and 50, but their son James was only 20. They arrived with high hopes. James' brother William had gone to Wellington in 1841, writing home enthusiastically the following year that there were 'very few cultivators in the colony'. He also noted that 'I have enjoyed the sweets of a sober life since I have been in New Zealand, which I intend to continue.'[17] This was wishful thinking. William died in the same year as his brother in an accident caused by his intoxication.

By 1855 were there more cultivators in the colony? James Dew's nursery business was not necessarily successful even before he died. His estate, divided equally between his wife and son, was worth less than £100. The latter was a drinker like his uncle: he fell into the River Avon after an evening's drinking in 1863 and drowned. The nursery limped on for 10 years until Elizabeth's death; her repeated applications for exemption from paying rates suggest it was not viable.[18] Similarly, Wellington's Theresa Briggs struggled after the death of her shoemaker husband Phoenix in 1891, chasing customer debts and eventually running a boarding house and then a hotel in Hokitika. Her premises had a propensity for going up in flames and she repeatedly appeared in court for debt.[19]

Businesses based on skilled trades were most difficult for widows to manage, unless they had trained sons or could find reliable partners or workmen. In Westport Mary Frank continued her husband's business as blacksmith, wheelwright and farrier in 1884, hoping for public support by 'employing the most competent workmen'.[20] When Lyttelton hairdresser Jacob Dash died in 1864, aged 32, his widow Mary relied on her husband's manager, Thomas McDonald. Nineteenth-century hairdressing was a male business, sometimes also offering shaving services and tobacco sales. Within a year Thomas had his own shop and Mary was advertising for a replacement. She married John Rice in 1868 and, perhaps with some relief, left her business.[21]

Sarah Bryant fared better with her inherited hairdressing business in Wellington. Her husband Josiah Jeffries Bryant, 'late of Regent Street', was a hairdresser and perfumer from their arrival in 1851 until he died two years later. Sarah had been a monthly nurse but made the hairdressing business her own, reopening after 'considerable alterations', continuing it after remarriage to Patrick Campbell and diversifying, adding books in 1856. She relinquished the business on moving to Nelson in the 1860s. When she died in 1907 aged 88 she had been a resident of Mahakipawa in rural Marlborough for 42 years, having married for a third time and applied her enterprise and determination to make a success of a farming life.[22]

Widows could take control of enterprises with gusto. Nelson's Elizabeth Lloyd inherited her husband Richard's 14-year-old bootmaking business in Bridge Street in 1856 and diversified to include a general store in 1858. By 1864 she was exploiting her longevity, advertising Lloyd's Old Established Boot Store. She was still in business in 1869 and passed it on to her son Henry in the 1870s.[23] When baker Isaac McEwan died in Auckland in 1863, his wife Janet took over, moving to High Street and becoming a more general store. When she died in 1904 her obituary, unusually, remembered that 'Mrs. McEwan, with that energy, which characterised so many of these old settlers, continued the business of her husband successfully for some time'.[24]

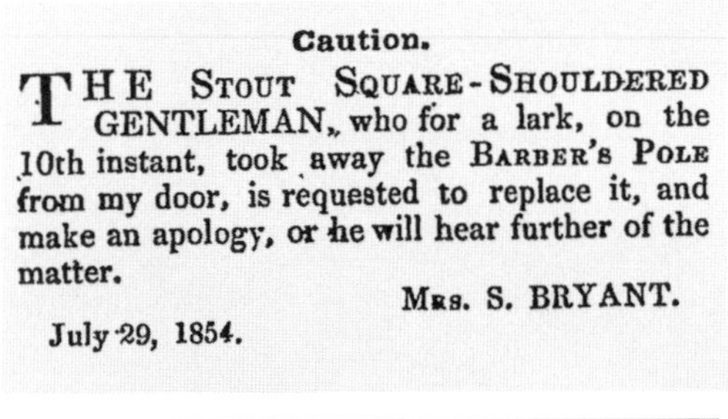
Caution.

THE STOUT SQUARE-SHOULDERED GENTLEMAN, who for a lark, on the 10th instant, took away the BARBER'S POLE from my door, is requested to replace it, and make an apology, or he will hear further of the matter.

MRS. S. BRYANT.

July 29, 1854.

Sarah Bryant stood no nonsense. Did she know the miscreant or was this sheer bravado? And was the pole returned?

New Zealand Spectator and Cook's Strait Guardian, 29 July 1854

Emma Jane Dixon, née Duck, was, like her mother-in-law Catherine, a key figure in the long history of the Dixon family aerated water and cordial manufactory business in Wellington.

Alexander Turnbull Library, PA-Coll 2971

After Annie Brown's husband William drowned in the Waimakariri River in 1891 while trying unsuccessfully to save their eldest son Charles, Annie survived by continuing the family grocery store, eventually passing it on to two remaining sons nearly 20 years later.[25] These women all ran businesses beyond their children's maturity, suggesting a sense of enjoyment or at least competency.

In January 1884 both Elizabeth Cooper and Emma Jane Dixon applied to register their trademarks for aerated waters and cordials in Wellington. Elizabeth's husband George had just died at the age of 40, leaving her his 16-year-old aerated water business on Thorndon Quay. Elizabeth became renowned for her disputes with other manufacturers over misusing trademarks – and she was more often in violation. When she married Charles Brodie in 1888, she quickly retired from the business, which became C.W. Brodie.[26]

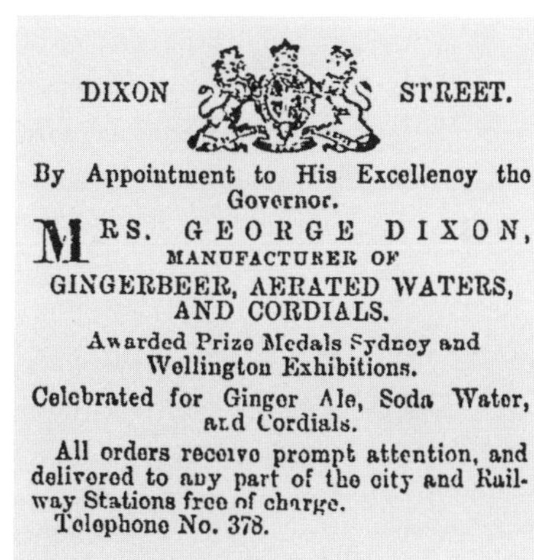

Emma Jane Dixon made this business her own, expanding, modernising and winning prizes.

Evening Post, 29 June 1889

Emma Jane Duck had a more positive experience after she married into the Dixon family cordial business in 1869. Family history suggests her mother-in-law Catherine had long been involved, having 'both energy and business tact'. She and her husband Edward had established a ginger beer business in Cuba Street in the 1850s. Edward retired after Catherine's death in 1875 and their son George took over. He died just eight years later in 1883, leaving Emma, aka 'Mrs George Dixon', who had 'learned the secrets of the family essences', in charge. She was no mere caretaker. She expanded and modernised, buying an old sawmill and converting it into a large factory with machinery 'of the latest possible description'. Her aerated waters and cordials won prizes at exhibitions in Sydney and Wellington and she remained in business for 14 years, before selling to Robert Ready and Alexander Bennett. Despite this, her 1908 *Evening Post* obituary described Emma merely as the widow of cordial manufacturer, George, and 'noted for many kindly deeds'.[27]

From wife-assistant to business owner

In 1881 Christchurch's Elizabeth Robinson was the first woman to register as a pharmacist under the 1880 Pharmacy Act. She was accredited because she had run a chemist's business since her husband Richard's death in 1871, although she had actually been taking charge of the chemist shop since 1864 while he was busy with his dentistry practice in an adjoining room. When Richard died he left her with five children, insolvent and, as the paper discreetly put it, 'in a delicate state of health'. The local community rallied round, collecting an impressive £90 within two weeks. Elizabeth continued in business for another 15 years until 1886, when she sold the pharmacy as a going concern and married widowed publican Charles Dann.[28]

Elizabeth was not the first New Zealand woman to have a chemist's business. Clara Macshane, widow of popular Nelson doctor and chemist Alexander Macshane, advertised in the 1850s. The couple had married a mere two days after the widowed Clara Durley and her three-year-old daughter had disembarked from the *Fifeshire* in 1842.[29] Popular legend immortalised Alexander's doctoring, recording that in 1843 he amputated the leg of a Māori patient who remained conscious and smoking a pipe throughout, though this seems as much a testament to the patient's fortitude as the doctor's skill. He and Clara had five children between 1843 and 1848, when Alexander was appointed as colonial surgeon at the newly built New Plymouth hospital. When he died of consumption a few months later, aged 38, his obituary in the *Nelson Examiner* was effusive: 'An ardent admirer of his profession, to which he brought

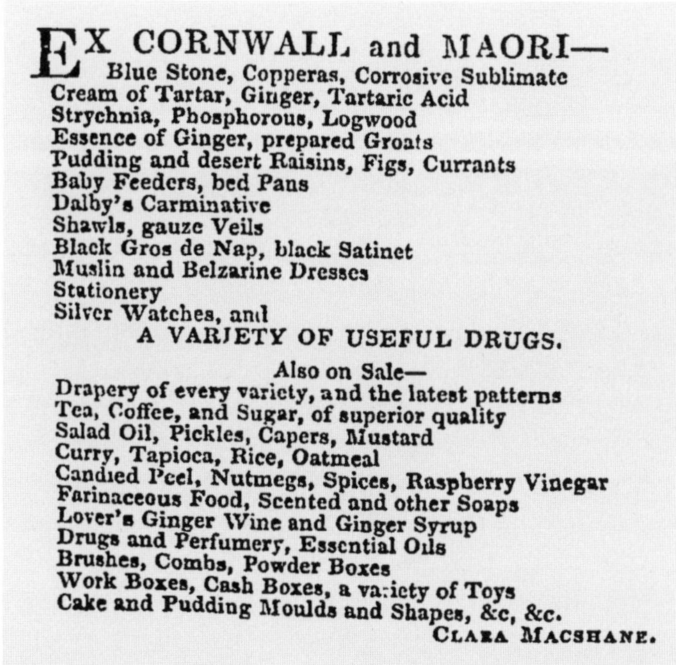

EX CORNWALL and MAORI—
Blue Stone, Copperas, Corrosive Sublimate
Cream of Tartar, Ginger, Tartaric Acid
Strychnia, Phosphorous, Logwood
Essence of Ginger, prepared Groats
Pudding and desert Raisins, Figs, Currants
Baby Feeders, bed Pans
Dalby's Carminative
Shawls, gauze Veils
Black Gros de Nap, black Satinet
Muslin and Belzarine Dresses
Stationery
Silver Watches, and
A VARIETY OF USEFUL DRUGS.
Also on Sale—
Drapery of every variety, and the latest patterns
Tea, Coffee, and Sugar, of superior quality
Salad Oil, Pickles, Capers, Mustard
Curry, Tapioca, Rice, Oatmeal
Candied Peel, Nutmegs, Spices, Raspberry Vinegar
Farinaceous Food, Scented and other Soaps
Lover's Ginger Wine and Ginger Syrup
Drugs and Perfumery, Essential Oils
Brushes, Combs, Powder Boxes
Work Boxes, Cash Boxes, a variety of Toys
Cake and Pudding Moulds and Shapes, &c, &c.
CLARA MACSHANE.

Clara Macshane, chemist of Nelson, stocked an immense array of items including tempting treats and potent drugs.
Nelson Examiner, 27 March 1852

talents of no mean order, and a man of perfect integrity and independence, his loss could not but be severely felt in any community, but more particularly so in the infant settlements of New Zealand.'[30]

Clara returned to Nelson where she could trade on the respect and approbation in which her husband had been held. And trade she did, opening a chemist's shop. She was not a pharmacist, but had probably assisted Alexander. In 1850 'C. Macshane' advertised 'a general assortment of drugs, perfumery, spices, sweetmeats & c'.[31] She also sold stationery, combs and brushes and an assortment of lotions and potions.[32] Alexander had left his entire estate to Clara, 'absolutely', trusting in her competency.[33] It is difficult to gauge her business's success although she was both solvent and a property owner. She deposited £400 in a bank account in 1854–55, maintaining a credit balance and ending the year with £18 12s 5d. This was considerably less than storekeeper Elizabeth Smith of Trafalgar Street in the same period (see Chapter 9), but it may not have been her only account.[34] Her chemist shop ran until at least 1861.[35]

The brutal business of butchery

Butchering, whether wholesale, carcase or retail, may not seem a particularly feminine business, but, as with other family businesses, women were involved. Across the Tasman in Sydney was the splendid Ritta Macnamara, witnessed by a young Randolph Bedford 'doing six bodies a week'. 'She handled the meat-axe and saw as if they were toys,' he recalled.[36] On this side of the ditch there were also female butchers. Jane Reese, for example, was a shipping and family butcher in Queen Street, Auckland, for ten years after her husband Robert died in 1852.[37]

Ann Bird, often remembered as 'the first white woman to step ashore' in Nelson in 1842, wins the prize for business longevity.[38] She inherited a six-year-old butchering business when her husband Reuben died in 1850, aged 32, although she may have been involved before his death. Her business became a Nelson landmark. Initially, in 1851, fellow butcher Henry Hargreaves killed the beasts for her.[39] Whether this was out of kindness or for a price, his support certainly helped. She did not advertise often but got free publicity from other businesses that stated they were 'across the street from Mrs Bird's butcher's shop'. Her sons joined her in the business but Ann was in charge until her death in 1891 leaving an estate worth £950.[40] Ann's sons included Thomas, who hanged himself when he was 25 in 1868 after being told he had an incurable heart condition. He left behind his pregnant wife of two years, Harriet, and a one-year-old son. Rather than join the family business, Harriet more conventionally advertised a 'day school for young children' and then a boarding house at her home in the Washington Valley. Four years later she sold up and moved to Melbourne, where she married Edward Wilkinson in 1874.[41]

Butchering was not limited to widows. Christina Pollock was in business for decades from 1842, nominally in partnership with her husband Alexander, but more often with her son as assistant. The 1868 directory listed Alexander Pollock as butcher but the shop was 'Mrs Pollock's' in the newspapers. Neighbour Philip Hannken remembered that 'Mrs Pollock's butcher shop' was near his parents' Queen Street drapery in the 1850s. Alexander himself farmed at Drury, supplying the shop.[42] Similarly, although Robert Giles advertised a butcher's stall at Auckland Markets in the 1870s and 1880s, another market dealer described her stall's location as opposite 'Mrs Giles' Butcher'.[43]

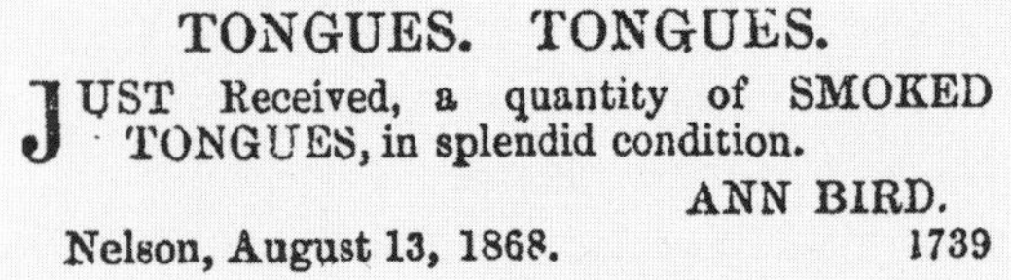
TONGUES. TONGUES.

JUST Received, a quantity of SMOKED TONGUES, in splendid condition.

ANN BIRD.

Nelson, August 13, 1868. 1739

Butcher Ann Bird rarely advertised, except when she had something special to sell. *Nelson Evening Mail*, 13 August 1868

Nelson butcher Ann Bird, looking a little weary of it all. She ran a 40-year business and brought up five children alone. Perhaps this photo was taken just after the suicide of her eldest son Thomas in 1868. Mrs Bird, Nelson Provincial Museum, Tyree Studio, 17353

With such a display of wares there was no mistaking Ann Bird's butcher's shop, an institution in Trafalgar Street, Nelson. It was run by the indomitable Ann, probably shown here with her two younger sons, Charles and Reuben, and another man.

Bird Butcher Shop, Nelson Provincial Museum, Bett Collection, 172

Gold rush 'widows'

The lure of gold in New Zealand, Australia or further afield often resulted in temporarily absent spouses, and wives stepped up. Charlotte Godley commented in 1850 that 'about fifty or sixty, mostly bad characters' from Wellington had gone to California. In particular, she noted 'our baker's wife has indeed a shade of sadness on her face', because her 'bad husband' had 'gone off to try his luck in California, and left her to carry on the business'.[44] The unnamed baker could have been one of two men, Peter Christison or Alexander Lyall, both of whom answered the siren call.

The eldest of Peter and Lydia Christison's five children, seven-year-old Sarah, had just died when Peter departed in March 1850, leaving Lydia to run their well-established bakery shop on Lambton Quay. Fortunately he realised his mistake quickly and was back in Wellington by October. In the late 1850s the family, with seven children, relocated south to Richmond, where they took over Edward Laney's bakery in 1859. It is likely Lydia was often in the bakery, because her husband continued his frequent excursions to goldfields.[45]

Alexander Lyall did not return from the goldfields, but left his wife and children to fend for themselves. A colourful character, he had emigrated from Dundee to Hobart in 1836, arriving in Wellington as a ship's steward on the *Olympus* in 1841. Captain John Whyte accused him of theft and desertion, leaving us with a description of Alexander as a '5ft 10in and stout made' man carrying a gun.[46] *Olympus* passengers hotly denied the charges and Alexander settled in Wellington, where he married fellow Scot, 20-year-old straw-bonnet maker Jane Malcolm, in 1842.[47] By 1845 Alexander had a bakery business, but four years later he sold up to Peter Laing and disappeared to Hobart and California. As his sister Margaret Mickle later recorded, 'Brother Alexander had gone to San Francisco and we saw him no more – we only heard in a casual way that he had died there – he left his wife and two sons at Wellington, New Zealand.' In August 1850 'Mrs J.C. Lyall' announced to 'her customers' that she had moved premises to Lambton Quay, where she would 'carry on the Business of BREAD and FANCY BISCUITBAKING, CONFECTIONERY, &c'.[48] She was listed in the directory for two years before a Mrs Townsend appeared in her place. Jane moved to Hobart with her two sons, perhaps hoping to find her husband or refuge with her in-laws. In 1858 she married 32-year-old David Holt, optimistically describing herself as a 31-year-old widow (she was at least 37 and not necessarily widowed), and gave birth to a daughter four months later.[49]

The Mrs Townsend who took over the bakery in 1852 was Jane's sister Isabella, also an experienced businesswoman with a colourful husband. She had married

25-year-old Chauncy Henry Townsend after a shipboard romance: she was in steerage, he in a cabin above. The Townsends opened refreshment rooms in their house on Karori Road in 1846, and by 1847 also had a shop, run by Isabella. She appeared in the directory as a baker just once when she took over her sister's business. She then vanishes from the records. When Chauncy was remarried in 1861 to Ellen Mason in Nottinghamshire, Isabella had probably died, although he would not have been the first to 'accidentally' wed a second spouse leaving the first alive and kicking on another continent.[50]

Who's the boss?

Some women were simply more business-minded than their spouses, and recognised as such by family and community. Elizabeth Betts was a 'greatly respected' seed store proprietor in Nelson. She arrived as a 17-year-old with her parents and siblings in 1842 and five years later married seaman Alfred George Betts. The couple moved to Auckland, where, for six years, Alfred was a commission agent and debt collector and Elizabeth produced four daughters. In 1854 Elizabeth advertised their genteel Wakefield Street residence and 'a few splendid gold brooches and silver pencil cases, direct from England' for sale. This was probably less a foray into business than a desperate attempt to liquidise assets.[51]

They retreated to Nelson with the support of Elizabeth's family, the Foys, and opened a seed store called Birmingham House. Taking advantage of gold fever, they diversified, recommending that 'no person should go to the diggings without one of Betts' cheap, lucky and good tents'. Alfred became custodian of the local fire engine, which was housed next door, and Elizabeth continued to produce daughters and was involved in the business. Trouble arose again in 1859. They sold their business and home and both appeared in court for assaulting the bailiff. Alfred was imprisoned and Elizabeth was fined £5, which she could ill afford. Her brother Thomas bought Birmingham House in 1861, announcing that it would be under Elizabeth's management.[52] Subsequent advertisements appeared in the name E.S. Betts. Alfred was not involved; his interest in the local fire brigade had become all-consuming, judging by his many letters to the newspaper.

In 1872, flying in the face of coverture, Elizabeth Betts was listed as a ratepayer, although Alfred was still living. She may have had a protection order, although they were still cohabiting. At least two of her daughters followed her example of economic independence. In 1873 daughter Elizabeth, having learned her trade with dressmaker Mrs Denne (and sued her for unpaid wages), advertised as a dressmaker from her sister Harriet Main's residence in Hope Street, where the latter also ran a boarding house.[53]

Alfred and Elizabeth were a fairly typical couple, except they reversed roles. Usually it was middle-class wives who were involved in such community activities as church fête committees and benevolent societies. The equivalent for Alfred was the Volunteer Fire Brigade. He may have been a useless businessman, but his funeral, when he died in 1877 was 'one of the largest' in Nelson, attesting to his popularity.[54]

Unlike Alfred Betts, Elizabeth Farmer's husband Alexander simply vanished from the records. He announced he was leaving the colony for a short while in 1850 and that his wife would continue the boot- and shoe-making business on Wellington's Lambton Quay. He returned briefly, became insolvent in 1852, and subsequent advertisements were in Elizabeth's name. In 1859 'Mrs Farmer's' business moved to Willis Street, where she diversified, adding groceries and eventually a butcher's shop. She advertised for boarders in 1879. The store lasted for over 30 years until 1887. Alexander's disappearance went unnoted and his invisibility in the records is particularly surprising because the Farmers were an extended family running multiple businesses in the city.[55]

Alice Townsend's husband William did not vanish but became a liability. He came to New Plymouth as a bugle major with the 43rd Light Infantry and married 20-year-old New Zealand-born Alice Wilkinson in 1865 when he was 23. They were both entrepreneurial. Over the next 15 years William advertised music and quadrille lessons and conducted local bands. In 1873, eight years after their marriage, with four children and another on the way, Alice began advertising in Devon Street as 'Mrs W.R. Townsend tobacconist', also selling 'musical instruments and music, stationery and fancy goods'. A year later, 'having purchased a tobacco cutting machine', she offered 'the best aromatic cut Tobacco'. She also sold the *Taranaki Herald* and tickets for the Taranaki Amateur Band concerts. Her business was successful: in 1880, pregnant

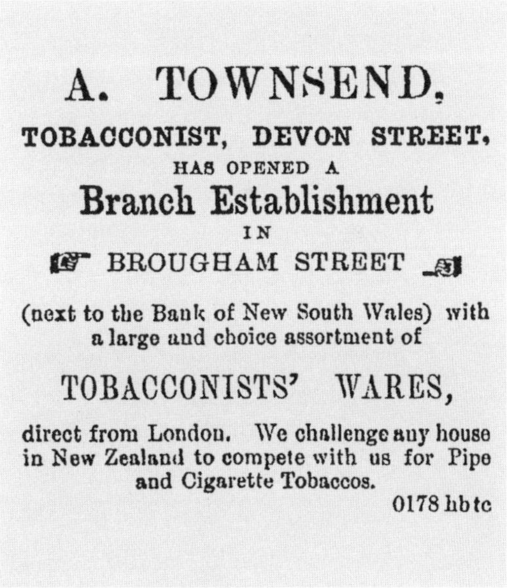
A. TOWNSEND,
TOBACCONIST, DEVON STREET,
HAS OPENED A
Branch Establishment
IN
BROUGHAM STREET
(next to the Bank of New South Wales) with a large and choice assortment of
TOBACCONISTS' WARES,
direct from London. We challenge any house in New Zealand to compete with us for Pipe and Cigarette Tobaccos.
0178 hbtc

Alice Townsend expanded her business with bold claims.
Taranaki Herald, 29 June 1880

Next to the bank in Brougham Street, New Plymouth, in the 1880s, 'A. Townsend, tobacconist' (Alice) and 'A.E. Cottier, newsagent' were both businesswomen. Spinster Annie Cottier's newsagency, servants' registry and fancy goods store lasted from 1875 into the twentieth century, when she retired and sold to Miss Weller. Puke Ariki, PHO2001-457

with her eighth child, she expanded, opening a branch in Brougham Street, while William sold pianos.[56] Although tobacconists could be fronts for brothels, catering to a male market, Alice's prized tobacco-cutting machine suggests she was serious about her business. Her diversification into stationery and fancy goods also indicates she was aiming beyond a male market.

Alice's life changed in the 1880s. Her seven-year-old daughter Emma died in 1881, just before baby number eight was born. William opened a United Service Club Billiard Room in the Devon Street shop but failed to prosper. By 1884 he had turned to drink and was bankrupt. Everything, the much-advertised tobacco-cutting machine and billiard table, as well as the piano, furniture and household goods, was sold. Alice opened Clarendon House, a temperance boarding house opposite the Beach House Hotel.[57] A year later William was charged with 'wilfully failing to provide' for his children. He left New Plymouth in 1886 and moved to Auckland and then Wellington, where he worked in the Postal Department. The couple had reconciled by 1893, when Alice gave birth to her last child in Wellington. William retained his optimistic entrepreneurialism, establishing a Post and Telegraph orchestra, devising a system by which, it was reported, 'each man was enabled within half an hour to perform satisfactorily upon an instrument with which, he was previously unfamiliar'.[58] Alice disappeared from business, but her daughter, also Alice, inherited her parents' entrepreneurial spirit. She and her husband Joseph Wallace ran an oyster saloon, with an illegal betting shop on the side, in Wellington in the 1890s, before she emigrated to Jacksonville, Florida, and ran a florist's shop.[59]

All in the family

Family and business networks were intertwined, and not only through father–son relationships. Ann White, 'bread and biscuit baker, pastry cook and confectioner' of Bridge Street, Nelson, was just 15 years old in 1849. Her business was connected with that of her stepfather, Edward Laney, who had another bakery in Nile Street, and, when he switched to manufacturing ginger beer, lemon syrup and peppermint, he sold his products through Ann White's shop. She was in business until her marriage to Joseph Bartlett in 1862, when she passed the business to her stepbrother, William Laney.[60]

Mothers and sons also worked together, or shared business premises. We have already seen how Mary Ann Warmoll's drapery business was linked with her son's mattress manufactory. Similarly, widowed Elizabeth Wrigglesworth had a circulating library and fancy goods business in Wellington in the early 1860s, at the same address as her son James Dacie Wrigglesworth's photography studio.[61] There is no evidence that Elizabeth assisted with the photography, but on the other side of the world in Yorkshire in 1861 Eliza Leaf was a photographer, working with her 18-year-old son Robert. After the family emigrated to Auckland in 1862, Robert advertised a long-lasting photography business. It would seem likely that Eliza continued to work with him.[62] If so, she might just squeeze out the woman usually claimed as New Zealand's first professional female photographer, Elizabeth Pulman. Elizabeth worked with her husband George at Pulman's Photographic Studios in Auckland from 1867 until his death in 1871, and continued the business through her second marriage to writer John Blackman until her death in 1900. She took scenic photographs as well as portraits, including of prominent Māori men and women. Her son Frederick assisted in the 1890s but allegedly declined to take over the business, which was sold. The New Zealand Government Tourist Bureau purchased her negatives.[63]

A career of her own

One of those captured on film by Elizabeth Pulman was Guide Sophia, 'the most famous woman of her time in Rotorua'. Unlike most married women, Sophia Hinerangi is better remembered than either of her husbands. She crossed cultural boundaries and participated in a highly public industry within the Pākehā world. Sophia ran a guiding business on Lake Tarawera from 1870 until the volcano erupted in 1886, destroying the popular tourist destination, the Pink and White Terraces. She was immortalised by painter Charles F. Goldie and numerous photographers. She later guided tourists at Whakarewerewa, and in her sixties she played herself in a theatre production touring Australia.[64] Sophia had her own career, exploiting her talents and culture.

Tourist guides pose for photographer Elizabeth Pulman outside the Hinemihi meeting house at Te Wairoa in 1881.

Pulman, Elizabeth, 1836–1900. Sophia Hinerangi, Kate Middlemass (Kati), and another guide, outside Hinemihi meeting house, Te Wairoa, Alexander Turnbull Library, 1/2-029217-F

Entrepreneurial Makereti Papakura, 'Guide Maggie', epitomises the modern Māori woman in this 1910 publicity shot, working at her desk, surrounded by books and draped in a feather cloak (over a European dress) inside her whare at Whakarewarewa.

Makereti in her whare Tukiterangi, Whakarewarewa. New Zealand News Ltd, Alexander Turnbull Library, PA1-q-012-39-2

Makereti Papakura was another tourist guide with entrepreneurial nous. Brought up by her Te Arawa relatives until her Pākehā father sent her to an English governess and then Hukarere Māori Girls' School, Makereti was ideally placed to move between two worlds, exploiting her Māori heritage and Pākehā education. She was a guide at Whakarewarewa before her marriage to surveyor Frank Dennan in 1891 and after its disintegration a year later, supporting herself and her small son. She successfully petitioned for divorce in 1900, taking advantage of the 1898 legislation which widened the grounds for divorce. But Makereti was not just a tourist guide. She also formed an international touring concert party with her sister and wrote a guidebook in the early twentieth century. After moving to England and a second marriage, Makereti enrolled as an anthropology student at the University of Oxford at the age of 57, although she died just weeks before her final thesis was due in 1930.[65] Makereti and Sophia exemplify the way some women exploited their culturally specific skills to create autonomous lives.

Other women also forged independent careers. Forty-year-old Norwegian Matilda Broderson advertised briefly in 1882 as a dentist on the West Coast. 'Prepared with all the newest improvements in Mechanical Dentistry [and] having studied under Professor Grogeson, eminent dentist of Copenhagen', she claimed to have been practising in Melbourne. When quickly informed that she needed to be registered under the 1880 Dentists Act, she cleverly advised customers that, having become aware of her mistake, she 'hastens to withdraw her advertisement pending registration'. She carefully added, however, that 'Madame B. is still to be found. Herbert Street.' A few months later, however, having been 'overtaken by paroxysms of mania', she was committed to the Hokitika Lunatic Asylum, where she remained until her death in 1901.[66]

A gruesome occupation for a woman?

In 1890 the *Auckland Star* painted an idyllic picture of an Auckland family business – taxidermist Jane Yandle stuffing birds, her daughters creating feather flowers and husband William making toys, all to be sold at a Christmas bazaar – but it hid a less than perfect reality. Jane was one of many women whose life was complicated by a problematic husband. Fortunately she had a trade to fall back on.

The art of taxidermy is not for the squeamish, but as historian Martha Sear has shown in her study of Sydney taxidermists Jane Tost and Ada Rohu, nineteenth-century women could be unexpectedly robust.[67] Jane Yandle was in business

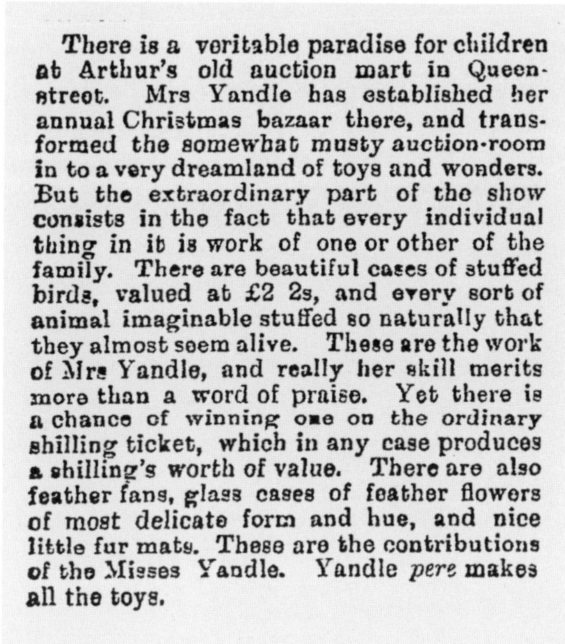

There is a veritable paradise for children at Arthur's old auction mart in Queen-street. Mrs Yandle has established her annual Christmas bazaar there, and transformed the somewhat musty auction-room in to a very dreamland of toys and wonders. But the extraordinary part of the show consists in the fact that every individual thing in it is work of one or other of the family. There are beautiful cases of stuffed birds, valued at £2 2s, and every sort of animal imaginable stuffed so naturally that they almost seem alive. These are the work of Mrs Yandle, and really her skill merits more than a word of praise. Yet there is a chance of winning one on the ordinary shilling ticket, which in any case produces a shilling's worth of value. There are also feather fans, glass cases of feather flowers of most delicate form and hue, and nice little fur mats. These are the contributions of the Misses Yandle. Yandle *pere* makes all the toys.

The 'veritable paradise' of the Christmas bazaar obscured a dysfunctional marriage.
Auckland Star, 20 December 1890

in Auckland from the 1860s with her husband William, who was variously butcher, taxidermist, furrier and carpenter. Jane was the real taxidermist, following in the footsteps of her mother, Mary Turle, 'the bird-stuffer of Taunton', who had reinvented herself from milliner to taxidermist. Jane's father Joseph, sometime musician and watchmaker, died in 1855 when she was 11. Her brother became a printer and her sister a milliner, but Jane was likely her mother's assistant until she married William Yandle in 1863 and immediately sailed for New Zealand.[68]

William became insolvent in 1877 and thenceforth Jane advertised the business alone. The problem was more serious than insolvency, however. In 1882, after the death of the couple's four-year-old daughter Annie, William was charged with 'brutally assaulting' his wife while drunk. Jane was 'too ill to tell the sad story of her wrongs', but explained to the court that her husband was 'seldom sober' and 'she was afraid he would take her life in one of his mad fits'. William himself admitted that 'that was about the truth of it'. It was probably because of his drinking that much of their stock was auctioned off under a distress warrant for rent a few days later.[69]

Jane moved to less fashionable premises and William, now a carpenter, had money troubles. Four years later things had not improved. William was in court for debt, explaining he was 'a vendor of toys but … really a butcher'. He did not 'stuff dolls'; that was 'Mrs Yandle's business'. She 'keeps the shop but she won't pay [my] debts', he complained.[70] William continued to drink and threaten his wife. In 1894,'having put up with his drinking for twenty years', and been prevented from earning a living, Jane demanded protection. Her 18-year-old son William agreed that his father had been drinking for as long as he could remember. William senior, who protested that the main cause of domestic trouble was that his wife would not let him in some rooms in the house, was bound over to keep the peace. Two years later the Yandles were in court again and this time the judge recommended that William seek employment elsewhere and not bother his wife and family again.[71] He seems to have done so.

Jane continued stuffing animals and restoring fur coats and hats at the 'reliable shop … established 1866' until she retired in 1908. Her married daughter Jane Greacen took over, advertising as a taxidermist, furrier and feather dresser in Mill Street in 1909, carefully reminding the public that she was 'née Miss Yandle'. That year, when her father was arrested yet again, the officer recommended his old age pension 'should be cancelled. It is simply providing him with money to waste on drink.'[72] Jane Yandle's business was unusual but her marital problems were not. In many cases, it was critical that these women were able to run a business to support their families, and some seemed to relish the opportunity.

A modern washerwoman

One such efficient and entrepreneurial wife with an independent business was Eliza Couchman, who started the first steam laundry in Petone in 1892. Although her business life began much later in the century than that of many women in this book, her story, like that of Emma Dixon and her cordial factory, illustrates how women adapted to changing times. It also shows that sharp business practices were not restricted to men.

Eliza and Charles Couchman arrived in Wellington in 1879. Charles was a carpenter at the railway workshops and then on his own account, while his wife had 10 children and, according to family history, made several trips to England to purchase equipment for a steam laundry. Although Charles' obituary declared he and his wife had established the business, Eliza was in charge. She promised that all laundry was 'under her personal supervision', emphasising the use of 'modern appliances' in the 'most up-to-date' local laundry.[73] Couchman's Petone Steam Laundry lasted

Residents of Wellington and Petone could not help but know of Eliza Couchman's steam laundry as her delivery cart did its rounds.

Henrietta Stuart Collection, Alexander Turnbull Library, PA1-q-1012-001

until 1922, when Eliza sold it to Timaru Steam Laundry proprietor George Burns. It employed numerous staff and, in the twentieth century, had its own liveried delivery truck.

Eliza's business was a far cry from those of earlier home-based laundresses like Lyttelton's Mrs Mahoney, who charged 2s 6d per dozen 'for every article of clothing, to be got up in the first style' in 1852,[74] or Elizabeth Stillwell, a decade later, whose charges of 4s per dozen for starched things and 2s 3d per dozen for plain laundry were insufficient for her to afford a doctor in her sixth confinement, which caused her premature

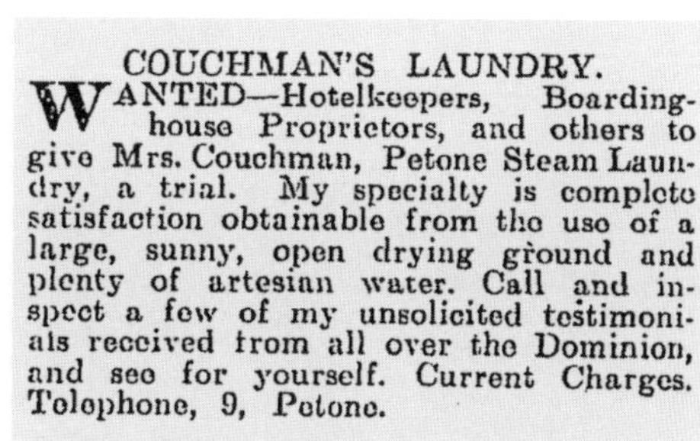

COUCHMAN'S LAUNDRY.

WANTED—Hotelkeepers, Boarding-house Proprietors, and others to give Mrs. Couchman, Petone Steam Laundry, a trial. My specialty is complete satisfaction obtainable from the use of a large, sunny, open drying ground and plenty of artesian water. Call and inspect a few of my unsolicited testimonials received from all over the Dominion, and see for yourself. Current Charges. Telephone, 9, Petone.

Mrs Couchman's specialty was complete satisfaction for her customers, although not, it seems, her employees.

Evening Post, 15 December 1909

death.[75] These women slaved alone over boiling coppers and scalding irons in their homes; Eliza Couchman's enterprise was large and industrial.

But Eliza's modern factory had a darker side. The women who worked there may not have felt that 'progress' and 'technology' had improved conditions much beyond those of earlier laundresses. For all Eliza's entrepreneurialism, she cannot be admired for her employment practices. She was fined in October 1906 for having women working through the night without the appropriate permit and failing to keep an overtime book, but the problems went further. A few months later her case was reported throughout the country. *New Zealand Truth* ran the headline 'Petone Sweating Den: Eliza Couchman's Laundry Lurk'. The Inspector of Factories, James Beveridge Lindsay, told the court that he 'had never come across a worse case' and 'a lot of ingenuity was employed to keep him out of the laundry'. Stories were told of girls locked inside and fainting at worktables. This was not the first time Eliza had been fined, but, Lindsay stated, the '£1 on a previous occasion had had no effect'. Indeed, it was posited, she seemed to 'find it cheaper to pay such a small fine and to carry out her system'. This time Eliza, or rather her husband, whom she sent to represent her, was fined £5 plus £18 costs. Whether this more substantial fine altered her business practices is unknown, but she did not make headlines again.[76]

Eliza's exploitation of female labour was not unique, as we have seen. Although the initiative, courage and entrepreneurialism of colonial businesswomen is admirable, sometimes their success was built on the exploitation of other women. Pursuit of profit could trump sisterhood.

Chapter 11

Pushing Boundaries: Exploiting 'accomplishments'

Playing minuets on the piano, singing solos at church fêtes, painting watercolours of flowers and keeping a diary were all prescribed activities for accomplished young ladies. Some women, however, went further, taking those accomplishments into the market place, not only teaching but performing and publishing. In this chapter we meet businesswomen whose businesses seem the antithesis of modest colonial femininity. They sang or danced or acted on the stage, not as employees but as independent stars or with their own companies. They published their words in authoritative black and white and exhibited their artwork. They gave public lectures to audiences of women and men.

'A most excellent amusement'[1]

One aspect of colonial women's much vaunted 'civilising' mission in the colonies was to offer the charm of music to relieve the tedium of everyday existence. Lady amateurs performed in polite company in drawing-room concerts, or for charitable causes, demurely decrying their talent. They learned their piano playing or singing from teachers, many of whom were also professional performers, combining teaching music with regular appearances in local halls and theatres, which provided publicity for their teaching. In Christchurch, Mrs Beechey gave 'finishing, singing and music lessons'. One of the few trained singers in the community, she was the stalwart of the local musical society for a decade. In late 1870, the *Lyttelton Times* suggested 'in the most friendly way' that she 'might now – perhaps ought to – withdraw from public solo-singing'. The *Star* agreed: 'she ought not, for the sake of her own reputation, attempt solos which require more compass and freshness of voice than she can now command.' Mrs Beechey ignored their advice and continued to perform and teach.[2] Further south in Dunedin, Louisa Clutsam, half-sister of touring bandmaster Alfred Labalestrier, also gave lessons and performed until 1886, when she moved to Auckland and continued to teach and occasionally appear in concerts. Her Australian-born son George Clutsam, claimed in 1873 as a budding 'New Zealand Mozart' by the local press, was one of her pupils.[3]

Other women made a living entirely from stage appearances. They were far removed from modest lady amateurs; these were truly transgressive show-women, boldly demanding attention for their talent, whether it be dancing, singing, acting or some other form of entertainment, and, perhaps even more boldly, demanding payment. Most led peripatetic lives, travelling around New Zealand and beyond. Many were part of theatrical troupes, often marrying or forming liaisons with their male colleagues, though they were frequently still referred to as 'Miss' regardless of their marital status. Some were employees but others were businesswomen: 'stars' travelling independently or running their own theatrical companies.

Women who travelled about as entertainers, venturing far beyond their local neighbourhoods and communities, challenged ideas of 'proper' feminine behaviour. One might expect that they would have been subject to tittle-tattle in the local press, dogged by scandal wherever they went, aspersions cast upon their character, morals and respectability. They certainly were in Britain, as historian Tracy Davis has shown. But in New Zealand they were not. Whatever shocking rumours were shared sotto voce in scandalised tones behind gloved hands in private, however many knowing nudges and winks were exchanged between men of the world over a pint in the local hotel about some visiting songbird or actress, the press, in the main, did not contribute, unless issues came to court. Instead, the likes of Madame Vitelli, the Misses Carandini and Anna Bishop were judged on their professional performances, in stark contrast to today's tabloids' obsession with scandal and scuttlebutt. Professional success was effective armour against scandal.[4]

Some women, such as Anna Bishop and the Carandinis, made long careers from performing, while others shone brightly for a moment and faded fast.[5] One less fortunate was Catherine (Kate) Redmayne. She and her sisters were all businesswomen after their arrival in Dunedin in 1857, her siblings Elizabeth and Anne more conventionally as dressmakers and running a ladies' school, before disappearing into matrimony.[6] Kate initially offered lessons in piano and singing, 'according to the principles taught in England', but quickly graduated to performance, becoming 'the Southern Vocalist' and delighting audiences across both islands in the 1850s and 1860s with her concerts and musical lectures. She was assisted by local amateurs and more seasoned performers, and sang traditional songs as well as new material, including the topical song, 'Pai Marire', which she wrote in 1865.[7] She was one of the earliest Pākehā female composers in New Zealand. Harriet Barlow in Wellington was the first, with the 'New Zealand Polka' in 1858, although she may not have earned any money from it.[8] Kate was entrepreneurial, offering a prize of 5 guineas in a singing competition in her first Dunedin concerts. She gave 'grand vocal entertainments' in Lyttelton in 1860, charging 5s for entry, and musical lectures in Otago and Canterbury.[9] She also toured England, performing in provincial towns. When she returned to Auckland in 1864, Kate exploited what had been a fairly unremarkable trip to England, styling herself 'late member of the Liverpool Philharmonic Mechanics Institute, Glee and Madrigal Societies ... recently returned from Great Britain'. The *New Zealander* described her as 'a talented and well-known vocalist ... about to start on a professional tour'. She worked her way south, giving concerts and lectures in Whangārei, Auckland, Napier, Wellington and Nelson. But by early 1865 the *New Zealander* had changed its tune, describing her unenthusiastically as 'a lady who has gained some celebrity in the country districts'. A review of her February performance in Parnell's Presbyterian schoolroom highlighted the problems that could face a travelling performer: 'We regret to say that the attendance ... was not so full as the clever and amusing lectures, as well as the exquisitely executed songs of this talented young lady deserved ... A large number of people enjoyed this concert free of expense, by standing close to the windows of the concert-room, from which place they could see and hear fully as well as those who had paid for admission.' The last mention of Kate performing was in a 'Drawing Room Entertainment, entitled Musical Mimical Character Sketches' at New Plymouth's Freemasons' Hall in 1866.[10]

Her next appearance in the newspapers was in 1869, when her death in Greymouth, where she was either living with or renting a room from organist and publican William Wood, attracted more column inches than her performances ever had. Apparently unaware of her pregnancy, and 'frequently seen the worse for drink', she died alone of an 'effusion of blood on the brain induced by excessive labor-pains, accelerated by previous drinking habits'. She had not made a will and her belongings were auctioned. As well as three boxes of clothes, ornaments, books and paintings, there were 'about 150 pieces of music', the only indication of her career as the 'Southern Vocalist', which went unmentioned in reports of her final days. Kate was just 44 years old.[11]

Show-womanship

Theatrical entrepreneur Mrs W.H. Foley was much more successful than Kate Redmayne. She was one of the first 'stars' of the New Zealand stage, reviews waxing lyrical about her 'genius'. When she first appeared in late 1855, the *Daily Southern Cross* declared that the performance of such an 'accomplished artiste' heralded 'a new era in the history of public amusements in Auckland'. Four years later, the *Wellington Independent* was also impressed: 'her acting [was as] elegant as it was perfect'. Theatre historian Peter Downes has described her range of roles as uncommonly diverse: she did indeed introduce a higher standard of acting to the country.[12] During the 1850s she appeared in her husband's circus and on stage in Sydney, Melbourne and in New Zealand. In the 1860s she toured New Zealand with her own theatrical company. She disappeared at the end of the 1860s, reappearing briefly in 1884 in Whanganui.

Until recently, nothing more was known about Mrs W.H. Foley, who could not even be credited with a Christian name in her entry in the 1990 volume of the *Dictionary of New Zealand Biography*. The recent development of searchable global digital archives allowed her identity to be uncovered in 2014. My serendipitous unearthing of a marriage notice buried in the columns of a Tasmanian newspaper led to the discovery of a whole history for Mrs Foley, a transnational tale involving multiple marriages, careers and reinventions, along with adulterous affairs, bigamy and child desertion.[13]

Catherine Huggins was born into an English theatrical family about 1820. Her parents Benjamin Huggins and Frances Pierce were both active in theatrical and lecturing circles, although it is unclear if their daughter performed. She married Lincolnshire chemist Daniel Caparn in 1845, having borne him a child, Charles Pierce Huggins, two years earlier. In 1847 Catherine's globetrotting began when she, Daniel and Charles emigrated to Hobart, where Catherine established a millinery business. Barely a year after they arrived their marriage was over. Catherine left for San Francisco in June 1849, just as gold was being discovered in California, and Daniel departed in September, leaving their six-year-old son in Tasmania, where he was 'adopted' by Launceston watchmaker and former Chartist leader, William Jones.[14]

By the time Daniel died in Honolulu in February 1851 Catherine was living in California with American circus impresario, William H. Foley. They married four months after Daniel's death and the newly minted Mrs W.H. Foley refashioned herself as an actress, making her Australian debut in Sydney in 1854. The couple toured the Antipodes with circus performances interspersed with theatrical engagements, and ran a boarding house in Christchurch in 1857. Sometime in 1858 Catherine and William Foley parted company, with William left holding their baby daughter, Kate Wilhelmina. William then took up with equestrienne 'Madame' Marie Tournear, with whom he had several children.[15]

Fêted as 'that distinguished American actress' in Sydney in 1859, Catherine established her own theatrical company, primarily of local amateurs, in New Zealand in 1860, touring until 1867. She was one of several women who travelled the world with their own companies.[16] Now in her forties, she apparently had a brief dalliance with 25-year-old photographer George Henry Swan, who acted in her productions and photographed her.[17] She found a new, more permanent leading man in Shakespearean actor Vernon Webster, who joined her company. The Foleys' split was amicable: for the next few years William's circus and Catherine's theatrical company appeared in different New Zealand towns as if in some carefully choreographed ballet, ensuring they were not competing for the same audiences. And when, unusually, they were both in Wellington in 1863, Catherine appeared at the Lyceum Theatre in a benefit performance for her estranged husband.[18]

Mrs Foley and Vernon Webster left New Zealand together in July 1867 for Valparaiso. A year later they were advertising a benefit performance so they could return 'to their own country' from Peru, 'having suffered severe pecuniary losses through the death of several members of the company of which they were at the head'.[19] Nothing was heard of Foley and Webster in New Zealand for the next 15 years. Then, in February 1884, the *New Zealand Mail* announced the return of Mrs W.H. Foley, who was living in Napier. Three months later, the *Wanganui Herald* advertised with great delight her reappearance, with Vernon Webster, at Whanganui's Princess Theatre.[20]

This was the last hurrah of 'Mrs W.H. Foley', but in Napier in February 1884, the memorably named Lowten Lowten and his wife Kate were at the Theatre Royal, playing the same roles as Foley and Webster.[21] They were, of course, one and the same. Lowten Lowten had adopted Vernon Webster as a non-de-plume when he began his acting career in Wellington in 1860.[22] The couple had married in West Derby in England in 1882, unaware or unconcerned that William Foley was alive and appearing at the Gaiety Theatre in Christchurch, New Zealand. Were they applying the 'seven years' disappeared' rule, or was there an official divorce?[23]

The simultaneous appearances of the Lowtens and Foley and Webster passed without comment in the newspapers, save for one brief report in the *New Zealand*

Mail in March 1884, acknowledging their dual identities. It is puzzling that they did not bother to advertise their appearances in Napier as Foley and Webster. Perhaps their pseudonyms were so well known it was unnecessary, or perhaps they were unsure of their reception. Neither of their performances received great acclaim – theatre had moved on since their heyday – and by 1885 they had swapped the stage for a more dependable source of income as hotelkeepers.[24]

PRINCESS THEATRE.
MONDAY EVENING, 21st APRIL.
Re-appearance of
MRS W. H. FOLEY,
AND
MR VERNON WEBSTER,
IN A
BRILLIANT PROTEAN ENTERTAINMENT!
For particulars see Programmes.

Mr and Mrs Lowten, the popular entertainers, will appear this evening at the Theatre Royal, in their performance entitled "A Brilliant Protean Drawing-room Entertainment," which has been given in the principal towns of England with much success.

'Brilliant Protean Entertainment'.

Wanganui Herald, 17 April 1884 and *Hawke's Bay Herald*, 29 February 1884

Although conducted in the public eye, Catherine's liaison with Vernon and her abandonment of her children, as well as her husband's liaison with Marie Tournear, were ignored by the press. As with other 'stars', it was Catherine's acting talent that was of public interest, not her private life, however titillating. Perhaps too, the frisson of sexual transgression was part and parcel of theatrical life, to be discussed in private but not in the pages of newspapers read over breakfast.

For leading ladies and theatre managers like Catherine, geographical mobility came with the job. Catherine's changes of names and husbands and her remakings of herself as milliner, circus performer, actress, singer, dancer, theatrical entrepreneur and publican both facilitated and were made necessary by her continual moving about. She was also self-sufficient. She attached herself to people who were useful to her – a keen emigrant, a circus proprietor, and a talented actor – and discarded those who were not – a six-year-old boy, a baby girl and a country-town photographer who outlived his appeal.

Eccentric performers

Singers and actresses were not the only businesswomen to take to the stage. Mesmerists, phrenologists and clairvoyants were active in the larger Australian markets from the 1850s. They included phrenologists Madame Sibley and Mrs Beer, and the entrepreneurial 'Madame Carole', 'Clairvoyante Physician' of Collins Street, Melbourne.[25] 'Madame Carole' also advertised in the *Wellington Independent* in 1861, offering remote diagnoses for the fee of £1. She was, in fact, Caroline Harper Dexter, famous 'bloomerist' and female activist, who diversified her portfolio of money-making activities with admirable energy.[26] In this case, she took full advantage of the growing popularity of pseudo-scientific fads, although whether any Wellingtonians availed themselves of her offer is unknown. New Zealand towns were too small to guarantee profitable audiences and only a few male phrenologists, fortune-tellers and mediums toured New Zealand before the 1870s.

New Zealand's first female performer of this ilk was 'Ida Bonifon', who arrived in 1874 with 'her astounding performance of SECOND SIGHT, or SUPERNATURAL VISION', accompanied by American 'conjurer and anti-spiritist' William A. Chapman. William's wife Emily in Melbourne advertised plaintively in New Zealand newspapers, begging him to 'write to your wife and child; they have had no communication for 18 months', but William paid no heed; in 1876 he was with Ida in Honolulu. One cannot feel too sorry for Emily Chapman, however. She had been a regular and colourful feature of newspaper columns since before her marriage. (She did not have the protection of being a professional star.) Then, as 'milliner and dressmaker' Emily Knox, 'a showily dressed young lady' who lived 'under a gentleman's protection', she was involved in frequent neighbourhood disputes. By 1877 she was the licensee of the Freemasons' Hotel in Swanston Street and still notorious, denying accusations of brothel-keeping and charging a newspaper proprietor with libel and extortion.[27]

Also gracing antipodean stages was Madam Cora de Lamond, aka Ohio native Ursula Bush (née Wainwright). 'The only Female Magician in the World' thrilled audiences in Australia and New Zealand in the 1860s and 1870s before going on a world tour. She was rumoured to have killed a young female member of her troupe in the Cape of Good Hope in 1877. Newspapers across the colonies ran wild with this story: murder was a step too far, even for stars of the stage. The rumours were thoroughly quashed when the alleged victim turned up alive and well in the United States. It nevertheless provided free advertising, keeping Madam Cora at the forefront of the public's mind. When she died in Durban in 1902 her second husband described her 'rank or profession' on her death notice as 'Professional. Known the World over as Madam Cora.'[28]

Madam Cora was the first of several female illusionists and fortune-tellers who were very popular by the end of the century, often combining public performance with private appointments. Mrs Dr Helen Burnaby (see Chapter 8) gave public lectures to women on medical matters, which were ideal advertisements for her private practice as an 'eclectic physician' and 'gynaecologist'. Whanganui-born Isabella Russell Sim married Danish phrenonologist Charles William Borreson in 1889 and immediately began practising herself. Within a few months she was being advertised as 'a deep and successful student of the science' of phrenology. The *Marlborough Express* 'strongly' recommended residents to consult her: 'Her system of classification of faculties, and her food, health and marriage tables are of quite a novel character.' She was also invited to lecture to local schoolboys, which the paper felt would be 'a very great treat and highly instructive'. The couple moved about together and separately in what was clearly a tumultuous relationship; they had a daughter in 1894 and eventually divorced in 1907; Charles claimed Isabella had wanted to leave him the day after the wedding. She gave lectures and offered consultations across the North Island until 1894, but how her money was earned subsequently is unclear. She came from a financially comfortable family – one brother became a well-known judge. Her ability to invent herself as a phrenologist was particularly impressive given that she was locally born rather than an exotic import.[29]

Show-womanship could also be exercised in the name of religion. Primitive Methodist Ruth Waters was in the business of saving souls and filling collection plates. She preached alongside her husband Charles around New Zealand from 1864 to 1874. Although, according to the *New Zealand Herald*, her sermons were 'not remarkable for any unusual display of originality and are perhaps somewhat wanting in that comprehensive methodical arrangement, vigour, and clearness of logic of the opposite sex', she was effective. The paper conceded that she had 'a certain self-possession and apparent earnestness that are calculated to invest her sermons with a good deal of impressiveness and interest, and which display a highly-cultivated intellect'. In New Plymouth in 1868 she attracted an audience of 200–300 people, although she did not please everybody: two young Primitive Methodist ministers threatened to resign if she preached.[30] For many, speech was clearly still 'the business of men', as Telemachus famously told his mother in *The Odyssey*, providing, according to Mary Beard, the first recorded example of a man telling a woman her voice should not be heard in public.[31] As she pointed out, 'when it comes to silencing women, Western culture has had thousands of years of practice'.[32] Nevertheless, women's voices were certainly audible across colonial New Zealand.

Ursula Wainwright, 'known the world over as Madam Cora' and 'The Only Female Magician in the World'.

Madam Cora (Cora de Lamond), magician, State Library of Victoria, Bk.11/No.110

The art of making money

In nineteenth-century rhetoric, sketching and painting were also framed as elegant accomplishments for young ladies. Women's art was rarely taken seriously enough to be sold or commissioned. Several women exhibited art and craftwork at the international exhibitions, but only a few made it a business. Like musicians, some combined teaching with the production of creative work. Although this is sometimes recognised today, it was not seen as marketable at the time, as in the case of Sarah Greenwood (see Chapter 5). (Sarah sent some work to London to be lithographed, but may not have benefited financially.)[33]

One of New Zealand's first female botanical artists was Martha King, who was commissioned by the Wellington Horticultural and Botanical Society in 1842 to produce watercolours of indigenous plants and woods for the New Zealand Company. Her primary sources of income, however, were the schools she ran with her sister Maria. They opened the first dame school in Whanganui in 1841 and another, with their sister-in-law, after the family moved to Taranaki in 1847. Whanganui settler Jessie Campbell was impressed with Maria, writing to her sister that 'her method is excellent, she is so kind and at the same time determined'. In New Plymouth theirs was the 'top school' according to their competitor Sarah Pratt. Martha's friend Emma Wicksteed also combined teaching with painting. In 1845 a lithograph of Emma's painting of New Plymouth was published, along with four lithographs of Martha King's botanical paintings, in Edward Jerningham Wakefield's *Illustrations to 'Adventure in New Zealand'*, although whether Emma received payment is unknown.[34]

Twenty-four-year-old Mary Townsend was already an accomplished and experienced painter when she arrived in Christchurch with her family in 1850. Charlotte Godley, who thought her 'the nicest of the Misses Townsend', commissioned her to paint her son and her husband, paying between 3 and 5 guineas per picture. According to Charlotte, Mary was surprised by the commission: 'It seems she used to take portraits professionally in London; but she did not expect to be asked for such things here.' Mary married 36-year-old Dr William Donald in 1851. Her flag, painted for the 1863 celebrations of the Prince of Wales' marriage in 1863, and carried in the procession, was chosen to be Lyttelton's permanent 'Banner of the Town'. She died in 1869, having suffered an attack of paralysis in 1867.[35] Later in the century Emily Cumming Harris of Nelson sold her paintings, exhibited at several exhibitions and published books of New Zealand flora, but, as with Martha King decades earlier, her earnings were insufficient. She ran a school in Nelson with her sisters from 1870 to 1886 and then took pupils for painting lessons at her 'studio' in Nile Street. By 1914 'Miss Harris' Studio' was 'open to the public'.[36] She exhibited frequently, and was well regarded.

Ink on a page

As with painting, middle-class girls were encouraged to scribble in diaries and journals, but it was another thing entirely to publish novels, plays, poems and travelogues.[37] And actually getting paid for one's writing, then, as now, was not always guaranteed; neither is it sometimes clear in the records. Some writers were clearly businesswomen, using their pen to make money, but others perhaps were not. Charlotte Lees Evans wrote romantic novels in Oamaru in the 1860s and 1870s. Her first efforts were serialised in the local newspaper in 1865, but whether she was paid is not clear.[38] Lady Mary Anne Barker was certainly paid. Her *Station Life in New*

Zealand (1870) was enormously successful. Lady Barker was prolific, exploiting her well-travelled life and penning several further books in the early 1870s.[39] Many of her works were part of a well-developed genre of female travel writing, although success was not guaranteed. Jane Hamilton Hope apparently published a *Narrative Relating to New Zealand* in 1857 in Dublin, but her book, if it existed, has left no trace. She probably hoped it would provide some financial relief. She had emigrated to Nelson four years earlier as a widow with three young sons, only to discover the land she thought she had bought did not exist. She persevered in New Zealand, including managing the Trafalgar Hotel, a position she held until she was 75 years old, but her literary ambitions went no further.[40] Maria Thomson published her *Twelve Years in Canterbury, New Zealand* (1867) as one of several moneymaking ventures (see Chapter 5). She wrote, however, that she had been 'induced to publish' her 'little work' of 'unadorned simplicity'. In reality a serious businesswoman, her self-deprecating words played to convention.[41]

Napier's Fanny Murdoch wrote the first 'proper' New Zealand cookbook in 1887, exploiting women's supposed domestic expertise. The title, *Dainties, or, How to please our lords & masters*, raised eyebrows even then. Later, as domesticity became a science involving new technologies, Elizabeth Miller made a career combining cookbook writing with teaching.[42]

Before women such as Louisa Baker were employed by newspapers as journalists they were considered 'freelance'.[43] Susan Nugent Wood was a contradiction. Although she earned money by contributing to newspapers and published literary collections, she held that 'women's work' was in the home and involved self-sacrifice to family.[44] Other women used journalism to espouse the cause of women's rights. In 1869 Nelson's Mary Ann Muller wrote *An Appeal to the Men of New Zealand*, a pamphlet in which she argued for the extension of the franchise to women. Published under the pseudonym 'Femina' in Nelson, it sold for a shilling. If Mary Ann herself was paid she had to hide her income, because her husband was apparently unaware of her feminist scribblings.[45]

In Wellington Mary Taylor vented her spleen in private letters to Charlotte Brontë and Ellen Nussey but did not publish until after she left New Zealand. Then, already with property investments and shopkeeping profits, she turned to her pen for additional income. Her publications reflected her feminist views. In the *Victoria Magazine* in the 1860s she wrote that 'the first duty … is for every woman to protect herself from the danger of being forced to marry'. She also published a novel, *Miss Miles*, which she had been writing in New Zealand.[46]

Auckland schoolteacher Frances Shayle George (see Chapter 5) was also a writer, publishing prose and poetry in Charles Dickens' weekly magazine, *Household Words*. The 'stated rate of payment' in *Household Words* for prose contributions was a guinea for a two-column page; poets were paid about twice that amount.[47] Frances's poem, 'An Emigrant's Glance Homeward', essentially a lament for home, was printed in 1852 and was reproduced throughout the British Empire. Settlers in Canada, Australia and Southern Africa could all 'glance homeward'. One of the lines in her poem was this comforting thought:

> Yet I am happy in my distant home;
> A sunny sky smiles over me;
> And let what will from God's good pleasure come,
> My friend, my husband I will always have *thee*.[48]

She was to be disappointed in her own husband, solicitor Thomas Shayle George, whom she had married four years earlier. He disappeared from Auckland in 1867, accompanied by rumours of fraud, and died a year later in the United States.[49] Frances was left to run her school, Wye Cottage, which she did successfully, and was celebrated as an educator when she died in 1890.

Frances was an outspoken advocate of girls' education although never a suffragist.[50] Her letter to the *New Zealand Herald* in 1872 echoed Susan Nugent Wood's sentiments. She declared that 'a woman's sphere is not the world, nor to govern the world – but to purify it; to be the leading principle of good order, peace and refinement, in man's sole remaining Paradise – his own Home'.[51] Just two years later, however, speaking to the Auckland Teachers' Association, she had modified her approach, perhaps appealing to an audience of fellow educators. She advised that girls should be given 'such an education as will best fit them to support themselves in whatever station of life they may be placed … surely nothing can be more prejudicial to the inner and higher life of any girl than to present continually before her eyes, as the highest hope and aim of her existence, the acquisition of a husband!'[52] Here she sounds more like Sarah Greenwood and her daughters, who did not limit women's activities to the home but were circumspect in their activism. Leading colonist Emily Richmond, in a speech in 1886 upon the Greenwood sisters' retirement from teaching, announced approvingly: 'They have taught and practised "woman's rights", not separated from her duties, as the way with some is.'[53] Those 'some' might have included Frances George's contemporary Mary Ann Colclough, who made the cause of women's rights her moneymaking business.

Speaking out

Mary Ann Colclough, who sparred with Frances Shayle George more or less politely through the columns of the local newspapers, is better known as 'Polly Plum'. She arrived in Auckland in 1857 as Mary Ann Barnes, an experienced 21-year-old governess, and in 1861 married Thomas Caesar Colclough, a farmer 30 years her senior.[54] By May 1862, already a few months pregnant with her first child, Mrs Colclough advertised her intention to open a school for young ladies 'in the healthy locality' of Papatoetoe. She variously ran her own schools and worked in state schools over the next decades, past Thomas's death in 1867.[55]

But Mary also had another life and another source of income: from 1868 'Polly Plum' began writing for newspapers. As she declared, in response to some criticism, she had taken up journalism 'to provide for my little fatherless children', noting that 'if I confined my attention solely to washing my dishes they would not often want washing, as there would seldom be food to put on them'.[56] Like Mary Taylor, 'Polly Plum' derided the idea that women's only work was to care for house and husband. She was an advocate of women's education, employment *and* suffrage. In particular, she spoke out in favour of married women's property rights. Her activism stemmed from personal experience: she had suffered from her husband's financial recklessness with money that she had earned. 'I was the breadwinner,' she wrote, 'whilst he had all the breadwinner's powers and privileges.'[57] In 1871, finally advertising as 'Mrs Colclough (Polly Plum)', she began giving popular public lectures.[58] The *New Zealand Herald* acknowledged in 1873 that she was an accomplished public speaker with 'a wonderful flow of language' and the ability 'to give full expression to her convictions', but was less approving of some of her content and her international exposure. The paper was concerned that 'her peculiarities [had] obtain[ed] publicity in the columns of the leading London journal', rather than locally, where her 'views are known, and accepted for what they are worth, [and] she can do no harm'. Was it any wonder that the *Herald* was disconcerted, given her lectures had titles such as 'Woman's Rights and Men's Wrongs Towards Them'?[59]

After being declared bankrupt in 1874 Mary moved to Melbourne, 'seeking to win a pleasanter livelihood', according to the *Auckland Star*. She had been invited by Martha Turner, recently appointed female pastor of the Melbourne Unitarian Church. New Zealand papers were quick to report Mary's failure to attract Australian audiences. She 'soon discovered that women's rights in Victoria are looked after tolerably well by themselves', as the *Daily Southern Cross* rather snarkily put it. In 1876 the *Auckland Star* announced that she was 'destitute' in Melbourne, with the *Argus* seeking subscriptions so that she could return to New Zealand. She returned quietly in the same year and took up teaching again in Rangiora, north of Christchurch. When she died in 1885 at the age of 49, the *New Zealand Herald* gave her a brief and uneffusive obituary, noting that 'her death would be regretted by many who knew her in the olden times', while the *Observer* remembered her as '"Polly Plum" (Mrs M.A. Colclough) formerly a clever contributor to the Auckland Press'.[60]

Pushing boundaries

The women in this chapter challenged ideas about women's place in New Zealand society by living their lives in the spotlight, confounding expectations of feminine modesty and decorum, by exploiting their accomplishments, whether music, art or writing, for profit, and by writing and speaking and arguing for the right of women to be financially independent from men, making a business of activism. Some were also geographically mobile, unsettling notions of stable domestic femininity. They were not, however, the only women to travel the world.

Chapter 12

Globetrotting

Nineteenth-century globetrotting was not restricted to white men, to a worldly elite, or to stars of the stage. Quite ordinary men and women criss-crossed the world, and not all those who migrated settled down. Rather, they moved on, moved about and moved back. They explored new horizons, were seduced by gold, or ran away from scandal, from debt or from unsatisfactory spouses.[1] For many, their ability to run a business enabled their mobility; for some, mobility was an integral part of their business strategy.

But mobility had two sides, especially for women. It could be admirable, offering opportunities to expand an enterprise, escape unpleasant situations or reinvent oneself. The *Auckland Star*'s obituary of the aged Eliza Rampling, of the Hanneken/Otto/Rampling family network, attributed her longevity to an 'adventurous life [that] seemed to strengthen her constitution'.[2] She had accompanied her first husband, British Army storekeeper George Otto, to the Peninsular War before moving to New South Wales, then to New Zealand with a second husband. Similarly, although more privately, Frederick Olson reported proudly to his family in 1858 that his new wife Eleanor Wallace was 'a far traveler shee has traveled Round The world shee left london when a small girl with a lady to the Cape of good hope'.[3]

Mobility, however, also contained suggestions of irresponsible rootlessness, and an unprotected female was looked upon askance. In 1850 the *Maori Messenger* 'remarked with great regret the departure of several native females for the shores of California'. They were following Pākehā lovers, the paper suggested, and it predicted a dire future: 'They will eventually be thrown desolate on a strange country whose people will despise them, and they will be left to die … like dogs in a ditch.'[4] Less alarmingly, Māori women had accompanied Pākehā husbands and partners on whaling expeditions, and Māori women and men were frequent visitors to Sydney from the eighteenth century.[5] Pākehā families were spread across both sides of the Tasman and business connections were strong. Melbourne and Sydney were metropoles for New Zealand towns, with businesswomen like draper Agnes Campbell making buying trips to the former. Some women rejected New Zealand in favour of Australia. Mary Grace Huxham's teaching venture in Nelson lasted barely six months before she was on a boat to Wellington in December 1842. She ended up in Tasmania and married Christopher Todd in 1851. In Australia she turned to hotelkeeping and then ran a servants' registry office.[6]

Tracking globetrotters

Women who moved around are sometimes easier to trace than those who settled, since they pop up in English censuses, or in newspapers across the world. As always, more unusual names are easier to find, although evidence is not necessarily conclusive. An 1854 gravestone in San Francisco for an 'Emily Chevassut, wife of Captain Joseph Wilson', suggests a sad end for a 21-year-old milliner who was in partnership with Hannah Losee in Auckland for six months in 1851. It is possible that Emily had been seduced by the charms of the captain of the barque *Hamlet*, which plied its trade through Auckland.[7] Other than placing them on the map as they travelled, however, understanding why women moved and what their experiences were can be difficult. Miss Agnes Dunlop Curl advertised a ladies' school in Nelson in 1849, taught in South Australia and then in 1855 was back in England after a whirlwind romance and marriage to the Royal Navy's William Philips on the Island of Ascension. Twenty years later she reappeared alone, running a school in Charleston, South Australia.[8] Beyond this her life is unrecoverable.

There are tantalising glimpses of women who were clearly strong personalities, but whose personal circumstances are frustratingly obscure, although they would have been familiar to contemporaries, if only briefly. Feather cleaner and milliner Jane McDonald did not stay long in Whanganui – her quirky advertisements in 1869 disappeared within the year – but she returned in 1886, boasting of having been 'twenty years in the trade'. She helpfully explained where she had been, hoping the cachet of being 'Late of Melbourne' would add to her marketability. She vanished again in July 1888.

In Melbourne, Jane McDonald advertised her glove and feather-cleaning services from Emerald Hill between 1880 and 1882. She diversified, promising 'Revelations,

Exciting and Amusing' for those who would send her '1s 8d stamps, Christian name, complexion age and address'. She also offered to 'carefully read and explain private papers' for the sum of 2s 6d. This may not have been successful, for in 1882 'McDonald 65 Clarendon Street' was wanting a 'Hotel … furnished unfurnished, must be bargain'. Was this Mrs McDonald or perhaps a husband, if he existed? Mrs McDonald obligingly resurfaced in Melbourne after leaving Whanganui in 1888, once again cleaning feathers. Although a woman of some character, Mrs McDonald's first name was elusive until an 1880 Melbourne street directory finally revealed Mrs *Jane* McDonald as a glove and feather cleaner. After moving around South Melbourne, Jane disappeared at the turn of the century.[9] We do not know why she flitted between Melbourne and Whanganui – was there family pulling (or pushing) her from one to the other? – but her ability to run a business facilitated her mobility. She may not, however, have found a market in the small New Zealand town for her revelations. Such frivolous, some might say fraudulent, enterprises were probably better suited to a more anonymous large city.

A combination of family ties and the search for prosperity motivated many women's (and men's) perambulations, and their business skills were critical to success. Clarissa Cazaly had a millinery business and a circulating library in New Plymouth from 1855, alongside her brother's commercial academy. Her general store operated from the same address until 1858, when Clarissa, her accountant husband James and their children moved to Nelson. Clarissa was again in business, first in a short-lived partnership with

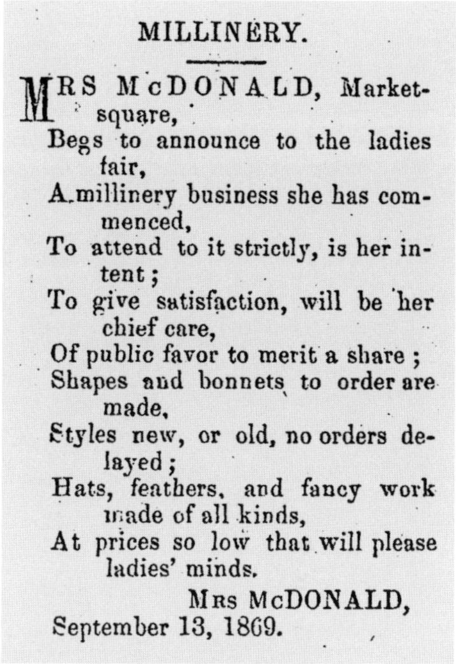
MILLINERY.

MRS McDONALD, Market-square,
Begs to announce to the ladies fair,
A millinery business she has commenced,
To attend to it strictly, is her intent;
To give satisfaction, will be her chief care,
Of public favor to merit a share;
Shapes and bonnets to order are made,
Styles new, or old, no orders delayed;
Hats, feathers, and fancy work made of all kinds,
At prices so low that will please ladies' minds.
MRS McDONALD,
September 13, 1869.

Jane McDonald's imaginative advertisements caught the eye.

Wanganui Herald, 16 October 1869

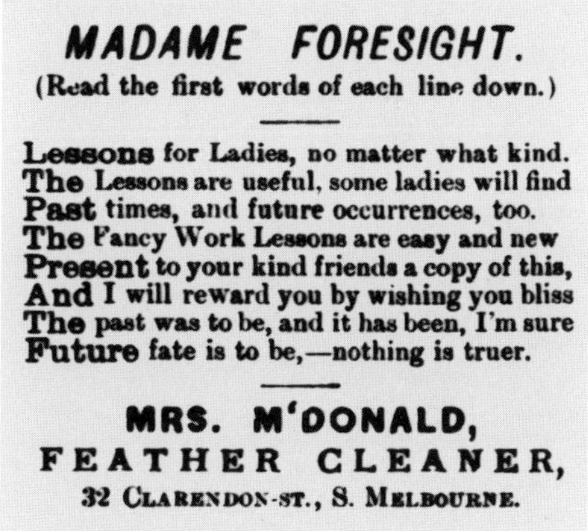
MADAME FORESIGHT.
(Read the first words of each line down.)

Lessons for Ladies, no matter what kind.
The Lessons are useful, some ladies will find
Past times, and future occurrences, too.
The Fancy Work Lessons are easy and new
Present to your kind friends a copy of this,
And I will reward you by wishing you bliss
The past was to be, and it has been, I'm sure
Future fate is to be,—nothing is truer.

MRS. M'DONALD,
FEATHER CLEANER,
32 Clarendon-st., S. Melbourne.

Jane McDonald's expanded enterprise in Melbourne.

Mercury and Weekly Courier, 16 October 1890

Alice Butiment and then independently, while James sold potatoes, cheese and other goods.[10] Between 1859 and 1871 the Cazalys were in Sydney, where Clarissa swapped millinery for boarding-house keeping in the Rocks, and James worked as an accountant. In February 1872 they returned to New Zealand, this time to Auckland where, seven months later, James committed suicide after losing money in a goldmining company. A relief fund raised £126 for Clarissa and her daughters and after a brief foray into boarding-house keeping and music lessons, in 1873 the family moved back to Sydney, joining Clarissa's brother and sister who had settled there. The Cazaly daughters ran a ladies' school at Auckland House in Manly and then in Surry Hills until 1885. Clarissa unsuccessfully tendered for the post office contract in 1875 in Manly, remaining there until her death in 1909.[11] As for many others, family was central to her mobility and her economic survival.

Some families seemed to specialise in spreading siblings around the globe. Selina Hurst lived in the Channel Islands, Wellington, Western Australia and Utah, ending her days in French Polynesia. She had emigrated to New Zealand in 1840 as a child, running a school for three years until her marriage to William Elias Taunton in 1854. He was the well-spoken black sheep of a good English family, sent down from Pembroke College Oxford after betting he would kiss the first woman he met in the street. Regrettably, that happened to be the dean's wife. Selina quickly became the stable breadwinner of the couple, resuming her school in 1866 after William became insolvent.[12] We do not know whose idea it was to move to Western Australia in the 1870s. Selina ran a boarding house in Perth, wrote articles for the local newspaper and later became the headmistress of the girls' school in nearby Northam. William, meanwhile, was wheeling and dealing, charming the good citizens of Northam with his manners and accent. He served on several local committees until he was accused of forgery and fraud while collecting school fees.[13]

When William died in 1877, Selina's brother Frederick 'heartily wish[ed] I could think of some redeeming quality in his character as a tribute to his memory, but alas I cannot'. Frederick and another brother Charles had joined the Mormons and although Selina had been 'full of abuse' against the church, by 1880 she was a teacher in Utah, living with Charles. Her travelling was not over, however. She died in 1894 in French Polynesia, living near a sister, Amelia Goltz.[14]

A life of mobility

Like the Hursts, the Liardet family moved around. Liardet men are associated with the development of Melbourne and New Plymouth. Less well remembered is a daughter, Josephine, whose entrepreneurial spirit was reflected both in her journeying, which took her as far as China, and her business activities that sustained her mobility.

The Liardet family was among the first to settle in Melbourne, where Wilbraham Liardet ran a hotel and sold paintings.[15] His daughter Josephine married Captain John Venables in 1854 and accompanied him to Hong Kong. This was a time of simmering tensions between the First and Second Opium Wars, and John left his wife in Hong Kong while he went to Whampoa (now Huangpu) in Guangzhou province to collect cargo. Josephine decided, against all advice, to follow him. As she wrote in the memoir of her derring-do, 'they said it would be suicidal to go'. Having dealt with her European protectors, she charmed a man-of-war captain, 'who told me ladies were not allowed on board', into taking her as a passenger. She reached her husband's ship, to find him 'dangerously ill and no one but the Doctor allowed to see him'. Naturally she took over, and, despite herself 'suffering terribly from the effect of the "stink pots" which the Chinese use to suffocate the people', she restored her husband to health. The doctor 'praised my nursing and said I had saved my husband's life'. Danger was all around: the 'rebels' 'practised terrible atrocities upon the British at every opportunity – de-capitation was the favourite method … and I was becoming extremely nervous'. She managed some sightseeing, despite feeling very anxious, especially on hearing the story of Captain Brown's wife, who had 'escaped near death by fighting off her attackers with her parasol'. Josephine herself did not have to resort to such measures. When confronted by some agricultural labourers she 'did not like the look of', she 'thought it best to make friends so I bowed first to one and then to the other and gave them my hand to help me up'. This behaviour apparently appealed to the men, who 'gave me a very pretty tray of ground nuts', which she was told was 'the highest compliment they could have paid me'. She finally departed some months later, with 'memories of many curious, alarming and altogether unusual events'.[16]

By 1859, having returned to Melbourne via England, Josephine was running a servants' registry office in St Kilda. In 1860 she diversified, adding dressmaking and sewing machine lessons. She again proved herself willing to stand up for herself and others. In 1862 she wrote to the *Argus*, publicly warning 'needlewomen at large' against the perfidy of Isodore Bernstein, who was 'conducting business in the name of Mrs Huffy'. He ran a scam offering work to women if they paid him a £1 deposit, and then refusing either to return the deposit or pay for the work.[17]

After John Venables died in 1864 at the Yarra Bend Lunatic Asylum, where he had been since 1859, Josephine crossed the Tasman to Auckland with her four young children, at least two of whom had been conceived during her husband's incarceration. She opened a servants' registry office in Wyndham Street before moving to bigger premises, offering luggage storage on the side, and advertising as far away as Napier. New Zealand was an obvious choice for Josephine. Her uncle Francis had been the New Zealand Company land agent for New Plymouth – credited with saving the life of Governor William Hobson, he had a street named after him – and her parents had migrated in the 1860s to Wellington, where her mother Carolina ran a boarding house in Willis Street. In 1866 Josephine also moved to what was by then the capital and opened yet another registry office.[18]

That year she married John Parker (or Poniatowski) Macdonald, moved to the West Coast and continued in business. In 1867 Ellen Bellinger sued John Macdonald for maintenance of her illegitimate daughter, Sophia Catherine Macdonald. Although the child was born before Josephine met John, the situation was awkward. When Josephine was convicted of 'striking [the daughter] on the back with a piece of wood' as she was being piggy-backed by her mother down the street, her lawyer contended that 'considerable ill-feeling existed' between the two women, with Ellen 'attempt[ing] in every way to annoy' Josephine, including 'hammer[ing] against the side of [her] house and abusing her'.[19] Ellen and her daughter disappeared from the records after this. Despite this challenge to her marriage and her respectability, Josephine remained with John and ran registry offices on the West Coast until 1873, when she briefly disappears from the records.[20]

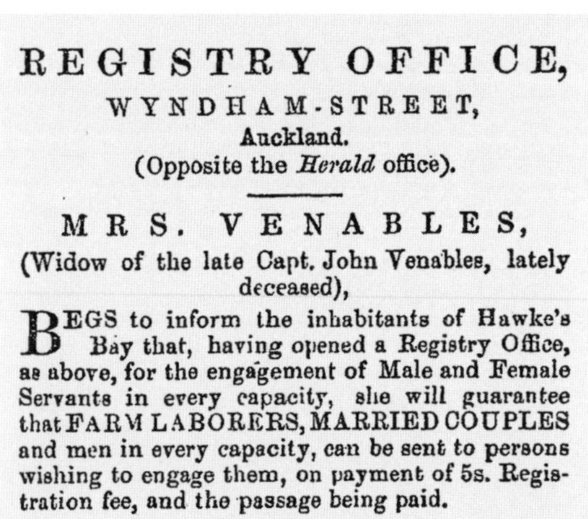
REGISTRY OFFICE,
WYNDHAM-STREET,
Auckland.
(Opposite the *Herald* office).

MRS. VENABLES,
(Widow of the late Capt. John Venables, lately deceased),

BEGS to inform the inhabitants of Hawke's Bay that, having opened a Registry Office, as above, for the engagement of Male and Female Servants in every capacity, she will guarantee that FARM LABORERS, MARRIED COUPLES and men in every capacity, can be sent to persons wishing to engage them, on payment of 5s. Registration fee, and the passage being paid.

Josephine Venables charged 5s to send servants to Napier from Auckland, using her widowhood and her husband's status to emphasise respectability and to exact sympathy.

Hawke's Bay Herald, 11 October 1864

She resurfaced in Wellington in 1879, starting 'a new industry … the manufacture of surgical belts, anti-rheumatic corsets (covered with wash-leather and lined with

Josephine Macdonald, late Venables, née Liardet, had multiple businesses enabling her mobility. Family stories suggest her West Coast servants' registry may also have been a brothel. (Tarja Walter) Private collection: Michelle Park flannel), Indian quilted cans, for summer wear, &c'. The *Evening Post* wished her 'all success in her undertaking, and hope that she will receive hearty and substantial support from the public'.[21] Josephine was the breadwinner: the 1883 directory listed her as a surgical belt maker, while her husband was merely a 'settler'. She remained in business for another 20 years. After John died in 1900, Josephine finally retired in 1901, at the age of 70, and passed her corsetry business to Miss Louisa Chant. The latter was not so successful, a victim of changing fashions perhaps, and was working as a charwoman when she died eight years later.[22]

Meanwhile Josephine Macdonald lived on, losing none of her vim. In 1916, aged 85, she organised a Red Cross sale of women's work for the benefit of disabled soldiers, even persuading her five-year-old great-granddaughter to make and sell dolls' clothes. She lived to be 97, dying in 1928 at her daughter's home in Wellington.[23]

A strategy of 'inventive' entrepreneurship

For some women, mobility was an integral part of their business strategy. Blessington Flood's husband, Charles, was a tailor in Nelson in 1866, having migrated from Mudgee in New South Wales, where he had become insolvent in 1860.[24] 'Some of the most respectable inhabitants of Mudgee' had given evidence that he had 'been living a very extravagant life both shortly before and since his insolvency', and had been 'in the habit of gambling and otherwise unlawfully expending the proceeds of his business'.[25] Blessington may have participated in the extravagance, but in Nelson she contributed to their support, recognising a business opportunity. She established a 'labor mart', proposing to provide local clients with domestic servants from Sydney and Melbourne. Although she cited experience 'in the Registry Offices of both Sydney and Adelaide', no record of this can be found in either city. She obtained the public support of Nelson's highest ranking official, Provincial Secretary Alfred Greenfield.[26] With this well-advertised sanction and having commanded sufficient local interest, Blessington went to Sydney and invited prospective servants to apply to her 'Registry Office' at the White Hart Hotel in George Street.[27] She made a much-anticipated return to Nelson at the end of April 1866 with 20 domestic servants.[28] She took another trip later in the year, having obtained orders for servants from as far afield as the West Coast. In February 1867 a second batch of 22 young ladies arrived from Sydney.[29] She endeavoured to expand her services to Wellington, approaching government officials there, but does not seem to have received encouragement.[30]

Blessington Flood was not unusual in running a servants' registry office. She *was* unusual in providing a transnational service. But, quick to exploit any commercial opening, that was not all she did. After her wax flowers were admired in August 1867 by the *Nelson Evening Mail*, which commented that it was an art 'not extensively practised by the lady members of this community', Blessington began to offer lessons, although in a later court case the judge suggested her prices were 'exorbitant'. Leatherwork lessons cost £1 10s, and seven wax flower-making lessons £3 3s, plus costs of materials.[31]

Blessington's eye for the main chance was also apparent when she was in Sydney in December 1866 gathering prospective servants. Seeking to profit from the gold rushes on the West Coast, she offered her services to 'Miners, Speculators, and others intending to proceed to New Zealand' as someone 'fully qualified to give all the necessary information to parties who may apply to her'. She had, she claimed, 'visited nearly the whole of the Provinces and all the principal Diggings of New Zealand' and had 'twelve years' experience in Victoria and New South Wales'.[32] It is unclear whether anyone availed themselves of her 'expertise'.

The Floods moved back to Sydney in 1868 after Charles became insolvent in Nelson. Blessington diversified again, starting a 'Clothing Club for Females' in conjunction with a similar business for men run by her husband in Pitt Street in 1870.[33] Charles was bankrupt again in 1883 and 1889.[34] It is impossible to say whether Blessington's entrepreneurial efforts contributed to Charles' insolvencies or offset them. Nevertheless, she was adept at exploiting her mobility and moneymaking opportunities when she found them. Her exaggeration of her experience was not unusual. Many businesswomen (and men) played a little fast and loose with the truth in advertising their services, and moving on to another town or colony provided ideal opportunities for reinvention.

Married to mobility

Some women married mobile men and found themselves dependent upon their own resources. Susannah Miller discovered her inner businesswoman when she ended up in Auckland with seven children. Her second husband, Moravian missionary Frederick Miller, had taken her from Manchester via New South Wales to a remote mission station on the Mokau River in the middle of New Zealand's North Island. After his death in 1847, the Wesleyan Missionary Society bundled her off to Tonga to marry another missionary, George Miller, whose Tongan wife had recently died leaving five children. In 1854 Susannah was back in Auckland, having added two more children to her brood, and was burying 46-year-old George.[35]

She spent the next seven years in business, starting by running a boarding house, then selling homeopathic medicines and finally establishing a draper's shop in 1857.[36] She married for a fourth time in 1859; Stephen Pain Brown was a recently widowed commission agent. That year, possibly with access to more capital through her marriage, Susannah employed 'a first class milliner from one of the leading Parisian establishments'. She sold the business to sisters Elizabeth Adlam and Sarah Anderton in 1861.[37] When she died aged 58 in 1869 she was buried next to her third husband, George Miller. Stephen remarried again within the year and eventually returned to England.[38] At first glance, Susannah seems to be a follower, traipsing around the world with missionary husbands, but her Auckland business life demonstrated that she could be self-reliant if required.

Wives of whalers, sailors and other seafarers were also well travelled and had to be independent. Some travelled both alone and with their husbands. Wellington boarding-house keeper Sarah Dougherty circumnavigated the globe, from New Brunswick in Canada, whence she had emigrated as a child, to England, Australia and the Bay of Islands. Very pregnant, she remained there with her husband's friends while he continued whaling. After giving birth, Sarah returned with her child to New Brunswick, via her in-laws in New Orleans. She and her husband were reunited in St John, then emigrated to New Zealand via London. Sarah's New Zealand garden included lemon-scented geraniums, lavender and strawberry plants, cultivated from seedlings carefully carried from her parents' home in Canada, while in her wardrobe hung treasured dresses from New Orleans, reflecting her international 'mind-map' of belonging.[39] Other seafarers' wives also found themselves alone in port cities, left to survive for various lengths of time, not knowing if their husbands would return.

Augusta Horton was a sea captain's daughter, so she knew what to expect when she married Herbert Ellis Danvers, master of the *Countess of Seafield*, in England in 1862. She accompanied him to Australia in 1864 with their young child but they were nearly wrecked near Hobart,[40] which forced Herbert into bankruptcy. They moved on to New Zealand. Augusta gave birth to a second child on board a ship in Lyttelton Harbour and they retreated to Napier, where Herbert's brothers were living and where Augusta took over as breadwinner, establishing a young ladies' school. By 1866 they were in Nelson, where Augusta again ran a school. When Herbert struggled to find employment in 1866, Augusta's aunt, Catherine Greenwood, wrote to her acquaintance, politician Donald McLean, requesting assistance in finding a 'situation' for the husband of her 'especial favourite' niece, who had 'left a comfortable home and fond parents' and borne 'severe troubles and hardships'. McLean's response is unknown, but by 1871 Augusta was back in England, where she and her four children were living spread between relations. Herbert had returned to sea. Augusta, who had another child in 1876, died three years later, aged 39, and Herbert four years after that in Singapore.[41] Their experiences encapsulate the fragility of lives lived at the whim of the sea, demanding long absences and financial contributions by both partners.

Escaping husbands

Some women used their abilities to run a business and move about to escape an unsatisfactory marriage. In the case of Madeline Nakin, it seems to have been not her marriage but her daughter's. 'Madame Nakin from Paris' started a millinery business with great aplomb in October 1855 in Auckland but in December was on a ship to Valparaiso with her husband Jacques and their 17-year-old daughter Octavie. Octavie's husband of just one year was left behind in Sydney.[42]

Dorothy Tomkies was used to travelling independently. Her husband Thomas was already in New Zealand when she followed him in 1847, bringing with her their two sons, aged five and six. Thomas, a leather merchant by trade, had been in Nelson since 1842, having migrated five days after the birth of his second boy.[43] Dorothy, who was from a teaching family, established a school in Nelson. Henry Daniell (see Chapter 5) was delighted to have found 'a sensible pious woman' to whom he could entrust his daughters' education and very sorry to lose 'our most intimate friend' when she returned to England in 1851. Dorothy's school was not advertised in the newspapers, and without the survival of Henry's letters its existence would be virtually unknown. Family history suggests that she and Thomas argued about their boys' upbringing. Leaving her husband behind, Dorothy took her children back to England and the family business, a ladies' school called Chaddock Hall at Astley near Manchester. All six Gretton sisters worked in the business and lived together in various combinations at different times. Thomas remained in New Zealand and at least one of their sons went back there and named his home Little Chaddock Hall. Dorothy's descendants spread as far afield as Canada and Australia.[44]

Dorothy's experiences show that running a business to survive independently of a male breadwinner was not restricted to the colonies, but part of a longer history in Britain and one that stretched across the empire. There may have been more economic opportunities in the new colonies, but family support was also critical. With four children under 10, a dysfunctional marriage and no immediate family in Nelson, Dorothy judged that a long sea voyage and a business enterprise with her sisters was preferable to going it alone in New Zealand.

The Married Woman's Advisor

It is perhaps unsurprising that the marriage of Dr Robert Porter Welch, author of *The Married Woman's Advisor and Young Mother's Guide,* published in London in 1838, did not live up to his expectations. He told his brother in 1874 it was 'an unfortunate one and the source of many a trouble since, for in travelling about to avoid it I took it with me'.[45] Robert, a 34-year-old doctor described disparagingly by one observer as 'short in stature, and very stout in person … coarse in his language, and uncouth in his demeanour', had married 19-year-old Helen Uther in Sydney in 1841. Over the next decade the family moved from Sydney to Murrurundi and then to West Maitland in the Hunter Valley, where by late 1852 Robert held the licence of the Northumberland Hotel. He also served as ship's surgeon on two voyages, one to London via China in 1847 and the other to Honolulu and California in 1851. He may have intended 'travelling about to avoid' his marriage, but Helen and their two children were also listed as passengers.[46]

By 1854 the family were in Lyttelton, where Robert was promoting his 'little book', *The Married Woman's Advisor.*[47] Designed for a married woman's boudoir, where she might consult it discreetly 'for her especial guidance', it purported to avoid 'profuse advice', fearing it 'tend[ed] rather to perplex than inform'. Nevertheless, Robert included a large amount of information in 116 pages, written in a florid and patronising style, on 'the treatment of those ailments which so frequently occur during the important period of pregnancy'.[48] He did have medical experience, but he wrote this while a bachelor and aged barely 30. No doubt he placed this 'little book' in Helen's hands during her own pregnancy.

Robert managed to escape his marriage in 1858, after the family had been in Wellington for three years. He moved to Greytown with their son, while Helen remained in Wellington with their daughter. This must have been a daunting moment for Helen, for she well knew how precarious life could be for a woman on her own. In 1826 her mother Maria had left Helen's father, Reuben Uther, in Sydney and moved to Tasmania. She drowned three years later, having, according to popular report, 'pursu[ed] a life of infamy, depravity and guilt', the latter presumed to have been caused by 'having eloped from her husband's protection, leaving him with two or three children'.[49] Helen Welch was more fortunate than her mother, and took care to ensure that she could support herself through her own enterprise. She opened a girls' school in Wellington with her daughter and for the next three decades moved between Wellington, Napier, Hamilton and Auckland, running schools and offering music lessons.[50] Her school business meant she was financially independent, but it was also portable, enabling her to relocate near her daughter in later years. She was one of many women for whom running a business was a means to escape an unfortunate marriage.[51]

Escaping social convention

Mary Taylor escaped a stultifying life as a vicar's spinster daughter in a small Yorkshire village, first to teach in Europe and then to New Zealand, where she became a shopkeeper. As Charlotte Macdonald and Frances Porter note, such a role back home would have 'jeopardised her status as a gentlewoman; it was a matter not just of social nicety but of social fabric'.[52] Nearly 50 years later, Isabel Cargill, granddaughter of the 'founder of Otago' and part of an extended, highly respectable middle-class Otago family, made the opposite journey to escape, finding Dunedin 'too provincial'. She and an English friend, Anna Maria Babington, travelled the continent. They spotted a business opportunity when they searched in vain to find 'a decent cup of tea' in central Rome. Babington's Tea Rooms, which opened in 1893, is still a well-known landmark at the foot of the Spanish Steps, run today by Isabel's great-grandchildren. Isabel also wrote 'Letters from Rome' for the *Otago Witness*. Both Isabel and Mary Taylor used a combination of travel and business to explore opportunities beyond the domestic. Mary Taylor avoided social convention by travelling to a 'new' society. For Isabel, Italy was sufficiently foreign to allow her to escape the growing middle-class consciousness of post-goldrush Dunedin.[53]

Forgetting scandal

Before improved communications later in the century made breaking from one's past more difficult, many women avoided scandal by moving on and reinventing themselves, particularly if they had the means to earn a living.

Babington's Tea Rooms in Rome, founded in 1893 by Englishwoman Anna Maria Babington and Isabel Cargill, granddaughter of the 'founder of Dunedin'. Isabel escaped provincial Dunedin with a long-lived Italian business and Italian painter husband.

Photo: Catherine Bishop

Amelia White's awkward predicament was not of her own making, although her later behaviour suggested a level of complicity. Living in London in 1841, happily married to a surgical instrument maker Charles Eagland and mother to a young son born in 1835, Amelia had her world turned upside down by the reappearance of Charles's first wife. As Amelia's great-niece recorded in her family history, Charles, 'faced by a blowsy middle-aged woman, could not deny that as a student he had married the cook of his college'. Quickly realising his mistake, he had fled 'this most unsuitable wife' and ended up in London. Unfortunately he had failed to obtain a divorce. Women were rarely granted custody of their children and Amelia was forced to leave her home, her 'husband' and her young son, who was already 'showing promise of a brilliant musical career', having performed at the court of Queen Victoria. In 1842 she boarded the *London* for Wellington with her sisters Sophia Thomas and Ann Worsley and their families. Fortunately, Amelia had a trade: she advertised in Wellington in 1843 as 'a stay and corset maker from Mrs Huntley's in

Regent Street'. Emigration so far away from her husband and son may have been her sisters' plan rather than her own, because she soon sailed for Sydney to 'join friends'. Those friends were, in fact, her husband and son. Family history suggests their reunion was by chance, Charles Eagland having travelled to find his 'true love' after the death of his unwanted wife. This seems a little serendipitous. Whatever the case, their happiness was short-lived. Charles died within a year, in 1845, just before his daughter Sarah was born. Amelia established another business as a dress and stay maker to support her family until her remarriage several years later.[54]

Straw-bonnet maker Sarah Masters also crossed the Tasman to escape an unsavoury past. From 1842 she and her husband Joseph, a cooper, ran well-patronised parallel businesses on Wellington's Lambton Quay. Politically active Joseph later became an early settler in Wairarapa, where the town of Masterton is named after him.[55]

Sarah's veneer of respectability, however, hid a scandal. In Hobart in 1835 she had appeared before the Supreme Court charged with murdering her newborn baby. The details of the case were so shocking that the *Hobart Town Courier* declared it 'not of a nature to lay before our readers; though it excited intense interest among numerous auditory'. The *Colonial Times* had no such prudish scruples and told all – of a suspiciously dark-skinned baby, an absent husband and a tearful confession by Sarah to a midwife of an extramarital affair with a non-European man followed by infanticide.[56] Medical evidence was unable to prove exactly how the child had died and Sarah was eventually acquitted. It was fortunate for the Masters that this story did not make it to interstate newspapers; it was certainly forgotten by the time the couple arrived in Wellington seven years later. Joseph married widow Sarah Bowler nine months after Sarah's death in 1859 and closed the lid on his first marriage, barely mentioning his first wife in his memoirs. When these were published in 2005, however, the editors rectified his omission, including the story of Sarah's misstep.[57]

Reinvention was central to Mary Ann Brown's mobility. 'Madame De Bar' had a millinery and dressmaking business, selling 'an elegant assortment of Parisian and English millinery' and offering lessons in 'the Art of Dress Making', alongside her husband's chemist shop in Auckland's Queen Street in 1858. After just six months she closed her shop, announcing 'she would 'resume business in a few days'.[58] She never did. Instead she vanished. 'Madame de Bar' was actually Mary Ann Harriet Hoare Brown, born in London where, aged 18, she had married Richard Cooke, aka 'Monsieur de Bar', in 1844. The couple had arrived in Auckland in December 1857. After their brief sojourn in New Zealand, they turned up in 1859 in Goulburn,

MADAME DE BAR,
AT APOTHECARIES HALL,
QUEEN-STREET, AUCKLAND,
MILLINER, DRESS AND MANTLE-MAKER,
From Bond-Street, London,

BEGS to acquaint the Ladies of Auckland and its vicinity, that she has brought from England an elegant assortment of Parisian an English Millinery; also, all the newest Fashions in Mantels, Lndies' and Children's Dresses; and that she has made arrangements with her Agents in England to forward the London and Paris Fashions monthly.

MADAME DE BAR having had great experience for many years in instructing young people, will undertake to teach the Art of Dress Making, &c., &c., in a Series of Lessons. Patterns given to Pupils. Ladies desiring to have their Patterns taken for their own use can depend upon the latest designs.

Apprentices and Improvers wanted, also a good first hand Dressmaker.

'Madame de Bar' advertised for six months before suddenly disappearing.

New Zealander, 23 January 1858

New South Wales, where 'M. De Bar' was again in business as a chemist and 'Madame de Bar' had reinvented herself. 'Having great experience in the Medical Profession', she could 'be consulted by ladies'. She sold fancy goods on the side. Their story then becomes more dramatic. In 1866 40-year-old 'Madame de Bar' skipped town with her husband's young assistant, 18-year-old Richard Bellamy, and 'a large amount of gold [she] had always kept concealed around her stays, and which she had carried away to enrich her transferred love'. A year later her husband had drunk himself to death and the runaways were married, Mary Ann recording her age optimistically as 32. Three days after the wedding she was dead, poisoned, it was said, by her new young husband to acquire the money she had inherited from her late spouse. He was tried but not convicted. The murder did not reach New Zealand newspapers, other than a brief comment on Richard Bellamy's acquittal by an *Otago Daily Times* correspondent. No one connected the sad story of the poisoned 'Anne Hoare Bellamy' to the Auckland milliner 'Madame de Bar' nine years earlier.[59]

Scandal following

As the century progressed and news travelled more quickly, the revelation of scandalous pasts, criminal dealings and bigamous marriages became more difficult to avoid, although, as Harriet Corston's case shows, public memory could still be mercifully short. Harriet Reed was only 17 when she arrived with her parents and five younger siblings on the *Jura* in Auckland in 1860, but within two years she had established a millinery and dressmaking business in popular Queen Street.[60] Less than 12 months later she sold off her stock and married Peter Corston, who took over the premises as a commission agent.

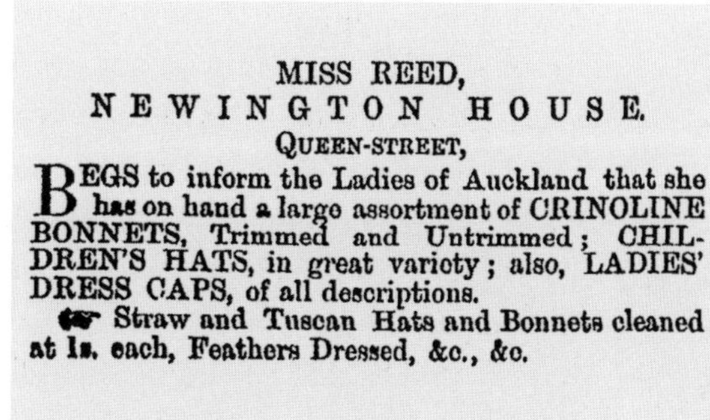
MISS REED,
NEWINGTON HOUSE.
QUEEN-STREET,
BEGS to inform the Ladies of Auckland that she has on hand a large assortment of CRINOLINE BONNETS, Trimmed and Untrimmed; CHILDREN'S HATS, in great variety; also, LADIES' DRESS CAPS, of all descriptions.
☞ Straw and Tuscan Hats and Bonnets cleaned at 1s. each, Feathers Dressed, &c., &c.

Daily Southern Cross, 4 December 1862

Over the next 20 years the Corstons moved around New Zealand, sometimes living together and sometimes apart. As Peter euphemistically explained, they changed address when his 'affairs became somewhat involved'. In addition to twice becoming insolvent, he was prosecuted for embezzling funds from an Auckland confectionery wholesaler and in 1872 had 'done a "little bit" of defrauding the Government of New Zealand' by smuggling tobacco on the Thames goldfields.

Meanwhile, Harriet brought up her children, moving between Auckland, Thames, Nelson and the West Coast.[61] In 1874 with the support of her mother, who lived with her, she opened Newington House Millinery and Dressmaking Establishment in Thames next door to her brother William Reed's photographic studio.[62] Although she often struck financial difficulties, she was adept at persuading men to lend her start-up capital.[63] She could also defend herself. When creditor Henry Campbell turned up on her doorstep demanding his money in 1878, she not only took him to court for assault but also 'used strong language', calling him a 'dirty old blackguard'. She was accused of 'pulling his whiskers', which she strenuously denied.[64] There was, of course, more to the story. Henry had taken Harriet to court two months earlier seeking £48 11s he claimed he had lent her. It became clear during the case that Henry had thought this was more than a business relationship. The judge found in his favour but commented that 'it only proved how silly gentlemen could make themselves. When they were in this silly state they were very generous with their money, but on reflection wanted it back again.'[65]

In 1882 Peter and Harriet were together again, as teachers at the Te Ngaere Native School in Northland. It was closed a year later, owing to a lack of support by local Māori.[66] Peter then disappeared to Melbourne in 1884 and Harriet went into business in Auckland. In 1886 she crossed the Tasman and married widower William Green Hibble, a justice of the peace and well-respected businessman she had known in Auckland. He was keen to marry Harriet 'because she was a good businesswoman'. Within six months, however, they separated; William would later claim that she was 'an expensive woman to keep'. Harriet, again using the name Corston, ran what was described in the social columns of one New Zealand newspaper as a 'high class boarding establishment' at Roslyn Hall in Darlinghurst Road. According to her son, Harriet was 'harassed' by William after their separation with 'repeated visits', provoking her to threaten to 'horsewhip him' if he turned up again.[67]

Missing here was a small but necessary detail – the death of Peter Corston. In 1889 he turned up in Sydney, having spent time at Her Majesty's pleasure in Pentridge in Victoria for receiving stolen goods.[68] During the ensuing bigamy trial, Harriet's name was splashed across newspapers throughout Australasia.[69] Readers were riveted by the 'he said/he said' allegations. She not only claimed that she had thought Peter Corston was dead but her defence, significantly, rested on the fact that 'there was no necessity for her to marry Hibble [as] she was in a position to make her own living'.[70] Nevertheless both she and William were found guilty. William was sentenced to 12 months' hard labour, but Harriet received a token imprisonment merely 'to the rising of the court', which meant literally until the end of that day. Clearly her charm had worked on the judge. Her real punishment perhaps was ending up saddled with Peter Corston until his actual death in 1894. She ran boarding houses and hotels in Sydney and the Blue Mountains before returning to New Zealand and to millinery in 1901.[71] Ever alert to business opportunities, in 1911 she petitioned parliament for a land grant on the basis of her entitlement to 40 acres as a single female immigrant in 1860. She died in 1918 aged 75.[72]

Harriet is an extreme case of the ways in which scandal, mobility, business and gender intersected. She was not alone, though, in being 'in a position to make her own living' and using that to facilitate mobility. We are used to reading about the travels of elite men and women, of 'remittance' men muddling their way around the globe, of luckless male gold seekers and of Miles Fairburn's 'rootless' male wanderers, but we are less used to imagining ordinary women circumnavigating the globe, engaging in business to make it possible.[73] Yet many did.

Chapter 13

Forgetting and Remembering

Forgetting

Tourists wandering along Wellington's Willis Street today can pause to admire an old house labelled 'Spinks Cottage c 1860' in the grounds of St John's in the City, on the corner of Dixon Street. Its heritage colours exude a recognisably 'historic' aesthetic: tourists know that they are seeing 'the past'. Until the mid-1880s, this was the home of storekeeper William Spinks, his wife Mary and their daughters Florence and Jane. But it was also a 20-year-long business premises. Florence ran a school there from 1860 until 1879, with Jane until she married in 1862, and then alone. As George Macmorran wrote in 1900, 'all old settlers remember well the popular school of the Misses Spinks, [where] … a large percentage of the Te Aro girls (and small boys) received … their early training'.[1]

Nothing at the site today recalls this long-lived enterprise. Although familiar while memories survived, it has also become almost invisible in the archive, appearing in only a few directories and rarely advertised in the newspapers before the 1870s. Jane's diaries are reticent about the *business* of the school, although students and lessons appear frequently.[2] Spinks Cottage exemplifies how female entrepreneurship and participation in the colonial economy can disappear from history.

Several factors contribute to the forgetting. Women's businesses tended to be small and seldom passed to the next generation or lasted into the twentieth century. When they did, it was usually through an injection of testosterone, as men took over and women's contributions were often downplayed. We tend, also, to celebrate businesses that grew and lasted, rather than the many little enterprises, run by men and women, which together made up much of the fabric of urban life. Another factor is the dearth of family memory. The achievements of women without progeny faded fastest. Long-time businesswomen the Jay sisters of Nelson had no local descendants to keep their memory alive. When the last Miss Jay, Winifred, died in August 1883, she was eulogised only as a 'much respected and aged settler'.[3] Such worthy women were entrenched figures in their local communities, frequently running businesses and often, like the Jays, stalwarts of the church, washing dishes, sewing pew cushions and baking cakes for bazaars. But they are seldom remembered after death, and are quickly replaced by another generation of loyal female workers.

Women's obituaries generally celebrated their 'self-sacrifice', community service, longevity and fecundity, and made much of the public or commercial achievements of their male relations. Obituaries acknowledging women's business acumen were rare. That of Matilda Ritchie, 'well-known grocer' and member of the Port Chalmers Old Identities Association, was one. Widowed at 38 and childless, she continued the bakery and grocery store she and husband Archibald had established in Port Chalmers in 1859. She invested in property and developed the business, obtained a bottle licence in 1875 and worked until a year before her death in 1918. The *Otago Daily Times* called her business 'one of the oldest' in Port Chalmers, celebrating her 'great interest in all that concerned the public life of the town'. Matilda Ritchie is, however, barely remembered today, probably because she was childless, although the building she had erected at 10 George Street, until recently the Port Royale Café, still stands.[4]

'A lifetime's washing and cooking leaves no monuments', noted Margaret Anderson and Kylie Winkworth.[5] Nor do many women's businesses. While men were carpenters or ironworkers, architects or jewellers, whose furniture, buildings and heirloom necklaces survive through generations, women ran schools, hotels, food stores and retail outlets, providing services, consumables or goods that were ephemeral, albeit essential, just like a lifetime of washing and cooking. Even surviving clothing is often anonymous – labelling began in the later nineteenth century – and tends to be items worn only rarely, 'best' clothes or those of the rich, which spent more time in wardrobes than on bodies. These lend themselves to stories of weddings and parties, rather than of working lives.[6]

Pākehā 'pioneer settler' memorials tend to depict men, endowing them with 'pioneering spirit' or 'entrepreneurialism'. Memorials to pioneer women stick to the 'colonial helpmeet' rhetoric, honouring 'pioneer mothers', who 'maintained their homes' with great 'self-sacrifice' and 'endurance'.[7] Only a few individual nineteenth-century women, such as Christchurch suffragist Kate Sheppard or Waimate doctor Margaret Cruickshank, have memorials. Emily McWilliam, erstwhile dressmaker and missionary wife, was celebrated for her contributions as nurse, homeopathist and Otaki Cottage Hospital fundraiser. Her memorial, a public clock in

The carefully preserved exterior of Spinks Cottage in Wellington gives no hint of its past as a school, run by businesswomen sisters Florence and Jane Spinks. Photo: Michael Hall

the post office, disappeared, however, when the building was demolished in the 1950s.[8] On the rare occasions Māori women appear, they are generally depicted as romantic heroines in pre-European 'Māori legends', attracting the tourist gaze at suitably scenic destinations.[9]

Individual men do have memorials. They often converted business clout into political power, wrote themselves into history and created lasting monuments. Despite winning the vote in 1893, women could not be members of parliament until 1919: their commercial power was expressed more often in community, charitable and social contexts. Businesswomen served alongside leisured middle-class matrons on ladies' committees, in benevolent societies and in temperance campaigns. Onehunga's Matilda Furley was one such businesswoman. While her husband Samuel dealt in real estate, Matilda from 1844 managed their general store, bakery, confectioner's and a hotel. After his death in 1878, Matilda continued to run the bakery into the 1890s. She was active in St Peter's Church and helped to found the local Ladies' Benevolent Society. Indeed, her intervention in the cause of destitute militia wives, who led 'a cheerless existence' in the local barracks which were 'in a very insanitary condition', led to the society's initial meeting. The society's first president was hotel owner Elizabeth George. The next generation of strong Onehunga women went one step further: in 1894 Elizabeth Yates became New Zealand's first female mayor.[10]

Some women did exercise political rights earlier in the century. In Nelson, butcher Ann Bird, chemist Clara Macshane and Jane Hamilton Hope were property owners and ratepayers and could vote in school board elections in the 1850s.[11] In Auckland in 1871 town clerk Frank Brodie explained that 'there was nothing in the [Municipal Corporations] Act to prevent females from being enrolled on the burgess roll', which included all ratepayers and entitled them to vote in local elections. Councillor Thomas Macready, husband of publican Ann, confirmed that women had indeed voted in past city board elections. A number of women were listed on the 1872 burgess roll, including publican Louisa Macmahon of the Nottingham Castle Hotel and Shortland Street milliner Miss Nicholas.[12] In 1880 shopkeeper Mary Ross appeared on the New Plymouth roll, which listed ratepayers entitled to vote in council elections.[13] In 1885 Matilda Meech, fruit-shop owner and later baths proprietor, successfully applied to be listed and was one of Wellington's earliest female burgesses. Her presence, and that of a number of other women, was entirely overlooked in the 1897 *Cyclopedia of New Zealand* which, although recognising that 'Women have equal privileges with the men', declared that 'so far, no woman has sought municipal distinction in Wellington'.[14] Through running businesses, these women gained entrée to the political periphery, an important step towards full enfranchisement and political power. There were many businesswomen's names on the suffrage petitions of the 1890s.

Remembering

If you know what you are looking for, New Zealand's city streets today offer numerous opportunities to remember nineteenth-century female enterprise. The lovely façade of Kirkcaldie & Stains recalls a long-lived department store run by men, although we could spare a thought for 'the best saleswoman in Wellington', Kate Kelly, who decamped to go into business with young Warnock and Adkin. 'James Smith's Corner' in Cuba Street is the site of Mary Taylor's shop. In Auckland the department store buildings of Marianne Smith and Charlotte and Mary Jane Milne still stand, although the McLaughlin sisters' store has long gone.

The Takaka Pioneer Memorial lists 69 pioneers, all men. More recently the Town Plaques project has highlighted historic buildings, recognising entrepreneurial women like Julia Byrne of the Byrne Family Butchery. Photo: Byrne Family and Heritage Golden Bay

Small towns have often been better at remembering pioneer businesswomen than cities. The museum in the tiny West Coast town of Ross has immortalised Ellen Gill's skill as a businesswoman. A display of the family Bible and a christening gown belonging to Richard and Ellen Gill might be expected to tell a story of Ellen's domestic and maternal activities, but instead the label describes her entrepreneurial skill: 'In New Zealand Ellen proved to be a superb businesswoman and amassed a considerable amount of money on the share market, whilst Richard worked the goldfields.'[15] In Takaka, Golden Bay, surviving heritage buildings bear plaques with photographs and stories of their erstwhile residents, including businesswomen. The label for Julia Byrne's butcher's shop, run with husband Henry in the 1890s, reads: 'Julia was known as a dynamic businesswoman. She regularly went by boat to Nelson with their own cured bacon and hams and even boxes of their popular home made soap utilising the tallow.'[16] Butcher Ann Bird and draper Sophia Anstice have prominent places in the Nelson Provincial Museum. Property owner and Greytown hotelier Elizabeth Hacker and her sister, shopkeeper Emma Jeans, have streets named after them.[17] At Hayes Engineering Works and Homestead in Otago, the remarkable

Hannah Hayes, repairing her bicycle, is immortalised on the coffee packet sold at Hayes Engineering and Homestead in Central Otago. The tagline celebrates her ingenuity and recalls nineteenth-century rhetoric that allowed women to be capable entrepreneurs within a framework of need rather than ambition.

Heritage New Zealand Pouhere Taonga

Hannah Hayes is front and centre: 'Dressed in ankle-length skirts, she made intrepid bicycle trips throughout the Maniototo and MacKenzie [sic] counties, seeking orders for Ernest's early inventions … A colourful example of creativity and determination in the face of hardship and isolation.' Hannah and her trusty bicycle even appear on the packets of coffee Heritage New Zealand produces for sale there.[18]

Heroes and villains: A final cautionary tale

The businesswomen in the pages of this book deserve acknowledgement in our history, but should not be placed on pedestals. Some were laudable; like some men they managed businesses, were devoted to their families and became embedded in communities, contributing to the building of a better society. Others seem less admirable, building their success on the exploitation of others or flouting the letter or the spirit of the law. Consider the highly entrepreneurial Mary Ann Macgregor. Pieced together, the scant evidence shows she suffered some misfortune as she reinvented herself from milliner to Chinese merchant in the 1880s. Her first husband, George Lester Simpson, probably drowned in 1865 on the West Coast; her second, Edward Higgins, was a bigamist. By 1873, Mary Ann was in Thames with two Simpson sons and four Higgins offspring all under nine. Her third partner, William Gibbons, added three more, all of whom died of scarlet fever in 1881. Mary Ann, meanwhile, became known in the Thames courts. In 1875 two sons were sent to the industrial school as neglected children: William Simpson was an 'associate of thieves'; Joseph Higgins, 'a very wee child of the London Arab type', was arrested for stealing. Two years later Mary Ann was imprisoned for assaulting her neighbour with a 'piece of scantling [timber beam] containing rough nails', after which sons John and Augustus Higgins were taken into care. When Mary Ann was released after three months, she and William Gibbons were immediately in court for larceny. In 1881, Mary Ann left Gibbons and seemed to pull herself together. She established a feather and hat cleaning and dying business in Brown Street, later moving to Pollen Street and adding new services, including ladies' millinery and making Panama hats for 'young men and youths'.

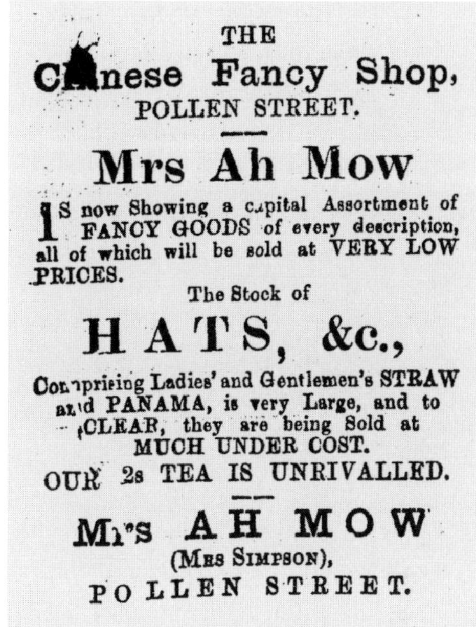

Was there ever a Mr Ah Mow, or was Mary Ann Macgregor trying to sound exotic? *Thames Star*, 5 January 1885

September 1884 saw the ultimate reinvention: Mrs Simpson became 'Mrs Ah Mow' with a 'Chinese Fancy Shop' selling fancy goods and fireworks. She also reconnected with her children, although one magistrate suggested her interest in 16-year-old John Higgins derived from his now being 'able to work'. 'Mrs Ah Mow' was in business for several years, donating Chinese curios to the Wesleyan Bazaar in 1888. There was no sign of a Mr Ah Mow.

In 1893, Mary Ann, 'better known as Messrs Ah Mow', a 'widow', was committed to the Auckland Lunatic Asylum for at least one year with 'chronic insanity'. Her record there reveals a sad state of affairs. She owned the land and shop in Pollen Street, but it was mortgaged to its full value of £120. The public trustee sold everything to pay for her maintenance in the asylum. Her five living children, scattered throughout the colony, were 'inactive in respect of their mother'. Perhaps she deserved no less.

Thirteen years passed and then she resurrected herself yet again as Mary Ann Macgregor, marrying William Stevenson in 1906. Seven years later she died in Rotorua, aged 75.[19] Mary Ann's story demonstrates that being in business guaranteed neither an adequate livelihood nor an admirable character, but it also shows the limitations of the archive. The piecemeal evidence can be read a number of different ways and often raises more questions than it provides answers. We do not know Mary Ann's real motivations or circumstances. In an age that told women to seek financial security through attachment to men she chose badly. Forced to fall back on her own resources, she discovered an entrepreneurial streak but seems to have sacrificed much along the way.

Women mean business

Colonial businesswomen did not pass laws or stand for parliament, construct railways or build monumental town halls, yet they played vital roles in shaping New Zealand society. They dealt with the stuff of everyday life: few New Zealanders could avoid dealing with or benefiting from a businesswoman's enterprise at some point in their week. They clothed and hatted and shod, birthed and nursed and buried, fed and watered and entertained the populace; they provided decorative stuffed birds and library books, butchered meat, baked goods and procured hard-to-get servants for needy ladies and companionable bodies for needy men. They educated the younger generation, sold the luxuries that distinguished living from existing and, through establishing places to relax, gossip and enjoy life, provided the social cement that made an urban community.

There was no typical businesswoman or typical female business. Women ran a wide variety of enterprises of varying sizes and for differing lengths of time at all stages of their lives, just as men did. Family support was often critical. Their sex sometimes restricted their activities but also occasionally provided opportunities for filling a niche market. Married women had to negotiate laws of coverture, would-be hotel proprietors the vagaries of licensing committees. Women were not educated to be entrepreneurial, may well have had less access to capital and were not expected to be ambitious in their businesses – few lasted beyond a generation or into the twentieth century. Women's primary responsibility for childcare and housekeeping also affected which businesses they operated, and how. There were opportunities, however, to cater to a female market, or exploit a 'female' skill. New Zealand, as a developing economy, offered business openings for those who might have been employees at home.

As the twentieth century approached, conditions for women gradually changed. Wives gained more control over their property, women obtained the vote and educational opportunities expanded. Universities began to admit women from the

1870s, widening the variety of jobs and professions available. There were more jobs, too, in the developing department stores, manufactories and public schools. It was not all positive, however. Women's businesses were vulnerable to this increased competition as well as to economic downturns. The hotel licensing system continued to discriminate against them.

The rhetoric of idealised female domesticity and respectability pervaded nineteenth-century New Zealand. It was there when missionary families first modelled the perfect nuclear Christian family for the benefit of local iwi; when Thomas Bracken, composer of New Zealand's national anthem, in parliament described women as 'the light of the home and genius of the fireplace'; when the suffragists argued for the vote because women guided families and ran households.[20] As the women in this book illustrate, however, the role of the 'colonial helpmeet' could quite respectably encompass moneymaking enterprises. Their circles of connection radiated out from the domestic to encompass wider family, neighbourly and business networks. If we remember that women had multifarious roles, including visible, respectable and sometimes successful places in the world of colonial business, any notion of New Zealand as a 'man's country' is unsettled.

According to a survey commissioned by the ANZ Bank, in 2013 women still owned only one-third of small businesses in New Zealand, although that may not have included husband–wife partnerships, which would increase the number substantially.[21] More broadly, statistics on senior business management suggest that female participation has actually gone backwards, down from 31 per cent in 2004 to 18 per cent in 2018.[22] The businesswomen in this book provide new role models – and cautionary tales – and another way of understanding women's participation in New Zealand history. In the nineteenth century, as now, being female did not necessarily mean being restricted to the home or low-paid employment; women could mean business.

Abbreviations

General

Ancestry: Genealogical website www.ancestry.com
Archives NZ: Archives New Zealand: Auckland, Wellington, Christchurch, Dunedin
ATL: Alexander Turnbull Library
AWMM: Auckland War Memorial Museum
Burke Manuscript: William Ellison Burke, Burke Manuscript, Christchurch City Libraries
DNZB: Dictionary of New Zealand Biography, Te Ara, the Encyclopedia of New Zealand
ENZB: Early New Zealand Books, Auckland University
FamilySearch: Genealogical website www.familysearch.org
FMCES: Female Middle Class Emigration Society
Macdonald Dictionary: George Ranald Macdonald, G.R. Macdonald Dictionary of Canterbury, Biographies, Canterbury Museum
NPM: Nelson Provincial Museum
NSWBDM: New South Wales Births Deaths and Marriages index
NZ Census: Census of New Zealand for various years
NZ Probate: New Zealand probate records, Archives NZ
NZBDM: New Zealand Births Deaths and Marriages website
NZETC: New Zealand Electronic Text Collection, Victoria University of Wellington
NZLII: New Zealand Legislation Information Institute, NZ legislation website
Papers Past: Papers Past, digitised newspaper website, National Library
SLNSW: State Library of New South Wales, Sydney
SLV: State Library of Victoria, Melbourne
Te Ara: Te Ara, the Encyclopedia of New Zealand
UKBDM: UK Births Deaths and Marriages Records
UK Census: Census for England and Wales for various years

Newspapers

Argus: The Argus (Melbourne)
AS: Auckland Star
Colonist: Colonist (Nelson)
DSX: Daily Southern Cross (Auckland)
DT: Daily Telegraph (Napier)
EP: Evening Post (Wellington)
ES: Evening Star (Christchurch)
FS: Feilding Star
GRA: Grey River Argus
HBH: Hawkes Bay Herald
HBT: Hawkes Bay Times
LT: Lyttelton Times

NEx: Nelson Examiner and New Zealand Chronicle
NEM: Nelson Evening Mail
NOT: North Otago Times
NZ Truth: NZ Truth (National)
NZer: New Zealander (Auckland)
NZG: New Zealand Gazette and Wellington Spectator
NZH: New Zealand Herald (Auckland)
NZMail: New Zealand Mail (Wellington)
NZSCSG: New Zealand Spectator and Cook Strait Guardian
NZT: New Zealand Times (Wellington)
OW: Otago Witness
ODT: Otago Daily Times
Press: The Press (Christchurch)
SMH: Sydney Morning Herald
Star: Star (Christchurch)
TA: Thames Advertiser
TH: Taranaki Herald
TS: Thames Star
WC: Wanganui Chronicle
WCT: West Coast Times
WH: Wanganui Herald
WI: Wellington Independent
WT: Westport Times

Notes

Chapter 1: Don't Assume It's a Man

1. *DSX*, 13 May 1859 p. 3.
2. *NZer*, 11 May 1859 p. 2.
3. Garth Houltham, *The James Q.C.E. Story* (Auckland: James Family History Society, 1984) p. 18; J.A. Mackay, *Life in Early Poverty Bay* (Gisborne: Gisborne Publishing Company, 1927) p. 114: http://nzetc.victoria.ac.nz/tm/scholarly/tei-MacLife-t1-body-d19.html; *WCT*, 8 November 1867 p. 2; *WT*, 8 June 1868 p. 2; *WH*, 21 July 1868 p. 2; *GRA*, 16 October 1869 p. 1; *Press*, 26 September 1871 p. 1; *Northern Territory Times and Gazette*, 13 March 1874 p. 2; *Express and Telegraph*, 4 December 1884 p. 2.
4. NZ Bank of New South Wales Current Account Ledger Books, Auckland 1861, 1862–63, Westpac Archives, Wellington; Houltham, *The James Q.C.E. Story*.
5. Raewyn Dalziel, 'The colonial helpmeet: Women's role and the vote in nineteenth-century New Zealand', *New Zealand Journal of History* 11, 1977, pp. 112–23.
6. For example, Brad Patterson, Tom Brooking and Jim McAloon, *Unpacking the Kists: The Scots in New Zealand* (Dunedin: Otago University Press, 2013).
7. Ruby Jones, Enid Hawker, Linda Bloomfield (eds), *Women of Westland and their Families*, vol. II (Greymouth: Westland Branch of National Council of Women, 1977). Significantly, the first volume, produced in 1960, had far fewer women of enterprise, adhering more strongly to the domestic helpmeet line.
8. See also Barbara Brookes, *A History of New Zealand Women* (Wellington: Bridget Williams Books, 2016); Charlotte Macdonald, Merimeri Penfold and Bridget Williams (eds), *The Book of New Zealand Women/ Ko Kui Ma Te Kaupapa* (Wellington: Bridget Williams Books, 1991); Caroline Daley, *Girls & Women, Men & Boys: Gender in Taradale 1886–1930* (Auckland: Auckland University Press, 1999); Charlotte Macdonald, *Women Writing Home 1700–1920*, vol. 5 (London: Pickering & Chatto, 2006); Melanie Nolan, *Breadwinning: New Zealand women and the state* (Christchurch: Canterbury University Press, 2000); Stephanie Wyse, 'Gender, wealth and margins of empire: Women's economic opportunity in New Zealand cities, c. 1890–1950', PhD thesis, King's College London, University of London, 2008. Across the Tasman, businesswomen have been investigated by some historians: Catherine Bishop, *Minding Her Own Business: Colonial businesswomen in Sydney* (Sydney: NewSouth, 2015); Maria Nugent, *Women's Employment and Professionalism in Australia: Histories, themes and places* (Canberra: Australian Heritage Commission, 2002); Glenda Strachan and Lindy Henderson, 'Assumed but rarely documented: Women's entrepreneurial activities in late nineteenth-century Australia', paper presented at the 'The Past is Before Us' Labour History Conference, Sydney, 2005.
9. Ian Hunter, *Age of Enterprise: Rediscovering the New Zealand entrepreneur 1880–1910* (Auckland: Auckland University Press, 2007), p. 6.
10. Margaret Walsh, 'Gendered endeavours: Women & the reshaping of business culture', *Women's History Review* 14, no. 2, 2005, p. 181.

11. Beatrice Craig, *Women and Business since 1500: Invisible presences in Europe and North America?* (New York: Palgrave Macmillan, 2016). Internationally, feminist business history scholarship dates from the 1990s in North America and more recently in Britain, Europe and South America. Examples include Jennifer Aston, *Female Entrepreneurship in Nineteenth-Century England: Engagement in the urban economy* (London: Palgrave Macmillan, 2016); Peter Baskerville, *A Silent Revolution?: Gender and wealth in English Canada, 1860–1930* (Montreal: McGill-Queen's University Press, 2008); Bettina Bradbury, *From Wife to Widow: Lives, laws and politics in nineteenth-century Montreal* (Vancouver: University of British Columbia Press, 2011); Nancy Christie 'Women in the formal and informal economies of late eighteenth-century Quebec, 1760–1820', *Gender and History* 29, no. 1, 2017 pp. 104–23; Nicola Foote, 'Rethinking race, gender and citizenship: Black West Indian women on the Atlantic coast of Costa Rica, c. 1920–1940', *Bulletin of Latin American Research* 23, no. 2, April 2004, pp. 198–212; Eleanor Gordon and Gwyneth Nair, 'The economic role of middle-class women in Victorian Glasgow', *Women's History Review* 9 no. 4, 2000, pp. 791–814; David Green and Alistair Owens, 'Gentlewomanly capitalism? Spinsters, widows, and wealth holding in England and Wales c. 1800–1860', *Economic History Review* 3, 2003, pp. 510–36; Alison Kay, *The Foundations of Female Entrepreneurship: Enterprise, home and household in London, c. 1800–1870* (New York and London: Routledge, 2009); Andrea Kwolek-Folland, *Incorporating Women: A history of women and business in the United States* (NY: Palgrave Macmillan, 1998); Anne Laurence, Josephine Maltby and Janette Rutterford, *Women and their Money 1700–1950: Essays on women and finance* (Abingdon, Oxon, New York: Routledge, 2009); Susan Ingalls Lewis, *Unexceptional Women: Female proprietors in mid-19th-century Albany New York 1830–1885* (Columbus: Ohio State University Press, 2009); Vanessa Oliveira, 'The gendered dimension of trade: Female traders in nineteenth-century Luanda', *Portuguese Studies Review* 23, no. 2, 2015, pp. 93–121; Nicola Phillips, *Women in Business, 1700–1850* (Woodbridge: Boydell, 2006); Pamela Sharpe, *The Nineteenth-Century Businesswoman in the British Isles: Work culture, adaptation and the lace trade* (Nedlands, WA: Centre for Women and Business, Graduate School of Management, University of Western Australia, 2003); Helen F. Siu (ed.), *Merchants' Daughters: Women, commerce and regional culture in South China* (Hong Kong: Hong Kong University Press, 2010); Galina Ulianova, *Female Entrepreneurs in Nineteenth-Century Russia* (London: Taylor and Francis, 2009); Mary Yeager (ed.), *Women in Business* (Cheltenham: Edward Elgar Publishing, 1999); Kari Zimmerman, '"As pertaining to the female sex": The legal and social norms of female entrepreneurship in nineteenth-century Rio de Janeiro, Brazil', *Hispanic American Historical Review* 96, no. 1, 2016, pp. 39–72. See also Jennifer Aston and Catherine Bishop (eds), *Female Entrepreneurs in the Long Nineteenth Century: A global perspective* (New York: Palgrave Macmillan, forthcoming).
12. This book extends my PhD research. Catherine Bishop, 'Commerce was a woman: Women in business in colonial Sydney and Wellington', PhD thesis, Australian National University, 2012.
13. Joseph A. Schumpeter, *Capitalism, Socialism and Democracy* (London: George Allen and Unwin, 1976), p. 132.
14. Hunter, *Age of Enterprise*, p. 18.
15. Joe Carlin, *A Brief History of Entrepreneurship: The pioneers, profiteers and racketeers who shaped our world* (New York: Columbia University Press, 2016).
16. Frank H. Knight, *Risk Uncertainty and Profit* (Boston and New York: Houghton Mifflen, 1921), p. 45, quoted in Ian Hunter, Peter Lineham and Marie Wilson, 'The entrepreneurial

immigrant', Business History and Europe Conference, University of Canterbury, 5–6 September 2003, p. 11; Mark Casson, 'Entrepreneurship': www.econlib.org/library/Enc1/Entrepreneurship.html

17. Joan Stevens (ed.), *Mary Taylor, Friend of Charlotte Brontë: Letters from New Zealand and elsewhere* (Auckland: Auckland University Press, 1972); *Dominion*, 27 August 1910, p. 10.
18. *AS*, 18 June 1874 p. 3; *NZH*, 15 November 1884 p. 3.
19. *TS*, 2 January 1885 p. 3, 12 November 1885 p. 1.
20. *AS*, 20 March 1876 p. 2.
21. *AS*, 4 April 1878 p. 2; Mrs Knight and Mrs McMath had vegetable stalls.
22. *HBH*, 13 July 1867 p. 2.
23. *DSX*, 11 November 1853 p. 2.
24. Jessie Campbell to Louisa Cameron, 27 June 1843; Jessie Campbell to Isabella (Cameron) Macgregor, 9 September 1845: 'Extracts from the letters of Jessie Campbell to her family from Petone and Wanganui 1841–45', (Typescript) qMS-0369, ATL, also available at 'Blenheim175': https://blenheim175.wordpress.com/2015/05/16/jessie-campbells-letters/; Bronwyn Daley, 'Migrant Groups and the Wine Industry', Te Ara, www.TeAra.govt.nz/en/wine/page-2. Although the original vines were pulled out in 1907, the vineyard was resurrected in 1998 by Derek Hagar as part of Lansdowne estate. John Saker, 'The story behind the world's best Pinot Noir': www.stuff.co nz
25. For later period see the Caversham Project: https://caversham.otago.ac.nz/resource/index.html; Barbara Brookes, Robin Law and Annabel Cooper, *Sites of Gender: Women, men and modernity in southern Dunedin, 1890–1939* (Auckland: Auckland University Press, 2003).
26. For UK see Cambridge University Drivers of Entrepreneurship project: www.campop.geog.cam.ac.uk/research/projects/driversofentrepreneurship. For issues of gender and the census see Marilyn Waring, *Counting for Nothing: What men value & what women are worth* (Wellington: Allen & Unwin/Port Nicholson Press, 1988); Kate McKegg, 'Gender, work and death registration in New Zealand', *Labour, Employment and Work in New Zealand* [S.I.], 1994, pp. 169–76: https://doi.org/10.26686/lew.v0i0.925; Desley Deacon, 'Political arithmetic: The nineteenth-century Australian census and the construction of the dependent woman', *Signs* 11, no. 1, 1985, pp. 27–47; Katrina Alford, 'Colonial women's employment as seen by nineteenth-century statisticians and twentieth-century economic historians', *Labour History* 51, 1986, pp. 1–10; Edward Higgs, 'Women, occupations and work in the nineteenth-century censuses', *History Workshop* 23, 1987, pp. 59–80; Bridget Hill, 'Women, work and the census: A problem for historians of women', *History Workshop* 35, 1993, pp. 78–94; Robert Sweeney, 'Gender, discrimination and housing in turn-of-the-century Montréal: What mapping the census returns of immigrants can tell us', *Frontiers in Digital Humanities* 3, no. 8, 2016, pp. 1–18.
27. See Erik Olssen and Maureen Hickey, *Class and Occupation: The New Zealand reality* (Dunedin: Otago University Press, 2005); 'Results of a census of the colony of New Zealand, taken for the night of the 1st of March, 1874', (NZ Census 1874).
28. See for example, 'Results of a census of New Zealand, taken for the night of the 27th February 1871', (Wellington: Government Printer, 1872), (NZ Census 1871).
29. NZ Census 1874, p. 13.
30. The category included hotel-keepers, boarding-house keepers, cooks (not in domestic service), servants, registry office proprietors, office keepers, nurses, coffee/eating- house keepers. NZ Census 1874, Table X.

31. See Deacon, 'Political arithmetic'.
32. *DSX*, 18 September 1860 p. 2.
33. This followed the example of New South Wales statistician Timothy Coghlan.
34. NZ Census 1871, VIII.
35. *The Wellington Almanack for the Year of Our Lord 1853* (Wellington: Wellington Independent, 1853).
36. *Chapman's New Zealand Almanac, for Leap Year 1860* (Auckland: George T. Chapman, 1860), ENZB.
37. This figure is a rough estimate based on multiple sources such as an analysis of the 1860 Auckland directory.
38. Catherine Bishop, 'The serendipity of connectivity: Piecing together women's lives in the digital archive', *Women's History Review* 26, no. 5, 2017, pp. 766–80. Few bankruptcy and court records survive from the mid-nineteenth century.
39. Philip Hannken, 'Reminiscences of Auckland 1858–1880': http://localhistorybartley.blogspot.com.au/2014/08/new-heritage-rating-in-lower-queen-st.html; *NZer*, 11 August 1855 p. 1 (Jones), 9 February 1859 p. 2 (Chapman), 9 March 1859 p. 2 (Edwards), 15 September 1860 p. 2 (Lorigan); *DSX*, 2 December 1851 p. 3 (Vercoe), 24 July 1860 p. 3 (Bruce), 10 June 1863 p. 1 (Spalding), 11 August 1868 p. 3 (Pollock); *NZH*, 7 March 1865 p. 6 (Holloway), 30 June 1870 p. 1 (Powley); Policy 73681, Northern Assurance Company Auckland Agency, Fire Policy Copybook 1855–1866, MF–331, AWMM (Cox).
40. *The Wellington Almanack for the Year of Our Lord 1853.*
41. Alice East, 'The story of Sophia or how we happen to be here', edited by C.E. Fordham, MS Papers 2855, ATL, p. 8; there are two references to a Mrs Thomas's boarding house in advertisements. *HBH*, 30 March 1865 p. 2, 1 April 1865 p. 1.
42. Raewyn Dalziel, 'Hirst, Grace', DNZB: www.teara.govt.nz/en/biographies/1h25/hirst-grace; Grace Hirst to Martha Bracken, 24 August 1852, Hirst Family Letters, ATL, quoted in Dalziel, 'Colonial helpmeet', p. 116.
43. Miss Peach(e)y: advertisement, *Laurance's Auckland Registry Office Almanac for 1860* (Auckland: G.R. Laurance, 1860); *AS*, 18 June 1870 p. 2; Miss Plumb: *DSX*, 28 March 1856 p. 2; *NZer*, 9 April 1856 p. 2; 4 February 1857 p. 2; *NSWBDM*, Emma Painter NZ Probate 1900; E. Campbell: Rates Books, Wellington; *EP*, 18 July 1865 p. 3.
44. *TH*, 10 December 1864 p. 3, 27 July 1887 p. 2; *NZH*, 10 August 1888 p. 5; *HBH*, 1 August 1899 p. 3.
45. *DSX*, 7 September 1855 p. 2.
46. Hazel Petrie, *Chiefs of Industry: Māori tribal enterprise in early colonial New Zealand* (Auckland: Auckland University Press, 2006), pp. 35, 46.
47. For example, Makuini Kahawai, who provided the capital for her brother-in-law Werahiko to establish what eventually became Lake House Hotel at Ohinemutu: Philip Hart, 'Hone Werahiko: The discoverer of gold at Te Aroha', *Te Aroha Mining District Working Papers* 61, revised 7 February 2017, University of Waikato, p. 8.
48. Eleanor Spragg, 'Te Rau-o-te-rangi, Kahe', DNZB: www.teara.govt.nz/en/biographies/1t73/te-rau-o-te-rangi-kah; *WI*, 16 September 1869 p. 3.
49. Mary Louise Ormsby, 'Matenga, Huria', DNZB: www.teara.govt.nz/en/biographies/1m24/matenga-huria. Other prominent women who dealt in land were Kate Wyllie and Nga-kahu-whero (see DNZB).
50. David A. Armstrong, 'Yates, Ngawini and Yates, Samuel', DNZB: www.teara.govt.nz/en/

biographies/3y1/yates-ngawini. The Māori word iwi refers to an extended kinship group, tribe, nation, people, nationality or race, or a large group of people descended from a common ancestor and associated with a distinct territory.

51. Laurie Barber, 'Faulkner, Ruawahine Irihāpeti', DNZB: www.teara.govt.nz/en/biographies/1f3/faulkner-ruawahine-irihapeti; Garry Hooker, 'Cummins, Piipi Raumati', DNZB: www.teara.govt.nz/en/biographies/4c46/cummins-piipi-raumati
52. *NZer*, 12 December 1846 p. 2. Benjamin Smith bought potatoes from a Māori woman for one shilling, refusing to pay an extra 6d when she returned to demand more money. After a confrontation, Benjamin was thrown in prison by the local constable and his two Māori deputies. He was most indignant.
53. Enga Washburn, *Courage and Camp Ovens: Five generations at Golden Bay* (Wellington: Reed, 1970), p. 28; Martha Adams also recorded that a Māori woman sold goods at her door. Martha Adams, 'Journal, transcription', 1850–52, MS 0006, ATL.
54. Susan Wall, 'Copy of a letter from Susan [sic] Wall to her sisters, 18 December 1842', Wall Collection, MS–Papers–1739, ATL.
55. Elizabeth Caldwell, 'Diary of Mrs E.P. Caldwell', MS91, AWMM, p. 21.
56. Angela Wanhalla, *Matters of the Heart: A history of interracial marriage in New Zealand* (Auckland: Auckland University Press, 2012), p. 75; Maida Barlow, 'Harrold, Agnes', DNZB: www.teara.govt.nz/en/biographies/1h10/harrold-agnes
57. These calculations are a lower estimate. They assume businesses in 1853 had only been in existence for one year. The survival of businesses beyond 1883 was not calculated. This means that while 1853 businesses could be recorded as surviving as much as 31 years, those started in 1866 were tracked for only 17 years. Likewise, the gap between the directories was such that a business started in 1863 but gone before 1866 was recorded as having only lasted one year, when in fact it might have survived up until the end of 1865 and have been started in late 1861. Nevertheless since the same disadvantages applied to both male and female businesses, with those run by women being further disadvantaged because of issues with the sources, I feel the results are still significant. The average length of businesses that appeared in the directory for 1853 was 12 and a half years for men and only five for women, but this was the exception.
58. Ministry of Business Innovation and Employment/Hikina Whakatutuki, *Small Business Sector Report and Factsheet*, 2016, p. 2.
59. Raewyn Dalziel, 'Emigration and kinship: Migrants to New Plymouth 1840–1843', *New Zealand Journal of History* 25, no. 2, 1991, pp. 112–28; see also Angela McCarthy (ed.), *A Global Clan: Scottish migrant networks and identities since the eighteenth century* (London: Tauris Academic Studies, 2006).
60. Elizabeth Bartley 'Early reminiscences of Auckland': http://localhistorybartley.blogspot.com.au/p/early-reminiscences-of-auckland-by-mrs-e.html; *DSX*, 6 January 1870 p. 1.
61. 'Mrs John Pilkington's story', Edith Mary Story, 'Our fathers have told us', pp. 253–58, qMS 1898-1899, ATL.
62. *DSX*, 14 October 1856 p. 2, 16 June 1857 p. 1, 16 July 1858 p. 1; *NZer*, 26 March 1859 p. 1, 2 May 1860 p. 1, 29 December 1860 p. 2, 18 February 1870 p. 3.
63. *NZH*, 24 January 1874 p. 1; *Bay of Plenty Times*, 7 November 1888 p. 2, 3 April 1890 p. 2, 30 January 1891 p. 3, 5 October 1894 p. 4, 13 January 1900 p. 3, 21 December 1906 p. 2.
64. Cordelia Fine, *Testosterone Rex: Unmaking the myths of our gendered minds* (Sydney: Allen and Unwin, 2017).

65. Catherine Ralfe, 'Reminiscences', MS–Papers–1129, ATL, quoted in Megan Hutching, *Over the Wide and Trackless Sea: The pioneer women and girls of New Zealand* (Auckland: Harper Collins, 2008), p. 209. Mrs Black was possibly Evirilda, wife of William, who later ran Cashel House, or Rachel, wife of Robert, draper in High Street.
66. Initially banks dealt in short-term loans, with the risk of longer-term loans delegated to local merchants. W.J. Gardner, 'A colonial economy', in W.H. Oliver (ed.), *Oxford History of New Zealand* (Wellington: Oxford Uuniversity Press, 1981), p. 69.
67. See 'Mortgagor: Mary Bruce – Mortgagee: William Buchanan. Allot 17 Sec 42 City of Auckland and Lot 25 of the subdivision of Allot 18 Sec 40 City of Auckland' 10103/A403/3/N707, and 'Mortgagor: Alice Glover – Mortgagee: Auckland Permanent Cooperative Building and Investment Society. Part of allot 19 Section 3 Suburbs of Auckland', 10103/A403/11/N2830, Discharged Mortgages – North Auckland, Archives NZ, Auckland.
68. Grace Hirst to Martha Bracken, 24 August 1852, Hirst Family Letters, ATL, quoted in Dalziel, 'Colonial helpmeet', p. 116.
69. Macdonald Dictionary (misspelled as Maria Thompson); Richard L.N. Greenaway, 'Maria Thomson', *Rich Man, Poor Man, Environmentalist, Thief: Biographies of Canterbury personalities written for the millennium and for the 150th anniversary of the Canterbury settlement* (Christchurch: Canterbury Public Library, 2000): http://christchurchcitylibraries.com/Heritage/Publications/RichManPoorMan/MariaThomson/
70. *NEx*, 21 November 1865 p. 4; *NEM*, 12 October 1868 p. 2, 7 October 1879 p. 3, 5 January 1877 p. 3, 31 July 1894 p. 2; *Colonist*, 27 August 1878 p. 4, 21 August 1879.
71. Mary Taylor (MT) to Ellen Nussey (EN), 15 August 1850, in Stevens, *Mary Taylor*, p. 102.
72. See for example Douglas Mary McKain, 'Diary and commonplace book, 1841–1872', transcribed by J.B. Moles, p. 2, MS–Papers–7262, 1852–53, ATL.
73. Ben Schrader, *The Big Smoke: New Zealand cities, 1840–1920* (Wellington: Bridget Williams Books, 2016).
74. Sarah Pratt to her sister Julia Rendall, 15 February 1858, in Frances Porter, Charlotte Macdonald and Tui MacDonald, *My Hand Will Write What My Heart Dictates: The unsettled lives of women in nineteenth-century New Zealand as revealed to sisters, family and friends* (Auckland: Auckland University Press, Bridget Williams Books, 1996), p. 163.
75. Charlotte Godley, *Letters from Early New Zealand 1850–1853*, edited with notes by John R. Godley (Christchurch: Whitcombe & Tombs, 1951), p. 36.
76. See Margaret Tennant, *The Fabric of Welfare: Voluntary organisations, government, and welfare in New Zealand 1840–2005* (Wellington: Bridget Williams Books, 2007).
77. Ruth Bentham NZ Probate 1890.
78. See Jenny Carlyon, 'New Zealand Friendly Societies, 1842–1941', PhD thesis, University of Auckland, 2001.
79. Stephen Symons, 'Criterion Hotel', *Poddimok*: https://poddimok.wordpress.com/087-the-watering-holes-an-historical-essay/criterion-hotel/
80. *LT*, 9 March 1867 p. 3, 27 May 1870 p. 3; *Star*, 9 June 1869 p. 3, 17 February 1870 p. 3.
81. *Press*, 8 September 1871 p. 3; *Star*, 13 February 1872 p. 2.
82. *Star*, 7 September 1870 p. 3.
83. *Press*, 1 July 1879 p. 3.
84. Porter et al., *My Hand Will Write;* Macdonald et al., *The Book of New Zealand Women.*
85. Edward Palmer Thompson, *The Making of the English Working Class* (London: Gollancz, 1963), pp. 12–13.

Chapter 2: Women's Place and Men's Responsibility

1. For migration to New Zealand see for example: Lyndon Fraser, *A Distant Shore: Irish migration & New Zealand settlement* (Dunedin: University of Otago Press, 2000); Lyndon Fraser and Katie Pickles (eds), *Shifting Centres: Women and migration in New Zealand history* (Dunedin: University of Otago Press, 2002); Angela McCarthy, *Irish Migrants in New Zealand, 1840–1937: 'The Desired Haven'* (Woodbridge: The Boydell Press, 2005); Angela McCarthy (ed.), *A Global Clan: Scottish migrant networks and identities since the eighteenth century* (London: Tauris Academic Studies, 2006); Jock Phillips and Terry Hearn, *Settlers: New Zealand immigrants from England, Ireland and Scotland 1800–1945* (Auckland: Auckland University Press, 2008). A demographic approach is provided by Ian Pool, Arunachalam Dharmalingam and Janet Sceats, *The New Zealand Family from 1840: A demographic history* (Auckland: Auckland University Press, 2007).
2. Susan Nugent Wood, *Woman's Work in Australia* (Melbourne: Samuel Mullen, 1862), p. 20.
3. Charlotte Macdonald, *A Woman of Good Character: Single women as immigrant settlers in nineteenth-century New Zealand* (Wellington: Allen & Unwin/Historical Branch, 1990), p. 4.
4. Annabel Cooper, 'Poor men in the land of promises: Settler masculinity and the male breadwinner economy in late nineteenth-century New Zealand', *Australian Historical Studies* 39, 2008, pp. 245–61 (257).
5. *NZH*, 20 November 1866 p. 4; *DSX*, 20 November 1866 p. 6.
6. William Williams to Henry Williams, Turanga, 27 December 1849, in Frances Porter (ed.), *The Turanga Journals: Letters and journals of William and Jane Williams* (Wellington: Victoria University Press, 1974), p. 553. George Rich was in fact a successful sheep farmer, although that might have been after Williams' comments were made.
7. Porter et al., *My Hand Will Write,* p. 447; Bobbie Amyes and Fiona Gray, 'It started with a painting – James Rollason', *New Zealand Genealogist* 20, no. 107, 2016. This article includes the bigamies. I am grateful to Bobbie Amyes for sharing her own and Fiona Gray's meticulous research.
8. *HBH*, 18 February 1860 p. 2; she was probably the Maria Elizabeth Forrest who married Charles Anderson in the same year.
9. *Colonist*, 27 July 1860 p. 2, 23 November 1860 p. 2, 12 February 1861 p. 2, 15 February 1861 p. 4, 23 June 1865 p. 2, 15 September 1865 p. 2; Rebecca's age from Rebecca Agnes Smith NZ Probate 1897; NZBDM (Agnes Smith); *NZT*, 15 March 1897 p. 3.
10. Heidi Whiteside, '"We shall be respectable": Women and representations of respectability in Lyttelton 1851–1893', (MA thesis, University of Canterbury, 2007), p. 28.
11. Frances Shayle George, 'From a settler's wife', *Household Words* 4, no. 103, 13 March 1852, p. 586.
12. Caldwell, Diary, p. 9.
13. MT to EN, 11 March 1851, in Stevens, *Mary Taylor*, p. 105.
14. Ibid.
15. Sarah Pratt to her sister Martha Powley, 1855, in Porter et al., *My Hand Will Write,* p. 163.
16. Adams, 'Journal', pp. 168–69; Sarah Pratt to sister Martha Powley, 1855, in Porter et al., *My Hand Will Write,* p. 163.
17. Adams, 'Journal', pp. 168–69; Ellen Ellis made a similar observation: Angela Caughey, *Pioneer Families: The settlers of nineteenth-century New Zealand* (Auckland: David Bateman, 1994), p. 128.

18. Such diaries and letters provide a vivid picture of colonial female life: Porter et al., *My Hand Will Write*; see also Jean Garner and Kate Foster, *Letters to Grace: Writing home from colonial New Zealand* (Christchurch: Canterbury University Press, 2011).
19. Schrader, *The Big Smoke*, p. 91.
20. Ibid., pp. xvii–xviii.
21. Ibid., p. 191–92.
22. Charles Terry, *New Zealand Its Advantages and Prospects as a British Colony* (London: T. and W. Boone, 1842), p. 259, ENZB.
23. John Wilson (ed.), *Reminiscences of the Early Settlement of Dunedin and South Otago: Dealing in the main with Clutha and neighbouring districts: Compiled from information supplied to the Clutha Pioneers' Association by early settlers, and matter taken from other sources* (Dunedin: J. Wilkie & Co Ltd, 1912), p. 311.
24. Charles Hursthouse, *New Zealand, or Zealandia, the Britain of the South*, vol. II (London: Edward Stanford, 1857), quoted in Annabel Cooper, 'Poor men in the land of promises', p. 249.
25. Pat McClunie, *A Far Traveller: Eleanor Mills and her Wallace descendants* (Hokitika: Pat McClunie, 2000), pp. 8–9; Olson Family, Letters from Members of Olson Family, MS229, AWMM.
26. Raewyn Dalziel, 'Colonial Helpmeet' p. 116; Brookes, *A History of New Zealand Women*; see also for masculinity: Miles Fairburn, *The Ideal Society and its Enemies* (Auckland: Auckland University Press, 1989) and the array of scholarship that followed, debating the nature of New Zealand society.
27. Sarah Greenwood to her mother and aunt, 13 May 1844, Greenwood Family Letters, qMS–0887, ATL.
28. Rebecca Lee Sinclair, 'A few recollections of my early life in Nelson, July 1932': www.genealogy.ianskipworth.com/pdf/rebeccasincinclair.pdf, also in Hodgson Family collection, NRAMB400, NPM, p. 3; see also June E. Neale, *The Greenwoods: A pioneer family of New Zealand* (Nelson: General Printing Services, 1984); Janet Paul, 'Greenwood, Sarah', DNZB: www.teara.govt.nz/en/biographies/1g19/greenwood-sarah
29. Robert Boddington, letter to Mr W. Boddington, Coventry, 28 May 1842, *Letters from Settlers & Labouring Emigrants in the New Zealand Company's Settlements of Wellington, Nelson, & New Plymouth, from February, 1842, to January, 1843* (London: Smith, Elder & Co, 1843), pp. 88–89, ENZB.
30. John Philps, letter 15 December 1842, *Letters from Settlers*, p. 54; David Harris, letter 1842, *Letters from Settlers*, p. 53.
31. William Henwood to relatives in St German's Cornwall, 2 March 1843, *Letters from Settlers*, p. 150.
32. MT to CB, 10 April 1859, in Stevens, *Mary Taylor*, p. 85.
33. Wall, 'Copy of a letter'.
34. Marjory F.E. Adams, *A Garland from Quatt: The story of a pioneering ancestor as told by her granddaughter* (Auckland: M. Adams, 2001); Emma Frances Adams, 'Our first 12 years in New Zealand from 1860–1872', 1937, pp. 11–13, 92/26, AWMM.
35. Jane Anderson née Spinks, 'Diary 1861–62', 12 February 1861, MSX–7831, MS Group 1538, ATL; Catherine Bishop, 'Spinks Cottage: Heritage, history and use', in Annabel Cooper, Angela Wanhalla & Lachlan Paterson (eds), *The Lives of Colonial Objects* (Dunedin: Otago University Press, 2015), pp. 72–77.

36. Sarah Greenwood to Mary Greenwood, June 1852, in Greenwood Family Letters, p. 64.
37. Caldwell, Diary, p. 9. Susan Waters (see Chapter 9) enjoyed the brief period in which she only had domestic responsibilities, but was quickly back in harness when required. Similarly, Sarah Pratt in New Plymouth felt the pressure of having a school as well as a household and family (see Chapter 5). From Mrs W-, Wellington, 10 January 1845, in 'Emigrant voices from New Zealand', in William and Robert Chambers, *Chambers Edinburgh Journal*, no. 257, 2 December 1848, pp. 354–58, p. 357; Sarah Pratt, letter to her sister Julia Rendell, 1858, in Porter et al., *My Hand Will Write,* p. 163.
38. Whiteside, 'We shall be respectable', p. 28.
39. Macdonald Dictionary; *LT*, 1 March 1851 p. 1, 20 September 1851 p. 8, 17 September 1853 p. 4.
40. William White, *Directory of Leeds and Clothing District* (Sheffield: William White, 1847), p. 446; William White, Directory of Leeds, Bradford ... (Sheffield: William White, 1854), both at Historical Directories of England and Wales: http://specialcollections.le.ac.uk/cdm/landingpage/collection/p16445coll4; UK Census 1851, 1871; *NZer*, 25 October 1854 p. 4, 25 December 1861 p. 3, 19 March 1862 p. 2.
41. UK Census 1841, 1851, 1861; UKBDM; *Post Office Directory of Gloucestershire with Bath and Bristol* (London: Kelly & Co, 1856) at Historical Directories of England and Wales; passenger lists of Cresswell (1858) and Ravenscraig (1862) at Denise and Peter Ourstuff: http://freepages.genealogy.rootsweb.ancestry.com/~ourstuff
42. 'Old Gloucestershire Diary', possibly by Paul Hawkins Fisher, author of *Notes and Recollections of Stroud*: www.johnhearfield.com/Dir/OldGlosDiary_home.htm
43. *London Gazette*, vol. 1, 1839, p. 396; *NEx*, 28 February 1857 p. 2.
44. 'Nelson: Schedule of nominated passengers for whom a guarantee of payment has been made 1855–1862 and 1872', Archives NZ, Wellington, ACFT 8249 IM–N4/1/1: www.nzpictures.co.nz/pandoraresearchANZ-IM-N-4-1-4.pdf; *Cheltenham Examiner*, 29 October 1856 p. 6.
45. Mary Taylor's biographers and publishers make the most of the Brontë connection, using the latter's name in book titles. On the front of the 1990 edition of her own novel, *Miss Miles*, she was described as 'life-long friend of Charlotte Brontë' (Mary Taylor, *Miss Miles, or, a Tale of Yorkshire Life 60 Years Ago, with an Introduction by Janet H. Murray* (New York: Oxford University Press, 1990, originally published 1890)). See also: Joan Bellamy, *'More Precious Than Rubies'. Mary Taylor: Friend of Charlotte Brontë, strong-minded woman* (Beverley: Highgate, 2002); Joan Stevens (ed.), *Mary Taylor, Friend of Charlotte Brontë: Letters from New Zealand and elsewhere* (Auckland: Auckland University Press, 1972).
46. MT to CB, April 1850, in Stevens, *Mary Taylor,* p. 94. See also Mary Taylor, *The First Duty of Women: A series of articles reprinted from the* Victoria *magazine, 1865 to 1870,* facsimile edn (London: Emily Faithfull, 1870); Taylor, *Miss Miles.*
47. Porter et al., *My Hand Will Write*, pp. 418–19.
48. MT to CB, June–24 July 1848, in Stevens, *Mary Taylor*, p. 78; MT to CB, April 1850, in Stevens, *Mary Taylor*, p. 95.
49. MT to CB, June–24 July 1848, in Stevens, *Mary Taylor*, p. 76; *NZSCSG*, 20 March 1847 p. 1.
50. MT to CB, 10 April 1849, in Stevens, *Mary Taylor*, p. 86; MT to CB, 5 April 1850, in Stevens, *Mary Taylor*, p. 88.
51. MT to CB, 5 April 1850, in Stevens, *Mary Taylor,* pp. 88–90.
52. Ellen Taylor (ET) to CB, 13 August 1850, in Stevens, *Mary Taylor*, pp. 99–100.
53. (My emphasis.) MT to CB, 5 April 1850, in Stevens, *Mary Taylor*, p. 88.

54. MT to EN, 11 March 1851, in Stevens, *Mary Taylor*, p. 104.
55. MT to CB, 1852, in Stevens, *Mary Taylor*, pp. 107–108.
56. MT to EN, 4–8 January 1857, in Stevens, *Mary Taylor*, p. 131.
57. MT to CB, June–24 July 1848, in Stevens, *Mary Taylor*, p. 77; MT to EN, 8 January 1857, in Stevens, *Mary Taylor*, p. 131; MT to CB, April 1850, in Stevens, *Mary Taylor*, p. 95; MT to CB, June–24 July 1848, in Stevens, *Mary Taylor*, p. 78.
58. MT to CB, June–24 July 1848, in Stevens, *Mary Taylor*, p. 77.
59. MT to EN, 9 February 1849, in Stevens, *Mary Taylor*, p. 82.
60. Grace Hirst to her sisters, February 1871, quoted in Peter A. Marshall and Kean K. Brown, 'The identification of the five ladies', in *Swiss Notes by Five Ladies* (first published 1875) (Lancaster: Peter A. Marshall, 2003), p. 115.
61. Grace Hirst, Letters, February 1871, July 1872, in Marshall and Brown, 'The Identification', pp. 119–20.
62. *WI*, 27 September 1866 p. 4.
63. *EP*, 1 March 1892 p. 2 .
64. Lyn Lofland, *The Public Realm: Exploring the city's quintessential social territory* (Hawthorne, New York: Aldine de Gruyter, 1998), pp. 10–14; I am grateful to Clare Hoare for this reference.

Chapter 3: 'This Outlandish Place at the End of the Earth'

1. From Mrs W-, Port Nicholson, 28 July 1842, in 'Emigrant voices from New Zealand', *Chambers' Edinburgh Journal* 257, 2 December 1848 p. 355.
2. See Ben Schrader, *The Big Smoke: New Zealand cities, 1840–1920* (Wellington: Bridget Williams Books, 2016).
3. See Lachlan Paterson and Angella Wanhalla, *He Reo Wahine: Māori women's voices from the nineteenth century* (Auckland: Auckland University Press, 2017).
4. Jim McAloon, 'The New Zealand economy, 1792–1914', in Giselle Byrnes (ed.), *The New Oxford History of New Zealand* (South Melbourne: Oxford University Press, 2009).
5. Charlotte Godley, *Letters from Early New Zealand 1850–1853*, edited with notes by John R. Godley (Christchurch: Whitcombe & Tombs, 1951), p. 40.
6. Russell Stone, 'Auckland business, 1841–2004: Myth and reality', in Ian Hunter and Diana Morrow (eds), *City of Enterprise: Perspectives on Auckland business history* (Auckland: Auckland University Press, 2006), p. 135.
7. Stone, 'Auckland business', p. 234; John Logan Campbell, 9 August 1841, in Russell Stone, *Makers of Fortune: A colonial business community and its fall* (Auckland: Auckland University Press, 1974), p. 5.
8. Elizabeth Bartley, 'Early reminiscences of Auckland': http://localhistorybartley.blogspot.com.au/p/early-reminiscences-of-auckland-by-mrs-e.html
9. William Swainson, *Auckland, the Capital of New Zealand and the Country Adjacent: Including some account of the gold discovery in New Zealand* (London: Smith, Elder & Co; Auckland: J. Williamson, 1853), pp. 65, 70.
10. See Philippa Mein Smith, *A Concise History of New Zealand* (New York, Port Melbourne: Cambridge University Press, 2005), pp. 53–63.
11. Frederick Mackie, Journal, vol. 1, 1852–1854, pp. 125–27, MS 0865, ATL.

12. Godley, *Letters*, pp. 32, 91.
13. Mackie, Journal, pp. 125–27.
14. Godley, *Letters*, p. 100.
15. Gerald T. Bloomfield, *New Zealand: A handbook of historical statistics* (Boston, Mass: G.K. Hall, 1984), p. 57.
16. *WH*, 26 February 1889 p. 2; *HBH*, 26 January 1892 p. 3. Earlier, the Waiwera River further north had enjoyed this sobriquet. *NZH*, 6 January 1865 p. 3.
17. There is considerable debate among historians about how to refer to these events at Wairau in 1843. Initially described by settlers as a 'massacre', usage which remained until the early 1980s, this is now seen as an unnecessarily loaded term. Historian and descendant of Te Rauparaha, member of Ngāti Toarangatira, Lloyd Carpenter, has done substantial research into what he terms the Wairau affray. The word 'affray' also appears more often than 'incident' in *Te Ara*, although other historians, including Angela Wanhalla of Ngāi Tahu, suggest 'incident' is preferred. In 2015 Te Papa curator Matiu Baker called it the 'Wairau conflict'. I have used all three more recent terms – affray, incident and conflict: https://blog.tepapa.govt.nz/2015/06/12/dirty-deeds-done-dirt-cheap/?fbclid=IwAR06qwT0_EpvYEgE9iE15LBumEJFiYQ-gZ8Cwx_tiSn7uny9UiVUydJEti4
18. See Ruth Allan, *Nelson: A history of early settlement* (Wellington: A.H. & A.W. Reed, 1965); Jim McAloon, *Nelson: A regional history* (Whatamango Bay: Cape Catley & Nelson City Council, 1997); Hilary and Maui John Mitchell and Wakatū Incorporation, *Te Tau Ihu o te Waka: A history of Māori of Nelson and Marlborough* (Wellington: Huia Publishers in association with the Wakatū Incorporation, 2004).
19. See Geoffrey W. Rice, *Christchurch Changing: An illustrated history* (Christchurch: Canterbury University Press, 1999), pp. 19–32.
20. Bloomfield, *New Zealand*, pp. 35–36, 57.
21. Julius von Haast, *Geology of the Provinces of Canterbury and Westland, New Zealand: A report comprising the results of official explorations* (Christchurch, 1879), p. 87, NZETC.
22. J.A. Mackay, *Life in Early Poverty Bay* (Gisborne: Gisborne Publishing Co., n.d.), p. 114, NZETC.
23. See for example Rosemary Killip, *To Find a Fortune: Women of the Thames goldfield, 1867–1893* (Wellington: Victoria University Women's Studies, 1995).
24. Swainson, *Auckland*, pp. 70, 71.
25. *NZer*, 15 November 1848 p. 2.
26. Eileen McSaveney, 'Historic earthquakes – the 1848 Marlborough earthquake', Te Ara – the Encyclopedia of New Zealand: www:teara.govt.nz/en/historic-earthquakes/2
27. *WI*, 4 November 1848 p. 3.
28. *NZer*, 7 July 1863 p. 1, 7 October 1865 p. 3; *NZH*, 26 September 1864 p. 3, 7 January 1867 p. 1.
29. Schrader, *The Big Smoke*, Chapter 4; Mackie, Journal, p. 125. He described seeing Māori in the streets and in shops, pp. 128, 197.
30. James Adams, tailor formerly of Earlston, to his parents, Dunedin, 20 November 1848, in G.B. Earp, *Hand-Book for Intending Emigrants to the Southern Settlements of New Zealand*, 2nd edn (London: W.S. Orr & Co, 1849), p. 228.
31. Angela Wanhalla, *In/Visible Sight: The mixed-descent families of southern New Zealand* (Auckland: Auckland University Press, 2010); Angela Wanhalla, *Matters of the Heart: A*

history of interracial marriage in New Zealand (Auckland: Auckland University Press, 2012); Barbara Brookes, *A History of New Zealand Women* (Wellington: Bridget Williams Books, 2016), passim.; Hazel Petrie, *Chiefs of Industry: Māori tribal enterprise in early colonial New Zealand* (Auckland: Auckland University Press, 2006); Shaunnagh Dorsett, *Judicial Encounters: Māori and the colonial courts, 1840–1851* (Auckland: Auckland University Press, 2017).

32. Jennifer Ashton, *At the Margin of Empire: John Webster and Hokianga, 1841–1900* (Auckland: Auckland University Press, 2015).
33. Clendon House Tour pamphlet, Heritage New Zealand; Alice Bennett, who was also governess to John Webster's children and scribe for John Marmon, is an intriguing character. In *Tides of Hokianga* (Wellington: Wingfield Press, 1956) Cecil and Celia Manson describe her as 'wayward', without offering any other explanation. Trevor Bentley says she was part-Māori, but I have been unable to find his source. Another possibility is that she was the widow, Alice Mary Bennett, who died in 1894, her probate papers revealing her to have had no relatives and 'entirely dependent on remittances [from] Mr Richard Beauchamp of Carlton Club, London' since 1884. Trevor Bentley, *Cannibal Jack* (Auckland: Penguin, 2010); Alice Mary Bennett NZ Probate 1894; *EP*, 8 September 1870 p. 3; Roger Wigglesworth, 'The myth and the reality: A study of the adaptation of John Marmon (1800?–1880) with comments on his three newspaper autobiographies', research essay, Massey University, 1974.
34. *Te Awamutu Courier*, 4 April 2006 p. 3.
35. From Mrs W-, 28 July 1842, 'Emigrant voices', p. 355. 'Te reo' refers to the Māori language.
36. Caldwell, Diary, p. 18; Charlotte Parkinson, 'Reminiscences of Mrs Parkinson', pp. 1–2, 89/140, AWWM.
37. Bartley, 'Early reminiscences'.
38. John Sidney Smith, 1808–1880: Account Book, qMS 1826, ATL.
39. *WC*, 24 June 1875 p. 2, 7 April 1886 p. 2.
40. *NZH*, 20 June 1867 p. 4; see also Alister Matheson, 'Early Maketu storekeepers', *Bay of Plenty Journal of History* 44, no. 2, 1986, pp. 91–118: www.lowerkaituna.co.nz/cmsAdmin/uploads/Vol-44-No-2.pdf
41. Bartley, 'Early reminiscences'; *Te Korimako*, 15 June 1885 p. 10; A.A. Ryan, photograph of 'Lake Rotorua – after eruption June 10 1886', C.010233, Photography Collection, Te Papa: https://collections.tepapa.govt.nz/object/20227
42. *Te Korimako*, 15 July 1884 p. 12.

Chapter 4: One Ring to Bind Them All

1. Numerous examples refer to this as a quote from William Blackstone. For example Susan B. Anthony Center for Women's Leadership, 'Susan B. Anthony and Elizabeth Cady Stanton', University of Rochester: www.rochester.edu/SBA/suffrage_sba_ecs.html. The real version can be found in William Blackstone, *Commentaries on the Laws of England*, vol. 1 (Oxford: Clarendon Press, 1765), pp. 442–45.
2. See also Bettina Bradbury, 'Colonial comparisons: Rethinking marriage, civilisation and nation in nineteenth-century white settler societies', in p. Buckner & D. Francis (eds), *Rediscovering the British World* (Calgary: Calgary University Press, 2005); Bettina Bradbury, 'From civil death to separate property: Changes in the legal rights of married women in

nineteenth-century New Zealand', *New Zealand Journal of History*, 29, no. 1, 1995, pp. 40–66; Charlotte Macdonald, 'Land, death and dower in the settler empire: The lost cause of "the widow's third" in nineteenth-century New Zealand', *Victoria University of Wellington Law Review* 41, 2010, pp. 493–518. For international literature see Catherine Bishop, 'When your money is not your own: Coverture and married women in business in colonial New South Wales', *Law and History Review* 33, no. 1, 2015, pp. 181–200; Catherine Bishop, 'Commerce was a woman: Women in business in colonial Sydney and Wellington', PhD thesis, Australian National University, 2012.

3. See 1854, 'Case of Widow Meurant', Bradbury, 'From civil death', pp. 45–46.
4. See especially Bradbury, 'From civil death'; Barbara Brookes, *A History of New Zealand Women* (Wellington: Bridget Williams Books, 2016); Angela Wanhalla, *Matters of the Heart: A history of interracial marriage in New Zealand* (Auckland: Auckland University Press, 2012); Angela Wanhalla, *In/Visible Sight: The mixed-descent families of southern New Zealand* (Auckland: Auckland University Press, 2010).
5. *An Act to Extend the Provisions of 'The Married Women's Property Protection Act 1860'* (33 and 34 Victoriae 1870, no. 37), NZLII.
6. *The Married Women's Property Protection Act 1860* (24 Victoriae 1860, no. 9); *Married Women's Property Act*, 1884 (48 VICT 1884, no. 10), NZLII.
7. *DSX*, 30 January 1867 p. 4.
8. *NZH*, 8 November 1867 p. 4; *DSX*, 8 November 1867 p. 4; see also *DSX*, 1 October 1868 p. 2, 2 October 1868 p. 5, 3 October 1868 p. 3.
9. *WH*, 8 November 1869 p. 3, 17 December 1869 p. 2, 14 February 1871 p. 2; *WC*, 24 June 1875 p. 2, 3 June 1880 p. 2; Athol Kirk, 'Ayrshire House', *Wanganui Historical Record* 19:1 (1991), pp. 21–22.
10. *NEx*, 20 April 1844 pp. 27, 25.
11. *NEx*, 24 August 1844 p. 99.
12. Family history sources say George died on 28 October 1856 in the immigration barracks: www.wikitree.com/wiki/Estcourt-44; *NEx*, 14 February 1857 p. 2, 27 October 1860 p. 2, 20 July 1861 p. 2, 11 September 1861 p. 9; *Colonist*, 27 January 1860 p. 2, 4 December 1860 p. 2.
13. *ODT*, 19 January 1866 p. 5.
14. *ODT*, 23 December 1867 p. 6.
15. *ODT*, 20 August 1867 p. 5; 'Brothel Surveillance Return – Dunedin June 1869', in Charlotte Macdonald, 'The "social evil": Prostitution and the passage of the Contagious Diseases Act (1869)', in Margaret Tennant, Charlotte Macdonald and Barbara Brookes (eds), *Women in History: Essays on European women in New Zealand* (Sydney, Wellington: George Allen & Unwin, 1986), p. 30.
16. *ODT*, 20 August 1867 p. 5.
17. *Colonist*, 20 January 1863 p. 2; *NEx*, 12 February 1863 p. 3.
18. For example, Margaret and Peter King, *NZG*, 12 June 1841 p. 3, 26 June 1841 p. 1.
19. For example, John Castle re Marie Castle, *NZG*, 28 May 1842 p. 1.
20. *WI*, 25 February 1865 p. 4, 20 September 1866 p. 6, 9 March 1867 p. 5; *EP*, 8 March 1867 p. 2.
21. See Margot Finn, 'Women, consumption and coverture in England, c. 1760–1860', *The Historical Journal* 39, no. 3, 1996, pp. 703–22.
22. *DSX*, 7 November 1863 p. 1, 17 November 1865 p. 5, 25 November 1865 p. 6, 22 May 1868 p. 4; *TA*, 2 June 1875 p. 3.

23. For example Nelson's Frederick Kent's wife Emma, who moved on to John Imrie in 1842, causing her husband to advertise his cuckoldry in order to avoid her debts. *NEx*, 31 December 1842 p. 169.
24. For example, Emma Wrey, who married Philip Deck in 1851 only 'to be married before her sister', according to Constantine Dillon, was separated by 1857 but in her obituary in 1903 was 'the relict of Deck'; *NEx*, 22 February 1851 p. 4, 28 March 1857 p. 2; *EP*, 4 July 1903 p. 6; Constantine Dillon to his wife Fanny, 20 February 1851, p. 321, Dillon, Constantine Augustus, Papers MS-0685, ATL. Note also William Berkett, who deserted wife Christina at Waimea East in 1861 but was living with her again when she died in 1903. *Colonist*, 7 January 1862 p. 2; *NEM*, 21 March 1903 p. 2.
25. *NEx*, 31 March 1849 p. 18, 9 June 1849 p. 57, 12 December 1865 p. 7; David Monro, 'Statement of My Property in New Zealand 1 July 1857', Entry in the front of diary of 1857, in R.E. Wright-St Clair, *Thoroughly a Man of the World: A biography of Sir David Monro MD* (Christchurch: Whitcombe & Tombs, 1971), p. 298; see also p. 54.
26. *NEM*, 29 July 1878 p. 2; *Colonist*, 16 September 1873 p. 2. See also Jenny Robin Jones, *No Simple Passage: The journey of the 'London' to New Zealand, 1842: A ship of hope* (Auckland: Random House, 2011), p. 185.
27. *Destitute Persons Act 1846* (10 Victoriae 1846 no. 9), NZLII.
28. *Married Women's Property Protection Act 1860* (24 Victoriae 1860 no. 9), NZLII. See for example Mary Brooks, *EP*, 18 April 1868 p. 2; Anonymous, *DSX*, 31 August 1869 p. 4.
29. 'The Deserted Wives and Children Act 1840 as Amended by the Act of 1858', NSW Legislation as Made: www.legislation.nsw.gov.au/acts/1858-9a.pdf
30. *DSX*, 6 November 1867 p. 3.
31. *WCT*, 28 February 1870 p. 1, 16 November 1870 p. 2; *GRA*, 20 August 1870 p. 3; Bobbie Amyes, 'Sergeant James William Reilly – A Bit of a Rogue', Dunedin Family History Group, *Irish Parents*, 2013, 33–46. I am grateful to Bobbie Amyes for sharing her research.
32. *Southland Times*, 1 August 1866 p. 3; Judith Bassett, 'Barron, Hannah Ward', DNZB: www.teara.govt.nz/en/biographies/2b7/1/barron-hannah-ward; Michael Bassett, 'Ward, Joseph George', DNZB: www.teara.govt.nz/en/biographies/2w9/ward-joseph-george
33. *Lake Wakatip Mail*, 7 November 1863 p. 5.
34. *ODT*, 11 April 1876 p. 3; *Brisbane Courier*, 14 May 1869 p. 1. See also Julia Bradshaw, 'Adjustable Marriages: Relationships, divorce and bigamy on the goldfields', *Echoes of Our Past, Proceedings of the 2018 Conference of the New Zealand Society of Genealogists*, June 2018. I am grateful to Julia Bradshaw and also Jenny Mayne for sharing their research with me.
35. *Divorce and Matrimonial Causes Act 1867* (31 Victoriae 1867, no. 94); *Divorce Act 1898* (62 VICT 1898, no. 42), NZLII. Before 1857, when the English Matrimonial Causes Act was passed legislating for divorce under some circumstances, it was possible to obtain marriage dissolutions in England through the Doctors' Commons and an Act of parliament, an expensive process that few pursued.
36. Birth year based on age at death and that of her younger sister, Mary Ann, who died in 1902 aged 55.
37. George's first wife Sarah died in Hobart in 1856 aged 24 after two years of marriage: *Tasmanian Colonist*, 26 June 1854 p. 2; *WI*, 17 March 1864 p. 2.
38. *HBH*, 7 January 1865 p. 2, 9 March 1865 p. 1; *EP*, 17 August 1883 p. 2.
39. Her sisters, Elizabeth Chapman, wife of Henry, and Lucy Eleanor Tiffen, wife of Frederick, were both in Napier: *HBH*, 22 April 1863 p. 1, 10 December 1869 p. 2, 26 June 1867 p. 2.

40. *EP*, 27 August 1873 p. 2, 3 June 1875 p. 2, 8 October 1880 p. 2; *HBH*, 21 August 1874 p. 4, 20 January 1877 p. 3, 18 April 1877 p. 2, 1 February 1878 p. 4, 4 April 1878 p. 2, 4 January 1882 p. 4.
41. *EP*, 1 March 1882 p. 3, 4 September 1882 p. 3, 25 October 1882 p. 2, 6 March 1883 p. 3, 19 April 1883 p. 3.
42. *EP*, 17 August 1883 p. 2. See Robyn Anderson, '"The hardened frail ones": Women and crime in Auckland, 1845–1870', MA thesis, University of Auckland, 1981.
43. *EP*, 20 December 1883 p. 2; *The Age* (Melbourne), 26 February 1884 p. 7.
44. *Daily Telegraph*, 2 May 1888 p. 1; *FS*, 22 July 1893 p. 2, 8 December 1893 p. 2, 4 January 1897 p. 3; *Hastings Standard*, 29 May 1897 p. 1; *Manawatu Times*, 8 January 1918 p. 4; Maria Duncan NZ Probate 1916; Walter Duncan NZ Probate 1956. Lilian disappeared from the records after 1897.
45. See Raewyn Dalziel, 'The privileged crime: Policing and prosecuting bigamy in nineteenth-century New Zealand', *New Zealand Journal of History* 51, no. 2, 2017, pp. 1–26. See also lawyer's opinion in Stanton case below.
46. *Mount Ida Chronicle*, 14 March 1873 p. 7, 21 March 1873 p. 6.
47. Reverend Robert Cole to George Grey, 27 November 1851, in Jenny Robin Jones, *Writers in Residence: A journey with pioneer New Zealand writers* (Auckland: Auckland University Press, 2004), p. 134.
48. *WH*, 23 August 1867 p. 4, 7 July 1869 p. 2, 12 September 1872 p. 2, 11 December 1872 p. 3; *Southland Times*, 16 January 1911 p. 6.
49. *NEM*, 5 December 1876 p. 2, 9 January 1877 p. 2; Marie Woods, 'The Stanton family: Silk weavers from Coventry', unpublished ms; I am grateful to Marie Woods and Jane Teal for sharing their research about Mary Lechner.

Chapter 5: 'Good Morning, Miss'

1. MT to EN, 9 February 1949, in Joan Stevens (ed.), *Mary Taylor, Friend of Charlotte Brontë: Letters from New Zealand and elsewhere* (Auckland: Auckland University Press, 1972), p. 81.
2. See Patricia Clarke, *The Governesses: Letters from the colonies, 1862–1882* (Melbourne: Hutchinson, 1985); A. James Hammerton, *Emigrant Gentlewomen: Genteel poverty and female emigration, 1830–1914* (Canberra: Australian National University Press, 1979); Kate Matthew, 'The Female Middle Class Emigration Society governesses in Australia: A failed vision?', *Journal of Australian Colonial History* 14, 2012, pp. 107–30; FMCES, Fawcett Library Collections microfilmed by the Australian Joint Copying Project, M2291–2314, SLNSW.
3. Cary, FMCES, Dunedin, 18 October 1863, pp. 101–04; Dunedin, 15 September 1864, pp. 133–35; Dunedin, 17 August 1865, p. 195; Whanganui, 2 October 1867, pp. 280–83 (all Bk1).
4. Isabella Cary (sometimes Carey), FMCES, 15 September 1864.
5. Cary, FMCES, 18 October 1863, 15 September 1864; *ODT*, 7 June 1864 p. 3, 5 July 1865 p. 2.
6. *ODT*, 23 May 1864 p. 3.
7. *ODT*, 6 July 1963 p. 3.
8. Cary, FMCES, 2 October 1867.
9. *ODT*, 5 July 1865 p. 6; Cary, FMCES, 17 August 1865, 2 October 1867.
10. Cary, FMCES, 15 September 1864.

11. Cary, FMCES, 2 October 1867; *WH*, 5 February 1868 p. 3.
12. Cary, FMCES, 2 October 1867.
13. Cary, FMCES, 18 October 1863.
14. Cary, FMCES, 2 October 1867.
15. Isabella Cary NZ Probate 1878; *TS*, 8 June 1874 p. 3, 22 March 1875 p. 3, 15 February 1876 p. 2, 4 March 1878 p. 2.
16. Doug Burgum, Susan Grant, pers. comm.; Susan Grant et al, 'Merritt family and gasworks Auckland': https://lists.rootsweb.com/hyperkitty/list/nz-auckland@rootsweb.com/thread/22559876/
17. Eliza Brook, FMCES, Dunedin, 20 January 1869, p. 331–33 (Bk1); (now Eliza MacDonnell) 27 July 1870, pp. 368–71 (Bk1).
18. Harriet Herbert, FMCES, Napier, 8 May 1879, pp. 55–59 (Bk2); *Poverty Bay Herald*, 3 July 1879 p. 2; *WC*, 23 March 1881 p. 2.
19. Herbert, FMCES, 8 May 1879.
20. Caroline Fox, FMCES, c. August 1879, pp. 72–73 (Bk2).
21. Herbert, FMCES, 8 May 1879, 26 January 1880 (Bk2); UK Census 1861. See also Kate Brind, FMCES, Nelson, 1 June 1873, 14 March 1875 (Bk1, pp. 436–37, 456–57).
22. *HBH*, 5 April 1878 pp. 2–3; 25 March 1878 p. 2. In 1874 Harriet selected and imported a whole shipload of immigrants of 'a very superior class' to Napier, much to the satisfaction of the local newspaper. *HBT*, 3 February 1874 p. 102.
23. School proprietors included Mrs Mary Ann Buxton, Mrs Constantia Davison, Mrs Fox, Mrs Green, Mrs Mary Harvey, Mrs Mary George, Mrs Ann Mudgway, Miss Ann Tilke, Miss Anna Maria Smith, Mrs Wakefield and Miss Emily Wakefield and Mrs (Dr) Young. George Macmorran, *Some Schools and Schoolmasters of Early Wellington* (Wellington: S. & W. Mackay, 1900).
24. Macmorran, *Some Schools*, pp. 69–70.
25. Rollo Arnold, 'Buxton, Mary Ann', DNZB: www.teara.govt.nz/en/biographies/1b56/buxton-mary-ann; Macmorran, *Some Schools,* pp. 36–39; Mary Ann Buxton, NZ Probate 1888.
26. Fanny L. Irvine-Smith, *The Streets of My City: Wellington New Zealand* (Wellington: Reed, 1948), part 2, ch. 4, p. 84: www.wcl.govt.nz/heritage/streetspart2chap. 4.html; Jeremy Lowe, '30 Ascot St', *Thorndon Society Newsletter*, no. 164, December 2012, p. 4, reprinted from no. 108, December 1995; *Wellington Almanack Directory Calendar and Diary for the Year 1871* (Wellington: Thomas McKenzie, 1871), p. 183; Marcus Marks, *Memories (Mainly Merry) of Marcus Marks* (Sydney: Endeavour Press, 1934). My thanks to Brett McKay of the Thorndon Society for sharing his research.
27. *DSX*, 11 November 1853 p. 2; Caldwell, Diary, p. 12.
28. None of these statistics were divided by sex or by stage of education.
29. *Colonist*, 1 June 1858 p. 2, 4 June 1858 p. 2.
30. *Education Act 1877* (41 Victoriae 1877, no. 21), NZLII; Statistics of New Munster 1841–48: http://archive.stats.govt.nz/browse_for_stats/snapshots-of-nz/digitised-collections/19th-century-collection.aspx; Census of New Zealand 1871–1881: http://archive.stats.govt.nz/browse_for_stats/snapshots-of-nz/digitised-collections/census-collection.aspx; Statistics of New Zealand for 1861: www3.stats.govt.nz/historic_publications/1861-statistics-nz/1861-statistics-nz.html#idsect2_1_1546
31. Helen May, *School Beginnings: A nineteenth-century colonial story* (Wellington: NZCER Press,

2005); Coral Chambers, *Lessons for Ladies: A social history of girls' education in Australasia, 1870–1900* (Sydney: Hale & Iremonger, 1986); Sue Middleton, *Women and Education in Aotearoa* (Wellington: Allen & Unwin, Port Nicholson Press, 1988); Alison Jones and Sue Middleton, *Women and Education in Aotearoa 2* (Wellington: Bridget Williams Books, 1992); J.C. Dakin, *Education in New Zealand* (Newton Abbot, UK: David & Charles, 1973).

32. Inward Letters – A. & J. Boughton, 12 Letters from Adeno [sic] Boughton and his wife Jane, 1868–1872 to Donald McLean, MS-Papers-0032-0167, ATL; see also May, *School Beginnings*, pp. 150–51; Frances Porter, Charlotte Macdonald and Tui MacDonald, *My Hand Will Write What My Heart Dictates: The unsettled lives of women in nineteenth-century New Zealand as revealed to sisters, family and friends* (Auckland: Auckland University Press, Bridget Williams Books, 1996), pp. 431–32.
33. Ruth Flashoff, 'Williams, Anna Maria', DNZB: www.teara.govt.nz/en/biogaphies/2w20/williams-anna-maria
34. May, *School Beginnings*, p. 150.
35. J. Webster to G.F. Russell, Letter 17, 13 June 1849; Letter 18, 16 July 1849, 1848–1850 NZMS 4/19, Sir George Grey Special Collections, Auckland Library. Later in the century, daughters of Thomas Porter and Te Rangi-i-paea attended Mrs Sheppard's Ladies School in Napier: Tony Chadwick, 'Howie, Fanny Rose', DNZB: www.teara.govt.nz/en/biographies/3h40/howie-fanny-rose
36. *Education Act 1877* Article 10; see May, *School Beginnings*, p. 152.
37. Elizabeth to William Colenso, 19 December 1853, in Porter et al., *My Hand Will Write*, p. 300.
38. Macmorran, *Some Schools*, pp. 18–19.
39. Ibid., p. 21.
40. *NEx*, 15 June 1844 p. 57.
41. *NZer*, 18 July 1856 p. 1, 1 July 1857 p. 1; *DSX*, 13 February 1857 p. 3.
42. *LT*, 1 November 1851 p. 8, 22 April 1854 p. 1, 10 January 1855 p. 1, 18 September 1858 p. 5, 18 July 1860 p. 6; *Press*, 5 September 1873 p. 1; Edward had another wife, wed in his youth in a 'Scottish marriage', who was in an English asylum. *NZ Truth*, 18 August 1927 p. 8.
43. *WI*, 7 January 1862 p. 6, 11 April 1863 p. 3, 22 October 1867 p. 5, 7 July 1868 p. 1, 10 April 1869 p. 7, 20 September 1871 p. 3, 12 October 1871 p. 3, 10 December 1870 p. 4; *EP*, 9 June 1869 p. 3, 12 October 1871 p. 3; *Manawatu Standard*, 10 December 1885 p. 2; *FS*, 31 January 1889 p. 2, 15 April 1890 p. 4; *WH*, 7 January 1893 p. 4.
44. Macmorran, *Some Schools*, p. 58; *WI*, 15 April 1846 p. 2.
45. William Williams, Diary, 13 December 1849, in Frances Porter (ed.), *The Turanga Journals: Letters and journals of William and Jane Williams* (Wellington: Victoria Unversity Press, 1974), p. 511; 1875 NZ Electoral Rolls; see Find-a-Grave: www.findagrave.com/memorial/157323562/frederick-brathwaite; *NZer*, 8 July 1848 p. 4, 5 October 1850 p. 4; *NZH*, 4 February 1868 p. 1; *AS*, 4 December 1878 p. 3, 8 September 1883 p. 2.
46. Sarah Platt to Julia Rendell, 15 February 1858, in Porter et al., *My Hand Will Write*, p. 163; Sarah Platt to Henry, 16 October 1858, p. 4, Pratt Family Correspondence Outward, MS Papers 0229-2, ATL; *TH*, 1 July 1871 p. 3.
47. Tosti Murray, *Marsden: The history of a New Zealand school for girls* (Wellington: The Marsden Old Girls' Association, 1967), p. 52, quoted in Jai Paterson, 'Among friends: Middle class Tasmanians who moved to New Zealand, 1855–1875', PhD thesis, University of Tasmania, 2015, p. 193; Beryl Hughes, 'Swainson, Mary Anne', DNZB: www.teara.govt.nz/en/biographies/2s55/swainson-mary-anne

48. *DSX*, 28 April 1870 p. 3; *AS*, 23 January 1884 p. 2.
49. *Ford's Sydney Commercial Directory for the Year 1851* (Sydney: W. & F. Ford, 1851); *The Asiatic Journal and Monthly Miscellany*, 1840, p. 76.
50. M.A. Brassey to J. Hall, 1865, MS Papers 1784 29, ATL.
51. School proprietors, as drawn from various advertisements on *Papers Past*, included Mrs Barnes, Mrs Brathwaite, Miss Chalmers, Mrs Colcough, Miss Conway, Mrs Davis, Miss Drabble, Miss Drury, Madame Du Fane, Mrs Glover, Mrs Hooper, Miss Lampriere, Mrs Lewis, Mrs Palmer, Miss Rich, Mrs Shayle George, Miss Taylor, Mrs Tester, the Misses Fisher and the Misses Vibert and Anstie. *Stevens and Bartholomew's New Zealand Directory, 1866–67* (Melbourne: G. Stevens and D.H. Bartholomew, 1866–67); *DSX*, 17 January 1867 p. 6.
52. M.A. Brassey to Hall, 1865; *NZH*, 7 May 1879 p. 1, 31 October 1892 p. 4.
53. *NZer*, 7 July 1860 p. 2; *DSX*, 1 July 1862 p. 1, 18 November 1871 p. 1; *AS*, 1 December 1881 p. 1, 24 March 1888 p. 6; Isabella Lewis, NZ Probate 1888.
54. *WH*, 10 July 1873 p. 3, 25 March 1876 p. 3; *WC*, 21 January 1885 p. 2; *Manawatu Standard*, 21 March 1885 p. 2.
55. Sarah Greenwood to Ellen, 23 February 1866; Sarah Greenwood to Rhoda Nelson, 27 November 1869, in Sarah Greenwood, 'Correspondence – Sarah Greenwood to Family and Friends', Greenwood Family Papers, 1843–1880, MS–Papers–0098–14 (MS–Copy–Micro–0194–2), ATL; June E. Neale, *The Greenwoods: A pioneer family of New Zealand* (Nelson: General Printing Services, 1984), p. 88.
56. *NZer*, 26 September 1863 p. 2.
57. *NZG*, 25 December 1841 p. 4. In Nelson Mary Grace Huxham charged similar fees. *NEx*, 31 May 1842 p. 41; 'Mrs Edward' Young (Caroline) charged annually: daily pupils £6/6/0 for English with extras of £4/4/0 for each subject. *NZG*, 11 December 1841 p. 1.
58. *NZG*, 4 October 1843 p. 1.
59. *NZ Colonist and Port Nicholson Advertiser*, 2 August 1842 p. 4.
60. *NEx*, 22 June 1844 p. 61, 28 December 1844 p. 169; she married W. Sharp (probably William).
61. Emma Evans to Francis Bradey from Prospect Cottage, Kawau, 22 August 1848, Papers relating to the Bradey Family, MS 91/61, AWMM.
62. *NZer*, 17 February 1855 p. 2, 17 June 1857 p. 1; *DSX*, 9 March 1855 p. 2, 28 December 1855 p. 2; 'Samuel Ludbrooke Clarke, 'Clarke family of Te Waimate': www.clarke.org.nz/?sid=12
63. *NZer*, 18 July 1856 p. 1, 01 July 1857 p. 1; *DSX*, 13 February 57 p. 3.
64. *NZer*, 7 July 1852 p. 4, 7 July 1858 p. 4; The Misses Anstie also understood the cachet of guineas. They charged three guineas per quarter for morning lessons including French and two extra guineas per quarter for afternoon lessons in Italian and German in 1863, *DSX*, 14 January 1863 p. 1.
65. *DSX*, 13 April 1858 p. 2.
66. In Wellington Sophia Askin charged 50 guineas in 1856; Miss Hunt charged £50 in 1863, *HBH*, 21 August 1858 p. 4; *WI*, 8 January 1863 p. 4. In Nelson Sarah Greenwood's boarding pupils paid £12 a quarter and in 1866 she had 13 day scholars paying £16 each a year. Neale, *The Greenwoods*, p. 79; Sarah Greenwood to Ellen 23 February 1866, 'Correspondence'.
67. *DSX*, 15 October 1852 p. 1.
68. *NZer*, 27 July 1861 p. 2, 27 January 1863 p. 1.
69. *Timaru Herald*, 28 April 1883 p. 1.
70. *DSX*, 29 September 1857 p. 1.

71. *NZer*, 23 July 1856 p. 1.
72. *NZH*, 30 March 1869 p. 1.
73. *DSX*, 18 May 1860 p. 2; *NZer*, 9 January 1861 p. 1.
74. *NZer*, 7 September 1861 p. 3.
75. *LT*, 18 December 1861 p. 5; Margaret Francis, 'Alabaster, Ann O'Connor', DNZB: www.teara.govt.nz.en/biographies/1a5/alabaster-ann-oconnor
76. Macdonald Dictionary.
77. *Star*, 30 September 1869 p. 4; *Press*, 11 September 1871 p. 1, 29 December 1874 p. 2, 16 December 1876 p. 5; *Globe*, 29 December 1874 p. 2; *LT*, 16 December 1875 p. 2, 24 January 1885 p. 7; Macdonald Dictionary.
78. *NZG*, 25 December 1841 p. 4, 28 October 1843 p. 1.
79. *NEx*, 22 May 1852 p. 18; December 1852 p. 169; *NEM*, 13 November 1911 p. 6.
80. *NEx*, 15 October 1856 p. 2.
81. UK Census 1841; William White, *History, Gazetteer and Directory of Leicestershire and Rutland 1846* (Sheffield: W. White, 1846), p. 195, University of Leicester, Historical Directories of Leicestershire: https://cdm16445.contentdm.oclc.org/digital/collection/p.15407coll9; *NEx* 13 August 1862 p. 2; *Colonist*, 28 August 1884 p. 3, 16 September 1884 p. 2; *NEM*, 28 August 1884 p. 2.
82. *NZer*, 14 January 1857 p. 2, 30 December 1857 p. 2.
83. *DSX*, 21 February 1862 p. 1; *NZer*, 14 July 1863 p. 2.
84. *DSX*, 18 January 1866 p. 1, 22 February 1866 p. 1, 5 November 1866 p. 1, 19 January 1867 p. 1, 18 November 1873 p. 1; *NZH*, 17 January 1884 p. 8.
85. *OW*, 21 April 1860 p. 6.
86. *LT*, 22 September 1858 p. 1.
87. *HBH*, 31 July 1858 p. 2; Alicia Willcocks offered places to boarders 'to whose comfort and happiness particular attention will be devoted, and their religious and moral training carefully attended to', *NZer*, 9 January 1861 p. 1.
88. *NZer*, 31 July 1858 p. 2.
89. *NZer*, 7 July 1852 p. 4.
90. *WI*, 4 October 1851 p. 2.
91. *NZer*, 9 January 1861 p. 1.
92. Flora Spurdle, *New Stories of Old Whanganui* (Whanganui: H.P. Willemsen, 1958), p. 17.
93. *NZer*, 16 January 1863 p. 1; UK Census 1851.
94. *WI*, 29 September 1863 p. 2.
95. *HBH*, 17 December 1867 p. 2, 11 January 1868 p. 2.
96. *WI*, 10 December 1870 p. 4.
97. *DSX*, 17 January 1872 p. 1. Little is known about Mrs Garland, or whether her claims were true. Susan Seaman became headmistress of Takapuna Primary School and published a volume of poetry. Susie Mactier, 'Takapuna Lake Poet', Auckland City Council, 'Takapuna Writers' Walk': https://57.myt.li/tours/1507970552/stops/1771181974/index.html
98. *NZer*, 7 November 1849 p. 2.
99. Brind, FMCES, 1 June 1873, pp 436–37, 14 March 1875, pp. 462–63.
100. *WH*, 14 December 1867 p. 3.
101. *NZH*, 26 July 1865 p. 1; she married Jean Aubin in 1867. 'Jean Aubin of Pirongia, New Zealand': www.theislandwiki.org/index.php/Jean_Aubin_of_Pirongia,_New_Zealand
102. *NZG*, 4 October 1843 p. 1.

103. *ODT*, 26 May 1863 p. 7; Stephen Glover (1812/13–1870) was a composer of popular songs and Sigismund Thalberg (1812–1871) a piano virtuoso.
104. *NEx*, 17 April 1858 p. 2; I am grateful to Fiona Hevey-Kenning and Lynn Macgyver for sharing their research.
105. Henri Herz, *My Travels in America* (translated by Henry Bertram Hall) (Madison: State Historical Society of Wisconsin for University of Wisconsin 1963) p. 34, (pp. 110–11 of original French).
106. *NZer*, 17 February 1855 p. 2.
107. *NZG*, 3 March 1841 p. 1.
108. Archdeacon Henry Jacobs would become dean; Dr James Somerville Turnbull was a local identity with his wooden leg; Rose Bealey was the wife of the Canterbury provincial superintendent, Samuel Bealey; and 'Mrs Macfarlan' was probably Mary Anne, wife of wine and spirit merchant Dugald Macfarlane in Cranmer Square. Macdonald Dictionary; *Press*, 19 February 1866 p. 4; Christchurch City Council, Town Planning Division, 'Cranmer Club', in 'Architectural heritage of Christchurch': www.Christchurchcitylibraries.com/Heritage/Publications/ChristchurchCityCouncil/ArchitecturalHeritage/CranmerClub/CranmerClub.pdf
109. *NZH*, 30 March 1869 p. 1; they were the Reverend James Buller, the Reverend John Whewell and Dr William Stockwell.
110. *LT*, 1 October 1853 p. 12 (Thomson), 18 September 1858 p. 5 (Taylor), 14 July 1860 p. 6 (Thomson), 18 July 1860 p. 6 (Taylor).
111. *NZH*, 30 March 1868 p. 1.
112. Fanny Cross, FMCES, Oamaru, 25 October 1881 (Bk2).
113. Sarah Pratt to her sister Ellen Adams, 1855; Sarah Pratt to Julia Rendell, 15 February 1858; both in Porter et al., *My Hand Will Write*, p. 163.
114. *NZG*, 29 May 1841 p. 2; *NZer*, 15 September 1847 p. 2, 29 June 1861 p. 4; *Argus*, 15 December 1873 p. 1, 7 October 1889 p. 1.
115. *DSX*, 14 January 1863 p. 1.
116. *AS*, 3 July 1875 p. 3.
117. Macdonald Dictionary; *LT*, 20 October 1873 p. 1; *Press*, 24 January 1939 p. 24.
118. Johanna Lohse left in 1890 and Annette Bowen was advertising for pupils the following year. There seems to have been no formal handover announcement, but both sets of pupils were included as 'Old Girls' in 1901. *LT*, 26 July 1890 p. 8; 21 January 1891 p. 1; *Press*, 11 October 1901 p. 1; *Star*, 19 October 1909 p. 3; *TH*, 10 January 1910 p. 5; Philip Hedgeland's Reminiscences in 'Wilson-Ross Family History', compiled c. 1936, private collection Geoff Bremner, London; Johanna Lohse, *Mistaken Views on the Education of Girls* (Christchurch: Whitcombe & Tombs, 1884).
119. Douglas Saxon Coombs, Anne G. Coombs and Elise Pickett, *Strangers and Pilgrims: The von Tunzelmann saga* (Dunedin: Douglas and Anne Coombs, 2006); *Colonist*, 6 July 1871 p. 6, 19 January 1872 p. 8; *NEM*, 13 January 1874 p. 2.
120. Gilbert Pickett to Donald Mclean, 3 August 1871, Object #1006285, MS–Papers–0032–0503, ATL: http://mp. natlib.govt.nz/detail/?id=1006285&recordNum=0&t=items&q=gilbert+pickett&l=en
121. *Colonist*, 10 July 1877 p. 3; *NEM*, 12 February 1878 p. 4, 16 January 1879 p. 2; Coombs et al., *Strangers and Pilgrims*, pp. 195–96.

122. *DSX*, 14 December 1849 p. 1.
123. J. Webster–G.F. Russell, 16 August 1849, Letter 19, NZMS 4/19, Sir George Grey Special Collections, Auckland Library.
124. *NZer*, 5 January 1850 p. 2.
125. *Southland Times*, 17 July 1867 p. 3, 16 June 1875 p. 2; *ODT*, 17 July 1875 p. 2.
126. *NZH*, 30 March 1869 p. 1.
127. *NZSCSG*, 19 January 1853 p. 2.
128. *NZSCSG*, 24 September 1853 p. 2; see also *NZer*, 14 January 1863 p. 2.
129. Caldwell, Diary, p. 12; Caldwell's school ran 1851–53, 1856–58. *NEx*, 20 December 1851 p. 169, 1 January 1853 p. 107, 11 October 1856 p. 4, 3 October 1857 p. 2, 6 February 1858 p. 4.
130. Janet Holm, *Nothing But Grass and Wind: The Rutherfords of Canterbury* (Christchurch: Hazard Press, 1992), p. 32; *HBH*, 31 July 1858 p. 2; *NEx*, 7 August 1858 p. 2; 'Liverpool and London Fire and Life Insurance Company Wellington Agents Life Insurance Policies Allen – Askin: Sophia Askin', Levin & Company Ltd, MS–Papers–1347–6–1–1, ATL.
131. *Timaru Herald*, 9 October 1874 p. 3, 28 April 1883 p. 1, 4 February 1897 p. 1, 1 January 1889 p. 2, 7 September 1897 p. 2; Edward Tate NZ Probate 1882; South Canterbury Museum, 'From the grave', *Timaru Herald*, 23 January 2007: www.pressreader.com/new-zealand/the-timaru-herald/20070123/282776352063578
132. Elizabeth Burbidge's name appears as both Burbridge and Burbidge in contemporary sources. Most newspaper accounts, and the NZBDM index, use Burbidge, although the index to probate records (but not the probate itself), and Smith's account book, refer to her as Burbridge. Unfortunately she did not leave a will so we cannot see how she herself spelt her name. Elizabeth Burbridge NZ Probate 1868; *NZer*, 6 November 1858 p. 2; *WI*, 20 June 1857 p. 3, 8 September 1858 p. 3, 2 October 1858 p. 3, 10 January 1865 p. 2; *EP*, 7 February 1868 p. 2; Jeremy Finn, 'The schoolgirl and the horse-whipped parson: An account of an early New Zealand cause celebre', *Australian Journal of Legal History* 9, 2005, pp. 1–29; John Sidney Smith, 1808–1880: Account Book, qMS 1826, ATL.
133. Caroline Newman, Letter, 7 December 1855, MS 483, AWMM; *NZer*, 17 February 1855 p. 2.
134. William Williams to Henry Williams, Turanga, 27 December 1849, in Porter (ed.), *The Turanga Journals*, p. 553.
135. Marjory F.E. Adams, *A Garland from Quatt: The story of a pioneering ancestor as told by her granddaughter* (Auckland: M. Adams, 2001); Adams, 'Our first 12 years in New Zealand from 1860–1872'; *AS*, 13 January 1872 p. 2, 15 January 1872 p. 3, 10 August 1875 p. 3; *DSX*, 15 January 1872 p. 3.
136. The Nelson School Society established a primary school in the 1840s with a male teacher, although it is likely that the wife of the first teacher, John Perry Robinson (later provincial superintendent), was also involved, as she was listed as a schoolmistress in the 1845 census, even though by then her husband was working in the Bay of Islands. Nelson Census Returns, January 1845, SSD 3 1/1, Micro 3632 Repro 56, Archives NZ, Wellington.
137. Henry Cooper Daniell, 'Letters 1841–54', MS–061, ATL; Ruth Alban, notes from Daniell's letters: 3 April 1846, 1 October 1846, 4 March 1848, 4 July 1851, 10 August 1852, 1 September 1853, 18 October 1853, in 'Primary Education 1842–50', Ruth Allan Papers, MS–Papers 205/29, ATL; Henry's wife Anna is invisible in public records, save for her support of the British Patriotic Fund in 1855 and her death notice in 1885. *NEx*, 21 March 1855 p. 2; *NEM*, 31 July 1885 p. 2.

138. Caldwell, Diary, p. 12.
139. *NEx*, 24 January 1863 p. 2; *WCT*, 25 April 1866 p. 1; *NEM*, 18 January 1869 p. 3, 15 January 1874 p. 2, 31 December 1879 p. 2, 8 September 1909 p. 3; *Colonist*, 21 June 1884 p. 2 (supplement).
140. *NEx*, 18 August 1860 p. 2, *NEM*, 10 July 1869 p. 3; Catherine Rentoul NZ Probate 1884.
141. Rebecca Lee Sinclair, 'A few recollections of my early life in Nelson, July 1932': www.genealogy.ianskipworth.com/pdf/rebeccasincinclair.pdf, also in Hodgson Family collection, NRAMB400, NPM.
142. Daniel Peddie, precentor to the Nelson Presbyterian Church, taught secular and sacred music in her schoolroom. UK Census 1841; *NEx*, 28 February 1852 p. 1, 19 June 1852 p. 65, 25 December 1852 p. 173.
143. *NEx*, 29 December 1855 p. 2, 13 September 1856 p. 2; Francis Sait NZ Probate 1873.
144. *NEx*, 19 September 1857 p. 2, 19 December 1857 p. 3.
145. *NEx*, 6 August 1864 p. 3.
146. *NEx*, 5 September 1868 p. 6; *NEM*, 22 December 1874 p. 2.
147. *Colonist*, 13 January 1876 p. 6.
148. The monitorial system consisted of one teacher and 'monitors', often older children using systemised materials. May, *School Beginnings*, p. 24.
149. *NEM*, 6 February 1879 p. 5.
150. Elizabeth Sait NZ Probate 1910.
151. *NEM*, 17 January 1910 p. 5; *EP*, 4 April 1910 p. 2. Women's occupations were not recorded in death registration data either until well into the twentieth century, Kate McKegg, 'Dying to be noticed: Gender, work and death registration in New Zealand', *Labour, Employment and Work in New Zealand* [S.I.], 1994, p. 173ff.
152. *NZH*, 30 March 1875 p. 2; *AS* 16 April 1879 p 3; *NZH*, 24 January 1883 p. 8; Raewyn Dalziel, 'George, Frances Shayle', DNZB: www.teara.govt.nz/en/biographies/1g8/george-frances-shayle
153. *EP*, 24 August 1876 p. 2; *Wairarapa Standard*, 11 June 1878 p. 2.
154. Richard L.N. Greenaway, 'Maria Thomson', *Rich Man, Poor Man, Environmentalist, Thief: Biographies of Canterbury personalities written for the millennium and for the 150th anniversary of the Canterbury settlement* (Christchurch: Canterbury Public Library, 2000); *EP*, 22 May 1929 p. 13.
155. *LT*, 4 January 1862 p. 5.
156. Mrs Charles Thomson, *Twelve Years in Canterbury, New Zealand, with Visits to the Other Provinces, and Reminiscences of the Route Home Through Australia etc. (from a Lady's Journal)* (London: Sampson Low, Son and Marston, 1867?), ENZB.
157. Popular myth has it that she took on a partner, Mrs Clark, described as 'a kindly soul' who, according to Leonard Hewland writing in the 1950s, taught girls to 'sew, read, write and do their sums in that order' at 'Richmond House Seminary'. Actually Mrs Clark, while she may indeed have emphasised needlework in her curriculum, was not associated with Maria's Avon House. She ran the competing Avonside House. Leonard Hewland, 'Girls' schools in early Christchurch recalled', *Press*, 30 April 1956, in Greenaway, 'Maria Thomson', *Rich Man, Poor Man*.
158. *The Southern Provinces Almanac, Directory and Year Book* (Lyttelton: Lyttelton Times Office, 1868); advertisements from various newspapers 1867–69, Papers Past.

159. *Press*, 27 June 1868 p. 1, 26 May 1875 p. 1; *LT*, 24 September 1853 p. 12, 6 July 1867 p. 1; Macdonald Dictionary (misspelt as Maria Thompson); Greenaway, 'Maria Thomson', *Rich Man, Poor Man*. Other women had already been celebrated in a suffrage centenary volume: Greenaway, *Unsung Heroines: Biographies of Christchurch women written to commemorate Women's Suffrage Year, 1993* (Christchurch: Canterbury Public Library, 1994): http://christchurchcitylibraries.com/Heritage/Publications/UnsungHeroines/
160. M.J. Greenwood to Caroline Abraham, Wellington, 29 May 1870, Caroline H. Abraham Papers, MS Papers–2305–2, ATL.

Chapter 6: A Stitch in Time

1. *WT*, 9 October 1869 p. 2.
2. See Jane Malthus, 'Dressmakers in nineteenth-century New Zealand', in Margaret Tennant, Charlotte Macdonald and Barbara Brookes (eds), *Women in History 2* (Wellington: Bridget Williams Books, 1992), 76–97; *OW*, 7 August 1852 p. 2; R.J. Bunce, *Slippery Jim or Patriotic Statesman: James Macandrew of Otago* (Dunedin: Otago University Press, 2018).
3. *OW*, 28 February 1852 p. 2, 27 November 1852 p. 1, 26 March 1863 p. 25, May 1855 p. 2; *Glasgow Herald*, 13 March 1865 p. 5.
4. The Youngs then settled in Southland and William opened a drapery business, in which his wife's expertise was doubtless invaluable. *Mary* passenger list 1849; *OW*, 13 December 1851 p. 2; *Southland Times*, 9 August 1864 p. 3; J. Wilson (ed.), *Reminiscences of the Early Settlement of Dunedin and South Otago* (Dunedin: Wilkie & Co., 1912), p. 162: https://archive.org/stream/reminiscencesofe00duneiala/reminiscencesofe00duneiala_djvu.txt
5. *OW*, 26 March 1853 p. 2, 1 February 1909 p. 4, 3 January 1912 p. 34.
6. *ODT*, 10 December 1859 p. 4, 30 July 1886 p. 3, 27 December 1893 p. 2; *OW*, 25 March 1854 p. 1, 30 August 1856 p. 2, 26 November 1859 p. 2, 19 January 1861 p. 2, 2 March 1861 p. 2.
7. 'Brown, Ewing & Co', *Cyclopedia of New Zealand Otago and Southland Provincial Districts* (Christchurch: The Cyclopedia Company Ltd, 1905), p. 401; reiterated in Helen Laurenson, 'Department stores and shopping malls: The rise of department stores', Te Ara: www.teara.govt.nz/en/department-stores-and-shopping-malls/page-1
8. *OW*, 25 February 1854 p. 2; sleeves and collars were removable and sold separately. They could be laundered separately (being the most likely to be dirty), but could also be replaced to update an outfit.
9. *OW*, 30 June 1855 p. 2.
10. *OW*, 25 October 1856 p. 2.
11. *OW*, 1 January 1859 p. 4.
12. *OW*, 1 December 1860 p. 10; Matilda's sister Amelia Headland married widower Edward Bland Atkinson within five months of arriving in Dunedin with the Bakers.
13. *ODT*, 12 November 1866 p. 1; *NOT*, 14 April 1864 p. 5; *Oamaru Mail*, 4 April 1890 p. 3; *Stevens & Bartholomew New Zealand Directory 1866–67*.
14. Barrie Macdonald, *Imperial Patriot: Charles Alma Baker and the history of Limestone Downs* (Wellington: Bridget Williams Books, 1993).
15. *OW*, 16 January 1858 p. 4.

16. *OW*, 21 September 1861 p. 4.
17. *OW*, 19 October 1861 p. 4.
18. *OW*, 6 October 1860 p. 4, 19 October 1861 p. 4; *ODT*, 5 December 1861 p. 3, 13 December 1861 p. 4; Miss Doran was previously employed by C.T. Ick; *OW*, 21 July 1860 p. 4.
19. *OW*, 28 July 1883 p. 2 (supplement).
20. *OW*, 5 July 1884 p. 10.
21. *ODT*, 23 July 1908 p. 8.
22. *Pioneers of Foxton: Book One* (Foxton: Foxton Historical Society, 1988), pp. 6–9: http://horowhenua.kete.net.nz/en/site/topics/74-amos-burr
23. Wendy Gamber, *The Female Economy: The millinery and dressmaking trades, 1860–1930* (Urbana: University of Illinois Press, 1997); See also Beth Harris (ed.), *Famine and Fashion: Needlewomen in the nineteenth century* (Aldershot and Burlington: Ashgate, 2005).
24. Malthus, 'Dressmakers'.
25. Florence Hartley, *Ladies' Book of Etiquette and Manual of Politeness* (Boston: G.W. Cottrell, 1860), p. 216.
26. *NZer*, 27 February 1861 p. 1.
27. *LT*, 22 August 1855 pp. 1 and 4, 2 July 1859 p. 3, 6 March 1861 p. 7, 10 August 1861 p. 1; *Press*, 14 January 1865 p. 1, 3 November 1875 p. 2; Macdonald Dictionary; Picture of Albion House, and Mary Ann wrongly identified as Elizabeth, who was John's second wife, Arts and Culture Oceania, 'Chancery Lane 1862': https://marapito.blogspot.com.au/2009/07/chancery-lane-1862.html
28. Madame Johanna Weigel was an entrepreneurial businesswoman based in Australia. See Veronica Lampkin, *Madame Weigel: The woman who clothed the Australasian colonies* (Carrara, Queensland: V. Lampkin, 2015).
29. *NZer*, 24 April 1847 p. 3.
30. *NZer*, 17 July 1852 p. 2.
31. Trimmings were all the rage in the 1860s and 1870s, as Adrian Forty points out in *Objects of Desire* (New York: Pantheon Books, 1986), p. 54.
32. *NZer*, 8 November 1856 p. 2.
33. *Colonist*, 5 April 1859 p. 2, 22 March 1883 p. 3, 11 August 1883 p. 3; *NEM*, 27 April 1880 p. 2.
34. *NZG*, 6 November 1841 p. 3, 13 November 1841 p. 1.
35. *OW*, 2 May 1857 p. 4.
36. MT to EN, 4–8 January 1857, in Stevens, *Mary Taylor*, p. 129.
37. ET to CB, 13 August 1850, in Stevens, *Mary Taylor*, pp. 99–100.
38. MT to CB, 5 April 1850, in Stevens, *Mary Taylor*, pp. 89–90.
39. ET to CB, 13 August 1850, in Stevens, *Mary Taylor*, p. 99.
40. *ODT*, 18 January 1865 p. 5; *WI*, 18 July 1865 p. 2.
41. *OW*, 13 August 1859 p. 2, 3 September 1859 p. 6, 20 October 1860 p. 7, 9 April 1864 p. 21; *ODT*, 18 March 1865 p. 5; Agnes Logan's niece would become Anna Stout.
42. *WI*, 3 January 1855 p. 3.
43. *WI*, 18 December 1858 p. 2, 24 February 1860 p. 2, 2 August 1861 p. 2, 17 January 1863 p. 2; *EP*, 1 November 1865 p. 3, 10 February 1877 p. 2; *NZ Times*, 5 January 1901 p. 5; Rachel F. Baskerville, *Jane Harvey and Solomon Levy: A New Zealand family* (Wellington: R.F. Baskerville, 2006).
44. *Colonist*, 5 April 1859 p. 2, 6 March 1860 p. 4; *NEx*, 29 January 1862 p. 2, 30 July 1862 p. 1.

45. *WH*, 15 March 1875 p. 2, 26 May 1893 p. 2; Agnes was in business from 1870 to at least 1887: *WH*, 12 November 1870 p. 1, 19 November 1887 p. 3.
46. *ODT*, 27 June 1863 p. 3; *NZT*, 8 September 1883 p. 4; *NZH*, 4 March 1865 p. 1; see L. Ward, *Early Wellington* (Auckland: Whitcombe & Tombs, 1928); he does not reference his claim but says the sewing machine was passed on to Miss Kinniburgh next door.
47. Catherine Ralfe, 'Life in New Zealand', MS Papers 1129, ATL; see also Malthus, 'Dressmakers', pp. 88–89; Megan Hutching, *Over the Wide and Trackless Sea: The pioneer women and girls of New Zealand* (Auckland: Harper Collins, 2008), pp. 201–43; Ellen Ellis, 'Ralfe, Catherine Hester', DNZB: www.teara.govt.nz/en/biographies/2r2/ralfe-catherine-hester
48. See Wendy Gamber, '"Reduced to science": Gender, technology, and power in the American dressmaking trade, 1860–1910', *Technology and Culture* 36, no. 3, 1995, pp. 455–82.
49. *NEM*, 28 September 1888 p. 4.
50. *EP*, 17 June 1879 p. 3; *NZH*, 22 March 1894 p. 1, 4 May 1895 p. 1; *AS*, 7 June 1898 p. 4.
51. *NZH*, 25 January 1892 p. 1.
52. *Employment of Females Act 1873* (37 Victoriae 1873 no. 71), *Employment of Females Amendment Act 1875* (39 Victoriae 1875 no. 89), NZLII.
53. *ES*, 17 March 1879 p. 2, 8 September 1879 p. 2; *ODT*, 18 March 1879 p. 2, 12 September 1879 p. 7.
54. *AS*, 13 June 1881 p. 2.
55. *Colonist*, 18 August 1883 p. 3, 28 January 1885 p. 3.
56. *NEM*, 28 September 1888 p. 4.
57. *ODT*, 19 April 1870 p. 1; *ES*, 9 May 1881 p. 3, 17 June 1889 p. 3, 8 July 1889 p. 2, 18 March 1897 p. 3; Supreme Court – Lunacy Case File No L102 – Elizabeth Keates, wife of Timothy Keates, DAAC D140 Box 270, Archives NZ.
58. Rutherford Waddell, D.P. Fisher and Colin Allan, *Addendum to the 1890 Sweating Commission*: www.teara.govt.nz/en/photograph/25561/1890-sweating-commission. Notably, the *Factories Act 1891* (54 and 55 VICT 1891 no. 32) did not address outwork either. NZLII.
59. *OW*, 31 August 1861 p. 2.
60. *WI*, 2 February 1859 p. 3, 25 October 1861 p. 2, 25 October 1864 p. 2, 5 January 1867 p. 6, 21 March 1867 p. 2, 23 May 1867 p. 1.
61. NZ Census 1859, 1864.
62. *HBH*, 15 January 1859 p. 1, 26 November 1859 p. 2, 18 February 1860 p. 2, 1 November 1861 p. 1, 1 July 1862 p. 2, 26 July 1862 p. 4.
63. *HBH*, 25 August 1860 p. 8; *WI*, 25 September 1862 p. 2.
64. *HBT*, 20 September 1864 p. 2.
65. *HBT*, 25 November 1864 p. 2; *HBH*, 29 November 1864 p. 4, 26 February 1867 p. 1, 17 September 1867 p. 2, 24 September 1867 p. 1, 10 March 1868 p. 1.
66. *DSX*, 29 August 1862 p. 1; *NZer*, 14 September 1864 p. 4; *HBT*, 21 January 1867 p. 3; *Daily Telegraph* (Napier), 12 April 1887 p. 4; *HBH*, 2 August 1887 p. 2; Mrs White 'with eight years experience in Manchester and Liverpool' advertised for a few months in Hastings Street Napier, *HBH*, 21 March 1868 p. 4, 14 November 1868 p. 1. Mrs Williams and Miss Lambert were also in Hastings Street.
67. *TH*, 26 August 1865 p. 4, 28 April 1866 p. 3.
68. *NEx*, 7 August 1858 p. 2, p. 1 (supplement); Robert Ross, 'Letter to a Gentleman in London', Nelson, 30 November 1842, *Letters from Settlers & Labouring Emigrants in the New Zealand*

Company's Settlements of Wellington, Nelson, & New Plymouth, from February, 1842, to January, 1843 (London: Smith, Elder & Co, 1843), p. 121; William Harley survived his imprisonment and lived until the ripe old age of 81, having had two wives.

69. *TH*, 24 December 1864 p. 5; 7 January 1865 p. 2, 29 July 1865 p. 1, 7 October 1865 p. 2, 2 June 1866 p. 1, 9 October 1872 p. 3.
70. *TH*, 28 February 1874 p. 1.
71. *TH*, 25 August 1878 p. 3, 11 October 1879 p. 4, 13 November 1880 p. 3, 27 September 1882 p. 3.
72. *TH*, 20 September 1882 p. 2, 21 September 1882 p. 2.
73. *TH*, 28 August 1891 p. 2.
74. *TH*, 17 May 1863 p. 1, 16 June 1866 p. 6, 12 December 1868 p. 1; Judy Hanline, 'Hood, Mary', DNZB: www.teara.govt.nz/en/biographies/2h48/hood-mary
75. Mary Hood NZ Probate 1902; Hanline, 'Hood, Mary', DNZB.
76. *WH*, 28 November 1873 p. 2; Bill Shipman, *Hogg Family History from Scotland to Wanganui* (Papatoetoe: W. Spence and B. Shipman, 1989).
77. Athol Kirk, 'Ayrshire House, Economic, D.I.C., Arthur Barnetts', *Whanganui Historical Record* 22, no. 1, 1991, p. 21; *WH*, 8 June 1867 p. 3, 17 December 1869 p. 2, 1 March 1871 p. 3, 19 January 1884 p. 3.
78. *WH*, 2 January 1886 pp. 2–3; *WC*, 28 September 1904 p. 4; Sarah Hogg NZ Probate 1901.
79. *WI*, 11 November 1869 p. 3, 28 July 1873 p. 3; *WH*, 12 June 1873 p. 2; see Julia Bradshaw, 'Adjustable marriages: Relationships, divorce and bigamy on the goldfields', *Echoes of Our Past, Proceedings of the 2018 Conference of the New Zealand Society of Genealogists*, June 2018; Margaret Long, 'Memorials to Emily McWilliam', *Otaki Historical Journal* 21, 1998, pp. 50–53; Rex Kerr, *Not Only Te Rauparaha and Hadfield, but also …* (Otaki: Black Pony Books, 2016), pp. 92–93.
80. *WH*, 31 January 1870 p. 2.
81. Goodfellow: *WH*, 3 July 1867 p. 4; Reilly: *WH*, 15 September 1868 p. 3; Potto: *WH*, 16 November 1868 p. 3; Tingey: *WH*, 14 December 1868 p. 5; Rankin: *WH*, 30 September 1869 p. 3; Craig, Gaites, Nash, Neville: *The Wellington Almanack and Diary 1866* (Wellington: T. McKenzie, 1866) pp. 177–78; Green, Thorpe, Wilton, *The Wellington Almanack and Diary 1866*.
82. *LT*, 15 November 1851 p. 8; *The Argus*, 18 July 1871 p. 3.
83. *NZer*, 22 March 1856 p. 2; UK census 1851.
84. *ODT*, 22 January 1863 p. 3; *LT*, 21 February 1868 p. 3.
85. *HBH*, 29 November 1864 p. 4.
86. *HBH*, 26 February 1867 p. 1.
87. *DSX*, 6 April 1855 p. 2; *NZer*, 15 August 1856 p. 1; *WI*, 8 April 1859 p. 3; *SMH*, 5 July 1919 p. 11; UK census 1851; David Stanton, 'Elizabeth Ann Jones nee Buller': www.mis.net.au/stanton/elizabeth_ann_buller.htm
88. *Colonist*, 10 April 1860 p. 1; *NEx*, 28 February 1852 p. 1, 13 March 1852 p. 9, 10 December 1859 p. 2, 12 May 1860 p. 2, 2 January 1861 p. 4.
89. *NEx*, 20 April 1861 p. 4, 15 January 1862 p. 1.
90. NSWBDM; Probate Packets NRS 13660, Records of NSW: www.records.nsw.gov.au; Betty Hunt, *The Acklands of Fiji* (Auckland: Betty Hunt, 2010). My thanks to Betty Hunt and also to Robyn Atherton of Harden.

91. *LT*, 11 January 1851 p. 5, 18 January 1851 p. 8; *Press*, 1 February 1862 p. 6; *LT*, 22 October 1862 p. 1.
92. *Press*, 3 November 1877 p. 1, 10 August 1882 p. 2.
93. She and her 17-year-old sister Elizabeth were both listed as domestic servants when they arrived with their parents, 45-year-old shoemaker Hugh and 39-year-old Mary Anne. Sisters Agnes, Catherine and Mary were already in Christchurch, having emigrated on the *Victory* in 1863. *LT*, 6 November 1868 p. 3; *Press*, 7 May 1867 p. 2.
94. Mrs Williams, Miss Lowther, Mrs Scott, Miss Moore, Mrs Waters, Mrs Culbert, Mrs Butler, Mrs Franks, Mrs Hobbs, Mrs Simpson, Mrs Sellars, Mrs Rowe, Miss Smith, Mrs Austin, Mrs Street, Mrs Roper, Mrs Pearce, Mrs Irving, Mrs Dalton, *Southern Provinces Almanac Directory and Yearbook for 1868* (Lyttelton: Lyttelton Times Office, 1868).
95. *Press*, 14 February 1871 p. 3, 2 September 1873 p. 1; *Star*, 7 October 1872 p. 1, 4 February 1893 p. 2.
96. *Manawatu Times*, 16 August 1883 p. 2.
97. *WH*, 5 October 1869 p. 3, 30 December 1873 p. 4, 19 May 1874 p. 4, 11 January 1882 p. 3.
98. *WH*, 9 June 1877 p. 2, 10 June 1878 p. 2.
99. *WH*, 3 January 1882 p. 3, 8 August 1883 p. 2; *WC*, 14 January 1882 p. 2, 7 October 1882 p. 2, 20 September 1883 p. 2; *Observer*, 25 August 1883 p. 3; Clara Rankin NZ Probate 1924; Clara Rankin and Lydia Burr of Foxton were sisters. John Notman: *Manawatu Times*, 8 August 1883 p. 2; obituary *WC*, 21 May 1909 p. 5.
100. 'Return of all the houses, cottages and warries with the names of their owners and occupiers in the district of Auckland 1845', IA1, 1845/1939, Microfilm 3630,5070, Repro 70, Archives NZ, Auckland.
101. *NZer*, 5 January 1848 p. 1, 30 June 1855 p. 4, 7 February 1857 p. 1.
102. *NZer*, 5 January 1848 p. 1, 7 June 1848 p. 2, 18 October 1848 p. 1.
103. *NZer*, 8 January 1848 p. 1, 19 February 1848 p. 1, 13 March 1850 p. 1.
104. Miss Jane Jennings and Mrs Maria Wardell, Mrs Elizabeth Lowson, Mrs King, Miss Hannah Brickwell, the Martin sisters, Miss Ann Hamer, Mrs Hegarty and Mrs Byrchmore were all advertising their services, along with Mrs Caroline Wethered, who made artificial flowers.
105. *NZer*, 7 April 1852 p. 1, 10 April 1852 p. 4, 29 April 1854 p. 2.
106. *NZer*, 26 April 1854 p. 2, 6 December 1856 p. 3.
107. *DSX*, 21 December 1852 p. 2, 23 May 1854 p. 2, 19 September 1856 p. 2, 23 September 1856 p. 2, 12 August 1857 p. 4; *NZer*, 28 January 1857 p. 3.
108. *TH*, 25 December 1858 p. 2, 7 December 1872 p. 3, 9 January 1875 p. 2; Elizabeth Webster NZ Probate 1897; Hartley Webster NZ Probate 1907.
109. Elizabeth and Alexander Mollison arrived with at least two Misses Forsyth in 1857; Ann and her brother David emigrated on the *Strathallan* in 1859. Brother Robert and sister Mary arrived in 1859 on the *Sevilla*; *OW*, 17 January 1857 p. 4, 16 January 1858 p. 4, 6 July 1861 p. 5; *ODT*, 1 August 1864 p. 8; New Zealand Electoral Rolls 1893, Transcription: www.findmypast.com.au
110. G. Clifton, *Directory of British Scientific Instrument Makers 1550–1851* (London: Zwemmer & National Maritime Museum, 1995), quoted in W. Orchiston, C. Romick and p. Brown, 'James Henry Marriott: New Zealand's first professional telescope maker', *Journal of Astronomical History and Heritage* 18, no. 3, 2015, pp. 261–76.

111. Mechanics' Institutes and schools of arts were established in Britain and its colonies in the nineteenth century to encourage adult learning among working men, providing lectures and libraries. Women were also known to attend lectures and occasionally to present them.
112. *WI*, 31 May 1864 p. 1.
113. *WI*, 1 August 1872 p. 2; *EP*, 5 October 1887 p. 3.
114. Peter Downes, 'Marriott, James Henry', DNZB: www.teara.govt.nz/en/biographies/1m15/marriott-james-henry; UK Census 1851; Emma Marriott NZ Probate 1898.
115. *Star*, 16 August 1881 p. 3.
116. *NEx*, 20 August 1859 p. 2, 28 May 1862 p. 1, 23 January 1866 p. 1, 13 August 1867 p. 2; *NEM*, 19 August 1868 p. 3.
117. *NEx*, 28 August 1852 p. 105, 22 September 1860 p. 1; *Colonist*, 2 May 1862 p. 4; 7 March 1883 p. 4; *Cornwall* passenger list 1851.
118. *NEx*, 25 April 1860 p. 2, 15 September 1860 p. 2, 12 May 1862 p. 3, 11 August 1862 p. 1, 31 December 1862 p. 1, 22 November 1864 p. 4. Theresa sold Bible tracts from her store in 1860, both were involved in the Order of Foresters, and when he died in 1913 William left most of his £2800 estate to Nelson's Christ Church Cathedral, establishing an organ fund. *NEM*, 25 February 1905 p. 2; *Colonist*, 27 February 1905 p. 2, 29 December 1913 p. 4.
119. *NEx*, 16 May 1855 p. 2, 11 February 1857 p. 1, 14 February 1857 p. 4, 3 July 1858 p. 2, 4 December 1858 p. 2, 13 June 1860 p. 1, 1 August 1860 p. 1, 3 October 1860 p. 2, 24 September 1869 p. 1, 14 July 1877 p. 3.
120. *NEx*, 1 December 1858 p. 2, 18 December 1858 p. 1.
121. *NEx*, 24 March 1860 p. 2.
122. *NEx*, 28 March 1860 p. 2, 15 December 1860 p. 2, 2 May 1860 p. 2, 24 May 1862 p. 1, 25 October 1862 p. 2; *Colonist*, 21 August 1860 p. 2, 21 September 1860 p. 2, 23 September 1862 p. 1, 14 February 1865 p. 2; *NEM*, 16 March 1866 p. 4, 21 September 1866 p. 3, 27 September 1869 p. 3.
123. Catherine Bishop, 'The serendipity of connectivity: Piecing together women's lives in the digital archive', *Women's History Review* 26, no. 5, 2017.
124. *NZer*, 12 February 1859, p. 1 (supplement).
125. Powley, Criminal Deposition Book, Police Office Auckland, 16 December 1852, in Robyn Anderson, '"The hardened frail ones": Women and crime in Auckland, 1845–1870', MA thesis, University of Auckland, 1981, pp. 91–92.
126. *NZer*, 17 November 1858 p. 2; *DSX*, 6 September 1862 p. 10, 19 October 1869 p. 4.
127. *NZer*, 7 May 1863 p. 3; *DSX*, 15 June 1863 p. 3, 17 June 1863 p. 1, 20 June 1863 p. 6.
128. *NZer*, 19 October 1869 p. 4, 30 June 1870 p. 1; *DSX*, 19 October 1869 p. 3; *NZH*, 26 September 1871 p. 1 (supplement); *AS*, 14 September 1871 p. 3.
129. *AS*, 8 September 1873 p. 3, 19 December 1901 p. 8; *NZH*, 29 January 1881 p. 7, 22 September 1902 p. 4.
130. Burke Manuscript, p. 122: http://christchurchcitylibraries.com/Heritage/Digitised/Burke/; *LT*, 25 December 1861 p. 6, 16 July 1862 p. 1; *Press*, 28 January 1864 p. 3, 16 October 1867 p. 3; *Globe*, 5 May 1882 p. 2; Harriett Ellen Lowther NZ Probate 1883; Mary Selina Lowther NZ Probate 1910.
131. *SMH*, 19 February 1855 p. 1, 23 April 1857 p. 4; *WI*, 27 October 1858 p. 2.
132. Anthony Dreaver, 'The draper's diary', unpublished ms., Chapters 9 and 12, based on W.G. Adkin's diary (in private hands). I am grateful to Anthony Dreaver for allowing me access to his research.

133. Mary Ann Basset, Rebecca Thompson, Kate Elisa Matts listed in *Historia* passenger list 1854, Victoria; *Argus*, 20 July 1864 p. 4, 19 March 1868 p. 2; *Avoca Mail* (Victoria), 27 May 1865 p. 3.
134. Dreaver, 'The draper's diary', Chapter 12, p. 6.
135. Letter from W.G. Adkin to his family in 8 November 1885 (held by Mrs D. Hodge), quoted in Dreaver, 'The draper's diary', Chapter 12, p. 1; *EP*, 13 October 1885 pp. 2–3.
136. Dreaver, 'The draper's diary', Chapter 12, p. 8.
137. Adkin, c. 17 January 1885, in Dreaver, 'The draper's diary', Chapter 9, pp. 7, 9.
138. Adkin, 8 November 1885, in Dreaver, 'The draper's diary', Chapter 12, p. 1.
139. *EP*, 17 September 1906 p. 5; Anthony Dreaver, Peter Warnock, Jocelyn Bond, pers. comm.
140. *WH*, 16 November 1868 p. 3, 18 March 1871 p. 2; Fiona G.,'Potto, McCaul and Pollock Families, Whanganui and Wellington', Digital NZ Story: https://digitalnz.org/stories/50ac828bfb002c6f36000001
141. UK Census 1851; *LT*, 15 March 1851 p. 5.
142. *NZSCGS*, 28 January 1854 p. 2; *WI*, 23 December 1857 p. 2, 3 April 1858 p. 2, 15 July 1859 p. 6, 26 December 1872 p. 3; *EP*, 15 February 1873 p. 3; 'Liverpool and London Fire and Life Insurance Company, Wellington Agents – Inward Correspondence – Martin – Wigglesworth: Elizabeth Willcox', Levin and Company Ltd, 1855, MS–Papers–1347–6/4/9, ATL.
143. *WH*, 30 November 1867 p. 3, 4 January 1870 p. 2; *EP*, 6 November 1893 p. 2, 27 December 1893 p. 3, 9 October 1894 p. 2; Macdonald Dictionary.
144. UK census 1841/51/61/71; Passenger lists: *Mermaid* 1868, *Celaeno* 1870; *Press*, 4 January 1868 p. 2.
145. *EP*, 28 December 1872 p. 2.
146. *EP*, 15 February 1873 p. 3; *WI*, 3 May 1873 p. 1.
147. *EP*, 28 July 1873 p. 3, 8 July 1876 p. 3, 17 June 1879 p. 3; Yarnacombe was at Lot 10 Britannia Street, where the library now stands.
148. *EP*, 15 February 1883 p. 3; *Wairarapa Daily Times*, 17 May 1886 p. 3.
149. *EP*, 20 December 1887 p. 3, 6 October 1893 p. 2, 5 November 1898 p. 8, 7 July 1899 p. 4; *Star*, 26 March 1894 p. 3.
150. *EP*, 19 October 1901 p. 1, 16 May 1903 p. 6, 29 June 1903 p. 4; Elizabeth Cowles NZ Probate 1903.
151. *EP*, 15 February 1883 p. 3, 13 January 1885 p. 3, 12 November 1888 p. 3.
152. See Ben Schrader, *The Big Smoke: New Zealand cities, 1840–1920* (Wellington: Bridget Williams Books, 2016), p. 149ff; Helen B. Laurenson, *Going Up, Going Down: The rise and fall of the department store* (Auckland: Auckland University Press, 2006).
153. *Star*, 23 August 1879 p. 2; *Press*, 18 March 1880 p. 3, 31 January 1944 p. 2, 14 June 1944 p. 5.
154. cf. Laurenson, *Going Up*, p. 60; Jennifer Aston and Catherine Bishop (eds), *Female Entrepreneurs in the Long Nineteenth Century: A global perspective* (New York: Palgrave Macmillan, forthcoming); Catherine Bishop, *Minding Her Own Business: Colonial businesswomen in Sydney* (Sydney: NewSouth, 2015).
155. *Auckland Industrial and Mining Exhibition: Opened December 1st 1898: Official handbook and catalogue*, Auckland, 1898, pp. 172–74, cited in Laurenson, *Going Up*, pp. 60–61.
156. Sandra Coney, 'Smith, Marianne', DNZB: www.teara.govt.nz/en/biographies/4s33/smith-marianne. I am grateful to Marianne's granddaughter Shirley-Ann and her husband Murray

Reid for information. 'About Smith & Caughey's': www.smithandcaugheys.co.nz/about-us.aspx

157. Fusedale Bloor Pope, Theft, 7 April 1856, Proceedings of the Old Bailey: www.oldbaileyonline.org/browse.jsp?div=t18560407-438; Royal Philanthropic Farm School Redhill, Admissions 1788–1906: www.geni.com/projects/Royal-Philanthropic-Farm-School-Redhill-Admissions-1788-1906/17360
158. *Press*, 8 August 1866 p. 1.
159. Robyn Gosset, *The History of Mrs Pope's Ltd* (Christchurch: Whitcoulls Ltd, 1979); Jo-Anne Smith, 'Pope, Maria Sophia', DNZB: www.teara.govt.nz/en/biographies/1p. 24/pope-maria-sophia
160. The popular story is that the store was named after Esther's birthplace in Bedfordshire. However, Esther McAveney was actually born and brought up in Kent. Gordon Ogilvie, *Ballantynes: The story of Dunstable House 1854–2004* (Christchurch: J Ballantyne & Co, 2004); *LT*, 13 December 1854 p. 7, 30 December 1854 p. 4, 14 January 1857 p. 8, 2 January 1864 p. 1; *Timaru Herald*, 30 July 1864 p. 5.
161. George Macdonald speculated that it was Elizabeth, not Esther, who was the real milliner, but William Burke noted that Esther started Dunstable House. Both were critical in shaping the business. Burke Manuscript, p. 254; Macdonald Dictionary; Gordon Ogilvie, pers. comm. January 2017; Stan Smith pers. comm. February 2017; Ogilvie, *Ballantynes*; *LT*, 3 July 1852 p. 1, 17 February 1855 p. 5, 16 January 1856 p. 9.
162. *DSX*, 6 July 1849 p. 1; *NZer*, 7 November 1855 p. 4, 27 September 1862 p. 2, 1 December 1864 p. 6; *NZH*, 8 June 1864 p. 2, 26 December 1865 p. 5, 1 February 1873 p. 2; *Duchess of Argyle* passenger list 1852; Charles Lowson NZ Probate 1884. Only by connecting a misspelt BDM entry for Elizabeth Lawson and a death notice for the wife of Mr C. Lowson was her Christian name uncovered.
163. *NZer*, 5 December 1860 p. 2; Ken Tucker, *Milne & Choyce: A one hundred year business history 1867–1967* (Auckland: Milne & Choyce, 1968); B.N. Norris, *The Milnes and Choyces of Early Auckland* (Auckland: J.R. Milne, R.S. Milne & J.S. Kidd, 1991).
164. Norris, *The Milnes and Choyces*, p. 8.
165. Tucker, *Milne & Choyce*, pp. 13, 16.
166. *AS*, 3 December 1873 p. 3, 1 March 1876 p. 3; *NZH*, 22 February 1876 p. 1, 7 October 1876 p. 5.
167. *AS*, 20 June 1874 p. 2, 31 August 1874 p. 2, 17 April 1876 p. 3.
168. Tucker, *Milne & Choyce*, p. 73.
169. H. Reid, 'Milne, Mary Jane', DNZB: www.teara.govt.nz/en/biographies/2m49/milne-mary-jane
170. Norris, *The Milnes and Choyces*, pp. 27–28.
171. *NZH*, 9 October 1916 p. 4.
172. *AS*, 14 October 1926 p. 4, cited in Laurenson, *Going Up*, pp. 60–61.
173. www.businesshalloffame.co.nz
174. *NEM*, 3 August 1880 p. 3, 27 January 1885 p. 3; 16 October 1885 p. 2, 12 November 1885 p. 2, 21 June 1886 p. 2, 3 September 1886 p. 2; *Colonist*, 2 September 1886 p. 2, 27 April 1891 p. 2, 23 January 1892 p. 2; C.B. Malone, 'Anstice, Sophia', DNZB: www.teara.govt.nz/en/biographies/2a10/anstice-sophia; Profile of Herbert Anstice qMS GRA, NPM; I am also grateful to Sharon Eyres for sharing her research about her ancestor.
175. *NEM*, 7 July 1876 p. 2.

176. *DSX*, 12 June 1855 p. 2; *NZer*, 11 October 1856 p. 2; *NZH*, 16 November 1864 p. 3.
177. *NZH*, 8 May 1890 p. 4, 9 March 1895 pp. 1, 5; *AS*, 19 March 1895 p. 8, 27 March 1895 p. 8.

Chapter 7: 'Personal Offices for Man'

1. For further discussion of New Zealand female publicans see Sandra Quick, '"The colonial helpmeet takes a dram": Women participants in the Central Otago goldfields liquor industry, 1861–1901', MA thesis, University of Otago, 1998; Sandra Quick, '"A magnificent stamp of a woman": Female sly grog sellers and hotelkeepers on the Central Otago goldfields 1861–1901', in Lloyd Carpenter and Lyndon Fraser (eds), *Rushing for Gold: Life and commerce on the goldfields of New Zealand and Australia* (Dunedin: Otago University Press, 2016), pp. 151–64; Julia Bradshaw, 'Forgetting their place: Women of abandoned character on the Otago goldfields', in Carpenter and Fraser (eds), *Rushing for Gold*, pp. 165–75; Susan Upton, *Wanted: A Beautiful Barmaid: Women behind the bar in New Zealand, 1830–1976* (Wellington: Victoria University Press, 2013).
2. *DSX*, 27 May 1843 p. 1.
3. Elizabeth Bartley 'Early reminiscences of Auckland': http://localhistorybartley.blogspot.com.au/p/early-reminiscences-of-auckland-by-mrs-e.html
4. Dean Wilson, 'Community and gender in Victorian Auckland', *New Zealand Journal of History* 30, no. 1, 1996, pp. 24–42, 37–38. His characterisation ignores the presence of women as barmaids and publicans, p. 36.
5. *OW*, 29 December 1860 p. 4; 19 January 1861 p. 10; *ODT*, 19 November 1863 p. 10 (supplement); *NOT*, 31 March 1864 p. 4.
6. *Colonist*, 9 December 1859 p. 2; *NEM*, 26 January 1870 p. 3.
7. Paul Hickford, 'On the Wright trail: London, Melbourne, Echuca, Hokitika …', *New Zealand Genealogist* 40, no. 319, 2009, pp. 231–34; I am grateful to Paul Hickford for sharing his research.
8. Jane Deans, *Letters to My Grandchildren* (Christchurch: Cadsonbury Publications, 1995, first published 1923); Jenny Betts, *The Mitre Hotel 1849–1899* (Christchurch: Mitre Tavern Historic Trust, 1999).
9. *ODT*, 24 April 1874 p. 3; *GRA*, 3 March 1875 p. 2.
10. *ODT*, 18 February 1885 p. 3; see also *EP*, 3 June 1884 p. 3; *WCT*, 6 June 1906 p. 3.
11. *WI*, 6 Sept 1851 p. 2.
12. *NEx*, 7 March 1855 p. 2.
13. Edith Sparks, *Capital Intentions: Female proprietors in San Francisco* (Chapel Hill: University of North Carolina Press, 2006).
14. *OW*, 27 April 1861 p. 1; *NOT*, 4 January 1866 p. 2.
15. *LT*, 11 April 1863 p. 5, 6 April 1865 p. 5; Macdonald Dictionary; nobblers were servings of beer and spirits.
16. *NZH*, 9 November 1864 p. 1; *DSX*, 14 May 1868 p. 4.
17. Eugene O'Conor, 1870, NZ Parliamentary Debates VII, p. 338 and Jane McBride's obituary, *Lake County Press*, 6 June 1918 p. 4, also quoted in Quick, 'The colonial helpmeet takes a dram', p. 24.
18. *WH*, 19 November 1867 p. 2, 8 April 1870 p. 2; *WC*, 6 June 1876 p. 2, 8 June 1876 p. 2; Laraine Sole, *The Early Hotels of Old Wanganui*, (Whanganui: Sole, 2016).

19. *WCT*, 20 July 1874 p. 3, 28 August 1877 p. 3; *Ashburton Guardian*, 18 May 1895 p. 2, 20 May 1895 p. 2.
20. *The Age* (Melbourne), 12 June 1856 p. 2; *ODT*, 31 July 1862 p. 3, 8 October 1862 p. 5; *WCT*, 18 December 1889 p. 4.
21. *ODT*, 1 December 1862 p. 6, 23 December 1862 p. 5, 14 April 1863 p. 2; *OW*, 10 September 1864 p. 13; *NOT*, 23 February 1865 p. 4.
22. *ODT*, 13 December 1861 p. 1, 12 June 1862 p. 3, 21 March 1863 p. 5, 4 December 1863 p. 3, 18 May 1864 p. 5.
23. *ODT*, 27 June 1862 p. 3, 25 September 1862 p. 5, 15 October 1862 p. 5; *OW*, 28 June 1862 p. 5.
24. *ODT*, 8 April 1863 p. 4, 9 July 1863 p. 3, 14 October 1863 p. 2, 18 May 1864 p. 5.
25. *Colonist*, 19 November 1867 p. 3; *Westport Times*, 7 January 1868 p. 2; *Marlborough Express*, 11 January 1868 p. 3; *Hawke's Bay Weekly Times*, 13 January 1868 p. 8.
26. This figure is based on a fairly unscientific sampling of lists of licensees in directories and newspapers over the period.
27. *NEx*, 18 June 1859 p. 4; Carol Kidd, 'The link in the chain', 1985, in 'Frederick Reid', Geni: www.geni.com/people/Fredrick-Reid/6000000035826858451
28. *NEx*, 16 April 1862 p. 2, 19 January 1864 p. 2, 6 March 1866 p. 3; *Colonist*, 27 May 1859 p. 2.
29. *WI*, 2 November 1867 p. 4.
30. *WI*, 8 December 1858 p. 3, 27 May 1865 p. 3, 5 July 1871 p. 2.
31. Susan Upton, pers. comm., February 2018; NZ Census 1874, 1881.
32. *TA*, 9 March 1896 p. 3.
33. Susan Upton, pers. comm., February 2018; for more on licensing history, although not female licensees, see Conrad Bollinger, *Grog's Own Country: The story of liquor licensing in New Zealand* (Auckland: Minerva, 1959, 1967).
34. *Licensing Act 1842* (5 Victoriae 1842, no. 12); *Licensing Amendment Act 1844* (7 Victoriae 1844, no. 21); *Licensing Act 1873 Amendment Act 1874* (38 Victoriae 1874, no. 10); *Licensing Act 1881* (45 Victoriae 1881, no. 21), NZLII.
35. *Licensing Act 1881 Amendment Act 1889* (53 VICT 1889, no. 22); *Alcoholic Liquors Sale Control Act 1893* (57 VICT 1893, no. 34); *Licensing Amendment Act 1952* (1952, no. 79), NZLII.
36. *Westport Times*, 2 September 1871 p. 2, 15 November 1871 p. 2.
37. *WC*, 22 April 1874 p. 2.
38. *WI*, 20 January 1858 p. 3; 25 July 1863 p. 2; *NZT*, 10 June 1875 p. 2; Hugh McPhail, 'Jane McKenzie', Blenheim 175: https://blenheim175.wordpress.com/2015/03/27/hugh-mckenzie-and-catherine-mcdonald/
39. *WI*, 25 July 1863 p. 2, 21 April 1864 p. 2, 9 August 1864 p. 3.
40. *Evening Star*, 13 November 1888 p. 3, 25 June 1889 p. 2; *EP*, 7 June 1889 p. 3, 11 June 1889 p. 2; *LT*, 11 June 1889 p. 3; *Press*, 22 October 1889 p. 6.
41. *ODT*, 24 April 1874 p. 3, 2 December 1874 p. 5 (supplement).
42. *GRA*, 3 March 1875 p. 2; *Inangahua Times*, 13 April 1891 p. 4, 18 June 1895 p. 2, 4 July 1895 p. 2; CerberusCoins, 'Descendants of William Searight, County Londonderry, Northern Ireland', Mawhinny Family History Research, 19 December 2014: https://cerberuscoins.wordpress.com/tag/mawhinney/
43. Upton, *Wanted: A Beautiful Barmaid.*
44. *WCT*, 3 November 1868 p. 2.
45. *WCT*, 29 May 1868 p. 3.
46. *WT*, 13 November 1869 p. 2.
47. *WT*, 9 October 1869 p. 2.

48. *NZH*, 14 June 1880 p. 4.
49. *Nelson Goldfields Licensing Ordinance* 1867 and 1868, NZLII.
50. *WT*, 14 May 1868 p. 2.
51. *ODT*, 8 June 1870 p. 3; See also Quick, 'The colonial helpmeet takes a dram'.
52. *GRA*, 3 May 1871 p. 2.
53. *GRA*, 12 January 1871 p. 3.
54. *WCT*, 11 January 1871 p. 2; *GRA*, 5 November 1873 p. 2.
55. *WCT*, 13 January 1871 p. 3.
56. *WCT*, 11 January 1871 p. 2.
57. *NZH*, 14 June 1880 p. 4.
58. *Kumara Times*, 24 June 1880 p. 3.
59. Angela McCarthy, *Irish Migrants in New Zealand, 1840–1937: 'The desired haven'* (Woodbridge, UK: Boydell, 2005), p. 44.
60. *WH*, 19 November 1867 p. 2, 8 April 1870 p. 2; *WC*, 6 June 1876 p. 2, 8 June 1876 p. 2.
61. *WI*, 20 April 1853 p. 2; Sandra Clarke and Neville Gilmore, 'Mata Pekamu Tamatuhiata', Wellington City Library: www.wcl.govt.nz/maori/wellington/tupunabeckham.html; James Bryant, Daybooks 1860–1863, MS-Papers-158311, 2, ATL; Hilda McDonnell, 'Mary Ann Ames of the South Sea Hotel', in *Publicans in the Port Nicholson District in the Colony of New Zealand* (Wellington: Vera Publications, 2014); Stephen Donaldson, 'Shore Whalers Wahine Project': www.whalerswahine.com, and pers. comm., 2011–17.
62. *Sydney Gazette*, 11 August 1825 p. 3; Andrew Kincaid, 'Whaler and hotelier: Mary Ann Ames (1817–1887)', *Otaki Historical Society Journal* 31, 2009, pp. 40–42.
63. *EP*, 22 November 1887 p. 2; *NZT*, 22 November 1887 p. 4.
64. *NZer*, 15 April 1848 p. 2; *DSX*, 21 April 1854 pp. 2–3.
65. *DSX*, 7 October 1856 p. 2, 14 April 1857 p. 2, 22 April 1863 p. 3, 26 July 1869 p. 5; *NZH*, 21 October 1872 p. 2.
66. Quick, 'The colonial helpmeet takes a dram', pp. 40–41; *Cyclopedia of New Zealand (Otago & Southland Provincial Districts)*, (Christchurch, 1905) p. 1026: http://nzetc.victoria.ac.nz/tm/scholarly/tei-Cyc04Cycl-t1-body1-d7-d85.html
67. Quick, 'The colonial helpmeet takes a dram', p. 37.
68. *NEx*, 26 March 1856 p. 2; *DSX*, 16 August 1861p. 1; Janice C. Mogford, 'George, Elizabeth', DNZB: www.teara.govt.nz/en/biographies/1g7/george-elizabeth
69. *WI*, 19 March 1863 p. 3.
70. Mary Ann Kennedy, NZ Probate 1875; *WI*, 21 April 1864 p. 2, 20 April 1865 p. 3, 19 April 1871 p. 2; *EP*, 10 November 1874 p. 3, 3 August 1875 p. 3, 19 August 1875 p. 3.
71. Hickford, 'On the Wright trail'; *EP*, 22 October 1892 p. 2.
72. Mary Power may have arrived in Auckland in 1863 with Sergeant William Power and two daughters on the *Devonshire* from London, although one daughter was born in Victoria. Perhaps William was the Wodonga policeman remembered by John Sadleir as 'most acute and observant', although 'one might easily take him to be a commonplace, perhaps even a dull man'. *Recollections of a Victorian Police Officer*, Ch. 26: https://www.redhodgestories.com.au/the-irish-in-australia-in-the-19th-century/recollections-of-a-victorian-poice-officer-by-john-sadleir/; *NZer*, 9 February 1862 p. 2; Ancestry; *ODT*, 22 March 1864 p. 4, 23 June 1865 p. 5; *Press*, 26 April 1866 p. 2; *EP*, 10 December 1875 p. 2, 4 December 1877 p. 2, 15 April 1882 p. 2, 27 November 1886 p. 2, 29 November 1886 p. 2; *WC*, 13 June 1883 p. 2; *WH*, 21 June 1883 p. 2; *NZ Mail*, 14 March 1884 p. 8; *WCT*, 7 May 1866 p. 2. Notably, the *West Coast Times* refrained from mentioning the race of either combatant, unlike the *Press*; John Leydon, 'Ups

and Downs', in Julia Bradshaw (ed.), *Carl J. Pfaff, the Diggers' Story: Accounts of the West Coast gold rushes* (Christchurch: Canterbury University Press, 2014), p. 108.

73. Marie Woods, 'The Stanton family: Silk weavers from Coventry', unpublished ms.
74. *NZH*, 3 June 1865 p. 5, 6 March 1867 p. 5; *DSX*, 29 May 1867 p. 4, 13 June 1867 p. 3.
75. *GRA*, 24 June 1871 p. 2.
76. Her first husband was Charles Madden, whom she married in 1849. It is unclear when Charles died but Jane married John Mounce in 1857.
77. *TS*, 8 February 1878 p. 3, 25 February 1878 p. 2.
78. *TS*, 17 June 1886 p. 2, 8 May 1893 p. 2.
79. *WH*, 8 March 1879 p. 3, 14 March 1879 p. 2, 27 May 1884 p. 2, 11 November 1884 p. 2; *WC*, 18 January 1881 p. 2, 11 December 1882 p. 2.
80. *NZT*, 15 March 1890 p. 4; *FS*, 1 December 1892 p. 3; *EP*, 1 June 1910 p. 7; Pat Lawlor, *Old Wellington Hotels: Some history, personalities and anecdotes* (Wellington: Millwood Press, 1974), p. 663.
81. *WC*, 22 August 1888 p. 3, 25 October 1888 p. 4, 21 May 1889 p. 3, 8 June 1892 p. 3; *WH*, 21 January 1890 p. 2, 16 June 1892 p. 3, 22 June 1892 p. 3; Emma Siddells, NZ Probate 1940.
82. Valerie Burr, 'Amos and Lydia Burr', *NZ Legacy* 2, 1990, pp. 23–24; Vera L. McLennan-Boman, *Glimpses into Early Manawatu* (Waikanae: Heritage Press, 1985); Foxton Historical Society, *Pioneers of Foxton: Book one* (Foxton: Foxton Historical Society, 1988), pp. 6–9: http://horowhenua.kete.net.nz/en/site/topics/74-amos-burr
83. *NZSCSG*, 2 February 1842 p. 1; *WI*, 7 July 1863 p. 4, 24 April 1869 p. 7, 30 January 1873 p. 3; *EP*, 14 January 1876 p. 3; *WH*, 21 June 1867 p. 3, 24 June 1867 p. 3, 10 September 1867 p. 41, 1 September 1874 p. 3; Burr, 'Amos and Lydia Burr'; McLennan-Boman, *Glimpses*; Foxton Historical Society, *Pioneers*.
84. *WH*, 31 August 1876 p. 2; *Manawatu Herald*, 29 February 1896 p. 2; *Manawatu Times*, 21 June 1897 p. 4; Burr, 'Amos and Lydia Burr'; McLennan-Boman, *Glimpses*; Foxton Historical Society, *Pioneers*.
85. Susan Upton, pers. comm.
86. Sarah Miles to Joseph Phipps Townsend, 9 July 1850, miscellaneous papers, 1847–1862, MLMSS 1461/3 CY2541, pp. 24–25, SLNSW.
87. Sparks, *Capital Intentions*; Wendy Gamber, *The Boardinghouse in Nineteenth-Century America* (Baltimore: Johns Hopkins University Press, 2007).
88. *NZer*, 30 June 1860 p. 2.
89. *LT*, 3 November 1860 p. 5, 10 July 1861 p. 1, 24 September 1862 p. 2, Macdonald Dictionary.
90. *NZer*, 3 March 1860 p. 2, 7 June 1862 p. 1; *DSX*, 22 January 1861 p. 1, 18 November 1862 p. 1.
91. *NZer*, 8 August 1846 p. 1.
92. *DSX*, 13 November 1855 p. 1, 28 March 1856 p. 2, 6 May 1856 p. 1; *NZer*, 25 March 1857 p. 2.
93. Celia Manson, *Widow of Thorndon Quay: Part 2 of the story of a New Zealand family* (Wellington: Pigeon Press, 1981); Hugo Manson, 'Dougherty, Sarah', DNZB: www.teara.govt.nz/en/biographies/1d18/dougherty-sarah; Catherine Bishop, 'Women on the move: Gender, money-making and mobility in mid-nineteenth century Australasia', *History Australia* 11, no. 2, 2014, pp. 38–59.
94. *Press*, 27 June 1868 p. 1, 26 May 1875 p. 1; *LT*, 24 September 1853 p. 12, 6 July 1867 p. 1; Burke Manuscript, p. 281; Greenaway, 'Susannah Bligh', *Unsung Heroines*: http://christchurchcitylibraries.com/Heritage/Publications/UnsungHeroines/SusannahBligh/
95. *TH*, 4 October 1854 p. 1, 14 March 1855 p. 2, 6 May 1865 p. 1, 3 August 1867 p. 2, 7

November 1868 p. 2, 14 September 1870 p. 1, 8 January 1873 p. 3, 10 November 1875 p. 2, 7 June 1878 p. 2; *Hawera and Normanby Star*, 5 July 1923 p. 12 (supplement).

96. *HBH*, 5 January 1867 p. 1, 20 April 1867 p. 2, 11 January 1868 p. 1, 14 March 1868 p. 2; *HBT*, 21 April 1871 p. 2.
97. *HBH*, 22 November 1870 p. 3, 8 March 1890 p. 2; *Daily Telegraph* (Napier), 30 June 1881 p. 3, 21 June 1886 p. 3, 21 October 1889 p. 3; for more on Phillippa Terrill (noting that deserted wives could claim protection from 1860 and not 1880 as suggested in the article) see also Sonia Sly, 'Beyond Kate: Women exercising their new rights', 5 October 2018: www.stuff.co.nz/life-style/107645571/beyond-kate-women-exercising-their-new-rights
98. In 1888 George A. Hill of Hastings advertised, looking for Charles A. Watson, his mother and sisters; *AS*, 2 August 1884 p. 7, 31 December 1884 p. 3; *NZH*, 14 October 1884 p. 1, 1 December 1884 p. 1, 6 December 1884 p. 1, 7 September 1885 p. 3, 13 March 1888 p. 1.
99. *DSX*, 5 October 1858 p. 3; *NZH*, 4 May 1866 p. 1, 16 October 1878 p. 3; *AS*, 15 October 1878 p. 3.
100. *ODT*, 23 March 1877 p. 3; I am grateful to Margaret Gillingham for bringing Catherine's story to my attention.
101. *ES*, 5 November 1912 p. 4; *Marlborough Express*, 7 November 1912 p. 3; *Poverty Bay Herald*, 8 November 1912 p. 5.
102. *LT*, 7 September 1869 p. 6, 29 January 1862 p. 5, 12 December 1866 p. 3, 29 December 1871 p. 1; *Press*, 4 January 1864 p. 4, 8 January 1864 p. 2, 8 January 1864 p. 1, 6 July 1864 p. 2, 15 September 1864 p. 1, 9 August 1866 p. 1; *Colonist*, 11 June 1864 p. 5.
103. *Press*, 5 October 1864 p. 2.
104. *LT*, 30 January 1866 p. 3, 10 April 1866 p. 3, 29 December 1870 p. 3, 7 March 1884 p. 8; *Press*, 16 March 1866 p. 1, 9 February 1867 p. 1, 30 January 1871 p. 2, 3 February 1874 p. 2, 7 June 1900 p. 7, 28 December 1900 p. 8.
105. Wall, 'Copy of a letter'.
106. *NEx*, 28 December 1859 p. 2; *Colonist*, 15 June 1869 p. 1, 25 June 1890 p. 4, 8 October 1891 p. 3; *NEM*, 2 November 1881 p. 2, 7 November 1889 p. 3; Susannah Lloyd, NZ Probate 1891.
107. UK Census 1851; *ODT*, 24 October 1874 p. 3; *OW*, 23 December 1887 p. 26.
108. UK Census 1851; *ODT*, 24 October 1874 p. 3; *OW*, 23 December 1887 p. 26.
109. *OW*, 31 March 1860 p. 4.
110. *ODT*, 22 September 1862 p. 3; *OW*, 21 April 1860 p. 6.
111. *ODT*, 31 December 1862 p. 8.
112. *ODT*, 28 April 1866 p. 6, 5 November 1867 p. 1.
113. *ODT*, 9 May 1868 p. 1; 3 December 1868 p. 1.
114. *ODT*, 26 October 1872 p. 1, 30 October 1874 p. 4; *ES*, 28 February 1874 p. 3.
115. *ODT*, 17 June 1875 p. 2.
116. *ES*, 5 July 1889 p. 2, 23 July 1889 p. 2; *ODT*, 6 July 1889 p. 3.
117. *AS*, 11 September 1886 p. 2.
118. In the census they were recorded in the 'criminal class' and probably represented only those who were serving sentences at the time. 1874 Census; 'Brothel Surveillance Return', in Charlotte Macdonald, 'The "social evil": Prostitution and the passage of the Contagious Diseases Act (1869)', in Margaret Tennant, Charlotte Macdonald and Barbara Brookes (eds), *Women in History: Essays on European women in New Zealand* (Sydney, Wellington: George Allen & Unwin, 1986), pp. 30–33; for further scholarship on brothels and prostitution see Stevan Eldred-Grigg, *Pleasures of the Flesh: Sex and drugs in colonial New Zealand 1840–1915*

(Wellington: A.H. and A.W. Reed, 1984); Bronwyn Dalley, 'Lolly shops "of the red light kind" and "soldiers of the king": Suppressing one-woman brothels in New Zealand 1908–1916', *New Zealand Journal of History* 30, no. 1, 1996, pp. 3–23; Bradshaw, '"Forgetting their place".

119. Wanhalla, *In/visible Sight*; Angela Wanhalla, *Matters of the Heart: A history of interracial marriage in New Zealand* (Auckland: Auckland University Press, 2012).
120. Macdonald, 'The "social evil"'.
121. Burke Manuscript, p. 218.
122. *DSX*, 30 September 1843 p. 2.
123. *DSX*, 17 March 1854 p. 3; see Anderson, 'Hardened frail ones', p. 92.
124. Anderson, 'Hardened frail ones', pp. 92–94.
125. *Star*, 4 July 1874 p. 2.
126. Macdonald, 'The "social evil"'.
127. *ES*, 5 June 1871 p. 2.
128. *EP*, 5 July 1881 p. 2.
129. *EP*, 13 December 1873 p. 2, 15 August 1876 p. 2; *NZT*, 7 January 1875 p. 5, 27 April 1875 p. 3.
130. *DSX*, 23 April 1869 p. 7.
131. *Colonist*, 14 March 1874 p. 3.
132. *Contagious Diseases Act 1869* (32 and 33 Victoriae 1869, no. 52), NZLII; Macdonald, 'The "social evil"'; Anderson, 'Hardened frail ones', Chapter 5.
133. *Press*, 29 March 1869 p. 4, 17 August 1869 p. 2; 16 November 1869 p. 2; *Star*, 15 November 1869 p. 2.
134. *WI*, 12 July 1872 p. 3.
135. *WCT*, 17 December 1870 p. 2.
136. *WCT*, 28 August 1871.
137. *ODT*, 23 August 1865 p. 5, 21 February 1866 p. 4, 12 June 1866 p. 5, 2 July 1866 p. 4, 10 October 1867 p. 5, 16 October 1867 p. 5, 3 December 1867 p. 5, 11 January 1868 p. 4, 17 April 1868 p. 4, 20 January 1869 p. 2, 20 October 1869 p. 2, 30 October 1869 p. 2, 13 January 1870 p. 2, 25 January 1870 p. 3, 28 January 1870 p. 2, 14 March 1870 p. 3, 19 October 1870 p. 3.
138. *ES*, 29 June 1869 p. 2; *ODT*, 30 June 1869 p. 3.
139. *ODT*, 10 May 1871 p. 2, 13 May 1871 p. 5; 16 May 1871 p. 2.
140. See Anderson, 'Hardened frail ones', Chapter 5.
141. *WI*, 16 June 1858 p. 6 (supplement), 18 August 1858 p. 3, 2 November 1860 p. 3, 26 July 1861 p. 5, 15 September 1863 p. 3; *EP*, 24 November 1865 p. 2, 28 December 1866 p. 2.
142. *EP*, 16 July 1867 p. 2; *WI*, 5 September 1867 p. 3.
143. *WI*, 5 September 1867 p. 3; *EP*, 27 May 1872 p. 2, 26 September 1882 p. 2, 14 April 1886 p. 2.
144. *EP*, 14 September 1874 p. 2; *NZ Times*, 11 January 1875 p. 2.
145. *WI*, 3 March 1864 p. 3.
146. *NZSCSG*, 1 June 1864 p. 3.
147. *WI*, 17 January 1867 p. 5, 19 March 1867, 16 April 1867 p. 5; see Anderson, 'Hardened frail ones', Chapter 5.
148. Dalley, 'Lolly shops'.
149. *AS*, 2 February 1880 p. 3; *NZH*, 3 February 1880 p. 6.
150. *WCT*, 30 June 1866 p. 2.
151. *WCT*, 19 August 1867 p. 7.
152. *WCT*, 31 July 1866 p. 2, 27 July 1867 p. 2, 30 July 1867 p. 2, 3 September 1867 p. 2, 14 September 1867 p. 4, 21 September 1867 p. 2, 12 March 1868 p. 2, 7 April 1868 p. 2, 9 May 1868 p. 3, 15 February 1872 p. 2.

153. *WCT*, 19 August 1867 p. 2, 5 April 1869 p. 2.
154. *WCT*, 27 November 1868 p. 2, 13 March 1875 p. 2.
155. *WCT*, 18 March 1869 p. 2.
156. *WCT*, 14 April 1868 p. 2.
157. *WCT*, 17 March 1873 p. 2.
158. *WCT*, 28 October 1871 p. 2, 12 March 1872 p. 2, 20 May 1873 p. 2, 22 August 1873 p. 2, 13 March 1875 p. 2, 16 September 1876 p. 2; *Westport Times*, 2 September 1873 p. 2.

Chapter 8: 'Personal Offices for Woman'

1. Alison Clarke, *Born to a Changing World: Childbirth in nineteenth-century New Zealand* (Wellington: Bridget Williams Books, 2012), pp. 48–51.
2. Robert H. Bakewell to Provincial Secretary, 10 October 1873, in Adelheid Wassner, *Labour of Love: Childbirth at Dunedin Hospital 1862–1972* (Dunedin: A. Wassner, 1999), p. 16, in Clarke, *Born to a Changing World*, p. 50.
3. *NZH*, 4 October 1865 p. 5.
4. Nurses' Registration Act (1 EDW VII 1901 No. 12); Midwives' Act (4 EDW VII 1904 No. 13).
5. Alice East, 'The story of Sophia or how we happen to be here', edited by C.E. Fordham, p. 5, MS Papers 2855, ATL.
6. Elizabeth McDiarmid, 'Early Woodside, West Taieri', MS–0579, Hocken Library, in Vivien Caughley, *New Zealand's Historic Samplers: Our stitched stories* (Auckland: David Bateman, 2014), p. 61.
7. Patricia Ann Sargison, '"Essentially a woman's work": A history of general nursing in New Zealand 1830–1930', PhD thesis, University of Otago, 2001.
8. Charlotte Parkinson, 'Reminiscences of Mrs Parkinson', p. 3, 89/140, AWMM.
9. Janet C. Angus, 'Carran, Catherine', DNZB: www.teara.govt.nz/en/biographies/2c9/carran-catherine
10. M.G. Patrick, 'Mckain, Douglas Mary', DNZB: www.teara.govt.nz/en/biographies/1m36/1; Douglas Mary McKain, 'Diary and commonplace book, 1841–1872', transcribed by J.B. Moles, p. 2, MS–Papers–7262, 1852–53, ATL.
11. *LT*, 14 October 1857 p. 5.
12. *DSX*, 3 June 1843 p. 2; see Clarke, *Born to a Changing World*, pp. 41–42.
13. *WI*, 12 June 1852 p. 2.
14. *NEx*, 15 October 1853 p. 4.
15. *TH*, 14 March 1855 p. 2, 20 September 1856 p. 2.
16. *NZer*, 4 July 1855 p. 1; *TH*, 6 March 1858 p. 2, 9 May 1857 p. 1, 3 August 1867 p. 2.
17. *OW*, 31 July 1858 p. 4; *NZH*, 9 March 1865 p. 6.
18. *AS*, 26 October 1876 p. 2; see Chapter 3.
19. *NEx*, 4 April 1857 p. 2.
20. *NEx*, 15 October 1862 p. 2, 11 May 1865 p. 5.
21. *ES*, 21 May 1870 p. 2.
22. *ODT*, 18 May 1870 p. 2; *Evening Star*, 21 May 1870 p. 2, 24 December 1870; *OW*, 11 February 1871 p. 17 p. 2.
23. *DSX*, 1 April 1859 p. 2.
24. *LT*, 5 November 1859 p. 5.

25. *OW*, 11 August 1860 p. 3.
26. *NEx*, 28 May 1856 p. 1.
27. *DSX*, 16 June 1865 p. 1.
28. *ODT*, 28 July 1866 p. 2; see Clarke, *Born to a Changing World*, pp. 44–48.
29. *ODT*, 10 April 1865 p. 8; Mrs Elizabeth Lowe switched midwifery in Wakapuaka Road in Nelson in 1859 for sewing and mantle-making in Bridge Street a year later, before her death aged 36 in 1860; *NEx*, 6 July 1859 p. 2, 4 January 1860 p. 2.
30. *LT*, 15 April 1880 p. 1.
31. *Press*, 17 July 1911 p. 9.
32. The first abortion case, involving 20-year-old Maria Hackett, was in Christchurch in 1868. Thomas Yates was prosecuted. *Star*, 30 December 1868 p. 2; see also Margaret Sparrow, *Rough on Women: Abortion in 19th-century New Zealand* (Wellington: Victoria University Press, 2014).
33. *WH*, 8 April 1886 p. 2, 11 June 1891 p. 2; *WC*, 9 October 1891 p. 2, *Marlborough Express*, 10 June 1891 p. 3; Sparrow, *Rough on Women*, pp. 125–30.
34. *Bay of Plenty Times*, 12 October 1891 p. 2; *WH*, 10 October 1891 p. 2.
35. *Oamaru Mail*, 24 April 1893 p. 1; for more on alternative therapies and medicines see Philippa Martyr, *Paradise of Quacks: An alternative history of medicine in Australia* (Sydney: Macleay Press, 2002).
36. *Evening News* (Sydney), 2 June 1890 p. 8.
37. *AS*, 19 October 1888 p. 1, 10 September 1892 p. 5, 23 February 1895 p. 5, 28 November 1896 p. 1; *Evening News* (Sydney), 2 January 1890 p. 8; *NZH*, 5 October 1894 p. 4 (supplement), 24 October 1896 p. 1.
38. *Truth*, 20 May 1900 p. 3.
39. *Argus*, 2 December 1867 p. 4; *Ballarat Star*, 8 August 1868 p. 3, 10 August 1868 p. 1, 1 September 1871 p. 2.
40. *AS*, 9 December 1891 p. 1; *WC*, 12 September 1892 p. 2; *Star*, 1 January 1898 p. 5.
41. *AS*, 7 May 1889 p. 2.
42. *FS*, 16 April 1891 p. 3; *WH*, 26 May 1891 p. 3; *TH*, 20 April 1892 p. 3; *TA*, 29 April 1892 p. 3; *TS*, 16 June 1894 p. 2; *WCT*, 18 April 1900 p. 3; Indictable Offences Summary Jurisdiction Bill 1894 (9–4), NZLII.
43. *NEx*, 2 December 1843 p. 361, 18 January 1845 p. 181; *London Gazette*, 1842 Part 3 p. 2042.
44. *NZer*, 31 March 1849 p. 4.
45. Susannah Brown – see Chapter 12.
46. *DSX*, 26 April 1861 p. 2.
47. *NZer*, 16 February 1861 p. 2, 6 March 1861 p. 1, 25 January 1862 p. 2.
48. *DSX*, 22 September 1862 p. 1, 1 January 1864 p. 1, 11 February 1865 p. 6, 26 August 1865 p. 3, 26 June 1866 p. 4.
49. *DSX*, 28 May 1867 p. 1.
50. *NZH*, 2 November 1872 p. 2; see also Michael Brown, '"A piano in every other house?" The piano in New Zealand trade statistics', *New Zealand Journal of History* 51, no. 2, 2017, pp. 26–52.
51. *NEx*, 23 January 1869 p. 3, 17 February 1869 p. 2.
52. *Press*, 14 September 1878 p. 1; UK Census 1861.
53. *Stevens and Bartholomew's New Zealand Directory 1866–67*; *LT*, 12 March 1869 p. 1.

54. *Press*, 14 September 1878 p. 1.
55. *Press*, 24 January 1879 p. 1.
56. *Southland Times*, 2 June 1882 p. 3.
57. *Press*, 1 February 1886 p. 2, 20 April 1888 p. 8, 8 April 1905 p. 13.
58. *Star*, 10 June 1905 p. 6.
59. *ODT*, 27 October 1862 p. 6.
60. Adams, 'Journal', p. 158; Charlotte Macdonald, *A Woman of Good Character: Single women as immigrant settlers in nineteenth-century New Zealand* (Wellington: Allen & Unwin/Historical Branch, 1990), pp. 120–21.
61. Jemima Martin, 16 August 1852, Martin Family Papers, MS 199, AWMM; see also Caroline Newman, 25 November 1854, Newman Family Letters, MS 483, AWMM.
62. Jessie Campbell to her sister Isabella, 9 September 1845, 'Extracts from the letters of Jessie Campbell to her family from Petone and Wanganui 1841–45', (Typescript) qMS–0369, ATL.
63. William Swainson, *Auckland, the Capital of New Zealand and the Country Adjacent: Including some account of the gold discovery in New Zealand* (London: Smith, Elder & Co; Auckland: J. Williamson, 1853), p. 69.
64. *OW*, 5 October 1861 p. 4.
65. *DSX*, 7 April 1866 p. 1.
66. *DSX*, 6 October 1866 p. 1.
67. *OW*, 26 July 1873 p. 12.
68. *NZer*, 4 January 1860 p. 4.
69. *WCT*, 22 October 1867 p. 1.
70. *ODT*, 6 January 1863 p. 4.
71. *OW*, 5 July 1851 p. 3.
72. *OW*, 24 November 1860 p. 4, 5 October 1861 p. 4.
73. *HBH*, 5 July 1864 p. 2, 15 October 1864 p. 4, 22 October 1864 p. 1.
74. *HBH*, 11 October 1864 p. 4.
75. *HBH*, 15 July 1865 p. 2.
76. *HBH*, 21 October 1865 p. 2, 28 May 1867 p. 2.
77. *LT*, 6 November 1868 p. 3; *Press*, 14 February 1871 p. 3.
78. *WC*, 12 January 1878 p. 2, 10 November 1879 p. 3; *WH*, 8 September 1879 p. 2, 24 April 1880 p. 2, 26 April 1881 p. 2.
79. Barbara (30), Betsy (21) and Jessie (14) arrived in Dunedin from Skye in 1859 on the *Alpine* with their widowed mother Mary (59). Brothers Colin and Alexander were already in the colony. Colin was a teacher and immigration agent and Alexander a teacher in the Dunedin suburb of Green Island. Their father had been a schoolteacher.
80. *ODT*, 14 January 1863 p. 8, 26 May 1866 p. 2.
81. *ODT*, 14 January 1863 p. 8, 5 April 1865 p. 2, 26 February 1878 p. 1, 11 May 1905 p. 6, 5 October 1907 p. 1; 11 June 1909 p. 1; Electoral Roll 1893: www.findmypast.com.au
82. Catherine Bishop, *Minding Her Own Business: Colonial businesswomen in Sydney* (Sydney: NewSouth, 2015), pp. 68, 78, 160, 249–50.
83. Charlotte Macdonald, 'Howard, Caroline Cadette', DNZB: www.teara.govt.nz/en/biographies/1h35/howard-caroline-cadette
84. Miss Marion Cane took over Caroline Alpenny's registry office business for a few years before passing it on to Mrs Mary Dick, *ODT*, 28 March 1871 p. 1, 21 June 1875 p. 1; *ES*, 16 June 1871 p. 2.

85. *WCT*, 5 July 1867 p. 1, 30 September 1867 p. 1, 17 October 1867 p. 1, 22 January 1868 p. 3, 3 November 1868 p. 2.
86. Margaret Kiddle, *Caroline Chisholm* (Melbourne: Melbourne University Press, 1969, first published 1950); Samuel Sidney, *Female Emigration As It Is – As It May Be: A letter to the Right Honorable Sidney Herbert, MP: With an Appendix* (London: William S. Orr, 1850).
87. *WCT*, 23 June 1871 p. 1; *ES*, 15 August 1871 p. 2; *WCT*, 5 December 1871 p. 2.
88. *WCT*, 1 November 1871 p. 2.
89. *WCT*, 14 May 1872 p. 2, 18 May 1872 p. 2, 21 May 1872 p. 2, 28 May 1872 p. 2, 4 June 1872 p. 2, 5 July 1872 p. 2, 16 July 1872 p. 2, 23 August 1872 p. 2, 27 August 1872 p. 3.
90. *ODT*, 27 September 1873 p. 2, 2 October 1874 p. 2.
91. *ES*, 19 September 1874 p. 3, 31 October 1874 p. 3, 6 November 1874 p. 3; *ODT*, 14 November 1874 p. 3, 16 November 1874 p. 2, 23 November 1874 p. 3.
92. *ES*, 24 June 1875 p. 3, 17 October 1917 p. 5; *ODT*, 27 September 1873 p. 2, 2 October 1874, p. 2, 14 November 1874 p. 3, 23 November 1874 p. 3, 8 June 1908 p. 1, 12 June 1913 p. 1, 29 March 1916 p. 8.
93. *Constabulary Force Act 1849* (13 Victoriae 1849, no. 9), NZLII.
94. *NZer*, 28 January 1857 p. 3.
95. *Star*, 20 November 1876 p. 2; *LT*, 22 November 1876 p. 1.
96. *NEx*, 3 November 1858 p. 2; Dawn Smith, 'Forget not the bath', *Journal of the Nelson and Marlborough Historical Societies* 1, no. 6, 1986, pp. 4–8: http://nzetc.victoria.ac.nz/tm/scholarly/tei-NHSJ04_06-t1-body1-d1.html
97. *Southland Times*, 11 November 1864 p. 1.
98. *DSX*, 20 September 1867 p. 1.
99. *Mount Alexander Mail* (Victoria), 26 February 1862 p. 3.
100. *NEM*, 14 February 1872 p. 2; *NEx*, 14 November 1873 p. 4; *Maitland Mercury and Hunter River General Advertiser*, 17 April 1875 p. 7; *Colonist*, 2 March 1880 p. 4; *Australian Town and Country Journal*, 29 October 1890 p. 17; *Wairarapa Daily Times*, 28 May 1891 p. 2.
101. Phillipa Templeton, 'Holland and Tye Families', Selling Hillcrest, www.sellinghillcrest.co.nz/Gallery/ID/4/HISTORY-Holland-and-Tye-Families. According to physician John Bell's 1859 *A Treatise on Baths*, patients sat upright in the sitz bath or 'sit tub', with their lower body immersed in warm water. Smithsonian Museum: http://americanhistory.si.edu/collections/object-groups/portable-bathtubs-tub-bathing-from-the-early-19th-and-20th-centuries
102. 'Professor' Aaron Ayers, hairdresser, tobacconist and entrepreneur, proposed establishing Turkish baths in Christchurch much earlier, in 1864, but it was not until 1877 that his were established, *Press*, 12 May 1864 p. 2; *Globe* (Canterbury), 29 December 1877 p. 2.
103. *ODT*, 29 September 1874 p. 2.
104. *AS*, 4 October 1875 p. 1; *EP*, 25 November 1882 p. 3.
105. *LT*, 23 March 1882 p. 3; *Star*, 24 May 1900 p. 3; Vivenne Morrell, 'Halls Turkish Baths Wellington', blog post, 25 June 2016: https://viviennemorrell.wordpress.com/2016/06/25/halls-turkish-baths-wellington/; John William Hall NZ Probate 1900; Ellen Cox Hall NZ Probate 1922.
106. *WI*, 11 November 1859 p. 4, 17 November 1868 p. 4; *EP*, 29 April 1870 p. 2.
107. *EP*, 3 October 1871 p. 3.
108. *WI*, 24 November 1873 p. 3.

109. Hilda McDonnell, 'Meech, Matilda', DNZB: www.teara.govt.nz/en/biographies/1m40/1/Meech-matilda; Hilda McDonnell, 'Early residents of Clyde Quay: Henry and Matilda Meech', *Heritage Link* 117 (Wellington Historical & Early Settlers' Association, October 2015).
110. *WI*, 22 November 1859 p. 2, 3 January 1860 p. 4, 6 July 1860 p. 3, 28 August 1860 p. 2, 16 May 1865 p. 5, 19 May 1866 p. 5, 2 August 1866 p. 6, 4 August 1866 p. 5, 21 September 1867 p. 5, 7 April 1868 p. 4, 14 July 1868 p. 5, 24 November 1873 p. 3; *EP*, 11 January 1866 pp. 3, 7, 6 May 1868 p. 3.
111. *EP*, 13 March 1891 p. 2; Redmer Yska, *Wellington: Biography of a city* (Wellington: Reed, 2006), p. 82.
112. *Dominion*, 18 November 1907 p. 8.

Chapter 9: The Corner Shop

1. Albeit with a smaller variety of goods on offer, the dairy remains on many corners in New Zealand, a popular source of ice creams and groceries.
2. *EP*, 24 December 1867 p. 2, 2 September 1869 p. 8, 30 December 1869 p. 7, 24 March 1875 p. 3, 15 February 1877 p. 3, 22 March 1877 p. 3, 23 March 1877 p. 4, 28 July 1877 p. 3.
3. John Sidney Smith, 1808–1880: Account Book, qMS 1826, ATL.
4. *EP*, 3 October 1877 p. 2, 5 October 1877 p. 4, 10 November 1877 p. 2, 26 August 1878 p. 2; 11 February 1880 p. 2.
5. M. Gray, 'Bibby, Mary Ann', DNZB: www.teara.govt.nz/en/biographies/2b22/bibby-mary-ann
6. Vera L. McLennan-Boman, *Glimpses into Early Manawatu* (Waikanae: Heritage Press, 1985), p. 54; Rob Knight, 'Scott, Thomas', DNZB: www.teara.govt.nz/en/biographies/1s2/scott-thomas
7. *Northern Advocate* (Northland), 25 July 1916 p. 1.
8. Advertisements for another Miss Donaldson, a 'machine sewer', may well have been Nancy, her unmarried sister, *AS*, 2 December 1880 p. 3, 26 August 1882 p. 3.
9. Susan Waters' identity was confirmed by examining the passenger list of the *Birman*, identified in the published letters and through comparison of Christian names mentioned.
10. From Mr W-, Port Nicholson, 11 December 1842, in 'Emigrant voices from New Zealand', in William and Robert Chambers, *Chambers Edinburgh Journal*, no. 257, 2 December 1848, p. 356; from Mrs W-, Wellington, 2 October 1842, in 'Emigrant voices', p. 355; from Mrs W-, Wellington, 4 September 1843, in 'Emigrant voices', p. 356.
11. From Mrs W-, Wellington, 10 January 1845, in 'Emigrant voices', p. 357; from Mrs W-, Wellington, 26 August 1846, in 'Emigrant voices', p. 357; from Mrs W-, Wellington, 18 September 1847, in 'Emigrant voices', p. 357.
12. *NZSCSG*, 10 April 1852 p. 2; one of the permits to buy gunpowder was issued in the name of S. Waters, *WI*, 11 July 1863 p. 2; *EP*, 16 October 1866 p. 3, 27 October 1873 p. 3; Bill from Mrs E. Waters 1859 in C.A. Vallance – Accounts and Receipts', Levin & Company Ltd Records, MS Papers 1347 5-17-21, ATL.
13. *EP*, 14 March 1865 p. 2; *WI*, 28 October 1873 p. 2.
14. *NZSCSG*, 12 October 1864 p. 2; *EP*, 23 May 1882 p. 3.
15. *EP*, 14 March 1883 p. 3.
16. W.R. Waters owned the premises. Mrs Durrant was advertising for dressmaking apprentices in Dixon Street the following year, *EP*, 6 January 1885 p. 3, 5 March 1886 p. 3.

17. *EP*, 13 January 1899 p. 5.
18. Hau Hau was another name for Pai Mārire, a Māori Christian religious faith that grew out of the wars in Taranaki.
19. Mrs Duff Hewett, *Looking Back or Personal Reminiscences by the Widow of a New Zealand Pioneer Settler* (Auckland: H.L. Thatcher, 1925) (first published 1911); *NEx*, 7 April 1858 p. 1, 25 November 1865 p. 1.
20. *London* passenger list 1842, at Nelson Early Settlers: www.museumnp. org.nz; Nelson Census Returns, January 1845, SSD 3 1/1, Micro 3632 Repro 56; Nelson returns for the year 1849, SSD 3/2 Part 1, Micro 6892, Archives NZ, Wellington; *NEx*, 28 February 1852 p. 1, 4 April 1855 p 2.
21. Nelson returns for the year 1849, SSD 3/2 Part 1; Micro 6892, Archives NZ, Wellington; *NEx*, 12 March 1853 p. 9, 2 July 1853 pp. 1, 4, 21 January 1854 p. 8; *Colonist*, 6 July 1858 1, 14 June 1859 p. 1; W.H. Cole, 'Birds eye view of the early days in Nelson, New Zealand 1842–48', [c. 1970], copy of a drawing, AC833, Bett Loan Collection, Nelson Provincial Museum.
22. *NEx*, 2 April 1856 p. 1; *NEM*, 26 October 1881 p. 3.
23. *NEx*, 20 July 1861 p. 2; *Colonist*, 23 July 1861 p. 2.
24. *Colonist*, 14 July 1884 p. 3; *NEM*, 30 July 1884 p. 2.
25. B.E. Dickinson and C.T. Kidson, 'Nelson names', *Nelson Historical Journal* 2, no. 1, 1966, p. 16.
26. 'William Stanton', in 'Biographical notes on settlers', V.R. Gunn, Papers on the History of Richmond, MS-Papers-0112-09, p. 153, ATL; *NEx*, 11 August 1855 p. 1, 15 October 1856 p. 1.
27. Betty Bint, 'Some early storekeepers of Waimea South', *Journal of the Nelson and Marlborough Historical Societies* 1, no. 4, 1984, pp. 10–13.
28. *NEx*, 22 September 1858 p. 2, 21 March 1868 p. 2, 25 April 1868 p. 2, 28 November 1868 p. 3; *NEM*, 23 September 1868 p. 2, 10 October 1868 p. 2, 24 October 1868 p. 3, 28 October 1868 p. 2.
29. *NEx*, 23 January 1847 p. 1, 23 November 1850 p. 153, 29 October 1853 p. 5, 7 January 1854 p. 1, 4 November 1854 p. 2.
30. *NEx*, 3 June 1854 p. 1, 10 June 1854 p. 4, 16 May 1957 p. 2, 20 October 1858 p. 2, 2 March 1860 p. 2.
31. *Colonist*, 27 November 1857 p. 4; one of the Te Anaroa Caves is now called Rebecca Cave; *NEx*, 9 March 1859 p. 2.
32. *NEx*, 3 May 1862 p. 2.
33. *Colonist*, 1 June 1860, 21 January 1862 p. 2, 22 May 1863 p. 3; *NEx*, 26 April 1862 p. 2, 23 May 1863 p. 2, 23 November 1865 p. 2, 7 December 1865 p. 2.
34. *NEM*, 13 July 1866 p. 2, 21 July 1866 p. 2; *NEx*, 4 June 1868 p. 5; *Westport Times*, 23 May 1871 p. 2.
35. Sandra Coney, 'Caradus, Elizabeth', DNZB: www.teara.govt.nz/en/biographies/2c7/caradus-elizabeth; Alice Caradus, *Courage and Perseverance: Russell–Caradus story* (Auckland, 1975), pp. 77–78.
36. Current Account Ledger, Nelson 1858, Union Bank of Australia, ANZ Archives, Wellington.
37. A Mrs Smith and Miss Smart were fellow passengers on a jaunt from Auckland on the *White Swan* in 1858 so they were possibly friends, *Colonist*, 8 October 1858 p. 2.
38. *Colonist*, 21 December 1858 p. 2, 26 April 1859 p. 2, 10 June 1859 p. 1, 31 August 1860 p. 2, 29 January 1861 p. 2; *NEM*, 13 August 1867 p. 3, 25 January 1868 p. 2–3, 21 March 1868 p. 3, 8 April 1896 p. 2.

39. Mary Ann was probably the wife of William Wells of Mangorei, although they may have been estranged. Samuel Crocker married William's youngest daughter Mary Ann Eliza Wells: *TH*, 3 November 1866 p. 3, 12 January 1870 p. 3, September 1872 p. 1, 9 January 1875 p. 2, 3 February 1875 p. 1, 11 May 1888 p. 2, 26 April 1890 p. 4, 28 September 1893 p. 2, 10 November 1893 p. 2, 26 January 1894 p. 3, 26 April 1915 p. 7; *Hawera and Normanby Star*, 1 November 1921 p. 4.
40. *Colonist*, 11 September 1860 p. 2; *TH*, 31 March 1860 p. 2, 10 December 1864 p. 2, 6 January 1866 p. 1, 29 February 1868 p. 1, 10 April 1868 p. 4, 10 October 1868, 5 November 1873 p. 3, 14 July 1875 p. 2, 13 September 1877 p. 2, 20 December 1898 p. 2; Edmund Dover NZ Probate 1875: www.ancestry.com/boards/thread.aspx?mv=flat&m=22&p=surnames.radford; I am also grateful to Terry McBeth for sharing information.
41. *TH*, 8 September 1860 p. 2, 3 February 1866 p. 2, 2 January 1869 p. 3, 23 January 1869 p. 1, 15 January 1870 p. 4, 22 January 1870 p. 2, 14 May 1870 p. 2, 6 August 1870 p. 2, 28 April 1875 p. 2.
42. *TH*, 9 January 1864 p. 2, 19 November 1873 p. 4, 22 July 1874 p. 2, 29 August 1874 p. 2, 11 August 1875 p. 3, 19 September 1879 p. 2, 9 July 1918 p. 2.

Chapter 10: Butchers and Bakers and Cordial Makers

1. E. Mairs, *The Wallis Family Children's Home, Motueka 1867–1887* (Westport: E. Mairs, 1989).
2. Charlotte Macdonald, 'Land, death and dower in the settler empire: The lost cause of "the widow's third" in nineteenth-century New Zealand', *Victoria University of Wellington Law Review* 41, 2010, pp. 493–518.
3. Erik Olssen, 'Families and the gendering of European New Zealand in the colonial period, 1840–80', in Caroline Daley and Deborah Montgomerie (eds), *The Gendered Kiwi* (Auckland: Auckland University Press, 1999), p. 43; Jane Hinkley, 'Pioneer widows of Otago, 1870–1900: A case study of independent women', (postgraduate diploma long essay, University of Otago, 1990), pp. 2–3, 40, quoted in Sargison, 'Essentially a woman's work', p. 36. See also Catherine Bishop, 'On their own in a "man's world": Widows in business in mid-nineteenth-century Australia and New Zealand', in Aston and Bishop (eds) *Female Entrepreneurs in the Long Nineteenth Century: A global perspective* (New York: Palgrave Macmillan, forthcoming); 'Lynne Bowd, 'On her own: Women as heads of family groups in the 1828 census', *Australian Historical Studies* 27, no. 107, 1996, pp. 303–22; Bettina Bradbury, 'Surviving as a widow in 19th-century Montreal', *Urban History Review/Revue d'histoire urbaine* 17, no. 3, 1989, pp. 148–60; Sue Hart, 'Widowhood and remarriage in colonial Australia', (PhD thesis, University of Western Australia, 2009); Susan Ingalls Lewis, 'Business widows in nineteenth-century Albany, New York, 1813–1885' in Rudolph P. Bell and Virginia Yans-McLaughlin (eds), *Women on Their Own: Interdisciplinary perspectives on being single* (New Brunswick: Rutgers University Press, 2007); Beatrice Moring and Richard Wall, *Widows in European Economy and Society, 1600–1920* (Woodbridge: Boydell and Brewer, 2017); Katie Pickles, 'Locating widows in mid-nineteenth-century Pictou County, Nova Scotia', *Journal of Historical Geography* 30, no. 1, 2004, pp. 70–86; Glenda Strachan and Lindy Henderson, 'Surviving widowhood: Life alone in rural Australia in the second half of the nineteenth century', *Continuity and Change* 23, no. 3, 2008, pp. 487–508.
4. Martha Adams, 'Journal, transcription', 1850–52, pp. 162–64, MS 0006, ATL.

5. Clendon House tour pamphlet, Heritage New Zealand.
6. Ellen Ellis, 'Bennett, Mary Jane', DNZB: www.teara.govt.nz/en/biographies/1b18/bennett-mary-jane; Ellen Ellis, 'A first and only for Pencarrow Lighthouse', *Historic Places in New Zealand* 16, 1987; William Lyall – Superintendent Province of Wellington 23 January 1860, old reference: WP Series2 60/47, now Inwards Letters 26 November 1855–24 October 1876, ACIA 16194 WP. 2 1, Archives NZ, Wellington, also quoted in 'Keepers of the Light', *Public Service Journal*, April 1959; I am grateful to Ellen Ellis for sharing her research.
7. UK Census 1871, 1881; Ellis, 'A first and only'.
8. *WI*, 15 June 1872 p. 3; *EP*, 28 September 1885 p. 2.
9. *NZer*, 23 November 1853 p. 2, 24 December 1862 p. 6, 2 April 1863 p. 6; *NZH*, 7 April 1868 p. 3, 27 November 1874 p. 2; I am grateful to Michelle Smith late of Papakura Museum for her assistance.
10. K.M. Matthews, 'Bates, Sophia Ann', DNZB: www.teara.govt.nz/en/biographies/1b14/bates-sophia-ann
11. *WI*, 9 September 1846 p. 2.
12. *WH*, 16 September 1871 p. 3; *The Wellington Almanack and Diary 1866* (Wellington: T. McKenzie, 1866).
13. *TH*, 21 December 1861 p. 2, 2 January 1875 p. 1, 3 April 1875 p. 3.
14. *WH*, 31 March 1875 p. 2, 19 February 1876 p. 2, 1 March 1876 p. 2; *WC*, 4 November 1881 p. 2; 'Hair Estate', Whanganui Regional Museum: https://whanganuiregionalmuseum.wordpress.com/tag/hair-estate/; 'Mt St Joseph Homestead', Register Item 362, Built Heritage Inventory, Whanganui District Council: http://maps.whanganui.govt.nz/Wanganui/Photos/HeritageInventory/362.pdf
15. George Johann Hanneke NZ Probate 1863; *WI*, 25 October 1865 p. 5; *EP*, 9 April 1867 p. 3.
16. *NEx*, 27 December 1854 p. 2, 6 January 1855 p. 2, 18 August 1855 p. 2, 18 July 1857 p. 2; *Colonist*, 5 February 1858 p. 1.
17. William Dew, letter to his brother James Dew Gardener, Ham near Richmond, Surry, Wellington, 2 October 1842, 25 December 1842, in *Letters from Settlers & Labouring Emigrants in the New Zealand Company's Settlements of Wellington, Nelson, & New Plymouth, from February, 1842, to January, 1843* (London: Smith, Elder & Co, 1843), pp. 37, 59.
18. Records also suggest James left a pregnant widow, Jane (née Kite, from Nelson), who remarried two years later, but there is no mention of her in the inquest reports. *Press*, 9 November 1863 p. 2, 19 February 1867 p. 2, 11 July 1871 p. 2; *LT*, 28 August 1866 p. 2; *Star*, 9 November 1869 p. 2, 22 July 1873 p. 1.
19. Lyndsay Rendall, 'Brown Briggs Family', unpublished notes on family history; thank you to Lyndsay for sharing her research.
20. *Westport Times*, 30 September 1884 p. 3.
21. *LT*, 8 March 1864 p. 6, 9 January 1868 p. 3.
22. *WI*, 28 February 1852 p. 2, 28 February 1855; *NZSCSG*, 22 May 1852 p. 2, 19 August 1854 p. 3; *Marlborough Express*, 21 July 1875 p. 2; *The Royal New Zealand Almanack and Commercial Calendar for 1859* (Wellington: George Watson, 1859); Denise Abbott and Peter Wells, 'Burial Register 1840 to 1866 St Paul's Church Molesworth St Thorndon': http://freepages.genealogy.rootsweb.ancestry.com/~ourstuff/StPaulsA-C.htm
23. *NEx*, 17 July 1858 p. 2; *Colonist*, 30 September 1864 p. 7; *Lucas's Nelson Almanac and Year-Book*, 1869, 1874 (Nelson: R. Lucas & Son, 1869, 1874).
24. *NZH*, 14 June 1904 p. 4.

25. Lyndsay Rendall, 'Brown Briggs Family'.
26. *EP*, 6 November 1883 p. 2, 4 January 1884 p. 2, 24 April 1884 p. 3, 10 February 1885 p. 2, 5 June 1885 p. 2; 15 September 1887 p. 4, 25 April 1890 p. 3; Wellington Antique Bottle & Collectibles Club, 'G. Cooper', 'T. Cooper', and 'C.W. Brodie': www.wellingtonantiquebottles.org.nz/companies/gcooper.shtml; www.wellingtonantiquebottles.org.nz/companies/tcooper.shtml; www.wellingtonantiquebottles.org.nz/companies/cwbrodie.shtml
27. *EP*, 19 November 1908 p. 7; 'Dixon, Mrs George', *Cyclopedia of New Zealand Wellington Provincial District* (Wellington: The Cyclopedia Company Limited, 1897), pp. 611–12: http://nzetc.victoria.ac.nz/tm/scholarly/tei-Cyc01Cycl-t1-body-d4-d39-d2.html; Lois Burleigh, *The Dixon Family in New Zealand: The first generations in 150 years* (Milton: Dixon Family Reunion Committee, 1992), pp. 99–110; Wellington Antique Bottle and Collectibles Club, 'Edward Dixon', 'George Dixon': www.wellingtonantiquebottles.org.nz/companies/edixon.shtml; www.wellingtonantiquebottles.org.nz/companies/gdixon.shtml
28. Louise Shaw, 'From family helpmeet to lady dispenser: Women pharmacists 1881–1939', *New Zealand Journal of History* 32, no. 1, 1998, pp. 23–42, pp. 24, 27; *Press*, 3 March 1864 p. 4; *LT*, 23 December 1871 p. 2; *Star*, 21 December 1871 p. 2, 6 October 1873 p. 1, 30 May 1874 p. 1; Macdonald Dictionary.
29. This may have been a particularly whirlwind romance but it is more likely that they knew each other already, although even then, they had worked fast. There was a window of about six months when they were both in England after Clara had returned from South Australia, and before Alexander set sail for Nelson on the *Whitby* in April 1841. Clara emigrated on the *Fifeshire* in 1842. Aged 19, she had married her previous husband William in 1837 and travelled to South Australia with him and her brother, Henry Pope, in the *Eden* in 1838. Her daughter Clara Adelaide was named for the city in which she was born, in 1839, the same year her father died. Clara and her daughter returned to England in the *Katherine Stewart Forbes* in 1840 before emigrating again, this time as cabin passengers, to Nelson: www.slsa.sa.gov.au/BSA/ShipLists%20Alpha%20by%20Year/1838A-F.htm; *Adelaide Chronicle and South Australian Advertiser*, 7 April 1840 p. 2; *South Australian Record and Australasian and South African Chronicle*, 3 October 1840 p. 14.
30. Max Lash, *Nelson Notables 1840–1940: A dictionary of regional biography* (ed. Dawn Smith) (Nelson: Nelson Historical Society, 1992), p. 102; *NEx*, 21 July 1849 p. 84.
31. *NEx*, 19 January 1850 p. 183.
32. *NEx*, 27 March 1852 p. 17.
33. Lash, *Nelson Notables*, p. 102; *NEx*, 15 July 1857 p. 1, 16 December 1857 p. 2.
34. Current Account Ledger, Nelson 1858, Union Bank of Australia, ANZ Archives, Wellington.
35. *NEx*, 9 December 1854 p. 3.
36. Randolph Bedford, *Naught to Thirty-Three* (Sydney: Currawong Publishing Company, n.d.), p. 34, in Catherine Bishop, *Minding Her Own Business: Colonial businesswomen in Sydney* (Sydney: NewSouth, 2015), pp. 153–54.
37. *The Auckland Almanack and Directory, 1856* (Auckland: W. Lambert, 1856); Chapman, *Chapman's New Zealand Almanac 1860*; *NZH*, 11 September 1882 p. 2.
38. The Birds travelled in steerage class. One might have imagined that cabin class passengers, among whom was Clara Durley, soon to be Mrs Clara Macshane, would have disembarked first.
39. Constantine Dillon to his wife Fanny c. 1851, p. 299, Dillon Papers, MS 0685, ATL.
40. *NEx*, 28 August 1868 p. 1; *Colonist*, 26 June 1891 p. 3; Ann Bird NZ Probate 1891.

41. *NEx*, 24 November 1868 p. 2, 8 March 1873 p. 2; *Colonist*, 3 September 1869 p. 1, 4 June 1874 p. 2; *NEM*, 23 April 1872 p. 2; *The Record and Emerald Hill and Sandridge Advertiser* (Victoria), 14 May 1874 p. 2.
42. *DSX*, 11 August 1868 p. 3, 3 March 1869 p. 1; Philip Hannken, 'Reminiscences of Auckland 1858–1880': http://localhistorybartley.blogspot.com.au/2014/08/new-heritage-rating-in-lower-queen-st.html
43. *AS*, 19 November 1880 p. 3; Catherine Giles had married Robert in 1876 after the sudden death of her first husband, Fred Hammond, who was also a butcher, *AS*, 8 March 1876 p. 2.
44. Charlotte Godley, *Letters from Early New Zealand 1850–1853*, edited with notes by John R. Godley (Christchurch: Whitcombe & Tombs, 1951), p. 37.
45. *WI*, 23 February 1850 p. 4; *NEx*, 26 March 1859 p. 2; Julie Ann Macdonald, 'The pot of gold: Christison biography', New Zealand Society of Genealogists 1990 Sesquicentennial Family Biography Competition Collection, Folder 034, MS Papers 4280, ATL.
46. *NZG*, 5 June 1841 p. 2.
47. *NZG*, 10 July 1841 p. 2, 1 October 1842 p. 1.
48. *NZSCSG*, 8 February 1845 p. 1 (supplement), 17 August 1850 p. 2; *WI*, 6 September 1848 p. 3, 4 August 1849 p. 2; Mary Cotter, pers. comm.
49. Libraries Tasmania, 'Tasmanian Name Index': https://librariestas.ent.sirsidynix.net.au/client/en_AU/names/
50. A property transfer in the names of Chauncy and Isabella was recorded in 1859, *NZG*, 12 June 1841 p 3; *NZSCSG*, 10 January 1846 p. 2, 20 March 1847 p. 3.
51. *DSX*, 28 April 1854 p. 3, 11 July 1854 p. 2.
52. *NEx*, 20 September 1859 p. 2; 7 December 1861 p. 2, 28 April 1864 p. 4.
53. *NEM*, 9 September 1873 p. 2.
54. *NEM*, 18 June 1877 p. 2.
55. *WI*, 13 March 1850 p. 4, 2 March 1859 p. 2, 26 March 1863 p. 2; *EP*, 1 December 1869 p. 3, 29 March 1873 p. 3, 28 June 1879 p. 3, 19 November 1887 p. 3, 28 January 1898 p. 6; John Cumming, Ken Ward, pers. comm.; Rates Books, Wellington City, 1863–1870, Series 00162 and 1870–1975, Series 00163, Wellington City Council Archives; Jane Anderson, Diary, 9 March 1861.
56. *TH*, 31 March 1866 p. 2, 29 April 1871 p. 3, 21 June 1873 p. 3, 20 December 1873 p. 3, 24 December 1873 p. 3, 28 February 1874 p. 1, 14 March 1879 p. 1, 26 June 1880 p. 3, 1 December 1880 p. 1.
57. *TH*, 5 August 1881 p. 1, 21 January 1882 p. 3, 25 April 1882 p. 2, 9 June 1882 p. 1, 22 June 1883 p. 2, 14 August 1883 p. 3.
58. *TH*, 10 March 1884 pp. 2–3, 23 June 1884 p. 1, 20 August 1884 p. 2, 1 September 1884 p. 2, 5 March 1885 p. 5, 7 March 1885 p. 6, 17 August 1898 p. 2; *EP*, 4 October 1894 p. 2.
59. *Fair Play* (National, Wellington), 16 December 1893 p. 6; *EP*, 5 January 1894 p. 3; Phil and Jill Bennett, pers. comm., 24 January 2018; I am grateful to both the Bennetts and Conal Townsend for sharing their research.
60. In 1866 after William had died at the age of 24, closely followed by his mother, William's father Edward resumed control of the business but sold it in 1867. *NEx*, 20 January 1844 p. 387, 29 December 1849 p. 171, 1 November 1851 p. 141, 8 November 1851 p. 145, 30 May 1857 p. 2, 23 February 1861 p. 4, 12 April 1862 pp. 2–4, 19 April 1862 p. 1, 19 April 1866 p. 2, 2 June 1866 p. 2, 30 October 1866 p. 1, 26 January 1867 p. 1.

61. *NZSCSG*, 5 July 1854 p. 3; *WI*, 6 February 1858 p. 2, 5 July 1859 p. 4, 26 March 1864 p. 2.
62. See Keith Giles, 'Robert Leaf': www.aucklandcity.govt.nz/dbtw-wpd%5Cphotographers%5Cessays%5Cleaf.pdf. Coincidentally, Eliza's daughter Annie was a prominent local singer and married William Reed, also a photographer, and brother of Harriet Corston (see Chapter 11); 'Robert Leaf', Early New Zealand Photographers: http://canterburyphotography.blogspot.com/2013/01/leaf-robert.html
63. Keith Giles, 'Fairs & Steel: Their impact on Auckland photography', *New Zealand Legacy* 19:3 (2007), pp. 8–12; Phillip D. Jackson, 'Pulman, Elizabeth', DNZB: www.teara.govt.nz/en/biographies/2p. 32/pulman-elizabeth
64. Jennifer Curnow, 'Hinerangi, Sophia', DNZB: www.teara.govt.nz/en/biographies/2h37/hinerangi-sophia
65. June Northcroft-Grant, 'Papakura, Makereti', DNZB: www.teara.govt.nz/en/biographies/3p. 5/papakura-makereti
66. *GRA*, 10 January 1882 p. 2, 2 February 1882 p. 2; *Kumara Times*, 4 May 1882 p. 2.
67. Bishop, *Minding Her Own Business*; Martha Sear, 'Tost, Jane Catherine (1817–1889)', Australian Dictionary of Biography: http://adb.anu.edu.au/biography/rohu-ada-jane-13285; Sear, '"Curious and peculiar"? Women taxidermists in colonial Australia', in Joan Kerr and Jo Holder (eds), *Past Present: The national women's art anthology* (Sydney: Craftsman House, 1999).
68. William Samuel Mitchell D'Urban, Murray Alexander Mathew and John Gerrard Keulemans, *The Birds of Devon* (London: R.H. Porter, 1892); Lisa Truttman, 'William and Jane Yandle, taxidermists', Timespanner: http://timespanner.blogspot.com.au/2011/05/william-and-jane-yandle-taxidermists.html; Pauline Leggat, Mary Fox and Joseph Turle, 'The Musicians': www.turle.name/the_musicians/indiI1099.html; www.turle.name/the_musicians/indiI1085.html
69. *NZH*, 11 December 1873 p. 1; 31 May 1877 p. 2; 5 December 1881 p. 6, 10 April 1882 p. 3; *DSX*, 31 May 1875 p. 4; *AS*, 14 July 1877 p. 3, 4 May 1878 p. 1, 8 April 1882 p. 3.
70. *AS*, 25 April 1882 p. 3, 1 November 1882 p. 3, 19 August 1886 p. 2.
71. *NZH*, 11 September 1894 p. 6; *AS*, 21 February 1896 p. 3.
72. *NZH*, 27 May 1905 p. 1, 21 June 1909 p. 1; *AS*, 17 December 1908 p. 2, 16 October 1909 p. 4.
73. *EP*, 3 May 1898 p. 6, 4 December 1909 p. 6; *NZT*, 9 June 1909 p. 1, 6 October 1909 p. 12; *Dominion* (Wellington), 1 January 1910 p. 1.
74. *LT*, 21 February 1852 p. 2.
75. *LT*, 7 December 1859 p. 4, 28 March 1860 p. 6, 20 September 1864 p. 4.
76. *NZT*, 27 October 1906 p. 11; *EP*, 15 February 1907 p. 6; *NZ Truth*, 16 February 1907 p. 4; *New Zealand FreeLance*, 23 February 1907 p. 6; *GRA* 19 February 1907 p. 3.

Chapter 11: Pushing Boundaries

1. Florence Hartley, *Ladies' Book of Etiquette and Manual of Politeness* (Boston: G.W. Cottrell, 1860); see also John MacGibbon, *Piano in the Parlour: When the piano was New Zealand's home entertainment centre* (Wellington: Ngaio Press, 2007); Kirstine Moffat, *Piano Forte: Stories and sounds from colonial New Zealand* (Dunedin: Otago University Press, 2011); Kirstine Moffat, 'The piano as cultural symbol in colonial New Zealand', *History Compass* 7, no. 3, 2009, pp. 719–41.
2. *LT*, 26 October 1870 p. 2; *Star*, 19 November 1870 p. 2.

3. *ODT*, 3 February 1873 p. 3, 3 April 1886 p. 2; *ES*, 15 January 1875 p. 1; *LT*, 21 February 1878 p. 2; *AS*, 7 June 1890 p. 3, 25 October 1890 p. 8; *Argus*, 10 January 1922 p. 1; George Skinner, 'Australharmony': http://sydney.edu.au/paradisec/australharmony/index.php
4. See also Catherine Bishop, *Minding Her Own Business: Colonial businesswomen in Sydney* (Sydney: NewSouth, 2015); for contrast with Britain and for employees see Tracy C. Davis, *Actresses as Working Women: Their social identity in Victorian culture* (London: Routledge, 1991); for a different argument on Australia see Jane Woollard, '"The elasticity of her spirits": Actresses and resilience on the 19th-century colonial stage', in R. Scollen and M. Smalley (eds), *Resilience: Revive, restore, reconnect. Australasian Association for Drama Theatre and Performance Studies* [ADSA] *2016 Conference Proceedings*, vol. 1, Artsworx, 2016.
5. Many of the women who performed in New Zealand were on the international circuit. Graeme Skinner's biographical dictionary of musicians, 'Australharmony', includes many female performers.
6. *OW*, 28 November 1857 p. 4, 9 January 1858 p. 2, 18 December 1858 p. 4. Annie Dyer worked as governess to the Jones family in the rural area of Tokomairiro. Her new husband was no stranger to the idea of women in business as his mother and sisters were milliners and dressmakers in Sydney, *OW*, 31 March 1898 p. 11; *Sydney Herald*, 24 February 1840 p. 1; *SMH*, 16 April 1850 p. 1.
7. Unfortunately we do not have a copy of Kate's song, which may have been inspired by Pai Mārire followers' ritual killing of missionary Carl Völkner in March 1865, or by more peaceable aspects of the religion: https://nzhistory.govt.nz/politics/pai-marire/pai-marire-intro
8. *WI*, 26 June 1868 p. 1; see also Elizabeth Nichol, '"Dedicated to the colonial music-loving public": New Zealand's published music 1840–1913', PhD thesis, University of Auckland, 2017; Elizabeth Nichol, 'Transplanting colonial traditions: Immigrant colonial composers in New Zealand', in Michael Brown and Samantha Owens (eds), *Searches for Tradition: Essays on New Zealand music past and present* (Wellington: Victoria University Press, 2017), pp. 25–45. Several Māori women were composers of traditional waiata. They were not businesswomen, however, as they do not appear to have received payment for their compositions. Te Ahukaramū Charles Royal, 'Māori composers: Ngā kaitito waiata': www.teara.govt.nz/en/maori-composers-nga-kaitito-waiata
9. *OW*, 23 January 1858 p. 4, 3 April 1858 p. 3, 24 April 1858 p. 3; *LT*, 11 April 1860 p. 5.
10. *WI*, 29 April 1865 p. 2; NZer, 14 September 1864 p. 4, 2 February 1865 p. 4, 9 February 1865 p. 4; *TH*, 14 April 1866 p. 2.
11. *GRA*, 2 November 1869 p. 2, 18 November 1869 p. 3.
12. *DSX*, 30 November 1855 p. 3; *WI*, 6 May 1859 p. 3; Peter Downes, *Top of the Bill: Entertainers through the years* (Wellington: A.H. & A.W. Reed, 1979), p. 27; Peter Downes, 'Foley, Mrs W.H.', DNZB: www.teara.govt.nz/en/biographies/1f13/foley-mrs-w-h; Peter Downes, *Shadows on the Stage. Theatre in New Zealand: The first 70 years* (Dunedin: J. McIndoe, 1975).
13. Catherine Bishop, 'Women on the move: Gender, money-making and mobility in mid-nineteenth century Australasia', *History Australia* 11, no. 2, 2014; Downes, 'Foley, Mrs W.H.', DNZB; *The Courier* (Hobart), 10 September 1851 p. 2. Thank you to New Zealand theatre historian Peter Downes and genealogist Ian Harding for their help in the search.
14. Ian Harding, pers. comm.; *The Courier* (Hobart), 18 December 1847 p. 2, 5 August 1848 p. 1; 22 November 1848 p. 3; *Colonial Times* (Hobart), 29 June 1849 p. 2; *Launceston Examiner*, 12 September 1849 p. 6; *Cornwall Chronicle* (Launceston), 19 July 1851 p. 452; Charles

married Mary Anne Egan and had at least three children, Eileen Annie Caparn Jones, Mary Cecelia Caparn Jones (b1877) and John Caparn Egan Jones (1871–1951). William Lloyd Jones (1809–1873) and Mary Anne Edwards seem to have adopted Charles. When Charles died in 1909 in Victoria he was recorded as Charles Caparn Jones, son of William and Mary Anne.

15. *Daily Alta California* (San Francisco), 14 March 1851 p. 2; *LT*, 17 June 1857 p. 8. The baby daughter was Wilhelmina Kate Foley. Her death certificate records her parents as William and Martha but her mother was likely to have been Catherine Foley. The birth certificate for William and Martha's first-born son in 1860 states that William had no other children with Martha but one, Wilhelmina, by his former wife. 'John William Foley Birth Certificate', Darrin Lythgoe, Foley Family History: http://genealogy.eproject.co.nz/foley_family_main/william_foley/

16. *SMH*, 24 July 1859 p. 1; Amelia Fisher also toured New Zealand with her own company in 1856–57 but she has been impossible to positively identify. She was, perhaps, a daughter of Dr Alder Fisher, who arrived with his family in 1864 and at least one of whose daughters gave French lessons in Parnel; but she might equally have been someone entirely different. See also Anna Clarke, active in England as an actress and then in Hobart as head of a company in the 1840s, and Marie Carandini, whose troupe toured Australia, New Zealand, the United States and India in the 1860s. Nicole Anae, '"A crowned and selected band of women": Tasmanian actresses/celebrities of the nineteenth century & "home-grown" identity', PhD thesis, University of Tasmania, 2005; Ann K. Wentzel, 'Carandini, Marie (1826–1894)', Australian Dictionary of Biography: http://adb.anu.edu.au/biography/carandini-marie-3162/text4729

17. Her involvement with George Swan has not been substantiated but appears in at least one biographical sketch of Swan. William Main, *Wellington Through a Victorian Lens* (Wellington: Millwood Press, 1972), pp. 9–12. George Swan later became a long-serving mayor of Napier and his youthful dalliance with the fascinating Mrs Foley, if true, was perhaps something he preferred to forget.

18. Vernon Webster was playing at a rival theatre at the time. *WI*, 19 September 1863 p. 2.

19. *WI*, 4 July 1867 p. 1; 24 November 1868 p. 2.

20. *NZMail*, 22 February 1884 p. 10; *WH*, 17 April 1884 p. 3.

21. *HBH*, 25 February 1884 p. 2; *EP*, 17 April 1884 p. 2.

22. There was also, rather confusingly, an actor in England at the time called Webster Vernon. Lowten Lowten may have chosen the name 'Vernon Webster' to cash in on the similarity. Lowten Lowten was in Wellington, using his own name, in July 1859 and apparently before that in Lyttelton. *LT*, 4 August 1858 p. 4; *WI*, 12 January 1859 p. 6 (supplement).

23. *Star*, 15 May 1882 p. 2; UK Census 1881; 'Certified Copy of an Entry of Marriage Lowten Lowten and Lucy Catherine Foley', 1882 (West Derby: General Register Office). I am grateful to Ian Harding for unearthing the marriage certificate and sharing his discovery. Nothing has been discovered about the activities of the Lowtens, or Foley and Webster, between 1868 and 1881. It is possible that the Foleys obtained an official divorce but no records have been located thus far. W.H. Foley died in Queensland in 1885. *Colonist*, 30 December 1885 p. 4; for more on W.H Foley and circuses see Mark St Leon, *Circus: The Australian story* (Melbourne: Melbourne Books, 2011) and research by Matthew Wittman: www.matthewwittmann.com

24. *NZMail*, 7 March 1884 p. 10; *WH*, 21 April 1884 pp. 2, 3, 22 April 1884 p. 2; Peter Downes, pers. comm.; I am grateful to my eagle-eyed editor, Anna Rogers, for finding the *NZ Mail* reference.

25. Bishop, *Minding Her Own Business.*
26. *WI*, 3 May 1861 p. 2; Bishop, *Minding Her Own Business*, pp. 183–84.
27. *The Age* (Melbourne), 22 August 1866 p. 4, 1 May 1867 p. 7, 8 February 1870 p. 2; *Marlborough Express*, 18 March 1874 p. 2; *LT*, 22 October 1874 p. 3; *TS*, 20 November 1874 p. 2; *Hawaiian Gazette*, 28 June 1876 p. 2; *Argus*, 15 June 1877 p. 6.
28. *Newcastle Chronicle* (NSW), 28 November 1871 p. 2; *ES*, 20 January 1873 p. 3; *Tuapeka Times*, 27 February 1873 p. 4; *Evening News* (Sydney), 15 January 1877 p. 2; *Adelaide Observer*, 25 May 1878 p. 6; Ursula Chisholm, Probate 1902, South Africa, Pietermaritzburg Estate Files 1846–1950, on FamilySearch.
29. *Marlborough Express*, 6 September 1889 p. 2, 9 September 1889 p. 2, 11 September 1889 p. 2; *Waikato Times*, 26 November 1892 p. 2; *Manawatu Standard*, 14 September 1907 p. 5; *SMH*, 7 May 1935 p. 10; Whanganui Museum Founders Index, Whanganui Regional Museum Archives; Nigel Jamieson, 'Sim, William Alexander', DNZB: www.teara.govt.nz/en/biographies/3s18/sim-william-alexander; SS *Tahiti* passenger list 1922, Familysearch.
30. *DSX*, 2 September 1867 p. 6; *NZH*, 2 September 1867 p. 6; *TH*, 14 March 1868 p. 2; *Evening News* (Sydney), 27 September 1893 p. 4; Verva Mossong, 'Remember the Primitive Methodists', Wesley Historical Society (NZ) Publication 63, 1996, p. 18: www.methodist.org.nz/files/docs/wesley%20historical/63(3)%20remember%20the%20primitive.pdf
31. Mary Beard, 'The public voice of women', in *Women & Power: A manifesto* (London: Profile Books, 2017), first published in *London Review of Books*, 20 March 2014.
32. 'Preface' in Beard, *Women & Power.*
33. Janet Paul, 'Greenwood, Sarah', DNZB: www.teara.govt.nz/en/biographies/1g19/greenwood-sarah
34. Moira M. Long, 'King, Martha', DNZB: www.teara.govt.nz/en/biographies/1k12/king-martha; Jessie Campbell, 8 May 1842, 'Extracts from the letters of Jessie Campbell to her family from Petone and Wanganui 1841–45', (Typescript) qMS–0369, ATL; Sarah Pratt to her sister Martha Powley, 1855, in Frances Porter, Charlotte Macdonald and Tui MacDonald, *My Hand Will Write What My Heart Dictates: The unsettled lives of women in nineteenth-century New Zealand as revealed to sisters, family and friends* (Auckland: Auckland University Press, Bridget Williams Books, 1996), p. 163; *New Plymouth in 1843*, artwork in Jock Phillips, 'Rural mythologies: Immigrant hopes', Te Ara: www:teara.govt.nz/en/artwork/20300/new-plymouth-in-1843
35. Charlotte Godley, *Letters from Early New Zealand 1850–1853*, edited with notes by John R. Godley (Christchurch: Whitcombe & Tombs, 1951), pp. 217, 221, 274; *LT*, 15 July 1863 p. 2; 'Dr William Donald', Macdonald Dictionary; Robert McDougall Art Gallery, *Concise History of Art in Canterbury 1850–2000* (Christchurch: Robert McDougall Art Gallery for Christchurch City Council, 2000).
36. *Colonist*, 8 April 1870 p 1, 23 December 1896 p. 2, 21 May 1919 p. 12; *NEM*, 15 July 1885 p. 3, 1 February 1887 p. 3, 7 August 1925 p. 4; Moira M. Long, 'Harris, Emily Cumming', DNZB: www.teara.govt.nz/en/biographies/2h15/harris-emily-cumming
37. See also J.E. Traue, 'Nineteenth-century New Zealand novels and novellas published as serials in New Zealand, Australian and British newspapers and periodicals and never published as monographs: A checklist', *Journal of New Zealand Studies* 20, 2015: https://doi.org/10.26686/jnzs.v0i20.3875
38. Anne D. Brown, 'Charlotte Lees Evans, 1841–1882', *Kotare* 7, no. 1, 2007: https://ojs.victoria.ac.nz/kotare/issue/view/111

39. Cherry Hankin, 'Barker, Mary Anne', DNZB: www.teara.govt.nz/en/biographies/1b5/barker-mary-anne
40. DNZB Biographical Database, pers. comm., November 2009; Helen Whelan, 'Jane Hope', in Max Lash, *Nelson Notables 1840–1940: A dictionary of regional biography* (ed. Dawn Smith) (Nelson: Nelson Historical Society, 1992), pp. 34–35.
41. Mrs Charles Thomson, *Twelve Years in Canterbury, New Zealand, with Visits to the Other Provinces, and Reminiscences of the Route Home Through Australia etc. (from a Lady's Journal)* (London: Sampson Low, Son and Marston, 1867?), ENZB, Preface. For other writers see also Helen Bones, *The Expatriate Myth: New Zealand writers and the colonial world* (Dunedin: Otago University Press, 2018).
42. *Star*, 30 November 1887 p. 2; David Burton, 'Cooking: Cookbooks, magazines and television shows', Te Ara: www.TeAra.govt.nz/en/cooking/page-3; Duncan Galletly, 'Bibliography of New Zealand cookbooks to 1922': www.aristologist.com/resources/cookery-books-to-1922.html
43. Janet McCallum, 'Baker, Louisa Alice', DNZB: www.teara.govt.nz/en/biographies/3b4/baker-louisa-alice
44. Rosemarie Smith, 'Wood, Susan', DNZB: www.teara.govt.nz/en/biographies/1w37/wood-susan; Susan Nugent Wood, *Woman's Work in Australia* (Melbourne: Samuel Mullen, 1862).
45. Raewyn Dalziel, 'Muller, Mary Ann', DNZB: www.teara.govt.nz/en/biographies/1m59/muller-mary-anne
46. Mary Taylor, 'Marriage', *The First Duty of Women: A series of articles reprinted from The Victoria Magazine, 1865 to 1870* (London: Emily Faithfull, 1870), p. 209; see also Kirstine Moffat, '"Devoted to the cause of woman's rights": The New Zealand new woman novel', *Women's Writing* online, 2017, DOI: 10.1080/09699082.2017.1282930; Kirstine Moffat, 'Agents of empire and feminist rebels: Settlement and gender in Isabella Aylmer's distant homes and Ellen Ellis's everything is possible to will', in T.S. Wagner (ed.), *Victoria Settler Narratives: Emigrants, cosmopolitans and returnees in nineteenth-century literature* (London: Pickering & Chatto, 2011), pp. 41–53.
47. Anne Lohrli, *Household Words: A weekly journal 1850–1859 conducted by Charles Dickens. Table of contents, list of contributors and their contributions based on The Household Words Office Book in the Morris L. Parrish collection of Victorian novelists, Princeton University Library* (Toronto: University of Toronto Press, 1973), quoted at www.victorianweb.org/periodicals/hw.html
48. *Household Words*, 10 April 1852, p. 80.
49. *DSX*, 7 March 1867 p. 4; *NZH*, 27 June 1868 p. 3.
50. *NZH*, 30 March 1875 p. 2, 24 January 1883 p. 8; *AS*, 9 September 1890 p. 8, 11 September 1890 p. 4.
51. *NZH*, 2 March 1872 p. 3.
52. Frances Shayle George, 'Education of Girls' (Auckland: Upton & Co, 1874), pp. 6–7: https://nzetc.victoria.ac.nz/tm/scholarly/tei-Stout33-t8.html; Raewyn Dalziel, 'George, Frances Shayle', DNZB: www.teara.govt.nz/en/biographies/1g8/george-frances-shayle; S. Simmonds, 'A Family History': http://simmondshistory.blogspot.com.au/2006/04/frances-southwell-shayle-george-1828.html
53. *EP*, 16 December 1886 p. 2.
54. Jenny Coleman, *Polly Plum: A firm and earnest woman's advocate: Mary Ann Colclough, 1836–1885* (Dunedin: Otago University Press, 2017); *NZer*, 24 July 1858 p. 1.

55. *NZer*, 7 May 1862 p. 2; *AS*, 26 January 1872 p. 1, 13 June 1874 p. 2.
56. *DSX*, 2 June 1870 p. 3.
57. Quoted in Judy Malone, 'Colclough, Mary Ann', DNZB: www.teara.govt.nz/en/biographies/2c25/colclough-mary-ann
58. *DSX*, 23 September 1868 p. 4, 24 December 1868 p. 5.
59. *NZH*, 14 April 1873 p. 2; 14 July 1873 p. 3.
60. *AS*, 26 September 1874 p. 2, 6 January 1876 p. 2; *ODT*, 5 February 1875 p. 2; *DSX*, 9 February 1875 p. 3; *NZH*, 14 April 1975 p. 2, 8 April 1876 p. 4; *Press*, 18 May 1878 p. 1, 26 January 1884 p. 3, 24 January 1885 p. 2, 10 March 1885 p. 4; *Star*, 5 February 1879 p. 2, 26 November 1881 p. 3; *Observer*, 14 March 1885 p. 4.

Chapter 12: Globetrotting

1. Catherine Bishop, 'Women on the move: Gender, money-making and mobility in mid-nineteenth century Australasia', *History Australia* 11, no. 2, 2014.
2. *AS*, 28 February 1877 p. 2.
3. Frederick Olson from Wellington, c. 1858, Letters from Members of Olson Family, MS229, AWMM. See also Pat McClunie, *A Far Traveller: Eleanor Mills and her Wallace descendants* (Hokitika: Pat McClunie, 2000).
4. *Maori Messenger*, 28 March 1850 p. 2.
5. Hazel Petrie, *Chiefs of Industry: Māori tribal enterprise in early colonial New Zealand* (Auckland: Auckland University Press, 2006), p. 64; Jo Kamira, 'Māori', *Sydney Journal* 3, no. 1, 2010, pp. 23–34; Rohan Howitt, 'Poihākena: Māori travellers and workers in New South Wales, 1793–1840', Honours thesis, University of Sydney, 2017.
6. *NEx*, 25 June 1842 p. 61; *Colonial Times* (Hobart), 4 June 1852 p. 2; *Mercury*, 31 December 1862 p. 1; *Tasmanian Tribune*, 11 May 1875 p. 2; *Tasmanian News*, 30 January 1886 p. 3.
7. *NZer*, 3 April 1850 p. 1, 29 November 1851 p. 2, 28 July 1852 p. 2; Emily Chevassut, Mission Dolores Cemetery, San Francisco, 1854, Find a Grave: www.findagrave.com/memorial/7720241/emily-chevassut
8. *NEx*, 15 September 1849 p. 109, 29 March 1851 p. 19; *SMH*, 5 April 1851 p. 4; *South Australian Register*, 16 May 1851 p. 5, 13 July 1852 p. 2, 29 November 1855 p. 2, 12 March 1875 p. 4; *Adelaide Times*, 14 February 1853 p. 3; *Evening Journal* (Adelaide), 10 June 1873 p. 3, 12 May 1874 p. 3.
9. *WH*, 13 September 1869 p. 2, 10 April 1886 p. 3; *Record and Emerald Hill and Sandridge Advertiser*, 4 June 1880 p. 1, 8 October 1880 p. 1; *Record* (Emerald Hill), 22 April 1881 p. 4, 10 Jun 1881 p. 4; *The Age*, 23 October 1882 p. 8; *WC*, 10 July 1888 p. 1; *Mercury and Weekly Courier* (Melbourne), 16 October 1890 p. 2: Melbourne Directories online, Melbourne History Workshop, University of Melbourne: https://omeka.cloud.unimelb.edu.au/melbourne-history/exhibits/show/melbournedirectories/browsemelbournedirectories; see 'Praises' by Jane McDonald, poem on General Gordon's death, *The Herald* (Melbourne), 17 February 1885 p. 2; Jane Mcdonald drunk and disorderly, *WH*, 22 June 1887 p. 2.
10. *TH*, 6 June 1855 p. 2, 19 September 1855 p. 1, 27 September 1856 p. 2; *Colonist*, 2 April 1858 p. 2, 21 May 1858 p. 1, 22 June 1858 p. 2; *NEx*, 26 May 1858 p. 2, 26 February 1859 p. 2.
11. *DSX*, 17 February 1872 p. 2, 25 September 1872 p. 3, 3 October 1872 p. 1, 8 October 1872

p. 1; *AS*, 25 September 1872 pp. 2–3, 29 October 1872 p. 3, 22 January 1873 p. 2, 20 May 1873 p. 3; *SMH*, 17 July 1873 p. 6, 30 December 1876 p. 15, 12 January 1877 p. 15, 7 January 1885 p. 11; JMacR, 'Auckland House and Mrs Cazaly', Manly Library Local Studies Blog: http://manlylocalstudies.blogspot.com/2013/09/auckland-house-and-mrs-cazaly.html

12. *Bolton* passenger list 1840; *WI*, 23 April 1851 p. 2, 13 August 1853 p. 4, 14 August 1869 5, *NZSCSG*, 27 May 1854 p. 3; William Garnett Taunton, *The Tauntons of Oxford* (London: Elliot Stock, 1902), pp. 9, 53.
13. *Western Australian Times* (Perth, 1874–1879), 25 August 1876 p. 3, 17 October 1876 p. 2; *Herald* (WA), 14 December 1872 p. 3; *The Inquirer and Commercial News*, 3 April 1872 p. 3.
14. *Western Australian Times* (Perth, 1874–1879), 30 August 1878 p. 2, 27 December 1878 p. 2, 7 January 1879 p. 2; *Herald* (WA), 27 December 1878 p. 2, 7 January 1879 p. 2; *Western Mail*, 21 September 1933 p. 10; Frederick William Hurst, 'Diaries', Brigham Young University (Utah): Selected material from the Archives of the Mormon Experience, [c. 1826] – 1918, MS-Group-0075, MS-Papers-4294-17 ATL, p. 7, April 1877 pp. 54, 203, 245, 246, also available at: http://joyceholt.com/FWHurst/download.html, 1880 United States Census, Familysearch.
15. Anon., 'Liardet, Wilbraham Frederick Evelyn (1799–1878)', Australian Dictionary of Biographies: http://adb.anu.edu.au/biography/liardet-wilbraham-frederick-evelyn-2358/text3087; see also Michael Hiscock, 'Wilbraham Frederick Evelyn Liardet: Romantic visionary of the beach 1839–62', *La Trobe Journal* 54, March 1995.
16. 'An Account of a Revolution in China 1854 by Josephine Liardet-Venables-Macdonald', typescript, MS-Papers 6304-2, ATL.
17. *The Argus*, 10 December 1859 p. 1, 16 August 1862 p. 3.
18. *The Argus*, 12 January 1864 p. 4; *WI*, 22 February 1868 p. 6; *Stevens and Bartholomew's New Zealand Directory, 1867–68* (Melbourne: G. Stevens and D.H. Bartholomew, 1867–68); 'Liardet Street', Kete New Plymouth: http://ketenewplymouth.peoplesnetworknz.info/site/topics/show/806-liardet-street-dn-24102009
19. *WCT*, 10 October 1867, 15 October 1867.
20. *WCT*, 11 March 1868 p. 1; *GRA*, 8 November 1870 p. 3, 27 May 1871 p. 3, 9 August 1873 p. 3.
21. *EP*, 29 September 1879 p. 2.
22. *EP*, 5 January 1901 p. 2, 14 January 1901 p. 6; *Dominion*, 21 May 1909 p. 6; Louisa Chant NZ Probate 1909.
23. *EP*, 5 June 1916 p. 9, 20 August 1928 p. 1; she also organised a sale for the Commercial Travellers and Warehousemen's Blind Soldiers and Sailors Fund in 1921, *EP*, 25 November 1921 p. 8.
24. *SMH*, 20 October 1860 p. 8; *NEM*, 2 August 1866 p. 2.
25. Charles Flood Insolvency 1860, 13654/5143, SLNSW.
26. *Colonist*, 2 March 1866 p. 4; *NEM*, 13 April 1866 p. 1.
27. *NEM*, 27 April 1866 p. 1; *Empire*, 6 April 1866 p. 1; *SMH*, 17 December 1866 p. 8.
28. *NEM*, 23 April 1866 pp. 1, 4.
29. *NEM*, 11 February 1867 p. 2; *GRA*, 4 August 1866 p. 3.
30. 'Mrs Charles Flood, Nelson, to Knowles – 21 May 1867 – requesting an answer to a previously made proposition about bringing female domestic servants into the province [and enclosures]', Wellington Provincial Government: General inwards letters and letters from the Commissioner of Crown Lands and the general government 1867, WP. 3 21/258, Archives NZ, Wellington.
31. *NEM*, 31 August 1867 p. 2, 5 September 1867 p. 2.

32. *SMH*, 17 December 1866 p. 8.
33. *SMH*, 12 May 1870 p. 1.
34. *NEM*, 13 March 1868 p. 3; 'Insolvency Index Compiled from NRS 13656 Supreme Court Insolvency Index 1842–87': www.records.nsw.gov.au/archives/collections-and-research/guides-and-indexes/bankruptcy-and-insolvency/indexes
35. Jill Weeks, 'Susannah Napier – Her Story', *Wesleyan Historical Society Journal* 61, 1994, pp. 46–47.
36. *DSX*, 2 January 1855 p. 2; *NZer*, 5 November 1856 p. 2, 29 August 1857 p. 1.
37. *DSX*, 19 November 1861 p. 3; *NZer*, 28 September 1859 p. 2, 4 January 1862 p. 2.
38. *NZH*, 6 November 1869, 6 February 1895.
39. Celia Manson, *Widow of Thorndon Quay: Part 2 of the story of a New Zealand family* (Wellington: Pigeon Press, 1981); Hugo Manson, 'Dougherty, Sarah', DNZB: www.teara.govt.nz/en/biographies/1d18/dougherty-sarah; Joan Druett, *Petticoat Whalers: Whaling wives at sea, 1820–1920* (Auckland: Collins, 1991); Bishop, 'Women on the move'; Desley Deacon, 'Location! Location! Location!: Mind maps and theatrical circuits in Australian transnational history', *History Australia* 5, no. 3, 2008, pp. 81.1–81.16.
40. Gary Danvers, 'Countess of Seafield: The painting': http://web.archive.org/web/20091021160749/http://geocities.com/garydanvers/CoS-painting.html
41. *Press*, 20 September 1864 p. 5; *LT*, 23 February 1865 p. 4; *HBH*, 24 June 1865 p. 1, 11 July 1865 p. 2, 23 September 1865 p. 1; *Colonist*, 10 July 1866 p. 2; Catherine S. Greenwood to Sir Donald McLean, 24 August 1866, Inward Letters, MS Papers 032 0301, ATL.
42. *DSX*, 26 October 1855 p. 2, 18 December 1855 p. 2; *Empire*, 30 September 1854 p. 4; *SMH*, 23 May 1855 p. 1; *Bendigo Advertiser*, 9 June 1857 p. 3.
43. Dorothy's sister-in-law Elizabeth was already in Nelson. She and husband Thomas had arrived in New Zealand in 1840, but Thomas had tragically drowned on a survey party in 1841. Elizabeth had been a housekeeper in Wellington but in 1844 married James Ladley in Nelson.
44. Jill Davison, Auckland, extensive family tree material, pers. comm.; Doreen King, John Tomkies: http://johntomkies.sites.simplehost.co.nz/Tompkins_family.html; http://johntomkies.sites.simplehost.co.nz/Gretton.html
45. Robert Porter Welch, 'Three letters written by Dr Robert Porter Welch from Wairarapa, New Zealand, in 1874 and 1875, to his brother John in England', 1874–75, p. 4, 06–144, Wairarapa Archive, Masterton; Robert Porter Welch, *The Married Woman's Advisor and Young Mother's Guide* (London: W. Grigg, 1838).
46. *SMH*, 13 June 1848 p. 2, 15 January 1852 p. 2; Welch, 'Three letters' p. 4; Charles Rooking Carter, *Life and Recollections of a New Zealand Colonist*, vol. II (London: R. Madley, 1866), p. 128, ENZB.
47. *LT*, 27 May 1854 p. 3.
48. Welch, *The Married Woman's Advisor*, p. 1; he had already written several books, including *Ten Minutes' Advice to Invalids in Search of Health Abroad* and a collection, *Songs, Ballads and Rhymes* (Sydney: T. Trood, 1841).
49. *The Australian*, 31 May 1826 p. 2; *Colonial Times* (Hobart), 23 January 1829 p. 3.
50. Welch, 'Three letters', pp. 9–10; 'Welch, Helen (Mrs) Receipt for dancing lessons in C.A. Vallance – Accounts and Receipts – T-Z', Levin & Company Ltd Records, 1860, 5/17/21, MS Papers 1347, ATL; *WI*, 15 September 1858 p. 2, 15 July 1859 p. 6, 17 August 1865 p. 4, 28 July 1873 p. 3, 21 March 1874 p. 4; *HBH*, 23 March 1861 p. 7, 1 November 1862 p. 4, 20 June 1863

p. 2, 22 July 1863 p. 1; *Waikato Times*, 4 July 1874 p. 2, 19 March 1881 p. 4; *TA*, 17 June 1876 p. 2; *AS*, 4 July 1882 p. 3, 11 July 1885 p. 7.

51. See also the example of Mary Elizabeth Small, who moved from Sydney to Canterbury to escape her husband. Her story was immortalised in Elsie Locke's *The Runaway Settlers: An historical novel* (London: Jonathan Cape, 1965).
52. Porter et al., *My Hand Will Write*, pp. 418–19.
53. Carla Massi, *Babingtons: I Primi 125 Anni. La storia del tè a Roma* (Rome: Babingtons, 2018); 'Babingtons': www.babingtons.com/en; *OW*, 26 March 1902 p. 71, 16 April 1902 p. 60, 17 September 1902 p. 60.
54. East and Fordham, 'The story of Sophia, or how we happen to be here', MS Papers 2855, ATL; *NZG*, 18 June 1842 p 2; Francis Low, *The City of Sydney Directory for 1844–45* (Sydney: Francis Low, 1845); Francis Low, *Low's Directory of the City and District of Sydney for 1847* (Sydney: F. Low, 1847); NSWBDM. See also Jenny Robin Jones, *No Simple Passage: The journey of the 'London' to New Zealand, 1842: A ship of hope* (Auckland: Random House, 2011), p. 112, although in this version Amelia meets her husband in Wellington.
55. G.H. Sutherland, 'Masters, Joseph', DNZB: www.teara.govt.nz/en/biographies/1m23/masters-joseph
56. *Hobart Town Courier*, 15 May 1835 p. 4; *Colonial Times*, 12 May 1835 p. 6. See also *The Morning Star and Commercial Advertiser*, 12 May 1835 p. 2.
57. Joseph Masters and Ian Fraser Grant, *The Memoirs of Joseph Masters: Founder of small farm settlements for the 'small man'* (Masterton: Wairarapa Archive, 2005).
58. *DSX*, 22 January 1858 p. 2, 30 July 1858 p. 1.
59. Kent Blackmore, 'Monsieur Philippe de Barr': www.sydneymagic.net/HISTORY/DE_BARR/de_barr.html; *Goulburn Herald*, 24 August 1859 p. 4; *Queanbeyan Age*, 15 August 1867 p. 3, 29 July 1869 p. 1; *Sydney Mail*, 17 August 1867 p. 4; *ODT*, 19 September 1867 p. 5.
60. *DSX*, 17 January 1860 p. 2.
61. *DSX*, 28 August 1862 p. 3, 15 April 1863 p. 1, 28 April 1863 p. 1; *TS*, 14 March 1889 p. 2; *SMH*, 8 March 1889 p. 4.
62. *TA*, 9 July 1874 p. 2; 'William Henry Reed', Early New Zealand Photographers: www.canterburyphotography.blogspot.com/2013/10/reed-william-henry.html
63. *AS*, 15 April 1886 p. 2.
64. *TS*, 22 January 1878 p. 2.
65. *TA*, 8 December 1877 p. 3.
66. *TS*, 14 March 1889 p. 2; *NZH*, 20 March 1889 p. 4; 'E-02 Education: Native schools', *AJHS*, Parliamentary Papers, 1884, Session 1: https://paperspast.natlib.govt.nz/parliamentary
67. *SMH*, 22 December 1887 p. 14, 8 March 1889 p. 4, 14 March 1889 p. 5, 24 April 1889 p. 11; *Observer*, 30 September 1893 p. 7.
68. *The Argus*, 7 August 1885 p. 7; *SMH*, 8 March 1889 p. 4.
69. Seventy-three reports in 29 papers across five colonies in Trove and 51 reports in 22 papers in Papers Past.
70. *SMH*, 14 March 1889 p. 5.
71. For Harriet's Australian adventures see Bishop, *Minding Her Own Business.*
72. *SMH*, 15 March 1901 p. 4.
73. Miles Fairburn, *The Ideal Society and its Enemies* (Auckland: Auckland University Press, 1989).

Chapter 13: Forgetting and Remembering

1. Catherine Bishop, 'Spinks Cottage: Heritage, history and use', in Annabel Cooper, Angela Wanhalla & Lachlan Paterson (eds), *The Lives of Colonial Objects* (Dunedin: Otago University Press, 2015), pp. 75–80; 'St John's in the City Presbyterian Church: Church complex': www.stjohnsinthecity.org.nz/about/complex.htm; George Macmorran, *Some Schools and Schoolmasters of Early Wellington* (Wellington: S. & W. Mackay, 1900), p. 71; *Wellington Almanack, Directory, Calendar and Diary for 1878* (Wellington: New Zealand Times Co Ltd, 1878); *EP*, 1 August 1908 p. 6; 'BNZ Share Register 1861–1863', Ac No 3968 [20], BNZ Archives, Wellington; Jane Anderson née Spinks, 'Diary 1861–62', 12 February 1861, MSX-7831, MS Group 1538, ATL. Florence Mary and Sarah Ellen Jane Spinks were known as Florence and Jane.
2. The diary has recently been donated to the National Library.
3. *Colonist*, 11 August 1883 p. 3.
4. *ODT*, 1 December 1882 p. 1 (supplement), 18 June 1918 p. 4; *ES*, 13 May 1884 p. 2, 18 June 1918 p. 4; David Murray, 'Matilda Ritchie's Building': https://builtindunedin.com/2015/04/28/matilda-ritchies-building/
5. Margaret Anderson and Kylie Winkworth, 'Museums and gender: An Australian critique', *Museum* 171, 43, no. 3, 1991, pp. 147–51 (147).
6. See Tanya Evans, 'The use of memory and material culture in the history of the family in colonial Australia', *Journal of Australian Studies* 36, no. 2, June 2012, pp. 207–28 (esp. 209); Elise Weinstein Dintsman, 'Tattered cloth tells more: Women's work and museum representation', PhD thesis, University of Toronto, 2012; a counter example is 'Australian Dress Register', Powerhouse Museum: www.australiandressregister.org
7. See 'Tree transformed into pioneer statue', *Western Bay of Plenty District Council News*, 28 December 2011: www.westernbay.govt.nz/Council/News/Media/Tree-transformed-into-pioneer-statue/; South Canterbury GenWeb, 'Churches at Cave, South Canterbury, New Zealand': www.rootsweb.ancestry.com/~nzlscant/cavechurches.htm; Thomas Davis Burnett, *St David's Pioneer Memorial Church: Cave, South Canterbury* (Timaru: The Timaru Herald, 1967, originally published in 1930); Emily H. Siedeberg McKinnon and Irene L. Starr, *Otago Pioneer Women's Memorial: Being a brief history of the foundation of a memorial building dedicated to the pioneer women of Otago to serve the interests of present and future generations of women and organised societies in civic welfare; founded 1939* (Dunedin: Otago Daily Times and Witness Newspaper, 1939): www.dunedin.govt.nz/your-council/dunedin-history/memorials/pioneer-womens-memorial-building; Katie Pickles, 'Naturalising Nightingale in the Ashburton Domain', in Annabel Cooper, Angela Wanhalla & Lachlan Paterson (eds), *The Lives of Colonial Objects* (Dunedin: Otago University Press, 2015), 236–41.
8. Margaret Long, 'Memorials to Emily McWilliam', *Otaki Historical Journal* 21, 1998, pp. 50–53; Rex Kerr, *Not Only Te Rauparaha and Hadfield, but also …* (Otaki: Black Pony Books, 2016), pp. 92–93.
9. For example, Hinemoa sits beside Lake Rotorua, waiting for her lover Tūtānekai. See also the statue of Tainui at Virginia Lake, Whanganui.
10. Charlotte Parkinson, 'Reminiscences of Mrs Parkinson', pp. 1–2, 89/140, AWWM, p. 1; Emma Frances Adams, 'Our first 12 years in New Zealand from 1860–1872', 1937, pp. 11–13, 92/26, AWMM; Janice C. Mogford, 'George, Elizabeth', DNZB: www.teara.govt.nz/en/biographies/1g7/george-elizabeth; Janice C. Mogford, 'Yates, Elizabeth', DNZB: www.teara.

govt.nz/en/biographies/2y1/yates-elizabeth; Janice C. Mogford, 'Furley, Matilda', DNZB: www.teara.govt.nz/en/biographies/1f20/furley-matilda

11. *NEx*, 14 November 1857 p. 1 (supplement).
12. *NZH*, 25 July 1871 p. 3; Burgess Rolls for the City of Auckland Database 1872–1892, Auckland City Council Archives: http://www.aucklandcity.govt.nz/dbtw-wpd/CityArchives/FamilyHistory/ACC396/searchburgessrolls.htm. After 42 years of marriage Louisa Macmahon/McMahon owned substantial property and went to court to protect it from her problematic husband Francis. *AS*, 3 October 1877 p. 2.
13. *TH*, 11 October 1879 p. 4, 13 November 1880 p. 3.
14. 'Application to be placed on Burgess Roll–Matilda Meech 15 July 1885', Early correspondence Wellington City Council Town Clerk's Department, 00233:12:1885/787; 1185 Burgess List 00296_0_11, p. 147, Wellington City Council Archives; 'The Burgess Roll', *Cyclopedia of New Zealand Wellington Provincial District*: http://nzetc.victoria.ac.nz/tm/scholarly/tei-Cyc01Cycl-t1-body-d4-d11-d10.html
15. 'Katherine Florence Gill's Bible and christening gown', Ross Goldfields Information and Heritage Centre, Ross, New Zealand.
16. 'Byrne Family Butchery Site – 1896', Site no. 4, Heritage Golden Bay, Takaka. In an indication of the difficulties of such memorialisation, recent research by Heritage Golden Bay suggests that the butcher's shop was located on the east side of Commercial Street next to Brown and Kerr jeweller and near the corner with Motupipi Street. I am grateful to Sally Gaffney of Heritage Golden Bay and the Byrne family for sharing their research.
17. Gareth Winter, 'Remarkable story of settler siblings', *Wairarapa Times-Age*, 7 January 2016; *WI*, 4 August 1864 p. 2.
18. Heritage New Zealand, 'Hayes Engineering Works and homestead': www.heritage.org.nz/places/places-to-visit/otago-region/hayes-engineering; see also Heritage New Zealand, 'Clendon House': www.heritage.org.nz/places/places-to-visit/northland-region/clendon-house
19. *TS*, 20 January 1875 p. 2, 26 March 1881 p. 3, 25 September 1883 p. 3, 23 September 1884 p. 3, 2 November 1885 p. 3, 4 March 1886 p. 2, 21 June 1888 p. 2, 22 November 1893 p. 2; *TA*, 10 March 1875 p. 3, 28 April 1877 p. 3, 8 May 1877 p. 3, 6 July 1877 p. 3, 31 January 1882 p. 2, 27 December 1882 p. 2; 'In the matter of the estate of Mary Ann Simpson', Lunacy case files, AAAR 25135 246/339, Archives NZ, Wellington. I am grateful to Debbie Macauley and Althea Barker for their assistance.
20. Raewyn Dalziel, 'The colonial helpmeet: Women's role and the vote in nineteenth-century New Zealand', *New Zealand Journal of History* 11, 1977, p. 65.
21. TNS Business Finance Monitor 2011–2013; survey commissioned by ANZ: https://bizhub.anz.co.nz/resources/women-in-business-infographic.aspx
22. 'Proportion of women in senior management roles has hit rock bottom': www.grantthornton.co.nz/press/press-releases-2018/proportion-of-women-in-nz-senior-leadership-roles-has-hit-rock-bottom/ – based on Grant Thornton International Women in Business Report.

Bibliography

Primary sources

ARCHIVES

Alexander Turnbull Library (ATL)

Abraham, Caroline H., Papers, MS Papers–2305–2

Adams, Martha, Journal, transcription, 1850–52, MS 0006

Anderson nee Spinks, Jane, Diary 1861–62, 12 February 1861, MSX–7831, MS Group 1538

Campbell, Jessie, 'Extracts from the letters of Jessie Campbell to her family from Petone and Wanganui 1841–45', typescript, qMS–0369

Dillon, Constantine Augustus, Papers, MS–0685

East, Alice, 'The story of Sophia or how we happen to be here', edited by C.E. Fordham, MS Papers 2855

Greenwood Family, Letters, qMS–0887

Greenwood Family, Papers, 1843–1880, MS–Papers–0098–14 (MS–Copy–Micro–0194–2)

Hurst, Frederick William, Diaries, Brigham Young University (Utah): Selected material from the Archives of the Mormon Experience [c. 1826]–1918, MS–Group–0075, MS–Papers–4294–17

Levin and Company Ltd, Records, MS–Papers–1347

Macdonald, Josephine, 'An account of a revolution in China 1854 by Josephine Liardet-Venables-Macdonald', typescript, MS–Papers 6304–2

Macdonald, Julie Ann, 'The pot of gold: Christison biography', New Zealand Society of Genealogists 1990 Sesquicentennial Family Biography Competition Collection, Folder 034, MS Papers 4280

Mackie, Frederick, Journal, vol. 1, 1852–1854, MS 0865

McKain, Douglas Mary, Diary and Commonplace Book, 1841–1872, transcribed by J.B. Moles, MS–Papers–7262

McLean Inward Letters, A. & J. Boughton, 12 Letters from Adeno [sic] Boughton and his wife Jane, 1868–1872 to Donald McLean, MS–Papers–0032–0167

McLean Inward Letters, Gilbert Pickett to Donald McLean, 3 August 1871, Object #1006285, MS–Papers–0032–0503

Pratt Family, Correspondence Outward, MS Papers 0229–2

Ralfe, Catherine, 'Life in New Zealand', MS Papers 1129

Smith, John Sidney, 1808–1880: Account Book, qMS 1826

Story, Edith Mary, 'Our fathers have told us', qMS 1898–1899

Wall Collection, MS–Papers–1739

Archives New Zealand (Archives NZ)

Discharged Mortgages – North Auckland, 10103, Archives NZ, Auckland

'Mrs Charles Flood, Nelson, to Knowles – 21 May 1867 – Requesting an Answer to a Previously Made Proposition About Bringing Female Domestic Servants into the Province [and Enclosures]', Wellington Provincial Government: General Inwards Letters and Letters from the Commissioner of Crown Lands and the General Government 1867, WP3 21/258, Archives NZ, Wellington

Nelson Census Returns, January 1845, SSD 3 1/1, Micro 3632 Repro 56, Archives NZ, Wellington
Nelson returns for the year 1849, SSD 3/2 Part 1, Micro 6892, Archives NZ, Wellington
Nelson: Schedule of nominated passengers for whom a guarantee of payment has been made 1855–1862 and 1872', ACFT 8249 IM–N4/1/1, Archives NZ ,Wellington
Probate Records, 1843–1998, (NZ Probate) multiple series, digitised at www.familysearch.org
'Return of all the houses, cottages and warries with the names of their owners and occupiers in the district of Auckland 1845', IA1, 1845/1939, Microfilm 3630,5070, Repro 70, Archives NZ, Auckland
Supreme Court – Lunacy Case File No L102 – Elizabeth Keates, wife of Timothy Keates, DAAC D140 Box 270, Archives NZ, Dunedin
William Lyall – Superintendent Province of Wellington 23 January 1860, old reference: WP Series2 60/47, now Inwards Letters 26 November 1855–24 October 1876, ACIA 16194 WP2 1, Archives NZ, Wellington

Auckland War Memorial Museum (AWMM)
Adams, Emma Frances, 'Our first 12 years in New Zealand from 1860–1872', 1937, 92/26
Bradey, Papers relating to the Bradey Family, MS 91/61
Caldwell, Elizabeth, Diary of Mrs E.P. Caldwell, MS91
Newman, Caroline, Letter 7 December 1855, MS 483
Northern Assurance Company Auckland Agency, Fire Policy Copybook 1855–1866, MF–331
Olson Family, Letters from Members of Olson Family, MS229
Parkinson, Charlotte, Reminiscences of Mrs Parkinson, 89/140

Nelson Provincial Museum (NPM)
Anstice, Herbert, Profile, qMS GRA
Cole, W.H., 'Birds-eye view of the early days in Nelson, New Zealand 1842–48' [c. 1970], Copy of drawing, AC833, Bett Loan Collection
Sinclair, Rebecca Lee, 'A few recollections of my early life in Nelson', July 1932, Hodgson Family collection, NRAMB400

Bank archives
BNZ Share Register 1861–1863, Ac No 3968 [20], BNZ Archives, Wellington
Current Account Ledger, Nelson 1858, Union Bank of Australia, ANZ Archives, Wellington
NZ Bank of New South Wales Current Account Ledger Books, Auckland 1861, 1862–63, Westpac Archives, Wellington

State Library of New South Wales, Sydney (SLNSW)
Female Middle Class Emigration Society (FMCES), Letterbooks nos 1 and 2, 1862–1882, Fawcett Library Collections, microfilmed by the Australian Joint Copying Project, M2291–2314
Townsend, Joseph Phipps, Papers, MLMSS 1461

State Records of New South Wales, Sydney (SRNSW)
Insolvency Index Compiled from NRS 13656 Supreme Court Insolvency Index 1842–87: www.records.nsw.gov.au/archives/collections-and-research/guides-and-indexes/bankruptcy-and-insolvency/indexes
Probate Packets NRS 13660
Supreme Court Insolvency Records NRS 13654

Newspaper archives

British Newspaper Archive: www.britishnewspaperarchive.co.uk

California Digital News Collection: https://cdnc.ucr.edu/cgi-bin/cdnc

Papers Past: https://paperspast.natlib.govt.nz/newspapers

Trove: www.trove.nla.gov.au

Miscellaneous archives

Bartley, Elizabeth, 'Early reminiscences of Auckland', NZ MS 1051, Sir George Grey Special Collections, Auckland Public Library, also available at http://localhistorybartley.blogspot.com.au/p/early-reminiscences-of-auckland-by-mrs-e.html

Burgess Rolls for the City of Auckland Database 1872–92, Auckland City Archives: www.aucklandcity.govt.nz/dbtw-wpd/CityArchives/FamilyHistory/ACC396/searchburgessrolls.htm

Burke, William Ellison, Burke Manuscript, Christchurch City Libraries: http://christchurchcitylibraries.com/Heritage/Digitised/Burke/

Fisher, Paul Hawkins, Old Gloucestershire Diary, possibly by Paul Hawkins Fisher: www.johnhearfield.com/Dir/OldGlosDiary_home.htm

Hannken, Philip, 'Reminiscences of Auckland 1858–1880': http://localhistorybartley.blogspot.com.au/2014/08/new-heritage-rating-in-lower-queen-st.html

Lowten, Certified Copy of an Entry of Marriage Lowten Lowten and Lucy Catherine Foley, 1882, West Derby: General Register Office

Macdonald, George Ranald, G.R. Macdonald Dictionary of Canterbury (Macdonald Dictionary), Biographies: https://collection.canterburymuseum.com/persons/10767

Old Bailey, Proceedings: www.oldbaileyonline.org/browse.jsp?div=t18560407-438

Royal Philanthropic Farm School Redhill, Admissions 1788–1906: www.geni.com/projects/Royal-Philanthropic-Farm-School-Redhill-Admissions-1788-1906/17360

Ryan, A.A., 'Photograph of Lake Rotorua – after eruption June 10 1886', C.010233, Photography Collection: https://collections.tepapa.govt.nz/object/20227

Webster, John–G.F. Russell, Correspondence, NZMS 4/19, Sir George Grey Special Collections, Auckland Public Library

Welch, Robert Porter, 'Three letters written by Dr Robert Porter Welch from Wairarapa, New Zealand, in 1874 and 1875, to his brother John in England, 1874–75', 06–144, Wairarapa Archive, Masterton

Wellington City Rates Books, 1863–70, Series 00162 and 1870–1975, Series 00163, Wellington City Council Archives

Whanganui Museum Founders Index, Whanganui Regional Museum Archives

Wilson–Ross Family History compiled c. 1936, private collection Geoff Bremner, London

Official records

Census of England and Wales (UK Census): www.freecen.org.uk; Familysearch: www.familysearch.org; and Ancestry: www.ancestry.com

Census of New Zealand 1871–81 (NZ Census): http://archive.stats.govt.nz/browse_for_stats/snapshots-of-nz/digitised-collections/census-collection.aspx

New South Wales Births Deaths and Marriages index (NSWBDM): https://familyhistory.bdm.nsw.gov.au

New Zealand Acts As Enacted, New Zealand Legal Information Institute (NZLII): www.nzlii.org

New Zealand Births Deaths and Marriages (NZBDM): www.bdmhistoricalrecords.dia.govt.nz/Home/

New Zealand Parliamentary Papers: https://paperspast.natlib.govt.nz/parliamentary
New South Wales Legislation As Made: www.legislation.nsw.gov.au
Statistics of New Munster 1841–48: http://archive.stats.govt.nz/browse_for_stats/snapshots-of-nz/digitised-collections/19th-century-collection.aspx
Statistics of New Zealand for 1861: www3.stats.govt.nz/historic_publications/1861-statistics-nz/1861-statistics-nz.html#idsect2_1_1546
UK Births Deaths and Marriages (UKBDM): www.freebmd.org.uk and Familysearch: www.familysearch.org

Genealogical and museum websites (electoral rolls, passenger lists etc)
Ancestry: www.ancestry.com
Australharmony, George Skinner: http://sydney.edu.au/paradisec/australharmony/index.php
Australian Dress Register, Powerhouse Museum: www.australiandressregister.org
Early New Zealand Books (ENZB): www.enzb.auckland.ac.nz
Find a Grave: www.findagrave.com
Find My Past: www.findmypast.com
Geni: www.geni.com/home
Kete Horowhenua: http://horowhenua.kete.net.nz
Kete New Plymouth: http://ketenewplymouth.peoplesnetworknz.info
Libraries Tasmania, 'Tasmanian Name Index': https://librariestas.ent.sirsidynix.net.au/client/en_AU/names/
Moorfield, John C., Te Aka Online Māori Dictionary, 2003–2019: https://maoridictionary.co.nz
Nelson Provincial Museum, 'Early Settlers' (for Nelson until 1850): www.museumnp.org.nz/early-settlers/
New Zealand Electronic Text Collection (NZETC): http://nzetc.victoria.ac.nz/
New Zealand Yesteryears: www.yesteryears.co.nz
Ngaio Press Passenger Arrivals at Port Chalmers (for Dunedin 1848–51): www.ngaiopress.com/drhocken.htm
South Australian Passenger Lists 1838: www.slsa.sa.gov.au/BSA/ShipLists%20Alpha%20by%20Year/1838A-F.htm
Wells, Denise and Peter Abbott, 'Denise and Peter Ourstuff': http://freepages.genealogy.rootsweb.ancestry.com/~ourstuff
Wikitree: www.wikitree.com

DIRECTORIES

Chapman's New Zealand Almanac, for Leap Year 1860 (Auckland: George T. Chapman, 1860)
Ford's Sydney Commercial Directory for the Year 1851 (Sydney: W. & F. Ford, 1851)
Laurance's Auckland Registry Office Almanac for 1860 (Auckland: G.R. Laurance, 1860)
Low's Directory of the City and District of Sydney for 1847 (Sydney: F. Low, 1847)
Lucas's Nelson Almanac and Year-Book, 1869 and 1874, (Nelson: R. Lucas & Son, 1869, 1874)
Melbourne Directories online, University of Melbourne: https://omeka.cloud.unimelb.edu.au/melbourne-history/exhibits/show/melbournedirectories/browsemelbournedirectories
Stevens and Bartholomew's New Zealand Directory, 1866–67 and 1867–68 (Melbourne: G. Stevens and D.H. Bartholomew, 1866–67, 1867–68)

The Auckland Almanack and Directory, 1856 (Auckland: W. Lambert, 1856)
The City of Sydney Directory for 1844–45 (Sydney: Francis Low, 1845)
The Royal New Zealand Almanack and Commercial Calendar for 1859 (Wellington: George Watson, 1859)
The Southern Provinces Almanac, Directory and Year Book (Lyttelton: Lyttelton Times Office, 1868)
The Wellington Almanack and Diary 1866 (Wellington: T. McKenzie, 1866)
The Wellington Almanack Directory Calendar and Diary for the Year 1871 (Wellington: Thomas McKenzie, 1871)
The Wellington Almanack for the Year of Our Lord 1853 (Wellington: Wellington Independent, 1853)
The Wellington Almanack, Directory, Calendar and Diary for 1878 (Wellington: New Zealand Times Co Ltd, 1878)
UK directories online, Historical Directories of England and Wales, University of Leicester: http://specialcollections.le.ac.uk/cdm/landingpage/collection/p16445coll4

CONTEMPORARY BOOKS AND PAMPHLETS

Asiatic Journal and Monthly Miscellany (London: William H. Allen & Co, 1840)
Bell, John, *A Treatise on Baths*, 1859, Smithsonian Museum: http://americanhistory.si.edu/collections/object-groups/portable-bathtubs-tub-bathing-from-the-early-19th-and-20th-centuries
Blackstone, William, *Commentaries on the Laws of England*, vol. 1 (Oxford: Clarendon Press, 1765)
Cyclopedia of New Zealand Wellington Provincial District (Wellington: The Cyclopedia Company Limited, 1897)
Cyclopedia of New Zealand Otago and Southland Provincial Districts (Christchurch: The Cyclopedia Company Ltd, 1905)
Carter, Charles Rooking, *Life and Recollections of a New Zealand Colonist*, vol. II (London: R. Madley, 1866)
D'Urban, William Samuel Mitchell, Murray Alexander Mathew, John Gerrard Keulemans, *The Birds of Devon* (London: R.H. Porter, 1892)
Dickens, Charles (ed.), *Household Words* (London: Bradbury and Evans, 1850–59)
'Emigrant voices from New Zealand', in William and Robert Chambers, *Chambers Edinburgh Journal*, no. 257, 2 December 1848
Earp, G.B., *Hand-Book for Intending Emigrants to the Southern Settlements of New Zealand*, 2nd edn (London: W.S. Orr & Co, 1849)
George, Frances Shayle, *Education of Girls* (Auckland: Upton & Co, 1874)
George, Frances Shayle, 'From a settler's wife', *Household Words* 4, no. 103, 13 March 1852
Godley, Charlotte, *Letters from Early New Zealand 1850–1853* (Christchurch: Whitcombe & Tombs, 1951)
Hartley, Florence, *Ladies' Book of Etiquette and Manual of Politeness* (Boston: G.W. Cottrell, 1860)
Herz, Henri, *My Travels in America* (trans. Henry Bertram Hall) (Madison: State Historical Society of Wisconsin for University of Wisconsin, 1963)
Hewett, Mrs Duff, *Looking Back or Personal Reminiscences by the Widow of a New Zealand Pioneer Settler* (Auckland: H.L. Thatcher, 1925, first published 1911)
Hursthouse, Charles, *New Zealand, or Zealandia, the Britain of the South*, vol. II (London: Edward Stanford, 1857)

Letters from Settlers & Labouring Emigrants in the New Zealand Company's Settlements of Wellington, Nelson, & New Plymouth, from February, 1842, to January, 1843 (London: Smith, Elder & Co, 1843)

Lohse, Johanna, *Mistaken Views on the Education of Girls* (Christchurch: Whitcombe & Tombs, 1884)

Marks, Marcus, *Memories (Mainly Merry) of Marcus Marks* (Sydney: Endeavour Press, 1934)

Murdoch, Fanny, *Dainties, or, How to Please our Lords and Master* (Napier: Dinwiddie, Walker & Co, 1887)

Sadleir, John, *Recollections of a Victorian Police Officer* (Melbourne: George Robertson & Co, 1913)

Sidney, Samuel, *Female Emigration As It Is – As It May Be: A letter to the Right Honorable Sidney Herbert, MP: With an appendix* (London: William S. Orr, 1850)

Taunton, William Garnett, *The Tauntons of Oxford* (London: Elliot Stock, 1902)

Taylor, Mary, *Miss Miles, or, a Tale of Yorkshire Life 60 Years Ago, with an introduction by Janet H. Murray* (New York: Oxford University Press, 1990, first published 1890)

Taylor, Mary, *The First Duty of Women: A series of articles reprinted from the Victoria Magazine, 1865 to 1870* (London: Emily Faithfull, 1870)

Terry, Charles, *New Zealand: Its advantages and prospects as a British colony* (London: T. and W. Boone, 1842)

Thomson, Mrs Charles, *Twelve Years in Canterbury, New Zealand, with Visits to the Other Provinces, and Reminiscences of the Route Home through Australia etc. (from a Lady's Journal)* (London: Sampson Low, Son and Marston, 1867?)

von Haast, Julius, *Geology of the Provinces of Canterbury and Westland, New Zealand: A report comprising the results of official explorations* (Christchurch, 1879)

Waddell, Rutherford, D.P. Fisher and Colin Allan, *Addendum to the 1890 Sweating Commission*: https://teara.govt.nz/en/photograph/25561/1890-sweating-commission

Wecker, Anna, *Köstlich new Kochbuch von allerhand Speisen …* or, *New Delightful and Useful Cookbook* (originally published 1596) (Basel: Verlag Emanuel Königs und Söhnen, 1679)

Welch, Robert Porter, *The Married Woman's Advisor and Young Mother's Guide* (London: W. Grigg, 1838)

_____, *Songs, Ballads and Rhymes* (Sydney: T. Trood, 1841)

_____, *Ten Minutes' Advice to Invalids in Search of Health Abroad* (published before 1838)

Wilson, John (ed.), *Reminiscences of the Early Settlement of Dunedin and South Otago: Dealing in the main with Clutha and neighbouring districts: Compiled from information supplied to the Clutha Pioneers' Association by early settlers, and matter taken from other sources* (Dunedin: J. Wilkie & Co Ltd, 1912)

Wood, Susan Nugent, *Woman's Work in Australia* (Melbourne: Samuel Mullen, 1862)

Woolley, Hannah, *The Queen-like Closet, or, Rich Cabinet: Stored with all manner of rare receipts for preserving, candying & cookery, very pleasant and beneficial to all ingenious persons of the female sex* (London: R. Lowndes, 1670)

Secondary Sources

Dictionary of New Zealand Biography (DNZB): https://teara.govt.nz/en/biographies

BOOKS, ARTICLES AND CHAPTERS

Adams, Marjory F.E., *A Garland from Quatt: The story of a pioneering ancestor as told by her granddaughter* (Auckland: M. Adams, 2001)

Alford, Katrina, 'Colonial women's employment as seen by nineteenth-century statisticians and twentieth-century economic historians', *Labour History* 51, 1986, 1–10

Allan, Ruth, *Nelson: A history of early settlement* (Wellington A.H. & A. W. Reed, 1965)

Amyes, Bobbie and Fiona Gray, 'It started with a painting – James Rollason', *New Zealand Genealogist* 20, no. 107, 2016

Amyes, Bobbie, 'Sergeant James William Reilly: A bit of a rogue', Dunedin Family History Group, *Irish Parents*, 2013, 33–46

Anderson, Margaret and Kylie Winkworth, 'Museums and gender: An Australian critique', *Museum* 171, 43, no. 3, 1991, 147–51

Anon., 'Liardet, Wilbraham Frederick Evelyn (1799–1878)', Australian Dictionary of Biography: http://adb.anu.edu.au/biography/liardet-wilbraham-frederick-evelyn-2358/text3087

Ashton, Jennifer, *At the Margin of Empire: John Webster and Hokianga, 1841–1900* (Auckland: Auckland University Press, 2015)

Aston, Jennifer, *Female Entrepreneurship in Nineteenth-Century England: Engagement in the urban economy* (London: Palgrave Macmillan, 2016)

Aston, Jennifer and Catherine Bishop (eds), *Female Entrepreneurs in the Long Nineteenth Century: A global perspective* (New York: Palgrave Macmillan, forthcoming)

Baker, Matiu, 'The Blenkinsop Indenture: Dirty deeds done dirt cheap!': https://blog.tepapa.govt.nz/2015/06/12/dirty-deeds-done-dirt-cheap/?fbclid=IwAR06qwT0_EpvYEgE9iE15LBumEJFiYQ-gZ8Cwx_tiSn7uny9UiVUydJEti4

Baskerville, Peter, *A Silent Revolution?: Gender and wealth in English Canada, 1860–1930* (Montreal: McGill-Queen's University Press, 2008)

Baskerville, Rachel F., *Jane Harvey and Solomon Levy: A New Zealand family* (Wellington: R.F. Baskerville, 2006)

Beard, Mary, 'The public voice of women', in *Women & Power: A manifesto* (London: Profile Books, 2017)

Bellamy, Joan, *'More Precious than Rubies': Mary Taylor: Friend of Charlotte Brontë, strong-minded woman* (Beverley: Highgate, 2002)

Bentley, Trevor, *Cannibal Jack* (Auckland: Penguin, 2010)

Betts, Jenny, *The Mitre Hotel 1849–1899* (Christchurch: Mitre Tavern Historic Trust, 1999)

Bint, Betty, 'Some early storekeepers of Waimea South', *Journal of the Nelson and Marlborough Historical Societies* 1, no. 4, 1984, 10–13

Bishop, Catherine, *Minding Her Own Business: Colonial businesswomen in Sydney* (Sydney: NewSouth, 2015)

______, 'On their own in a "man's world": Widows in business in colonial New Zealand and Australia', in Jennifer Aston and Catherine Bishop (eds), *Female Entrepreneurs in the Long Nineteenth Century: A global perspective* (New York: Palgrave Macmillan, forthcoming)

_____, 'The serendipity of connectivity: Piecing together women's lives in the digital archive', *Women's History Review* 26, no. 5, 2017, 766–80

_____, 'Spinks Cottage: Heritage, history and use', in Annabel Cooper, Angela Wanhalla & Lachlan Paterson (eds), *The Lives of Colonial Objects* (Dunedin: Otago University Press, 2015), 75–80

_____, 'When your money is not your own: Coverture and married women in business in colonial New South Wales', *Law and History Review* 33, no. 1, 2015, 181–200

_____, 'Women on the move: Gender, money-making and mobility in mid-nineteenth-century Australasia', *History Australia* 11, no. 2, 2014, 38–59

Blakeley, Katherine, 'E.B. Miller': https://nzhistory.govt.nz/suffragist/e-b-miller

Bloomfield, Gerald T., *New Zealand: A handbook of historical statistics* (Boston, Mass: G.K. Hall, 1984)

Bollinger, Conrad, *Grog's Own Country: The story of liquor licensing in New Zealand* (Auckland: Minerva, 1959, 1967)

Bones, Helen, *The Expatriate Myth: New Zealand writers and the colonial world* (Dunedin: Otago University Press, 2018)

Bowd, Lynne, 'On her own: Women as heads of family groups in the 1828 census', *Australian Historical Studies* 27, no. 107, 1996, 303–22

Bradbury, Bettina, 'Colonial comparisons: Rethinking marriage, civilisation and nation in nineteenth-century white settler societies', in P. Buckner & D. Francis (eds), *Rediscovering the British World* (Calgary: Calgary University Press, 2005)

_____, 'From civil death to separate property: Changes in the legal rights of married women in nineteenth-century New Zealand', *New Zealand Journal of History* 29, no. 1, 1995, 40–66

_____, *From Wife to Widow: Lives, laws and politics in nineteenth-century Montreal* (Vancouver: University of British Columbia Press, 2011)

_____, 'Surviving as a widow in 19th-century Montreal', *Urban History Review/Revue d'histoire urbaine* 17, no. 3, 1989, 148–60

Bradshaw, Julia, 'Adjustable marriages: Relationships, divorce and bigamy on the goldfields', *Echoes of Our Past, Proceedings of the 2018 Conference of the New Zealand Society of Genealogists*, June 2018

_____, 'Forgetting their place: Women of abandoned character on the Otago goldfields', in L. Carpenter and L. Fraser (eds), *Rushing for Gold: Life and commerce on the goldfields of New Zealand and Australia* (Dunedin: Otago University Press, 2016)

Brookes, Barbara, *A History of New Zealand Women* (Wellington: Bridget Williams Books, 2016)

Brookes, Barbara, Robin Law and Annabel Cooper, *Sites of Gender: Women, men and modernity in southern Dunedin, 1890–1939* (Auckland: Auckland University Press, 2003)

Brown, Anne D., 'Charlotte Lees Evans, 1841–1882', *Kotare* 7, no. 1, 2007

Brown, Michael, '"A piano in every other house?" The piano in New Zealand trade statistics', *New Zealand Journal of History* 51, no. 2, 2017, 26–52

Bunce, R.J., *Slippery Jim or Patriotic Statesman: James Macandrew of Otago* (Dunedin: Otago University Press, 2018)

Burleigh, Lois, *The Dixon Family in New Zealand: The first generations in 150 years* (Milton: Dixon Family Reunion Committee, 1992)

Burnett, Thomas Davis, *St David's Pioneer Memorial Church: Cave, South Canterbury* (Timaru: The Timaru Herald, 1967, first published 1930)

Burr, Valerie, 'Amos and Lydia Burr', *NZ Legacy* 2, 1990, 23–24

Burton, David, 'Cooking: Cookbooks, magazines and television shows', Te Ara: www.TeAra.govt.nz/en/cooking/page-3

Byrnes, Giselle (ed.), *The New Oxford History of New Zealand* (Melbourne: Oxford University Press, 2009)

Caradus, Alice, *Courage and Perseverance: Russell–Caradus story* (Auckland, 1975)

Carlin, Joe, *A Brief History of Entrepreneurship: The pioneers, profiteers and racketeers who shaped our world* (New York: Columbia University Press, 2016)

Carpenter, Lloyd and Lyndon Fraser (eds), *Rushing for Gold: Life and commerce on the goldfields of New Zealand and Australia* (Dunedin: Otago University Press, 2016)

Caughey, Angela, *Pioneer Families: The settlers of nineteenth-century New Zealand* (Auckland: David Bateman, 1994)

Caughley, Vivien, *New Zealand's Historic Samplers: Our stitched stories* (Auckland: David Bateman, 2014)

Chambers, Coral, *Lessons for Ladies: A social history of girls' education in Australasia, 1870–1900* (Sydney: Hale & Iremonger, 1986)

Christchurch City Council, Town Planning Division, 'Cranmer Club': www.christchurchcitylibraries.com/Heritage/Publications/ChristchurchCityCouncil/ArchitecturalHeritage/CranmerClub/CranmerClub.pdf

Christie, Nancy, 'Women in the formal and informal economies of late eighteenth-century Quebec, 1760–1820', *Gender and History* 29, no. 1, 2017, 104–23

Clarke, Alison, *Born to a Changing World: Childbirth in nineteenth-century New Zealand* (Wellington: Bridget Williams Books, 2012)

Clarke, Patricia, *The Governesses: Letters from the colonies, 1862–1882* (Melbourne: Hutchinson, 1985)

Clarke, Sandra and Neville Gilmore, 'Mata Pekamu Tamatuhiata', Wellington City Library: www.wcl.govt.nz/maori/wellington/tupunabeckham.html

Coleman, Jenny, *Polly Plum: A firm and earnest woman's advocate: Mary Ann Colclough, 1836–1885* (Dunedin: Otago University Press, 2017)

Coombs, Douglas Saxon, Anne G. Coombs and Elise Pickett, *Strangers and Pilgrims: The von Tunzelmann saga* (Dunedin: Douglas and Anne Coombs, 2006)

Cooper, Annabel, 'Poor men in the land of promises: Settler masculinity and the male breadwinner economy in late nineteenth-century New Zealand', *Australian Historical Studies* 39, 2008, 245–61

Craig, Beatrice, *Women and Business Since 1500: Invisible presences in Europe and North America?* (New York: Palgrave Macmillan, 2016)

Dakin, J.C., *Education in New Zealand* (Newton Abbot, UK: David & Charles, 1973)

Daley, Caroline, *Girls & Women, Men & Boys: Gender in Taradale 1886–1930* (Auckland: Auckland University Press, 1999)

Daley, Caroline and Deborah Montgomerie (eds), *The Gendered Kiwi* (Auckland: Auckland University Press, 1999)

Dalley, Bronwyn, 'Lolly shops "of the red light kind" and "soldiers of the king": Suppressing one-woman brothels in New Zealand 1908–1916', *New Zealand Journal of History* 30, no. 1, 1996, 3–23

_____, 'Migrant groups and the wine industry', Te Ara: www.TeAra.govt.nz/en/wine/page-2

Dalziel, Raewyn, 'The colonial helpmeet: Women's role and the vote in nineteenth-century New Zealand', *New Zealand Journal of History* 11, 1977, 112–23

_____, 'Emigration and kinship: Migrants to New Plymouth 1840–1843', *New Zealand Journal of History* 25, no. 2, 1991, 112–28

_____, 'The privileged crime: Policing and prosecuting bigamy in nineteenth-century New Zealand', *New Zealand Journal of History* 51, no. 2, 2017, 1–26

Davis, Tracy C., *Actresses as Working Women: Their social identity in Victorian culture* (London: Routledge, 1991)

Deacon, Desley, 'Location! Location! Location!: Mind maps and theatrical circuits in Australian transnational history', *History Australia* 5, no. 3, 2008, 81.1–81.16

_____, 'Political arithmetic: The nineteenth-century Australian census and the construction of the dependent woman', *Signs* 11, no. 1, 1985, 27–47

Deans, Jane, *Letters to My Grandchildren* (Christchurch: Cadsonbury Publications, 1995, first published 1923)

Dickinson, B.E. and C.T. Kidson, 'Nelson names', *Nelson Historical Journal* 2, no. 1, 1966

Dorsett, Shaunnagh, *Judicial Encounters: Māori and the colonial courts, 1840–1851* (Auckland: Auckland University Press, 2017)

Downes, Peter, *Shadows on the Stage: Theatre in New Zealand: The first 70 years* (Dunedin: J. McIndoe, 1975)

_____, *Top of the Bill: Entertainers through the years* (Wellington: A.H. & A.W. Reed, 1979)

Druett, Joan, *Petticoat Whalers: Whaling wives at sea, 1820–1920* (Auckland: Collins, 1991)

Eldred-Grigg, Stevan, *Pleasures of the Flesh: Sex and drugs in colonial New Zealand 1840–1915* (Wellington: A.H. and A.W. Reed, 1984)

Ellis, Ellen, 'A first and only for Pencarrow lighthouse', *Historic Places in New Zealand* 16, 1987

Evans, Tanya, 'The use of memory and material culture in the history of the family in colonial Australia', *Journal of Australian Studies* 36, no. 2, June 2012, 207–28

Fairburn, Miles, *The Ideal Society and its Enemies* (Auckland: Auckland University Press, 1989)

Fine, Cordelia, *Testosterone Rex: Unmaking the myths of our gendered minds* (Sydney: Allen and Unwin, 2017)

Finn, Jeremy, 'The schoolgirl and the horse-whipped parson: An account of an early New Zealand cause celebre', *Australian Journal of Legal History* 9, 2005, 1–29

Finn, Margot, 'Women, consumption and coverture in England, c. 1760–1860', *The Historical Journal* 39, no. 3, 1996, 703–22

Foote, Nicola, 'Rethinking race, gender and citizenship: Black West Indian women on the Atlantic coast of Costa Rica, c. 1920–1940', *Bulletin of Latin American Research* 23, no. 2, April 2004, 198–212

Forty, Adrian, *Objects of Desire* (New York: Pantheon Books, 1986)

Foxton Historical Society, *Pioneers of Foxton: Book one* (Foxton: Foxton Historical Society, 1988)

Fraser, Lyndon, *A Distant Shore: Irish migration & New Zealand settlement* (Dunedin: University of Otago Press, 2000)

Fraser, Lyndon and Katie Pickles (eds), *Shifting Centres: Women and migration in New Zealand history* (Dunedin: University of Otago Press, 2002)

Gamber, Wendy, *The Boardinghouse in Nineteenth-Century America* (Baltimore: Johns Hopkins University Press, 2007)

_____, *The Female Economy: The millinery and dressmaking trades, 1860–1930* (Urbana: University of Illinois Press, 1997)

_____, '"Reduced to science": Gender, technology, and power in the American dressmaking trade, 1860–1910', *Technology and Culture* 36, no. 3, 1995, 455–82

Gardner, W.J., 'A colonial economy', in W.H. Oliver (ed.), *Oxford History of New Zealand* (Wellington: Oxford University Press, 1981)

Garner, Jean and Kate Foster, *Letters to Grace: Writing home from colonial New Zealand* (Christchurch: Canterbury University Press, 2011)

Giles, Keith, 'Fairs & Steel: Their impact on Auckland photography', *New Zealand Legacy* 19, no. 3, 2007, 8–12

_____, 'Robert Leaf': www.aucklandcity.govt.nz/dbtw-wpd%5Cphotographers%5Cessays%5Cleaf.pdf

Gordon, Eleanor and Gwyneth Nair, 'The economic role of middle-class women in Victorian Glasgow', *Women's History Review* 9, no. 4, 2000, 791–814

Gosset, Robyn, *The History of Mrs Pope's Ltd* (Christchurch: Whitcoulls Ltd, 1979)

Green, David and Alistair Owens, 'Gentlewomanly capitalism? Spinsters, widows, and wealth holding in England and Wales c. 1800-1860', *Economic History Review* 3, 2003, 510–36

Greenaway, Richard L.N., *Rich Man, Poor Man, Environmentalist, Thief: Biographies of Canterbury personalities written for the millennium and for the 150th anniversary of the Canterbury settlement* (Christchurch: Canterbury Public Library, 2000)

_____, *Unsung Heroines: Biographies of Christchurch women written to commemorate women's suffrage year, 1993* (Christchurch: Canterbury Public Library, 1994)

Hammerton, A. James, *Emigrant Gentlewomen: Genteel poverty and female emigration, 1830–1914* (Canberra: Australian National University Press, 1979)

Harris, Beth (ed.), *Famine and Fashion: Needlewomen in the nineteenth century* (Ashgate: Aldershot and Burlington, 2005)

Hart, Philip, 'Hone Werahiko: The discoverer of gold at Te Aroha', *Te Aroha Mining District Working Papers* 61, rev. 7 February 2017, University of Waikato

Hickford, Paul, 'On the Wright trail: London, Melbourne, Echuca, Hokitika …', *New Zealand Genealogist* 40, no. 319, 2009, 231–34

Higgs, Edward, 'Women, occupations and work in the nineteenth-century censuses', *History Workshop* 23, 1987, 59–80

Hill, Bridget, 'Women, work and the census: A problem for historians of women', *History Workshop* 35, 1993, 78–94

Hiscock, Michael, 'Wilbraham Frederick Evelyn Liardet: Romantic visionary of the beach 1839–62', *La Trobe Journal* 54, March 1995

Holm, Janet, *Nothing but Grass and Wind: The Rutherfords of Canterbury* (Christchurch: Hazard Press, 1992)

Houltham, Garth, *The James Q.C.E. Story* (Auckland: James Family History Society, 1984)

Hunt, Betty, *The Acklands of Fiji* (Auckland: Betty Hunt, 2010)

Hunter, Ian, *Age of Enterprise: Rediscovering the New Zealand entrepreneur 1880–1910* (Auckland: Auckland University Press, 2007)

Hutching, Megan, *Over the Wide and Trackless Sea: The pioneer women and girls of New Zealand* (Auckland: Harper Collins, 2008)

Irvine-Smith, Fanny L., *The Streets of My City: Wellington New Zealand* (Wellington: Reed, 1948)

Jones, Alison and Sue Middleton, *Women and Education in Aotearoa 2* (Wellington: Bridget Williams Books, 1992)

Jones, Jenny Robin, *No Simple Passage: The journey of the 'London' to New Zealand, 1842 – a ship of hope* (Auckland: Random House, 2011)

_____, *Writers in Residence: A journey with pioneer New Zealand writers* (Auckland: Auckland University Press, 2004)

Jones, Ruby, Enid Hawker and Linda Bloomfield (eds), *Women of Westland and their Families*, vol. II (Greymouth: Westland Branch of National Council of Women, 1977)

Kamira, Jo, 'Māori', *Sydney Journal* 3, no. 1, 2010, 23–34

Kay, Alison, *The Foundations of Female Entrepreneurship: Enterprise, home and household in London, c. 1800–1870* (New York and London: Routledge, 2009)

Kerr, Rex, *Not Only Te Rauparaha and Hadfield, but also …* (Otaki: Black Pony Books, 2016)

Kiddle, Margaret, *Caroline Chisholm* (Melbourne: Melbourne University Press, 1969, first published 1950)

Killip, Rosemary, *To Find a Fortune: Women of the Thames goldfield, 1867–1893* (Wellington: Victoria University Women's Studies, 1995)

Kincaid, Andrew, 'Whale and hotelier: Mary Ann Ames (1817–1887)', *Otaki Historical Society Journal* 31, 2009, 40–42

Kirk, Athol, 'Ayrshire House, Economic, D.I.C., Arthur Barnetts', *Whanganui Historical Record* 22, no. 1, 1991

Kwolek-Folland, Andrea, *Incorporating Women: A history of women and business in the United States* (New York: Palgrave Macmillan, 1998)

Lampkin, Veronica, *Madame Weigel: The woman who clothed the Australasian colonies* (Carrara, Queensland: V. Lampkin, 2015)

Lash, Max, *Nelson Notables 1840–1940: A dictionary of regional biography* (Nelson: Nelson Historical Society, 1992)

Laurence, Anne, Josephine Maltby and Janette Rutterford, *Women and their Money 1700–1950: Essays on women and finance* (Abingdon, Oxon, New York: Routledge, 2009)

Laurenson, Helen, 'Department stores and shopping malls: The rise of department stores', Te Ara: www.teara.govt.nz/en/department-stores-and-shopping-malls/page-1

_____, *Going Up, Going Down: The rise and fall of the department store* (Auckland: Auckland University Press, 2006)

Lawlor, Pat, *Old Wellington Hotels: Some history, personalities and anecdotes* (Wellington: Millwood Press, 1974)

Lewis, Susan Ingalls, 'Business widows in nineteenth-century Albany, New York, 1813–1885', in Rudolph P. Bell and Virginia Yans-McLaughlin (eds), *Women on Their Own: Interdisciplinary perspectives on being single*, (New Brunswick: Rutgers University Press, 2007)

_____, *Unexceptional Women: Female proprietors in mid-19th-century Albany New York 1830–1885* (Columbus: Ohio State University Press, 2009)

Leydon, John, 'Ups and downs', in Julia Bradshaw (ed.), *The Diggers' Story: Accounts of the West Coast gold rushes* (Christchurch: Canterbury University Press, 2014)

Locke, Elsie, *The Runaway Settlers: An historical novel* (London: Jonathan Cape, 1965)

Lofland, Lyn, *The Public Realm: Exploring the city's quintessential social territory* (Hawthorne, New York: Aldine de Gruyter, 1998)

Lohrli, Anne, *Household Words: A weekly journal 1850–1859 conducted by Charles Dickens. Table of contents, list of contributors and their contributions based on The Household Words Office Book in the Morris L. Parrish Collection of Victorian novelists, Princeton University Library* (Toronto: University of Toronto Press, 1973)

Long, Margaret, 'Memorials to Emily McWilliam', *Otaki Historical Journal* 21, 1998, 50–53

Lowe, Jeremy, '30 Ascot St', *Thorndon Society Newsletter*, no. 164, December 2012, 4

Macdonald, Barrie, *Imperial Patriot: Charles Alma Baker and the history of Limestone Downs* (Wellington: Bridget Williams Books, 1993)

Macdonald, Charlotte, 'Land, death and dower in the settler empire: The lost cause of "the widow's third" in nineteenth-century New Zealand', *Victoria University of Wellington Law Review* 41, 2010, 493–518.

_____, 'The "social evil": Prostitution and the passage of the Contagious Diseases Act (1869)', in Margaret Tennant, Charlotte Macdonald and Barbara Brookes (eds), *Women in History: Essays on European women in New Zealand* (Sydney, Wellington: George Allen & Unwin, 1986)

_____, *A Woman of Good Character: Single women as immigrant settlers in nineteenth-century New Zealand* (Wellington: Allen & Unwin/Historical Branch, 1990)

_____, *Women Writing Home 1700–1920*, vol. 5 (London: Pickering & Chatto, 2006)

Macdonald, Charlotte, Merimeri Penfold and Bridget Williams (eds), *The Book of New Zealand Women/Ko Kui Ma Te Kaupapa* (Wellington: Bridget Williams Books, 1991)

MacGibbon, John, *Piano in the Parlour: When the piano was New Zealand's home entertainment centre* (Wellington: Ngaio Press, 2007)

Mackay, J.A., *Life in Early Poverty Bay* (Gisborne: Gisborne Publishing Company, 1927)

Macmorran, George, *Some Schools and Schoolmasters of Early Wellington* (Wellington: S. & W. Mackay, 1900)

McSaveney, Eileen, 'Historic earthquakes: The 1848 Marlborough earthquake', Te Ara: www.teara.govt.nz/en/historic-earthquakes/2

Main, William, *Wellington through a Victorian Lens* (Wellington: Millwood Press, 1972)

Mairs, Elspeth, *The Wallis Family Children's Home, Motueka 1867–1887* (Westport: E. Mairs, 1989)

Malthus, Jane, 'Dressmakers in nineteenth-century New Zealand', in Margaret Tennant, Charlotte Macdonald and Barbara Brookes (eds), *Women in History 2* (Wellington: Bridget Williams Books, 1992), 76–97

Manson, Celia, *Widow of Thorndon Quay: Part 2 of the story of a New Zealand family* (Wellington: Pigeon Press, 1981)

Manson, Cecil and Celia Manson, *Tides of Hokianga* (Wellington: Wingfield Press, 1956)

Marshall, Peter A. and Kean K. Brown, 'The identification of the five ladies', in *Swiss Notes by Five Ladies* (Lancaster: Peter A. Marshall, 2003, first published 1875)

Martyr, Philippa, *Paradise of Quacks: An alternative history of medicine in Australia* (Sydney: Macleay Press, 2002)

Massi, Carla, *Babingtons: I Primi 125 Anni. La storia del tè a Roma* (Rome: Babingtons, 2018)

Masters, Joseph and Ian Fraser Grant, *The Memoirs of Joseph Masters: Founder of small farm settlements for the 'small man'* (Masterton: Wairarapa Archive, 2005)

Matheson, Alister, 'Early Maketu storekeepers', *Bay of Plenty Journal of History* 44, no. 2, 1986, 91–118

Matthew, Kate, 'The Female Middle Class Emigration Society governesses in Australia: A failed vision?', *Journal of Australian Colonial History* 14, 2012, 107–30

May, Helen, *School Beginnings: A nineteenth-century colonial story* (Wellington: NZCER Press, 2005)

McAloon, Jim, *Nelson: A regional history* (Whatamango Bay: Cape Catley & Nelson City Council, 1997)

_____, 'The New Zealand economy, 1792–1914', in Giselle Byrnes (ed.), *The New Oxford History of New Zealand* (South Melbourne: Oxford University Press, 2009)

McCarthy, Angela (ed.), *A Global Clan: Scottish migrant networks and identities since the eighteenth century* (London: Tauris Academic Studies, 2006)

_____, *Irish Migrants in New Zealand, 1840–1937: 'The desired haven'* (Woodbridge: Boydell Press, 2005)

McClunie, Pat, *A Far Traveller: Eleanor Mills and her Wallace descendants* (Hokitika: Pat McClunie, 2000)

McDonnell, Hilda, 'Early residents of Clyde Quay: Henry and Matilda Meech', *Heritage Link* 117 (Wellington Historical & Early Settlers' Association, October 2015)

_____, 'Mary Ann Ames of the South Sea Hotel', in *Publicans in the Port Nicholson District in the Colony of New Zealand* (Wellington: Vera Publications, 2014)

McKegg, Kate, 'Gender, work and death registration in New Zealand', *Labour, Employment and Work in New Zealand*, [S.I.] 1994: https://doi.org/10.26686/lew.v0i0.925

McKinnon, Emily H. Siedeberg and Irene L. Starr, *Otago Pioneer Women's Memorial: Being a brief history of the foundation of a memorial building dedicated to the pioneer women of Otago to serve the interests of present and future generations of women and organised societies in civic welfare; founded 1939* (Dunedin: Otago Daily Times and Witness Newspaper, 1939)

McLennan-Boman, Vera L., *Glimpses into Early Manawatu* (Waikanae: Heritage Press, 1985)

Mein Smith, Philippa, *A Concise History of New Zealand* (New York, Port Melbourne: Cambridge University Press, 2005)

Middleton, Sue, *Women and Education in Aotearoa* (Wellington: Allen & Unwin, Port Nicholson Press, 1988)

Ministry of Business Innovation and Employment, Hikina Whakatutuki, *Small Business Sector Report and Factsheet*, 2016

Mitchell, Hilary and Maui John and Wakatū Incorporation, *Te Tau Ihu o te Waka: A history of Māori of Nelson and Marlborough* (Wellington: Huia Publishers/Wakatū Incorporation, 2004)

Moffat, Kirstine, 'Agents of empire and feminist rebels: Settlement and gender in Isabella Aylmer's distant homes and Ellen Ellis's everything is possible to will', in T.S. Wagner (ed.), *Victoria Settler Narratives: Emigrants, cosmopolitans and returnees in nineteenth-century literature* (London: Pickering & Chatto, 2011), 41–53

_____, '"Devoted to the cause of woman's rights": The New Zealand new woman novel', *Women's Writing*, DOI: 10.1080/09699082.2017.1282930

_____, 'The piano as cultural symbol in colonial New Zealand', *History Compass* 7, no. 3, 2009, 719–41

_____, *Piano Forte: Stories and sounds from colonial New Zealand* (Dunedin: Otago University Press, 2011)

Moring, Beatrice and Richard Wall, *Widows in European Economy and Society, 1600–1920* (Woodbridge: Boydell and Brewer, 2017)

Mossong, Verva, 'Remember the primitive Methodists', *Wesley Historical Society (NZ) Publication* 63, 1996: www.methodist.org.nz/files/docs/wesley%20historical/63(3)%20remember%20the%20primitive.pdf

Murray, Tosti, *Marsden: The history of a New Zealand school for girls* (Wellington: Marsden Old Girls' Association, 1967)

Neale, June E., *The Greenwoods: A pioneer family of New Zealand* (Nelson: General Printing Services, 1984)

Nichol, Elizabeth, 'Transplanting colonial traditions: Immigrant colonial composers in New Zealand', in Michael Brown and Samantha Owens (eds), *Searches for Tradition: Essays on New Zealand music past and present* (Wellington: Victoria University Press, 2017), 25–45

Nolan, Melanie, *Breadwinning: New Zealand women and the state* (Christchurch: Canterbury University Press, 2000)

Norris, B.M., *The Milnes and Choyces of Early Auckland* (Auckland: J.R. Milne, R.S. Milne & J.S. Kidd, 1991)

Nugent, Maria, *Women's Employment and Professionalism in Australia: Histories, themes and places* (Canberra: Australian Heritage Commission, 2002)

Ogilvie, Gordon, *Ballantynes: The story of Dunstable House 1854–2004* (Christchurch: J Ballantyne & Co, 2004)

Oliveira, Vanessa, 'The gendered dimension of trade: Female traders in nineteenth-century Luanda', *Portuguese Studies Review* 23, no. 2, 2015, 93–121

Olssen, Erik, 'Families and the gendering of European New Zealand in the colonial period, 1840–80', in Caroline Daley and Deborah Montgomerie (eds), *The Gendered Kiwi* (Auckland: Auckland University Press, 1999)

Olssen, Erik and Maureen Hickey, *Class and Occupation: The New Zealand reality* (Dunedin: Otago University Press, 2005)

Orchiston, W., C. Romick and P. Brown, 'James Henry Marriott: New Zealand's first professional telescope maker', *Journal of Astronomical History and Heritage* 18, no. 3, 2015, 261–76

Paterson, Lachlan and Angella Wanhalla, *He Reo Wahine: Māori women's voices from the nineteenth century* (Auckland: Auckland University Press, 2017)

Patterson, Brad, Tom Brooking and Jim McAloon, *Unpacking the Kists: The Scots in New Zealand* (Montreal: McGill-Queens University Press; Dunedin: Otago University Press, 2013)

Petrie, Hazel, *Chiefs of Industry: Māori tribal enterprise in early colonial New Zealand* (Auckland: Auckland University Press, 2006)

Phillips, Jock, 'Rural mythologies: Immigrant hopes', Te Ara: www.teara.govt.nz/en/rural-mythologies/page-2

Phillips, Jock and Terry Hearn, *Settlers: New Zealand immigrants from England, Ireland and Scotland 1800–1945* (Auckland: Auckland University Press, 2008)

Phillips, Nicola, *Women in Business, 1700–1850* (Woodbridge: Boydell, 2006)

Pickles, Katie, 'Locating widows in mid-nineteenth-century Pictou County, Nova Scotia', *Journal of Historical Geography* 30, no. 1, 2004, 70–86

_____, 'Naturalising Nightingale in the Ashburton Domain', in Annabel Cooper, Angela Wanhalla & Lachlan Paterson (eds), *The Lives of Colonial Objects* (Dunedin: Otago University Press, 2015), 236–41

Pool, Ian, Arunachalam Dharmalingam and Janet Sceats, *The New Zealand Family from 1840: A demographic history* (Auckland: Auckland University Press, 2007)

Porter, Frances (ed.), *The Turanga Journals: Letters and journals of William and Jane Williams* (Wellington: Victoria University Press, 1974)

Porter, Frances, Charlotte Macdonald and Tui MacDonald, *My Hand Will Write What My Heart Dictates: The unsettled lives of women in nineteenth-century New Zealand as revealed to sisters, family and friends* (Auckland: Auckland University Press, Bridget Williams Books, 1996)

Quick, Sandra, '"A magnificent stamp of a woman": Female sly grog sellers and hotelkeepers on the Central Otago goldfields 1861–1901', in Lloyd Carpenter and Lyndon Fraser (eds), *Rushing for Gold: Life and commerce on the goldfields of New Zealand and Australia* (Dunedin: Otago University Press, 2016), 151–64

Rice, Geoffrey W., *Christchurch Changing: An illustrated history* (Christchurch: Canterbury University Press, 1999)

Robert McDougall Art Gallery, *Concise History of Art in Canterbury 1850–2000* (Christchurch: Robert McDougall Art Gallery for Christchurch City Council, 2000)

Royal, Te Ahukaramū Charles, 'Māori Composers: Ngā Kaitito Waiata', Te Ara: www.teara.govt.nz/en/maori-composers-nga-kaitito-waiata

Schrader, Ben, *The Big Smoke: New Zealand cities, 1840–1920* (Wellington: Bridget Williams Books, 2016)

Schumpeter, Joseph A., *Capitalism, Socialism and Democracy* (London: George Allen and Unwin, 1976)

Sear, Martha, '"Curious and peculiar"? Women taxidermists in colonial Australia', in Joan Kerr and Jo Holder (eds), *Past Present: The national women's art anthology* (Sydney: Craftsman House, 1999)

_____, 'Tost, Jane Catherine (1817–1889)', Australian Dictionary of Biography: http://adb.anu.edu.au/biography/rohu-ada-jane-13285

Sharpe, Pamela, *The Nineteenth-Century Businesswoman in the British Isles: Work culture, adaptation and the lace trade* (Nedlands, WA: Centre for Women and Business, Graduate School of Management, University of Western Australia, 2003)

Shaw, Louise, 'From family helpmeet to lady dispenser: Women pharmacists 1881–1939', *New Zealand Journal of History* 32, no. 1, 1998, 23–42

Shipman, Bill, *Hogg Family History from Scotland to Wanganui* (Papatoetoe: W. Spence and B. Shipman, 1989)

Singley, Blake, '"Not such a bad speculation": Women, cookbooks and entrepreneurship in Australia', in Aston, Jennifer and Catherine Bishop (eds), *Female Entrepreneurs in the Long Nineteenth Century: A global perspective* (New York: Palgrave Macmillan, forthcoming)

Siu, Helen F. (ed.), *Merchants' Daughters: Women, commerce and regional culture in South China* (Hong Kong: Hong Kong University Press, 2010)

Smith, Dawn, 'Forget not the bath', *Journal of the Nelson and Marlborough Historical Societies* 1, no. 6, 1986, 4–8: http://nzetc.victoria.ac.nz/tm/scholarly/tei-NHSJ04_06-t1-body1-d1.html

Sole, Laraine, *The Early Hotels of Old Wanganui* (Whanganui: Sole, 2016)

Sparks, Edith, *Capital Intentions: Female proprietors in San Francisco* (Chapel Hill: University of North Carolina Press, 2006)

Sparrow, Margaret, *Rough on Women: Abortion in 19th-century New Zealand* (Wellington: Victoria University Press, 2014)

Spurdle, Flora, *New Stories of Old Whanganui* (Whanganui: H.P. Willemsen, 1958)

St Leon, Mark, *Circus: The Australian story* (Melbourne: Melbourne Books, 2011)

Stevens, Joan, ed., *Mary Taylor, Friend of Charlotte Brontë: Letters from New Zealand and elsewhere* (Auckland: Auckland University Press, 1972)

Stone, Russell, 'Auckland business, 1841–2004: Myth and reality', in Ian Hunter and Diana Morrow (eds), *City of Enterprise: Perspectives on Auckland business history* (Auckland: Auckland University Press, 2006)

_____, *Makers of Fortune: A colonial business community and its fall* (Auckland: Auckland University Press, 1974)

Strachan, Glenda and Lindy Henderson, 'Surviving widowhood: Life alone in rural Australia in the second half of the nineteenth century', *Continuity and Change* 23, no. 3, 2008, 487–508

Swainson, William, *Auckland, the Capital of New Zealand and the Country Adjacent: Including some account of the gold discovery in New Zealand* (London: Smith, Elder & Co; Auckland: J. Williamson, 1853)

Sweeney, Robert, 'Gender, discrimination and housing in turn-of-the-century Montréal: What mapping the census returns of immigrants can tell us', *Frontiers in Digital Humanities* 3, no. 8, 2016, 1–18

Tennant, Margaret, *The Fabric of Welfare: Voluntary organisations, government, and welfare in New Zealand 1840–2005* (Wellington: Bridget Williams Books, 2007)

Tennant, Margaret, Charlotte Macdonald and Barbara Brookes (eds), *Women in History 2*, (Wellington: Bridget Williams Books, 1992)

———, *Women in History: Essays on European women in New Zealand* (Sydney: George Allen & Unwin; Wellington: Port Nicholson Press, 1986)

Thompson, Edward Palmer, *The Making of the English Working Class* (London: Gollancz, 1963)

Traue, J.E., 'Nineteenth-century New Zealand novels and novellas published as serials in New Zealand, Australian and British newspapers and periodicals and never published as monographs: A checklist', *Journal of New Zealand Studies* 20, 2015: https://doi.org/10.26686/jnzs.v0i20.3875

Tucker, Ken, *Milne & Choyce: A one-hundred year business history 1867–1967* (Auckland: Milne & Choyce, 1968)

Ulianova, Galina, *Female Entrepreneurs in Nineteenth-Century Russia* (London: Taylor and Francis, 2009)

Upton, Susan, *Wanted: A Beautiful Barmaid: Women behind the bar in New Zealand, 1830–1976* (Wellington: Victoria University Press, 2013)

Walsh, Margaret, 'Gendered endeavours: Women & the reshaping of business culture', *Women's History Review* 14, no. 2, 2005)

Wanhalla, Angela, *In/Visible Sight: The mixed-descent families of southern New Zealand* (Auckland: Auckland University Press 2010)

———, *Matters of the Heart: A history of interracial marriage in New Zealand* (Auckland: Auckland University Press, 2012)

Ward, L., *Early Wellington* (Auckland: Whitcombe & Tombs, 1928)

Waring, Marilyn, *Counting for Nothing: What men value & what women are worth* (Wellington: Allen & Unwin/Port Nicholson Press, 1988)

Washburn, Enga, *Courage and Camp Ovens: Five generations at Golden Bay* (Wellington: Reed, 1970)

Weeks, Jill, 'Susannah Napier – her story', *Wesleyan Historical Society Journal* 61, 1994, 46–47

Whanganui District Council, 'Mt St Joseph Homestead', Register Item 362, Built Heritage Inventory: http://maps.whanganui.govt.nz/Wanganui/Photos/HeritageInventory/362.pdf

Wilson, Dean, 'Community and gender in Victorian Auckland', *New Zealand Journal of History* 30, no. 1, 1996, 24–42

Woollard, Jane, '"The elasticity of her spirits": Actresses and resilience on the 19th-century colonial stage', in Rebecca Scollen and Michael Smalley (eds), *Resilience: Revive, restore, reconnect, Australasian Association for Drama Theatre and Performance Studies*, 2016 Conference Proceedings, vol. 1, Artsworx, 2016

Wright-St Clair, R.E., *Thoroughly a Man of the World: A biography of Sir David Monro MD* (Christchurch: Whitcombe & Tombs, 1971)

Yeager, Mary (ed.), *Women in Business* (Cheltenham: Edward Elgar Publishing, 1999)

Yska, Redmer, *Wellington: Biography of a city* (Wellington: Reed, 2006)

Zimmerman, Kari, '"As pertaining to the female sex": The legal and social norms of female entrepreneurship in nineteenth-century Rio de Janeiro, Brazil', *Hispanic American Historical Review* 96, no. 1, 2016, 39–72

NEWSPAPER ARTICLES AND PRESS RELEASES

Saker, John, 'The story behind the world's best Pinot Noir': www.stuff.co.nz

Sly, Sonia, 'Beyond Kate: Women exercising their new rights': www.stuff.co.nz/life-style/107645571/beyond-kate-women-exercising-their-new-rights

South Canterbury Museum, 'From the grave': www.pressreader.com/new-zealand/the-timaru-herald/20070123/282776352063578

'Tree transformed into pioneer statue', Western Bay of Plenty District Council News: www.westernbay.govt.nz/Council/News/Media/Tree-transformed-into-pioneer-statue/

Thornton, Grant, 'Proportion of women in senior management roles has hit rock bottom': www.grantthornton.co.nz/press/press-releases-2018/proportion-of-women-in-nz-senior-leadership-roles-has-hit-rock-bottom/

Winter, Gareth, 'Remarkable story of settler siblings', *Wairarapa Times-Age*, 7 January 2016

THESES

Anae, Nicole, '"A crowned and selected band of women": Tasmanian actresses/celebrities of the nineteenth century & "home-grown" identity', PhD thesis, University of Tasmania, 2005

Anderson, Robyn, '"The hardened frail ones": Women and crime in Auckland, 1845–1870', MA thesis, University of Auckland, 1981

Bishop, Catherine, 'Commerce was a woman: Women in business in colonial Sydney and Wellington', PhD thesis, Australian National University, 2012

Carlyon, Jenny, 'New Zealand Friendly Societies, 1842–1941', PhD thesis, University of Auckland, 2001

Dintsman, Elise Weinstein, 'Tattered cloth tells more: Women's work and museum representation', PhD thesis, University of Toronto, 2012

Hart, Sue, 'Widowhood and remarriage in colonial Australia', PhD thesis, University of Western Australia, 2009

Howitt, Rohan, 'Poihākena: Māori travellers and workers in New South Wales, 1793–1840', Honours thesis, University of Sydney, 2017

Nichol, Elizabeth, '"Dedicated to the colonial music-loving public": New Zealand's published music 1840–1913', PhD thesis, University of Auckland, 2017

Paterson, Jai, 'Among friends: Middle-class Tasmanians who moved to New Zealand, 1855–1875', PhD thesis, University of Tasmania, 2015

Quick, Sandra, '"The colonial helpmeet takes a dram": Women participants in the Central Otago goldfields liquor industry, 1861–1901', MA thesis, University of Otago, 1998

Sargison, Patricia Ann, '"Essentially a woman's work": A history of general nursing in New Zealand 1830–1930', PhD thesis, University of Otago, 2001

Whiteside, Heidi, '"We shall be respectable": Women and representations of respectability in Lyttelton 1851–1893', MA thesis, University of Canterbury, 2007

Wigglesworth, Roger, 'The myth and the reality: A study of the adaptation of John Marmon (1800?–1880) with comments on his three newspaper autobiographies', Research essay, Massey University, 1974

Wyse, Stephanie, 'Gender, wealth and margins of empire: Women's economic opportunity in New Zealand cities, c. 1890–1950', PhD thesis, King's College London, University of London, 2008

UNPUBLISHED MANUSCRIPTS AND CONFERENCE PAPERS

Davison, Jill, family tree material

Dreaver, Anthony, 'The draper's diary'

Hunter, Ian, Peter Lineham and Marie Wilson, 'The entrepreneurial immigrant', Business History and Europe Conference, University of Canterbury, 5–6 September 2003

Rendall, Lyndsay, 'Brown Briggs family', notes on family history

Strachan, Glenda and Lindy Henderson, 'Assumed but rarely documented: Women's entrepreneurial activities in late nineteenth-century Australia', paper presented at 'The Past is Before Us' Labour History Conference, Sydney, 2005

Woods, Marie, 'The Stanton family: Silk weavers from Coventry'

HISTORY BLOGS

Anon., Early New Zealand Photographers: http://canterburyphotography.blogspot.com

Arts and Culture Oceania, 'Chancery Lane 1862': https://marapito.blogspot.com/2009/07/chancery-lane-1862.html

Bisson, Mike, 'Jean Aubin of Pirongia, New Zealand': www.theislandwiki.org/index.php/Jean_Aubin_of_Pirongia,_New_Zealand

Blackmore, Kent, 'Monsieur Philippe de Barr', 'Magic in Sydney': www.sydneymagic.net/HISTORY/DE_BARR/de_barr.html

CerberusCoins, 'Descendants of William Searight, County Londonderry, Northern Ireland', Mawhinny Family History Research, 19 December 2014: https://cerberuscoins.wordpress.com/tag/mawhinney/

Clarke, Samuel Ludbrooke, 'Clarke family of Te Waimate': www.clarke.org.nz/?sid=12

Danvers, Gary, 'Countess of Seafield: The painting': http://web.archive.org/web/20091021160749/http://geocities.com/garydanvers/CoS-painting.html

Donaldson, Stephen, 'Shore Whalers Wahine Project': www.whalerswahine.com

G., Fiona, 'Potto, McCaul and Pollock families, Whanganui and Wellington', Digital NZ Story: https://digitalnz.org/stories/50ac828bfb002c6f36000001

Galletly, Duncan, 'Bibliography of New Zealand cookbooks to 1922': www.aristologist.com/resources/cookery-books-to-1922.html;

Grant, Susan et al, 'Merritt family and gasworks Auckland': https://lists.rootsweb.com/hyperkitty/list/nz-auckland@rootsweb.com/thread/22559876/

JMacR, 'Auckland House and Mrs Cazaly', Manly Library Local Studies Blog: http://manlylocalstudies.blogspot.com/2013/09/auckland-house-and-mrs-cazaly.html

Kidd, Carol, 'The link in the chain', 1985, in 'Frederick Reid', Geni: www.geni.com/people/Fredrick-Reid/6000000035826858451

King, Doreen and John Tomkies: http://johntomkies.sites.simplehost.co.nz

Leggat, Pauline, 'The musicians': www.turle.name/the_musicians/home.html

Lythgoe, Darrin, Foley Family History Website: http://genealogy.eproject.co.nz/foley_family_main/william_foley/

McKee, Alison, 'Hunter Henry Murdoch', My Jacob Family: www.myjacobfamily.com/favershamjacobs/hunterhenrymurdoch.htm

McPhail, Hugh, 'Hugh McKenzie and Catherine McKenzie', Blenheim 175: https://blenheim175.wordpress.com

Mactier, Susie, 'Takapuna Lake poet', Auckland City Council, 'Takapuna Writers' Walk': https://57.myt.li/tours/1507970552/stops/1771181974/index.html

Morrell, Vivenne, 'Halls Turkish Baths Wellington': https://viviennemorrell.wordpress.com/2016/06/25/halls-turkish-baths-wellington/

Murray, David, 'Matilda Ritchie's Building': https://builtindunedin.com/2015/04/28/matilda-ritchies-building/

Simmonds, S., 'A family history': http://simmondshistory.blogspot.com.au/2006/04/frances-southwell-shayle-george-1828.html

South Canterbury GenWeb, 'Churches at Cave, South Canterbury, New Zealand': www.rootsweb.ancestry.com/~nzlscant/cavechurches.htm

Stanton, David, 'Elizabeth Ann Jones nee Buller': www.mis.net.au/stanton/elizabeth_ann_buller.htm

Symons, Stephen, 'Criterion Hotel': https://poddimok.wordpress.com/087-the-watering-holes-an-historical-essay/criterion-hotel/

Templeton, Phillipa, 'Holland and Tye Families, selling Hillcrest': www.sellinghillcrest.co.nz/Gallery/ID/4/HISTORY-Holland-and-Tye-Families.

Truttman, Lisa, 'William and Jane Yandle, taxidermists': http://timespanner.blogspot.com.au/2011/05/william-and-jane-yandle-taxidermists.html

Whanganui Regional Museum 'Hair Estate': https://whanganuiregionalmuseum.wordpress.com/tag/hair-estate/

OTHER WEBSITES

Babingtons: www.babingtons.com/en

Business Hall of Fame: www.businesshalloffame.co.nz

Cambridge University Drivers of Entrepreneurship project: www.campop.geog.cam.ac.uk/research/projects/driversofentrepreneurship

Casson, Mark, 'Entrepreneurship': www.econlib.org/library/Enc1/Entrepreneurship.html

Caversham Project: https://caversham.otago.ac.nz/resource/index.html

Heritage New Zealand, 'Clendon House': www.heritage.org.nz/places/places-to-visit/northland-region/clendon-house

Heritage New Zealand, 'Hayes Engineering Works and homestead': www.heritage.org.nz/places/places-to-visit/otago-region/hayes-engineering

New Zealand History: Nga Korero a Ipurangi o Aotearoa, New Zealand Ministry of Culture and Heritage: https://nzhistory.govt.nz

Smith & Caughey's: www.smithandcaugheys.co.nz/about-us.aspx

St John's in the City Presbyterian Church, Church Complex: www.stjohnsinthecity.org.nz/about/complex.htm

TNS Business Finance Monitor 2011–2013. Survey commissioned by ANZ: https://bizhub.anz.co.nz/resources/women-in-business-infographic.aspx

Wellington Antique Bottle and Collectibles Club: www.wellingtonantiquebottles.org.nz

Index

Page numbers in **bold** refer to illustrations